Contents

Part III. LEGAL LITERATURE OF OTHER LEGAL SYSTEMS

Part IV. LAW LIBRARY PRACTICE

Manual of Law Librarianship

MANUAL OF LAW LIBRARIANSHIP

The Use and Organization of Legal Literature

Second Edition

Edited by ELIZABETH M. MOYS, BA, FLA

Published for the British and Irish Association of Law Librarians

Gower

First edition published 1976 by André Deutsch Limited
This edition published by
Gower Publishing Company Limited
Gower House
Croft Road
Aldershot
Hants GU11 3HR
England

British Library Cataloguing in Publication Data
Manual of law librarianship: the use and
  organisation of legal literature.——2nd ed.
  1. Law libraries
  I. Moys, Elizabeth M. II. British and
  Irish Association of Law Librarians
  026'.34   Z675.L2

ISBN 0 566 03512 X

Printed in Great Britain by
Redwood Burn Limited, Trowbridge, Wiltshire

Foreword

W. A. F. P. STEINER, LLM, MA, FLA
President, British and Irish Association of Law Librarians

The first edition of the *Manual of Law Librarianship* was welcomed, in his foreword, by Professor Owen Hood Phillips, the then President of the British and Irish Association of Law Librarians. It gives me great pleasure to follow the precedent set by him.

The *Manual* was a pioneering work in that for the first time in the English-speaking world it combined the bibliography of law in all its aspects with a detailed treatment of the methods and procedures of law librarianship. It was designed to provide for the needs of practising law librarians, and quickly established itself as a standard work. The *Manual* was published about seven years after the British and Irish Association of Law Librarians had been founded, and it had been in the making for several years before that. This was a creditable achievement for a newly established and still very small association and it enhanced its reputation. The imprint of BIALL, on the other hand, conferred a certain authority on the *Manual*. It should not be thought that the publications programme of BIALL is concentrated on a single book. It has published or sponsored several works and it has been publishing *The Law Librarian* three times a year from its foundation.

The success of the *Manual*, on the one hand, and the need to update it, on the other, have combined to render the publication of a second edition necessary. The general character of the work has remained unchanged, but experience has shown the need for some shifts of emphasis; these are explained by the Editor in her Preface. She has been responsible for both editions, and many of the contributors to the first edition have contributed to the second edition also. The excellent co-operation between the Editor and the contributors and among the contributors themselves, which was a significant feature of the first edition, has been characteristic of the second edition also. I trust that, in expressing my appreciation of their work, I voice the feelings of all users of the *Manual*.

9 May, 1986   W. A. STEINER

Preface

The first edition of this *Manual* was inevitably somewhat experimental. The Editorial Board believes that certain lessons have been learnt. Furthermore, the Association was about ten years older and more experienced when the second edition was being planned. Therefore there have been some changes of emphasis in the new edition. While primacy has still been given to the legal literature of the British Isles, the coverage of other parts of the world has been extended. We have tried to give an indication of the type of legal system likely to be found in any modern area, without specifically mentioning all modern nation states. The most notable changes are:

    the allocation of a whole chapter to the European Communities;

    the allocation of one chapter to be shared between Commonwealth and United States legal literatures;

    the addition of a section on socialist legal systems;

    a substantial reorganization of the bibliographical chapters into two main Parts: Common law and Others;

    a reduction of the space devoted to law library practice, telescoping the contents of eight original chapters into five revised chapters.

The *Manual* is intended to be a book to help all people dealing with legal material in libraries, both general and specialized. The pattern adopted is:

    Part One: two introductory chapters explaining the general context of law librarianship in the British Isles;

    Part Two: the literature of the Common law, its various types and their uses, in the British Isles and in overseas jurisdictions;

    Part Three: the literature of other systems of law, ancient and modern, treated in a broadly similar fashion;

    Part Four: library techniques, with special reference to their application in law libraries.

As it is somewhat unusual for a library manual to allocate such a high proportion of its space to subject literature, an explanation is offered.

For many years law libraries have been recognized, albeit reluctantly, as being 'different'. The legal profession is undoubtedly different in detail from the other learned professions, such as medicine. However, experience suggests that, from the point of view of those serving them, the older professions have a great deal in common, such as innate conservatism in their professional outlook and their attitude to members of newer professions. It is not, therefore, the users of law libraries that single them out from other libraries, so much as their contents. The law books themselves are different from other subject literatures, not only in their subject matter, but also in their own internal forms. It is this knowledge that law books are somehow different (and are therefore presumed to be difficult to understand and deal with), that can sometimes lead to a willingness on the part of general librarians to set aside their normal centralist tendencies and segregate law books and their users into separate or semi-autonomous libraries.

Hence the emphasis placed on the literature of law in this *Manual*. No one can be an efficient law librarian unless he has acquired a good knowledge of the types of material that make up a law library and how best to obtain access to the information recorded there. A knowledge of the substance of the law itself is undoubtedly useful, but is less so than a good practical knowledge of library techniques, and in any case the librarian is debarred by the nature of his office from giving legal aid or advice. What he must have, in order to provide the service his readers require, is a sound knowledge of basic legal texts (legislation and law reports), reference books, indexes, bibliography, citation methods, databases and the organization of legal literature.

In planning the volume, the Editorial Board decided to include all types of legal material and all systems of law which might be represented in a law library anywhere in the British Isles. As Professor Cornish has pointed out on page 39, this involves at least six jurisdictions within the geographical area that could be called 'British Isles': England and Wales,

Scotland, Northern Ireland, the Isle of Man, the Channel Islands (where Jersey and Guernsey have some differences) and the Republic of Ireland. There is no implication that all British and Irish law libraries should have full (or any) coverage of all these jurisdictions – indeed many libraries serve restricted local interests and rarely need to look beyond the law of their local jurisdiction, whichever it may be. However, both individual and corporate persons are becoming increasingly mobile. Any law librarian could suddenly be faced with enquiries about, for example, company laws in tax havens or the validity of a will or a divorce originating almost anywhere in the world.

Over the centuries, successive waves of immigrants from Europe, and other continents, have brought with them additional laws and customs, notably those of religious origin. Academic or commercial lawyers may, of course, be concerned with yet other systems of law, such as classical Roman law or the laws of East European countries. The *Manual* therefore contains short statements and selective bibliographies to give elementary guidance on virtually all foreign and non-jurisdictional legal systems. Although much of the law of the European Communities is also the law of the United Kingdom and of the Republic of Ireland, it is not basically 'common law' and so has been placed in the 'other laws' section.

The remainder of the *Manual* deals with the organization and operation of law libraries. Contributors were asked to cover briefly the whole range of topics in their respective chapters, so that the volume would provide a complete outline of the subject. Efforts have been concentrated on practical, rather than theoretical aspects of librarianship, giving special attention to those matters where legal literature requires some variation from general librarianship practices. Readers who require more information are referred to further literature on each group of topics in the reading lists at the end of chapters.

Law librarianship is such a vast subject that, even in a volume of this size, it is not possible to give a total statement. However, a great deal of information has been assembled by the team of contributors and consultants, providing at least some clue to the solution of any problem likely to occur in a British or Irish law library and, where space restrictions prohibited a full discussion of a topic, references to further sources of information. Even so, most contributors have had to be highly selective in their chapter bibliographies. Readers will soon find that reference to the volumes cited in the *Manual* will lead them to still further literature.

A few themes pervade the chapters, showing how important they are to law librarians. One is the fact that the most important legal texts are in serial form. Unless otherwise specified, the term 'law books' in this volume includes these basic and vital serial publications. Another is that no law book, however old, is useless merely by reason of its age. The fact that some thirteenth-century legislation (*eg* some parts of *Magna Carta*) and legal principles enunciated in some of the medieval law cases are still valid today neatly combines these two themes. Every law librarian needs to develop a sense of historical perspective if he is to begin to understand the books and readers with whom he is working. There are many subject areas in which periodical literature plays an important part, but the degree of use of legal serials, dozens, or even hundreds of years after publication, is unique.

At the same time, law libraries have a vital need to keep up to date. While it is no longer true that a client's life depends on the preparation of a case by his legal representatives, it is still true that their reliance on superseded precedents could lose an otherwise good case. Law has always been a well-documented subject, provided with a substantial array of commercially produced indexes, bibliographies and other tools. It has also been in the forefront of modern automated information technology. Full-text databases are particularly well developed in the legal field, as outlined throughout the volume and especially in Chapter Sixteen. But all this in no way absolves the law librarian from the need to be on top of his subject by scanning in-coming serial literature and maintaining whatever current information indexes and services are appropriate for his readers. These and other aspects of the special needs of law libraries in the organization and representation of their contents are dealt with at some length.

In his Foreword, Mr Steiner has referred to the co-operation between the various contributors which was essential for the successful completion of this volume. I most sincerely wish to thank all the contributors for their efforts, and particularly the three Consultants. They each read almost every word of the authors' drafts in order to advise on the particular area of interest that involved them. I also wish to pay a special tribute to the members of the Editorial Board, who put in a great deal of effort, before, during and after meetings of the Board, in working out the shape the volume was to take and advising the Editor on a wide range of consequential problems. Finally, and perhaps most specially of all, I wish to thank the Assistant Editor, Barbara Tearle, for taking charge of the detailed work on the 'other systems' sections and for taking part in innumerable and lengthy sessions helping to sort out general editorial problems. A number of other members of BIALL helped with the *Manual* in various ways, and we thank them too. The names of people outside the Association who have given help are separately listed.

The text of the *Manual* is, in general, up-to-date to late April 1986. It is hoped to achieve limited further up-dating during the course of printing.

17 May, 1986   ELIZABETH M. MOYS

Contributors

MRS MARION BIRCH, BA, DIPLIB, ALA, Assistant Librarian, Institute of Advanced Legal Studies, London.

MISS D. MARY BLAKE, Law Librarian, Harding Law Library, University of Birmingham.

MR WALLACE BREEM, Librarian and Keeper of the Manuscripts to the Honourable Society of the Inner Temple, London.

DR JENNY BRINE, PHD, BA, DIPLIB, Librarian, Centre for Russian and East European Studies, University of Birmingham.

PROFESSOR W. R. CORNISH, LLB, BCL, Professor of English Law, London School of Economics and Political Science.

MISS SHEILA M. DOYLE, BA, DIPLIB, Assistant Librarian, University of Durham.

MR JOHN GOODWILLIE, BA, DIPLIBSTUD, ALA, Official Publications Librarian, Trinity College Library, Dublin.

MR JOHN JEFFRIES, BA, ALA, FRSA, MIINFSC, Head of Information Services, National Youth Bureau, Leicester.

MISS JUDITH M. KING, BA, ALA, Librarian, Denton Hall Burgin & Warrens.

MR ROBERT G. LOGAN, LLB, FLA, Assistant Librarian, Bodleian Law Library, Oxford.

MRS CHRISTINE MISKIN, LLB, DIPLIB, ALA, Director, Legal Information Resources Ltd.

MISS ELIZABETH M. MOYS, BA, FLA, Librarian, University of London Goldsmiths' College.

MR ALEX NOEL-TOD, MA, DIPLIB, Senior Assistant Librarian, University of East Anglia, Norwich.

MR PAUL NORMAN, BA, MA, ALA, Assistant Librarian, Institute of Advanced Legal Studies, London.

MISS DAPHNE A. PARNHAM, Deputy Librarian, Inner Temple Library.

MR DAVID E. PERROW, MA, MA(LIB), ALA, Assistant Librarian, Crookesmoor Library, University of Sheffield.

MRS SALLY PHILLIPS, BL, ALA, Librarian, Law Commission, London.

MS BARBARA M. TEARLE, LLB, ALA, Sub-Librarian, University College, London.

MR DEREK J. WAY, MA, FLA, Sub-Librarian, Faculty of Law, University of Liverpool.

MR JULES R. WINTERTON, BA, DIPLIB, ALA, Assistant Librarian, Institute of Advanced Legal Studies, London.

CONSULTANTS

MR GEORGE H. BALLANTYNE, MA, FLA, Librarian, Signet Library, Edinburgh (Scottish Consultant).

MISS ELIZABETH A. P. GLEESON, BA, Barrister, DIPLIB, Law Librarian, Trinity College, Dublin (Irish Consultant).

MRS LYNN V. QUINEY, BA, DIPLIB, ALA, Academic Services Librarian, South Bank Polytechnic, London (Automation Consultant).

Acknowledgments

The Editor and Contributors wish to acknowledge help provided by the following in the compilation of this Manual:

Miss Sally Bolton, Lloyd's Life Assurance (IOM) Ltd
British Library: Preservation Service
Ms A–M. Conway, Editor, Aslib Publications
Miss J. Dawson, Barrister, Butterworths Telepublishing
Mr W. D. Hines, Law Librarian, University College of Wales
Miss B. P. Knowles, Barrister, Butterworths Telepublishing
Mr A. D. E. Lewis, Faculty of Law, University College, London
Library Association: Publications Department
Mr Jack Mills, Bliss Classification Association
Rev. T. A. Myers, Ushaw College, Durham
Dr D. S. Pearl, Fitzwilliam College, Cambridge
Public Record Office: Conservation Department and Technical Services Department
Mr A. M. Rowland, Law Commission, London
Mrs C. M. Short, Hon. Secretary, Society of Archivists

Abbreviations

AACR 1967	Anglo-American Cataloguing Rules, 1967
AACR2	Anglo-American Cataloguing Rules, 2nd ed., 1978
AAL, SED	Association of Assistant Librarians, South East Division
AALL	American Association of Law Libraries
AC	Law Reports, Appeal Cases
ACAS	Advisory Conciliation and Arbitration Service
ACP	African, Caribbean and Pacific countries
ACT	Australian Capital Territory
ADP	Automatic data processing
AIR	All India Reporter
AJ	Architects' Journal
ALA	(1) Associate of the Library Association (2) American Library Association
All ER	All England Reports
ALR	American Law Reports
ALT	Association of Law Teachers
Am.Jur.2d	American Jurisprudence, 2nd ed.
ARTTEL	Automated Request Transmission by Telephone
BBC	British Broadcasting Corporation
BBIP	British Books in Print
BC2	Bliss Bibliographic Classification, 2nd ed.
BCS	British Computer Society
BGB	Bürgeliches Gesetzsbuch
BIALL	British and Irish Association of Law Librarians
BIDR	Bulletino dell'Istituto di Diritto Romano 'Vittorio Scialoja'

BIP	Books in Print (US)
BLAISE	British Library Automated Information Service
BLAISE/ADRS	British Library Automated Document Request Service
BLAISE/LOCAS	British Library Local Cataloguing Service
BLCMP	Birmingham Libraries Co-operative Mechanization Project
BLib	Bachelor of Librarianship
BLLD	British Library Lending Division
BLRD	British Library Reference Division
BM	British Museum
BNA	Bureau of National Affairs (US)
BNB	British National Bibliography
BS(I)	British Standard(s Institution)
BTR	Brewing Trade Review
BUCOP	British Union Catalogue of Periodicals
BW	Burgelijk Wetboek
C	(1) Celsius
	(2) Command papers (1870–1899)
CA	Cases on Appeal
CAT	Cases on Appeal Transcript
CBI	Cumulative Book Index
CCH	Commerce Clearing House
Cd	Command papers (1900–18)
CELEX	Communitatis Europaeae Lex
CFR	Code of Federal Regulations (US)
Ch	Chancery
CIO	Church [of England] Information Office
CJEC	Court of Justice of the European Communities
CL	Current Law (UK)
CLI	Current Law Index (US)
CLIC	Canadian Law Information Council
CLIRS	Computerized Legal Information Retrieval Service
CLYB	Current Law Year Book
Cmd	Command papers (1919–56)
CMLR	Common Market Law Reports
Cmnd	Command papers (1956–)

COM	(1) Computer output microform
	(2) [EC] Commission documents
COPOL	Council of Polytechnic Librarians
cps	Characters per second
CPU	Central processing unit
CRD	Court Recording Department
CUG	Closed user group
CUP	Cambridge University Press
D	Digest (Justinian)
DDC	Dewey Decimal Classification
DEP	Depository Library [for EC documents]
DIANE	Direct Information Access Network for Europe
DLR	Dominion Law Reports
DPB	Department of Printed Books, British Library
DPP	Director of Public Prosecutions
EAEC	European Atomic Energy Community
EAS	Executive agreement series [US]
EC	European Community/ies
ECJ	European Court of Justice
ECOSOC	Economic and Social Council
ECR	European Court Reports
ECSC	European Coal and Steel Community
ECST	Eighteenth Century Short Title Catalogue
EDC	European Documentation Centre
EEC	European Economic Community
EP	European Parliament
ER	English Reports
ERC	European Reference Centre [for EC documents]
Euratom	European Atomic Energy Community
ex rel.	ex relatione
F	(1) Fahrenheit
	(2) Federal
FAO	Food and Agriculture Organization
FAX	Facsimile (transfer)
FID	Fédération International de Documentation
FIRA	Fontes Iuris Romani Anteiustiniani

FLA	Fellow of the Library Association
GATT	General Agreement on Tariffs and Trade
GmbH	Limited company (Germany)
GPSL	Government publications sectional list
HC	House of Commons
HL	House of Lords
HLRO	House of Lords Record Office
HMC	Historical Manuscripts Commission
HMCR	Historical Manuscripts Commission Reports
HMSO	Her/His Majesty's Stationery Office
HULS	Heads of University Law Schools
HURIDOCS	Human Rights Information and Documentation System
I	Institutes (Justinian)
IAEA	International Atomic Energy Agency
IALL	International Association of Law Libraries
IALS	Institute of Advanced Legal Studies
ICAO	International Civil Aviation Organization
ICJ	International Court of Justice
ICLQ	International and Comparative Law Quarterly
ICLR	Incorporated Council of Law Reporting for England and Wales
ICLR(I)	Incorporated Council of Law Reporting (Ireland)
ICLR(NI)	Incorporated Council of Law Reporting (Northern Ireland)
ICR	Industrial Court Reports
IFLA	International Federation of Library Associations
IFLP	Index to Foreign Legal Periodicals
ILO	International Labour Organization
ILR	Indian Law Reports
ILSI	Incorporated Law Society of Ireland
ILTR	Irish Law Times Reports
INION	Academy of Sciences' Institute for Information in the Social Sciences (USSR)
Inst	Institutes (Justinian)

Interdoc	International Association for Legal Documentation
IoM	Isle of Man
IPSS	International Packet Switch Stream
IR	(1) Ireland
	(2) Irish Reports
IRMA(E)	Ius Romanum Medii Aevi
ISBD(G)	International Standard Book Description (General)
ISBN	International Standard Book Number
ISDS	International Serials Data System
ISSN	International Standard Serial Number
J	Justinian's Institutes
JJ	Judgments of the Royal Court of Jersey
JO	Journal Officiel des Communautés Européennes
JP	Justice of the Peace
JSPTL	Journal of the Society of Public Teachers of Law
Just	Justinian's Institutes
K	A thousand units (especially in connection with computer hardware and storage capacity)
KB	King's Bench
KWIC	Key word in context indexing system
KWOC	Key word out of context indexing system
LA	Library Association
LASER	London and South Eastern Region
LC	Library of Congress
LEd	Lawyers' edition of the US Supreme Court Reports
LJCC	Law Journal County Court Reporter
LRI	Legal Resource Index
M & W	Meeson and Welby
MARC	Machine-readable catalogue
MEP	Member of the European Parliament
MS	Manuscript
N	Novels (Justinian)
NBT	Notable British Trials
NI	Northern Ireland

NIJ & LG	New Irish Jurist and Local Government Review
NILR	Northern Ireland Law Reports
NS/ns	New series
OCLC	Online Computer Library Center [formerly Ohio College Library Center]
OECD	Organization for Economic Co-operation and Development
OJ	Official Journal of the European Communities
OJC	Official Journal: Information and Notices series
OJL	Official Journal: Legislative series
OSAR/OSALL	Organization of South African Law Libraries
OUP	Oxford University Press
PC	Privy Council
PCIJ	Permanent Court of International Justice
PL	Public Law (US)
POLIS	Parliamentary Online Information Service
PRO	Public Record Office
PSS	Packet Switch Stream
QBD	Queen's Bench Division
R	Rex; Regina; Regem; Reginam
RCJ	Royal Courts of Justice
Rec.	Receuil de la Jurisprudence de la Cour [ECJ]
RIDA	Revue Internationale des Droits de l'Antiquité
RR	Revised Reports
RS	(1) Revised Statutes (2) Rolls Series [of Year Books]
RSC	Revised Statutes of Canada, 1970
SA	South Africa
SCAD	Central Documentation Service of the Commission of the European Communities
SCCR	Scottish Criminal Cases Reports
SCL	Society of Computers and Law

SCOLPIS	Standing Committee on Library Provision and Information Services, BIALL
SCt.	Supreme Court Reporter [US]
SDHI	Studia et Documenta Historiae et Iuris
SDI	Selective dissemination of information
SEC	Secretary-General [EC documents]
SI	Statutory Instrument
SIGLE	System for Information on Grey Literature in Europe
SII	Integrated Information Systems [EC Commission]
SOQUIJ	Société Québecoise d'Information Juridique
SLS	Servicing the Legal System (NI)
SLT	Scots Law Times
SLTR	Scots Law Times Reports
SPTL	Society of Public Teachers of Law
SR & Os	Statutory Rules and Orders
SS	Selden Society
SSC	Society of Solicitors in the Supreme Courts of Scotland
STATUS	Statute search project
STC	Pollard, A. W. and Redgrave, G. R.: A short-title catalogue of books printed ... 1475–1640
SUC	Slavonic Union Catalogue (BLLD)
TIAS	Treaties and other International Acts Series (US)
TIS	Treaty Information Service (United Nations)
TRHS	Transactions of the Royal Historical Society
TvR	Tijdschrift voor Rechtsgeschedenis
UDC	Universal Decimal Classification
UGC	University Grants Committee
UK	United Kingdom of Great Britain and Northern Ireland
ULS	University of London Union List of Serials
UN	United Nations
UNBIS	United Nations Bibliographic Information System

UNDEX	United Nations documents computer-assisted indexing programme
UNDI	United Nations Documents Index
Unesco/UNESCO	United Nations Educational, Scientific and Cultural Organization
Unidroit	International Institute for the Unification of Private Law, Rome
UP	University Press
US(A)	United States (of America)
USC	United States Code
USCA	United States Code Annotated
USCS	United States Code Service
UST	United States Treaties and other International Agreements
UWIST	University of Wales Institute of Science and Technology
VAT	Value added tax
VDU	Visual display unit
WHO	World Health Organization
WLR	Weekly Law Reports
WS	Society of Writers to Her Majesty's Signet, Edinburgh
YB	Year Books (medieval)
ZSS Rom.Abt.	Zeitschrift der Savigny-Stiftung für Rechtsgeschichte. Romanistische Abteilung

Glossary

Abridgment: older form of digest or encyclopedia.

Accessioning: process of cross-checking contents of parcels, order records, invoices, etc., to ensure accuracy, and the subsequent taking into stock of the newly-received material.

Acoustic coupler: a piece of equipment which allows a telephone handset to be connected to the data communications network (usually up to 30 cps)

Administrative tribunals: quasi-judicial bodies set up under numerous statutes and entrusted with the investigation and decision of matters in controversy and disputes arising out of the functioning of public administration.

Analysis (cataloguing/classification): the process of preparing a bibliographic record which describes a part or parts of a larger item.

Back-up: the means of maintaining a service when the main machinery for providing that service is out of action (notably a duplicate copy of a machine-readable file).

Balance area: space within a building that is not assigned to specifically library functions, but is essential for services, circulation, toilets, etc.

Baud: a measure of signal speed in data communication.

Bay (shelving): group of shelves one shelf wide; may be single- or double-faced.

Blanket/block order: standing order with a supplier for all materials published in a special category.

Boolean logic/operators: an algebraic term used to identify logical relationships in information work using the operators 'and', 'or', 'not'.

Breviate: short account.

Bull: edict or mandate issued by a Pope or bishop.

By(e)-laws: subordinate legislation promulgated by local authorities and other bodies under statutory authority.

Canon: rule, law or decree of the Church, especially one laid down by an ecclesiastical council.

Carrel: small individual study or screened table; may be allocated to a serious worker who requires the uninterrupted use of certain books for long periods.

Casebook: compilation of extracts from leading cases (and sometimes other sources) on a particular subject, designed as a teaching aid.

CELEX: inter-institutional computerized documentation system for Community law.

Charging: process of recording loans in a library.

Citation order: order in which the various facets of a complex subject are dealt with in a classification scheme.

Citator: volume or section of a volume containing tables of cases or legislation, with reference to their published sources and tables of cases and legislation that have been judicially noticed in subsequent cases.

Civil law: (1) private rights of action for redress, contrasted with criminal law;
(2) the family of legal systems where the influence of Roman law has been strong.

Class mark: notation symbol representing the total subject of a book or document.

Codifying Acts: Acts passed to codify the whole of the existing law, both statutory and case law, on a subject.

Collating: checking all pages, plates, maps, or other contents of a publication to ensure that the text is complete, undamaged and in the correct order.

Collation: (1) make-up of a book from the printer's sections, etc.;
(2) part of a catalogue entry giving full or part details of the collation.

COM: computer output microform; can be either microfilm or, more usually, microfiche.

Command papers: papers presented to Parliament on the initiative of the Government.

Common law: (1) judge-made law, as distinct from legislation and the rules of equity;
(2) family of legal systems deriving from the law of England.

Concordance: a word index which records the position of words in a text and indicates their context within the text.

Concordat: treaty or agreement with the force of international law, between the Roman Catholic Church and a secular government.

Conflict of laws: that part of the law of a country which governs cases involving a foreign element. Also known as Private international law.

Consolidating Acts: Acts passed to consolidate the statute law only on a subject, without altering the substance of the law, and to supersede and repeal the statutory provisions consolidated.

Constitutions (Roman law): collective term for decrees of the Roman Emperors which had the force of law.

Convention: agreement between states, of less formality or importance than a treaty.

Cutter number: filing symbol ensuring alphabetical arrangement consisting of letters and numbers (after C. A. Cutter).

Dáil Eireann: lower house of the Irish Parliament.

Database: a collection of interrelated information stored on a computer.

Dataline: special type of telephone line used exclusively for transmitting data to and from computers.

Decretals: rulings by Popes and decrees of church councils.

Delegated legislation *see* Subordinate legislation.

Digest: (1) in common law jurisdictions: a compilation of the headnotes of decided cases, arranged alphabetically or systematically by subject;
(2) collection of principles of rules of law, compiled privately;
(3) major part of the Corpus Juris Civilis of Justinian.

Disk: a data storage device consisting of one or more flat circular plates coated with magnetizable material.

Documentation: recording the contents of a library collection, usually detailed analysis of the subject content for the purpose of specialist information retrieval.

Downloading: in computing, the transfer of data from a remote location into local storage, using a communications line.

Equity: body of rules and remedies developed by the Court of Chancery parallel to but separate from the common law.

EUROVOC: a thesaurus concerning Community matters.

Facet (classification): one of the constituent categories of a complex subject, *ie*, the group of divisions produced by the application of a single characteristic of division (*eg* place) to a subject.

Filing title: word or words inserted before the title statement in a catalogue entry, to ensure correct filing order for entries under the same heading; may be a uniform title or some other word(s) selected by the cataloguer.

Floppy disk: a small single disk usually designed for use with a microcomputer.

Flow-chart: diagrammatic representation of the logical steps in the task to be performed.

Fore-edge: edge of a volume opposite to the spine.

Foxing: brown stains caused by the growth of mould in paper, due to dampness in the atmosphere.

Free-text searching: the use of ordinary language, as opposed to a controlled vocabulary, in a computer search.

Gateway: a means in telecommunications which allows users of one network to access another.

Grey literature: material not issued through the normal commercial publishing channels, *eg* theses, conference papers, report literature, working papers, etc.

Hard disk *see* Disk.

Hardware: the physical equipment used in computing or audio-visual activity.

Head-note: concise statement of the legal principles contained in a law report.

Hospitality (classification): ability of a classification scheme to accommodate changes, especially additional subjects, after initial publication.

Host: a network provider, usually giving access to many databases produced by other organizations, *eg* DIALOG.

House of Commons Papers: papers dealing with House of Commons business or presented to the House as required by legislation or on request of the House.

House of Commons Sessional Papers: public bills, House of Commons papers and Command papers, sometimes assembled on a sessional basis.

House-keeping routines: routine library operations, such as ordering and cataloguing, as distinct from textual scanning, usually in connection with mechanization.

Imprint: (1) publisher's name and address as printed on the title page;

      (2) part of a catalogue entry giving place and date of publication and publisher's name.

Information broker: an independent person or organization hired to obtain information.

Information retrieval system: that part of a library's organization designed to give access to the subject information contained in its stock *eg* catalogues, indexes, shelf arrangement, etc. Frequently used to refer to automated systems.

Interest profile: definition of the information requirements of a person receiving SDI service(s).

Interface: the connection or junction between two systems or parts of the same system.

International law: (1) private: *see* Conflict of laws;

      (2) public: law concerning the rights and duties of sovereign states towards each other, both in peace and war.

Interpolations: alterations, either deliberate or accidental, in the texts of (mainly) classical Roman law jurists by later writers or by Justinian's Commissioners who prepared the Digest, Institutes and Code.

Keywords: significant words in a document which can be used as search terms.

Leges publicae: statutes passed by the vote of the Roman people in the popular assemblies, most of which were of temporary political interest.

Level: in information retrieval, the search request input at one time; can be modified and refined at subsequent levels.

Light pen: light sensitive fibre optic reader used to read barcoded labels.

Local and Personal Acts: Acts of Parliament with restricted local or personal application, enacted on petition from the local or personal sponsor.

Menu: a display of options in a computer system.

Mid user services: independent organizations offering online searches on payment of a fee.

Modem: modulator-demodulator, a device that translates digital signals to or from a computer so that they can be sent via a telecommunications link.

Municipal law: law of an individual sovereign state, as contrasted with public international law.

Non-parliamentary publications: HMSO publications other than sessional papers, parliamentary proceedings, etc.

Noting up: noting that a reported case has been cited, and with what effect, in a later reported case, by means of a manuscript annotation, printed label, card index, printed supplement, etc. (*see also* Shepardize).

Oireachtas: Parliament of the Republic of Ireland.

Online: direct access from a terminal to a computer's central processing unit enabling virtually immediate processing of input.

Packet switching: a method in data communication which arranges messages in self-contained 'packets' and reassembles them at the destination.

Palingenesis: the recreation or reconstruction of Roman law texts which have only survived in fragments or references.

Periodical: serial publication usually produced at regular intervals of less than a year and containing at least some articles and/or news items, as distinct from legislation and case reports.

Phase (classification): relationship between two subjects or two facets of one subject.

Practice book: volume devoted to the practice of a court or category of courts; usually includes court rules, court forms, practice directions, etc.

Practick: in Scots law, a precedent that is not necessarily binding.

Praetorian edicts: yearly Roman proclamations in which the new praetors made known those legal rules which they would apply to the administration of justice.

Precedent book: volume containing standard legal forms, precedents or other documents.

Prelims: all parts of a volume preceding the main text; may include half-title, title, contents list, foreword, introduction, etc.

Primary materials: texts consisting wholly or substantially of the law itself, *eg*, legislation, codes, law reports.

Private Acts: Acts of Parliament not held to be of general application; may be local or personal.

Private international law *see* Conflict of laws.

Program: set of instructions to a computer to perform a specific task.

Promulgation: official publication of a new law.

Range: a series of bays of shelving joined together; may be single- or double-faced.

Reception: (1) adoption in whole or part of the law of one jurisdiction by another jurisdiction.

   (2) the process whereby Roman law and canon law were adopted by some European countries, c.1400–1700.

Record: any document that is specially created as being authentic evidence of a matter of legal importance.

Roman-Dutch law: system of law of Holland from the mid-fifteenth century to the early nineteenth century, based on a mixture of Germanic customary law and Roman law as interpreted in medieval law schools.

Seanad Eireann: Upper House of the Irish Parliament.

Secondary legislation *see* Subordinate legislation.

Secondary materials: texts consisting of commentary on the law, rather than the law itself, *eg*, exposition, criticism, history, philosophy, teaching materials.

see also reference: reference linking catalogue entries under one or more related headings.

see reference: reference from a heading not used in the catalogue to the heading selected for use.

Selective dissemination of information: information service tailored to the specialized interests of individual readers.

Senatus consulta: advice from the Roman Senate which had no legal weight, although it was usually followed, until the second century AD, when it became the expression of the imperial will.

Serial publication: any publication issued at intervals over a long period, *eg*, any newspaper or journal, most law reports, legislative and treaty series; many libraries treat annuals and looseleaf and other encyclopedias as serials.

Shelf list: form of catalogue, arranged strictly in shelf order, with one entry only per item.

Shepardize: in United States practice, to produce a complete citator for a series of court reports.

Sizing: strengthening water-stained or soft leaves of a book by passing them through a bath of hot glue size, after which they are hung to dry.

Slip laws: individual pamphlets containing one enactment in each.

Software: (1) the program or set of instructions which tell a computer what tasks to perform;

(2) slides, records and other audio-visual items containing information, visual or audible, or both.

Sources of law: those repositories of legal rules to which lawyers, especially judges, turn in order to discover what the law is.

Stand-alone: a description of a computer or microcomputer system which can operate independently of other computer systems.

Stop words: common words, such as 'the', 'and', etc., which are nonsearchable in information systems.

Subordinate legislation: legislation made by a person or body, other than the legislature itself, by virtue of powers conferred either by statute or by legislation which is itself made under statutory powers.

Tag: form of coded label attached to an element of information input to a computer to distinguish one category of information from another, *eg*, order number, author, title, etc.

Tail-stamp: stamp bearing the library's insignia embossed at the base of a book's spine.

Telenet: a United States packet switching system.

Textbook: volume containing opinions, and sometimes texts, on the law, having no legal authority.

Thesaurus: a controlled vocabulary used in indexing and/or to provide search terms in a database.

Title-page title: the chief name of an item, including any alternative title but excluding parallel titles and other title information.

Treaty: a written agreement by which two or more states or international organizations create or intend to create a relation between themselves operating within the sphere of international law.

Tymnet: a United States packet switching network.

Uniform title: version of the title of a work selected as the filing medium for all editions and versions of the work, whatever the title-page title may be.

Unit entry: standard catalogue entry, to which may be added headings for co-authors, editor, title, series, subject, etc.

Videotex: generic term covering teletext, *eg*, Ceefax, viewdata, and similar systems.

Viewdata: an interactive information service using a telephone link between a host computer and the user who has a TV set or microcomputer adapted to display information and controlled by a keypad.

Visual display unit: a TV type monitor screen where data can be displayed.

Word-processor: special purpose hardware and software system which provides fairly sophisticated techniques for the input, editing, formatting, storing, output and possibly searching of text.

Year Books: notes made anonymously of debates by judges and counsel of the points at issue in cases, rather than reports of the decisions, during the period c.1270–1535.

Zoom: command in the ESA–IRS host language which analyzes, searches and suggests useful related terms from its thesaurus.

Part I Introduction

1. Law Libraries and Their Users

R. G. LOGAN

Law libraries in the British Isles have a long history (the library of Lincoln's Inn, for example, can be traced back to 1475) and today they form a distinct group in the field of librarianship characterized by their common interest in a specific subject area. At the same time they vary considerably in size, in the category of user to be served, and in their administration and finance. Most law libraries are but one department in a much larger organization. They cannot be said to be autonomous and it is not really possible yet to speak of a network of law libraries. Nevertheless such libraries are sufficiently different for their librarians to band together naturally as a group to exchange experience and seek further means of co-operation.

The purpose of this chapter is to examine the various types of law libraries, so that the chapters which follow may be seen in the context of the pattern of libraries whose staff this *Manual* is intended to assist.

The term 'law library' has been regarded loosely so that it includes general libraries with large or distinctive legal collections.

NATIONAL LIBRARIES

At a time when even the largest law libraries cannot claim self-sufficiency or indeed anything like it, the value of the law holdings in the national libraries as a back-up resource seems obvious. Yet despite certain recent efforts to improve knowledge of these resources they remain under-used. It is possible to find reasons which help to explain this and to suggest how matters could be improved with better understanding on both sides.

The very size of the collections impedes access for lawyers, who are accustomed to libraries arranged to facilitate quick reference. The great research libraries are geared more to readers who wish to retrieve a specific item and consult it at some length. The need to preserve material in perpetuity brings inevitable space and storage problems which are often solved by systems of closed access. Staff are required to devote their main efforts to building and maintaining collections, which are not necessarily arranged on a subject basis, rather than in developing reader services in detail.

None of this really accords with the normal pattern of law library usage. Most legal enquiries are either practical or relate to cross-references already discovered; few lawyers are engaged in leisurely long-term research. The national libraries should therefore be seen by law readers as a supplementary research resource rather than a first resort.

Theoretically the national libraries are open to all but, in practice, security and pressure on reader places means that there are some restrictions on admission. It is therefore usually necessary to show that access is required to material not readily available elsewhere.

England

There is no national law library in the United Kingdom as exists, for example, in the United States; but because it is a legal deposit library (under the Copyright Act 1911 s.15) the British Library Reference Division in London (still widely known by its previous name – the British Museum Library) possesses rich resources in English law. Its holdings of English legal periodicals, for example, are probably the best in the country. Unfortunately the legal material is not kept together as a separate law library but is dispersed throughout the library's holdings. Much of it is in the repository at Woolwich, with a 24-hour delay in delivery to the Reading Room. Neither are there specially qualified subject staff (as in its American counterpart). The result is that, despite the extent of its stock in law, the library is of limited practical value to all but the most determined research worker.

However, there is a small open access law collection in the Official Publications Library (formerly the State Paper Room), which includes good holdings of legislation and some legal digests but not law reports. This reading room has an enquiry desk which deals with legal queries amongst others.

Another part of the British Library is the Science Reference Library. Its Holborn branch in Chancery Lane incorporates the former Patent Office Library. It has strong holdings of patent law and other aspects of intellectual property law. Most recent material is on open access and there are specialist subject staff. The stock includes relevant legal journals and a basic collection of law reports. All of this material is for reference only (though photocopying facilities are available). The British Library Lending Division in Boston Spa, Yorkshire, provides borrowing facilities to libraries (for more details see Chapter 15).

Further information about the legal collections in the British Library can be found in the *Report of the British Library Working Party on Provision for Law*, 1983. One of its recommendations which has been implemented is the establishment of a consultative group to advise the British Library.

Two other legal deposit libraries, the Bodleian Library at Oxford and Cambridge University Library, perform many of the functions of a national library. They are treated in the section on academic libraries below.

Other parts of the British Isles

In Wales the privilege of legal deposit (with minor exceptions in respect of books with short print runs) is accorded to the National Library of Wales. In Scotland the legal deposit collection in law is housed in the Advocates' Library in Edinburgh. Non-members of the Faculty of Advocates can consult books upon application to the National Library of Scotland.

Both the above libraries are basically reference collections. Loan facilities are available to libraries through BLLD.

In the Republic of Ireland the National Library, being an Irish deposit library, holds a good collection of Irish law. In addition, Trinity College, Dublin is a British and Irish deposit library.

PROFESSIONAL LIBRARIES

This group comprises the libraries which are attached to the governing bodies of the legal profession. These collections have a long history and several are housed in buildings of architectural merit. The combination of antiquity and character is attractive to scholars, but it is important to remember that the libraries are funded by their members and are intended to be for their benefit. Most of them are generous in welcoming serious scholars who make prior enquiries but this should not obscure the fact that their first duty is to attend to the needs of their own members.

England and Wales

In England and Wales the legal profession is divided into two branches: barristers (collectively known as the Bar) and solicitors. The Bar is traditionally the senior of the two branches. Barristers are chiefly concerned with drafting legal documents, writing opinions, advising clients, and the preparation and pleading of cases heard in courts of law. The Bar has the monopoly of pleading before the higher courts. Barristers do not seek business directly but have to be 'briefed' by solicitors. There were approximately 5,000 barristers in practice in 1983, the majority of which were to be found in London, although the numbers practising in the provinces are growing. All barristers are members of one of the four Inns of Court (Lincoln's Inn, Inner Temple, Middle Temple, Gray's Inn) whose origin can be traced back to the fourteenth century. The Inns are independent entities with the legal status of unincorporated associations. They were originally founded to provide legal instruction for prospective lawyers. Apart from providing focal points for the profession and space within their confines for the establishment of chambers, they are, through their Senate and the Bar Council (the representatives of the practising barristers) responsible for many important matters affecting the profession, such as discipline and education – though the actual teaching and examination is performed by the Council of Legal Education on behalf of all the Inns.

The Law Society was founded in 1825 (though an earlier body known as the Society of Gentlemen Practicers in the Courts of Law and Equity preceded it in the eighteenth century) and now regulates the solicitors' branch of the profession by conducting qualifying examinations, granting annual certificates of practice, and maintaining a code of professional ethics. In addition, many of the other functions expected of a professional society are provided (*eg*, publications, social facilities and – not least important – a library). Solicitors are much more numerous than barristers (there were approximately 44,000 in practice in 1983) and are found in nearly every town. Because of this geographical scatter provincial law societies exist in most of the larger centres of population and some provide library services to their members.

It may be noticed that the professional libraries are concentrated in 'legal' London. This is due to the fact that the major courts in England and Wales have been located in that area since the thirteenth century and the professional bodies naturally wished to establish themselves nearby. Since the Inns and (later) the Law Society were also responsible for the education of their members – in the absence of academic courses in law at the universities (see page 19) – their libraries assumed a wider role than that of merely providing day to day information for the practising solicitor or barrister. The net result has been, in a sense, an over-provision of legal resources in the capital while many other parts of the country lag far behind.

Inns of Court

The exact dates of the foundations of the Inn libraries are uncertain, but the records available indicate that such were in existence in 1475 (Lincoln's Inn), 1506 (Inner Temple), 1521 (Gray's Inn) or, in the case of the Middle Temple, some time in the early sixteenth century. Their collections are sizeable and rich in rare historical material, although owing to the depredation of enemy bombs during the Second World War much that was irreplaceable was destroyed. In common with many other society libraries whose origins precede the present century, their collections are much more cosmopolitan than their present subject interests would indicate; apart from a wide range of legal material there can be found holdings in history, literature, topography, biography, and similar subjects. Unfortunately modern financial limitations no longer permit such excursions into alien territory and indeed the Inns struggle to maintain adequate coverage of the legal literature which may be required by the Bar. There has been some co-operation in the acquisition of Commonwealth law and Middle Temple has a special collection of American law which is strong on law reports. More formal co-operation is illustrated by the Inns of Court European Communities Law Library, established in 1972 and also housed in the Middle Temple Library. It has a comprehensive collection of community law material together with selective coverage of the laws of the original six member states. It is open to the Bar and to solicitors, by arrangement with the Law Society.

The Inn libraries principally serve two groups of user. Firstly, they exist to meet the needs of their members, most of whom are practising barristers. Since the majority of these practise in London, the Inns act as working libraries for them in the form of back-up facilities to the books they possess in chambers. The library stock is for reference use only, though special arrangements may be made to take material into court if it is not readily available elsewhere. Like many other special libraries, they give emphasis to assistance to readers, and since information is frequently required at short notice there is need for assistance with speed – the user cannot wait until next week if the case is being heard tomorrow!

Considering their relative shortage of staff (with the intermittent exception of Middle Temple) the Inn libraries can be proud of their achievements in assisting readers. Inner Temple, Lincoln's Inn and Middle Temple provide various forms of indexing services, the last two in some detail. Inner Temple has staff in the library to answer enquiries and Middle Temple has a service point. The Middle Temple library staff have written a most helpful series of guides to the use of the library.

The second group of users served is that of students studying for the Bar examinations. For them, the Inn libraries provide a place of study where, because of their reference nature, all of the standard works, reports, statutes, etc. are always to hand. There is little attempt, however, as in other libraries serving students, to make special provision for student needs. Lincoln's Inn has a special collection of textbooks for students and a separate students' reading room with law reports. Gray's Inn is used extensively by students due to its proximity to the Council of Legal Education.

It has already been mentioned that these libraries will do their best to help serious research scholars who give prior notice of their needs. In addition there is another class of user, best described as the general public, who are attracted to the libraries by their nature and location. Any assistance given to such users must obviously depend on the staff time left after the Inns' own members have received adequate attention.

The libraries also attract users interested in the areas in which they specialize under the co-operation scheme. These areas are: European Community law and American law (Middle Temple), Commonwealth law reports (Inner Temple), Commonwealth legislation (Lincoln's Inn) and international law (Gray's Inn).

Law Societies

In addition to the Law Society in London which regulates the solicitors' profession, there are a large number of London and provincial local law societies. These are independent of the Law Society (although in general they co-operate closely with it) and exist to provide a forum and some services to their members. In a few cases these services include a library.

The development of a significant library was one of the purposes behind the creation in 1825, of the body which later became the Law Society. The library was founded in 1828 on the same site in Chancery Lane on which it stands at the present day. The holdings now amount to 70,000 volumes, a large amount of non-legal material having been disposed of in the last twenty years. The library has a comprehensive collection of English law, omitting the more basic student textbooks, and adequate holdings of Scottish and Irish law together with a limited amount of European Communities material. It retains copies of old editions of textbooks and also has a good set of Local, Personal and Private Acts (the only comparable sets are in the British Library Official Publications Library, the Bodleian Law Library and the House of Lords Record Office) and other parliamentary papers. Current purchasing policy is geared to the needs of a modern practitioners' reference library. In general, use of the library is restricted to solicitors and their clerks and there are no loan services. It is comparatively well staffed by professional librarians, who operate an enquiry service for members, whether by personal visit, telephone, telex or letter, and a photocopying service. Various indexes are maintained in the library. About half the enquiries received by the library come from provincial members.

It is difficult to determine how many local law society libraries are still in existence. Quite a number are known to have been disposed of in recent years as the costs of upkeep have risen. Those that survive vary considerably in size and level of service, some being little more than a collection of books in an office.

Perhaps the largest and most active local law society library is that at Birmingham. Founded in 1818, it has the distinction of being the oldest law society library in the country, and contains some rare and valuable early legal material. There are also active libraries at Bristol and Liverpool. A number of other such libraries can be identified by consulting the *Directory of law libraries*, 2nd edn., 1984.

In some areas where there is no substantial practitioners' library the legal profession has formal or informal links with the local university law library.

Scotland

In Scotland the Faculty of Advocates governs the senior branch of the profession; Scottish solicitors come under the aegis of the Law Society of Scotland, but they may also belong to any one of various local societies for law agents, the best known of which are the Society of Advocates in Aberdeen and the Royal Faculty of Procurators in Glasgow. There are two national professional law societies in Scotland, namely, the Society of Writers to Her Majesty's Signet (WS Society) and the Society of Solicitors in the Supreme Courts of Scotland (SSC Society).

Scottish professional law libraries have tended to accumulate more general collections than similar libraries in England, perhaps due to the much smaller corpus of Scottish legal literature. The original Advocates' Library, which was founded in 1682 and enjoyed copyright privileges, was presented to the nation by the Faculty in 1925 and became the National Library of Scotland. The law books were retained to form the nucleus of the present library, now totalling some 100,000 volumes, and most legal publications received by the National Library under the copyright provisions are deposited in the Advocates' Library. These are available to the public at the National Library, so that, in a sense, the Advocates' Library may be said to be the national law library for Scotland.

The Signet (or WS) Library in Edinburgh, founded in 1722, was in its time the most important private general library in Scotland. However, in recent years many of the non-legal and non-Scottish books have been sold and the library now comprises some 65,000 items, about half of which pertain to law. The library is famed for the splendour of its Upper Library, which now houses the collection of Scottish books.

Similarly, the general books in the SSC Library in Edinburgh, the Advocates' Library in Aberdeen, and the Procurators' Library in Glasgow have been sold and the libraries are now devoted exclusively to law. The last-named is open to university teachers as well as to members and their staffs, and it operates a branch library at the Sheriff Court in Glasgow for the use of sheriffs and judges. It may be noted that the WS and SSC Libraries lend many volumes for use in the Court of Session.

Other parts of the United Kingdom

In Northern Ireland judges and members of the profession have access to the Law Faculty Library of Queen's University,

Belfast. The Northern Ireland Law Society is a reference library for the use of solicitors.

The Isle of Man Law Society and the Jersey Law Society have libraries specialising in local laws which are available to their members.

Republic of Ireland

King's Inns serves a similar function for the Irish Bar as is performed by the Inns of Court in London. Its origins are as old as its English counterparts but the library can be traced back only to 1787. Its present stock contains strong holdings of Irish and English law. Its facilities are extended to members of the Honourable Society of King's Inns including judges, barristers and students. Like its English and Scottish equivalents it is housed in premises in Dublin which reflect the glories and splendours of a bygone age.

The Incorporated Law Society of Ireland, also situated in Dublin, is similar in function to the Law Society in London and its library operates in a similar fashion, although on a smaller scale.

COURT LIBRARIES

Court libraries serve the judges who sit in those courts and the counsel who appear before them. Under the provisions of the Courts Act 1971 the Lord Chancellor's Office has overall responsibility for the administration of library services to the Supreme Court and the county courts. These court libraries vary considerably in their provision; some courts in fact have no library at all. But recent years have seen some improvements in the court library system. In 1977 the post of Supreme Court Librarian was created with the additional responsibility of Libraries Adviser to the Lord Chancellor's Office. A few years later this post was divided by the further creation of a post of Librarian to the Lord Chancellor's Office. In 1983 the three libraries housed within the Royal Courts of Justice were merged into one unified system under the direction of the Supreme Court Librarian.

Information on court libraries was previously hard to obtain but there is a good account in the British Library report by Miskin, 1981, at pp. 24–28.

The Supreme Court of Judicature for England and Wales – consisting of the Court of Appeal and the High Court of Judicature – sits at the Royal Courts of Justice in the Strand, London, and it is here that court library provision is most comprehensive. The library system comprises the Supreme Court Library, the Bar Library and the Probate Library. The Lord Chancellor's Department has responsibility for their administration and staffing but the Senate of the Inns of Court makes a substantial financial contribution to the maintenance of the collections and retains ownership of the Bar Library stock.

The most recently founded of the three libraries, the Supreme Court Library, is now the most important and ranks as one of the major law libraries in the country. Its stock includes considerable duplication (Miskin quotes 275 sets of the *Supreme Court Practice* and 112 sets of the *Law Reports*). Books are lent to judges, court officers and other staff of the Lord Chancellor's Department. Counsel may borrow books for use in court and they and litigants in person may use the library for reference. The library, which also maintains various smaller libraries scattered through the courts, has made a successful effort to extend its services in recent years. It issues a library bulletin and maintains an index to the Court of Appeal transcripts. The library was established in 1968 and is housed in modern premises in the Queen's Building.

Within the same building is situated the Probate Library, which was originally established in 1831. This is a subscription library for members of the Bar and all material may be borrowed.

The Bar Library was founded in 1883 as a joint venture by the four Inns of Court. It provides a basic working collection on English law. It is principally a reference library, although material may be borrowed for use in court.

In London other notable court libraries are those at the Central Criminal Court (the Old Bailey), which serves a similar purpose on a reduced scale to the Bar Library and includes a good collection on criminal law, and the Judicial Committee of the Privy Council, which is available only to members of their Lordships' Board and to barristers engaged in cases before the Board. Mention should also be made of the House of Lords Library (see page 18) which serves as the court library for the highest appellate court in the land.

Outside London, library provision in the courts is sparse and many of the smaller collections are provided for the judges only rather than for the Bar. These libraries are tabulated by circuit in the Miskin report. In Birmingham, Sheffield and Leeds the public libraries provide a service to the courts. Special mention must be made of the range of services provided at the library of Manchester Crown Court.

In other parts of the British Isles court libraries are as undeveloped as they are in the English provinces. In Ireland there is the Law Library at the Four Courts in Dublin, which is administered by the General Council of the Bar of Ireland and ranks as a substantial library. And in Guernsey there is a small Royal Court Library.

LAW FIRM LIBRARIES

In the first edition of this *Manual* law firm libraries rated only a single paragraph under the heading of 'miscellaneous libraries'. It is a measure of their growth in the last decade that they now fully merit a section of their own. Indeed few, if any, areas in the whole field of librarianship have shown such expansion in terms of the recruitment of professional staff within that period.

The reasons for this include: the removal of partnership restrictions (see Companies Act 1967 s.120), resulting in the development of much larger City firms able to support ancillary staff; the existing and successful example of firm libraries in America; the increasing specialization of City firms with a corresponding demand for more detailed information work; and the increasing complexity of legal and commercial information retrieval. Once the idea of employing professional library staff had been tried by a few of the largest firms and seen to work, others were bound to follow. Much is owed to the dedicated hard work of those appointed to those first posts.

The actual number of firms employing librarians is difficult to calculate as reliable information is not available. Probably about forty firms in the City do so. Provincial firms were slow to follow but a number have now done so, including firms in Birmingham, Manchester and Cardiff and in smaller legal centres such as Bedford and Bradford. Some of the more established firm libraries employ additional professional library staff.

These are very much private libraries in that they exist solely to serve the needs of the firm and are not available to litigants or outside users. Their purpose is to improve the profitability of the firm by the efficient management of its information resources which, in addition to the bookstock, normally include such materials as information files, commercial notices and in-house precedents. The bookstock is usually quite small (about 5,000 volumes is average) and consists of law reports, legislation and standard texts on the subjects in which the firm practises.

Library practice in firm libraries shows marked differences from that in other types of law library. There is less emphasis on the custodial role and more on the provision of a rapid information service. Budgeting and financial constraints are less of a problem because it is in the firm's interest to buy what it really needs. Thus all purchases are expected to be justified by use; duplicate copies are bought as required. The limited stock means that much reliance is placed on inter-library co-operation and contacts with the larger libraries. In London the firm librarians have formed themselves into the City Law Librarians Group, which meets regularly and maintains a union list of foreign and less usual holdings in member libraries. In addition to such mutual co-operation these libraries make regular use of facilities such as the City Business Library, the Guildhall Library, the Law Society Library, the Institute of Advanced Legal Studies Library and the Law Notes Lending Library. Another regular duty is to locate or purchase relevant new government publications.

Because of their private nature it would be invidious to mention individual libraries. The better established ones are well known to BIALL members through the professional activities of their staff.

GOVERNMENT LIBRARIES

Unlike some other countries, the United Kingdom does not possess a major government law library. All official libraries, however, have some legal connotations in that their primary function is to serve the various organs of state. Hence official documents and basic legal materials in their specialist fields are to be found within their collections. For example, the library of the Board of Inland Revenue contains material on tax law and the direct taxation systems of different countries; the Department of Trade and Industry contains a major reference library on commercial law; the Foreign and Commonwealth Office Library has special collections on international law, Community law and the law of Commonwealth countries – including a virtually complete set of Commonwealth legislation; the Home Office Library is particularly strong on criminal law and has a special collection of penal codes and codes of criminal procedure of overseas countries. Other special collections are to be found in the libraries of the Department of the Environment and the Department of Education and Science.

Among non-Departmental libraries which have legal collections, mention may be made of the Office of Fair Trading in London (consumer legislation of other countries), the Health and Safety Executive in London and Sheffield (law on health and safety at work) and the Equal Opportunities Commission in Manchester (sex discrimination and equal pay).

There are three government libraries principally devoted to law: those at the Law Commission, the Treasury Solicitor's Department and the Lord Chancellor's Department.

The Law Commission for England and Wales and a similar body for Scotland were established by the Law Commissions Act 1965 'to take and keep under review all the law with which they are respectively concerned, with a view to its systematic development and reform, including in particular the codification of such law, the elimination of anomalies, the repeal of obsolete and unnecessary enactments, the reduction of the number of separate enactments and generally the simplification and modernization of the law'. The Law Commission established a library almost immediately in London with the aim of building up a collection geared to the current work of the Commission and ultimately to house an important collection of law reform material obtained from other Commonwealth countries. It now contains a substantial collection, mainly on English Law – though general social science materials form a significant part of the stock (for it is difficult to consider reforms in the law without studying the relevant social background). Starting, as it did, from scratch the library was not hamstrung by procedures from the past and it is interesting to note that it was the first British library to adopt the *Classification scheme for law books* devised by E.M. Moys (see page 786).

The library of the Scottish Law Commission is similar in scope to its English cousin but smaller in size. However, it now has a full-time librarian and considerable expansion has taken place.

The office of Treasury Solicitor dates back to at least 1655 and his department provides a legal service for government departments not possessing their own legal sections. The library acts as a working library for the legal staff of the department. For some years it issued its own printed *Catalogue*, 6th edn.1977.

The Lord Chancellor's Department maintains a small law library and its librarian acts as libraries advisor to the Department.

Government libraries in other parts of the British Isles include those of the Department of the Director of Public Prosecutions in Belfast and the Attorney General's Chambers in the Isle of Man. The latter compiles a current awareness service on Manx law.

Government libraries were set up to serve the staffs of those particular departments and offices and are therefore not open to the public in the same way as national libraries. Many government libraries, however, are prepared to admit research workers and others who have a special interest in their holdings, generally upon prior application only.

PARLIAMENTARY LIBRARIES

In most countries the libraries of the legislature – as the main law-making body in the land – have extensive holdings of legal literature. In the United States, for example, the Law Library of Congress is the largest law library in the country. While no legislative body within the British Isles can boast of such a collection, each does contain within its library a significant amount of legal material, for access to legal information is obviously of great importance to our legislators.

The two most notable legislative libraries are those of the House of Commons and the House of Lords at the Palace of Westminster. The Commons Library provides for Members of Parliament a working law library, *ie* current editions of the more important texts and reference books on all major aspects of English and Scots law, together with reports, statutes and other such material relevant to those countries. There is a natural emphasis on statutory material. This and similar items on the law of the European Communities is exploited by a highly sophisticated information service, the smooth functioning of which is ensured by a realistic level of staffing which enables proper research assistance to be given to Members. The public are not admitted to the library but the associated Public Information Office answers telephone enquiries relating to current Bills and Acts and Parliamentary proceedings by reference to the retrieval system POLIS.

The law collection in the Lords Library is far more comprehensive than that in the Commons since the Lords of Appeal in Ordinary, sitting in the House, form the highest court of appeal in the land and the library is in effect their court library. This does have the effect of inflating the apparent size of the law holdings, for the Lords of Appeal sit as a court of five and each judge must have his copy of the volumes cited, so five copies of the more usual series are held. The library has particularly good holdings of early legislation.

In other parts of the British Isles, Stormont in Northern Ireland, the Dáil in the Irish Republic and their counterparts in the Isle of Man and the Channel Islands possess libraries for their respective members which contain, among other subjects, material on law.

ACADEMIC LIBRARIES

In the first edition of the *Manual* academic law libraries were described as 'the most rapidly expanding sector of the law library network today'. Only a decade later almost the reverse is true. Public expenditure limitations have led to reductions in book budgets, staffing ratios, opening hours and binding. There has been some investment in new technology but this is insufficient to sustain the initiative of the early 1970s. The mantle of 'most expanding sector' has long since been passed to the law firm libraries. Nevertheless the libraries grouped hereunder contain some outstanding collections, often housed in buildings of architectural merit.

Background

From their earliest days the Inns of Court had been teaching institutions; but their staple subject had been English Law for practitioners. Civil law was outside their field of interest but, as early as the thirteenth century, Roman law (upon which civil law is based) was being taught as a subject in the two ancient universities at Oxford and Cambridge. It was not, however, until the time of Henry VIII that such teaching was organized on a proper footing with the foundation of chairs of civil law at those institutions in 1538. The common law continued to be excluded from their curricula, however, until 1753 when Blackstone, who was a Fellow of All Souls, gave the first of a series of formal lectures at Oxford on the subject. This was originally a private venture, but thanks to the generosity of Viner – who left the proceeds of his *Abridgement*, 1742–58, and other monies to the University – a chair in common law was endowed there in 1758, and Blackstone became the first Vinerian Professor. From then until his resignation in 1756 he delivered lectures which were later to form the basis of his famous *Commentaries*, 1765–9; but after his resignation the teaching of common law at Oxford again fell into abeyance. In the early nineteenth century attempts were again made to initiate courses in common law at the universities. Thus in 1800 the Downing Professorship of the Laws of England was founded at Cambridge, but it was not until the foundation of University College London in 1826 that the first modern university law school appeared in this country. A chair of law was also established at King's College, London, in 1831. However, it was not until the second half of the century that law teaching as we now know it took firm root in English universities, when several courses were established and new professorial chairs installed at the above mentioned institutions. By 1908, with the growth of the civic universities, there were eight law faculties in England and Wales. But most were relatively small and, even by 1938, there were only 1,500 undergraduate students reading law in this country. By 1970 this number had risen steadily to 5,000. The next few years saw a period of rapid expansion as the *Report of the Committee on Legal Education,* (Ormrod), 1971, was followed by swelling law faculties and the creation of new polytechnic law departments. By 1977 numbers had reached a plateau of around 12,000, where they remain.

There are now 34 universities and 22 non-university institutions, mainly polytechnics, in England and Wales offering undergraduate courses in which law is the sole or principal component. In addition five universities in Scotland, one in Northern Ireland and four university colleges in the Republic of Ireland do so. In each of these institutions there is a law library (either as a separate entity or as part of the main library), providing not only collections of legal materials but also – of equal importance – places in which to study.

There are a number of other universities, polytechnics and colleges of higher education which teach law as a constituent part of non-legal degree courses, *eg* business studies or town planning. These institutions also have law collections in their libraries.

Academic law libraries number three particular groups among their users: undergraduates, who need access to the basic materials required for their first degree course – multiple copies of the most commonly cited items are often needed to make adequate provision for the numbers of students involved; postgraduate students, who require detailed provision in their special fields of study; and the teaching staff, whose needs are broadly similar to those of the postgraduates, and who need in addition to be kept abreast of the latest developments in the law in general as well as in their own particular subject fields.

Such libraries can also expect to receive requests for access to their collections from neighbouring academic institutions, the local legal profession, and the general public, including litigants in person. How much assistance is rendered to such groups is a matter of internal policy. It is becoming more common to levy a charge on non-members, especially corporate ones. But in many cases an academic law library is much the largest law library in the area and may be regarded as having some public responsibilities on account of this.

Standards of provision

In the 1960s and 1970s a considerable influence was exerted on the development of law libraries in universities (and latterly polytechnics) by the Society of Public Teachers of Law's *Statement of proposed minimum library holdings for law libraries in England and Wales*. This was first published in September 1958 as a result of the deficiencies revealed by a survey conducted the previous year. The *Statement* had no binding authority but since it gave law faculties a realistic standard to aim at it was widely adopted, resulting in a planned expansion of university law libraries. (It is doubtful if similar standards would have been so readily accepted if proposed by librarians.)

Apart from stock, the original *Statement* dealt with staff, seating accommodation, finance and other matters which are discussed elsewhere in this *Manual*. The revised statements of 1970 and 1975 in the *Journal of the Society of Public Teachers of Law*, n.s., vol. 11, 1970–1, pp. 90–103 and vol. 13, 1974–5, pp. 332–41 were less comprehensive and concentrated on up-dating the recommended minimum stock provision. The revisions were a consequence of changes in academic law teaching which reflected a trend towards broader syllabuses and of the expansion in student numbers following the Ormrod Report and the foundation of polytechnic law schools. However, these later standards were less readily achieved by newer institutions, particularly in terms of multiple copies and seating accommodation, as they soon encountered budgetary and storage problems. The rapid inflation of the 1970s soon rendered the SPTL *Statement* meaningless as a price guide.

A further SPTL statement of the provision of European Communities material in the *Journal of the Society of Public Teachers of Law*, n.s., vol. 13, 1974–5, pp. 113–41 appeared conveniently at a time when university law libraries received special funding to establish European Communities collections following the accession of the United Kingdom in 1973. This statement included textbook material and extended to coverage of the laws of the continental member states. Revised SPTL standards were published in *Legal Studies*, vol. 6, 1986.

In terms of holdings, academic law libraries vary considerably, both in size and coverage. The SPTL *Statements* suggest a basic minimum stock, which has generally been achieved, but beyond that differences are determined by many factors which include the size and wealth of the organization, the length of time that the law library has been established, the variety of courses taught, the relationship of the law school to other academic departments within the institution, the existence of special subject collections, and participation in shared acquisition schemes. A large percentage of the stock in most of these libraries is for reference only, being composed of law reports, legislation, sets of periodicals, and standard textbooks. Duplication of textbooks provided is common in order to meet the pattern of users' requirements.

Academic legal education today tends to be based on lectures and tutorials, the latter being supplemented with detailed required reading each week. Because generally only a single statute or case is required from each volume consulted, the process of working through a reading list can involve the student in using a great many volumes in a relatively short time. This brings with it pressure on reading places in the law library and pressure on particular items for a defined period. Many libraries have countered the latter problem by introducing controlled access collections which are under the control of library staff who issue items against a signature for limited periods only.

Centralization versus decentralization

One of the main differences within this group is that of the relationship with the main university or polytechnic library, *ie* whether the law collection is placed in a separate departmental library or within the central library. Today financial consider-ations are paramount in determining the choice but in an ideal world it is debatable which option librarians and law teachers would now favour. The tradition that librarians favour cen-tralization and law teachers favour decentralization seems over-simplistic. The SPTL evidence to the Parry Committee (University Grants Committee, *Report of the Committee on Libraries*, 1967), and the preamble to their minimum holdings list both came down on the side of departmental libraries, although that view was not reached unanimously. They stressed that law books, reports, etc., are essential to the law student and teacher in the same way that laboratory equipment and materials are essential in science teaching. Because of this the law library should be within the law school building. This argument still has some merit but it has been weakened by the increasingly inter-disciplinary nature of legal studies, which refers students to various official publications and materials in fields such as sociology, criminology, business studies, political science, linguistics and philosophy. Most of this material is more conveniently kept in the central library.

The case for independent law libraries is ever harder to justify, particularly in terms of staffing and opening hours where costs soon mount. There is no real evidence as to which form of provision provides the better service. What is appar-ent is that law students spend about half of their working time during the day in lectures and tutorials and the other half in fairly intensive use of the library. Thus, there are considerable logistical advantages in having the library stock adjacent to the teaching facilities. One solution is to have a separate law school library. Two other solutions which have proved quite success-ful are to provide a basic undergraduate reference collection in the law department with the major part of the law stock in the central library and to site the law school next to or nearby the central library.

Most institutions will by now have found the solution best

suited to their needs and the pace of change in this area has slowed virtually to a halt.

Educating the user

Various methods of teaching use of the law library are used at present, *eg* lectures, practical projects, tape/slide presentations, tape-recorded self-instruction sessions, videotapes, etc. There is a good basic textbook for beginners in Dane, J. and Thomas, P. A., *How to use a law library*, 1979. For details see Chapter 15.

There is no doubt that such instruction should form an integral part of every undergraduate law course and therefore that academic law librarians should regard this as one of the most significant duties which they can perform for their users.

England and Wales

Out of all the academic law libraries in the United Kingdom there are three which predominate in terms of their collections and facilities: the Bodleian Law Library at the University of Oxford, the Squire Law Library at the University of Cambridge, and the Institute of Advanced Legal Studies Library at the University of London.

The Bodleian Law Library is the largest law library in the United Kingdom (and probably in the Commonwealth). It is housed in fine premises, built with the financial assistance of the Rockefeller Foundation and opened in 1964. It is administratively part of the main Bodleian Library and thus receives virtually all law books deposited there under the provisions of the Copyright Act. This includes criminology and many law books for non-lawyers. Unlike most of the other deposit libraries the law collection is available on open access as a classified unit and all the looseleaf services are filed up to date. The holdings, apart from English Law, are particularly strong in legal materials from the Commonwealth and primary materials from the United States of America (the library has the most complete collection of state legislation in the country). There are also above-average collections of Roman

Law and jurisprudence and adequate holdings of foreign law. The library is for reference use only, like the main Bodleian. The latter still contains most pre-1800 law books, canon law, and many official papers of interest to lawyers.

The Codrington Library at All Souls College also has a fine law collection which often supplements the Bodleian in respect of older material. Its magnificent Great Library, some 200 feet in length, provides a memorable and unusual environment for research scholars. It is dominated by a bust of Blackstone, once a Fellow of All Souls.

The Squire Law Library at Cambridge has had a confusing history in recent years. Until 1982 it was a faculty library, although for some years it enjoyed an arrangement with the University Library whereby it acquired the law books deposited there under the Copyright Act unless those books were deemed to be of interest to readers other than lawyers. This arrangement, never completely satisfactory, eventually resulted in unacceptable delays in book supply and was abandoned. However, in 1982 administrative control of the library passed from the Faculty of Law to the University Library, again giving it access to the deposit collection when required. This erratic history has not helped either the development of the Squire or the building up of a unified law collection in the University Library, where a large part of the deposited books remain. The Squire has also been hampered by being housed in old premises unsuitable for a quick reference library and by relatively ungenerous staffing levels. Nevertheless it has fine all-round holdings and is particularly good on international law. The library's *Catalogue* was published in fourteen volumes in 1974, including the classification scheme devised by Mr W. A. Steiner. Unfortunately it has not proved possible so far to maintain the computer catalogue which he established.

Although there are a number of significant collections of legal material in the various libraries within the University of London, among which there is a marked measure of co-operative provision, the library of the Institute of Advanced Legal Studies is by far the most prominent. The Institute itself is unique in British legal education in that it is solely for postgraduate students (the University has a number of such institutes in various subject fields). It was set up in 1947, with the aid of grants from such bodies as the Ford and Nuffield Foundations for special collections of American and Commonwealth materials. The establishment of an adequate research library was regarded as a priority and has been pursued so vigorously that it now ranks second in size amongst British law libraries. In 1969, together with the Middle Temple Library, it was designated by the Foundation for Overseas Libraries of American Law as one of the two centres in London which would receive material with a view to establishing special collections in American law. The library has good all-round holdings, including West European law. It probably has the best collection of legal bibliographies in the country. The Institute's library staff have made a notable contribution to professional developments in law librarianship in Britain. After being housed for nearly thirty years in a building which, while retaining its own quaint character, was far from adequate for this purpose, the library moved into new premises in Charles Clore House in 1975.

The Institute is perhaps best known to law librarians for its bibliographical activities. Unfortunately this work has largely fallen victim to the cuts in public expenditure, as there is no money to provide the additional staff that would be necessary now that the library has increased in size and usage. Nevertheless the achievements of the past programme remain solid. Publications include the series of union lists, the most widely used of which is the *Union list of legal periodicals*, 4th edn., 1978, the *List of legal research topics*, 3rd edn., 1985, which gives details of theses completed or in progress for higher degrees in law in the United Kingdom, and the *Index to foreign legal periodicals*. The latter was published in co-operation with the American Association of Law Libraries at the Institute from 1960 to 1983, when the office moved to the University of California. The planning, and later the editing, of the *Index* reflect the abilities of the Institute's two outstanding law librarians, the late Mr K. Howard Drake and Mr W. A. Steiner.

The colleges in the University of London which offer undergraduate courses in law all have substantial law libraries of their own. In addition they specialize in particular subject areas: King's College (German and Italian law, medical ethics, military law), British Library of Political and Economic Science at the London School of Economics and Political Science (European Communities Documentation Centre, depository library for United States federal documents and United Nations publications), Queen Mary College (European Communities, commercial law, intellectual property law), School of Oriental and African Studies (Oriental and African law) and University College London (Roman law, Soviet law).

Provincial university law libraries are housed in a variety of settings *eg*, separate libraries (within their university library systems) at Birmingham and Nottingham, the major part of a site library at Sheffield, a separate reading room with shared security facilities at Bristol, and an integral part of the main library at Hull, Kent, Leicester and East Anglia.

Polytechnic law libraries are generally integrated within the main library or, in several cases, a site library. Polytechnic law librarians have consulted as a group on an occasional basis under the auspices of COPOL (Council of Polytechnic Librarians).

Other parts of the British Isles

Academic libraries in other parts of the British Isles closely resemble those in England and Wales. Where there is a law department there is a collection of legal material either in a separate library, as in Edinburgh University, or as part of the main library, as at the University of Strathclyde. In Wales there can be found at Cardiff the unusual spectacle of two law libraries in the same building, serving University College Cardiff and UWIST, although there are proposals for a merger in existence. In Northern Ireland there are two law collections within Queen's University, Belfast, administered by the University Library and by the Institute of Professional Legal Studies, which caters for graduates preparing for entry into the legal profession. In the Republic of Ireland the most comprehensive law library is that of Trinity College, Dublin, which has legal deposit privileges similar to those enjoyed by Oxford and Cambridge. University College Dublin has a good collection of British and Irish law in addition to American and European materials.

PUBLIC LIBRARIES

Little comprehensive information has been collected about law collections in public libraries and with the present interest in access to the law for the layman this would appear to be a fruitful field for research. Law librarianship poses obvious problems for public librarians in terms of budgeting, access to current material and, most important of all, the distinction between bibliographic and legal advice.

Nevertheless the coverage of law by public libraries is often surprisingly good and most municipal libraries have at least a basic collection of a set of statutes, a set of law reports, a digest and some leading textbooks. If this material is not always exploited as it might be this is scarcely the fault of the staff, who either lack training in legal enquiry work or lack exposure to the regularity of enquiries which builds confidence in handling them.

In London there are good legal collections at the City Business Library, the Guildhall Library, and the London Borough of Camden (Holborn Reference Library), Hammersmith and Westminster. Hammersmith at one time had responsibility for law under the co-operative acquisition scheme LASER (London and South-Eastern Region library scheme) but responsibility for this was moved to Buckinghamshire County Library at the beginning of 1976. The coverage provided by the scheme appears to have lapsed. However Hammersmith still tries to maintain a good law collection. The Holborn Reference Library is situated in 'legal London' and is heavily used by students from the nearby College of Law.

Outside London the best coverage is provided by the large city libraries of Birmingham (Social Science Department of the Reference Library), Liverpool (Commercial and Social Sciences Library), Manchester (Social Sciences Library) and Sheffield (Commerce and Technology Library). The relevant enquiry points are given above, although the collections may be scattered. At Leeds there is a Law Library in the courts building. Although in theory 'public', access is restricted to the legal profession while the courts are sitting and in general non-lawyers have to request items for consultation in the City Reference Library.

In Scotland there are good holdings of law at the Mitchell Library in Glasgow (Social Sciences Department).

In some public libraries legal information enquiries from businesses are handled as part of the commercial information service. In general there are few posts in which the principal part of the job involves law librarianship. Leeds has a Law Librarian who administers the library at the courts. Sheffield has a Commerce and Law Librarian and the Holborn Reference Library has a Commercial and Legal Information Officer.

MISCELLANEOUS LIBRARIES

Apart from the major groups of law libraries described above there are a number of other libraries with legal collections which should be noted.

The Law Notes Lending Library in Chancery Lane, London, is one of the very few commercial lending libraries left in the country and is the only one devoted to law books (perhaps the Probate Library in the Royal Courts of Justice could also be regarded as a commercial library, but it has a very restricted clientele and therefore can best be regarded as a practitioners' library). The advantages of such a library include: no restriction on membership other than payment of the requisite subscription; all material is available for loan (many law libraries are for reference use only); books may be kept out indefinitely, provided the subscription has not expired; the ability to borrow new books very shortly after publication, etc. The advantage of this type of library service to those remote from other law libraries is obvious, but the service is also of value to practitioners who wish to supplement their own libraries or to borrow material not loaned by their Inn or Law Society library. Even other libraries can find that a subscription is a useful way of supplementing their own holdings, and it is noticeable that law firm libraries make good use of this facility. The success of such a fee-paying library is indicative of the need which it meets.

The Radzinowicz Library of Criminology at the Institute of Criminology, University of Cambridge, provides excellent coverage of its topic and related matters. Its catalogue was published in six volumes in 1979.

The Reference Library of the US International Communication Agency at the United States Embassy in London provides information on United States government agencies, foreign and domestic policies, social and economic issues, and legislative developments. It has access to much federal material not readily available in this country.

The European Communities Office Library in London has a collection which covers European documentation and the legal system of the Communities.

There are a number of society, professional association, industrial and educational libraries which include law as a subsidiary part of their collection but are worthy of note for their special subject interests. Their identities can be traced through the *Directory of law libraries*. Some examples are: Royal Commonwealth Society, Royal Institution of Chartered Surveyors, National Coal Board, and Bramshill Police Staff College.

PROFESSIONAL ASSOCIATIONS FOR LAW LIBRARIANS

BIALL

The British and Irish Association of Law Librarians was founded in 1969. Earlier initiatives to establish such a group had foundered because of small numbers, the difficulty of reconciling the interests of staff from diverse types of library, and poor staffing levels with the resultant difficulty in obtaining time off for meetings. Few law librarians were members of the Library Association and it was thus necessary to start an independent group. The impetus for this came from two workshops held in 1968, one at Harrogate organised by Don Daintree for the Leeds College of Commerce (later Leeds Polytechnic) and one at Cambridge organised by Willi Steiner for the International Association of Law Libraries. The benefits gained by the participants excited a determination that such gatherings should continue and BIALL was founded at a second Harrogate workshop a year later.

By 1986 BIALL had grown to over 300 members, personal and institutional, from both home and overseas. It draws its members from many different types of library and from legal publishers. Perhaps one of BIALL's strengths is that it has never been dominated by one particular group of libraries.

BIALL is now administered by a Council, comprising five elected members and the four elected officers: Chairman, Secretary, Treasurer and Editor. It maintains standing committees on cataloguing and classification, education and training, library provision and information services, official publications, and publications. It organizes a duplicate exchange scheme, runs an annual conference, and plans other visits and short courses, often in association with other bodies. It keeps a watching brief on all matters of professional interest to law librarians and has prepared various reports and evidence for official committees.

For a small association BIALL has achieved much. The two activities which are given priority, because of their enduring influence on the development of law librarianship, are publications and conferences.

Publications

The journal *Law Librarian*, 1970–, is issued three times a year and includes news, articles and conference reports. Recently a newsletter has also been circulated to members between issues of the journal. In 1973 a bibliography on *Community law* was published under the editorship of Charlotte Lutyens. A much more ambitious undertaking was the first edition of this *Manual of law librarianship*, 1976, edited by Elizabeth Moys. Two editions of the *Directory of law libraries* have been prepared by Barbara Mangles, 1976, and Christine Miskin, 1984. An *Index to legal essays 1975–79* edited by Barbara Wells [*née* Tearle] was published in 1983.

Other associations

Apart from BIALL there are national or regional associations of law librarians in the United States of America, Canada, the Federal Republic of Germany, Australia, Japan, South Africa, Netherlands, Nigeria, the Philippines, and the Caribbean.

The American Association of Law Libraries, founded in 1906, is much the oldest and largest of these bodies. It organizes an annual convention attended by up to two thousand delegates from all over the world and publishes the quarterly *Law Library Journal*, 1908–.

There is also the International Association of Law Libraries, founded in 1959. It organizes courses in member countries in various parts of the world at regular intervals, sometimes in conjunction with the annual meeting of IFLA. These courses generally cover the law and legal bibliography of the host country and are intended for law librarians from abroad. IALL has published the *IALL Bulletin*, 1960–72, the *International Journal of Law Libraries*, 1973–81 and the *International Journal of Legal Information*, 1982–. The latter is published three times a year and currently contains mainly reviews and book notes.

LAW LIBRARIANSHIP AS A CAREER

The total number of law library posts has shown a gradual expansion since the late 1960s. The increase in academic posts which followed the *Report of the Committee on Legal Education*, 1971, has been halted and even reversed by the public expenditure cuts but opportunities in the private sector, principally in law firm libraries, are still growing. The catalyst for this seems to have been the removal of certain partnership restrictions enabled by the Companies Act 1967 s. 120, which has resulted in the creation of much larger City firms which are better able to employ skilled support staff.

Law librarianship now offers quite an attractive career to those who like the idea of such specialization and are content to remain within the middle ranks of the library profession. Some lateral movement between posts is possible, especially in the early years, and this can continue to be the case for law firm librarians of above-average ability who have the opportunity to demonstrate their worth to a firm.

There are a small number of senior and prestigious posts within specialist law libraries, although in the present financial climate such posts are liable to restructuring when they fall vacant. They are so few in number that they can scarcely be said to represent realistic career goals at the apex of a net-worked structure. In any case appointing committees are often more interested in a candidate's administrative abilities rather than his or her skills as a subject librarian. In law, as in general librarianship, it is difficult to prove all-round ability whilst maintaining expert subject bibliographical knowledge.

Little use has so far been made of law library consultants in making appointments, but those institutions sufficiently far-sighted to commission such a person have generally derived considerable benefit from the exercise.

BIALL has produced a short leaflet on careers in law librarian-ship, which is obtainable from the Hon. Secretary (current address published in the *Law Librarian*).

LAW LIBRARIES OVERSEAS

This survey has of necessity been confined to the law libraries of the British Isles, since any attempt to do adequate justice to law libraries in other countries would require a much larger chapter. A bibliography of recent references to law libraries in other countries is appended. The pattern of law libraries in any country is determined by the structure of the legal profession and the system of education and training for the law. Many common law countries, therefore, possess a pattern of law libraries similar to our own, the most important collections being those in the universities or held by the professional bodies.

The other countries which are most active in the field of law librarianship are the United States of America, Canada, Australia and the Federal Republic of Germany.

In the USA the law library network has developed to a degree undreamt of elsewhere and there are probably more law libraries there than in the rest of the world put together. The network includes court, law firm and public law libraries as well as the more usual national, university and bar association libraries. The great law libraries are to be found at the Library of Congress and the Universities of Harvard, Columbia, Yale, New York, Michigan, Texas, Minnesota, and California (Berkeley). There are interesting new buildings at Stanford and Texas (Tarlton Law Library, Austin).

FURTHER READING

GENERAL

Blunt, A. *Law librarianship*, Bingley, 1980. (*Outlines of modern librarianship*).
Directory of law libraries in the British Isles, 2nd edn.
Law Librarian: bulletin of the British and Irish Association of Law Librarians, 1970–.
Leinbach, A. E. 'An American in London law libraries', *Law Library Journal*, vol. 73, 1980, pp. 591–610.
Miskin, C. *Library and information services for the legal profession*, 1981. (*British Library Research and Development Reports*, 5633).
Moys, E. M. 'Law libraries' in *British library and information science, 1971–1975*, 1977, pp. 224–30.

NATIONAL LIBRARIES

British Library Working Party on Provision for Law *Report*, British Library, 1983.

PROFESSIONAL LIBRARIES

Breem, W. W. S. 'Professional law libraries in Great Britain', *Law Library Journal*, vol. 64, 1971, pp. 278–90.
Ballantyne, G. H. *The Signet Library, Edinburgh, and its librarians, 1722–1972*, 1979. (*Scottish library studies*, 6).
Barclay, J. B. 'The Society's library', in *The S.S.C. story, 1784–1984*, pp. 108–24.

ACADEMIC LIBRARIES

Boucher, H. 'Law collections in polytechnic libraries', *Law Teacher*, vol. 13, 1979, pp. 173–82.

Way, D. J. 'University law libraries of Great Britain', *Law Library Journal*, vol. 64, 1971, pp. 291–301.

PROFESSIONAL ASSOCIATIONS FOR LAW LIBRARIANS

Dahlmanns, G. 'Serving legal information: twenty-five years of IALL', in *Courts, law libraries and legal information in a changing society*, 1984, pp. 4–23.

Houdek, F. G. *Introducing the American Association of Law Libraries*, 1983.

Moys, E. M. 'BIALL: landmarks of the first ten years', *Law Librarian*, vol. 11, 1980, pp. 3–5.

Schwerin, K. 'The International Association of Law Libraries: its beginnings', *International Journal of Legal Information*, vol. 12, 1984, pp. 1–6.

Sprudzs, A. 'The International Association of Law Libraries and its twenty-five years of activities', *Law Librarian*, vol. 15, 1984, pp. 50–3.

LAW LIBRARIES OVERSEAS

Australia

Jordan, R. 'Australian law and law libraries, 1977', *Law Librarian*, vol. 8, 1977, pp. 39–42; vol. 9, 1978, pp. 5–6.

Wilson, B. *National survey of law libraries in Australia*, 1984.

Canada

Scott, M. 'Law libraries in Canada', *Law Library Journal*, vol. 64, 1971, pp. 314–22.

Scott, M. 'Law library resources and planning in Canada', *International Journal of Law Libraries*, vol. 3, 1975, pp. 78–90.

Europe

European law libraries guide, prepared by the International Association of Law Libraries, 1971.

France

Germain, C. M. 'France: libraries of law and librarians', *Law Library Journal*, vol. 72, 1979, pp. 235–44.

Germany

Lansky, R. 'Libraries for law in the Federal Republic of Germany', *International Journal of Law Libraries*, vol. 3, 1975, pp. 49–78.

India

Agrawala, S. K. 'Development and planning of law libraries in India', *International Journal of Law Libraries*, vol. 3, 1975, pp. 2–25.

New Zealand

Edwards, A. 'Our law libraries: a brief report', *New Zealand Libraries*, vol. 43, 1980, pp. 57–60.

Nigeria

Ogbeide, N. A. 'Law librarianship in Nigeria: history, development and problems', *International Journal of Law Libraries*, vol. 4, 1976, pp. 19–26.
Olaitan, M. O. 'Law librarianship in Nigeria, history and problems: a rejoinder', *International Journal of Law Libraries*, vol. 4, 1976, pp. 202–5.

Philippines

Feliciano, M. S. 'Law libraries and legal documentation in the Philippines', *International Journal of Law Libraries*, vol. 4, 1976, pp. 176–87.

United States

Borgeson, E. C. 'The Library of Congress and its influence on law librarianship: a panel', *Law Library Journal*, vol. 69, 1976, pp. 554–75.
Dobbs, K. W. and Haun, K. A. *The Law Library of the Library of Congress: its history, collections and services*, 1978.

Foust, J. M. 'Pennsylvania County law libraries', *Law Library Journal*, vol. 73, 1980, pp. 143–217.

Kavass, I. 'Law libraries of the United States: development and growth', *International Journal of Law Libraries*, vol. 3, 1975, pp. 25–49.

Mersky, R. M. 'Bicentennial history of American law libraries: a panel', *Law Library Journal*, vol. 69, 1976, pp. 528–53.

Taylor, R. M. *Federal court libraries*, 2 vols., 1981.

Union of Soviet Socialist Republics

Tearle, B. 'The dissemination of legal information in the Soviet Union', *Law Librarian*, vol. 15, 1984, pp. 3–6.

2. Legal Systems and Legal Literature

PROFESSOR W. R. CORNISH

The unsuspecting foreign visitor who enquires about the legal system of the United Kingdom is generally nonplussed by the answer. Justice, he is told, is separately administered in England and Wales, in Scotland and in Northern Ireland. Each has its own system of courts and the law applied in them differs in many important respects. To add to our foreigner's confusion, if he looks beyond the United Kingdom he will discover the separate legal systems of the Isle of Man and the Channel Islands.

No sooner has he learnt to regard them all as distinct, than he will have his attention drawn to their many similarities. He will learn, for instance, that the United Kingdom Parliament has legislative authority over all these territories; that the comparatively advanced state of English case-law on many subjects makes it frequently an exemplar in the other jurisdictions; that a host of similar attitudes have been bred out of a common approach to the role of judges and lawyers. The long historical association of the territories, for all its difficulties, has produced many unifying characteristics in fundamental legal matters. These similarities, indeed, make it sensible to link the legal system of the Irish Republic with the others so far mentioned, despite the severance of that state from the United Kingdom in 1922. For Ireland, like the many countries that once were British colonies but have now attained sovereign independence, developed legal institutions that closely resembled the English model. Accordingly she shares with England, Wales and Northern Ireland, as well as with many countries of the British Commonwealth and the United States, a 'common law' legal system, as distinct from the 'Romanist' (or 'civil law'), 'Scandinavian' and 'socialist' systems of different parts of Europe. The term 'common law' has a number of different usages. Here it is used to distinguish the family of legal systems deriving from England. We shall also see that it is used to describe the rules of law developed by the judges as opposed to legislation. Sometimes, according to context, 'common law' has a more specific historical sense: it refers to judge-made law developed in the former courts of the common law, as distinct from the rules of equity developed in the Court of Chancery. So too 'civil law' has distinct meanings. Here it identifies the family of legal systems where the influence of Roman law has been strong. But 'civil law' or 'civil proceedings' are terms which also distinguish, in any legal system, private rights of action for compensation and other redress from 'criminal law' or 'criminal proceedings', which are concerned with the infliction of punishment in the name of the state.

This chapter, which outlines the principal characteristics of the six legal systems of the British islands, tries to emphasize the interplay of differences and similarities between them. To attempt such a comparison in any depth would be beyond the scope of this *Manual*. Much of what follows is conceived as a very general sketch, though some matters are dealt with in more detail in later chapters. Apart from this the reader must be referred to the more complete accounts of the different systems in the works listed in the chapter bibliography.

Our attention will largely be concentrated upon two matters: the various structures of courts that exist to deal with civil actions and criminal prosecutions in the six jurisdictions, and the sources from which is derived the law applied in those courts. By 'sources of law' is meant those repositories of legal rules to which lawyers (and in particular, judges) turn in order to discover what the law is. We can at once say that there are two main sources of law in modern times – legislation and case-law – though we shall see the former influence of other sources, such as the Institutional writers in Scotland. To begin this investigation, we look at the development of the courts and make some preliminary observations about the law that is applied in them. Then certain basic characteristics of some or all of the six systems will be elaborated in more detail: the role of trial by jury, the organization of the legal profession and legal education, and the distinction between common law and equity. With this background, something more about the sources of law can be said in the last main section of the chapter.

EVOLUTION OF THE COURTS

We shall see that until the nineteenth century, the decisions of the judges formed the one regular source from which the general principles of English law were fashioned. And because the early judges and lawyers in Ireland were all trained in England the same principles were carried there. In both places there developed the twin branches of law that we know as common law and equity. This characteristic is still shared by the legal systems of England and Wales, Northern Ireland and the Irish Republic, and these legal systems will therefore be treated together as a group distinct from the systems of Scotland, the Channel Islands and the Isle of Man. For, in the latter group, English common law and equity were not a direct model, important though English case law may now be as a source from which legal rules may be generated.

England, Wales and Ireland

Let us start with a simplified picture of the court system operating in England and Wales today. The principal courts which hear civil actions may be represented thus:

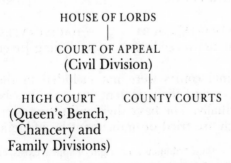

Most civil actions are tried in one of the divisions of the High Court or else in a County Court. County Courts may hear actions involving amounts up to certain monetary limits. The High Court has no such limits imposed upon it, but a litigant who prefers the High Court when he might have sued in the County Court may find himself penalized in costs. In this way the cases are divided up with reasonable flexibility. In addition, certain civil matters may be tried in other general courts: thus magistrates' courts have jurisdiction over certain important family and tenancy matters. Moreover, many disputes of a non-criminal character are handled by specially created tribunals – disputes, for example, over national insurance benefits, fair rents, planning and restrictive practices.[1]

From the decision reached at the trial there is a two-tier system of appeals: first to the Court of Appeal, and from there to the House of Lords.[2] This structure was largely erected when the administration of justice was modernized by the Judicature Acts 1873–5, and the separation between the courts of common law and equity was abandoned.

A diagram of the courts dealing with criminal cases is rather more elaborate:

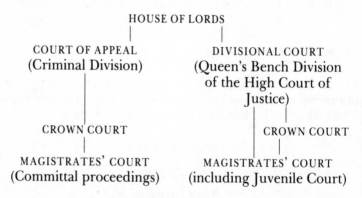

The criminal courts were not included in the Judicature Acts 1873–5 and their present structure has been built up more gradually. The basic division in the system is between cases which are tried on indictment by judge and jury in a

[1] From most of these tribunals some right of appeal exists, either to another special tribunal or person, or to the general courts.
[2] In limited circumstances, it is now possible to appeal directly to the House of Lords, 'leap-frogging' over the Court of Appeal.

Crown Court and those disposed of summarily in a magistrates' court. Again a fairly flexible system exists to determine whether a particular case goes to a higher court or a magistrates' court. Factors that *may* be taken into account include the intrinsic seriousness of the offence, the seriousness of the particular charge and the preference of the accused for one or other mode of trial.

A case that is tried on indictment may be the subject of an appeal by a convicted defendant to the Court of Appeal and then, in certain limited circumstances, to the House of Lords.[1] If a matter of law is involved in a case tried summarily there are certain rights of appeal by either side to a Divisional Court of the High Court and then to the House of Lords. Alternatively, a defendant who is convicted after pleading not guilty has a right to have his case completely retried in a Crown Court, sitting without a jury.

The pattern has been to divide cases into two groups according to their seriousness. Then, whether they are tried at the superior or the inferior level, there is the possibility of a two-tier appeal. The upper tier is constituted by a single court, the House of Lords, which is thus able to give the most authoritative rulings on legal questions that can be obtained from a court. It is also the supreme court of appeal for Northern Ireland and, in civil matters, for Scotland, so that on questions where the same law applies in these places the Lords may lay down a consistent rule for all three jurisdictions. (See also page 61.)

Edward I's conquest of Wales determined that no distinctive legal system would evolve in the principality. For a long period there were separate Welsh courts, but English influence was always strong and they were absorbed into the English judicial system in the nineteenth century. Henry II's conquest of Ireland, though more nominal in fact, led to the introduction of English common law and legal institutions which eventually, in the early seventeenth century, entirely superseded the native Irish Brehon law. An Irish Parliament developed from the late thirteenth century, but much English legislation came to apply directly or indirectly to Ireland. Though subordinate

[1] The prosecution has also recently acquired the right to have a question of law reviewed on appeal, but the result cannot affect the acquitted defendant.

to Westminster this body was given greater independence in 1782, only to be abolished by Pitt's Act of Union 1800. Direct rule was to rankle as one of the deepest and most persistent grievances in all the troubled Anglo-Irish relations that followed. The ultimate decision to partition the country not only created a separate state in the south, but created a subordinate parliament for the six counties of Ulster that became Northern Ireland. This Parliament at Stormont continued to exercise legislative power in most spheres of domestic government until the imposition of direct rule from Westminster in 1972.

Because the Irish courts had come so closely to resemble those of England the new system of the Judicature Acts was applied to them, the House of Lords constituting the final appellate court from the Irish Court of Appeal. In Northern Ireland after partition, the court structure retained its existing form: trial courts and the first tier of appeal courts were local; the House of Lords, sitting at Westminster, constituted the second tier. In detail, however, the structure varies somewhat from that of England. It may be thus represented (in simple form):

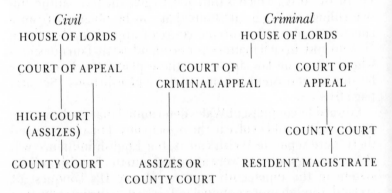

Civil		*Criminal*	
HOUSE OF LORDS		HOUSE OF LORDS	
COURT OF APPEAL		COURT OF CRIMINAL APPEAL	COURT OF APPEAL
HIGH COURT (ASSIZES)			COUNTY COURT
COUNTY COURT	ASSIZES OR COUNTY COURT		RESIDENT MAGISTRATE

In particular, it should be noted that the right of appeal from the County Court to the High Court in civil matters may involve a complete rehearing.

Events in Southern Ireland stand witness to the capacity of a basic legal structure to survive the most bitter political conflict. Given the intensity of anti-British feeling that brought about the creation of the Irish Free State, it was not surprising that both the system of courts and the common law applied in them came under heavy fire. In the period of 'the troubles', Sinn Fein, or Dáil, courts were set up in competition with the existing courts to administer law based on Irish custom, Roman or continental jurisprudence – any source other than English law. However, they scarcely survived the creation of the Free State under its Constitution of 1922.

The established judicial system was reconstituted in 1924, the Irish Supreme Court becoming the ultimate court of appeal from the High Court. The reorganization involved the creation, for the first time, of a Court of Criminal Appeal (seven years in advance of the equivalent court in Northern Ireland). District courts replaced the petty sessions of justices of the peace and resident magistrates, and circuit courts amalgamated the work of county courts and county quarter sessions. An appeal may be made from the county court, by way of complete rehearing, to a visiting judge of assize; and from him or directly from the county court, on a question of law, to a Divisional Court of the Supreme Court. Attempts were made, notably by Gavan Duffy, judge and then President of the High Court, to loosen the ties of English precedents and to allow the selection of rules appropriate to the conditions of the new state. But on the whole, the attitude of the judges proved conservative. Such was the respect for the English system of case-law, that even single decisions of the House of Lords before 1922 were held to bind the Supreme Court.

One casualty in the partition of Ireland was the High Court of Appeal for Ireland. Created by the Government of Ireland Act 1920, it was intended as an appeal court for both north and south. When the Canadian and Australian federations were created as independent dominions they were each given a federal superior court that could have a unifying effect over the law of the different provinces or states. The High Court of Appeal was an attempt to provide a similar body for the two Irelands. But such an experiment could not survive in a political atmosphere of such hostility and the court sat for only a year before the creation of the Free State.

In many important matters the courts in both parts of Ireland, as in England and Wales, continue to work on very similar lines. The rules which determine whether a civil or criminal case shall be tried in the superior or the inferior jurisdiction, and the rules which specify the grounds on which an appeal may be brought, though they may have grown apart in matters of detail, have retained the same general character. A lawyer trained in one of the systems can go to the others with the expectation (though no certainty) that similar principles of this nature will apply. This is the sense in which a family relationship survives between them. If he were to raise such a question in the context of (say) the French or Swedish legal systems, he could make no guess as to what the immediate answer or its ramifications might be. He would have to turn to an expert in the national law.

Scotland

By contrast with the close dependence of Irish common law upon that of England, the foundations of Scots law remain distinct. When the two kingdoms were joined by the accession of James I to the English throne, Scots law had already left behind its dark age. The rediscovery and interpretation of Roman law sources that had swept western Europe during the Renaissance had taken root in Scotland.

In England the native common law was too strong a growth to give much place to such foreign seed, and the difference became a means of marking Scots independence in legal matters. During the seventeenth century Scotland kept her own Parliament, but the Act of Union 1707 left Scotland without even a subordinate legislature equivalent to the Irish Parliament. At a time when statute was still only an occasional source of general law, the Romanist reception proved an ample buffer against any widespread penetration of English legal notions. Scots lawyers brought back to their homeland the learning of their student days in the great continental schools of law, particularly in France and the Low Countries. With time their own institutional writers emulated the European masters and provided the Romanized Scots law with texts that were treated in the courts as being of high authority.

It was therefore not until the rapid economic and social change of the nineteenth century, when law had to be made on an unprecedented scale, that English influences became more pronounced. In the first place statute became a substantial source of law. By no means all enactments applying to England were extended to Scotland and many Acts were passed to deal with exclusively Scottish matters. None the less many were common to the two countries. (The same was true of Ireland during the years of direct rule.) Secondly, the jurisdiction of the House of Lords, as the final court of appeal in civil matters, which it had asserted immediately after the Act of Union, began to acquire increasing importance. While the modern form of the judicial body in the Lords allows for the appointment of Scots and Northern Irish, as well as English, Law Lords, there was, particularly in the early nineteenth century, a tendency to treat the concepts of Scots law as though they were simply English transplants. The cavalier disregard which English judges have from time to time shown for the nuances of Scots doctrine continues to rankle.

Thirdly, the Scots tradition of studying law on the continent changed as codification spread through Europe. Legal education became less international and more directed towards the interpretation of a particular national text. The era of Romanist influence in Scotland thus drew to a close. The Scottish judges began to attach increasing importance to judicial precedents, a source of law so dear to the hearts of their English counterparts.

Civil and criminal jurisdiction in Scotland today may be represented (in simplified form) thus:

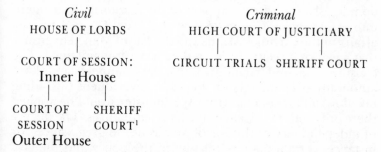

Civil	*Criminal*
HOUSE OF LORDS	HIGH COURT OF JUSTICIARY

COURT OF SESSION: CIRCUIT TRIALS   SHERIFF COURT
    Inner House

COURT OF   SHERIFF
SESSION   COURT[1]
Outer House

---

[1] Unlike the English county courts, the sheriff is under no monetary limits in the civil cases that he hears. If a case is heard by the sheriff an appeal may first be taken to the sheriff-principal.

While the system for trying civil cases bears some resemblance to the English, the criminal system is more distinctive. At the trial stage the cases tried 'in solemn form' with a jury are not sent to a different court from those tried summarily. Trials on circuit and some cases in the sheriff court are tried by jury, while the sheriffs also have an extensive summary jurisdiction. All summary trials are heard in the sheriff court. Moreover, there is only one tier for appeals. The House of Lords does not deal in criminal appeals from Scotland.

Channel Islands

The islands came to the English Crown as part of the Duchy of Normandy and remained English after the last of the French possessions had been given up. Their constitutional status is peculiar, being shared only with the Isle of Man. The two territories form no part of the United Kingdom, and they send no representatives to the United Kingdom Parliament. Parliament does have legislative competence over them which is superior to that of the local legislative bodies – the States of Jersey, Guernsey and Alderney, the Chief Pleas of Sark and the Tynwald of the Isle of Man. In this the islands resemble British colonies, such as Hong Kong.

Yet there are important respects, particularly in matters such as citizenship, in which the islands are accorded a special status by British legislation. Moreover, there exist special procedures that are in practice followed before United Kingdom legislation, when it applies to the territories, is brought into effect there. Committees of the Privy Council for the affairs of the Channel Islands and the Isle of Man help ensure that a working relationship on the matter is maintained. The constitutional understanding is that the Channel Islands have autonomy over matters of domestic government (including taxation) and legislation from Westminster would be applied there only with the assent of the local legislatures. The degree of independence of the Isle of Man is not so great, since, for instance, certain matters relating to the police and the civil service are reserved to the United Kingdom government, which is accordingly represented by a Lieutenant-Governor invested with active executive duties.

The history of the Channel Islands has left its stamp upon their legal system, for the applicable common law remains that of the Duchy of Normandy. The sources in which that law is set down, however, are very imperfect. They comprise the late thirteenth-century *Grand Coutumier du Pays et Duché de Normandie*, together with the *Coutume Reformée* of 1585. In addition, there were codifications of the laws of Guernsey (1583) and Jersey (1771) which were given legislative force, and certain expositions of the law that acquired the status of important legal authorities. Yet the problem of ascertaining principles of the Norman customary law as it applies, particularly, to rights over land in the Channel Islands, has remained a considerable problem.

The chief courts of the Islands are the Royal Courts of Jersey and Guernsey. In addition there is the Court of Alderney and the Court of the Seneschal in Sark, from which appeal may lie to the Royal Court of Guernsey. As well as the Bailiff who acts as judge in each of the Royal Courts, substantial use is made of jurats, their number depending on whether the court is sitting as a civil court of first instance, a criminal court of trial, or an appellate court. Above both Royal Courts there is a Court of Appeal with civil and criminal jurisdiction. An additional tier in the structure is provided by the possibility of appealing to the Judicial Committee of the Privy Council. The Judicial Committee may be composed of Privy Councillors from the Commonwealth with judicial experience as well as of British Lords of Appeal in Ordinary (appointed to hear appeals to the House of Lords). But normally the latter predominate upon the Committee, when they do not entirely make it up. So as final courts of appeal, the House of Lords and the Judicial Committee are generally homogeneous in character, while remaining distinct in form.

The Isle of Man

The legal system of the island is discussed together with those of Scotland and the Channel Islands out of respect for the Manx tradition that the system preserves its distinct origins. The island indeed had Viking and Scots rulers before passing to the English Crown. From 1406, it acquired greater stability of government than it had previously enjoyed when Henry IV granted its administration to the Stanleys as Lords of Man and the Isles. Not until 1765 and 1828 did the Crown, under statutory authority, purchase the feudal rights of its grantees. The feudal relationships that developed in the customary law of the Isle of Man were transmitted largely by oral tradition, though some were embodied in statutes of the local legislature, Tynwald. They continue to determine certain basic rules of the land law, but otherwise the law, so far as it is not to be found in statutes of Westminster or Tynwald, is mostly taken from English judicial precedents. The absorption of English common law, while not so complete as in Ireland, went to the extent of recognizing the special characteristics of English equity. The common law of the Isle of Man thus may be placed between that of England and Ireland on the one hand and that of Scotland and the Channel Islands on the other.

The fact that a Judicature Act was passed in 1883 to bring together the administration of law and equity in the island is one indication of the extent of English influence. Another is to be found in the composition of the present courts. The island's High Court consists of two judges called deemsters, who sit separately to try civil and serious criminal matters. From the deemster an appeal lies first to the Judge of Appeal (a Queen's Counsel of the English Bar) who sits together with the other deemster. From them, as with the Channel Islands, a second appeal is possible to the Judicial Committee of the Privy Council. Each deemster may sit as the Court of General Gaol Delivery in criminal cases, with appeal to a court consisting of all three judges. Summary trials are conducted by the High Bailiff and justices of the peace.

SOME BASIC CHARACTERISTICS

So far our discussion has scarcely touched upon English legal history, though we have indicated something of the evolution of the other five systems. The omission has been deliberate. There are aspects of the English story that tell a great deal about the distinctive character of common law systems today.

Accordingly they deserve separate treatment. As we turn now to discuss three of them, we shall find that the most interesting comparisons lie with Scots law, providing as it does the most developed contrast within the British islands.

Trial by jury

The jury system has done much to determine the characteristic form of litigation in common law jurisdictions. As an institution it has displayed a remarkable capacity for adaptation. The first jurors who appeared in judicial proceedings reached their verdicts on their own knowledge of local affairs. Gradually, however, as society became more complex, witnesses were introduced to give evidence in court to the jurors. Eventually the principle became that the jurors were to decide only upon what they learnt from witnesses at court. The trial (or petty) jury first became popular in England during the thirteenth century, when it was used as a substitute for methods of trial – for instance, by battle or ordeal – which appealed for divine revelation of justice. A century later the jury system spread to Scotland where it acquired certain distinctive characteristics.[1] It did not, however, as in the English common law courts, acquire a dominant position in the trial of civil actions; as though to mark the resurgence of English influence, the civil jury was specifically reintroduced in 1815 by legislation.

In the Middle Ages, the English judges found that unpaid, local jurors could be used for the rapid despatch of justice at a time when judicial manpower was short. Developments in France and elsewhere in Europe provide a contrast of long-lasting importance. There monarchs looked to their royal judges to conduct their own investigations as the means of determining the truth of matters in dispute. Justice became

---

[1] Scots juries in criminal cases have fifteen members and may reach a verdict by a bare majority; the verdict may be guilty, not guilty or not proven. English juries are twelve and had until very recently to return a unanimous verdict; now they may discount a small minority (*eg*, 10–2). The not proven verdict is not recognized in English law. In civil cases a Scots jury numbers twelve (Court of Session) or seven (Sheriff Court); in Northern Ireland and the Irish Republic the seven-man civil jury is also used.

inquisitorial and so an embodiment of royal power that was easily abused. Though juries proved capable of corruption, the system proved to have a certain resilience against the naked misuse of the judicial process. To eighteenth-century liberals trial by jury stood as a bulwark of liberty, discouraging governments from mounting mere show trials of their political opponents.

Our interest, however, is not so much in the constitutional role of this form of 'government by rotation'. The presence of the jury did much to shape the nature of the trial process, civil and criminal. Of necessity a trial became accusatorial, short and oral. By *accusatorial* is meant a process in which one side is obliged to make out his accusation against the other by putting forward his own evidence. The judge is a mere arbitrator, securing orderly procedure and informing the jury of the relevant law. He bears no responsibility for investigating the issue raised before him. The evidence of witnesses is principally tested by the opponent's cross-examination. The need for brevity, dictated by the jury's limited capacity to understand, remember and evaluate oral evidence, led to the development of severe and technical rules for the exclusion of irrelevant and unduly prejudicial evidence. In civil process, the jury was also a cause of the important procedure of pleading. One purpose of this procedure was to fine down the cause between the parties so that the jury would only be concerned with facts really in dispute. The heavy reliance on oral evidence at the trial – essential when there could be no certainty that the jurors would be literate – came thus to be counterbalanced by elaborate written preliminaries. These proved vital to the formation of common law principle in England, for it was the form in which judges permitted parties to express their pleadings that determined the content of the law.

With time the contents of the pleadings gave place to reported judgments as sources of the law. But for a long period of English legal history the judges in the common law courts were shaping the law so that it could be both understood and applied in a reasonable fashion by jurors who had no legal training or experience. That flavour has remained characteristic of so much of our law. For instance, the judges have laid a duty upon all persons to take such care as would a reasonable man to avoid harm to others. They mean by the term 'reasonable man' the collective good sense of the twelve jurors in the jury-box. Today the amount and complexity of litigation and the need to secure conformity in similar cases have led to the virtual replacement of juries in civil cases by judges sitting alone. Yet it will be long before the characteristic forms which the jury gave to both the substantive law and the court procedures of English common law will be lost.

How different legal process could become without jury trial is illustrated not only by the inquisitorial systems of Continental Europe, but even by the English Court of Chancery with its jurisdiction in equity. Chancery did not use juries and when it determined questions of fact for itself it relied upon documents where possible, even reducing the testimony of witnesses to written form by having them separately examined under oath.[1] The absence of a short, conclusive trial as a culminating focus to litigation contributed to the notorious dilatoriness and expense of Chancery proceedings in the time of Dickens.

The legal profession and legal education

Where a legal system depended upon the judges themselves to enquire into disputes, it was likely that a large body of judges would be built up. Indeed, in continental systems, judgeship became a lifetime's occupation. A young lawyer chose between entering the service of the state as a junior judge (expecting then to climb the judicial tree) and going into private practice.

In the various parts of Britain, the royal courts were able to operate with remarkably few judges. This was possible partly because of the limited role of the judge sitting with a jury, but partly also because of the extensive use that came to be made of another kind of unpaid lay judge – the justice of the peace.[2]

---

[1] The procedures followed in trying Chancery actions were brought closer to those of the common law in the reforms of the mid-nineteenth century which culminated in the Judicature Acts 1873–5.
[2] While the justice of the peace flourished in the social organization of pre-industrial England, in Scotland he failed to gain the same wide powers in face of the well-established sheriffs. In Ireland, the lack of a landlord class to fill the position led to the evolution of the resident magistrates.

The justices sat at their quarter sessions with a jury to dispose of serious criminal charges, as well as dealing with many matters of local administration. Increasingly they were given power to sit in petty sessions to try minor crimes, and from this has developed the modern notion of summary criminal trial.

It thus remained practicable to draw the royal judges from the ranks of senior advocates practising before the courts. The progress from bar to bench, so characteristic of the British systems, had many consequences. It was an important factor in determining how work should be divided between the two sections of private practice (barristers and solicitors in England and Ireland; advocates and solicitors in Scotland).[1] It created a close rapport between judges and the advocates who appeared before them. This working relationship helped support the high degree of respect that has come to be shown to British judges.

Their special position is in its turn closely associated with the fact that, in England, preservation and development of the law was kept within the grasp of the practising lawyers. The precedents set by judges and stored up by practitioners were the sources of law that weighed with later courts. Not for the judges in England the great deference shown by their continental counterparts for the teaching of doctrine by the professors of the universities. As we have already seen, the inbred English profession showed little interest for the Renaissance revival of Roman law principle. Even the Scots lawyers, who for more than two centuries learned so much from the Dutch and other schools of jurisprudence, did not establish a system of legal education that, in the nineteenth century, could give the teachers of law in the Scots universities the status of their French or German counterparts.

In England the training of lawyers had always been re-

---

[1] The division of legal practice into two branches is neither unique to common law systems, nor, as events in the United States and elsewhere demonstrate, is it necessary to the efficient functioning of the profession. Where it is maintained within the common-law world, the dividing line gives the advocate a specialist function in litigation in the higher courts, with which is associated the giving of opinions on difficult matters of law. The advocate is not directly employed by the client but is engaged by the client's solicitor. This gives to members of the bar a certain aloofness; a close-knit fraternity lightens the tasks of maintaining professional standards and selecting judges.

garded as a craft skill to be learnt from practitioners rather than an academic science to be studied at a distance. To this tradition Scotland returned in the nineteenth century. That century did, indeed, see the roots of legal studies beginning to extend in the universities of both countries and in Ireland. Today a degree in law has become a well-recognized route to the practice of the law. But, save in Scotland, it is not a sufficient professional qualification. For the most part a person may become a legal practitioner purely by taking the examinations set by the relevant professional bodies and completing the prescribed period of practical training. The graduate is merely given exemption from all or part of the academic side of these requirements.

Common law and equity

We have already made passing reference to the distinction between common law and equity, which is so basic to the legal history of England. It is a division that must be further elucidated, not only for its past importance, but also because it retains its significance today in major fields of civil law, such as property and contract.

In the centuries after the Norman Conquest three courts – Exchequer, Common Pleas and King's Bench – came to be treated as distinct from the Curia Regis. The legal principles recognized and enforced by them were in this context the 'common law'. However, it remained possible to petition the King himself, as the fountain of justice, for redress against a wrong. In the later Middle Ages he deputed the hearing of these petitions to his Chancellor, who granted relief in 'equity' beyond that available in the courts of common law. Numerous causes contributed to the popularity of this equitable jurisdiction in Chancery. With time it lost its discretionary character and hardened into a body of rules that supplemented or qualified the common law in settled ways.

For instance, the common law courts could, in most cases, only order the payment of money by way of relief to a successful plaintiff. But in equity it was possible to obtain such orders as an injunction against a course of conduct, or specific performance requiring a contract to be carried out. Common law required a borrower of money to repay on the exact day due, if he did not wish entirely to forfeit land that he had transferred to the lender by way of mortgage security. Equity gave the borrower more time to pay. Above all, equity developed that distinctive conception of property ownership known as the trust. The person who owned property (in the sense that the common law courts would recognize him as owner) might become the trustee of it for another. Equity declared that the latter should be treated as the beneficial owner. His right to whatever benefits the property produced would be recognized and enforced in a court of equity. In its modern form, the trust was first developed to accommodate the elaborate property arrangements of the landed aristocracy. But it was also adapted to such varied purposes as the organization of joint-stock companies, the administration of charities, and the property holdings of trade unions.[1]

The presence of equity beside common law is perhaps the most distinctive characteristic of the developed legal system of England and one that was implanted in its direct descendants – in Ireland, the American colonies and other British possessions that had no recognized legal system of their own.

One evident difference in Scots legal history is the absence at any stage of a separate court administering its own distinctive forms of equitable relief. Yet principles have developed in Scots law which have been justified by reference to reason, fairness, natural justice and which have been referred to as 'equitable'.[2] The Court of Session today administers both common law and equity and there is a family resemblance between principles developed in the English Court of Chancery and Scots equity. In particular, the trust concept took root in Scots law and proved there an equally useful formula in matters of property.

---

[1] However, most companies are today organized under a different legal scheme prescribed by the Companies Acts; charities (though not trade unions) may adopt a corporate form of this kind, or they may still use the trust.

[2] In addition the Court of Session has a special equitable jurisdiction, the *nobile officium*.

THE SOURCES OF LAW

English common law and equity, as we have now seen, were
built over many centuries by a small central band of judges
who worked with, and were drawn from, a compact body of
advocates. At the dawn of the nineteenth century most of this
law related to civil rights and touched the lives of only the
thin strata of propertied classes. The law they needed could
be wrought slowly by the pragmatic, practical technique of
judicial precedent. This English tradition was strong enough
to exert an increasing influence upon the separate system of
Scots law. But with growing speed of economic and social
change, the requirements of government and the need for
new law were too pressing to leave most of the work to the
judges. Legislation emerged in fact, as already it was in principle, the dominant source of law. Accordingly it is with
legislation – the enactments of Parliament, the subordinate
legislatures and other governmental bodies furnished with
legislative power – that we turn first in discussing the different
sources of law.

Legislation

The great constitutional struggles between the Stuarts and
their Parliaments determined where the ultimate power of
government should lie. The first principle upon which the
Revolution of 1688 was founded was that Acts of Parliament –
enactments passed in due form by King, Lords and Commons
– were law beyond challenge. Subordinate legislatures, such as
those of the Isle of Man, the Channel Islands and the colonies,
can today pass valid enactments only within the powers allowed them by United Kingdom legislation. In those former
colonies that have acquired dominion status or become republics under written constitutions, the legislatures must ensure
that their ordinary legislation complies with the higher dictates of the constitution. In all such cases, an enactment which
exceeds the limits of the legislature's power can be declared
void by the courts: it is *ultra vires*. The Republic of Ireland is
the obvious example for our purposes, but the same is true of

the Dominion of Canada, the Commonwealth of Australia and the United States of America.

But courts in Britain have had no such power in relation to the statutes of Parliament – for Parliament is sovereign. All a court may do is to interpret the meaning of an Act in relation to a case before it. The principles upon which the judges approach this task of interpretation are by now elaborate. There have been instances where judges have given a meaning to the words of a statute which prevents it achieving its purpose. The judicial coach-and-horses of interpretation may leave behind only the crumbling frame of a statute. But the United Kingdom Parliament may always make a further attempt to express it more clearly. By contrast, the Supreme Court of Ireland is entitled to say, once and for all, that the legislature may not pass a statute of a given character; its constitutional power has a significance of a wholly different order.

As nineteenth-century legislation on poor relief, education, public health, factories, pollution, police, prisons and so forth, swelled the pages of the statute book, new bodies, both central and local, were given power to carry the legislation into execution. Nor were the powers of these organs of government confined to administration. With growing frequency they became entitled to add details to the legislation itself under powers delegated by Parliament. What was novel was not the concept of such *delegated legislation* but the extent to which it came to be used. Because the bodies who exercised delegated legislative powers – ministries, local councils, and many others – can legislate only within the scope accorded them by Parliament, the courts may not only interpret the meaning, but may consider the validity, of their enactments.

Acts of Parliament and delegated legislation (sometimes referred to as 'subsidiary', 'subordinate' or 'secondary' legislation) thus form the most compelling source of law. If a statutory rule lays down a clear prescription for a particular situation, it prevails over any rule of case-law that may be at variance with it. Judges have no qualifying power to say when and where the legislation is not to apply.

So much for the accepted legislative forms. But when the United Kingdom and the Irish Republic joined the European

Economic Communities novel constitutional questions were raised. The law of the Communities – the treaties and the regulations, directives and decisions of the Community organs – became a source of law in both countries. In particular, some treaty provisions and regulations made by the Council of Ministers or the European Commission are 'directly applicable'. They confer rights and impose duties upon individuals, without the need for national legislation, which are enforceable in national courts. It is the opinion of the European Court of Justice that Community law prevails over inconsistent national law. But it remains an open question whether national courts will take this view when after a Community enactment there is passed a national statute that is beyond question inconsistent with it. In Ireland, moreover, there is the question whether community law can prevail over the constitution. To these questions no clear answers can be returned until they are raised in the courts. One thing, however, is sure: the highest judicial organ of the Communities, the European Court of Justice, has no power to declare any national legislation void. In this sense, at least, the sovereignty of the legislatures continues.

Judicial precedent

In nineteenth-century Europe, the movement to express the most general and basic principles in the form of a code progressed rapidly. Many governments, in support of their own legitimacy or in order to express a sense of national identity, promoted codes of civil, criminal, commercial and procedural law. Britain, which, in the person of Jeremy Bentham, had produced the foremost advocate of the cause of codification, nevertheless did not follow suit. The survival of both English and Scots law within the United Kingdom presented a difficulty, but a relatively minor one. The chief opposition to codification in England undoubtedly arose from the entrenched faith of the legal profession in the virtues of case-law, that is, in principles developed from the decisions of judges on the law applicable to the cases before them. Bentham objected vehemently to the obscurity of precedent –

a form of law, as he saw it, capable of extraction only by those trained in the mystery of the lawyer's craft. To its protagonists, however, precedent allowed the law to remain flexible – capable of being adapted to fit unanticipated circumstances and changed social conditions in a manner often impossible within the set phrases of a code. The development of common law and equity in England by means of judicial decision already had a long history and the technique was gaining importance in Scotland as continental influences receded. The close-knit profession of England, in particular, was consistently hostile towards plans to codify the criminal law and no serious attempts to codify either the law of contract or tort were ever made. Only in certain branches of commercial and property law were substantially complete statements of the law in legislative form achieved. Case-law has thus remained a vital source of fundamental principle in all the legal systems of the British islands and the many 'common-law' systems overseas.

The law-making content of a case is defined by the principle of *stare decisis* (let the decision stand). The essence of this conception may be stated thus: the decision of a court in a single case may be enough to settle that a general rule has the force of law and must be applied by judges to the determination of comparable cases. But there are two basic qualifications: first, it is only the *ratio decidendi* (the reason for deciding) that has this legally binding effect, and second, the decision of a particular court can only bind lower courts in the same hierarchy and, in some instances, the court itself.

In England, quite elaborate rules were laid down by each appellate court concerning the conditions in which that court would be bound by its own previous decisions. In 1965, however, the House of Lords abandoned its rule that it was always bound by its own precedents. Today it is only the Court of Appeal which, unless certain conditions are fulfilled, regards itself as bound by its earlier decisions. Scots and Irish courts have always been reluctant to lay down general rules of this character, though the Court of Appeal of Northern Ireland has said that it follows the same principle as the English Court of Appeal.

Ratio decidendi is a notion of some subtlety. It is best understood by beginners as the principle of law upon which a judge relies in order to reach his judgment. In particular, the *ratio decidendi* is to be distinguished from *obiter dicta* – remarks made by judges about principles of law that are not directly relevant in deciding the issues before them. A court is never obliged to apply *obiter dicta* from earlier decisions, though it may do so. The *dicta* of the foremost judges do indeed carry considerable weight. But they never constitute more than persuasive precedents.

By careful manipulation, it is often possible for a later court to avoid applying a precedent that it dislikes. It may perhaps find the precedent to be *dictum* rather than *ratio* and for that reason not binding. It may find that there is something about the facts of the case before it that makes the *ratio decidendi* of the precedent inapplicable; the earlier case is then said to be *distinguished*. The rule that a contract is complete upon posting an acceptance would be restrictively distinguished if a judge said that it only applied when the acceptance was expected to be by post, and not, for instance, by telephone. The court may even find that the principle set forth in the precedent was put in terms that were unduly wide of the subject-matter in hand: this process of reasoning is known as *restrictive distinguishing*. Suppose the precedent lays down that a contract is formed when a letter accepting an offer is put in the post. That rule would be distinguished by a judge who said that it is not enough to hand the letter to a postman instead of posting it in the normal way. It is not unknown for a court to dispose of an apparently binding precedent which it thinks incorrect by saying that it was a decision reached only in relation to the particular facts before it. Since facts very rarely repeat themselves exactly, this disposes of the precedent. But so cavalier a technique has been not unfairly described as 'distinguishing out of existence'. All these possibilities, imaginatively used, can allow a desirable fluidity in the development of the law. In the wrong hands they open the gateway of legal indeterminacy on a grand scale.

A precedent can never be more than persuasive upon a higher court in the same hierarchy or any court in a different hierarchy. The British islands provide no less than six separate hierarchies of courts, three (England and Wales, Scotland,

Northern Ireland) culminating in the House of Lords,[1] two in the Judicial Committee of the Privy Council, and the Irish system in the Supreme Court of the Republic. A decision of the English Court of Appeal can bind neither the House of Lords nor the Court of Session in Scotland. The precedent would constitute persuasive authority. The House of Lords might choose to *overrule* it as wrongly decided. The Court of Session, not belonging to the same set of courts, could not declare it wrong in this fashion; but it could choose *not to follow* it. In either case, the later court would doubtless look for a sufficient reason before departing from the precedent. This, however, is merely to recognize that, as far as possible, it is desirable to preserve the continuity and certainty of the law.

Compared with legislation, case-law is difficult material to conserve and make available to lawyers. It has become possible to apply *stare decisis* with increasing rigidity over the past century because the methods of reporting judicial decisions have become more substantial and more careful. Even at the end of the eighteeeth century the standards of the private reporters in England were frequently slap-dash, and it was still very much a novelty for reports to be made of judicial pronouncements out on the assize circuits, as opposed to those of the full benches sitting at Westminster.

In the nineteenth century reporting rapidly improved in accuracy and the range of courts covered was broadened. By the time that the Incorporated Council of Law Reporting was established in 1865 to publish semi-official case-reports of the superior courts of common law and equity a full report had reached its usual modern form. (For a fuller account of the history of law reporting, see Chapters 4 and 7.)

While a case in *The Law Reports* has special authority in that it will have been checked by the judge or judges involved, many additional series of reports, general and specialized, flourish today and may be cited in court.

In Scotland improvements in reporting follow a roughly parallel path. As early as 1705, however, the Faculty of Advo-

---

[1] It has never been finally determined whether a decision of the House of Lords in an appeal from England binds the courts in Scotland (where there is no acknowledged difference in Scots law) or in Northern Ireland. If the precedent is not technically binding, it will in any case be highly persuasive.

cates (the professional bar organization) intervened by appointing its own reporter. This practice developed into the various series reporting the decisions of the Court of Session. Since 1907 referred to simply as *Session Cases*, these are now the responsibility of the Scottish Council of Law Reporting and are also checked by the judges. In Ireland the growth of law reporting was slower but equivalent series of modern reports now exist.

In the different jurisdictions a law report generally conforms to a standard pattern. A subject heading list is followed by an epitome of the facts and the decision in the case. This is known as the head-note. Then comes a full statement of the facts at issue, and often a summary of the arguments presented by counsel. The judgment or judgments delivered by the court follow, and finally there is a report of the order made to express the result of the judgment.

Especially in the appeal courts, where the judges are regularly preoccupied with general principles of law, British judgments have in modern times acquired two important characteristics. One is that they are written in a relatively free and discursive style; they have none of the rigid formalism that so limits the scope of, for instance, a French judgment and stands as an impediment to the formation of general principle out of a particular decision. The other is that the discussion generally concentrates upon the previous case-law and other legal sources. This preoccupation with 'authority' is part of a tradition that is opposed to the overt discussion of the practical consequences that will ensue if one rule rather than another is adopted. In the United States the courts have been much readier to air such issues of policy in their judgments. This is one reason why particular precedents have not acquired such compulsive force in that country. English judges have long presented judgments stating the law as though they had an inevitable quality about them generated by an abstract sense of right.[1] It would be wrong to suggest that our judges have no

---

[1] English common lawyers, led by Coke and Blackstone, have been partial to the notion that in laying down precedents the judges do not make, but only declare, the law. Whatever the reality of such a theory when the royal courts were first making general rules out of established local customs, it is today rarely treated as more than a convenient fiction that 'explains' why a novel precedent applies to the very case in which it is laid down.

concern with the consequences of their judgments, just as it would be misleading to suppose that most of them acknowledge a higher moral order, such as a system of natural law, from which particular rules are to be deduced. But their 'authority-dominated' form of reasoning, together with the standing that is accorded even to isolated precedents, are but part of a larger phenomenon. Both contribute to the legal profession's own conception of the high and independent constitutional position of the judges. They contribute to that sense of distance that is thought to breed a respect for the law and its institutions amongst the lay public.

Texts and other legal writings

In many legal systems, the treatises and commentaries of legal scholars are treated by their courts as significant sources of law. The most authoritative writers may well be given greater weight by the courts than the decisions of judges, at least until a whole line of judicial precedent has been built up. This has been a characteristic, for instance, of the European states affected by the revival of Roman law. Thus, during its Romanist reception, Scots law was significantly developed and consolidated by the works of her own institutional writers. Today, on civil matters the works of Craig, Stair, Bankton, Erskine and Bell, and on matters of criminal law, those of Mackenzie and Hume, are universally conceded a special status, and in default of other authority would be treated as settling the law. English law has had its commentators, most notably Coke and Blackstone, whose writings have exerted considerable influence in their time upon the courts. Today, their interest is chiefly historical. More recent writers have not been accorded by judges a status that can compare with that of a clearly-expressed judicial decision. Writings may be cited in court to show what the law is, but it is unlikely that they will be given much weight unless the law to be extracted from statutory or case-law sources is contradictory, confusing or non-existent.

We may distinguish three kinds of legal writing. The first is the textbook prepared as a statement of what the law is for the use of legal practitioners. The widest-ranging of these is

Halsbury's Laws of England, but almost every subject has at least one practitioners' text devoted to it. The tendency is for these works to be written and edited by practising lawyers. The second is the introductory textbook, designed primarily for students of the law. The third, the critical commentary upon an aspect of the law, has been a product particularly of the expansion of academic legal education in the universities. Here the tendency is for authors, whether they produce books or write articles or notes in legal periodicals, to have some connection with law teaching. Of course these three kinds of writing are not mutually exclusive categories. A few practitioners' texts, for example, have a critical and speculative tone; and many books written primarily for the instruction of students contain much that is purely descriptive of the existing law. It can safely be said that, when courts do look to legal writings for legal authority, their preference is for works of the first kind. It is not often in Britain that one sees the judicial imagination being fired by the critical analysis of an academic article. Even when such writings are referred to, the ideas expressed in them acquire status as a legal authority at second-hand – that is, because a judge expresses his approval of them in a judgment.

Custom

For the sake of completeness, it must be said that custom has a recognized place as a source of law, though today it is much less important than formerly. Much of what became the 'common law' of the whole territory amounted to a generalization of the custom of localities. But there remains the possibility that a purely local custom, constituting a variation in the general law, may be treated as the applicable rule in that locality. The custom must be both definite and certain, fair and reasonable, and of substantial antiquity.[1] The only circumstances in which such a custom is at all likely to arise today is in connection with local land rights. The use of custom as a

[1] In English and Irish law the custom must have existed 'from time immemorial' – an elaborate concept. In Scots law the custom does not have to be shown to have existed for any particular period.

source of law in this way needs to be distinguished from the role that trade practices and similar evidence may be given to explain what is meant in an ambiguous situation. By this means it may be possible to prove that 'a dozen' means 'thirteen' in a baker's contract. But no question of varying an otherwise applicable rule of law is involved; merely the explanation of what was meant in a particular agreement.

COMMON LAW AND CIVIL LAW

At the outset, we drew a distinction between 'common law' and 'Romanist' or 'civil' legal systems, as well as others. These are broad groupings of national legal systems which suggest no more than a family likeness. But just as bone structure is often more important than superficial markings to a zoologist, so also with the investigator of legal institutions.

The traditions and techniques that developed in the English legal system were not merely influential in other parts of the British Islands. Wherever the British settlers colonized unoccupied territory without an established legal order they took with them English common law and so much of the existing statute law as was appropriate to the environment. In this way, a legal system was built in most of the American colonies which subsequently became parts of the United States, in all of Canada save Quebec, in Australia and New Zealand, and in the British colonies in East and West Africa.

By contrast, territories which became British by cession or conquest kept their own law unless and until altered by legislation. Thus in the Indian sub-continent, the regimes of Hindu and Mohammedan law were, during the nineteenth century, supplemented by statutory codes of criminal law, criminal procedure and evidence, contract and land law. There too, the judges were able to develop a law of tort based largely on principles of English common law. In South Africa and Sri Lanka, the inherited legal system, Roman-Dutch law, derived from earlier European colonization. In both countries, English influences arrived piecemeal by statutory change and the influence of practitioners, rather in the way that Scots law acquired English inflexions. To some extent the same has occurred in the French system of Quebec, though its separate character was strengthened by the adoption of the *Code Napoléon* shortly before the Canadian federation came into being.

The 'common law' family of legal systems now has two main branches, those of the various United States and those of countries that are or have been members of the British Commonwealth. The two centuries which now separate us from the Declaration of Independence have seen the growth of many important differences between the two. The protection of individual rights guaranteed by the Constitution of the United States, for instance, has had a profound influence there. But many foundations remain common: basic concepts of substantive law, attitudes to judicial precedent as a source of law, relationships between bench and practising profession – all the matters, indeed, which we have already seen to be most characteristic of the common law of England.

We have been able to glean from the course of events in Scotland some measure of the character shared by so many legal systems of Western Europe. In the sixteenth century, Roman law, as it had come to be interpreted by medieval scholars, began to be 'received' into them in addition to, or in place of, local customs. This meant that, in varying degrees, the common principles derived from this single source were adapted into the law of many kingdoms and republics scattered over the map of Europe. The reception of Roman law was much fostered by the teaching of the great university schools of law, whose international influence remained very considerable until the nineteenth century. Hence these 'civil law' systems, as they are often called, are also known to comparative lawyers as 'Romanist'.

The incorporation of law into national codes in these countries has in modern times made the influence of Roman law less direct. But it has left a pronounced mark upon many of the codes of European nations. And, as we have said already, the tradition has survived of placing considerable value upon scholarly commentaries as a source of law rather than upon the decisions of judges, at least when those decisions have not built up into an established line of authority. This difference is marked in the form which each takes. The scholarly treatise or commentary is expository in style, the judgment tends to be formal and elliptical; and accordingly it may be less useful as a source of general principle. Equally, while the regular study of common law in the English universities has mainly developed over the last century, the reporting of judgments in civil law countries has grown only over much the same period. As this suggests, the methods of common law and civil law are growing together. In France, for instance, decisions of the highest court, the Cour de Cassation, have a force not dissimilar to that of appellate courts in England. The differences that remain tend to be not so much of technique as of the substance of the law.

FOR THE FUTURE

In less than two centuries Britain and Ireland have changed from an agricultural to a largely urban, industrial society. In that time all institutions of government, including the legal system, have undergone many reforms. But much also has been allowed to stand unaltered. How much can perhaps be suggested if, in conclusion, we mention three novel ways in which law and its services are now beginning to be changed.

Jeremy Bentham not only believed in a complete codification of the law. He thought that the code should be kept under constant review and he devised institutional procedures by which those who administered the law in the courts might forward suggestions for revision of the Codes. At various times since there has been pressure for a permanent body concerned with law reform. This has sometimes taken the form of a plea for a Ministry of Justice in which could be centred the present responsibilities of various central departments for matters of legal administration and substantive law, as well as developing a section specifically concerned with law reform. For long this desire was met by a response typical of the British system: part-time bodies, composed of judges, practitioners and law teachers, were set up to report on desirable reforms. In addition, there were many *ad hoc* enquiries. Inevitably progress was slow and unsystematic. But the situation at last changed in 1965 when the English and Scottish

Law Commissions were set up 'to take and keep under review all the law with which they are respectively concerned with a view to its systematic development and reform'. Already they have been responsible for many desirable changes, most extensively in the field of family law. The English Law Commission is also well advanced in a modern project to codify the criminal law. Since reform of this kind must needs be by legislation, the more that the law commissions achieve, the more law takes statutory form. Increasingly the judge's role in law-making is that of interpreting legislation. If a defect in a statute emerges, the machinery for correction is now more efficient than it was, though the great difficulty of finding Parliamentary time for amendments makes it far short of perfect.

The self-regarding character of English law has been apparent in much that has been said already. There have, of course, been occasions when English lawyers have looked to Western Europe for inspiration in dealing with particular problems, but compared with the development of Scots law the degree of foreign influence has hitherto been slight. But membership of the European Communities is producing a flow of legal ideas from (and to) Continental Europe on a scale previously unknown. Not only is a great deal of Community law now directly applicable on the particular matters of economic regulation with which the Communities are currently concerned, but there are projects completed or afoot for the harmonization of national laws or the introduction of Community laws concerning companies, insolvency, insurance, banking, advertising and intellectual property. More fundamental still, native conceptions of judicial control of administrative bodies and public policy in relation to contracts may well, with time, be affected.

Let us end, however, not with law-making but with its application. So much of the law that is administered in the ordinary courts has, in the past, been devised for the needs of litigants who could afford to go there. The problem of making courts truly accessible to the community as a whole – a problem common to most legal systems – has, since the Second World War, been attacked with increasing vigour. In 1949 statutes covering England and Wales and Scotland made provision for state-aided legal assistance, both in and out of court, for those unable to afford it, on a much more substantial basis than ever before. These Acts have gradually been extended to cover more and more types of proceedings, though legal aid is still not available to secure representation before tribunals. Ways of providing cheap and simple redress have recently been introduced, and the opportunities for obtaining free advice from a solicitor have increased not only within the legal assistance scheme but by the development of neighbourhood law centres and legal services at citizens' advice bureaux. In an age when the complexities of ordinary life are constantly growing, it is clear that the legal system must continue these first developments towards providing a real and usable service to the community. For without access justice has no meaning.

FURTHER READING

LEGAL SYSTEMS

England

Baker, J. H. *An introduction to English legal history,* 2nd edn., 1971.
De Smith, S. A. *Constitutional and administrative law,* 4th edn., 1981.
Jackson, R. M. *The machinery of justice in England,* 7th edn., 1977.
Manchester, A. H. *A modern legal history of England and Wales, 1750–1950,* 1980.
Milsom, S. F. C. *Historical foundations of the common law,* 2nd edn., 1981.
Radcliffe, G. R. Y. and Cross, Sir G. N. *The English legal system,* 6th edn., Butterworth, 1977.
Walker, R. J. and Walker, M. G. *The English legal system,* 6th edn., 1985.
Williams, G. L. *The proof of guilt,* 3rd edn., 1963.
Wilson, G. P. *Cases and materials on the English legal system,* 1973.
Zander, M. *Cases and materials on the English legal system,* 4th edn., 1984.

Zander, M. *The law making process,* 1980 (*Law in context*).

Scotland

Walker, D. M. *The Scottish legal system,* 5th edn., 1981.

Ireland

Calvert, H. *Constitutional law in Northern Ireland,* 1968.
Donaldson, A. G. *Comparative aspects of Irish law,* 1957 (*Duke University Commonwealth Studies Center Publication no. 3*).
Dickson, B. *The legal system in Northern Ireland,* 1984.

Channel Islands

Sheridan, L. A. 'Channel Islands' in Keeton, G.W. and Lloyd D. *The British Commonwealth: The United Kingdom,* vol. 1, pt. 2, 1965.

Isle of Man

Holland, D. C. 'The Isle of Man' in Keeton, G. W. and Lloyd, D. *The British Commonwealth: The United Kingdom,* vol. 1, pt. 1, 1955.

JURIES AND JUSTICES OF THE PEACE

Cornish, W. R. *The jury,* 1968.
Devlin, Lord *Trial by jury,* new edn., 1970.
Moir, E. *The Justice of the Peace,* 1969.
Willock I. D. *Origins and development of the jury in Scotland,* 1966.

LEGAL PROFESSION

Abel-Smith, B. and Stevens, R. B. *Lawyers and the Courts,* new edn., 1970.

Megarry, R. E. *The lawyer and litigant in England,* 1962 (*Hamlyn lectures*).
Zander, M. *Lawyers and the public interest,* 1968.

CIVIL LAW

Lawson, F. H. *A common lawyer looks at the civil law,* 1955.
Yiannopoulos, A. N. *Civil law in the modern world,* 1965.

Part II Legal Literature of the British Isles and Other Common Law Systems

3. Primary Sources: Legislation

D. J. WAY

The whole body of legislative materials of the United Kingdom, excluding subordinate legislation, is often referred to conveniently as The Statute Book or, more concisely still, The Statutes. Individual items from the Statute Book are also referred to sometimes as Statutes or, more frequently, as Acts of Parliament. Unlike the legislative materials of many other countries, our Statute Book has grown over a period of several centuries without any overall plan, and hence is a body of exceptional size and complexity. We find, for example, that the current edition of the *Chronological Table of the Statutes* still begins with the Statute of Merton, 1235, and even after the recent extensive programme of law revision four sections of Magna Carta still remain on the Statute Book. The whole Statute Book in fact consists of specific Acts on specific topics, enacted by Parliament to remedy specific grievances, and often themselves amended by other Acts within a further twelve months.

PARLIAMENTARY BILLS

In considering this mass of material, we should start where it all begins, in Parliament. It is common knowledge that a new government is brought into power by a general election every four or five years with a mandate to bring into effect a certain programme, usually contained in a party manifesto published just before the election. Upon the new government taking office after the election, and again each year at the beginning of the new parliamentary session, it announces its legislative programme in the Queen's speech, which is indeed read by the Queen, but is of course drafted by the Cabinet. Then comes the first stage in legislation, which is the publication of

Wages

A

BILL

To make fresh provision with respect to the protection of workers in relation to the payment of wages; to make further provision with respect to wages councils; to restrict redundancy rebates to employers with less than ten employees and to abolish certain similar payments; and for connected purposes.

Presented by Mr. Kenneth Clarke
supported by
Mr. Chancellor of the Exchequer,
Mr. Secretary Hurd,
Mr. Secretary Edwards,
Mr. Secretary Rifkind,
Mr. Secretary Channon and
Mr. David Trippier

Ordered, by The House of Commons,
to be Printed, 30 *January* 1986

LONDON
Printed and published by
Her Majesty's Stationery Office
Printed in England at St Stephen's
Parliamentary Press

£4·70 net

[Bill 70]   (307064)   49/3

Figure 1

Wages Bill

EXPLANATORY AND FINANCIAL MEMORANDUM

The Bill repeals the Truck Acts 1831 to 1940 and other enactments imposing restrictions connected with the payment of wages. It establishes restrictions on deductions from wages and on the payments that may be received from workers by employers, and establishes a new right of access to industrial tribunals over claims relating to such deductions and payments. It restricts the operation of wages councils to workers who are aged 21 or over; provides powers for councils to set statutory minimum remuneration for workers within their scope; and provides for enforcement of the statutory minimum remuneration provisions. It restricts the payment of statutory redundancy rebates by the Secretary of State to employers with less than ten employees.

PART I

Clause 1 provides that deductions from pay, or payments received by employers, will be lawful where provided for in or by virtue of a statutory provision or in any relevant term of a worker's contract, or agreed to by a worker in writing in advance. The clause defines a relevant term of a contract for this purpose, and makes certain supplementary provisions.

Clause 2 provides that where a worker's employment involves selling directly to the public any deduction from his wages on account of a cash shortage or stock deficiency shall not exceed one-tenth of the gross amount of the wages payable to him.

Clause 3 provides for comparable protection in relation to payments received by an employer on account of a cash shortage or stock deficiency from a worker whose employment involves selling directly to the public.

Clause 4 provides that the limitation in clauses 2 and 3 will not apply to the final payment of wages made to a worker. It clarifies the interaction of the provisions with civil proceedings,

[Bill 70]   *a*   49/3

Figure 2

Parliamentary Bills embodying the measures forecast in the Queen's speech. These Bills have to pass through both Houses of Parliament by means of an agreed procedure, which usually consists of three readings, a Committee stage and a Report stage in each House, and then – somewhat later in the session and often somewhat amended – they receive the Royal Assent and so become Acts of Parliament.

Format of Bills

As law librarians, we are less concerned with the details of the legislative process than with the appearance which Parliamentary Bills have when they arrive in the law library. By placing a standing order with HMSO, it is possible to receive copies of every Bill (except those of a personal or local nature) coming before either House of Parliament. These will include all amendments as and when tabled and all revised prints issued after amendments have been made during the later stages of the Bill. Alternatively, if so desired, selected Bills may be purchased individually.

The main parts of a Parliamentary Bill may be seen in the specimen, Figs 1 and 2. Firstly, you will always find on the title page the date on which the Bill was ordered by the House of Commons to be printed, and you will also see the names of those by whom the Bill is proposed. You are thus enabled to keep your Bills in correct date order, by distinguishing between earlier and later prints of the same Bill, which is useful when several bundles arrive together from HMSO. You can also distinguish – by looking at the names of the promoters – between government Bills and those proposed by back-bench Members of Parliament or peers, which may be of far less importance. (Many Private Members' Bills never get beyond a first reading during the course of a parliamentary session, and are often presented only so as to focus public attention on a particular topic.) Another feature to note about Bills is that they nearly always contain an *Explanatory and Financial Memorandum*, which outlines briefly and in simple language the main purpose of the Bill and which also states the additional charge likely to be incurred by the public expenditure as a result of the Bill. This seems such an obvious insertion as to call for no particular comment, yet we shall find later that no statute – once it is enacted – has any such explanatory memorandum.

Each Bill has a serial number for citation purposes in the lower left-hand corner of the title page, enclosed within square brackets in the case of versions presented to the House of Commons and within round brackets in the case of versions presented to the House of Lords. The serial number is different for each stage of the Bill, and progresses throughout the session, so that the later versions of the Bill have higher serial numbers than the earlier. If citing a version of a Bill by its serial number, the session should also be indicated, as a new sequence of serial numbers is started at the beginning of each session. The examples, Figs 1 and 2 may be cited as H.C. Bill 1985–6 [70].

Library uses of Bills

The amount of use made of Parliamentary Bills depends very much upon the type of law library concerned. In a practitioners' law library, it is the final form taken by the Act that is alone of interest. For a practising lawyer to read a Bill at an earlier stage, when details in it still remain to be amended, would only confuse him unnecessarily, and he will as a rule leave it alone until it becomes an Act. In an academic law library, on the other hand, the situation is different. An academic lawyer teaching students a particular branch of the law must be able to give them forewarning of impending changes in that branch, because if a Bill is already on its way through Parliament, then it will be enacted and so part of the law by the time the students are qualified. For the same reason, an academic lawyer beginning to write a textbook on a particular topic must know what changes in the law are likely to be made while his textbook is under way, so that they may be incorporated as far as possible into the completed work. Given also that some academic lawyers have been associated with the work of the Law Commission and other law reforming bodies, you will see that in a university law library there is likely to be quite a lively interest in and use of Parliamentary Bills.

Progress of Bills through Parliament

A query often received in law libraries is how far a particular Bill has gone on its way through Parliament. This may be answered by reference to the *House of Commons Weekly Information Bulletin*, which appears weekly while Parliament is sitting and which indicates the title of each Bill before the House of Commons and the present state of its progress. If the library does not subscribe to this list, then the enquirer may have to be referred to the section headed 'Parliament' in the monthly issues of *Current Law* or to the appropriate sections in the *New Law Journal* or *Solicitors' Journal*. Very full information is also available on POLIS (see p. 695).

ACTS OF PARLIAMENT (THE STATUTES)

Queen's Printer's copies

Assuming now that our Bill has passed through all its stages in both Houses of Parliament, at the end of this process it receives the Royal Assent and so becomes an Act. As such, it will first appear in a paper copy published by HMSO, which is often known as a 'Queen's Printer's copy'. All new Acts are published by HMSO separately in this form, and unless the Act is of exceptional length and complexity, it should appear thus within a month of receiving Royal Assent. As with Bills, so with Acts, a standing order can be placed with HMSO, and a copy of each new Act received as published, or alternatively selected Acts may be purchased individually.

Parts of an Act

A quick glance at the illustrations shown (Figs 3–5) of a Queen's Printer's copy of an Act will indicate the main parts of a Statute, which may be referred to again during the course of the chapter. The Statute, unless very short, begins with the Arrangement of Sections, or table of contents. On the next page, there follows the short title ('Trade Union Act 1984' in

Trade Union Act 1984

CHAPTER 49

ARRANGEMENT OF SECTIONS

PART I

SECRET BALLOTS FOR TRADE UNION ELECTIONS

PART II

SECRET BALLOTS BEFORE INDUSTRIAL ACTION

PART III

POLITICAL FUNDS AND OBJECTS

Resolutions under 1913 *Act*

A

Figure 3

ELIZABETH II

Trade Union Act 1984

1984 CHAPTER 49

An Act to make provision for election to certain positions
in trade unions and with respect to ballots held in connection with strikes or other forms of industrial action;
to require trade unions to compile and maintain
registers of members' names and addresses; to amend
the law relating to expenditure by trade unions and
unincorporated employers' associations on political
objects; and to amend sections 1 and 2 of the Employment Act 1980.   [26th July 1984]

B E IT ENACTED by the Queen's most Excellent Majesty, by and
with the advice and consent of the Lords Spiritual and
Temporal, and Commons, in this present Parliament
assembled, and by the authority of the same, as follows:—

PART I

SECRET BALLOTS FOR TRADE UNION ELECTIONS

1.—(1) Subject to the following provisions of this Part of this Duty of trade
Act, it shall be the duty of every trade union (notwithstanding union to hold
anything in its rules) to secure— elections for
certain
(a) that every person who is a voting member of the princi- positions.
pal executive committee of the union holds that position by virtue of having been elected as such a member

Figure 4

26   c. **49**   *Trade Union Act 1984*

PART IV   (4) In subsection (5) (ballots to be conducted so as to secure that those voting may do so in secret) the word " may ", where it last occurs, shall be omitted.

(5) In section 2(2)(*b*) of the Act of 1980 (ballots to which section 2 applies to be conducted so as to secure that those voting may do so in secret), the word " may " shall be omitted.

Expenses.

1980 c. 42.

21. There shall be defrayed out of money provided by Parliament any increase attributable to this Act in the sums payable out of money so provided under section 1 of the Employment Act 1980 (payments in respect of secret ballots).

Short title, commencement and extent.

22.—(1) This Act may be cited as the Trade Union Act 1984.

(2) Section 4 shall come into force on the day on which this Act is passed.

(3) Save as aforesaid, Part I shall come into force on such day as the Secretary of State may by order made by statutory instrument appoint.

(4) Part II shall come into force on the expiry of the period of two months beginning with the day on which this Act is passed.

(5) Part III shall come into force on 31st March 1985.

(6) Parts I and II and sections 18 and 20 of this Act do not extend to Northern Ireland and Part III does not apply in relation to any trade union which has its head or main office in Northern Ireland.

PRINTED IN ENGLAND BY W. J. SHARP
Controller and Chief Executive of Her Majesty's Stationery Office and
Queen's Printer of Acts of Parliament

LONDON: PUBLISHED BY HER MAJESTY'S STATIONERY OFFICE
£3.30 net
ISBN 0 10 544984 9

Figure 5

the example shown); then we have the citation ('1984 Chapter 49'), the long title ('An Act to make provision for election . . .'), the date of Royal Assent (within square brackets), and the enacting formula ('Be it enacted . . .'). Sometimes in old Acts, there is also a preamble before the enacting formula, usually beginning with the word 'Whereas' and setting forth the mischief which the Act is intended to remedy; but this is rarely used today. Note that there is no explanatory memorandum, which is dropped from the Bill after it has been enacted.

The text of the Act follows, beginning with Section 1. As a matter of nomenclature, it should be noted that an Act has sections and subsections, whereas a Bill has clauses and sub-sections.

At the end of the statute, we normally have a section dealing with 'Citation, commencement and extent', or 'Short title, commencement and extent'; often, there are also preceding sections on 'Interpretation' and on 'Consequential amendments, repeals, savings, etc.'. Then follow the Schedules, which among other things prescribe forms to be used, furnish illustrations, and list consequential amendments in more detail. The Schedules also always contain a table of repeals, indicating which Acts or sections of Acts have been repealed by the new Act.

The official editions of the Statutes

The Queen's Printer's copies of the Statutes, because of their format, are not suitable for permanent preservation, but for this there is a choice of several bound series. The first to be mentioned inevitably is the official series, now known as *Statutes in Force*. This was completed between 1972 and 1981, and it contains with certain exceptions (to be mentioned later) all the public general Acts currently in force, arranged in groups and sub-groups according to their subject matter. At the time of completion of the series, there were 131 titles contained within 84 binders according to the officially suggested arrangement. All of the binders are looseleaf, so that new Acts can be inserted as and when published, and similarly repealed Acts can be removed. Further, it is the intention that new prints of heavily amended Acts shall be provided as and when required.

Libraries can subscribe to the whole of the series or to part of it only, as suits their requirements. A subscription can be taken out to all the Acts relating to a particular jurisdiction within the United Kingdom (England and Wales, Scotland, or Northern Ireland), and all Acts published are marked according to the jurisdiction or jurisdictions to which they relate. In addition, subscribers whose subject interests are restricted may sub-scribe to certain groups only, according to their needs.

The Acts not included in the series are Consolidated Fund, Appropriation, Expiring Laws, Statute Law Revision and Statute Law (Repeals) Acts, Acts relating to certain taxes no longer exigible, Acts extending only to territory outside the United Kingdom, Acts of a local or personal nature, and Acts of the Parliament of Northern Ireland.

The method of compiling *Statutes in Force* ensures that all the Acts relating to a group are placed together in the same binder and theoretically are kept up to date. Thus, all the Acts relating to sale of goods will be found within one binder, with a filing instruction and contents list at the front indicating which are included and when the latest Acts on the subject were filed into the binder. There is also a cumulative supplement to each group, providing a list of amendments, repeals and corrections, which is updated each year. An alphabetical list of groups, and alphabetical and chronological lists of Acts and Measures, are published each year as guides to the series.

Annotations to *Statutes in Force* are limited to footnotes indicating amendments to the text made in later Acts. Repealed sections are simply omitted, and a list of repealed sections with authority for their repeal is given after the text of the Act concerned.

It should be noted that, despite the hopes expressed when the series was first launched, replacement copies of amended Acts are not provided particularly lavishly, and it is therefore always necessary to check from the text of the Act itself to the cumulative supplement. A letter from Sir Theodore Ruoff to the *Law Society's Gazette*, vol. 80, 1983, p. 2,963, drew attention to the delay after numerous amendments in providing an updated copy of the Land Registration Act 1925, which may serve as a warning in this respect.

Statutes in Force, then, while an advance on its predecessor *The Statutes Revised*, the third edition, 1951, of which began to go out of date as soon as published, still has certain drawbacks. Users of the series are advised always to check that the library where they are consulting it has subscribed to all the groups and classes, and to remember that the Acts themselves are revised only as far as the dates indicated on their title pages. As the series is looseleaf, the possibility always exists that Acts may be removed by unscrupulous users, while from the librarian's point of view the series like all looseleaf publications needs regular servicing.

To supplement *Statutes in Force*, the annual series of bound volumes called *Public General Acts and Measures* continues to be published by HMSO, as it has been since 1831. Each year's volume contains the full texts of the Statutes and Church Assembly or General Synod Measures for the year, alphabetical and chronological lists of the Acts and Measures for the year, an alphabetical list only of the Local and Personal Acts for the year (up to 1919 and since 1962), a table showing the effect of the year's legislation, tables of derivations (since 1967) and destinations (since 1974) of Consolidation Acts for the year, a table of textual amendments by statutory instruments (since 1976), and an index.

The authoritative nature of *Statutes in Force* and of the *Public General Acts and Measures* is buttressed by section 19 of the Interpretation Act 1978 (1978 c. 30), which provides that any reference to an Act by a later Act 'shall, unless the contrary intention appears, be read as referring – (a) in the case of Acts included in any revised edition of the statutes printed by authority, to that edition ... (c) in any other case, to the Acts printed by the Queen's printer, or under the superintendence or authority of Her Majesty's Stationery Office'.

Other collected editions of the Statutes

As alternatives to the official series of the Statutes, there are several series issued by commercial publishers, who are permitted to reprint them by arrangement with HMSO. Most of these series are annotated to a greater or lesser extent, so as to convey additional information not available in the official editions. A brief guide to the respective merits of the various series now follows.

Halsbury's Statutes

Halsbury's Statutes (4th edition announced by Butterworths for 1985–9, 50 vols) is the most important privately issued series, and has several advantages in a law library over the official series. Besides being fully comprehensive, it is well annotated; the annotations usually follow each section of an Act, relating it to earlier legislation (stating, for example, whether it is a re-enactment), providing statutory definitions of terms used, giving cross-references where required, and mentioning any delegated legislation made under the authority of the section concerned.

Halsbury also has various time-saving arrangements for keeping up to date. The third edition has provided a looseleaf *Current statutes service* containing statutes of the current year in chronological order, which is replaced in due course by annual hardback continuation volumes. In the fourth edition, it is proposed greatly to expand the *Current statutes service*, which will remain in looseleaf form and which will contain all Acts passed since publication of the main volumes and not yet incorporated in re-issue volumes. These Acts will be arranged by subject. Instead of annual continuation volumes, re-issue volumes will be supplied as required to replace fourth edition volumes which have become substantially out of date.

The fourth edition, like the current third edition, will also provide a looseleaf noter-up service in order to record the effect of new legislation on already published material. The noters-up will be cumulated as before into an annual cumulative supplement. Subscribers to the new edition will also re-ceive a user's guide and an annual volume entitled *Is it in force?* giving the commencement dates of sections of post-1945 statutes in force as at 1 January of the current year. It can be assumed that the fourth edition of Halsbury like the third will also provide an index volume.

The method of arrangement in Halsbury, as in *Statutes in*

Force, is by subject, although the same subject headings are not always used in the two series. For instance, the headings 'Church of England' and 'Environment' in *Statutes in Force* become respectively 'Ecclesiastical law' and 'Open spaces and historic buildings' in Halsbury. Users should be aware of these differences when consulting either series.

A drawback to Halsbury is that certain Acts covering more than one subject are split to an excessive extent. For instance, in the third edition the Local Government, Planning and Land Act 1980 is split between seven headings in different parts of the 1980 continuation volume, and will therefore presumably be split between seven different volumes in the fourth edition. Another drawback to Halsbury is that Acts applying to Scotland only are omitted, although Acts applying to Northern Ireland only are included.

A new feature promised for the fourth edition of Halsbury is the use of LEXIS as the source of up-to-date texts of all Acts included in the work. It is noted that fourth edition subscribers will be entitled to receive print-outs from LEXIS of any statutes on request, at a special rate. For details of LEXIS, as regards statutes generally, see below.

Current Law Statutes Annotated

Current Law Statutes Annotated is another publisher's series of current statutes only from 1948 onwards, arranged in chronological order. The statutes originally appeared in paper sections, which were then replaced by bound volumes at the end of each year. From 1982 onwards, however, the initial issue of Acts has been in parts in a looseleaf binder, which enables the publishers to be more flexible in the order of publication. The looseleaf parts are replaced by bound volumes during the year, and can then be kept as duplicate copies or discarded. The annotations included are somewhat less detailed than those in Halsbury; but, unlike Halsbury, this series includes Acts pertaining to Scotland, where it is published with the prefix '*Scottish*'.

The series is supplemented by *Current Law Statutes Citator 1947–1971*, which indicated all repeals and amendments during that period, and also case-law in which the Acts listed had been judicially considered during the same period. This is continued by *Current Law Legislation Citator*, which is cumulative for the years since 1972.

A number of Acts of special importance are reprinted afterwards as *Current Law Statutes Reprints*, and are advertised by the publishers under the names of the editors responsible for the annotations.

Law Reports Statutes

The Law Reports Statutes, 1865 to date, are taken by a large number of law libraries, probably because they can be obtained on the same subscription as *The Law Reports*. They are not a wholly independent series, however, being in effect the Queen's Printer's copies reprinted under an Incorporated Council of Law Reporting imprint and with the same tables and indexes as *Public General Acts and Measures* at the end of the year. They are thus not annotated, and they have the further drawbacks (from the law librarian's point of view) that they are somewhat late in appearance and that they have to be bound by the subscriber.

Butterworths Annotated Legislation Service

Butterworths Annotated Legislation Service, 1947 to date, began as the continuation of a wartime looseleaf series by the same publishers entitled *Butterworths Emergency Legislation Service Annotated*. The aim of the series is to provide practitioners with a working guide to those statutes which are of everyday importance. Hence, it is selective rather than comprehensive in its coverage; but it contains the most detailed annotations of any series for those Acts which it does cover. Each volume contains either one Act only, or a selection of a few Acts at a time, and many of the former have been reprinted as separate publications later. Every two years a cumulative index to the series is produced, and this indicates which Acts to date have been printed in the series and where they may be found.

Collections of statutes by subject

The collections of statutes described have all been general ones, covering the whole legislative field. There exist also some very useful subject collections of statutes, which have been compiled for the law publishers. These include, for example, *Sweet and Maxwell's Property Statutes*, *Scots Mercantile Law Statutes* and *Butterworths Property Law Handbook*. Their main market is amongst law students, who are thus enabled to buy the statutes they most need in convenient format and at a reasonable price, but they also have their uses in law libraries.

It is interesting to note that the various subject collections of statutes issued by Messrs. Butterworths, including the example cited above, are now being prepared directly from LEXIS, so enabling new editions to be produced more economically.

Older statutes

All of the series of statutes mentioned so far have been current ones, suitable for tracing new or recent Acts, or older Acts still in force. Occasionally, however, it may be necessary to trace a nineteenth-century Act which has been repealed. Because it has been repealed, it will not be found in the third edition of *The Statutes Revised*, in *Statutes in Force*, or in the latest edition of Halsbury. In this case, the best means of obtaining a copy of the Act concerned is through the earlier volumes of *Public General Acts and Measures*, a series which, as already indicated, commenced in 1831 (at first under the title *Public General Acts*). For all editions of the statutes during the period prior to 1800, see Chapter 7.

The statutes in information retrieval systems

So much for the main series of statutes published in book form. Nowadays, however, the statutes, in common with other legal materials, are finding their way onto the databases of information retrieval systems, and no account of legislation tion can therefore be complete without mentioning these.

Far and away the most important information retrieval system covering law and the legal system is LEXIS, which is marketed in the United Kingdom by Butterworths Telepublishing. It includes all Public General Acts currently in force, together with those enacted but not yet in force. LEXIS is a full text system, so that the whole of any Act covered, including its Schedules, can be made available on the screen.

Another information retrieval service, LAWTEL, which is a closed user group of Prestel, offers information on statutes but is not full text. By special arrangement, users of this system can have access to LEXIS, at a cost.

For detail of additional information available on POLIS see p. 695.

Special types of statutes

The law librarian should be aware of the various types of statutes that exist, quite apart from their publishing arrangements. Thus, the Public General Acts can be divided according to their purpose. The largest class, and that requiring the least comment, consists of those described in an old term as 'remedial Acts', in the sense that they are passed in order to remedy defects in the existing law or defective social situations. Such, for example, are the numerous Landlord and Tenant Acts or Housing Acts that have been passed over the years. Another class requiring no comment here consists of the Finance Acts and others concerned with raising revenue for the government. Other types of Acts will be described briefly below.

Constitutional statutes

In some countries, constitutional laws form a special class of their own, and often require special procedures to be used for their amendment or repeal. This is not the case in the United Kingdom, where constitutional statutes go through Parliament on exactly the same basis as all other statutes. The differing situation in this respect in the Republic of Ireland is set on p. 119.

Codifying Acts

Codification of the law is a process which has been used in a number of other countries, for instance, in the case of the *Code Napoléon* in France or the German Civil Code. There has been no general codification in the United Kingdom, but there have been a number of codifying and consolidating Acts. To quote from an authoritative source, 'Codifying Acts are Acts passed to codify the existing law, both statutory and common law, *ie*, not merely to declare the law upon some particular point, but to declare in the form of a code the whole of the law upon some particular subject'. (Craies, W. F. *Craies on statute law*, 7th edition, 1971, p. 59.) Examples often quoted of Codifying Acts are the Bills of Exchange Act 1882, the Partnership Act 1890, the Sale of Goods Act 1893, and the Marine Insurance Act 1906.

Consolidating Acts

Consolidating Acts, on the other hand, only consolidate the statute law on a subject, and do not necessarily affect the case-law. Their object is to consolidate in one Act the provisions contained in a number of statutes, sometimes with minor amendments, so as to make the law more accessible to the practitioner. A number of consolidating statutes are passed each year now, a special procedure being used in Parliament to enable them to go through without debate. This procedure has been extended since 1967 to consolidating Bills giving effect to recommendations made by the Law Commission. Examples include the Highways Act 1980, the Income and Corporation Taxes Act 1970, and the Road Traffic Act 1972.

Statute Law Revision Acts

Another type of Act consists of the Statute Law Revision Acts or Statute Law (Repeals) Acts, which represent a tidying up operation on the Statute Book. The first Statute Law Revision Act at present in the Statute Book was passed in 1861, and others have continued at intervals to the present day. Activity in this field has become more systematic since the inception of the Law Commission and Scottish Law Commission. These bodies have been specifically charged with, among other duties, a review of the law 'with a view to its systematic development and reform, including in particular the codification of such law, the elimination of anomalies, the repeal of obsolete and unnecessary enactments, the reduction of the number of separate enactments, and generally the simplification and modernization of the law'. (Law Commissions Act 1965, s. 3.)

Geographical extent of statutes

So far, apart from brief references, we have been dealing with Acts covering the whole of the United Kingdom. Normally, in the case of Public General Acts, there is a presumption that the Act extends to the whole of the United Kingdom, unless stated otherwise. Any statement to the contrary will appear in the last section of any statute, which nearly always deals with the matters of 'Short title, commencement and extent'. Here, the word 'extent' means geographical extent, and the section will specify whether any portions of the United Kingdom are excluded. Thus, certain Acts, such as the Local Government Finance Act 1982, extend to England and Wales only, while others may extend to Scotland only or to Northern Ireland only; or alternatively, Scotland or Northern Ireland may be expressly excluded from the operation of the Act. Acts applying to Scotland or to Northern Ireland only are often identifiable as such from their titles, as for instance, the Local Government and Planning (Scotland) Act 1982 or the Northern Ireland Act 1982. Normally, England and Wales are treated as one unit, but occasionally there are separate provisions for Wales, as in the Local Government Act 1972, or Acts applying to Wales only, such as the Welsh Language Act 1967.

The statute laws of Scotland and of Northern Ireland are dealt with in more detail in the Scottish and Irish sections below.

Local and Personal Acts

All of the statutes referred to in the last section are public general statutes, even though only extending to part of the United Kingdom, but there is a parallel series of Local and Personal Acts (known before 1948 as Local and Private Acts), which must now be considered. These are Acts of Parliament, the application of which is limited to certain localities or individuals, for instance, by enabling local authorities to promote or prohibit certain activities in their areas. An example of a Local Act is the Merseyside Metropolitan Railway Act 1975, which gave the Merseyside Passenger Transport Executive and British Railways Board power to construct works and acquire land as necessary for a new underground railway in Liverpool. An example of a Personal Act is the Hugh Small and Norma Small (Marriage Enabling) Act 1982, which enabled a stepson and stepmother to be married legally to each other. Personal Acts are now rare, and there were none shown in the indexes between the Lucas Estate Act 1963 and the Wellington Estate Act 1972.

To make things more confusing, however, not every Act which is local or personal in its nature or application is a Local or Personal Act. Thus, the Conwy Tunnel (Supplementary Powers) Act 1983, which enabled the Secretary of State for Wales to acquire land and carry out works for the construction and maintenance of a road tunnel under the Conwy Estuary, has appeared in the Public General series, although clearly local in its application. Similarly with Mr Speaker King's Retirement Act 1971, which was an Act of a personal nature providing a pension to the retired Speaker of the House of Commons. So a further point of distinction may be made, which is that Public General Acts arise from Bills proposed by the Government or (occasionally) by private Members of Parliament, whereas Local or Personal Acts in England and Wales arise through a different procedure by petition from the promoters, who may be a local authority, a nationalized industry or public utility, or (very occasionally) a private individual. Because Local Acts originate in this way, all copies of the proposals in the Bill stage have to be printed by the promoters, and hence are not available from HMSO.

Historically, the distinction between Public General and Public Local and Personal Acts was first made in 1798. For the complicated history of their classification since that date, reference should be made to *Craies on statute law*, 7th edition, 1971, pp. 55–8, or, more briefly, *Halsbury's Laws of England*, 4th edition, vol. 44, footnote 2 to paragraph 806.

All the Local and Personal Acts (previously Local and Private Acts) have been published by HMSO since 1924. Before that date, as shown in the works referred to in the preceding paragraph, there were some exceptions as regards Private Acts. HMSO also publishes an annual table and index to the Local and Personal Acts, and it is possible to obtain all the Local and Personal Acts for the year on standing order as they come out. Few libraries in fact do obtain them all, so that a full collection of these Acts going back into the nineteenth century is extremely valuable. As we have already seen, there is also an alphabetical list of Local and Personal Acts of the year in the preliminaries to the volume of the Public General Acts and Measures for each year.

A major rationalization of local legislation is now under way, following the provisions of the Local Government Act 1972, s. 262, and the Local Government (Scotland) Act 1973, s. 225. Both sections authorized the continuance in force of local legislation in the areas to which it already applied, subject to a ministerial order extending it to the whole of a new local government area. It also provided that, except where a local Act was continued in force by ministerial order, all existing Local Acts were to cease to operate in metropolitan counties at the end of 1979 and in other areas at the end of 1984 (both dates since extended). It was intended that this period of grace should be used to enable local legislation to be pruned quite substantially and re-enacted in a more manageable form for the new local government areas. This task is proving even greater than was anticipated, as is shown by the successive extensions to the transition period, and it will be some time before local legislation will settle down in its new shape.

The re-indexing of local legislation is also under way. At present, there exist two useful retrospective indexes produced by HMSO, a main index covering the years 1801 to 1947 and a supplementary index covering the years 1948 to 1966. The main index is a classified subject index of all Local and Personal Acts during the period, broad subject headings being used such as Railways, Canals, Enclosures, and so on. The supplement has a similar arrangement, with only slight modifications to the subject headings used, and also contains separate alphabetical and chronological lists of all Local and Personal Acts passed during the nineteen years that it covers (a feature not contained in the main volume). Some repeals are shown in the entries in the main index, but not exhaustively, so that it is necessary to refer to the Acts themselves for certainty in this respect. At the same time, the indexes are a useful starting point in tracing Acts referring to a particular locality, and will at least suffice to give adequate references for inter-library loan, should the Acts required not be in your own library.

Apart from the limited amount of information given in the two indexes described above, there has been till recently no means of knowing which of the Local Acts on the Statute Book are still in force except by research on the Acts themselves. Because of the chaotic state of the Local Acts, the Law Commission was directed by the Statute Law Committee in 1974 to begin work on a *Chronological table of local legislation*. The aim of the project has been to produce complete chronological tables of Local and Personal Acts from 1797 to 1973 and of Private Acts from 1539 to 1973, showing the effect on them of later legislation. As a first stage in the project, a *Chronological table of local legislation* covering the fifty years from 1925 to 1973 has been produced and became available at the Law Commission early in 1985. This records the effect on Local, Personal and Private Acts passed between 1539 and 1973 of all legislation passed within the fifty-year period except local Statutory Rules and Orders, local Statutory Instruments and Acts of the Parliament of Northern Ireland. It should be noted that the *Chronological table of local legislation* is not for sale generally, but a limited number of copies are being made available to law libraries with extensive collections of this material.

Legislation passed during and since 1974, with effect on previous Local or Private Acts, is now noted in the *Chronological table of the statutes*.

Church Assembly and General Synod Measures

Another form of legislation, that it is convenient to mention here, are the Church Assembly Measures (known as General Synod Measures from 1972 onwards). Since the beginning of 1920, the National Assembly of the Church of England (now the General Synod of the Church of England) has been able to legislate for the Church, subject to the approval of the Ecclesiastical Committee of Parliament, under the terms of the Church of England Assembly (Powers) Act 1919. These Measures, as they are called, have the same binding force on the laity of the Church as statutes, and they are printed in the same volumes as the Public General Acts. Church Assembly Measures and General Synod Measures also appear in the group headed 'Church of England' in the series *Statutes in Force*. For further details about ecclesiastical law, see Chapter 13.

Citation of statutes

Having described the various series of statutes, our next task is to discuss the problems which the law librarian is likely to encounter when using statutory material. One of the most important of these is the citation of statutes. This arises because statutes are frequently cited in the official manner in references that you may be given, and in fact you might even be required to find statutes identified only by their citation.

Citation by regnal year

Any statute, or Act of Parliament, then, may be cited by its short title and calendar year, which is in fact the way in which it is commonly referred to in normal speech. Alternatively, it may be cited more precisely in the official way, but this form of citation differs according to whether the Act was passed before or after the last day of 1962. Any Act passed before the close of 1962 should be cited by its regnal year and chapter number. Thus, the Highways Act 1959 is cited officially as 7 &

8 Eliz. 2 c. 25. This means that it was the 25th Act to receive the Royal Assent during the parliamentary session taking place in the seventh and eighth years of the present reign. The regnal year and the parliamentary session almost never coincide, and both differ from the calendar year. The regnal year begins always on the date of the monarch's accession, which is 6 February in the case of the present Queen, whereas the parliamentary session normally runs from about the last week in October or first week in November. On account of the commencement of the parliamentary session in November, we find that chapter numbers of a few statutes at the extreme end of the calendar year (that is, the beginning of the new session) are lower than those earlier in the calendar year. Thus, to return to the year 1959, the closing Act of the session 7 & 8 Eliz. 2 was the Legitimacy Act 1959 (7 & 8 Eliz. 2 c. 73), which received Royal Assent on 29 July 1959. The next Act in the Statute Book, Mr Speaker Morrison's Retirement Act, received Royal Assent on 17 December 1959, and is cited as 8 Eliz. 2 c. 1.

Sometimes, it should be noted, the parliamentary session ends before its time, owing to an election, and then there is a much longer second sequence of Acts at the end of the year. For instance, in 1955, Parliament was dissolved for a General Election on 6 May, so closing the parliamentary session 3 & 4 Eliz. 2. The new Parliament assembled on 9 June, and 22 Public General Acts passed by it before the close of the year 1955 appear in the Statute Book, under the heading 4 Eliz. 2. This session, which became known as 4 & 5 Eliz. 2 as soon as the anniversary date of the Queen's accession on 6 February was passed, lasted until November 1956, so was considerably longer than a normal calendar year.

A further complication arises in the case of volumes of the Public General Acts prior to 1940. Each volume before that date contained all the Acts of a parliamentary session, not of a calendar year, so that the short second sequence of Acts at the end of a calendar year went in effect into the volume for the following year. One well-known example, which is often difficult to locate on this account, is the Public Order Act 1936. This Act was Chapter 6 of the parliamentary session 1 Edw. 8 & 1 Geo. 6, and it received Royal Assent on 18 December 1936. Because it came at the beginning of the new parliamentary session, it was included in the volume of the Public General Acts for 1937, not 1936. Another example where this practice had an odd effect is a volume of the Public General Statutes which runs over three calendar years, from 1914 to 1916, as it covers a parliamentary session extending from November 1914 to January 1916. It is thus most important, in the case of Acts passed before 1940, to have the citation to hand, in case difficulties such as these should arise.

Citation by calendar year

These complications were all brought to an end by the Acts of Parliament Numbering and Citation Act 1962 (10 & 11 Eliz. 2 c. 34), which laid down that the chapter numbers assigned to Acts of Parliament passed in the year 1963 and subsequently should be assigned by reference to the calendar year and not the session in which they were passed. This brings Britain into line with other Commonwealth countries and makes the whole method of citing statutes much easier to understand and to follow. The sequence of chapter numbers is now continuous throughout the whole calendar year, regardless of parliamentary session. Thus, the last Act of the parliamentary session 18 & 19 Eliz. 2 was the Indecent Advertisements (Amendment) Act 1970, which received Royal Assent on 29 May 1970 and is cited as 1970 c. 47; and the first Act of the new session of Parliament after the General Election was the Appropriation (No. 2) Act 1970, which is cited as 1970 c. 48. It should be noted also that many pre-1963 statutes are now being cited by calendar year retrospectively in official publications, although this is not obligatory.

Citation of Local and Personal Acts, and Church Assembly Measures

There are special methods of citing Local Acts, Personal Acts and Church Assembly Measures. Local and Personal Acts up to the end of 1962 were cited, like Public General Acts, by their regnal year and chapter number. The chapter numbers, however, ran in a different sequence from those of the Public

General Acts, and so the citation was by means of a roman numeral in the case of Local Acts and by an italicized arabic numeral in the case of the few Personal Acts that remain. For instance, whereas the citation 7 & 8 Eliz. 2 c. 25 referred to the Highways Act 1959, as already mentioned, the corresponding roman numeral citation 7 & 8 Eliz. 2 c. xxv refers to the North Devon Water Act 1959, which of course is in the local series. After 1962, Local Acts are cited, like Public General Acts, by year and chapter number, but again the chapter number is in roman numerals. For example, whereas the Finance Act 1972 was 1972 c. 41, on the other hand the citation 1972 c. xli refers to the Liverpool Corporation Act 1972 in the local series. The one and only Personal Act passed in 1972, the Wellington Estate Act 1972, is cited as 1972 C. *1*.

Church Assembly Measures and General Synod Measures are cited similarly, with regnal year up to 1962 and calendar year since 1962, but with numbers instead of chapters. Thus, the Truro Cathedral Measure 1959 was 7 & 8 Eliz. 2 No. 1, and the Sharing of Church Buildings Measure 1970 was 1970 No. 2.

Coming into force of statutes

Another topic, on which library queries also arise, is the coming into force of statutes. The layman may think that an Act of Parliament automatically comes into force as soon as it is passed, but in fact the position is not quite as simple as that. Section 4 of the Interpretation Act 1978 (1978 c. 30) states that 'An Act or provision of an Act comes into force – (a) where provision is made for it to come into force on a particular day, at the beginning of that day; (b) where no provision is made for its coming into force, at the beginning of the day on which the Act receives its Royal Assent'.

When checking to see whether an Act has come into force, therefore, we should first of all look within the Act itself. If a date is provided within the Act, it will usually be found in the last section of the Act, which as mentioned earlier, nearly always deals with the matters of 'Short title, commencement and extent' or 'Citation, commencement and extent'. (Occasionally, this rule is broken, an exceptionally bad example being the Local Government, Planning and Land Act 1980, in which commencement provisions were scattered throughout the Act.)

If no date of commencement is provided within the Act, then as stated above it will come into force on the date on which it receives Royal Assent. This may be found within square brackets at the beginning of the Act after the long title (see Fig. 4). The dates of Royal Assent and of commencement usually coincide only in the case of short Acts or of Acts with few complications. An example is the Island of Rockall Act 1972, which specifically states, 'As from the date of the passing of this Act, the Island of Rockall ... shall be incorporated into that part of the United Kingdom known as Scotland ...' Here, the date of Royal Assent is given as 10 February 1972.

Many Acts, for which a date of commencement is provided within the Act itself, come into force after a short fixed period, now usually two months, and therefore present few problems to the enquirer. An example of this type of commencement provision is to be found in the Occupiers' Liability Act 1984, Section 4(2) of which states, 'This Act shall come into force at the end of the period of two months beginning with the day on which it is passed'. The date of Royal Assent for this Act was 13 March 1984, so that it may be regarded as coming into force on 13 May 1984.

Many Acts, however, provide real difficulty to the enquirer seeking a date of commencement. These are usually Acts of considerable length and complexity, requiring administrative machinery to be set up, and on this account it is often left to the Minister concerned to prescribe by order when the various sections of the Act shall come into force. An example here is the Wildlife and Countryside Act 1981, the provisions for commencement of which occur as usual near the end. Certain portions of the Act are specified as coming into force after one month, but Section 74(3) of the Act then goes on to state, 'The remaining provisions of this Act shall come into force on such day as the Secretary of State may by order made by statutory instrument appoint and different days may be appointed under this subsection for different provisions, different purposes or different areas'. The commencement orders bringing the remaining provisions of the Act into force as stated are published as part of the Statutory Instruments series, which will be described below.

A useful summary of the dates of commencement of recent statutes is to be found near the beginning of each monthly issue of *Current Law*. Some Acts take many years to come into force, and occasionally never come into force. A well-known example is the Easter Act 1928, which is still on the Statute Book, but which has never been brought into force.

As a result of the complaints from The Law Society and the Statute Law Society about the difficulty in tracing commencement provisions, a *Note of new guidance on preparation and commencement of legislation* was issued by the Management and Personnel Office (formerly the Civil Service Department) in 1982 and received some publicity in the legal press. (*Law Society's Gazette*, vol. 79, 1982, p. 968; *Statute Law Review*, 1983, p. 42.) This suggested, among other things, the commencement of Acts not less than two months after Royal Assent, the grouping of commencement provisions at the end of an Act wherever practicable, and an attempt to minimize the number of separate commencement orders for each Act. Each commencement order should include a note as to earlier orders relating to the same Act, so that the enquirer could see at once how much of the Act had been brought into force. It is to be hoped that this Note will clear up the worst of the difficulties, which have been experienced in previous years in tracing the implementation of Acts of Parliament.

Apart from tracing the commencement orders themselves, enquirers who wish to check whether a particular Act is in force can also try the cumulative supplement to *Halsbury's Statutes*, 3rd edition, which notes the commencement orders for each statute up to the end of the previous year. As already noted, this information will be given in future in more easily accessible form in the new publication *Is it in force?*, which first appeared in 1985 as an auxiliary to the 4th edition of *Halsbury's Statutes*. However, the legal information retrieval services enable one to check much closer to the current date.

LEXIS includes in its database all the information needed by enquirers regarding commencement dates. Searches may be made in the system to find the date in force of a particular section of an Act, or alternatively which sections of an Act are or are not yet in force. The information on the database is updated weekly and is up to date to within two or three weeks. LEXIS does not at present give information on the progress of Parliamentary Bills.

LAWTEL reports on the progress of Bills through Parliament, and also indicates Royal Assents and commencement dates.

Determining whether statutes are still in force

Having ascertained whether our statute has come into force, the next thing to do logically is to find out whether it is still in force, and many queries may centre round this point. Here, it is necessary to consult one of the indexes to the Statutes.

Chronological Table of the Statutes

The *Chronological Table of the Statutes* is the best work to use for a quick-reference answer. It is published in July each year, and goes up to the end of the last but one preceding year. It lists all the Public General Acts from 1235 onwards section by section, showing which sections have been repealed (and by what authority) and which have been amended in any way by subsequent legislation. Acts still wholly or partially in force have their titles printed in heavy type, while Acts now wholly repealed have their titles printed in italic type.

As already mentioned, a separate section at the end of the *Chronological Table* gives a chronological table of Local and Personal Acts showing the effect on them of the Public General and Local and Personal Acts from 1974 onwards. There are also similar tables at the end of the volume for pre-1707 Acts of the Parliament of Scotland and for Church Assembly and General Synod Measures.

Index to the Statutes in force

The *Index to the Statutes in Force*, which similarly appears each year (with a longer delay), is a research tool rather than a quick reference guide. Its function is to index all the public general statute law still in force at the end of a given year under detailed subject headings. A recent innovation is the inclusion, after most of the Acts cited in a heading, of numerical references to the groups or sub-groups in which the relevant texts of the Acts may be found in the series *Statutes in Force*.

Keeping up to date

As always, there is an awkward gap for the last few months, where the indexes leave off. The table of *Effect of legislation*, compiled for the annual volumes of the *Public General Acts and Measures*, helps a little, as this appears in March each year, four months ahead of the *Chronological Table of the Statutes*, which is in fact revised with its aid (*Law Librarian*, vol. 1, 1970, p. 8). The table of *Effect of legislation* lists in chronological order all Acts repealed or amended by Acts passed during the last preceding year. Alternatives which can be used are the annual cumulative supplement to *Halsbury's Statutes* and the looseleaf noter-up to Halsbury, which appear more promptly still.

If it is suspected that an amendment to an old Act has been made by a statute passed in the current year, then even these aids will not suffice, and as a last resource reference may have to be made to *Current Law*, or to the latest Queen's Printer's copies of the Acts themselves.

Enquirers may also have recourse to the legal information retrieval systems. As before, LEXIS is the most comprehensive of these. The texts on LEXIS are updated weekly and are up to date to within two or three weeks. Searches may be made to confirm which sections of an Act are still in force.

LAWTEL is also kept comprehensively up to date, and as noted previously users of this system have access to LEXIS should they wish to search the full text.

Searching for statutory material

The beginner to law librarianship should not be put off too much by the complicated nature of statutory material. Many enquiries will be quite easy, and will be simply requests for a specific Act or part of an Act. If the year and title of the Act have been quoted correctly, it will then be quite easy to find it. Alternatively, the enquirer may think that there has been a new Act on such and such a subject, and it will then be a case of taking the latest material first and working your way backwards – and also of consulting digests such as *Current Law*. If you are short of statutes for a particular year, it is always worth remembering that many legal textbooks are little more than reprints of the Acts on their subjects, with some annotations, and so you can if necessary fall back on these, where you know that the subject fits. It is also important in this connection not to forget the looseleaf encyclopedias, which are described on pages 197–9. Providing that you use all your sources intelligently, you should always be able to find a copy of the Act that you want in some form or other.

SUBORDINATE LEGISLATION

At the beginning of the chapter, a brief reference was made to the division of United Kingdom legislative materials into statutes and subordinate legislation. The latter category, to quote *Halsbury's Laws of England* (4th edition, vol. 44, paragraph 981), is 'legislation made by a person or body other than the Sovereign in Parliament by virtue of powers conferred either by statute or by legislation which is itself made under statutory powers'. To continue from Halsbury, 'it is frequently referred to as delegated legislation in the former case and subdelegated legislation in the latter'.

From the law librarian's point of view, it is sufficient to know that any items referred to as Orders, Regulations, Rules, Schemes, Directions or Warrants are likely to be subordinate legislation, and that far and away the greater part of these will be found nowadays in the *Statutory Instruments* series. This series was set up under the authority of the Statutory Instruments Act 1946, which replaced the old term 'Statutory Rule' by the new term 'Statutory Instrument', and which laid down the procedure as regards publication, numbering and citation of Statutory Instruments.

Statutory Instruments

Statutory Instruments exist to deal with matters too detailed to be included in an Act of Parliament, and they also have the advantage that they can be revoked or amended at short notice by the Minister concerned, in order to meet changing circumstances. Like the Acts of Parliament themselves, Statutory Instruments cover every field of activity, and range from local or routine orders dealing with rights of way or customs and excise, to quite important items, such as the Building Regulations or the Motor Vehicles (Construction and Use) Regulations. These latter, to take an example, have been made by the Secretary of State for Transport in exercise of the powers conferred by the Road Traffic Act 1972 and have been amended frequently so as to enable fresh provisions regarding size or weight of vehicles to be brought quickly into effect. Other Statutory Instruments appear from time to time modifying fees and charges, or other prescribed sums of money. Examples of these, in different fields, are the *Local Land Charges (Amendment) Rules* 1983 (S.I. 1983 No. 1591) and the *Family Provision (Intestate Succession) Order* 1981 (S.I. 1981 No. 255). Statutory Instruments such as these may often be referred to in the law library.

Orders, regulations and rules are all contained in the Statutory Instruments series. The Donoughmore Report (Committee on Ministers' Powers, 1932) (Cmd. 4060), tried to distinguish between these terms, not very successfully. The difference between regulations and orders thus remains rather vague, but on the other hand the term 'Rules' has been restricted to those Instruments appertaining to procedural matters, as for instance, the *Rules of the Supreme Court* or the *County Court Rules*.

An Order in Council is the highest form of subordinate legislation, and is made at a meeting of the Privy Council presided over by the Queen. Orders in Council are normally used for the matters remaining within the royal prerogative, such as the constitutions of dependent territories. These, together with Royal Proclamations, are usually printed in the annual volumes of the *Statutory Instruments* at the end of each year although they are not numbered in the *Statutory Instru-*

ments series. Occasionally, there are lapses. Thus, the *Territorial Waters Order in Council 1964* was printed in full in the *London Gazette*, but was not reprinted in the *Statutory Instruments* series until the final volume of 1965, because it was not brought to the editor's attention until then. Hence, it is necessary to subscribe to the *London Gazette* as well as to the *Statutory Instruments* series to be absolutely certain that you have complete coverage of all this type of material.

One or two more mundane regulations, also, have from time to time missed inclusion in the *Statutory Instruments* series or its predecessor the *Statutory Rules and Orders* series, whether through accident or design. Two noteworthy absentees, which are both still in force, are the Electricity Supply Regulations 1937 and the Children Act (Appeal Tribunal) Rules 1949. More recent absentees are the various statements of Immigration Rules, which have been issued as House of Commons Papers in 1973 and 1980. Fortunately, all are referred to in the series *Halsbury's Statutory Instruments* and may be obtained from HMSO.

Publication of Statutory Instruments

Like the statutes, the Statutory Instruments are first of all published individually in paper copies by HMSO, and then in annual volumes. These now appear in three parts a year (bound as six volumes) and exclude only those Instruments which are of a purely local character and those which have already been revoked by the end of the same year. The annual volumes were arranged by subject up to the end of 1960, but since then the Instruments contained in them have been arranged chronologically in their order of registration, so enabling the volumes to be published more promptly. Each part contains a list of Instruments published in that part, a table showing modifications to legislation, and an index. The final part for the year also contains a fuller table of effect of legislation, a numerical list for the whole year, and also a classified list of local Instruments with reference particulars.

Some observations may be made here on the indexing of the *Statutory Instruments*. In general the headings are obvious or relate to the names of the Acts under which the respective orders have been made. Some headings, however, are not so easily apparent. One example, to which attention should especially be drawn, is the heading 'Terms and conditions of employment', under which occur all the references to orders made under the various Employment Acts and on related topics. In the past, this has confused many enquirers.

The non-availability of local Statutory Instruments in the normal published series is also sometimes a cause for concern, as they can be difficult to trace once copies go out of print at HMSO. The Law Commission, in its introduction to the *Chronological table of local legislation*, reports that the Statutory Publications Office has a complete set of local Statutory Rules and Orders made between 1922 and 1947, and of local Statutory Instruments made after 1947, which is in process of being transferred to the Public Record Office. The Law Commission reports on the other hand that no single complete collection of local Statutory Rules and Orders made between 1890 and 1921 has yet been traced.

The official edition of the Statutory Instruments

A collected official edition exists of *The Statutory Rules & Orders and Statutory Instruments revised to December 31, 1948*. The arrangement within the volumes is by subject, while the index volume contains a numerical table in chronological order. A new collected edition is needed very badly, since, not only have many Rules and Orders or Instruments contained in the 1948 edition already been revoked or amended, but also many of the annual volumes published since 1948 are now out of print. It is unlikely, however, that any new edition will be provided within the foreseeable future.

Halsbury's Statutory Instruments

Fortunately, there also exists a privately issued series of Statutory Instruments, namely, *Halsbury's Statutory Instruments* published by Butterworths. The volumes in this series are constantly being replaced by up to date re-issues, and in addition there are the looseleaf service volume and additional texts volume, which contain the latest material. A user's guide tells the enquirer how to trace items in the series. The series is arranged by subject, so that all the references to all the Statutory Instruments on a given subject are set out in the form of a table at one point, usually at the beginning of the section dealing with that subject. Unfortunately, many of the Instruments are only printed in Halsbury in an abbreviated form, so that it can in no sense be regarded as a full substitute for the official series. It is, however, a useful adjunct to it, since you can use it to look up the outline of a particular Instrument quickly under its subject, obtain the correct citation, and then refer with the aid of this to the fuller version in the official volume. One other point to remember when using *Halsbury's Statutory Instruments* – always look in the service volume as well as in the subject volume, in order to take in the latest developments.

Other sources

Other sources of Statutory Instruments on the subjects covered include the various looseleaf encyclopedias, which are described more fully in Chapter 5. For instance, in a search for the latest Motor Vehicle (Construction and Use) Regulations already referred to, it might be quicker to look them up in the looseleaf *Encyclopedia of road traffic law and practice* rather than in the official *Statutory Instruments* series, because there the possible field of search is so much narrower. The same will apply to any of the other subjects covered by this series.

Statutory Instruments are also contained in the legal information retrieval systems. LEXIS covers all except local Statutory Instruments full text, and keeps its files up to date in the same way as the Statutes. LAWTEL gives a daily update of Statutory Instruments coming into force, but does not have a complete list of all Statutory Instruments in force.

Citation of Statutory Instruments

Citation of Statutory Instruments is regulated by section 2 of the Statutory Instruments Act 1946, and is very much simpler than that of statutes. They are referred to either by title, or by year and running number. Thus, the Motor Vehicles (Variation of Speed Limit) Regulations 1984 are referred to by that title, and can be cited as SI 1984 No. 325. This citation is always indicated prominently at the head of the front cover of the Statutory Instrument concerned.

There is also a secondary series number used in the headings of Statutory Instruments of certain restricted classes. These classes include commencement orders (indicated with a 'C'), Instruments relating to fees or procedure in courts in England and Wales (indicated with an 'L') and Instruments which apply to Scotland only (indicated with an 'S'). Thus, the County Court (Amendment) Rules 1983 have the heading '1983 No. 275 (L.1)', indicating that they were the first Instrument relating to fees or procedure to be issued during the year. These series numbers are of interest, but are not of great practical importance – it is the main part of the citation that matters. Similarly, departmental reference marks printed on the bottom right-hand corner of some Instruments may be ignored by librarians outside those departments.

The date when a Statutory Instrument comes into force is always indicated prominently at the beginning, and at its close there is always an explanatory note indicating its general purport.

Indexes and tables of Statutory Instruments

As with statutes, so with Statutory Instruments, HMSO has published a number of reference indexes and tables in order to help their users.

The *Index to Government Orders in force* is published every two years, and is for Statutory Instruments the equivalent to the *Index to the Statutes in Force*. The main sequence gives, under subject headings, particulars of the statutory powers under which all Instruments are made and lists of the Instruments made in exercise of those powers, thus in effect acting as an alphabetical subject index to the series. A subsidiary sequence gives a chronological table of statutes with references to subject headings in the main sequence, thus enabling one to trace

Instruments made under a particular section of a particular Act.

The *Table of Government Orders* is the equivalent to the *Chronological Table of the Statutes*. This appears annually, and lists all the general Statutory Rules and Orders and Statutory Instruments in chronological and numerical order from 1671 to date, showing which of them have been revoked or amended, and by what. Orders in Council and Royal Proclamations are also included at their appropriate point in the chronological sequence. Where an Instrument has been amended, particulars are given of the affected article or section.

HMSO also publishes separate monthly and annual *Lists of Statutory Instruments*, giving under subject headings the names and numbers of the latest instruments. Since 1983, these have also included a separate *List of Statutory Rules of Northern Ireland*.

Byelaws

It is convenient here to add a mention of local authority byelaws. These, too, are subordinate legislation of a kind, although they are not often thought of as such. Byelaws generally comprehend such matters as good behaviour in public places and good rule and governance, and are made by the local council and confirmed by the Minister responsible at the time for local government (at present, the Department of the Environment in England or the Welsh Office in Wales, formerly the Ministry of Local Government and Planning). Under section 236(8) of the Local Government Act 1972, byelaws normally have to be printed and supplied on request to enquirers for a small fee. The best source, from which to enquire about the byelaws of a particular area, is naturally the local authority concerned, either through its administrative offices, or through its public library service.

Quasi-legislative materials

A certain amount of quasi-legislative material, sometimes described in the past as 'sub-delegated legislation', remains to be dealt with. This includes ministerial circulars and codes of practice.

Ministerial circulars consist of administrative directions, instructions and advice sent out from the various ministries, usually to local authorities. They are not in themselves legislation, but they are often concerned with the implementation of legislation. The most important series likely to be asked for in a law library are those issued by the Home Office, Department of Education and Science, Department of the Environment, and the Department of Health and Social Security. These vary greatly in their accessibility. A large number of circulars from the Department of the Environment are reproduced in the relevant looseleaf encyclopedias on the law of town and country planning, housing law, environmental health law and practice, and so on; for fuller details of these works, see Chapter 5. Many Department of Education and Science circulars appear in *The new law of education* by G. Taylor and J. B. Saunders, 9th edn., 1984.

Only Department of the Environment circulars are listed fully in the HMSO catalogues. Circulars issued by the other departments mentioned above are listed in the *Catalogue of British official publications not published by HMSO*, usually after some delay.

Other quasi-legislative materials include the various codes of practice. The first of these to appear with legislative authority was the code of practice issued under the Industrial Relations Act 1971, dealing comprehensively with the whole field of industrial relations. Subsequently, parts of this were superseded by three separate codes issued under the Employment Protection Act 1975 by ACAS in 1977–8; these, as their titles indicate, covered *Disciplinary practice and procedures in employment, Disclosure of information to trade unions for collective bargaining purposes*, and *Time off for trade union duties and activities*. Separate codes of practice on *Picketing* and on *Closed shop agreements and arrangements* were issued with the authority of Parliament in 1980. All of these industrial relations codes, together with the *Code of practice for the elimination of racial discrimination and the promotion of equality of opportunity in employment* (known for short as the *Race relations code of practice*), are to be found included in the *Encyclopedia of labour relations law* and in *Harvey on industrial relations and employment law* (both looseleaf).

A code of practice in an allied field of public law is the *Housing (Homeless Persons) Act 1977 code of guidance (England and Wales)*, which has now reached its second edition. This may be found in the section for ministerial circulars in the *Encyclopedia of housing law and practice*.

More recently, four codes of practice dealing with police powers have been issued under the authority of section 66 of the Police and Criminal Evidence Act 1984, and have been published by HMSO. These include the *Code of practice for the exercise by police officers of statutory powers of stop and search*, the *Code of practice for the searching of premises by police officers and the seizure of property found by police officers on persons or premises*, the *Code of practice for the detention, treatment and questioning of persons by police officers*, and the *Code of practice for the identification of persons by police officers*.

SCOTLAND

Statutes

As mentioned above, in the section on 'Geographical extent of statutes', Acts referring specifically to Scotland have been included in the United Kingdom series for each regnal year since the Act of Union in 1707. In addition, several collections have been compiled during this period of Scottish Acts only.

In 1848, the Edinburgh publishing firm of William Blackwood and Sons commenced annual publication of *The public general statutes affecting Scotland*. The need for a comprehensive set of Scottish statutes from 1707 to 1847 was met by the same firm in 1876, when three volumes covering that period were issued. The annual volumes, known as *Blackwood's Acts*, continued for a century, save one year, terminating in 1947 with the Acts for 1946.

At the end of the nineteenth century another Edinburgh publishing firm, William Green, which specialized in law, commenced publication of *The Scots Statutes Revised*. This set contained all the Acts applicable to Scotland still in force in 1900. From 1901, Green also brought out an annual volume of statutes pertaining to Scotland, parallel to the Blackwood series. These continued until 1948, when they were replaced by *Scottish Current Law Statutes*, which have since been issued annually. The difference between the two sets published by Green is accounted for by the inclusion of all United Kingdom statutes in the later set, as distinct from those affecting Scotland only. The *Scottish Current Law Statutes* are essentially similar to *Current Law Statutes*, except that they also contain the Acts of Sederunt and Adjournal. The official *Statutes in Force* may also be consulted for up to date details.

A very useful practical tool for solicitors and law librarians which largely comprises statutes is the *Parliament House Book* published annually by Green between 1824 and 1981. Since 1982 it has been issued in looseleaf form, now in three volumes. These cover most questions of law likely to arise from day to day and have the double advantage of both assembling Acts, Statutory Instruments and other relevant material on one topic together, and being always up to date. The various sections cover fees, stamps and capital taxes; the Upper and Lower Courts; Court of Session practice; criminal procedure; solicitors; legal aid; bankruptcy and mercantile; companies; conveyancing; family law; landlord and tenant; succession; tribunals; and valuation for rating. Most of these are available as offprints for purchase separately and are used mainly by students.

There are a few other types of legislation peculiar to Scotland which need to be mentioned. Local and personal Bills may be introduced under the Private Legislation Procedure (Scotland) Act 1936; under this, any private individual or local authority desirous of obtaining an Act applies to the Secretary of State for Scotland for a provisional order. Subject to the need for a local enquiry to meet objections, if any, the order is issued and a Confirmation Bill is introduced into Parliament, which, once passed, is placed on the Statute Book.

Subordinate legislation

Acts of Sederunt are rules passed by the Court of Session, in modern times relating exclusively to procedure in that court and the Sheriff Courts. Various codifying Acts of Sederunt have been issued, the latest in 1965 known officially as *Rules of the Court of Session*, or more familiarly as *Rules of Court*. An Act of Adjournal is one passed by the High Court of Justiciary for regulating procedure in that court and in the inferior criminal courts. It should be noted that the *Rules of Court*, brought up to date, appear in the *Parliament House Book* each year, and that this section is now issued separately in 'Scots Courts' Statutes'. A new edition of the *Rules of Court* is in preparation.

Other subordinate legislation in Scotland takes the same form as elsewhere in Britain, *ie*, through Statutory Instruments. Orders of a local nature are not printed by HMSO, and to check these it is necessary to consult *The Edinburgh Gazette*, issued twice weekly.

IRELAND

At the beginning of the period covered by this chapter, the separate Parliaments of Ireland and of Great Britain were merged as the Parliament of the United Kingdom, which came into existence on the first day of 1801. This legislated for the whole of Ireland, as for Great Britain also, up to 1921, when the Government of Ireland Act 1920 came into effect. Thereafter the ways of Northern and Southern Ireland diverged, and must be dealt with separately.

Northern Ireland

Statutes

From 1921 to 1972, the Parliament of Northern Ireland (often known colloquially as 'Stormont') legislated on matters within its competence as laid down in the Government of Ireland Act 1920. Its Bills and Acts were issued on the Westminster pattern by HMSO Belfast. Annual volumes of Northern Ireland statutes have been issued since 1921, and there are also a *Chronological Table* and an *Index to the Statutes in force*, both triennial. Tables in the annual volumes may be used for years not yet covered by these last two works.

When the Parliament of Northern Ireland was dissolved in March 1972, the province passed under direct rule from Westminster. Legislation applying to Northern Ireland only was then passed by Orders in Council, issued as a sub-series of the United Kingdom *Statutory Instruments* series. Thus, as well as having its SI number, each order has an additional number relating to Northern Ireland only. These orders are included in the annual volumes of the Northern Ireland statutes from 1972, and are not published in the annual volumes of United Kingdom *Statutory Instruments*.

During direct rule, Bills were replaced by Draft Orders in Council, the first stage of which was a Proposal for a Draft. The Proposals were issued by HMSO Belfast, while the Drafts were published by HMSO London. The Drafts and the Orders in Council were all recorded in the British *Daily Lists* of government publications and also in the Northern Ireland monthly and annual lists.

The new Northern Ireland Assembly came into being in July 1973 and, until its prorogation in May 1974, had passed four 'Measures'. These were published singly by HMSO Belfast. Since 1974 government has again been by direct rule from Westminster and legislation has reverted to the pattern described above.

Statutes Revised, Northern Ireland, 2nd edn., HMSO, 1982, contains the public general legislation in force in Northern Ireland on 31 March 1981, with one important exception. The series includes Acts of the Parliaments of England, Ireland, Great Britain and the United Kingdom passed before 1921, Acts of the Northern Ireland Parliament and Measures of the Northern Ireland Assembly, and Orders in Council made under the Northern Ireland Act 1974 and the Northern Ireland (Temporary Provisions) Act 1972. It does not include Acts passed by the United Kingdom Parliament after 1920 relating to Northern Ireland, for which reference should be made to *Statutes in Force*. Like *Statutes in Force*, the format is looseleaf, in order to facilitate updating.

The *Bulletin of Northern Ireland Law* 1981– , includes summaries and commencement dates of all new legislation applicable in Northern Ireland and relevant developments in EEC law; and the Northern Ireland section of *Current Law* contains digests of all Northern Ireland Acts and Orders. The title 'Constitutional Law' in volume 8 of the 4th edition of *Halsbury's Laws of England* contains a summary of the situation in Northern Ireland as at 15 May 1974, that is, just before the prorogation of the Northern Ireland Assembly.

Subordinate legislation

Statutory Rules and Orders have been published singly, and subsequently in annual volumes, by HMSO Belfast since 1922. They first appear in the *Belfast Gazette*. This procedure was not altered by direct rule. Rules and Orders are noted in the *Bulletin of Northern Ireland Law*, and in *Current Law* under 'Northern Ireland', and an *Index to the Statutory Rules and Orders of Northern Ireland* is published every three years.

Citation

Generally speaking, citation is similar to that in England, sometimes with an indication of origin in the form (NI) or (Northern Ireland). The position of the words 'Northern Ireland' in the title enables one to distinguish between a Westminster Statute applying to Northern Ireland, *eg*, the Criminal Appeal (Northern Ireland) Act 1968, and a Northern Ireland Statute, *eg*, the Criminal Procedure Act (Northern Ireland) 1951. Since 1943, earlier than at Westminster, Northern Ireland statutes have been cited by calendar year and chapter number.

An example of the citation of an Order in Council made under the Northern Ireland Act 1974 is The Family Law Reform (Northern Ireland) Order 1977, SI 1977 No. 1250 (NI 17). This may be cited more briefly as 1977 (NI 17).

A full citation of a Statutory Rule and Order would be, for example, The Children (Performances) Regulations (Northern Ireland), 1971 (SR & O (NI) 1971 No. 25, p. 146). They can be cited briefly by number and calendar year.

For full details regarding citation at that time, one should refer to the *Manual of legal citations, Part 1, the British Isles* (1959), at pp. 32–5 under 'Ireland'.

Republic of Ireland

Statutes

The present legislative body (since 1922) is the Oireachtas, or Parliament, which consists of the Dáil (lower house) and the Senate. Bills and Acts are published in a pattern not unlike that at Westminster, statutes appearing singly and in annual volumes in Irish and in English. (Bound volumes for the years 1980–4 are available in the English version only.) There have been various consolidated indexes, the current one published in 1978 covering the period 1922–75. Annual volumes contain tables of the effect of legislation, and tables of latest collective citations.

Irish Current Law Statutes Annotated, 1984– , is a new looseleaf service which aims to provide the full text of every statute from 1 January 1984 with detailed annotations to the more important ones.

Subordinate legislation

Orders were published as *Statutory Rules and Orders* until 1947, and annual volumes had running numbers. (Sets of collected orders appeared as follows: volumes 1–23, 1922–38, index volume 24; volumes 25–34, 1939–45, index volume 35; volumes 36–9, 1946–7, index volume 40.) From 1948, they have been called *Statutory Instruments*. Annual bound volumes are published about eight years after the printing of the individual Instruments. Index volumes, non-cumulative, were published in 1962, 1965, 1973, 1977 and 1982 covering the periods 1948–60, 1961–3, 1964–70, 1971–4 and 1975–9 respectively.

Citation

To distinguish the English form of the Acts of the Oireachtas from Westminster Acts, the abbreviation (RI) may be used after the short title and date. Acts are cited by serial numbers instead of chapter numbers, for instance, the Higher Education Authority Act 1971, which is cited as No. 22 of 1971 or 22/ 1971. For full details, including the citation of Acts of the Irish Parliament before 1801, reference may be made to Part 1 of the *Manual of legal citations.*

Statutory Instruments may be cited by the abbreviation SI and a number, and also by the short title, for instance, the Restriction of Imports (Fertilizers from East Germany) Order 1967 (SI (RI) No. 254 of 1967) or (SI (RI) 1967 No. 254). Since 1958, pagination is not continuous, so that there can be no full reference to volume and page numbers as previously.

Constitution

The Republic has a written constitution, enacted in 1937 by plebiscite, to replace the original one of 1922. Amendments to the constitution require a referendum; for example, that on entry to the European Communities which was held in 1972.

CHANNEL ISLANDS

The most accessible account of the legal bibliography of the Channel Islands and the Isle of Man is contained in *A bibliographical guide to the law of the United Kingdom, the Channel Islands and the Isle of Man*, 2nd edn., Institute of Advanced Legal Studies, 1973, edited by A. G. Chloros, from which are taken the extracts cited below. The Isle of Man, but not the Channel Islands, is also covered by a chapter in *Law publishing and legal information: small jurisdictions of the British Isles*, 1981, edited by W. Twining and J. Uglow.

The statutory materials of the three main islands are best considered separately.

Jersey

'Legislation is normally effected at the present time by the States, but an Act passed by the States requires confirmation by the Sovereign in Council before it can acquire the force of law. Such legislation is published in a series of "Recueils des Lois" commencing in 1771' (Chloros, p. 232). The series of *Recueils des lois* from 1771 to 1950 were republished as Tomes 1–7 in three volumes in 1963–77. Since then, the series has been continued in biennial volumes published by the States' Greffe, described as *Orders in Council, laws, etc.* on the title page and as *Recueil des lois* on the spine. Apart from the spine title and occasional amendments to earlier laws, they have appeared wholly in English. The series has become looseleaf from 1979.

There is also a separate series of *Regulations and Orders*, commencing in 1939 and appearing annually. These correspond to the *Statutory Instruments* series on the mainland.

Guernsey

The principal legislative series in Guernsey is the *Ordinances of the States*, Volume 1 to date, 1533/1800 to date, printed by the *Guernsey Herald*. The spine title is *Recueil d'ordonnances*. These were published either annually or every two or three years, according to the amount of material to be incorporated, up to Tome xx for 1975–6. Since then, the series has been published in separate paper copies of the various ordinances.

The subsidiary legislative series for Guernsey has the title *Orders in Council, and other matters of general interest registered on the records of the Island of Guernsey*, and commences with Volume 1, 1803–. The spine title is *Ordres en conseil*. Volumes usually appeared every two or three years up to Volume xxvi for 1976–8, since when the series has consisted of separate paper copies of the various orders.

Both these Guernsey series appear wholly in English.

ISLE OF MAN

'The Isle of Man is governed by an ancient legislature known as Tynwald ... The Manx legislature is empowered to enact statutes concerning matters not transcending the frontiers of the island. Legislation in relation to certain matters falling outside this category is normally enacted by the Parliament at Westminster and extended to the Isle of Man' (Chloros, p. 237).

The revised edition of *Statutes of the Isle of Man*, commencing from the year 1417, was published at Douglas from 1883 onwards and 'is supplemented by annual volumes entitled *Acts of Tynwald*. Periodically these annual volumes are revised and incorporated in the series of Statutes' (Chloros, p. 242). Since 1977, the annual volumes have been discontinued and have been replaced by looseleaf binders, into which the individual Acts can be inserted. A new complete reprint of the *Statutes in force of the Isle of Man*, incorporating current amendments with annotations, has been promised shortly.

The Isle of Man statutes are indexed in the *Subject guide to Acts of Tynwald revised to 31st October 1984*, which it is anticipated will now appear annually. Two other indexes published in 1978 gave a subject guide and chronological table of the Acts of Parliament and of the subordinate legislation of the United Kingdom extending or relating to, or having effect in, the Isle of Man.

Subordinate legislation takes the form of government circulars, which are now issued as xerox copies rather than printed. They are indexed by a looseleaf chronological table into which insertions can be made and by a more permanent compilation called the *Subject guide and chronological tables to the subordinate legislation of the Isle of Man (as at 31.12.81)*.

FURTHER READING

GENERAL

There are two recent guides to government publications as a whole written for librarians:

Butcher, D. *Official publications in Britain*, Clive Bingley, 1983.
Rodgers, F. *A guide to British government publications*, H. W. Wilson, 1980.

PARLIAMENTARY PROCEDURE

Two standard books on constitutional law give an outline of parliamentary procedure:

Phillips, O. H. *Constitutional and administrative law*, 6th edn., 1978.

Wade, E. C. S. and Phillips, G. C. *Constitutional and administrative law*, 10th edn., 1984.

Other scholarly books cover the same ground at a more popular level:

De Smith, S. A. *Constitutional and administrative law*, 5th edn., 1985.

Hanson, A. H. and Walles, M. *Governing Britain: a guidebook to political institutions*, 4th edn., 1984.

Hartley, T. C. and Griffith , J. A. G. *Government and law: an introduction to the working of the constitution in Britain*, 2nd edn., 1981.

PRIMARY LEGISLATION

The ramifications of statute law are dealt with in detail in:

Bennion, F. A. R. *Statute law*, 2nd edn., 1983.

Craies, W. F. *Craies on statute law*, 7th edn., 1971. See especially Chapter 4: 'Classification of statutes'.

Halsbury's Laws of England, 4th edn., vol. 44, 1983. See especially 'Statutes', starting at paragraph 801, and 'Subordinate legislation', starting at paragraph 981.

Miers, D. R. and Page, A. C. *Legislation*, 1982.

Walker, D. M. *The Scottish legal system*, 5th edn., 1981. See especially 'Legislation', pp. 346–63; 412–16.

Walker, R. J. and Walker, M. G. *The English legal system*, 6th edn., 1986. See especially 'The legal and literary sources of English law', pp. 89–126.

Zander, M. *The law-making process*, 2nd edn., 1985. See especially Chapter 1, 'Legislation', and Chapter 2, 'Statutory interpretation'.

Discussion about statute law reform has been extensive in the last few years, and many articles have appeared on the subject in legal periodicals. These can be located via the periodical indexes. The following works deserve special mention:

Great Britain. Lord President of the Council. *The preparation of legislation: report of a committee* (Chairman: Sir David Renton), 1975 (Cmnd. 6053).

Statute Law Society, *Renton and the need for reform*, 1979.

Statute Law Review, 1980–.

Statutes in Force

Dunlap, M. L. 'The arrangement of Statutes in Force', *Law Librarian*, vol. 13, 1982, pp. 3–6.

The Statutes in information retrieval systems

Harrison, R. N. G. 'The statutes on Lexis', *Statute Law Review*, 1982, pp. 51–5.

Local and Personal Acts

The rationalisation of local legislation is described in this article:
Study of Parliament Group 'Private bill procedure: a case for reform', *Public Law*, 1981, pp. 206–27.

SUBORDINATE LEGISLATION

Subordinate legislation is described in some of the general works already listed and in:
Great Britain. Committee on Ministers' Powers, *Report*, 1932. (Cmnd. 4060.) Chairman: Lord Donoughmore.
Great Britain, Parliament, House of Commons, Library, *Access to subordinate legislation* 1963, (*Document* no. 5).
Great Britain, Parliament, Joint Committee on Delegated Legislation, *Report*, 1972 (HL 184, 1971–2) (HC 475, 1971–2).
The work of publishing the statutes and Statutory Instruments and preparing their indexes is described in:
Lyons, A. B. 'The Statutory Publications Office, past, present and future', *Law Librarian*, vol. 1, 1970, pp. 5–8, 20–1 and 27.

Byelaws

Freeman, C. A. 'Local authority byelaws: creation and control', *Law Librarian*, vol. 14, 1983, pp. 19–23.

NORTHERN IRELAND

The standard work is still:

Calvert, H. *Constitutional law in Northern Ireland: a study in regional government,* 1968.

For more recent assessments see the following:

Boyle, C. K. *et al. Law and State: the case of Northern Ireland,* 1975.

Palley, C. *The evolution, disintegration and possible reconstruction of the Northern Ireland constitution,* 1972. (Also published in *Anglo-American Law Review,* vol. 1, 1972.)

REPUBLIC OF IRELAND

Kelly, J. M. *The Irish constitution,* 2nd edn., 1984.

4. Primary Sources: Law Reports

W. W. S. BREEM

No statutory obligation exists as regards the reporting of cases heard before the judiciary in courts of law and none is published under government authority, excepting only the *Reports of Tax Cases* and *Reports of Patent, Design and Trade Mark Cases,* which are issued by the relevant government departments concerned and are official publications. It is axiomatic, therefore, that only cases of interest to the legal profession are reported in any of the established series of law reports. Of concern will be such cases as those which extend the law, modify it or break new ground. Broadly speaking, reports may be divided into two categories: primary – which enunciate a general principle; and secondary – which are glosses providing applications of authority. Among the latter may be included cases which turn exclusively on their own special facts. Some nine-tenths of all reported cases, it is said, concern statutory definition; hence the importance of case-law.

The purpose of a modern law report has been defined as 'the production of an adequate record of a judicial decision upon a point of law in a case heard in open court, for subsequent citation as a precedent'. A law report then records only the issues and the facts considered necessary to the decision of the court. As of necessity there is a difference between the reporting of a case heard in a lower court as against one heard on appeal. In the lower court it is the duty of the judge to ascertain the facts if these are in dispute; and it is the reporter's obligation to provide a concisely edited transcript of only a part of the hearing. All irrelevancies, all repetitious matter is excised. In cases on appeal there is as a rule no dispute over the facts; the dispute concerns the effect of the law as applied to that particular situation. Then, it is the reporter's obligation to provide a transcript which is a contracted representation of the court's proceedings.

The report becomes a legal instrument of great precision. It records the decision of the court from which principles may be inferred, and from the mass of collective and related decisions emerges the corpus of judicial law known as case-law.

The authority of a decision resides in the judge(s) presiding over the proceedings in court. For citation purposes it is essential that either the decision be reported by a barrister and formally published above his signature, or that a barrister, acting as an *amicus curae,* shall inform the judge of a relevant decision lying within his own knowledge.

COMPOSITION OF A REPORT

A report is composed of a number of well-defined parts as follows:

1. The title. This is normally the surnames of the parties (see also page 151), together with the date of the hearing, the name of the court and the name or names of the judges presiding.

2. The catchwords. These are placed below the title. The first is usually a legal term, such as 'Tort', but not always and it forms the index head to the head-note. It is also employed subsequently as the key word in the digest. It will be of wider meaning than the remaining catchwords, since it is the practice of a reporter to go from the general to the particular.

3. The head-note. This is not a précis of the report but a digest of the law contained in it. Head-notes are either factual or propositional, the former being more common than the latter. Brevity is the hallmark of a good head-note. The best contain the material facts, the conclusion, and the proposition to be drawn from them.

4. Arguments of counsel. These may or may not be quoted; seldom in cases reported in the lower courts, occasionally in cases reported on appeal.

5. The judgment. In reports of cases on appeal more than one judgment may be recorded, but the reporter will take care to ensure that those parts of the second or other judgments which merely cover the same ground are excised.

Other information included will be the names of counsel and solicitors concerned and, as required the *holding,* the points of law which are held, and the *per curiam*, a statement of law not considered essential, a list of cases referred to in the judgment and cited in argument (the former normally much shorter than the latter) and, lastly, the name of the reporter who has reported the case.

Citation in court

The authority which renders a report citable in court is the signature of the reporter, who alone must accept responsibility for its accuracy. This authority, long accepted, found formal recognition in 1889 when Lord Esher, MR, delivering judgment, said, 'We will accept *The Times Law Reports* because they are reports by barristers who put their names to their reports.' A barrister, however, may not vouch a report solely on the basis of having read a transcript of the judgment and if he does so he abuses the privilege accorded him as a law reporter.

Reports from the superior courts of Ireland, the Commonwealth and the United States of America may be cited and, though not binding, are entitled to the utmost respect.

The superior courts in England are obliged to follow a unanimous decision of the Court of Session of Scotland on a statute equally applicable to England and Scotland. It would seem that these decisions are equably applicable to the courts of Northern Ireland.

When multiple reporting of a case occurs there is a recognized though largely unwritten order of precedence which governs the choice of series to be selected for citation purposes. The pre-eminence of *The Law Reports* was reinforced by the Law Reporting Committee who in 1940 recommended that 'the general rule of exclusive citation of a Report in the "Law Reports" should be enforced'. *The All England Law Reports* follow in order of selection. Other series fall naturally into order, much depending upon the case and the court in which it will be heard. If a suitable case cannot be found in any series it may be necessary to turn elsewhere:

1. to *The Times* newspaper reports. It should be noticed that these are of necessity résumés compiled at speed and should never be regarded as an adequate substitute for a proper law

report. Although not appearing above the printed signature or initials of their authors, they are generally understood to be compiled by barristers on the ICLR staff and are acceptable to the superior courts.

2. to legal journals. These may contain the only reports on points of practice and are acceptable to the superior courts as well as the Court of Appeal.

3. to quasi-legal journals of repute, such as *The Estates Gazette.* Cases reported therein have been cited in the High Court since the 1940s, usually with approval and on occasion in the Court of Appeal.

4. to other legal publications. Notes of cases in *Current Law* have from time to time been cited in the Court of Appeal.

5. to textbooks. While those by living authors should not be cited, many are cited and looked at by the courts.

Few, if any series of law reports are mutually exclusive. If overlapping is inevitable in respect of the two general series, *The Law Reports* and *All ER,* it occurs also in the specialist field where reports of a like-kind are established in competition and overlap with each other as well as with the general series. Overlapping is at its most extensive in the field of periodicals. The *Criminal Law Review, Law Society's Gazette, New Law Journal, Solicitor's Journal* and *The Times* contain a high proportion of repetitive matter. Yet each may notice some case that is not held elsewhere. If *Meecher v. Meecher* (1972) can be found only on LEXIS, *Smith v. Manchester Corporation* (1974) in 17 KIR p. 1 will not (as yet) be found elsewhere in print.

MODERN REPORTS: 1865 TO DATE

Official

The Law Reports of the Incorporated Council of Law Reporting for England and Wales date from 1865 and are issued in monthly parts which usually obtain publication eight to ten weeks after the conclusion of the period covered. Though a bound-volume service is not available, the Council will handle the binding of subscribers' copies. Additionally, uncut copies are available for those subscribers who prefer to bind their own. The service also includes the issue of a weekly series as well as annual indexes, a table of cases judicially noticed, and digests to the main series. For details of the statutes series issued by the Council see page 88.

Originally *The Law Reports* were divided into eleven sets covering all the superior courts of the day. Changes in the number of sets issued took place thereafter, corresponding with the changes in the organization of the courts. The first series of eleven sets runs from 1865 to 1875, the second series of six sets runs from 1876 to 1890, and the third series from 1891 to date, containing four sets: the Appeal Cases (of the House of Lords and of the Privy Council), Queen's and King's Bench Division, Chancery Division and Probate Division (reconstituted as the Family Division from 1972). Subsequently the restrictive practices cases were issued as an additional set, but closed after seven volumes. Thereafter these cases will be found in the *Industrial Court Reports* now *Industrial Cases Reports,* 1975– , a new series issued by the Council, but not as a part of their main series.

The recorded decision includes the arguments of counsel. The Queen's Bench Division reports include admiralty, commercial, Court of Appeal criminal division, Court of Appeal civil division and divisional court cases. The following have also been included as required: Courts-Martial appeals, Ecclesiastical cases, Employment Tribunal appeals, National Industrial Relations Court cases (1972–5) and Restrictive Practice cases on appeal.

Digests and indices, 1865–1950, followed by consolidated decennial indices, 1951–80, have been issued to date. Monthly and annual cumulative indices, 1981– are also issued.

The unique authority of the series lies in the fact that the reported decisions are read by the judiciary prior to publication; a privilege shared only, and then not consistently, by two other series, the *Law Journal Reports* (now defunct) and *The Reports of Patent, Design and Trade Mark Cases.*

The weekly series, known as *The Weekly Notes,* was designed as a holding series to provide for full publication with the least possible delay. To achieve this the arguments of counsel were not included. This series contained many reports of temporary concern, not subsequently printed in the main series. *The Weekly Notes* ran from 1866 to 1952, when it was curtailed, to be continued by *The Weekly Law Reports* which, while serving the same function, offers a superior service. The weekly issue consists of two parts. Part one contains decisions of points of minor or transitory interest which do not merit reprinting in the main series; part two contains reports of major concern worth reprinting, after revision, with the addition of counsels' arguments. Each issue contains a cumulative table of cases and an index of the subject matter. Annual cumulative indexes are also issued. Cases reported by ICLR from 1945 are available on LEXIS. WLR is also on CLARUS.

Commercial

The commercial publishing of law reports did not effectively commence until the nineteenth century, when legal journalism began to proliferate.

Some series commenced their existence independently of the journal with which they were associated and maintained their independence until they ceased publication; others began their existence as an integral part of the journal in which they were published, only to obtain independent publication at a subsequent date. Others again were independent one moment and merged the next. It was common practice to issue reports as a section at the back of a journal, but with a separate title page, and sometimes, though not always, a separate pagination. In some instances, through the need to keep the bound volume of the journal to a manageable size, the reports, if there were sufficient, might be pulled out by the subscriber to form a physically separate and apparently independent series, yet with others this justification has never arisen. Bibliographically speaking therefore, the history and status of commercial reports is confusing in the extreme, a subject for continuous debate between cataloguers, reflecting not only the varied policy decisions and commercial fortune of publishers, but also the fortuitous actions of librarians when faced with arbitrary changes in policy, size of format and physical bulk.

Only those general reports still of major concern to the profession require notice below.

The Law Journal newspaper commenced existence as a monthly, and issued reports of cases in the King's Bench and Chancery, 1803–6. In 1806 it ceased publication, but the reports were re-issued in three volumes under the name of the editor, J. P. Smith. *The Law Journal Reports,* the first general series of reports were commenced independently in 1822 (initially weekly, then monthly from 1830) and the first series lasted till 1831; the new series followed in 1832, ran to 118 volumes and was discontinued in 1949, when it was technically incorporated with *The All England Law Reports* (*All ER*) which had commenced thirteen years previously.

The Jurist, a weekly periodical containing reports in all the courts commenced publication in 1837 and continued till 1866, when it became defunct partially as the result of the publication of *The Law Reports.*

The Law Times, a weekly newspaper, commenced in 1843, including in its pages what is now known as the old series of *The Law Times Reports.* The latter began an independent existence in 1859, ran to 177 volumes and ceased publication in 1947, when it was technically incorporated with *All ER.* Volumes 1 to 11 of the new series had a second title page on which they were termed 'The Law Reporter', while volumes 12 to 23 (issued monthly) had altered titles and were headlined as 'Bar Reports, vols. 1–12'. Volume two ends with page 320, contains a title page and table of cases, but lacks an index. General indexes were issued in twelve volumes, covering volumes 1 to 120 only.

The Weekly Reporter was established in 1852 as a journal containing reports. It effectively ceased any independent existence when in 1906 the reports were incorporated within *The Solicitors' Journal and Reporter,* lasting thus until 1927.

The New Reports, a weekly, established in November 1862, became a casualty as a result of the emergence of *The Law Reports* and ceased publication in 1865, six volumes only being issued.

The Times newspaper (formerly *The Universal Register*) began publishing reports in their daily issues in 1785. From 1885 *The Times* also commenced publication of *The Times Law*

Reports. These were issued weekly and at first merely re-printed condensed reports which had appeared in the news-paper. Subsequently, verbatim transcripts of the judgments were recorded. By 1936 there was usually a six-week de-lay between judgment and publication. The series ceased in 1953 by arrangement with the Incorporated Council of Law Reporting, upon the commencement of *The Weekly Law Reports.* Three digests were issued, covering the years 1884–1905.

Delay in the issue of the monthly parts of *The Law Reports* and dissatisfaction with the service offered by *The Weekly Notes* were two of the reasons that lay behind the publication of what may with justice be termed the most satisfactory series of general reports yet issued commercially.

The All England Law Reports commenced in 1936 and are issued in weekly parts, the aim being to print cases as soon as possible after decision. The majority, still, are published with-in four weeks of judgment being given. The arguments of counsel are not usually reported and the judgments are not always quoted. The reports so printed include not only cases involving fresh principles of law but also those illustrating the application of established principles to modern circumstances. The House of Lords, the Privy Council, both divisions of the Court of Appeal and all divisions of the High Court are fully covered. Selected decisions of the Court of Justice of the European Communities, the Employment Appeal Tribunal and the Consistory Courts are also included. A digest of cases appears in each weekly issue while cross-references are made to *Halsbury's Laws, Halsbury's Statutes, Halsbury's Statutory Instru-ments* and *The Digest.* Thus the background of relevant law may be traced. For the noter-up service see page 162. A consoli-dated index, 1936–81, has been issued to date. Current cumu-lative tables and indices are issued every eighth week to be followed by annual cumulative indices 1982 to date. For *The All England Law Reports Reprint* see page 138–9; for details of *The All ER Annual Review,* provided free to subscribers to the bound volume service.

The following, noticed above – *LJR, TLR* and *All ER* – are available from 1945 on LEXIS.

Specialist series

Certain series deal solely with limited topics, or record cases heard before courts not normally covered by the series of general law reports noticed above.

Topics covered by series in progress include admiralty and shipping (*Lloyd's Law Reports*, 1919–), company law (*Palmer's Company Cases*, 1985–), domestic relations (*Family Law Reports*, 1976–), patents (*Reports of Patent, Design and Trade Mark Cases*, 1884–), property (*Property and Compensation Reports*, 1949–), rating (*Rating and Valuation Reporter*, 1961–), and taxation (*Reports of Tax Cases*, 1875/83–). Other series now closed have dealt with such varied topics as banking, bankruptcy, copyright, friendly societies, licensing, registration, weights and measures, and workmen's compensation.

Cases on special subjects will also be found in practitioners' treatises. These are usually compressed versions of cases reported elsewhere, but gathered together to illustrate the author's argument or theme. The second volume of Chitty's *Bills of Exchange*, 1834, is devoted to such cases; Elme's *Ecclesiastical and Civil Dilapidations*, 1929, has an appendix of cases; Montagu's *Law of Set-Off*, 1828, also contains an appendix of cases. Contemporary treatises continue this practice.

Magistrates' courts are covered by the *Local Government Reports* (formerly *Knight's Local Government and Magisterial Cases*), 1903– , county courts were reported by the *Law Journal Newspaper County Court Reports (formerly the LJCC Reporter)*, 1912–47, while the Court of Criminal Appeal is recorded by *Cox's Criminal Cases*, 1843–1948, by *The Criminal Appeal Reports*, 1908– , and by the *Criminal Appeal Reports (sentencing)*, 1979 to date.

The reports of cases heard before special courts now defunct but of concern primarily to legal historians, will generally be found in the publications of learned societies, either national or local. Such courts include forest courts, palatinate courts, seignorial courts (manor courts, courts baron and courts leet), the Star Chamber and coroners courts. Certain special courts still sit, but infrequently as a result of their nature: the Court of [Coronation] Claims in 1952, the High Court of Chivalry in 1954. The Court of Ecclesiastical Causes

Reserved (established by statute in 1963) first sat in 1984, while the sittings of the Court of Referees produced two volumes of *Locus Standi Reports,* 1936/7– .

Problems can arise over the cessation, apparent or actual, of a series as well as over the commencement of a series in an unusual format. Some change title – the *Planning and Compensation Reports* became the *Property and Compensation Reports* after eighteen years in 1949 and the *Property, Planning and Compensation Reports,* in 1986; some are absorbed in another series – *Annotated Tax Cases* 1922–75 were incorporated from 1976–81 in *Taxation Reports,* 1939–81; others are absorbed into another style of publication – the *Commercial Law Reports,* 1981–3, were incorporated in 1984 in a journal *Business Law Brief,* 1984– , and *Legal Decisions affecting Bankers,* 1879–1966, were continued by a textbook, Chorley and Smart's *Leading cases in the law of banking,* 5th edn., 1983. Some commence within a textbook – Bennion's *Consumer Credit Control,* a looseleaf publication, 1976– , contains the *Consumer Credit Law Reports,* 1976– . Others again have a more complicated metamorphosis. The *Brewing Trade Review Licensing Law Reports,* 1913–35 (originating in the BTR) were continued by the *Brewing Trade Review Law Reports,* 1936–53, the *Law Reports,* 1954–7, and were incorporated once more in the *Brewing Trade Review,* 1959–*c.*1973 re-titled the *Brewing Review c.* 1974–6.

Traditionally, cases in law report volumes are arranged chronologically. A recent development has been the arranging of cases by subject, as in the *Insurance Law Reports,* 1982– , and in *Employment Law Cases,* 1984– . The latter, together with the *Building Law Reports,* Vol. 1 [1976]– , illustrate a second development – the inclusion of previously unreported cases. In both, the cases are summarized and, in the latter, each case has a commentary added. A third development has been the widening of coverage to include selected Commonwealth cases considered to be of concern to the practitioner, as in *Butterworth's Company Law Cases,* 1983– , and (again) the *Building Law Reports*

Of the reports noticed above, the following are held on LEXIS: *Lloyds L. R., Family L. R., Rpts. of Patent Cases, Rpts. of Tax Cases, Local Government Rpts., Criminal Appeal Rpts., Crim. App. Rpts. (sentencing), Property, Planning and Compensation Rpts., Legal*

Decisions affecting Bankers, Insurance L.R., Building L.R. and *Butterworths Company Law Cases*; while RPC and BR are on LAWTEL.

THE NOMINATE REPORTS: 1571–1865

The long run of reports called 'nominate', but better known to practising lawyers as simply 'the old reports', has a publishing history that covers 328 years, during which time over 260 separate series, many running into numerous editions, were issued. For 248 of these years the reports were published as collections, the date of issue bearing little or no relationship to the period spanned by the cases gathered within a volume. The nominate reports extend from 1220 for a case in the Exchequer to 1881 for a case dealing with canals.

Though the majority of the reports published between 1571–1704 were issued in French (later editions often having English translations) a number were in English, Hobart's of 1641 being the earliest. The last in French was by Lutwyche in 1704. Thereafter all were in English.

Of the many reports issued only four require notice here: three for their role in developing the potentialities of law reporting; the fourth for its unparalleled influence upon the course of English law.

Reporting proper commenced with *Les commentaires, ou les reports de dyuers cases* ... by Edmund Plowden. First published in 1571, they cover cases heard 1550–71 in the courts of King's Bench, Common Pleas and Exchequer. This was Part one. Part two, covering cases heard 1571–80 was issued in 1579, according to the title page.

Plowden's reports, the first to be issued, remain a model of the act of reporting. They contain the arguments of counsel and the opinions of the judges. Plowden reported nothing at second hand, often submitted his drafts to the judiciary, and included in the final script only what was essential to his purpose. His reports ran into a number of editions and if his success encouraged others to try likewise, few cared to emulate the principles that led to it.

Sir Edward Coke's reports, often cited simply as 'The Reports', cover Queen's Bench cases, 1572–1616. Parts one to eleven were issued 1600–15, while the final two parts appeared posthumously, 1656–9. An English translation of the whole appeared in 1658, while numerous editions of the various parts followed, as well as abridgments and tables prepared by other writers.

Technically the reports are poorly structured. The first eleven parts contain approximately 500 cases, but it is often difficult to know precisely where fact ends and comment begins, for the work is as much a commentary upon the law as a series of reported cases. Coke's learning was prodigious, but is here ill-digested and ill-arranged. None of this matters. The author's reputation was such that his reports were cited more than any other series and acquired immense authority, for they stated the principles of the law and did much to shape the legal system of his time.

Burrow's reports of cases in the King's Bench cover the period 1756–72 and were issued in five volumes, 1776–80. There were four subsequent English editions, the last being in 1812.

Then, as now, it was customary for the judiciary to deliver oral opinions. Burrow did not write shorthand and his reports could not be based on official transcripts, these not then being taken. He was a careful note-taker, however, and any loss in accuracy was minimized, for he took pains to heed the sense rather than the words. His reports are lucid as to style and orderly in arrangement; the results of painstaking editing. He took care to ensure that each report was preceded by a statement of the case. This, being by the reporter, set out the facts and issues in a form that separated it from the opinion of the court, which then followed. Burrow would seem to have been among the first to realize the importance of clear divisions being required between the facts, the arguments of counsel, and the judgment of the court. And he invented the head-note.

As the volume of business before the courts increased, the need developed for the regular reporting of important judicial decisions which should be published without undue delay. This need was initially met by Durnford and East, whose *Term reports of cases in the King's Bench* span the years 1785–1800 and were first published as a set of eight volumes,

1787–1800; though original publication took the form of parts issued at the end of the legal term covered. Their example was to be followed by other reporters in other courts.

Dissatisfaction with the private reporting system was to develop however. The multiplicity of reports requiring purchase, their growing cost and increasing delays in publication – these were among the contributing factors that led to a demand for the Bar to set up its own reporting system. This it did in 1865, when the Council of Law Reporting in England and Wales was established. As a result, the private reporting system died, only to be replaced by the commercial publisher.

Collections

As a result of publishing practice, the great majority of reports printed prior to the middle of the eighteenth century were issued in quarto- or folio-size volumes. Those which did not merit numerous printings seldom or never obtained publication in octavo format. Complete collections of nominate reports in original editions lack uniformity of size, prove awkward of shelf arrangement and are costly of space. Their indexing can prove inadequate and the dates on title pages, showing coverage of the cases contained therein, are often inaccurate.

Two major reprints exist:

The Revised Reports (1786–1866), edited by Sir Frederick Pollock, was issued in 152 volumes, 1891–1920. It is a selected republication only of those reports, chronologically ordered, of the superior courts of common law and equity which were considered at the time of publication to be of value still to the profession. Also included are Irish reports held to be authoritative in the English courts and reports of the Admiralty Court and the Privy Council. In general, criminal cases are excluded. The editorial work is not inconsiderable: references have been added to later relevant decisions, the head-notes revised and obsolete matter omitted, whilst each volume's preface constitutes a guide to the leading cases contained therein. A table of cases in one volume and an index-digest in two volumes is also included. To facilitate use, the names of the relevant reporters are to be found on the spine of the appropriate volumes. The series contains two interesting curiosities. The data on the spine of volume 51 records the names of reporters whose cases will not be found within that volume, though this may be because the reporters in question are the authors of collateral reports, that is of cases which may be found elsewhere. This explanation cannot, however, explain the listing of Murphy and Hurlstone's reports of cases in the Exchequer, these not being collateral. Potton's index volume to the series indicates on the title page that it lists 'the cases retained and (from vol. 90 to vol. 149, *c.* 1851–66) those omitted from the Revised Reports'. Tables of cases omitted are rare in legal publishing.[1]

The English Reports reprint, 1220–1865, was issued in 178 volumes, 1900–32 and is in general a straight reprint in which the original footnotes are given. Notes in square brackets have been inserted, as required, above the head-notes, giving references to Mews' *Digest of English Case Law,* while in some instances editorial notes in square brackets have been added. Where pages of the original have been omitted this is usually stated and editorial notes indicate those decisions affected by subsequent legislation. Volume 12 records that references to Mews will be given by titles and sub-titles and that notes will be recorded at the conclusion instead of the commencement of cases. The reprint contains over 100,000 cases, representative of 265 separate series of reports, arranged by courts. The whole includes a two-volume index of cases, and citations are recorded as they appear in the original reports. A table was also printed listing the nominate reports included in the series, keying them to the volume(s) in which they are to be located. Collateral reports in Admiralty and Ecclesiastical courts, Common Pleas, Exchequer and King's Bench are excluded, together with those in bail and bankruptcy courts.

The only revised collection of modern times is *The All England Law Reports Reprint*. This consists of thirty-six volumes containing selected cases from the period 1558–1935, chosen for their present-day value to the legal profession. Up to date head-notes and annotations are provided, references to

---

[1] For a comprehensive analysis of *RR* see R. Logan's article: 'The Revised Reports' *in The Law Librarian,* vol. 13, no. 2, 1982, pp. 23–4.

Halsbury's Laws of England being given where necessary. The work contains approximately six thousand cases. The first eight volumes cover the nominate reports. The later volumes include material selected from *The Law Times Reports*. Publication commenced in 1957 and was concluded in 1968. Coupled with this are the *Extension Volumes*, issued 1968–71 and covering the period 1861–1935. This, a parallel series, consists of sixteen volumes and contains some 2,000 cases, many drawn from *The Law Reports* which have been relied upon extensively as important precedents, especially in the Australian courts.

OTHER REPORTS

Notes of cases

Summary reports and notes on cases may be located in many legal periodicals. Maxwell and Brown's *List of British and Colonial Law Reports and Legal Periodicals,* 1937, lists 168 such titles, of which forty contain reports of cases. This list is now known not to have been complete at the time of compilation. While a supplement to the work, issued in 1946, adds another twenty-one titles to the list, this only partially rectifies the many omissions. Though the majority of these have ceased publication, numerous new titles have appeared in the decades since 1937.

In the early nineteenth century the reporting of cases in periodicals was, in general, the work of barristers engaged on the staffs of the periodicals concerned, many of which sponsored their own separate series of reports. Today the tendency, amongst a number of leading periodicals anyway, is to report in note form, and with due acknowledgment, cases that have been reported, sometimes more fully, elsewhere. With these may be included notes of cases not otherwise noticed.

Among the major legal periodicals, *The Law Journal,* 1893–1965, continued as *The New Law Journal* in 1965/6, *Law Notes,* 1882– , *The Law Society's Gazette,* 1903– , and *The Law Times,* 1843–1965, concentrate in general on civil causes, while *Legal Action,* 1984– (formerly the *LAG Bulletin,* 1972–83) is invaluable for noticing matters not covered by its contemporaries. Specialist interests are met by periodicals whose titles display their concerns: *The Criminal Law Review*, 1954– , and the *Journal of Criminal Law*, 1937– ; *Family Law*, 1971– , and *Public Law*, 1956– .

Legal notes of cases may also be found in periodicals of concern to other professions as well as industry and commerce: the *Estates Gazette*, 1858– , and the *Chartered Auctioneer and Estate Agent*, 1921–70, amalgamated with the *Chartered Surveyor*, 1970– ; *Accountancy*, 1890– , and the *Certified Accountant*, 1965– ; the *Journal of the Institute of Bankers*, 1880–1982, replaced by *Banking World*, 1983– ; *The Secretary*, 1904–60; *Professional Administration*, 1971– , formerly the *Chartered Secretary*, 1961–71; and the *Brewing Review*, 1974– , formerly the *Brewing Trade Review*, 1959–73.

Transcripts of cases recorded in a proportion of the periodicals noticed above are held on LEXIS. For journals containing notes of tribunals' cases, see page 150.

Not all the notes of cases commented upon are signed nor do all acknowledge their source of origin.

Judgments and opinions

A number of the nominate reports confined their reporting to cases heard by a single judge, and other nominate reports are based on the notes of a particular judge. Alternatively, a judge's decisions may be collected and published in order to prove or consolidate his reputation. That they record cases of importance is supplementary to this purpose. Evans' *Decisions of Lord Mansfield*, 1803, and Birkenhead's *Judgments*, 1923, compiled by the author, are cases in point.

Counsel's opinions have also been published; the material usually being drawn from the notebooks and papers of deceased barristers. Burton's *Cases with opinions of eminent counsel*, 1791, Chalmers' *Opinions of eminent lawyers*, 1814, and Forsyth's *Cases and opinions on constitutional law*, 1899, being notable examples. Opinions of general application may be retained by solicitors' firms but remain private property. Opinions, however, are not a part of any court proceedings and must not be so regarded.

Unreported cases

While a proportion of the case-law material noticed below has been either printed for limited use, published, or made available on a database, none constitutes a formally constructed law report. Reports of court proceedings are not law reports. Nor can a shorthand writer's transcript be so regarded.

Appeals collections

Under this heading are noticed five major collections, three of which consist of documents relating to cases, individually issued in the first instance for the sole benefit of the courts concerned, and subsequently made available only to selected libraries. Not all the cases concerned are necessarily to be found reported elsewhere, and, in any event, the material recorded provides a valuable supplement to the condensed reports of the law reports.

The proceedings in peerage cases, also known as peerage claims and heard before the House of Lords, consist of a series of separate prints, the earliest of which dates from the eighteenth century. Initially unbound, these are available as collections, in whole or in part, in a number of the older libraries, such as the Inns of Court, the British Library and other public libraries. The cases include the claimant's statement of proofs, and documentary evidence such as pedigrees, together with appendices containing miscellaneous evidential documents. The best collection is almost certainly that in the House of Lords Library, for details of which see Bond, M. F., *Guide to the Records of Parliament*, 1971, p. 163.

The reporting of cases heard by the House of Lords was not permitted till *c.* 1812. As a result, the nominate reporters, whose earliest HL case is dated 1694, provide an inadequate coverage and there are reporting gaps between 1801–11 and 1822–6. As from 1865 cases appear regularly in *The Law Reports*. The Act of 1876 gave the Lords the duty of receiving appeals from the newly created courts of appeal in civil cases. In 1907 criminal cases were added. Printed texts of material relating to cases are available in a number of libraries as special collections, dating from the 1660s onwards. Today the papers for each individually printed case include the case(s) for the appellant(s) and for the respondent(s), an appendix containing a record of the previous proceedings and relevant documents, and the judgment. Transcripts of recent judgments are available on LEXIS; summaries on LAWTEL. *The Calendars of Manuscripts of the House of Lords* contain papers on appeal and cases in error. The best guides to these are the indices to the Lords and Commons *Journals*.

The reporting of cases on appeal to the Privy Council effectively commenced when Acton's reports for 1809–11 were issued in 1811–12. The printing of earlier cases for the period 1243–1783 did not commence till 1834. As from 1865 cases appear regularly in *The Law Reports*. In 1833 the judicial committee of the Privy Council was re-organized and the individually printed cases were made available to libraries as from the 1840s. The material contained within each individually printed case is similar to that contained in the Lords' appeals. At least twenty-five per cent of the cases in this collection have not been reported in any series of law reports published either in the UK or the Commonwealth. PC cases may also be located in digests and indices issued by the Commonwealth countries concerned. Such in their day have been published in Canada, India, etc. Transcripts of recent judgments are available on LEXIS.

Up to 1950, decisions of the civil division of the Court of Appeal were not officially recorded. In April 1951 the Lord Chancellor directed that an official note of all judgments in the court should be made, a copy to be filed in the Inns of Court Bar Library in the Royal Courts of Justice. Now held by the Supreme Court Library of the RCJ (see also page 154) the typed transcripts are approved by the judiciary prior to filing and are kept in one of two sequences according to their direction. The bound sequence comprises cases for permanent retention, these being numbered by the calendar year and domestically cited thus: Smith v. Brown, CAT, no. 81 of 1985. The unbound sequence comprises cases not requiring permanent retention (a matter now under reconsideration), these being numbered consecutively, regardless of year and are domestically cited thus: Jones v. Smith, UB 215 of 1985.

Availability is confined to those professionally concerned. Being Crown Copyright the transcripts may not be photocopied on site though manual copying is permitted. Applications for photocopies must be made to the Institute of Shorthand Writers, 2, New Square, Lincoln's Inn, London, WC2 3RU, or Room 392 (their 'office') in the RCJ. A microfiche edition of the transcripts, 1951–80, is available from HMSO. The transcripts are also available on LEXIS. Summaries of selected transcripts appear in *Current Law*, 1973–. These contain a brief outline of the facts, the date of judgment and the case name. A cumulative list of these will be found at the back of the monthly case citator. Summaries will also be found in the *New Law Journal*, 1976– , and in *Halsbury's Laws* (abridgment volumes and monthly series).

Despite the Lords' decision of 1981 to deny the citation of transcripts of the CA civil division, it would seem likely that citation will still be permitted at the level of the Court of Appeal and certainly at High Court and Divisional Court level, provided the judgments cited are either relevant or helpful.

Typed transcripts of decisions of the criminal division of the Court of Appeal, 1960 onwards, are held by the Criminal Appeals Office (Room 205) in the RCJ. These are also approved by the judiciary and photocopying is permitted in the office to those professionally concerned, thus making available that proportion not officially reported elsewhere.

Textbooks and periodicals

Cases otherwise unreported may on occasion be found in treatises, usually in a compressed form. Some fifty-one unpublished cases are noticed in Duke's *Law of charitable uses*, 1805, while Sugden's *Law of property*, 1849, contains over 600 cases heard in the House of Lords, 1814–48, a period not covered by any other reporter. Hudson's *Compensation*, 1905, Challis' *Real property*, 1911, Jones and Proudfoot's *Notes on hire purchase law*, 1937, and Cripps' *Compulsory acquisition of land*, 1950, include such cases also. Others, usually relating to negligence and damages, may be located in *Current Law*. These are of interest as a guide to the damages awarded by the courts.

Other cases possessing a transitory interest may be noted

briefly in both legal and quasi-legal periodicals, usually those of concern to the professions, commerce and industry. Their location can be difficult, since they are not always recorded in the relevant annual indexes, while cumulative indexes are rarely issued, if at all.

Newspapers

National newspapers often report cases of 'national interest' as news items, not all of which necessarily justify the attention of the law reporter. These, whether civil or criminal, can usually be traced through the files of the appropriate newspaper. *The Times Index* may, for the purpose of locating a case about which imprecise information has been supplied, be of use as a general index to the major national newspapers. Of these, it may be noticed that the news reports of proceedings in both *The Times* and the *London Standard* are usually the most comprehensive; and whilst the standard of reporting in both is usually held to be reliable, news reports' transcripts are never an adequate substitute for an official transcript. For cases of local interest only, reference should be made to the files of newspapers covering the area in which the case was heard, the incident took place, or the parties resided. Similarly, cases of no legal concern that yet may become *causes célèbres* may be subsequently published in book form, as noted on pages 182–5.

Transcripts

From 1980, transcripts of all unreported cases in the following courts have been available on LEXIS, HL, PC, CA (civil division), Admiralty, Commercial, Patent and Revenue, together with transcripts of cases summarized or reported in over twenty-five periodicals.

If an unreported case cannot be located anywhere in print or on computer, then recourse must be made to the official transcript of the proceedings, subject to the limitations set out below.

It was only after 1908 that the employment of shorthand writers was commenced in all divisions of the High Court, as well as the criminal courts, following the practice already obtaining in the divorce courts. And not until after 1936 did this practice spread to include the Supreme Court. Until their (partial) replacement by mechanical recording the major firms of shorthand writers held a franchise in respect of the proceedings held in particular courts and their addresses may be located in the appropriate *Law Lists* of the period. Transcripts, if extant, may be obtained upon payment of a fee. For causes heard in London, failing the address of the firm in question, enquiries should be put to the Institute of Shorthand Writers (see page 143); in causes heard outside London, to the firm attached to the court.

On 2 October 1968 the Mechanical Recording Department (now the Court Recording Department) was established in the RCJ and by 1975 was covering thirty-seven courts. The CRD now makes tape recordings, as required, of proceedings in all the various courts previously covered by shorthand writers, excluding only the Court of Appeal, civil division, and the Crown Office, these still remaining the province of the shorthand writer. Transcripts are available to those concerned upon payment of a fee. Application should be made to the Court Recording Department, Room 525, Royal Courts of Justice. Transcription is undertaken by shorthand writers and the time taken to produce a transcript is variable; it may range from three to four weeks or longer.

In addition to the work described above, the shorthand writer now principally covers courts outside London.

Official recordings are taken in every action or proceeding heard in the Queen's Bench or Chancery Division which is tried or heard with witnesses and in every cause in the Admiralty courts, unless the judge directs otherwise. It is rare, however, for everything uttered in the court to be noted in the transcript. Certainly in criminal proceedings it is the duty of judge, counsel and court officers to ensure that the evidence and summing-up is properly recorded, and if no recording is made, care must be taken to ensure that an unchallengeable note is taken. Yet if proceedings are recorded the opening or closing addresses may be omitted at the discretion of the judge. In the divisional court in bankruptcy, shorthand notes on a motion of appeal are taken only upon a successful application by one or both of the parties concerned, who must then bear the costs; whilst in the county court shorthand notes are not taken officially, it being the duty of counsel to take a note of a judgment and make it available in all cases likely to go on appeal. The proceedings in magistrates' courts are also not recorded by official shorthand-writers.

Transcripts are not always accurate as to detail. The speaker may err and his mistake be recorded, but no correction noted. Alternatively, the shorthand-writer or transcriber may hear incorrectly what has been said and thus report it. The judge's summing-up in the NBT publication of the trial of Mrs Maybrick (1889) contains a number of mistakes in dates, besides mis-quoting the quantity of arsenic in the body.

The availability of transcripts is the prerogative of the Lord Chancellor's Department, which may impose restrictions in the public interest. In practice this power is seldom exercised: almost never in the case of civil proceedings (with the exception of the proceedings in family courts, certain libel actions and hearings in chambers in Chancery) and only occasionally in criminal proceedings – the trial of Stephen Ward (1963) for example, as well as cases involving contravention of the Official Secrets Act.

It can be seen therefore that it is not always possible to obtain a written report of the proceedings of any case that is not officially reported in a law report, Nor, if such a report is obtainable, will it necessarily be a verbatim report of the entire proceedings.

ADMINISTRATIVE TRIBUNALS

Tribunals may be designated as arbitrators, authorities, boards, commissioners, committees, courts, referees, trib-unals or umpires. As quasi-judicial bodies exercising some of the functions of courts of law, though outside the conventional legal system, they have existed in their modern form ever since the establishment of the Railway and Canal Commission in the second quarter of the nineteenth century. This was to reappear in 1921 as The Railway Rates Tribunal and then metamorphosed into the Transport Tribunal in 1947. Reports of *Proceedings under the Conciliation (Trades Disputes) Act, 1896,* were issued in sixteen volumes between 1896–1920. The First World War increased the number of tribunals, courts being established to deal with matters of compensation, munitions, and military service. *Civil Service Arbitration Board Awards* were published between 1917 and 19 and *Industrial Court decisions* (afterwards *Industrial Arbitration Board awards,* 1971–6, subsequently *Central Arbitration Committee awards,* 1976–) cover the period 1919–71. Tribunals did not multiply significantly, however, until after 1945. Their creation since has been an acknowledgment by government of the social obligations of a highly complex, industrial society.

In 1958 the Council on Tribunals was established, its principal purpose being to keep under review the constitution and working of the tribunals placed under its general supervision. Other functions include reporting on Bills and statutes that may be referred for attention, being consulted before procedural rules are made for any tribunal specified in the schedule to the Tribunals and Enquiries Act 1971, and the handling of complaints. The Council's statutory role is advisory only, not executive. At present, some 67 separate authorities (48 in England and Wales, 19 in Scotland) are in existence, and between them they control the activities of over 2,000 actual tribunals or courts. Those authorities vary considerably in function, structure, purpose and 'status'. Some are single, London-based tribunals with national jurisdiction, such as the Betting Levy Appeal Tribunal, and the Civil Aviation Authority; the Immigration Appeal Tribunal, hearing appeals against the decisions of adjudicators throughout the country; the Transport Tribunal which is a court of record in that its proceedings are permanently recorded and may have power to fine and imprison, and whose Scottish cases are, for convenience, heard before a special panel in Edinburgh; the Commons Commissioners, settling disputes for all time over the use of common land; the Special Commissioners of Income Tax; and the Lands Tribunal. The latter has been likened to a specialized court of law: its membership comprises both lawyers and valuers, and it is both a tribunal of first instance in respect of a proportion of the cases heard, and an appellate tribunal hearing appeals from local valuation courts as well as other matters. These last two go 'on circuit'. The Pension Appeal Tribunals are nominally London-based for administrative purposes but in fact have tribunal sittings not only in London but also in regional centres throughout the country. Other tribunals are wholly regionally based. Industrial Tribunals comprise 16 separate offices and hear cases brought under 10 statutes. The Traffic Commissioners have 10 tribunals in England and Wales, and one in Scotland. There are 155 Social Security Tribunals, while rent tribunals are appointed *ad hoc* from 13 regional Rent Assessment Panels in England and Wales. The Crofters Commission in Scotland, however, is confined to the seven northern counties, and National Health Service Committees are usually based by local authority areas.

All tribunals under the Council's supervision operate under statutory authority. Only some are required to have legally qualified chairmen (these may be overruled by lay assessors sitting with them) but preference is almost always given to the appointment of a lawyer as chairman. The subject fields of tribunals are bewildering in their variety and attempts to classify them into satisfactory divisions are rarely successful. They may deal with agriculture, consumer credit, dairy produce quotas, education and mental health on the one hand or performing rights, plant varieties, prevention of fraud, vaccine damage payments and wireless telegraphy on the other.

The rules of procedure for each tribunal are issued as SIs and lists may be found in the Council's annual reports, mentioned below. Procedures vary considerably to enable a specific tribunal to conduct its hearings in the manner considered most suitable for clarifying the issues and for handling the proceedings justly. The usual arrangement in two-tier tribunal systems is for appeals in the first instance to lie to the second-tier tribunal, as with immigration appeals, but if the appeal is on a point of law it shall lie to the High Court. There is an exception. The Social Security Commissioners are the only second-tier tribunal from whose decisions such right of appeal has not been provided, while there is also a minority of tribunals from whose decisions no appeal is possible.

Tribunals are under no obligation to issue reports of their proceedings and decisions, though in fact a number do so. They are not bound by the rules of procedure that govern courts of law and are not bound by precedent. They do not make decisions that affect the substantive law of the land, and such decisions cannot in any way be compared with those of courts of law. As a result, little useful purpose is served by publishing their decisions. Indeed, as in the case of domestic tribunals set up by professional bodies (though not all) publication may prove harmful to those appearing before them and thereby nullify the purpose for which they exist. Finally, it must be stressed that administrative decisions are not 'of authority', and the decisions of a tribunal may not be cited before the superior courts of record. The only exception to this statement would seem to be the *Immigration Appeals* [Reports] which 'do supply case-law' (see the Council's annual report, 1979–80 at para 5.6).

Of those tribunals whose function appears to warrant the publication of their decisions, some are issued for limited circulation as cyclo-styled paper parts (*Commons Commissioners' Decisions*, 1978– , in which the arrangement is by counties) or sheets ([*Transport Tribunal Appeals*], 1955–); others are printed for publication. Those issued by HMSO (the leading publisher in this field) include *Immigration Appeals* [*Reports*] 1970/71–, *Value Added Tax Tribunal Reports*, 1973– (containing *c.* 25 per cent of the decisions heard) and [*Social Security Commissioners' Decisions*], 1979– . These were formerly known as [National Insurance Commissioners Decisions] issued in two series: the 'blue series', 1948–76, being merged with the 'red series', 1957– , as from 1977 when their title change was effected. These, classified as 'reported', are the ones establishing points of law, but other decisions, known as 'numbered decisions', which are circulated to selected officials, are obtainable at regional offices of the DHSS or from the Commissioners. Selections from those published may be found in the *Encyclopaedia of Social Security law*, 1980–5, vol. 2. Decisions issued by other publishers include *Lands Tribunal Rating Appeals*, 1950/51–1960/61, *Knights Industrial Reports*, 1966/7–74 (formerly entitled *Knights Industrial and Commercial Reports*), and *Lands Tribunal Cases*, vol. 1 [1972–3]– .

Volume 1 of the latter re-issues all cases noticed in the *Local Government Review* for the period covered. Volume 6 (issued in 1979), described as the 'sixth edition', is the last published to date. Selected decisions will also be found in the *Estates Gazette* and *Estates Gazette Digest*. Confusion may arise from the inclusion of tribunal hearings in series principally devoted to reporting High Court actions. *Ryde's Rating Cases,* 1956/7–1976/9, contain both High Court and Lands Tribunal Cases, while ICLR's *Industrial Case Reports,* 1976– , cover HL, QBD and Ch. cases, together with Employment Appeal Tribunal hearings on appeal from Industrial Tribunals.

Immigration Appeals, Rating Appeals, Rating and Income Tax Reports, Rating and Valuation Reports, Ryde's Rating Cases and *Value Added Tax Tribunal Reports,* together with transcripts of all unreported Employment Appeal Tribunal cases, and Lands Tribunal cases, and full transcripts of selected VAT Tribunal decisions, are available on LEXIS.

Information concerning availability of decisions is hard to come by. The *Annual Reports,* 1959– of the Council on Tribunals lists those with which it is concerned but not their addresses, which may change with frequency. And, while it notes the statutory authority under which the tribunal is to be established, the date of this is not necessarily the date upon which the tribunal commences its duties. A difference of five or six years may elapse before the one follows the other. Those decisions printed by HMSO may be located by reference to HMSO official publication lists; the existence of others not so printed may be located by searching *Current Law,* appropriate legal and quasi-legal journals, and specialist law reports. And the existence of others may become known only by chance.

The British Journal of Administrative Law, 1954–8 contains a section entitled Administrative Law Reports which records the decisions of some eleven major tribunals. This series ceased when the journal was merged with *Public Law* in 1959.

It must be remembered that the object of the tribunal system is to provide a judicial process which is speedy, informal and inexpensive. Legal aid is available only in a minority of tribunals. Hearings may be in public or private. Some tribunals have full transcripts made of selected proceedings but this is usually done only when there is an appeal against the decision or when an interested party requests a transcript. Not all tribunals are required automatically to provide a statement giving reasons for their award or decision, and the use of tape recorders is subject to the discretion of the president of the hearing.

Important tribunals, not under the survey of the Council and so not covered by this section, include the Attendance Allowance Board, Criminal Injuries Compensation Board (this has issued summaries of its cases since 1964), Foreign Compensation Commission, Gaming Board, Law Societies' Legal Aid Committees, Parole Board, and Race Relations Board.

CITATIONS AND REFERENCES

Almost all law reports are known either by the name of the reporter(s) or editor(s), as in the case of the nominate reports issued before 1865 in England (see page 135), or by their title, as is the case with most post-1865 reports in the United Kingdom (see page 129). In practice all such reports are referred to in print by their citation. This is always an abbreviation of the name of the reporter(s) or of the title.

Cases

In general, citations of judicial decisions contain five elements, usually written in the following order: the name of the case, *ie*, that of the party or parties concerned; the date of the decision; the volume number of the relevant report; the name of the report, usually tersely abbreviated; and the page number of the volume at which the case is reported.

Name

A case is always cited by the surnames of the parties given at the head of the report, the Christian names being omitted. Thus: *Smith v. Jones*, the versus being abbreviated. In speech, however, the profession will refer to the case as 'Smith and Jones'. In actions where there are a number of plaintiffs and/ or defendants, the names of all parties except the one first mentioned on either side are omitted and the case printed thus, *Smith et al. v. Jones et al.* will be cited as *Smith v. Jones*.

In the instance of either party possessing a title of honour or an official designation which is recorded at the head of the report, this will be included in the citation. Thus *Leicester (Earl of) v. Wells-next-the-Sea Urban District Council* or *R. v. Recorder of Oxford*.

In criminal actions where the prosecution is conducted by or against the Crown, *R.* is the abbreviation employed for 'Rex', 'Regina', 'Regem' or 'Reginam'. Thus *R. v. Smith, Brown v. R.* Again in speech the case will be referred to as 'The King against Smith' or 'Brown against the Queen'. In some criminal prosecutions, however, the action is brought by the Director of Public Prosecutions who, since 1920, has represented the Crown in appeals to the House of Lords. So a case commenced as *R. v. Brown* in the lower court becomes *Brown v. Director of Public Prosecutions* when on appeal.

In instances where the Crown is a party to civil litigation, English is preferred to Latin and the case will be referred to as *The King v. Smith,* or *Brown v. The Queen,* whilst in civil appeals the names of the parties as recorded in the lower court are often reversed in the House of Lords.

The names of corporations and other bodies are given in full, the definite article alone being omitted. Thus *Rhokana Corporation, Ltd v. Inland Revenue Commissioners.* In Admiralty cases involving shipping, the ship becomes a party even though the action is in fact brought or defended by its owners, and then the definite article is retained. Thus *The 'Midhurst' v. The 'Lake Atlin'*.

Special forms of citation, however, are used in certain types of proceedings, as follows:

1. Where a particular estate, person or matter forms the matter to which proceedings relate, particularly in Chancery and bankruptcy cases, *eg*: *Warren in re Wheeler v. Mills* (the trustee in bankruptcy), the phrase *'in re'* meaning 'in the matter of'. For citation purposes the title may be shortened to *Re Wheeler*.

2. Where a person voluntarily intervenes in proceedings in the Family Division; *eg: Thompson otherwise Hulton v. Thompson (Causton intervening)* may be shortened to *Thompson (orse Hulton) v. Thompson.*

But where the phrases 'In the estate of' and 'In the goods of' appear in clear they are not abbreviated. Yet *'In bonis'* meaning 'In the goods of' may be abbreviated as *in b. Jones.*

3. Where an application is made by a person who is not a party to the proceedings but who has an interest in the matter which entitles him to make an application; *eg: Regina v. Criminal Injuries Compensation Board, Ex parte Reinisch,* the phrase *Ex parte* meaning 'on the application of' may be abbreviated, as in *Ex. p. Reinisch.*

4. Where anonymity is permitted, as in certain actions such as annulments of marriage, the names of the parties are suppressed and initials only used; thus: *B v. B.*

5. Where, as in the early nominate reports, the reporter has titled the case by its popular title, either the name of the party or even the subject, it must be so cited; thus: *Brown's Case,* or *The Case of Heresy.*

Date of decision

In certain nominate reports and some more modern reports the date is omitted from the citation. Where this is given in a modern citation it will usually be within round brackets; thus: *Steadman v. Arden* (1846) 15 M&W 587. In *The Law Reports* and certain other series, the date is given in square brackets; thus: *Welden v. Smith* [1924] AC 484. The date is almost always the date on which the decision is awarded, but this need bear no relation to the date of the actual hearing; thus: *Thomson v. Cremin* (1941) [1956] 1 WLR 103n indicates that judgment was given in 1941, but the decision was not reported till fifteen years later.

Name of the report

There are conventional abbreviations for the majority of these and the best lists in print will be found in the works listed on pages 155–6.

Volume and page number

Where the volume of a series is numbered consecutively, its number is always given; thus: 12 QBD. Not all series, however, are numbered, in which case the volume is identified by the year of coverage. The *Appeal Cases* series in *The Law Reports* are an example; *eg*: [1893] AC. The page number is normally that of the page on which the case commences; thus: 12 QBD 715. But where the reference is to a passage later in the text of the report it will read thus: 9 QBD 245 at 249; or 9 QBD 245,249.

The court in which a case is heard is not normally cited. Exceptions, however, are made in respect of courts established or reconstituted since 1875, particularly the higher appellate courts, in which case the reference will end with the initial letters in capitals of the court concerned; *eg*: [1892] AC 105, HL.

Unreported cases are cited in the same manner as a reported case, but using such detail as may be available. Thus: *Haigh v. A. Lewis & Co.* (unreported) cited in *Dorber v. London Brick Co. Ltd.* [1974] ICR 270 at 271. *Walton on the Naze U.D.C. v. T. J. Moran* (1905) as reported in Hudson, *Law of Building Contracts* (1914) II, 376. *Bastile Properties Ltd. & Another v. Cooper* (1966) *The Times,* October 6.

Cases available only in transcripts held in the Supreme Court Library are sometimes cited as follows (particularly in textbooks): *Dean v. Woods* (1953, CA; unreported; Bar Library, no. 203). But the serial number allotted, though domestic, can be employed as an aid to locating the case in question.

For the usual form of citation in regard to court rolls see pages 281–2. For further information refer to: Institute of Advanced Legal Studies, *Manual of Legal Citations,* Part 1, The British Isles, 1959. This contains the best exposition in print on the subject of citations.

Reports

England and Wales

Little uniformity in the citation of legal sources exists, though attempts have been made in recent years to establish standard forms of abbreviations for, in particular, law reports. New series sometimes print the citation which it is hoped will be used for the reference to the reports. This was not always the case, however, while authors of treatises have, throughout the centuries contrived to construct their own citations, paying little heed to the form adopted by others. This individuality of approach has meant (and still means) that a legal citation may have an abbreviated form that may be any one of a number of variants. This variation of form can be so violent that the reader may recognize the abbreviation in one form and fail completely to do so when confronted with it in another form. As a result, this diversity can cause extreme difficulty over tracing a much needed reference and may prove expensive of staff time.

The major treatises will contain lists of abbreviations of reports referred to in the main text and these should be consulted first in any case of difficulty. More general lists will be found in the standard law lexicons, particularly in Osborn's *Concise law dictionary* and Stroud's *Judicial dictionary*. Excellent lists will also be found in the following:

1. Sturgess, H. A. C. and Hewitt, A. R. *Dictionary of legal terms: statutory definitions and citations*, 2nd edn., 1940. This contains abbreviations of the reports of the UK and Empire.

2. Sweet and Maxwell's *Guide to law reports and statutes*, 4th edn., 1962. This contains a list of abbreviations covering the UK, Irish and Commonwealth law reports, with dates denoting the period covered by the reports.

3. *Where to look for your law*, 14th edn., 1962. This contains the best basic list of abbreviations for UK and Irish law reports, and also provides coverage dates.

4. *The Digest*, re-issue edn., 1971– . The cumulative supplements and replacement volumes provide an up-to-date series of lists covering British, Commonwealth and European abbreviations cited in the text.

5. Price, M. O. and Bitner, H. *Effective legal research*, 4th edn., 1979. This contains a comprehensive list of abbreviations in Anglo-American law.

These various lists, however, suffer from a number of common defects. Their alphabetical arrangements are variable and not always consistent with their own chosen plan, and, regardless of dates of publication, each is likely to contain some references that are not to be found in the others. In addition none has attempted to give more than one form of an abbreviation for a specific report. As a result, it may often be necessary to consult more than one list before the required abbreviation is identified, if at all.

The most complete list to date, and one that aims to avoid the limitations noticed above is D. Raistrick's *Index to legal citations and abbreviations,* 1981. This contains over 1,900 citations covering Anglo-American law, Ireland, the Commonwealth and Europe.

Scotland

Scottish cases are cited in a style similar to English cases. In verbal citation the form employed is Smith *against* Jones. A married woman, though, is named in the heading to the report by both her names, the maiden preceding the married name. In citing the case her maiden name is omitted.

Ireland

Irish cases are also cited in the same style as English cases, but the abbreviations may, for the sake of clarity, often be followed by 'Ireland' in brackets, shortened thus: (Ir.). In the Republic, the state prosecutes in the name of the people, thus: *The People (Attorney General) v. O'Donoghue.*

Channel Islands

Cases to be found in *Judgments of the Royal Court of Jersey* 1950– , are to be cited JJ followed by the page number. Cases will also be found in *Table des décisions de la cour royale de Jersey* for the period 1885– , the reference being given by date, series and page.

Isle of Man

Cases are cited in the same style as English cases.

DIGESTS AND INDEXES

Digests aim at recording reported cases in such a manner as to provide a ready guide to the case-law on a given topic. The reports are presented in a highly compressed form and the notes on them seek to provide an abstract of the legal principles which may be inferred from them. Cases are usually arranged under titles, alphabetically ordered, according to their subject matter; the order of presentation of the cases normally being a chronological one. Digested cases, however, are not an adequate substitute for the reports themselves.

Digests may be general, aiming to record all the cases in all the courts, or limited, confining themselves to a particular series of reports, branch of the law or merely to cases that have been judicially noticed. For the latter see page 160.

Among the earliest digests must be noticed those abridgments which included the cases of the nominate reporters. Henry Rolle's *Un Abridgment des plusieurs cases et resolutions del common Ley,* 1668, was written in Law French, runs to some 1,700 pages, and in it the case-law is abridged under alphabetical heads divided into sub-titles. The work is still cited from time to time. A *General Abridgment of Cases in Equity,* by a Gentleman of the Middle Temple, 1732–56, ran to five editions and aimed to contain all equity cases then in print. Charles Petersdorff's *Practical and Elementary Abridgment of Cases in the Courts of King's Bench, Common Pleas, Exchequer, and at Nisi Prius,* 15 volumes, 1825–30, was the first to approximate to a modern digest, containing as it did a series of catchwords or phrases under each title. Supplementary volumes were subsequently issued.

Of early modern general digests the first was Fisher's *Digest of Reported Cases,* 1756–1870, issued in five volumes 1870. Continuation volumes were added to 1879. The continued history of the work, credited to T. W. Chitty and J. Mews, is bibliographically confusing. It is sufficient to say that Mews was the *de facto* author of the new edition of Fisher, issued in seven volumes in 1884 and known as Fisher's *Common Law Digest*, that he issued annual digest volumes up to 1897, and that the first edition of Mews' *Digest of English Case Law*, in 16 volumes, appeared in 1898. A second edition followed in 1925 and was kept up to date by annual volumes to 1970, when it ceased publication. The original edition of Mews contained over 30,000 references to decided cases, but editorial policy precluded the inclusion of 'every case that ever has been reported'.

The English and Empire Digest was first issued in 49 volumes, 1919–32 and a second replacement edition, the 'blue band' re-issue, was published in 56 volumes, 1950–70 followed by the 'green band' re-issue edition, 1971– . As from 1981 the work was retitled *The Digest*. The scheme of arrangement and classification is, in so far as is possible, modelled on *Halsbury's Laws of England*, for which it was designed to become a companion work. This digest purports to be a comprehensive digest of every case reported from early times and claims to contain over three-quarters of a million cases, principally English, together with cases from the courts of Scotland, Ireland, Canada, Australia, New Zealand, India and other countries of the Commonwealth and South Africa. The titles are arranged alphabetically and the cases under them are, in general, presented in chronological order, each section of cases being keyed to both *Halsbury's Laws* and *Statutes*. The work is kept up to date by continuation volumes of cases and annual cumulative supplements.

The Law Reports' Digest of Cases was first issued in 1892 in three volumes covering the period 1865–90, volume 1 being the index volume to the cases. Later supplements appeared at ten-yearly intervals till 1931. The Second World War caused a break in publication and the last supplement to be issued covered the period 1931–50 and was issued in 1952. Since then consolidated indexes have been published covering cases printed 1951–80. As from 1912, the digest widened its scope to include other series of standard English reports, both general and special, as well as *Indian Appeals* and Scots reports, but until 1947 excluded all references to *All ER*. The indexes 1971– , include cases reported in *All ER, Criminal*

Appeal Reports, Lloyds L.R., Local Government Reports, Road Traffic Reports, Reports of Tax Cases, and *Tax Cases Appeals. Knights Industrial Reports,* 1961–76 (subsequently continued in *Managerial Law*) were also included.

The monthly issues of *Current Law* also digest selected cases in some thirty series, either reports or notes in journals; emphasis being given to *The Weekly Law Reports* and *The All England Law Reports.* In these digests the *ratio decidendi* is extracted from the decisions and set out in a separate paragraph. Cases from specialist series are more compressed, giving only the facts and the decision. In addition, reported case-notes of decisions in county courts and crown courts, not otherwise reported, are printed from time to time, while persuasive cases from reports and journals published in the Commonwealth, Scotland, Ireland, South Africa and the United States may also appear. All the latest cases authentically reported, even though not yet appearing in print in a series, are summarized in a special section at the back of each issue, as well as being referred to in the text. The decisions of a number of tribunals are also digested. The indexes to the monthly parts are cumulative but cases are best located by reference to the relevant topic, all topics being alphabetically ordered in the main text.

A useful update service is available through LAWTEL. This provides summaries of House of Lords decisions as well as of 'significant' decisions of the courts and more important tribunals, reported in some 30 law report series as from November 1980 onwards. Over 1,000 cases are noticed annually and the service provides daily information on yesterday's decisions. LAWTEL also provides summaries of quantum damage awards in cases of death and personal injury.

Tables of cases will be found also in the annual *Current Law Year Book,* usually issued each April and in the *Current Law Consolidation,* 1947–51 as well as the later *Master Volumes,* issued every five years until 1971 as supplements to the latter.

Among specialist series, *Lloyd's Law Reports* issue decennial digests and indices, while Harrison's *Tax Finder and Digest,* an index to the *Reports of Tax Cases* was issued in looseleaf format in 1982. The *Index to Periodical Case Reports,* issued monthly from November 1984, covers seven major titles, including the

New Law Journal, Family Law, and the *Financial Times. The Times* law reports are also covered by the latter as well as by the *Index to the Times Law Reports,* 1984– . This is issued monthly and a back-run is in progress. The *Estates Gazette Digest,* 1902–84, contains annual statements on editorial policy changes.

NOTING UP

In most series of modern reports, at the end of the preliminary matter that precedes the first or only judgment of each recorded case, there will be found a list of references to cases in other series of reports, usually currently published and which have been referred to (*ie,* judicially noticed in the judgment(s) that follow(s)). The case in which the reference is found (or cited) is known as the annotating case and the case referred to is known as the annotated case. The different expressions used to describe the effect of the annotating case have particular meanings and the terms most commonly used to describe these are as follows:

Affirmed (affd.), applied (appld.), approved (apprd.), considered (consd.), disapproved (disap.), distinguished (distd.), doubted (dbtd.), explained (expld.), extended (extd.), followed (folld.), not followed (n.f.), overruled (overd.), referred (refd.), reversed (revsd.). These terms are defined in appropriate legal dictionaries.

There exists in the United Kingdom no central index or citation system in published form for the recall of those cases that have been judicially noticed. Such a system would enable a lawyer to locate with facility all leading cases relevant to the case-law of the topics requiring his attention. Failing this, recourse must be made to a number of works whose inclusion of a citation system is, with one exception, incidental to their primary function.

Early works that attempted to meet this need require notice in passing. Dale and Lehmann's *Digest of cases overruled, not followed, disapproved,* [etc.] from 1756 to 1886, 1887, was superseded by Woods and Ritchie's *Digest of cases overruled, approved* [etc.] 3 volumes, 1907. The 30,000 cases were arranged under alphabetical topics and extracts from the more important judgments included. Talbot and Fort's *Index of cases judicially noticed* was issued in 1891, ran to three editions and recorded in the last edition all cases cited in judgments published 1865–1905. Its arrangement was inferior to that of Woods and Ritchie. More ambitious in scope was Campbell's *Ruling cases*, issued in 27 volumes, 1894–1908 and containing American notes by I. Brown.

In Mews' *Digest*, volume 23 contained an *Index of cases judicially noticed*. This included cases noticed in 1926 and a citation search would commence with this volume, continue through the cumulative supplements for 1925–35, 1936–45, and then the twenty-four annual volumes to 1970 when publication ceases.

The Law Reports Digest may similarly be consulted, but the cases digested are not earlier than 1865, though cases referred to may, of course, be of earlier date.

The most profitable digest for citation searches is undoubtedly *The Digest*. The location of the case in question in the table of cases will give a reference to the appropriate volume in which the case is digested. The digest of the case is followed by the relevant citations which indicate how the case has been annotated in later cases. Reference should then be made to the later supplements where, under the same reference number as was given to the case in the original volume, will be found any later cases, together with digests of additional relevant cases.

It must be noticed however that a given case may be digested under more than one head and it must be looked for, in the first instance, under the head most appropriate to the searcher's requirements.

The *Current Law Citator*, issued annually since 1947, periodically consolidated, is a case citator. This lists in strict alphabetical order every English case reported since 1947; every case of whatever date which has been judicially considered in a case reported since 1947, giving also the reference to the paragraph in which the amending case or statute is digested in the CLYB; every case of whatever date which has been the subject of an article or substantial case-note in any of the legal periodicals covered by *Current Law* since 1947; and every Scots, Irish, Commonwealth or South African case similarly digested in *Current Law* since 1947. It also gives full references to every English case reported since 1947. The monthly parts of *Current Law* also contain a case citator section at the commencement of the part. If digested during the current year, the name of the case is printed in standard type; if written about or judicially considered, it is printed in italics; if the case is going to appeal it is marked with an asterisk.

Individual series of law reports such as *The Law Reports* and *All ER* issue tables of cases judicially considered, and these may also be of value as a means of ascertaining the status of a case.

Cases may also be searched on LEXIS.

LOCATION OF CASES

Printed sources

No central index to cases exists. The nearest approximation to such an index is that to *The Digest* which claims to contain every English case reported from early times to the present day, with additional cases from the courts of Scotland, Ireland and the Commonwealth. Similarly, the *Current Law Citator* claims to list every English case reported since 1947. In both, the lists are alphabetical.

If the correct citation is known there is rarely any problem, except that of identifying the relevant series of reports. It is possible, however, that a printed reference may be inaccurate, owing to typographical errors or poor proof-reading, in which case, if there is certainty as to the series, it may be advisable to examine alternative combinations of pages and volume numbers, or years.

Difficulty usually arises only when inadequate information is available.

If the name of a case is known but not its date or any citation, it may be traced:

1. by searching the consolidated table of cases (vols. 52–54, 'blue band' edition) to *The Digest* (if before 1967). This provides references to the relevant volume, subject and page

number of the 'blue band' edition. If the 'blue band' volume has been replaced, locate the case in the table of cases at the front of the appropriate 'green band' volume;

2. through the table of cases at the front of the cumulative supplement to the same digest (if after 1 Jan 1967);

3. through the *Current Law Citator* (if after 1947). Should these not yield results, indexes to the other digests may be consulted in the same manner. If still not located, it is likely to be a recent case not covered by the latest volume of the major digests. In this instance:

4. by consulting the *Current Law Consolidation* (if after 1947) and then the subsequent *Current Law Year Books*.

If the case (whatever is known about it) is of too recent origin to have been noticed in the latest monthly issue of *Current Law,* then trace it:

1. through the latest issue of *All ER* and/or the *Weekly Law Reports*;

2. through the latest issue of the *Solicitors' Journal* and/or *New Law Journal*;

3. through recent issues of *The Times* if no custom built cut-out service with running index is operated.

If the name of a case and the report in which it appears is known but not its date, then trace it in the index volume of the appropriate series. *The All England Law Reports* have a con-solidated index for all cases in the series since 1936, and there is an annual consolidated index to *The Law Reports* and *The Weekly Law Reports,* issued since 1953.

If the date of a modern case is known, but not its name, then trace it:

1. through Mews' *Digest of English Case Law* (if after 1924); or

2. through *Current Law* (if after 1947).

If the date of a case and/or its name but not its citation is known (and it is before 1865), then it may be traced through the index volumes to *The English Reports*.

But if the case is prior to 1865 and is not listed in the index to *The English Reports* then, provided the date, name and type of case is known (*eg,* King's Bench or Admiralty) reference should be made to Maxwell and Brown's *List of British and Colonial Law Reports and Legal Periodicals,* 1937. In this work reports are arranged chronologically by dates of coverage under courts and subjects, *ie,* Admiralty and taxation.

Cases are occasionally reported long after being decided, usually those heard before the House of Lords or as a result of a brief note made *ex. rel.* a member of the Bar and printed in a journal, subsequently cited, thus requiring insertion in an official series of reports. Such belated reports are normally full reports. *Cremin v. Thomson* originated as an incident in 1938. The case was heard by the Court of Session, 26 July 1940, but not reported. It went to the Lords, 14–24 July 1941, judgment being given on 20 October 1941. It was not reported in *The Law Reports* but was reported in *Lloyds LR* 1941, vol. 71, subsequently in *All ER* 1953, vol. 2 and finally in *W.L.R.* 1956 vol. 1 as a note.

If none of the above methods proves successful, it is likely that the case has not been reported in any established series of reports and it should be treated as an unreported case, for which see page 141.

Computerized sources

With the absorption in 1985 of EUROLEX by LEXIS there exists one major computerized legal service providing current awareness facilities with full text in the field of case-law. Such services may be likened either to electronic libraries or subject indices, but more sophisticated in construction, more compact in their deployment of space, and providing recall facilities denied to any sheaf, card or printed index. To the skilled user they offer two benefits: a speed of search superior to that undertaken by conventional means; and certainty that, out of the material held, no case relevant to the enquiry has been overlooked. If full text is stored they can provide the same primary sources for a lawyer in his study, office or chambers as are available in a printed books library. Only two of their disadvantages require notice here. The case-law held in the database does not, currently, cover a wide enough time span to satisfy the needs of the most exacting user. And it may, apparently, take as long to update the material held as it does to produce *Current Law*. But it must be noticed that the availability of up to date judgments on a full text service is necessarily limited by the availability of transcripts. Their production cannot be hurried.

LEXIS includes recall facilities for over thirty-five official, commercial and specialist law reports series, as well as full transcripts of cases reported or summarized in over twenty periodicals and news letters. For unreported cases see p. 141. While cases may be searched for by name, or for references to statutes and regulations or for any references to any material, legal or non-legal, special searches may also be undertaken. These include searches for the decision of a particular court, the judgments of a particular judge, and counsel involved. Searches may also be made for cases decided before, after, or on a given date or between any two dates.

For services offering restricted information see pages 159, 174 and 180. Enquiries about computerized sources should be made either direct to the organization concerned or to the Online Information Centre, Aslib.

A computer search, therefore, even if unsuccessful, can eliminate a great range of material and narrow the field left to be searched with a speed incapable of realization by traditional means.

SCOTTISH REPORTS

The influences that shaped the development of Scottish law reporting do not, as may be expected, mirror that of their English counterpart. Apparent similarities must not be explored too closely. There are no convenient cut-off dates marking changes in its history. In some important respects Scotland was ahead in ideas, in others merely different.

One major variant requires notice. The doctrine of the precedent as a means of influencing the course of Scots law did not begin to burgeon until the last half of the eighteenth century. Up to that time, and later, decided cases imposed no obligation upon the judiciary; they might influence but were not authoritative.

Modern reports

Official

Cases decided in the Court of Session, familiarly known as *Session Cases,* report the actions of the supreme civil court of Scotland

and commenced publication in 1821. Initially they were a result of private enterprise and the first five series, each separately numbered, are often referred to and are sometimes better known by the name of the principal reporter for each series: Shaw, Dunlop, Macpherson, Rettie and Fraser. Volume 10 (1847–8) of the second series began to include cases in other courts, such as the Teind Court, and Court of Exchequer; volume 13 (1850–1) began to include House of Lords cases with a separate pagination, while volume 1 (1873–4) of the fourth series began to include justiciary (criminal) cases, the latter also separately paginated.

In 1907 responsibility for publication of the session cases was assumed by the Faculty of Advocates, who in turn handed this over to the Scottish Council of Law Reporting in 1957. Now, the *Session Cases* are published in parts throughout the year and include lands valuation appeal decisions in addition to those of courts already mentioned.

As a result of the separate pagination, the justiciary cases as from 1917 are occasionally to be found separately bound, generally five years to a volume and having their own distinctive citation are often regarded as a separate series. The House of Lords appeals appearing in the *Session Cases*, also with a separate pagination and an equally distinctive citation are similarly regarded. They are, however, rarely bound separately owing to the paucity of the material. Neither the Lords nor justiciary cases are accorded the dignity of a title page. This is reserved for the session cases alone.

It is usual for the recorded decisions to be submitted to the judiciary for correction and approval prior to printing. As a result, the series is held to be of the highest authority and the accuracy of its reporters is rarely if ever questioned. *Session Cases* are also available on LEXIS.

The *Session Notes* were issued weekly 1925–48 under the authority of the Faculty of Advocates. They contained notes of cases decided in the Court of Session, Court of Justiciary and the House of Lords, and effectively provided an interim service whilst publication of the relevant part of the *Session Cases* was awaited. Not all such notes however were subsequently followed by full reports in the *Session Cases* and publication was discontinued, their purpose being already adequately met by the Notes of Recent Decisions to be found in *The Scots Law Times,* noted below.

Commercial

Commercial publication of reports had commenced in the nineteenth century. Deas and Anderson's reports appeared in five volumes covering 1829–32. These dealt mainly with cases decided in the Court of Session, but additionally had Jury Court and justiciary reports. For the same period the same publishers issued *The Law Chronicle* which included a few reports. Both contained analogous cases decided in England. Of particular importance were the *Scottish Jurist,* 46 volumes, 1829–73 and the *Scottish Law Reporter,* 61 volumes, 1865–1924, the latter thereafter incorporated with *The Scots Law Times.* The former contained session, justiciary, teind and Lords cases from its commencement and, at its conclusion, was also reporting decisions reached by the railway and canal commission, the valuation appeal court, provisional order committees and the Privy Council.

The Scottish Law Review commenced publication in 1885 and was issued monthly. It included reports of decisions in the Sheriff Courts from 1885 to 1963 as well as notes of English cases held to be of relevance. The former have their own citation and are occasionally to be found separately bound. From 1913 to 1963 (when it ceased publication) a supplement contained decisions of the Scottish Land Court, also bound separately.

With the demise of the *Scottish Jurist* and the *Scottish Law Review* only one main commercial series remains in progress.

The Scots Law Times Reports are issued within the weekly parts of *The Scots Law Times* but with a separate pagination. The make-up of the *SLT* is a complicated one and the various series of reports to be found within its published parts form such an integral part of this publication that its composition demands elucidation. Each has its own separate title page and pagination.

The Scots Law Times commenced publication in 1893–4 and the first two volumes contained brief signed notes under the heading 'Reports' of cases heard in the Court of Session, House of Lords and Sheriff Court. As from volume 3 (1895–6) *Scots Law Times Reports* appeared in the journal, entitled volume 3, 1895–6, with their own separate title page and pagination. The *SLTR* covered Lords, justiciary and session cases. Volumes 1 to 16 only were numbered. As from 1909 the volume numbering was dropped and citation was by the year, two volumes of reports being issued each year until 1922, when reversion was made to a single volume of reports. In 1922 the *SLT* commenced the *Sheriff Court Reports,* while an index of cases and annual digest appeared at the back of the *SLTR*. In 1932 the *SLT* added another series, the *SLT Poor Law Reports.*, continued till 1941, when it ceased. In 1946 the *SLT* started a new series *Notes of Recent Decisions.* Cases in the Notes are often expanded into full reports in subsequent issues. Again, in 1950, a further series commenced, the *SLT Lyon Court Reports.* This series, published only intermittently, lasted till 1959, was discontinued, and revived only twice since in 1966 and 1977. In 1964 the *SLT Scottish Land Court Reports* commenced and in 1971 the *SLT* started the *Lands Tribunal for Scotland Reports.* In 1984 there began *European Court Case Notes.* The *SLT* with its various reports series is also available on LEXIS.

Other reports

Selected Scottish appeals to the House of Lords will be found in the following English series of reports: the two volumes of Scotch and Divorce Appeals, 1866–75, in the first series of *The Law Reports* (see pages 128–9), from 1876 onwards in the *Appeal Cases* of the later series, and *The All England Law Reports,* 1936 to date.

Decisions by the Scottish courts on such specialist matters as elections, income tax, and pensions are reported from time to time and may generally be located either in the series recorded above or in appropriate specialist reports whether English or Scottish. For example, important Scottish cases on commercial and maritime law are to be located in *Lloyd's Law Reports* but matters affecting local government will be found in the *County and Municipal Record,* 1903 to date. Likewise, Scottish tribunal decisions may be recorded in for example *Knights Industrial Reports,* 1966–75 (continued in *Managerial Law*) or appropriate government publications (see also page 149).

Early reports

The earliest reports were either notes made for personal use or notes of cases to be found in volumes of Practicks. Private reporting commences with a case of 1540, not printed however till 1741, and the authors of the majority of the early reports were judges, whose notes, made initially for private use, were seldom intended for publication.

Session reports

Of early reports the most important are the twenty-one private or original reports, separately printed, which cover cases in the Court of Session from 1621 to 1822, commencing with Durie's *Decisions of the Lords of Council and Session,* 1641– 42, issued by Sir A. Gibson of Durie, and concluding with David Hume's *Decisions,* 1781–1822, issued in 1839. Other notable reporters in this group were Sir James Dalrymple, 1st Viscount Stair, and Henry Home, Lord Kames.

Durie's was the earliest volume of reports in any court to be printed. The professional reporter did not appear till 1705, when William Forbes was appointed by the Faculty of Advocates to report the decisions of the Court of Session and his only volume, covering cases heard 1705–13, appeared in 1714. Lacking judicial encouragement, this venture to produce a systematic official series was temporarily abandoned. The judiciary were hostile to the suggestion of allowing more than mere decisions to be published and Robert Bell, the first independent reporter, met with animosity and obstruction when he announced his intention of reporting without an official appointment. His *Cases decided in the Court of Session,* 1790–5 was published in 1794–6, the judges being denoted in the text only by letters. His reward was a summons to the robing room and the reproof of the judiciary. It was over a decade before they changed their views.

If the absence of the binding authority of a decided case had delayed over-long the arrival of the professional reporter, his continued activity until the first quarter of the twentieth century was due, perhaps, to the failure of the second attempt by the Faculty of Advocates at an official series. Their *Decisions, 1752–1808*, issued in fourteen volumes, 1760–1815, was entitled 'Old Faculty Reports', the cases being reported by a Committee of the Bar. A new series was subsequently issued, bringing the period of cases covered down to 1841. The composite set of twenty-one volumes is best known as the 'Faculty Collection', more familiarly the 'Faculty Collection folios' to distinguish them from the later octavo set, covering the period 1825–41. The delay in their production proved unpopular and the session case series initiated by Patrick Shaw and his colleagues in 1821, and continued without a break by his successors until 1908, was to result in their closure.

Justiciary reports

Also of importance as a group are the eleven reporters of criminal cases who recorded decisions in the Court of Justiciary for the period 1670–1916, broken by a gap, 1774–1818. They commence with John MacLaurin, Lord Dreghorn's *Arguments and Decisions*, 1670–1773, issued 1774, and close with Adam's *Justiciary Cases*, 1893–1916, issued in seven volumes. Collections of early cases, principally of concern to legal historians, have been published by the Scottish History Society and the Stair Society. For collections of criminal trials refer to Trials at page 182–5. As from 1874, commencing with the fourth series, edited by Rettie, justiciary cases have been reported in the annual volumes of *Session Cases*, which are noticed above. The *Scottish Criminal Case Reports*, 1981–, issued in 1981 is the first attempt to produce a separate set of reports of criminal cases since Adam's *Justiciary Cases* of 1916 (noticed below). While the *SCCR* is expected to contain mainly appellate decisions it is hoped that other decisions, including those dealing with sentencing will also be included. The *SCCR* is available on LEXIS.

House of Lords' appeals

The reporting of Lords' decisions in Scottish appeals commenced with Robertson's *Reports of Cases on appeal from Scotland, decided in the house of peers from 1707–27*, issued 1807. It continued in private hands till 1879 when Paterson published in two volumes his *Reports of Scotch Appeals in the House of Lords*, [1851–73]. This was in fact a revision of reports that had already appeared in the *Scottish Jurist*. Of this group of ten reporters, Macqueen's *Reports* alone were subsequently reprinted in the *English Reports*. Certain English nominate reports recording English House of Lords cases also contain Scottish appeals, for details of which see Leadbetter, J. S. 'The printed Law Reports', in *Sources and Literature of Scots Law*, Stair Society 1, 1936, pp. 57–8.

Collections: 1540–1816

The majority of the early cases were reprinted in two major collections, which also printed for the first time a number of important manuscript series. Kames and Woodhouselee's *Decisions of the Court of Session*, abridged in the form of a dictionary, covered the period 1540–1796 and was issued in five volumes, 1741–1804. More comprehensive was Morison's *Decisions, Court of Session* [1540–1808] *in the form of a Dictionary*, issued in twenty-two volumes, 1801–15. The dictionary contains some reports earlier than 1540, taken from Balfour's *Practicks*; volumes 20 and 21 are a synopsis or digest of the cases recorded; volume 22 has supplemental matter; and two appendices were subsequently added, the first containing decisions reported whilst the work was in progress. A supplement in five volumes by Brown was subsequently issued adding material omitted by Morison. For the location of material (the arrangement in Brown differs, the cases being arranged chronologically under each reporter) reference should be made to Tait's *Index*, 1823, which alone provides an adequate key as well as a full account of the complicated bibliographical make-up of Morison's work.

The most modern collection to date, noted here for

convenience, is the *Scots Revised Reports,* a re-issue of many Scots decisions prior to 1873, published in forty-five volumes, 1898–1908. It is selective, drawing upon Morison's *Dictionary,* the Faculty's *Decisions,* Appeals to the House of Lords, the first three series of *Session Cases* and cases reported in the *Scottish Jurist.*

A microfilm edition of *Scottish Law Reports,* reproducing over 300 volumes, and a near complete collection of the early reports was issued in 1973–4.

Digests and indexes

The purpose and construction of Scottish law digests is so similar to that of their English counterparts as to require no elucidation.

Because of the order of their arrangement a number of the early published works noticed above at page 171 are sometimes treated as being digests of case-law. They are not so regarded here.

A number of the earlier digests are still of value, but since there is a lack of uniformity in the style of headings used, searches must often be made under a variety of headings in order to locate the required material. Brown's *Synopsis of decisions in the Court of Session, including House of Lords appeals, 1540–1827* was issued in four volumes, 1827–9. This work covers all the cases in Morison's *Dictionary,* Brown's *Supplement,* the reported decisions of Elchies, Hailes and Bell, and the first four volumes also of the Faculty of Advocates' *Decisions* down to 1827. Bell's *Compendium of decisions of the court of session from 1808–33,* was issued in two volumes in 1841–2. Shaw's *Digest of cases decided,* issued [1869] was a consolidation of two previous digests and included cases decided in the Supreme Courts, 1800–68 and on appeal by the House of Lords, 1726–1868. It was in three volumes and included criminal cases under the heading Crime.

There are two major modern digests. The first is the Faculty of Advocates' *Digest* (a continuation of Shaw), covering 1868–1922 and issued in six volumes, 1924–6, which was continued up to 1950 by three supplementary volumes, and thereafter by annual parts. It includes all cases reported in the *Session Cases*, excluding Sheriff Court decisions, the *Scottish Law Reporter*, the *Scots Law Times* and the *Justiciary Reports*. The titles are arranged alphabetically, criminal cases being grouped under justiciary. The second is *The Scots Digest*, first published in four volumes, 1908–12 and digesting cases in the Lords from 1707 and in the Supreme Courts, 1800–73. A second series was issued in two volumes in 1905 and continuations appeared thereafter. The 1946 volume for the period 1937–44 covers *Session Cases, Session Notes*, the *Scots Law Times*, the *Scottish Law Reporter* and *Justiciary Cases*.

It should be noted that the last part-issue of the *Faculty Digest* (publication of which was assumed by the Scottish Council of Law Reporting after 1957) covers the year 1963 and was issued in 1967. Subsequent issues were projected but are unlikely to appear. The last part-issue of *The Scots Digest* for 1946–7 was issued in 1948. Both are unofficially supplemented by the Scottish edition of *Current Law*.

Digests, usually annual, will be found in the *Scots Law Times Reports* and the *Scottish Law Reporter*. Occasionally consolidations are issued. *A Digest of cases decided in the Sheriff Courts of Scotland* covered the period 1885–1944 while the *Scottish Law Reporter Digest*, issued in 1898, digested nearly 1,300 cases reported in the first thirty-two volumes of the *Scottish Law Reporter, 1865–95*.

A selection of Scottish cases are digested in English publications such as Mews' *Digest of English Case-Law* and footnote references will be found in *The English and Empire Digest*, continued as *The Digest*.

The best printed reference guide to modern cases however must remain the Scottish edition of *Current Law*. Those sections applicable to the United Kingdom give an identical coverage to that in the English edition (see page 159), but the section giving material information applicable to Scotland contains references to cases reported in all the major series of Scottish law reports. Indexes to monthly parts are cumulative, but cases are best located by reference to the relevant topic, all topics being alphabetically ordered in the main text.

Tables of cases will be found also in the annual *Current Law Year Book*, which contains a special Scottish section, but for convenience these are general to the whole volume. Master volumes are issued quinquennially, giving coverage over the previous five years, the last covering 1967–71.

LAWTEL provides summaries of significant cases from November 1980 to date in some nine series of law reports, principally those published in the *Scots Law Times* and in *Session Cases*.

Noting-up

The general principle regarding the noting-up of cases is identical with that for English material (see page 160). No Scots digests specifically concerned with cases judicially noticed have been published, however. Reference must be made to the indexes of appropriate digests and to the *Scottish Current Law Citator*, whose case citator, periodically consolidated, is divided into two sections. The first section relates to English cases and the second to cases reported in Scotland, together with cases of whatever date which have been judicially considered in the Scottish courts during the period under review. It is thus possible to trace the history of any case of whatever date which has been judicially considered since 1948 except Court of Appeal cases.

IRISH REPORTS

Republic of Ireland (Eire)

The Irish Reports, which now record the decisions of the High Court, the Court of Criminal Appeal and the Supreme Court of Eire, commenced publication in 1894. Until 1926, two volumes were issued per year, the first covering the Chancery, the second the King's Bench division. Initially the courts reported included the Court of Appeal, High Court of Justice, Court of Bankruptcy and Irish Land Commission. In 1898 for bankruptcy was substituted Crown cases reserved, and in 1923 (after independence) the reports covered the courts of the

Irish Free State and Northern Ireland. As from 1925, reporting was confined to the Irish Free State alone, cases on appeal in the then new Supreme Court being first recorded in volume 1 for that year, criminal appeals appearing in volume 2. Land Commission cases have not been reported since 1968. Now, *The Irish Reports* are issued quarterly, though two parts are frequently combined in one, and there are unavoidable publication delays. Unlike the *Session Cases*, the volumes contain a single pagination system. A verbatim reprint for the period 1894–1912 was issued in twelve volumes, 1913–15. In 1983 the ICLR (I) issued *Judgments of the Court of Criminal Appeal, 1924–78*. Those in part one represent one third of the unpublished judgments delivered during the period covered, while part two contains selected judgments published in the *Irish Reports* of the day. Volume 2, covering 1979–83 was published in 1984.

The *Irish Law Times and Solicitors Journal*, 1867–1980 (new series, 1983–) is still issued weekly, and initially reported cases appearing in the miscellaneous part of the journal in the form of weekly notes of cases, these being supplied by the reporters of the Council of Law Reporting in Ireland. As from volume 5 (1871), a supplement with a separate title page and its own pagination was issued, entitled the *Irish Law Times Reports*. Notes of cases, however, continued to appear in the journal. Initially the *ILTR* included reports of cases in the Supreme Court of Judicature, bankruptcy and the county courts. The *Irish Law Reports Monthly*, 1981– was published in 1981 to replace the *ILTR* and aims to provide a complete coverage of the superior court judgments.

The *Irish Jurist* commenced publication in 1849. After seven volumes a new series, volumes 8 to 18, 1855–66, was issued. Volume 19, pt. 1 is said to have been issued also. Both series contained reports of decisions in all the courts. Between 1901–5, appeared *The New Irish Jurist and Local Government Review*, which contained the *NIJ* and *LG Reports* for 1900–5. *The Irish Jurist* was re-born in 1935, initially issued monthly and then quarterly. The periodical and law report sections were separately paginated and thirty-one volumes were issued, 1935–1965. A new series commenced in 1966 and continues. While the first series contains reports of decisions in all the courts, the new series contains a digest of selected cases only from both jurisdictions.

Northern Ireland

The Northern Ireland Law Reports commenced publication in 1925 under the authority of the newly-established Incorporated Council of Law Reporting for Northern Ireland. Prior to 1925, relevant cases appeared in *The Irish Reports,* as noticed above. The reports are issued in quarterly parts and cover cases in the High Court of Justice and Court of Appeal in Northern Ireland. As from 1970, cases on appeal therefrom in the House of Lords have been included. An *Index to Cases decided in the courts of Northern Ireland and reported during the period 1921 to 1970,* edited by D. F. Greer and B. A. Childs, was published in 1975, a supplement to 1975 being issued in 1976. In 1972 the ICLR (NI) commenced the *Northern Ireland Judgments Bulletin,* issued as a mimeograph production, approximately monthly. The *Bulletin* covers civil judgments delivered in the High Court, Court of Appeal and Court of Criminal Appeal. Distributed on a restrictive basis, it is accepted for citation in court, and includes a proportion of cases not subsequently reported in the *Northern Ireland Law Reports.*

The *Northern Ireland Legal Quarterly* commenced publication in 1936 and the first part issued contained notes on case-law. As from the second part of volume 1, this title was changed to 'a survey of recent case-law'. As from volume 15 (volume 1 NS) the *Quarterly* was published from the Law Faculty, Queen's University and acquired a title page, a table of cases noted, a section entitled 'notes of cases', and a digest of unreported NI cases, the latter being dropped from volume 16. It should be noticed that in the later volumes the notes of cases section contains digests of special tribunal decisions as well as digests of unreported cases.

Selected appeals to the House of Lords will be found in the Appeal Cases of *The Law Reports* as well as in *NILR.*

The courts of Northern Ireland, while respecting the decisions of the English courts, are not bound by them, though they are bound by decisions of the House of Lords as the supreme court of appeal. Pre-1921 Irish decisions are said by some to be binding, particularly in the case of decisions of the Court of Appeal, and are at least accorded the same respect as English decisions below the House of Lords. Decisions of the courts of Eire are, naturally, not binding on Northern Ireland, but would in certain circumstances (*eg* when interpreting the statutes in force in Northern Ireland) be treated with the utmost respect.

Earlier reports

Law reporting in Ireland did not effectively commence until the last quarter of the eighteenth century, though the earliest reporter would seem to have been Sir John Davies, whose *Le primer report des cases et matters en Ley ... en les courts del roy en Ireland* covering cases 1604–12, was issued in 1615. These are reprinted in *ER*, volume 80. Exchequer cases were first reported by Howard in 1760; he was also the first to report Chancery cases in 1772 in a work entitled *Rules and practice of the High Court of Chancery*. The nineteenth century saw a considerable increase in private reporting and some fifty reporters (or pairs of reporters) produced over one hundred volumes of reports during this period. Of later reporters Fitzgibbon was the most prolific. His *Irish Land Reports, 1895–1920*, in twenty-five volumes, 1895–1920 was issued almost concurrently with his *Irish Local Government Orders and Legal Decisions, 1899–1919*, in seventeen volumes, 1899–1919.

The earliest attempt to record cases in all the courts was the product of commercial enterprise. *The Law Recorder, containing reports of cases in the courts of law and equity, 1827–31*, a weekly publication, was issued in five volumes, 1828–32; a new series, 1833–8, in six volumes followed, issued 1833–8.

In 1839 were published two series, both covering the period 1838–50 in thirteen volumes and issued 1839–52. The first, *Irish Law Reports*, reported cases in the Queen's Bench, Common Pleas and Exchequer; the second, *Irish Equity Reports*, cases in Chancery, Rolls court and Equity Exchequer. Both were subtitled 'Third Series of The Law Recorder'. These were followed by the *Irish Chancery Reports, 1850–66*, in seventeen volumes, 1852–67, and the *Irish Common Law Reports*, 1849–66, also in seventeen volumes, 1852–67

In 1867 was established the Council of Law Reporting in Ireland. The *Irish Reports* were then first issued, publication following the pattern of their English equivalent. Initially there were two main series, the *Common Law Series* and the *Equity Series* covering decisions reported 1867–78 in eleven volumes each. In addition, a volume of registry appeals was published in 1879. This series was continued by *The Law Reports (Ireland)*, 1878–93, issued in thirty-two volumes, 1879–93, which in turn was to be continued by *The Irish Reports*, 1894–, already noticed above. A reprint of all series of *Irish Reports*, 1838–1974 was issued in 1976, and a microform edition of this is also available.

Collections

No reprint collection devoted solely to Irish reports has yet been produced in volume form, though a selection of Irish reports held to be authoritative may be located in *The Revised Reports* (see page 137).

A micro-film edition of the earlier reports is in the course of preparation. This aims to include the series in Maxwell and Brown to 1900 and the main series to 1894.

Digests and indexes

The purpose and construction of Irish law digests is identical to that of their English counterparts and require no additional exposition.

The earliest digest would seem to have been Finlay's *Digested index to all Irish reported cases in law and equity from the earliest period*, issued in 1830. This also included cases dealing with ecclesiastical and criminal law and a variety of original cases from authentic sources. Thereafter, numerous digests, analytical and otherwise were published, few aiming to be all-inclusive and the majority fated to be superseded when rationalization of law reporting took place. Kinahan's *Digested index to the reports of . . . courts of equity in Ireland,* issued 1830 requires notice because it included cases upon appeals from Ireland to be found in the *English Reports*. Similarly, Millin's *Digest* of reported cases relating to petty sessions between 1875–98 is useful, since it contains seventeen unreported cases.

The first inclusive digest and one which remains unsuperseded was Brunker's *Digest of Cases Superior and other Courts of Common Law and Court of Admiralty from Sir F. Davies' reports to the present time*. This was issued in 1865.

In 1879 was issued the first *Digest of Cases* published by the Incorporated Council of Law Reporting for Ireland and covering the period 1867–77. Two extension volumes were issued, the first in 1890, covering 1867–88, the second in 1899 covering 1867–93. In 1899 another digest was issued for the period 1894–8 and digests have continued to be issued to date covering consecutive periods of time, not always decennially. The most recent, issued in 1974, covers the period 1959–70. In 1921 the *Digest of Cases,* by arrangement, included also cases printed in the *Irish Law Times* and *New Irish Jurist* (subsequently the *Irish Jurist*), while as from 1930 the *Digest of Cases* has also included, by arrangement, the *Northern Ireland Law Reports*. It is now therefore a digest to all reported cases in the geographical area of Ireland. In 1984 was issued an *Index to cases decided in the Supreme Court, Court of Criminal Appeal and High Court,* 1976–82. Confined to those cases 'in which written judgments were available for circulation' this work (entitled on the spine: Index to Irish Superior Court written judgments) is in fact a digest, originally published in current parts of the *Gazette of the Incorporated Law Society of Ireland*.

The Irish Jurist digest, edited by Blackham in 1852, digested cases in volumes 11–13 of the *Irish Law Reports*, the first volume of the new series and volumes 2–4 of the *Irish Jurist*.

The Irish Law Times Digest of Cases, compiled by Stubbs, covering cases reported in the *Irish Law Times Reports* and the *Irish Law Times and Solicitors Journal* for the period 1867–1903, was published 1895–1905 in two volumes, and as with the 'official' *Digest of Cases* noted above, employed the same system of arrangement as that which was adopted by the Incorporated Council of Law Reporting of England and Wales.

As with Scottish cases, a selection of Irish cases, usually those of a persuasive nature, are digested in English publications such as *The English and Empire Digest*, and its continuation, *The Digest*.

The English *Current Law* (see page 159) contains a section on Northern Ireland, but also contains references to cases of a persuasive nature reported in *The Irish Jurist*, *The Irish Law Times* and *The Irish Reports*, as well as *Northern Ireland Land Tribunal Decisions* and *Northern Ireland Law Reports*. LAWTEL however, provides summaries of significant cases from November 1980 to date in the *Northern Ireland Law Reports*, *Northern Ireland Judgments Bulletin* and the *Northern Ireland Legal Quarterly*.

Tables of cases will be found also in the annual *Current Law Year Book* and in the annual notices of the *IR* and *NILR*.

Noting-up

The general principle regarding the noting-up of cases is identical with that for English material. Reference should be made to the indexes of the appropriate digests noticed above, as well as to *The Digest*.

The Current Law Citator should also be consulted. This contains every Irish decision of a persuasive nature digested in *Current Law* since 1947.

CHANNEL ISLANDS

Jersey

The principal court is the Royal Court of Jersey whose more recent decisions will be found published in *Judgments of the Royal Court of Jersey and of the Court of Appeal of Jersey*, 1950–. There were no printed reports prior to 1950 but a classified summary of decisions has been issued since 1885, entitled *Table des décisions de la Cour Royale*, 1896–.

Appeals lie to the Privy Council and a number of decisions relative to Jersey will be found in *Ordres du conseil et pièces analogues enregistrés à Jersey*, edited by H. M. Godfray and A. Messeroy, 1536–1867, issued in six volumes, 1897–1906.

Guernsey

In 1814 was published *Causes heard and determined at St Peter Port in the Island of Guernsey before . . . His Majesty's Commissioners, 16 October to 20 December, 1607*. With this exception no reports of decisions have been printed.

In 1961 a Court of Appeal was set up to obviate the necessity of carrying appeals to the Privy Council, though such access still remains if needed. The Court hears both civil and criminal appeals and these are published in *Guernsey Court of Appeal (Civil Division)* [Reports], 1965–, and *Guernsey Court of Appeal (Criminal Division)* [Reports], 1964–.

ISLE OF MAN

The principal civil court is the High Court of Justice, which includes Chancery and Common Law divisions, together with a Court of Appeal. The principal criminal court is the Court of General Gaol Delivery. Appeals in civil and criminal cases lie to the Privy Council's Judicial Committee.

The Manx Law Reports, 1981–3, were published in 1985 and the series aims to contain reports back to 1884. Case notes of recent or current cases may be located in the *Manx Law Bulletin*, 1982/3–. Cases may also be located in the Island's newspaper. In 1948, there was published Farrant's *Digest of Manx cases heard and decided during the period, 1925–47*. The more important decisions on appeal will be found in the relevant series of English law reports.

Early cases may be found in Talbot's *Manorial Roll of the Isle of Man*, issued 1924 and covering the period 1511–15, and in Bluett's *The Advocate's Notebook, being notes and minutes of cases heard before the judicial tribunals of the Isle of Man*, 1847.

For unpublished cases it may be necessary to consult the typed transcripts of the Reasons for Judgment given by the Deemsters, while the legal records in the General Registry at Douglas include House of Keys judgments prior to 1865.

TRIALS

Under this head come verbatim reports of the proceedings of actions in civil and criminal courts. These by definition cannot be classed as law reports. The printed transcripts have normally been abridged, but will include counsel's opening and closing speeches, examinations-in-chief and cross-examination of witnesses, concluding with the judgment or sentence of the court. Being verbatim reports they are of value to practising lawyers, legal historians and students of advocacy. But they are not to be confused with works about trials which are narrative accounts, subjectively written, usually more concerned with the crime or cause of action then the trial itself. Dependent upon their importance, such cases may or may not be found reported elsewhere. It is unfortunate that there exists in print no adequate bibliography of this material.

Civil

Reports of civil actions are usually issued as individual works. Publication (at its height in the eighteenth and nineteenth centuries) may be general or private. It may originate at the instigation of one of the interested parties; a legal journalist may be concerned to draw attention to the state of the law; or an editor be commissioned to record an historic event. The proceedings in the case of the *City of Manchester v. Manchester Palace of Varieties*, heard in the High Court of Chivalry in 1954 and published by the Heraldry Society, are an example.

Criminal

Reports of criminal actions, issued either in collections or as individual works, far outweigh civil actions, since public demand inevitably encourages the promotion of private gain. Criminal pamphlets and broadsides, allegedly relating the life, trial and execution of notorious criminals had been printed as early as the time of Elizabeth I. Enduring through the seventeenth and eighteenth centuries, they influenced the compilation of a number of remarkable works, some of which are noticed below. Attention however must first be given to the availability of official material.

The principal judicial records relating to the higher criminal jurisdiction are held in manuscript by the House of Lords' Record Office.

For printed records relating to proceedings in impeachment, reference should be made to the *Journals of the House of Lords,* 1621–1806. This run also contains related documents such as articles of impeachment, answers of the accused, and petitions and orders. For evidential documents, 1617–1795, not printed, reference must be made to the original manuscripts. The judgments, 1621–1806 are included in the *Journals* and reprinted in various collections of state trials as noted below.

For records of proceedings relating to the trials of peers, reference must again be made to the *Journals of the House of Lords,* 1678–1935. These also contain related records – petitions, 1641–1776, orders of the House, 1641–1935, writs of certiorari and commissions appointing the Lord High Steward, 1678–1935, indictments and inquisitions for the same period, and miscellaneous petitions and orders 1641–1935. For recognizances of witnesses, not printed, reference must be made to the original manuscripts. The proceedings of peerage trials were ordered to be printed in 1693. For accounts of trials to 1776, see the various collections of state trials as noted below. For trials from 1841 reference should be made to the House of Lords sessional papers. It should be noted that the privilege of peers to be tried by the Lords was abolished by statute in 1948.

Though numerous works with titles which include the wording State Trials have been published, the term is most commonly used with reference to the collection initially edited by Thomas Salmon and issued in 1719. Of this work four editions were published, the last by Francis Hargrave. The best-known edition, based on Hargrave, is that credited to the two Howells: *Complete Collection of State Trials and Proceedings for High Treason,* edited by T. B. Howell and T. J. Howell, 34 volumes, 1809–28. This includes cases from 1163 to 1820. In fact, the first twelve volumes were edited by W. Cobbett, who is seldom credited except by professional bibliographers. This edition was continued by a new series in eight volumes, covering 1820–58 and issued 1888–98. In general, the trials record the prosecutions of notable English, Scottish and Irish personages, are of historic as well as legal interest and deal not only with impeachments, treason, sedition and other criminal matters, but also with cases of constitutional and public concern. The cases are chronologically arranged. Not all are strictly verbatim reports, the earliest ones being based on chronicles, histories and records. The proved reliability of the work, however, has given it a semi-official status and it is so regarded.

The Old Bailey Session Papers, 1729–1834, issued in seventy-six volumes, 1715–1834, were continued by the *Central Criminal Court Session Papers*, 1834–1913, issued in 158 volumes, 1834–1913. Together these remarkable series illustrate the work of the court and of criminal justice over a period of 140 years. The reports, however, may be heavily compressed and cases heard may be excluded, *eg*, the three trials in 1895 of Oscar Wilde.

Of commercial publications the following require special notice: the *Notable British Trials* series, comprising eighty-four volumes under the general editorship of J. H. Hodge and issued 1905–59. Each volume deals with an individual action and the series (unnumbered) covers cases heard 1586–1953. The majority are criminal, but some civil actions are included. The series incorporates the *Notable Scottish Trials*, originally a separate series, of which a number of volumes were issued, distinguished by their own series title and a distinctive green binding. Later editions of the Scottish series were re-issued in the NBT format. A supplementary series under the same general editorship was issued after 1945, dealing with selected war crimes trials held under British jurisdiction and published in nine volumes, 1948–52. For detailed information relating to these and other war crimes trials reference should be made to the UN's *History of the United Nations War Crimes Commission*, compiled by the Commission, issued in 1948. This details the trials held, names of defendants, the courts' decisions and dates of sentences, as required.

In general, individually issued and commercially-backed

reports of proceedings contain introductory essays of variable length and quality. Often, though not in the NBT, the verbatim passages (their sources not always defined) are of the briefest and are linked by editorial commentary. The latter can also be suspect since information may be introduced that was not put in evidence at the trial. An exception is S. Bedford's *The best we can do,* 1958, an account of the trial of Bodkin Adams (1957).

For information on published criminal cases, refer to Sir J. Cummings' *Contribution towards a bibliography dealing with crime and cognate subjects,* 1935. The section entitled 'criminal trials' does not unfortunately differentiate between commentaries and transcripts. For summary details of newsworthy crimes and trials, refer to the relevant annual volume of *Whitaker's Almanack*; for details on published English, Scottish and Irish trials and causes, refer also to the subject indexes in the relevant volumes of Sweet and Maxwell's *Legal Bibliography*.

FURTHER READING

ADMINISTRATIVE TRIBUNALS

Way, D. J. 'Tribunals: an outline of the literature', *Law Librarian*, vol. 3, 1972, pp. 10–14.
Wraith, R. E. and Hutchesson, P. G. *Administrative Tribunals,* 1973.

CITATIONS AND REFERENCES

Axele-Lute, P. 'Legal citation form: theory and practice', *Law Library Journal*, vol. 75, 1982, pp. 148–56.
Cooper, B. D. 'Anglo-American legal citations: historical development and library implications', *Law Library Journal*, vol. 75, 1982, pp. 1–35.
Marion, P. C. 'Sources for determining citation practice for court reports throughout the world', *Library Resources and Technical Services*, vol. 25, 1981, pp. 139–48.

COMPUTERIZED SERVICES

Bing, J. (ed.) *Handbook of legal information retrieval*, 1984.

GENERAL

Twining, W. L. and Uglow, J. *Law publishing and legal information: small jurisdictions in the British Isles*, 1981. Covers Scotland, Republic of Ireland and the Isle of Man.

IRISH REPORTS

O'Higgins, P. *Bibliography of periodical literature relating to Irish law*, 1966 and supps. 1972 and 1983. Contains a section on law reports and reporting. There is no legal literature of any substance on Irish law reports and reporting.

LAW REPORTING

Burrow, R. 'Law reporting', *Law Quarterly Review*, vol. 58, 1942, pp. 96–106.

Ellis, C. J. 'Law reporting today', *Law Librarian*, vol. 6, 1975, pp. 5–8.

Goodhart, A. L. 'Reporting the law', *Law Quarterly Review*, vol. 55, 1939, pp. 29–34.

Great Britain, Lord Chancellor's Office, *Report of the Lord Chancellor's Committee on Law Reporting*, 1940.

Lindley, Lord. 'History of the Law Reports', *Law Quarterly Review*, vol. 1, 1885, pp. 137–49. A review of Daniel (see 'Modern Reports'), in which the author formulates principles of contemporary law reporting.

Mews, J. 'The present system of law reporting', *Law Quarterly Review*, vol. 9, 1893, pp. 179–87.

Moran, C. G. *Heralds of the law*, 1948. The best work on the responsibilities of the reporter and the composition of a modern report.

MECHANICAL RECORDING

Great Britain. Lord Chancellor's Office, *Report of a Working Party on Recording Court Proceedings*, 1972.

MODERN REPORTS

Daniel, W. T. S. *History and origin of the Law Reports*, 1884. A history of the founding of ICLR.

Latey, W. *A short history of the Law Reports*, 1865–1965 [1966] [Pamphlet. An abridged version of Daniel].

Pollock, F. 'English law reporting', *Law Quarterly Review*, vol. 19, 1903, pp. 451–60. A critical assessment of *The Law Reports*.

NOMINATE REPORTS

Abbott, L. W. *Law reporting in England, 1485–1585*, 1973.

Holdsworth, W. S. *History of English law*, various edns., 1936–72, vol. 5, pp. 355–78 and 6, pp. 531–73 and 616–19 (1485–1700) contain an assessment of the reports, with accounts of the reporters; vol. 12 (1701–1875) deals with reports and abridgments at pp. 101–78; vol. 13 (1701–1875) contains a section on the reports at pp. 424–43, with a list of authorized reporters at pp. 434–43; vol. 14 (1832–75) contains a section on the courts, and specialized tribunals, at pp. 180–7; vol. 15 (1832–75) at pp. 248–75 deals with reports, abridgments, digests, indexes and collections of cases.

Logan, R. 'Revised reports', *Law Librarian*, vol. 13, 1982, pp. 23–4.

Logan, R. 'Checklist of reports used in compiling the Revised Reports', *Law Librarian*, vol. 14, 1983, pp. 3–9.

Pollock, F. *First book of jurisprudence*, 6th edn., 1929. Chapter 5 deals with the history of the reports, and Chapter 6 with the relation of one judicial decision to another.

Wallace, J. W. *The reporters*, 4th edn. [by] F. F. Head, 1882. Gives bibliographical data, with critical assessments of the reporters to the time of George III.

Winfield, P. H. *Chief sources of English legal history*, 1925. 'Case law' contains a valuable assessment of some of the early reporters.

UNREPORTED CASES

Andrews, N. H. 'Reporting case law: unreported cases, the definition of a *ratio* and the criteria for reporting decisions', *Legal Studies*, vol. 5, 1985, pp. 205–32.

Harrison, N. 'Unreported cases: myth and reality', *Law Society's Gazette*, vol. 81, 1984, pp. 257–66.

Megarry, R. E. 'Reporting the unreported', *Law Quarterly Review*, vol. 70, 1954, pp. 246–52.

SCOTTISH REPORTS

Gloag, W. M. and Henderson, R. C. *Introduction to the law of Scotland*, 8th edn., 1980, pp. x–xi. Useful bibliographical and citation notes.

[Hannay, R.] *Letter to the Dean of the Faculty of Advocates relative to a plan ... for reporting the decisions of the Court of Session*, 1823.

[Hannay R.] *Address to the ... Lord President Hope ... on the method of collecting and reporting decisions*, 1821.

Leadbetter, J. S. 'The printed law reports' in *Sources and literature of Scots Law*, 1936, pp. 42–58 (Stair Society 1).

Tait, W. *Index to decisions, Court of Session, ... and in Morison's Dictionary of decisions*, 1823. Contains 30 pages of valuable notes on reporters and reporting.

Walker, D. M. *The Scottish legal system*, 5th edn., 1981. Chapter 11 'Repositories of the law', pp. 412–42 is the best account.

TRIALS

Bond, M. F. *Guide to the records of Parliament*, 1971. Invaluable for information on original material.

Langan, P. St J. 'Irish material in the State Trials', *Northern Ireland Law Quarterly*, vol. 18, 1967, pp. 428–36; vol. 19, 1968, pp. 48–53, 189–97, 299–309.

5. Secondary Sources

D. J. WAY

TEXTBOOKS

The place of textbooks in legal literature

The distinction between a textbook and a primary source is well defined in a popular work for law students: 'A textbook differs from a statute or a law report in that it is not an original literary source of law. Textbooks, even if of the highest authority, contain only opinions as to the state of the law. In short they are descriptive rather than creative.' (Walker, R. J. and Walker, M. G. *The English legal system*, 6th edition, 1985, p. 162.)

There are, however, two types of textbooks, viewed as sources of law. The first type are the so-called 'books of authority', the last of which is generally agreed to be Blackstone's *Commentaries on the Laws of England* in the mid-eighteenth century, and the second type are modern textbooks. Most of the books of authority were written by judges, and many of them appeared before law reporting had been fully developed; they are therefore accorded intrinsic authority in their own right. They are described in more detail in Chapter 7. A modern textbook, on the other hand, to quote Walker and Walker again (p. 162), 'is not a source of law and is only of use in that it indicates where a direct source, such as a statute or a law report, may be found'.

Judicial attitudes to textbooks

The judicial attitude to textbooks has been illustrated most clearly in recent years in the case *Cordell v. Second Clanfield*

Properties Ltd, in Mr Justice Megarry's judgment reported at [1969] 2 Ch. 9. Counsel had quoted to Mr Justice Megarry a passage from his own book (Megarry, R. E. and Wade, H. W. R. *The Law of Real Property*, 3rd edition, 1966), written before he became a judge. After making the point that words in a book written or subscribed to by an author who was or became a judge had the same value as words written by any other reputable author, neither more nor less, Mr Justice Megarry continued: 'I would, therefore, give credit to the words of any reputable author in book or article as expressing tenable and arguable ideas, as fertilizers of thought, and as conveniently expressing the fruits of research in print, often in apt and persuasive language. But I would do no more than that, and in particular I would expose those views to the testing and refining process of argument. Today, as of old, by good disputing shall the law be well known.'

It has been pointed out by legal writers that judges have not hesitated on several occasions to set aside statements in long-established textbooks, where they felt that these were inaccurate. To take only one example, the House of Lords in *R. v. Button and Swain* [1966] A.C. 591, drew attention to errors in Archbold's *Pleading, Evidence and Practice in Criminal Cases* and in Russell on *Crimes and Misdemeanors*, both standard works. On the other hand, there have been many more occasions on which statements in textbooks have been approved by the courts, and in particular the old practice that a living author must not be cited in court is no longer valid. Both Walker and Walker (p. 166) and Hood Phillips (*A first book of English law*, 7th edition, 1977, pp. 242–6) give several examples of cases in which statements by both textbook writers and the writers of articles in legal periodicals have been accepted by the courts in their own lifetime. Indeed, the law is changing so rapidly at present that it would be strange if a dead author were to be preferred to a living one.

Some features of legal textbooks

Practitioners' books and students' books

In general, legal textbooks are published at two levels – there are practitioners' books and students' books. The two levels are distinguished very obviously by their depth of treatment of the subject, and hence by their size and price. There is also a less obvious internal distinction. Practitioners' books are intended for reference and for consultation, rather than for continuous reading. Students' books, on the other hand, are meant for continuous reading, and are likely to contain much clearer statements of principle. The distinction is well set out by Lord Denning (then Sir Alfred Denning) in a review of Winfield's *Textbook of the Law of Tort* in the *Law Quarterly Review*, vol. 63, 1947, p. 516. It can, however, easily become blurred. Gibson's *Conveyancing*, for example, is regarded primarily as a students' textbook, and it has appeared as such on lists issued by the Council of Legal Education and the College of Law; but it is also sufficiently detailed to be referred to by many practitioners in their early years.

As regards external appearance, practitioners' books, which are intended to last four or five years with the aid of supplements, are normally still bound in hardback. Students' textbooks on the other hand have become almost exclusively paperback during the past few years, only sufficient hardback copies being bound to meet the expected sale to libraries.

Authorship

As already mentioned, it was the practice at one time that a living author could not be cited in court, and perhaps it is on this account that so many legal textbooks still bear the names of their original authors, even though these may have long since been dead and gone. For instance, the original author of Woodfall's *Law of Landlord and Tenant*, now in its 28th edition, died as long ago as 1806. In contrast, however, it is becoming increasingly usual nowadays for new legal authors to write under their own names and even usurp the place of past favourites. Thus, Lushington's *Law of Affiliation and Bastardy* was replaced by Chislett's *Affiliation Proceedings*, and Burnett's *Elements of Conveyancing* by Bowman and Tyler's *Elements of Conveyancing*, a deliberate decision being made by the publisher in each case to make a new start rather than to continue with extra editions of an already existing work.

The credentials of the author – that is, stating whether he is a barrister or a solicitor – normally appear on the title page. Books by authors with only academic qualifications are unlikely to commend themselves to practitioners.

The preface

The preface of a legal textbook always repays investigation. In the case of a completely new title, the author will use the preface to say what he is trying to do, while in a new edition of an old title, he will mention in it what has been excised or replaced and what has been retained, and will often summarize briefly the main changes in the subject of the book since the last edition. At the end of the preface, or immediately following it, there is usually the all-important statement giving the date up to which all new developments in the law have been covered by the book. This is naturally more important than the date on the title page, since there is always a certain lapse of time between completion of the work and publication.

The tables of cases and statutes

A textbook should always have full tables of cases and statutes, and nothing so much marks off the second rank of law publishers as their tendency to economize in this respect. A table of statutes may either be alphabetical or chronological, but ideally should always give the correct citations of the Acts concerned, as well as their short titles. A table of cases should give, not only the title of the case and the page reference to it in the textbook, but also the full reference back to where it is reported in the original. A table of abbreviations is also often desirable, especialy for textbooks which cite cases from unfamiliar law reports belonging to other jurisdictions.

Arrangements for keeping textbooks up to date

Keeping a work up to date is as important from the point of view of the author or publisher as from that of the librarian, since, once a work has lost its freshness, sales will drop and the stocks remaining in the publisher's hands will lose their value. There are several methods that a publisher may use, in order to keep up to date.

New editions

The publisher may, first of all, print new editions of his works much more frequently, possibly putting them on an annual basis. This can be done where changes in the law are frequent and continuous, so that sufficient copies can be sold of each edition to make the exercise worthwhile. Examples that come to mind are the various practice books (see below). Textbooks on revenue law also frequently appear on an annual basis, this being made possible by the demand from students working for the various professional examinations. A recent example has been *A Practical Approach to Revenue Law*, by Stephen Mayson, which has had a new edition each year since first being published in 1980.

Supplements

For practitioners' books as a whole, new editions each year are not economically possible. They represent a much larger investment to their purchasers than students' books, since the price of many of them (due to inflation) now runs almost into three figures in pounds. Also, whereas there is a new generation of students to study revenue law each year, the market for new editions of practitioners' books only changes and grows slowly. Hence, the most favoured method of keeping practitioners' books up to date is to issue a paperback supplement, which is only a fraction of the price of the original hardback volume. A space for insertion of the supplement is often left at the end of the volume, so that the two may be carried together as one unit. The supplement is arranged with chapter or key numbers similar to those in the original volume, so that reference to it for new developments may be quickly made. Supplements of many textbooks now appear on an annual basis; each issue is cumulative, so that the earlier supplement may be discarded on receiving the later one.

Looseleaf format

In some subjects, even the method of issuing an annual paperback supplement is not sufficient to keep a book adequately up to date. In these cases the legal publishers have taken to issuing whole works in a looseleaf form, which can then be kept up to date by periodically inserting and discarding pages according to the instructions supplied. Usually fresh sets of pages with instructions are sent out three or four times a year for this type of work, occasionally (as with De Voil's *Value Added Tax*) rather more frequently. These looseleaf works comprise a special genre of textbook (see page 197).

Special types of books

Encyclopedias

Encyclopedic works covering the whole of the law of England in a single volume or series of volumes are nothing new, and they can be traced back historically to the first abridgments (see Chapter 7). The outstanding representative today of the legal encyclopedia is *Halsbury's Laws of England*, which is in its fourth edition. This work owed its origin to Stanley Shaw Bond, of Messrs Butterworth's, who conceived the idea of a collection of writings covering the whole range of English law by the best legal minds of the day, with the Lord Chancellor as editor-in-chief. By great pertinacity, he persuaded the then Lord Chancellor, Lord Halsbury, to lend his name to the project, and the volumes of the first edition started to appear in 1907.

The fourth edition of Halsbury, following the same basic pattern, started to appear in 1973, and the full work of 52 volumes is now complete. To these will be added four volumes of tables and index. Again a Lord Chancellor, Lord Hailsham, has agreed to be editor-in-chief. As in previous editions, the whole of the law has been covered, including the law of the European Communities so far as it forms part of English law. Again as before, elaborate arrangements are being made for keeping up to date, including an annual cumulative supplement, a monthly current service issue, and replacement of individual outdated volumes, if this seems necessary. A separate user's guide completes the service. A good description of the planning and early progress of this edition may be read in the *Law Society's Gazette*, vol. 70, 1973, p. 1,839.

There is also an *Annual Abridgment* to *Halsbury's Laws*, which has appeared each year since 1974 and which provides a survey of the year's case-law and statute law; it also includes references to articles in selected legal journals, indexed under their subject headings. The material, which appears in the *Annual Abridgment*, is cumulated from the *Monthly Review*, part of the monthly current service referred to in the previous paragraph.

Halsbury's Laws of England is encyclopedic in scope, but in its internal arrangement it contains fewer and therefore broader subject headings than the conventional non-legal encyclopedia. In the fourth edition, for instance, the list of subjects begins with the new title *Administrative Law*. There are copious references to authorities after each paragraph, and the work is so comprehensive that it has been said that a legal office could if necessary function on Halsbury alone, which is more than could be said for any other single work.

In the law library, Halsbury fills a key position. It plays a useful role for the librarian as the first port of call for any legal enquiry, of which the precise subject is not immediately apparent. Halsbury is especially useful to the novice law librarian, in suggesting to him the headings under which he should look for further information on any subject requested, and can thus help out in areas where the subject index of the law library may be deficient.

One other general legal encyclopedia, namely, Green's *Encyclopaedia of the Laws of Scotland*, is mentioned on page 211.

Precedent books

In law libraries frequented by practitioners, precedent books are among the most used items. A lawyer who has, for example, to prepare a conveyance or a will does not have to draft the wording out of his head afresh each time. Instead, he can take a standard form from the book, and if necessary adapt it to the circumstances of the particular case. Requests for precedents can therefore arise quite often in practitioners' law libraries; some may be easy to find, while others may need a considerable amount of research. It is of course possible that there may be no particular precedent at all for the situation that the enquirer has in mind, but naturally every possible source must be checked before one can come to that conclusion. The following are some of the main collections of precedents, that can be tried in such an enquiry.

The *Encyclopaedia of Forms and Precedents*, known familiarly to practitioners as the *Encyclopaedia*, is now appearing in its 5th edition. This will consist of 42 volumes, including three volumes each on company law, landlord and tenant, and sale of land. Other topics in which the *Encyclopaedia* is strong, and which may be the subject of frequent enquiries, include contracts for services, mortgages, and wills and intestacy. New titles covered by this edition of the *Encyclopaedia* will include such subjects as computer contracts and intellectual property. The *Encyclopaedia* will be kept up to date by means of looseleaf service binders, and individual volumes in the edition will be revised and replaced as and when required. Selections of precedents from the new edition will also be made available on floppy discs for use in word processors.

The *Encyclopaedia* does not cover litigation, and this is taken care of by the parallel work, Atkin's *Encyclopaedia of Court Forms in Civil Proceedings*, known familiarly as 'Atkin'. It may be noted that some titles already seen in the *Encyclopaedia* recur in Atkin, for instance, companies or landlord and tenant. Whereas the precedents in the *Encyclopaedia* include the original draft agreements under the respective subject headings, those in Atkin cover situations where litigation has intruded. For instance, the landlord and tenant section of the *Encyclopaedia* contains numerous specimen leases, whereas this section in Atkin contains actions for breach of agreement for a lease. Atkin is undergoing continuous revision, and some of the most used volumes, such as that on divorce, have been re-issued more than once since the edition first appeared. Additional volumes provided after the end of the main series include an annual supplement, a consolidated index revised annually, and a user's guide.

Another precedent book, which deserves separate mention, is the looseleaf work *Precedents for the conveyancer*, now appearing in two volumes. This covers the same ground as the *Encyclopaedia*, but offers a different selection of material, often more up to date because of the possibilities for revision provided by the looseleaf format. It succeeds a section on precedents formerly included in the journal *The Conveyancer*.

There are many other precedent books covering smaller and more specialized fields which naturally cannot all be described in detail. Quite apart from books with the word 'precedent' in the title, precedents on specific subjects can often be found in textbooks on those subjects. Sometimes, the precedents may be hidden away in an appendix, but are none the less useful. Examples that come to mind, for instance, are Tristram and Coote's *Probate Practice*, and Potter and Monroe's *Tax Planning*. In assessing the usefulness of a legal textbook, therefore, a factor to be taken into account is the presence or otherwise of an appendix of precedents relating to the subject.

Precedents also appear from time to time on the 'Practitioner' pages of the *New Law Journal*, and these are indexed at the end of each year's set of issues. These precedents, like those formerly contained in *The Conveyancer*, enable the practitioner to keep abreast of new situations not yet provided for in the textbooks. For instance, the *New Law Journal* published promptly a set of the forms prescribed for use under the *Employment Appeal Tribunal Rules*, 1980.

Looseleaf encyclopedias

Looseleaf encyclopedias, which have already been mentioned briefly above, are now sufficiently numerous to warrant inclusion as a separate class of work. *Simon's Taxes*, previously *Simon's Income Tax*, was one of the first textbooks to go partly looseleaf, no doubt because revenue law is especially susceptible to frequent and unpredictable changes. Since then, Messrs Sweet and Maxwell in particular have adopted this type of work with enthusiasm and have published a whole range of looseleaf encyclopedias in the *Local government library* series, covering not only revenue law, but also housing law, road traffic law, town and country planning, compulsory purchase and compensation, highways, factories and offices, public health, and labour relations.

Each encyclopedia contains all the Acts, Statutory Instruments and ministerial circulars relating to its subjects. To take one example, the *Encyclopedia of Planning Law and Practice* contains five parts in its four volumes. These parts contain respectively a general statement of the law relating to town and country planning, statutes pre-1970 (so far as they are still in force), statutes post-1969, rules and orders (*ie*, Statutory Instruments relating to the subject), ministerial circulars, and decisions of selected planning appeals. Each of these parts is preceded by a complete list of contents, and there is an index to the whole work in each of the three volumes.

The releases containing new material to be inserted in the various looseleaf encyclopedias in most cases come out three or four times a year. Usually, the instructions simply provide for the insertion of new pages and taking out of the corresponding old pages; the latter are then to be destroyed after checking, as provided for in the instructions. One or two looseleaf works issued by HMSO include further complications; here, there are occasionally little slips to be gummed in where it is deemed inappropriate to issue a whole new page, and occasionally there are also instructions for annotations to be written in by hand. The commercial publishers have fortunately omitted these additional refinements.

The advantages of looseleaf encyclopedias are obvious, as are the disadvantages. If they are kept up to date, they often provide the most recent material available on their respective subjects. Their arrangement is usually so clear that it is often easier to trace Acts and Statutory Instruments on a subject through its looseleaf encyclopedia (if it has one), than through the official publications described in Chapter 3. The compensating disadvantage of looseleaf works is the amount of staff time swallowed up in their periodic servicing.

Practice books

Practice books form another sub-division under the general heading of textbooks, and like precedent books are used especially in law libraries devoted to the needs of practitioners. They usually appear annually, or alternatively have frequent supplements, and their purpose is to keep their users up to date in the practice of the courts.

The most important work of this genre is the *Supreme Court Practice*, sometimes known as the 'White Book', which now appears every three years, with a cumulative supplement two or three times a year during the period in between editions. The *Supreme Court Practice* (formerly the *Annual Practice*) contains not only the revised text of the Rules of the Supreme Court, but also the prescribed forms, orders relating to court fees and stamps, practice directions, and other rules and orders sufficient to enable the practitioner to find his way through court procedure.

The *County Court Practice*, known sometimes as the 'Green Book', is the corresponding work for county court practice and procedure, and this appears annually.

Stone's Justices' Manual appears annually in three volumes, and contains a selection of the Acts most likely to be referred to in magistrates' courts, such as the Road Traffic Acts, the Betting, Gaming and Lotteries Act, and so on. A selection of relevant Statutory Instruments is included in an appendix. Because of the nature of its contents, Stone is one of the few law books suitable for use in a public reference library, since it covers those sections of the law that impinge most directly on the layman.

Paterson's Licensing Acts which also appears annually, is devoted specifically to the needs of practitioners attending licensing sessions.

Finally, Archbold's *Pleading, Evidence and Practice in Criminal Cases* (42nd edition, 1985), known more briefly as Archbold's *Criminal Pleading*, is the most comprehensive work on criminal practice. A new edition appears every three or four years, and in addition there is a cumulative supplement three times a year.

Casebooks

So far, all the various types of books described have been devoted to the needs of practitioners. Casebooks, on the other hand, are designed especially to meet the needs of students and are more important in academic law libraries.

Although the so-called 'casebook' method of teaching law students originated in the universities in America, casebooks as such have been published over a long period in this country, and owe nothing in their origin to transatlantic influence. The first edition of Smith's *Leading Cases*, for example, appeared as long ago as 1837. It would be true to say, however, that the use of casebooks has expanded in recent years, and university law faculties now generally expect their students to buy their own copies of these for their main subjects. The chief justification of the casebook is that the head-notes and the most relevant extracts from a whole series of reports can be placed together in one volume, together with comments by the editor, so enabling the students to have the materials which they need constantly to hand. Although ideally students should always pursue their references in the original reports, time in a university year is limited and the use of the casebook enables them to short-circuit this process – and, incidentally, also saves wear and tear on the original volumes of the reports in the library.

A large number of casebooks have been issued by the main legal publishers, covering most of the subjects on the universities' law degree syllabus. Although the general pattern of all of these is as described above, the proportion of a case that is reproduced can vary a great deal according to publishing policy and the decision of the individual editor. One tendency noted increasingly is for casebooks to bear the title 'Cases and materials on . . . ', leaving the individual editors free to include materials other than cases as appropriate, for instance, extracts from statutes or from government White Papers.

Some casebooks are more abbreviated. Instead of giving extracts from the originals, they merely give brief summaries by the editor of the cases concerned. These are essentially 'sweat books' for students, and are of little use from the point of view of libraries. Examples of this type of casebook include the *Cracknell's Law students' companion series* published by Messrs Butterworth and the *Concise college casenotes series* published by Messrs Sweet and Maxwell.

Recent developments in textbook publishing

The last ten years, since the first edition of this *Manual*, have seen both a considerable increase in the number of legal books published and a widening of the circle of publishers responsible for their appearance. The established law publishers, such as Butterworths, Oyez Longman, and Sweet and Maxwell, have kept hold of substantial sections of the market, but at the same time a number of new names have made their presence felt. These have included new all-round publishers of law books, such as Professional Books or Weidenfeld and Nicolson, and also others within specialized fields. Examples that come to mind are those of Edward Arnold, Gower or Martin Robertson in the field of socio-legal studies, European Law Centre or ESC Publishing in the field of EEC law and Ravenswood Publications in the field of medical and National Health Service law. As a result, the law library book selectors have to make their choice nowadays from an ever-increasing quantity of material.

Despite the overall growth in the number of titles published, there have been some deficiencies in legal publishing during the past decade. These have been highlighted in the interim and final reports of the Society of Public Teachers of Law Working Party on Law Publishing, references to which are given in the list of further reading at the end of this chapter. The Working Party were especially concerned at the difficulty in getting published works dealing with relatively narrow topics, as contrasted with whole fields of law, and also works which sought to change established ideas or ways of thinking. A remedy for this was sought in a link-up between the Society of Public Teachers of Law and a commercial law publisher in order to establish an *SPTL Law Series*, giving the opportunity for works to be published that would not otherwise appear.

Another concern of the Working Party was the difficulty encountered in publishing books in small jurisdictions, and this will be referred to again in the Scottish and Irish sections at the end of the chapter.

PERIODICALS

Periodicals rank after textbooks as an important secondary source of legal information. As with other subjects, so with law, periodicals are used for current professional news and as a means of disseminating the latest information well ahead of its appearance in book form. Additionally, some periodicals contain law reports, albeit abbreviated ones, which means that they have a continuing value.

Types of periodicals, by readership

Legal periodicals are best studied in connection with the audience at which they are aimed. Four types of audience are involved, namely, academic lawyers, practising lawyers, law students, and law librarians, and it will be seen that each group attracts different journals. In addition, a growing number of specialist legal journals are now appearing, which draw their readers from both academics and practitioners.

Academic lawyers

The main periodicals of interest to academic lawyers are the *Law Quarterly Review*, the *Modern Law Review* (published six times a year) and the *Cambridge Law Journal* (published three times a year). These appear relatively infrequently compared to practitioners' journals, and they contain long articles in depth and shorter notes on selected topics, but relatively little up-to-the-minute news. All have good book review sections, the usefulness of which is vitiated (for law librarians) by the fact that the books reviewed have often been published for a year or more before the reviews appear. Each of these journals covers the whole legal field, although there is a tendency for the *Modern Law Review* to concentrate more on socio-legal topics (for instance, it always contains a section headed 'Reports of Committees', with reviews of current White Papers), while the *Law Quarterly Review* is stronger in articles on legal history.

Also worthy of mention are *The Law Teacher* and *Legal Studies*, which are the journals respectively of the Association of Law Teachers and of the Society of Public Teachers of Law. Of these, *The Law Teacher* has kept closest to its original objective by retaining a substantial number of articles on legal teaching methods and on legal education generally. The *Journal of the Society of Public Teachers of Law*, in its old format, also contained articles relating to both legal education and law libraries, such as the *Second Survey of Legal Education in the United Kingdom* by J. F. Wilson and S. B. Marsh and the *Statement of Minimum Holdings for Law libraries in England and Wales* (both in vol. 13, new series, 1974–5). More recently, it was decided to wind up the existing series of the *Journal* and to relaunch it in a new format. This began to appear in 1981 with the title *Legal Studies* and it has become a general academic law journal, giving an additional outlet for full-length academic articles similar to those appearing in the three journals mentioned in the last paragraph.

There are also a number of journals produced by the various law schools, some of which have become firmly established. On the whole, however, they have as yet neither the size nor the prestige of their American counterparts.

Practising lawyers

The main periodicals of interest to practising lawyers are the *New Law Journal, Solicitors' Journal* and *Law Society's Gazette* which all appear weekly. The type of information contained in all three of these follows a similar pattern. Each leads with editorial comments on current legal topics, and all contain articles on new legislation and other subjects (with a practising rather than an academic audience in mind), correspondence, book reviews, news about the profession, and practice sections.

The contents of these practice sections repay special investigation, as they contain useful reference aids. The *New Law Journal*, for instance, devotes the central section of each weekly issue to Practitioner pages printed on yellow paper. Among other things, these contain details of the progress of Parliamentary Bills, new Statutory Instruments, a selection of circulars issued by the Home Office and the Lord Chancellor's Department and summaries of Court of Appeal transcripts. The specimen precedents also included on these pages from time to time have already been referred to.

In the *Solicitors' Journal*, there are somewhat similar pages with features headed 'Solicitors' Journal case reports', 'Westminster and Whitehall', 'Practice directions' and 'Notes and news'. The *Solicitors' Journal* also publishes an office management supplement under the title of *Practice Today* several times a year.

The *Law Society's Gazette* duplicates much of the same type of information in its practice pages, but in addition it gives details of such things as administrative changes in The Law Society, arrangements for the issue of practising certificates, admissions of new solicitors, and disciplinary proceedings under the Solicitors' Acts. A practice management section appears frequently to keep solicitors up to date with developments in technology affecting the running of their offices. After appearing for several years in an awkward oversize format, the *Law Society's Gazette* reverted to a more normal A4 size in 1983.

Law students

All of the periodicals already described can and do contain articles and features of interest to law students from time to time. Nevertheless, there are two journals aimed specially at a student audience. The first of these is *Law Notes*, which is published monthly by the College of Law. This contains items similar to those in many of the journals already mentioned, such as current topics, case notes, new statutes, book reviews, and so on, but it is written throughout in a simpler and more concise style. Many practitioners, it may be noted, continue to take *Law Notes* as a refresher, even after they have qualified.

Another journal aimed at the student market, the *Students'*

Law Reporter, appears three times a year, and contains a full selection of case notes of recent cases.

The *Law Society's Gazette* is the first source of information for any changes in the regulations dealing with the education and training of articled clerks. It also contains a monthly section called 'Trainee solicitors' forum', containing news and views of interest to articled clerks.

Law librarians

Periodicals aimed especially at law librarians are naturally much fewer in number than those aimed at either academic lawyers or practitioners. The only British journal in this field is the *Law Librarian* (published three times a year), which has appeared since 1970. English-language journals for law librarians published abroad include the *Law Library Journal* from America (published quarterly) and the *International Journal of Legal Information* (published three times a year), formerly the *International Journal of Law Libraries*.

Specialist legal periodicals

No account of legal periodicals would be complete without mentioning the enormous growth in recent years of specialist journals, covering particular aspects of the law. This process has gone on continuously, regardless of recession. A recent analysis by J. N. Adams in the *Law Librarian*, vol. 15, 1984, p. 7, showed that, out of 54 new legal periodicals initiated during the five years up to 1983, only 11 could be described as of general practitioner or traditional academic interest, while no fewer than 29 were specialist in nature. (The balance was made up of pressure group publications and periodicals covering crime and criminology.) It would seem that before very long each branch of law will have its own journal, and the inference made by J. N. Adams in the same article (*Law Librarian*, vol. 15, 1984, p. 9) is that the general legal journal of the type of the *Law Quarterly Review* will, in time, become extinct.

It is naturally impossible in a work such as this to list all the specialist legal periodicals of note, but their details will be found in the periodical directories and indexes mentioned in Chapter 9.

Use and function of periodicals in the law library

The first use of periodicals from the point of view of the law librarian is in keeping abreast of his subject. The publishers' notices and book reviews contained in periodicals are an important aid to book selection. At the same time, by scanning quickly the more important periodicals as they come in, the law librarian can keep in touch with current topics and developments, so that he is less likely to be at a loss when some new and unexpected query arrives on his desk.

Secondly, the practice sections of current periodicals form an invaluable quick reference aid. The type of material to be found in these sections has already been indicated. Although of course *Current Law* is normally the first source of information to which any law librarian goes, there is always a gap of two to six weeks (according to the time of the month), which is not covered by the last issue of *Current Law*. The latest issues of the weekly periodicals fill this gap and bring coverage of any particular query right up to date.

Thirdly, the articles in the periodicals form a source of reference to both students and practitioners, and, as has already been mentioned, may provide information on subjects which are too new or too specialized to have been written about in books. To take one example, an article in the *Law Society's Gazette* entitled 'Buying property in Spain' (vol. 81, no. 25, 4 July 1984, pp. 1898–1904) gives useful information not yet available in book form about the pitfalls on which a solicitor should advise a client wishing to settle in that country. Again, an article in the *Solicitors' Journal* on 'Law Society's Conditions of Sale (1984 Revision)' (vol. 128, No. 36, 7 September 1984, pp. 605–6) gave readers an early opportunity to note the differences between the latest edition of the Conditions of Sale and its predecessors. Again, such information will take a long time to appear in book form. Articles such as these will be a continuous source of reference over a longer period than the material in the practice sections of the journals, and hence obviously the need for maintaining back files of periodicals in law libraries.

In order to exploit periodicals fully, a knowledge of how the main periodical indexes work is clearly necessary, and for this the reader should refer to Chapter 9.

SECONDARY SOURCES

Theses and legal research

Theses form a separate class of legal literature, since unlike books they may be completed without being published in the normal sense of the word. Because the majority of them remain unpublished, restrictions exist on access to them, and permission may have to be sought both from the author and from the institution concerned before they may be consulted.

About fifty to a hundred legal theses and dissertations are listed each year in a section of the *Index to theses accepted for higher degrees by the universities of Great Britain and Ireland and the Council for National Academic Awards*, which is published twice a year by Aslib. The entries, which are listed in author order within each subject, give details of the title, place and date of each thesis, and state whether it is available on fiche. A separate section on availability of theses at the beginning of each volume gives the terms on which each institution allows access to theses and dissertations. This section is of special value, since such a large number of theses remain unpublished.

An annual survey published by the Institute of Advanced Legal Studies called the *List of current legal research topics* gives a list of topics of all legal research work for theses and dissertations currently in hand in universities and polytechnics in the United Kingdom. In contrast to the Law section of the Aslib list, the IALS list contains several hundred items, but it must be remembered that these consist of work in progress, not completed theses. Many of the items on this list remain there from one year to another and some projects are never completed. The items are listed in alphabetical author order, but there are also useful subject and geographical indexes, and an index under names of sponsoring institutions.

Another work issued by the Institute of Advanced Legal Studies, its *List of legal research topics completed and approved since about 1935*, 1961, with a supplement for 1961–6, lists completed research retrospectively. A new edition: *Legal research in the United Kingdom, 1905–1984*, was published in 1986.

Academic research in progress is also listed in an annual publication of the British Library, *Current Research in Britain*, one volume of which covers the social sciences including law. This however is a list of research projects rather than of theses, and as with the IALS list there is no indication as to which projects reach fruition and when.

AUDIO-VISUAL MATERIALS

No account of secondary legal sources would be complete now without a reference to audio-visual materials. Audio-cassettes appeared on the market first, in the early 1970s, and their contents have been reviewed from time to time in the legal journals. The College of Law in particular has sought to provide cassette study packs for the practitioner to add to the transcripts of crash courses and refresher lectures which it already issues in book form. Two series, the *New Law Cassettes* and the *All England Quarterly Law Cassettes*, were also produced for some years by Butterworths, but were later relinquished by them. (*All England Quarterly Law Cassettes* are still being published by Discourses Ltd of Tunbridge Wells.)

The mixed success of audio-cassettes is perhaps due to the limitations in their format. These were described succinctly some years ago in a review appearing in the *New Law Journal*: 'The cassette can be played in the car at the traffic lights, whilst shaving and at all other times the family permits. Its disadvantages are that it cannot be studied nor turned to easily for reference. Nor can it be taken to court and played in support of an argument' (*New Law Journal*, vol. 126, 1976, p. 1,194).

Video-cassettes have appeared much more recently than audio-cassettes, and these seem likely to take a greater share of the market, because of their suitability as a medium for certain forms of student instruction. These include the induction of new students into the use of legal materials generally, and instruction in court work, which can benefit greatly from a visual presentation. It is noteworthy that recently both of the two major law publishers have begun to issue this type of material. Butterworths have published a series of interviews with Lord Denning on videotape, while Sweet and Maxwell have produced the first of what is promised will be a series of *Lawfilms* on *The Sunday Times case*.

Other law video programmes have been distributed by specialist suppliers, such as Concord Films Council Ltd or the Higher Education Film and Video Library, and others again have been produced by the television units at various universities. A useful guide to the wealth of material already available was published in 1984 by the British Universities Film and Video Council under the title of *Audio-visual Materials on Law: a select list of programmes recommended for degree-level use*. This catalogue in fact contains two lists of material; the items on the first list have been viewed and commended by law teachers, and a brief review of each item is therefore included. The second list includes items which have not yet been evaluated, and there is also a short bibliography on the use of video in law teaching generally.

A quotation from another review may conclude this summary of the present position as regards the use of audio-visual materials: 'Video and audio cassettes have not yet replaced law books in their main function as authoritative recorders of sources of law, something which books have been doing successfully for centuries. However, if there is a dull topic such as civil procedure, or a complex or difficult one such as composite restatement or company law, audio-visual aids are invaluable' (*Solicitors' Journal*, vol. 126, 1982 p. 756).

SCOTLAND

Textbooks

The position of textbooks in Scottish law is similar to that in England: 'The function of the textbook is to collect and present in logical form a statement of the rules of law on a given topic, drawn from the authoritative sources, the relevant statutes and scattered cases, and to suggest their cumulative effect and how they appear to the author to apply in different circumstances ... Textbooks are, in general, therefore, only secondary authorities and useful in so far as they completely and accurately present rules laid down in the primary authorities, *ie*, the statutes and cases, on any topic' (Walker, D. M. *The Scottish legal system*, 5th edn., Green, 1981, pp. 344–5). There are likewise books of authority in Scotland, known as the institutional writings, the best known being Viscount Stair, *The Institutions of the law of Scotland*, 1681.

The actual number of textbooks dealing with Scots law is very much smaller than in England, largely because of the economics of law publishing, which make it difficult for a legal title to be a commercial success. Thus there are several successful books issued many years ago which normally would have gone through a number of editions, but which still await revision. On the other hand, some have been kept up to date, notably Gloag, W. M. and Henderson, R. C. *Introduction to the law of Scotland*, which in 1980 reached its 8th edition. A textbook of high standard is Walker, D. M. *Principles of Scottish private law*, 3rd edition, in 1982–3, in 4 volumes. A development in 1960 was the establishment of the Scottish Universities' Law Institute, the avowed purpose of which is to 'encourage, stimulate and advance the scientific study of the law of Scotland'. To this end, the Institute is endeavouring to re-state the main branches of the law in some fifteen to twenty separate treatises. Eleven of these volumes have been published, with several having gone into second editions, and others are in hand.

The problem of publishing literature relevant to smaller countries is a worldwide one. Cognizance of the position in the British Isles was made in 1981 with the appearance of Twining, W. and Uglow, J. *Law publishing and legal information: small jurisdictions in the British Isles*, in which Scotland is dealt with on pages 5–43. The conclusion is reached that 'at the moment Scotland cannot boast comprehensive legal literature at a variety of levels ... [but] there does seem to be a lively awareness of the problem' (p. 23).

This awareness became evident in the late 1970s, since when

there has been a welcome growth in the number of law books published in Scotland. Both Green and Hodge, the two main publishers, have increased their output so that there are now several volumes in each of Green's 'Concise College Texts' and 'Casebooks' series. Hodge have issued texts on such subjects as banking, housing and planning, all areas previously neglected. Occasional important volumes from other sources have also appeared, *eg*, Maxwell's *Practice of the Court of Session*, produced by the Scottish Courts Administration in 1980. The Law Society of Scotland began a publishing programme in 1980 and this has resulted in several small, compact guides to such topics as professional ethics, medical negligence and accounting for executries and trusts. Thus the position regarding up to date information is considerably improved compared with the 1960s and 1970s.

However, Scotland's chief legal encyclopedia is very much out of date. The *Encyclopaedia of the laws of Scotland*, more familiarly known as *Green's Encyclopaedia*, was first issued in fourteen volumes between 1896–1904. After the First World War the need for revision was evident, and a 3rd edition in sixteen volumes appeared between 1926–35; a supplementary volume in two parts was published in 1949–51, with an appendix in 1952. A complementary work is the *Encyclopaedia of Scottish legal styles* in ten volumes, also published by Green, between 1935–40. Both encyclopedias are badly in need of revision. In 1981 the Law Society of Scotland announced that a new edition of *Green's* was to be undertaken. In 1985 it was stated that this would comprise 25 volumes, to be published over a five-year period and be known as the *Stair Memorial Encyclopedia*. It is anticipated that volume one may appear during 1987.

The chief current practice book in Scotland, which has already been mentioned on page 114 as it includes certain statutes, is the *Parliament House Book*. This is now published in looseleaf form, and amongst its diverse contents are sections on companies, family law and landlord and tenant. Modern precedents, or styles as they are known in Scotland, had a limited appearance in a 'Workshop' insert to the *Journal of the Law Society of Scotland* between 1979–83. Most other style books require revision.

Periodicals

Those periodicals published in Scotland may conveniently be considered under a single heading, as they are few in number. The only independent journal which is general in its scope is the *Scots Law Times*, first issued in 1893, and which for most of its existence has appeared in several sequences, the chief two being *News* and *Reports*. The *Scottish Law Review*, also general in its coverage, was published regularly from 1885–1963, and included *Sheriff Court Reports* as an appendix (now in *Scots Law Times*). Following the setting up of the Law Society of Scotland in 1949, the Society's *Journal* has appeared monthly since 1956 and, as well as Society news and events, etc., it features articles, commentaries, reviews, and similar matter. A sister periodical is the *Scottish Law Gazette*, published quarterly since 1933. This is intended for circulation among members of the Scottish Law Agents Society, but is of limited value to the law librarian. Since 1975, *Scolag: the bulletin of the Scottish Legal Action Group* has been issued monthly.

The sole Scottish journal aimed at an academic audience is the *Juridical Review*. Sub-titled when it first appeared in 1889 as a *Journal of Legal and Political Science*, in 1956 this became *The Law Journal of the Scottish Universities* (from 1968 the second definite article was dropped). This was as a result of an arrangement between Green, the publishers, and the then four Scottish University law faculties, which wished to have a journal but which saw little point in producing a rival title. It should be noted, for citation purposes, that the first series, from 1889–1955, was numbered volumes 1–67, but that the fresh series begun in 1956 is unnumbered.

A convenient summary of current British legal periodicals and indexes appears in Walker, D. M. *The Scottish legal system*, 5th edn., 1981, p. 441.

IRELAND

Textbooks

The status of textbooks in Irish courts is the same as in England. See Delany, *Administration of justice in Ireland*, 4th edn., p. 11.

Ireland, like Scotland, has encountered the previously described difficulties affecting legal publishing in small jurisdictions. Up to a few years ago, the publication of legal textbooks in both Northern and Southern Ireland was very limited, but in each case the position is improving. In the Republic of Ireland, the growth of the legal profession has provided an increased market for legal books, and as a result more titles are now being produced. The Incorporated Law Society of Ireland has been commissioning the publication of law books since the early 1970s, and has been followed recently by a number of commercial publishers including Professional Books, Sweet and Maxwell, and Butterworths. Assistance to legal publishing has also been provided by the Arthur Cox Foundation, a trust which has made grants to potential authors or publishers of law books, such grants to be repaid out of royalties after publication.

In Northern Ireland, with an even smaller potential market, the problem was tackled by the inauguration in 1980 of the 'Servicing the Legal System' programme. This was set up in the Faculty of Law at Queen's University, Belfast, with outside financial support from the legal profession and elsewhere, and has aimed to produce texts on Northern Ireland law that would not otherwise be viable, under the imprint of 'SLS Legal Publications (NI)'. Where a separate text has not proved possible, a supplement to a recognized English work has been produced instead, for instance, the *Northern Ireland Supplement to Smith and Hogan on criminal law* by J. E. Stannard, which is designed to be used with the fifth edition of Smith and Hogan.

English law textbooks also still have to be used in some areas in the Republic of Ireland, but to a far less extent than previously. Again, adaptation by way of supplement may be available, although not always consistently. For instance, a supplement may be available only for one or two editions of the main work, as in the example of *The law of trusts* by Keeton and Sheridan (8th and 9th editions). The extent of coverage is not always clear from the title. *Bibliography on British legal education* by A. W. Green covers both the United Kingdom and the Republic of Ireland, despite its title, while some textbooks published in England such as the later editions of *Salmond on torts* include Irish cases. Where the word 'Irish' is included in the title, it is not always clear whether the book applies to both Northern Ireland and the Republic of Ireland. For example, *The Irish law of torts* by McMahon and Binchy applies to the law of the Republic of Ireland only, whereas *Irish land law* by J. C. W. Wylie applies to both jurisdictions.

Practice books

For the Republic of Ireland, the main source is Rules of the Superior Courts, amended by the Superior Courts Rules Committee from time to time, new rules being published as Statutory Instruments. The Superior Court Rules are at present being revised. The Committee on Court Practice and Procedure under the chairmanship of Mr Justice Brian Walsh published 20 reports up to 1978, covering such topics as the jurisdiction and practice of the Supreme Court, liability for professional negligence, on-the-spot fines, interest on judgment debts, and desertion and maintenance.

In Northern Ireland, the Rules of the Supreme Court were published in looseleaf form in 1980 (S.R. No. 346 of 1980).

Periodicals

The Irish Law Times and Solicitors' Journal was published weekly from 1867 to 1980. A new series has been published monthly from 1983. The *Gazette of the Incorporated Law Society of Ireland* has been published monthly since 1907. The *Irish Jurist* new series has been published since 1966. The *Dublin University Law Journal* (1976–) and the *Journal of the Irish Society for Labour Law* (1982–) are also published in the Republic of Ireland.

The *Northern Ireland Legal Quarterly* (1936–) has been published from the Law Faculty of Queen's University since 1964, before which it was published by the Incorporated Law Society of Northern Ireland. It provides a detailed commentary on major developments in the law of the province, as well as academic legal articles and reviews.

The *Bulletin of Northern Ireland Law* (1981–), another product of the 'Servicing the Legal System' programme, appears ten times a year and gives a monthly digest of all new law in Northern Ireland, both legislation and case-law, on the model of *Current Law*. The latter still provides, in its 'Northern Ireland' section, a further source of information on the law of the province, in rather less detail.

The *Gazette of the Incorporated Law Society of Northern Ireland*, which has been published since 1964, covers the professional field.

The *Irish Jurist*, the *Northern Ireland Legal Quarterly* and the *Dublin University Law Journal* are indexed in the *Index to Legal Periodicals*. For Irish material and articles by Irish legal writers, O'Higgins, P. *A bibliography of periodical literature relating to Irish law*, 1966 and supplements 1973 and 1983, is invaluable as both legal and non-legal journals have been used as source materials.

ISLE OF MAN

Textbooks

A bibliography of textbooks on Isle of Man law published since the beginning of the nineteenth century is given in the appendices to *Law publishing and legal information: small jurisdictions of the British Isles*, by W. Twining and J. Uglow.

Periodicals

The first legal periodical in the Isle of Man, the *Manx Law Bulletin*, was published from the Attorney General's Chamber in Douglas in 1984. The first issue covers the eleven months from October 1982 to August 1983, and contains references under appropriate subject headings to new Manx legislation and case law.

FURTHER READING

GENERAL

Legal textbooks and periodicals have been much less written about than either the statutes or the law reports. The best short accounts, which have already been referred to in the text, are:

Phillips, O. H. *A first book of English law*, 7th edn., 1977. See especially, Chapter 15, 'Books of Authority', pp. 238–59.

Walker, D. M. *The Scottish legal system*, 5th edn., 1981. See especially 'Secondary sources – legal literature', pp. 427–42.

Walker, R. J. and Walker, M. G. *The English legal system*, 6th edn., 1985. See especially Chapter 7, 'Textbooks', pp. 162–7.

Chapters 1 and 6, in particular, of the symposium below contain material of considerable interest. (Chapter 6 has been reprinted in *The Law Librarian*, vol. 5, 1974, pp. 21–4 and 41–3.)

Sweet and Maxwell. *Then and now, 1799–1974: commemorating 175 years of law bookselling and publishing*, 1974.

The following is a recent comparative account of the history of the legal treatise in Britain and America:

Simpson, A. W. B. 'The rise and fall of the legal treatise: legal principles and the forms of legal literature', *University of Chicago Law Review*, vol. 48, 1981, pp. 632–79.

LOOSELEAF ENCYCLOPEDIAS

Gokkel, H. R. W. 'Publications à feuilles mobiles', *International Association of Law Libraries Bulletin*, no. 26, May 1971, pp. 3–6.

Armstrong, A. 'Industrial library news', *New Library World*, vol. 76, 1975, p. 64.

PERIODICALS

Daintree, D. 'The legal periodical: a study in the communication of information', MA thesis for the University of Sheffield, 1975.

RECENT DEVELOPMENTS IN TEXTBOOK PUBLISHING

The two reports referred to in the text under this heading are as follows:

SPTL. Working Party on Law Publishing and Legal Scholarship, *Interim Report*, 1975.

Society of Public Teachers of Law. Working Party on Law Publishing, *Final report on law publishing and legal scholarship*, 1977.

SMALL JURISDICTIONS

Twining, W. and Uglow, J. *Legal literature in small jurisdictions*, 1981.
Twining, W. and Uglow, J. *Law publishing and legal information: small jurisdictions of the British Isles*, 1981.

6. Government Publications

Section 1: Great Britain, Channel Islands and Isle of Man

J. JEFFRIES

All law libraries contain some British government publications and large libraries will have substantial collections, yet this remains a difficult literature. Despite these difficulties, the significance and content of British government publications are as wide-ranging as the activities of the government they reflect. The various forms in which government publications appear make bibliographic control difficult, and the complexity of bibliographic description makes conventional library cataloguing a time-consuming process. What is worse, the complicated records which result may not be particularly helpful to the user of a government publications' collection. For example, at page 854 of *Government Publications 1973* there are two documents listed each with titles ten lines long. There are few subjects which are not touched upon in British government publications, and law is not the least of those dealt with in some depth. The aim of this chapter is to chart a course through what many librarians do regard as a most intractable body of literature, excepting legislation which is dealt with in Chapter 3.

There are some useful categories of publications which can be identified. It used to be the case that the overwhelming number of British government publications were handled by Her Majesty's Stationery Office, or HMSO as it is usually known. And at one time, nearly all HMSO publications were issued as Parliamentary papers. Unfortunately, such assumptions no longer hold good, though happily, for recent material at least, bibliographic control is satisfactory.

HMSO CATALOGUES

The most recent HMSO publications, and publications sold but not published by HMSO (for HMSO acts as a bookseller for a number of bodies especially international organizations) are entered on the *Daily List of Government Publications from Her Majesty's Stationery Office*. This information is also recorded on PRESTEL, and in future may be available as an online database. An additional aid is the *List of Non-Parliamentary Publications sent for printing together with forthcoming Acts of Parliament* which is useful for those who wish to order material from HMSO in advance of publication. There is also a *Weekly List of Government Publications from Her Majesty's Stationery Office: a selection of interest to local authorities*. The *Daily List* is available from HMSO on subscription, the others can be obtained free of charge. Eventually the entries from the *Daily List* are superseded by the monthly catalogue, *Government Publications of ... *. The *Daily List* is produced on a 'common sense' basis – without reference to any recognized cataloguing code, but the monthly catalogue follows AACR2. Whereas the *Daily List* records Statutory Instruments, these are omitted from the monthly catalogues, separate lists being produced by the Statutory Publications Office. Later, sometimes much later, an annual catalogue is produced, *Government Publications of ... *. The monthly and annual catalogues are divided into two main sections: the first is devoted to Parliamentary publications and the second is a classified list which records all HMSO publications and some non-HMSO works under the name of the appropriate body with a great many '*see*' references. Thus, all documents which emanate from the Law Commission, whether Parliamentary or non-Parliamentary are entered under that heading, and there is a reference from the Lord Chancellor's Department. It must be said that sometimes the headings selected are rather obscure. Other features are a detailed subject index, an ISBN index and a periodicals list.

The annual catalogue also records the addresses of those libraries which receive the HMSO Selected Subscription Service. Like the *Daily List*, the monthly catalogue lists the material sold but not published by HMSO, but in the annual catalogue the entries for the publications of international organizations are consigned to a supplement, *International Organisations Publications* . . . . Throughout the annual catalogue, publications sold but not published by HMSO are noted as 'sold by HMSO' and are readily distinguished from HMSO publications by different ISBNS. HMSO has two ISBN publisher codes: 10 for Parliamentary papers and 11 for non-Parliamentary publications. In 1976 HMSO abandoned the 'common sense' method of listing publications in its annual catalogues, and adopted AACR2, though it has never adopted AACR2 for the *Daily List*. Since 1935 the annual catalogues have been paginated over five-year periods, and quinquennial cumulative indexes are produced.

The *Annual Catalogues of British Official and Parliamentary Publications* have been reprinted in two volumes by Chadwyck-Healey covering the years 1894–1919. The same company has also reprinted the *Annual Catalogues of Government Publications*, together with the seven quinquennial indexes, in five volumes covering 1920–70. For a detailed treatment of the various sales catalogues of British government publications, see K. A. Mallaber's article: 'The sales catalogues of British government publications, 1836–1965', *Journal of Librarianship*, vol. 5, 1973, pp. 116–131.

Thirty-three *Sectional Lists*, actually numbered between 1 and 69, are handy, and frequently revised, lists of the material currently available from HMSO. Some continue to list material which is noted as out of print, and some record a quantity of non-HMSO items, especially commercial reprints of HMSO publications. The following *Sectional Lists* are likely to be particularly useful in law libraries:

  3 *Energy, Trade and Industry*
  5 *Department of the Environment*
 11 *Department of Health and Social Security*
 18 *Health and Safety Executive*
 21 *Department of Employment*
 22 *Department of Transport*
 26 *Home Office*
 29 *Board of Inland Revenue*
 43 *Land Registry*

Publications of the Law Commission, Law Officers' Department and the Lord Chancellor's Department are to be found in *Sectional List*: 50 which is entitled *Miscellaneous*. *Sectional Lists* are available free of charge on application to HMSO.

NON-HMSO PUBLICATIONS

Apart from the enormous quantity of material issued by the Patent Office, there are still many thousands of government publications which appear each year but are not published or sold by HMSO. It should be remembered that HMSO is obliged to publish certain categories of material, especially Parliamentary papers, but for the rest it is required to act only on a commercial basis. Whilst it may act as a printer for government departments, or make arrangements for the printing of a document, this does not necessarily mean that it will act as the publisher and bookseller for that document. In the case of the greater number of non-Parliamentary publications, it makes decisions solely upon the basis of the likely commercial return. It is confusing enough that HMSO should have the three functions of printer, publisher and bookseller – as well as mixes of these functions – which are usually quite distinct in the commercial world. Moreover, it is hard to explain to a third person why a work which has on the back such words as 'printed by ... for HMSO' is not an HMSO publication.

Until 1980 the position was most unsatisfactory. Very many non-HMSO government publications are too slight or too ephemeral to be recorded in the *British National Bibliography* or the usual trade bibliographies, and most are not sales publications anyway. Indeed, it was most irritating when shown a newspaper cutting stating that such and such a minister had produced a consultative document to find that it was listed in no HMSO catalogue.

From 1980 onwards we can turn to the *Catalogue of British Official Publications not Published by HMSO*, produced by Chadwyck-Healey. This is part of an impressive microfiche document delivery service which currently records about 10,000 items each year. The catalogue is published bi-monthly with annual cumulations. Since October 1983 there has also been a COM microfiche keyword index. The Chadwyck-Healey catalogue has the additional feature that it gives the full address of the organization from which each document may be obtained in hard copy. It is now essential to check both the Chadwyck-Healey and the HMSO catalogues for recent material. Chadwyck-Healey may soon be searchable online.

HMSO periodical titles are listed in the HMSO monthly and annual catalogues, but a more exhaustive list, including many non-HMSO titles can be found in the *Checklist of British Official Serial Publications* which is issued by The British Library Reference Division.

GUIDES TO THE LITERATURE

J. E. Pemberton, *British official publications*, 2nd edn., 1973, though now very dated must still be regarded as a standard work. E. Johansson, *Current British government publishing*, 1978, is a useful commentary though it ante-dates the Chadwyck-Healey initiative. F. Rodgers, *A guide to British government publications*, 1980 is the most comprehensive text. From an entirely practical point of view, S. Richard, *Directory of British official publications: a guide to sources*, 2nd edn., 1984, is a most valuable work with plenty of incisive comments in the introduction. Also worth noting is D. Butcher, *Official publications in Britain*, 1983. Though notoriously North American in bias, *Government publications review*, 1974– does carry articles on British official publishing from time to time, often by American writers.

LISTS OF COMMITTEE CHAIRMEN

In view of the frequency with which one finds the reports of committees and commissions cited only by the name of the chairman, it is very helpful to have access to some of the tools which assist in supplying the full bibliographic details. None the less, this does not solve the problem of the same name, frequently the same individual, being associated with a number of different reports.

HMSO publishes the quarterly *Index to Chairmen of Committees*, but this work has only appeared since 1983. S. Richard has compiled *British government publications: an index to chairmen of committees and commissions of inquiry*, vol. 1, 1982, covers the nineteenth century and vols 2 to 4 cover 1900–40, 1941–78 and 1979–82 respectively. Annie Mary Morgan compiled *British government publications: an index to chairmen and authors, 1941–1966*, 1969, and with Lorna R. Stephen compiled *British government publications: an index to chairmen, 1967–1971*, which was published in 1976. In 1977 John Kite brought these last mentioned lists up to date to the end of 1975 with *British government reports 1971–1975: indexes of chairmen and subjects*.

PARLIAMENTARY PAPERS

Throughout the nineteenth century, admittedly with awkward exceptions, government publications and Parliamentary papers were virtually synonymous. It was not until 1883 that HMSO took over the publication of Parliamentary papers from Eyre and Spottiswode. In 1887 HMSO also took over the publication of Acts of Parliament, but it was not until 1909 that it took over the publication of *Hansard*. It is probably true that only in the 1930s and 1940s had HMSO anything like a near monopoly of British official publishing. But at no time has it ever enjoyed a complete monopoly.

Nineteenth-century Parliamentary papers are a most important resource to scholars of many disciplines and the ways in which they can be located and exploited are relatively well known. They are also relatively easy to deal with because they fall into fairly easily identifiable categories with an acceptable degree of bibliographic control. Thus, it is not really surprising that the main categories of Parliamentary papers are better known than most other features of British official publishing. Moreover, Parliamentary papers are usually more generally available in libraries than other official publications.

Command papers

The term 'command paper' arises from the unlikely fiction that such documents are laid before Parliament by command of the sovereign. However, this device really signifies that a minister wishes to present a document to Parliament, but has no particular authority for so doing. Command papers first appeared during the eighteenth century, but they were not so readily identifiable as a separate category of publication from other sessional papers until 1833, when contract printing was introduced. The following numbered series have appeared:

First series	[1]	– [4222]	1833–69
Second series	[C.1]	– [C.9550]	1870–99
Third series	[Cd.1]	– [Cd.9239]	1900–18
Fourth series	[Cmd.1]	– Cmd.9889	1919–56
Fifth series	Cmnd.1	–	1956–

The unnecessary practice of placing the numbers in square brackets was abandoned in 1922. By one of those exquisite peculiarities with which the literature of official publications abounds, command papers are not protected by Parliamentary privilege.

Of the various types of document which appear as command papers there are very many of relevance to law libraries. These include 'white papers' – which are really statements of ministerial intent to introduce certain legislation – though in a more general sense could be any document so insubstantial that it does not require a cover; 'green papers' or consultative documents – though it must be remembered that many consultative documents are non-HMSO items; the United Kingdom *Treaty Series* and many other Foreign and Commonwealth Office documents; the reports of Royal Commissions as well as some, but by no means all, reports of departmental and other investigatory committees; the annual reports of some statutory bodies, as well as some statistical returns. But, one cannot emphasize enough that there appear to be no hard and fast rules which determine whether a document appears in one category of publication rather than another, and one can make few safe assumptions.

House of Commons papers

These cover the whole spectrum of Parliamentary activity, and include amongst many other things, the reports of the various select committees of the House, together with many other documents which might equally have appeared as command papers – except that they are returns required by an Act of Parliament (sometimes referred to as 'Act papers'). These papers are numbered consecutively within a Parliamentary session – the number appearing in the bottom left-hand corner of the front cover and title page of the document. That is, except for *Her Majesty's most gracious speech to both Houses of Parliament* which is not given a number at all. House of Commons papers always carry the legend 'ordered by the House of Commons to be printed'.

House of Commons Bills are a separate series and are printed on pale green paper. They are numbered within a Parliamentary session, but are distinguished from House of Commons papers by the number appearing in square brackets.

House of Lords papers and Bills

These are numbered consecutively within a Parliamentary session, but the number which appears in the bottom left-hand corner of the cover and the title page is enclosed in round brackets. Although very many of the documents in this category are Bills and amendments to Bills, there is an increasing number of select committee reports which are worthy of note – such as those of the Select Committee on the European Communities.

Published collections of sessional papers

Command papers, House of Commons papers, and House of Commons Bills are sometimes known collectively as sessional papers. Sheila Lambert has edited the *House of Commons sessional papers of the eighteenth century*, published in 147 volumes by Scholarly Resources, 1975–6, complete with its own index. The Irish University Press attempted to publish a full reprint of the nineteenth-century House of Commons sessional papers in a series of subject volumes. This project was never completed, and was perhaps over-ambitious in concept, but the still very

considerable number of volumes which were published –
1,000 – are of lasting value and are to be found in some
libraries. The principal drawback in turning to this set is that
few of the supporting indexes were produced. The Readex
Microprint Corporation has produced a microcard edition of
sessional papers (1801–), reproduced from the set in New
York Public Library. Some libraries hold a microform edition
of the nineteenth-century sessional papers produced by
Chadwyck-Healey. Oceana have commenced a reprint of the
extant House of Lords papers.

   Some longer-established libraries have the sets of sessional
papers as published originally, but bound together according
to the scheme devised by the House of Commons Library. It
should be remembered that binding together in these sets
depended upon the use of a standard paper size. Since papers
published in a different size were invariably omitted from the
bound sets, it is essential, when using such sets, to consult the
sessional indexes described below.

Indexes to sessional papers

Since 1801 the House of Commons Library has produced
indexes to the House of Commons sessional papers. These
appear first as indexes for each Parliamentary session. They
are then cumulated into decennial and eventually fifty-year
general indexes. The indexes should be used to trace documents in any bound sets which follow the scheme devised
by the House of Commons Library – and this includes the
Readex Microprint set. It is from the sessional indexes that
one finds the volume and page numbers which the House of
Commons Library gives to each document.

   The earliest extant House of Commons sessional papers can
be traced using a number of sources. *Printing for Parliament
1641–1700*, by Sheila Lambert appeared as vol. 20 in a List and
Index Society special series published in 1984. One can refer
also to *Hansard's breviate* as it is generally known, or to give it its
full title: *Catalogue of Parliamentary reports and a breviate of their
contents: arranged under heads according to the subjects 1696–1834*.
This appeared first as a House of Commons paper in 1834,

and was reprinted by Blackwell in 1953 with a new introduction by Percy and Grace Ford. The Scholarly Resources reprint of eighteenth-century papers contains the index prepared by Sheila Lambert which covers 1715–99. Percy and Grace Ford produced a *Select list of British Parliamentary papers 1833–1899*, published by Blackwell in 1953. This is continued by three volumes of breviates published as follows:

A *breviate of Parliamentary papers*, 1900–1916, 1957
A *breviate of Parliamentary papers*, 1917–1939, 1951
A *breviate of Parliamentary papers*, 1940–1954, 1961

Lastly, there is Percy Ford *et al. Select list of British Parliamentary papers 1955–1964*, 1970.

Frank Rodgers records all the above works, describes them in considerably more detail, and includes a number of other bibliographic aids in his section on catalogues and indexes in *A guide to British government publications*, pp.107–14. Another useful source to note is *Serial publications in the British Parliamentary papers 1900–1968: a bibliography*, 1971, also by Frank Rodgers.

Parliamentary debates

Frank Rodgers has a chapter on 'Parliamentary debates', and another on 'Journals' and 'Votes and proceedings' in *A guide to British Government publications*, pp. 69–94. 'Parliamentary debates' and those other related publications ('Journals' are the formal minute books of Parliament) are all published currently by HMSO. They should be regarded as Parliamentary papers but they are not sessional papers. D. Menhennet has described the House of Commons 'Journals' in *The Journals of the House of Commons*, 1971.

There is plenty of room for confusion. For example, the standing committee debates are published alongside other Parliamentary debates – though not of course as a part of *Hansard* itself – but the minutes of proceedings of standing committees (which debate Bills clause-by-clause) appear as House of Commons papers.

Hansard, which is published in two series – House of

Commons, and House of Lords – first appeared in 1803. The difference between *Hansard* and the *Journals* is that one records what was said and the other what was done. The 5th series of *Hansard* commenced in 1909 when HMSO took over its publication, and the reports became verbatim for both Houses. Answers to written questions can also be found in *Hansard* as well as the texts of the debates themselves.

The Parliamentary Online Information Service, POLIS, is an indexing service for much of the documentation relating to the work of Parliament, and *Hansard* is now available in full text.

NON-PARLIAMENTARY PUBLICATIONS

In 1922 the Treasury initiated a move to reduce the volume of material issued as Parliamentary papers – and hence with a large free distribution list – by creating the category of departmental publications which would be available only for sale. Since 1950, the number of non-Parliamentary publications has been swelled appreciably by those which are not HMSO either.

In 1972 it was decided that the annual reports of various statutory bodies – like nationalized industries – need not appear as House of Commons papers. These will not necessarily be published by HMSO, though they have to be laid before Parliament. Usually they are sold by HMSO and consequently they are listed in the HMSO annual catalogues. Of course, libraries which receive the HMSO Selected Subscription Service will be sent only the material actually published by HMSO – so such non-HMSO items will be excluded.

All the material in the Controller's Library (that is HMSO's archival collection) for the years 1922–72 has been microfilmed by the Historic Documents Institute, and made available with a new hard copy index.

Statistics

The best guide to official statistics is entitled a *Guide to official statistics* and is prepared by the Central Statistical Office. The

4th edition was published by HMSO in 1982. There are several sections of direct interest to law libraries: 'civil and criminal proceedings', pp. 71–7; 'the police service', pp. 77–82; and 'the treatment of offenders', pp. 82–8. Since this guide deals with both HMSO and non-HMSO material it helps to sort out some of those bibliographic curiosities which exist in large numbers. For example, *Criminal Statistics, England and Wales* appears annually as a command paper, but most of the data are presented in the non-HMSO Home Office publication *Criminal Statistics, England and Wales, Supplementary Tables*. Details of specific statistical sources are given below.

Gazettes

Many countries other than the United Kingdom have an official gazette which is the vehicle for the communication of a great deal of public information, and which frequently includes legislation. The *London Gazette* (1665–), and its sister publications, the *Edinburgh Gazette* (1793–) and the *Belfast Gazette* (1921–), do contain a great deal of miscellaneous public information, but they are not of the same standing as say the French *Journal Officiel*. Even the *London Gazette* is likely to be found in only the minority of law libraries. Some of the commercial information it contains may be of significance to law firms, such as petitions for the compulsory winding up of companies, and the names of companies struck off the Register of Companies. Since 1893 it has also been the vehicle for the publication of some statutory material as described in Chapter 3.

PUBLICATIONS OF GOVERNMENT DEPARTMENTS

The material actually collected by individual law libraries will of course be a matter for local decision, and it is hard to identify all those categories of official publications which might be of interest to most of them. In the final analysis, any British government publication may be of interest at some stage. Some individual publications which emanate from government departments are worthy of special note and some of them are described below whatever their form of publication.

A persistent problem which must be noted results from the changes of structure and nomenclature within the government service. For example, within a fifteen-year period there have been the following sequence of changes: Board of Trade–Department of Trade and Industry–Department of Trade–Department of Trade and Industry. These changes have obvious implications for bibliographic description.

Board of Inland Revenue

The *Inland Revenue Statistics* are published annually, and the *Report of the Commissioners* is published annually as a command paper. There is a set of the Taxes Acts as in force for each fiscal year, and a multi-volume looseleaf work on *Income Taxes outside the United Kingdom*. *Tax cases: appeals to the High Court etc.* are published as individual leaflets. *Tax cases reported under the direction of the Board* has so far appeared in fifty-four volumes covering 1938–84, and new volumes appear irregularly. Some Capital Transfer Tax cases are published as individual leaflets and are listed in the Chadwyck-Healey catalogue.

Charity Commission

The *Report of the Charity Commissioners for England and Wales* is a House of Commons paper.

Central Office of Information

This body produces a selection of general information publications which includes a series of *Reference pamphlets*. Worth remembering are: 'Criminal justice in Britain', *Reference pamphlet*: 129, 1979, and 'Justice and the law in Britain', *Reference pamphlet*: 173, 1983.

Criminal Law Revision Committee

Twelve reports appeared as command papers between 1959 and 1973. There have also been some unnumbered working papers.

Department of Health and Social Security

The Decisions of the Commissioners in respect of questions arising from the various categories of social security payments are issued individually in a number of different series. The *Reported decisions* are reprinted in nine volumes covering 1948–82. In addition there is the looseleaf *Social Security Case Law: digest of Commissioners' decisions.* Two further looseleaf works are also worthy of note, namely: *The law relating to social security and child benefit* (the 'brown' book) and *The law relating to supplementary benefits and family income supplements: the statutes, regulations and orders as now in force* (the 'yellow' book). Another valuable work, frequently revised, is the *Supplementary Benefits handbook: a guide to claimants' rights*, 7th edn., 1985.

Department of Trade and Industry

This department issues a number of publications concerned with commercial and industrial organization. The Companies Legislation Division issues an *Annual Report* under the Companies Acts, and the reports of investigations under sections 164 and 172 of the Companies Act 1948. Reports of the Monopolies and Mergers Commission appear as command papers. The weekly *British Business* is useful to libraries of most kinds.

HM Customs and Excise

A notable publication is the series *Value Added Tax Tribunal Reports*, 1973–.

Home Office

The Home Office is the government department concerned with crime, punishment and the police service, amongst other responsibilities. The department deals mainly with matters in England and Wales, while Scottish matters are dealt with by the Scottish Home and Health Department.

So far as the police service is concerned, there are three annual reports to note: the *Report of Her Majesty's Chief Inspector of Constabulary* and the *Report of the Police Complaints Board* both of which appear annually as House of Commons papers; and the *Report of the Commissioner of Police of the Metropolis* which appears annually as a command paper. The *Triennial Review of the Police Complaints Board* is also a command paper.

There are several series of reports issued by the Advisory Council on the Penal System and the Advisory Council on the Treatment of Offenders, and a series entitled *Studies in the causes of delinquency and the treatment of offenders*. *Prison Statistics*, the *Report of Her Majesty's Chief Inspector of Prisons for England and Wales*, and the *Report on the work of the Prison Department*, together with *Criminal Statistics, England and Wales*, are all published annually as command papers. The annual *Report of the Parole Board* is a House of Commons paper.

Criminal Statistics, England and Wales, Supplementary Tables has appeared in four volumes since 1980 as a non-HMSO publication:

    vol. 1 'Proceedings in Magistrates' Courts',
    vol. 2 'Proceedings in the Crown Court',
    vol. 3 'Tables by Police force areas and some Court areas',
    vol. 4 'Convictions, cautions, DPP prosecutions, mentally disordered offenders, appeals, prerogatives of mercy, legal aid'.

Data prior to 1980 is hard to come by, though some libraries may hold the volumes of statistics which were prepared by the Home Office but not sold.

Up to 1985 the Home Office Research Unit had issued eighty-seven *Research studies*. These cover the entire range of Home Office responsibilities but a number are specifically legal or criminological in content.

The Chadwyck-Healey catalogue for 1983 lists 383 non-HMSO publications from the Home Office, and a substantial number of these are of legal interest.

Law Commissions

The Reports of the Law Commission and the Scottish Law Commission, and their respective *Annual Reports* are published variously as command papers and House of Commons papers, though they have additional numbering in the series *Law Com.* and *Scot. Law Com.* Between 1965 and 1985, 153 Law Commission *Reports* and 99 Scottish Law Commission *Reports* were issued. Professional Books have published a 13-volume reprint of the first 120 Law Commission *Reports* under the editorship of Donald Raistrick, who has also written the *Law Commission Digest*, 1979, which is intended to give an outline of all law reform proposals put forward by the Law Commission in its reports, with notes on resulting legislation.

As well as the *Reports*, the Law Commission has produced a series of *Working Papers*, 94 of which had appeared up to the end of 1985. Nos. 1–84 have been reprinted by Professional Books, again under the editorship of Donald Raistrick. Nos. 1–49 were not published by HMSO and are rather fugitive in their original form. The Scottish Law Commission equivalent publications are entitled *Memoranda*, a list of which appears in each *Annual Report*. Some are also listed in the Chadwyck-Healey catalogues.

Law Reform Committee

Twenty-three reports were issued between 1953 and 1982 as command papers. They are listed in *Sectional List: 50*.

Lord Chancellor's Department

As might be anticipated this department prepares a number of publications of interest to law libraries. *Judicial Statistics,*

England and Wales now appears annually as a command paper, and replaces *Statistics on Judicial Administration* (1972–4). *The Annual Report of the Lay Observer* is a House of Commons paper, as is the *Annual Report of the Council on Tribunals*, though the latter was issued as a non-Parliamentary publication from 1959 to 1966. The *Supreme Court Rules* appeared as a looseleaf work in 1965 and 46 supplements had appeared up to 1985. The *Legal Aid Handbook*, 1983 is another non-Parliamentary publication, though the *Annual Report of the Lord Chancellor's Advisory Committee on Legal Aid* and the annual *Accounts* for the Legal Aid Fund are both House of Commons papers.

Ministry of Defence

The Ministry of Defence issues a number of looseleaf works of legal interest:

> *Manual of Air Force law*, 6th edn.
> *Manual of military law*, 12th edn.
> *Queen's regulations for the Army*, 1975
> *Queen's regulations for the Royal Air Force*
> *Queen's regulations for the Royal Navy*
> *Regulations for the Ulster Defence Regiment*, 1980
> *Territorial Army regulations*, 1978.

Ombudsmen

There are five so-called ombudsmen who issue regular reports. Those of the Parliamentary Commissioner for Administration and the Health Services Commissioner appear as House of Commons papers. The reports of the Commission for Local Administration in England, and the Commission for Local Administration in Wales are not published by HMSO, and can be traced in the Chadwyck-Healey catalogues. The annual report of the Commissioner for Local Administration in Scotland is a non-Parliamentary publication of HMSO.

Registry of Friendly Societies

The Registry has issued a *Guide to the law relating to Industrial and Provident Societies*, 1978.

SCOTLAND

Although HMSO has an office in Edinburgh, and a number of HMSO publications appear exclusively with the Edinburgh imprint, it would be wrong to overstate the significance of this. Whereas the publications of HMSO Belfast do not usually appear in the HMSO catalogues described above, HMSO Edinburgh publications always do.

The Scottish Office has issued a useful booklet prepared by members of the legal staffs of the Scottish Law Commission and the Office of the Solicitor to the Secretary of State for Scotland. A third edition appeared in 1981, entitled *The legal system of Scotland*. The Scottish Home and Health Department issues the *Annual Report of the Law Society of Scotland on the Legal Aid Scheme*. The Department of the Registers of Scotland has issued a looseleaf work entitled *Registration of title practice book*, 1981. A further looseleaf work to note has been issued by the Crown Office 'primarily for use by members of the Procurator Fiscal Service' entitled *Criminal Procedure (Scotland) Act as amended* .... Volume 1 is 'solemn procedure', and volume 2 'summary procedure'. It was first published in 1976 with an amended second edition in 1983.

Annual publications include the *Report of the Parole Board for Scotland* and the *Annual Report of the Scottish Lay Observer*, both of which are House of Commons papers. The *Report of Her Majesty's Chief Inspector of Constabulary for Scotland*, the *Report of Her Majesty's Chief Inspector of Prisons for Scotland*, and the *Report of the Scottish Land Court* are all command papers. The *Report of the Scottish Valuation Advisory Council* is issued by the Scottish Office. The Scottish Courts Administration issues *Civil Judicial Statistics, Scotland*, and the Scottish Office issues *Criminal Statistics, Scotland*, both of which are command papers.

The Law Reform Committee (Scotland) issued fourteen reports as command papers between 1957 and 1964 when it went out of existence. Its work has been taken over by the Scottish Law Commission whose publications are described above under the heading Law Commissions.

ISLE OF MAN

Manx official publications are listed in *Government Publications: a short list of some of those available*, which appears quarterly and can be obtained free of charge from the Central Reference Library, the Central Government Offices, Douglas, Isle of Man. The Printing Committee of Tynwald issues the reports of the debates of Tynwald and the Keys and the Legislative Council. The *Tynwald Companion* gives notes on the rules and procedures of Tynwald as well as listing members of committees and giving biographies of current members of the House of Keys and Members of the Legislative Council. *Standing Orders of Tynwald, House of Keys and Legislative Council* are available looseleaf. *Notes for Isle of Man Justices of the Peace* is a looseleaf publication produced for the guidance of Justices. Coroners, who have a different function from those in England and Wales, have a *Coroners' Handbook*. Forthcoming legislation can be traced in the *Monthly Bulletin* produced by the Government Office, and available on subscription.

CHANNEL ISLANDS

The States of Jersey published the *Development of the Government of Jersey, 1771–1972*, by R. G. Le Hérissier, in 1974. S. Richard says that there is no central source for the publications of the departments of Jersey, but he lists 19 departments and organizations from which information can be obtained in his *Directory of British Official Publications: a guide to sources*, 2nd edn., 1984, pp. 386–90.

The States Office, Guernsey publishes a few titles. For example, the States Advisory and Finance Committee issued a report on the 1981 census.

FURTHER READING

Bellot, H. H. 'Parliamentary printing, 1660–1837', *Bulletin of the Institute of Historical Research*, vol.11, 1933–34, pp. 85–98.

A bibliography of Parliamentary debates of Great Britain, 1956.

Bond, M. F. *Guide to the Records of Parliament*, 1971.

Butcher, D. *Official publications in Britain: an outline of modern librarianship*, 1982.

Ford, P. and Ford, G. *A guide to Parliamentary papers*, 3rd edn., 1972.

Kemp P. *Votes and Standing Orders of the House of Commons: the beginning*, 1971.

Lambert, S. 'Guides to Parliamentary printing, 1696–1834', *Bulletin of the Institute of Historical Research*, vol. 38, 1965, pp. 111–17.

Lambert, S. 'House of Commons papers of the eighteenth century', *Government Publications Review*, vol. 3, 1976, pp. 195–202.

Lambert, S. 'Printing for the House of Commons in the eighteenth century', *The Library*, ser. 5, vol. 23, 1968, pp. 25–46.

Law, W. *Our Hansard, or, the true mirror of Parliament*, 1950.

Mallaber, K. A. 'The House of Lords sessional papers', *Journal of Librarianship*, vol. 4, 1972, pp. 106–14.

Marshallsay, D. M. *British government publications: users' guide*, 1975.

Marshallsay, D. M. *Official publications: survey of the current situation*, 1972.

Parsons, K. A. C. *A checklist of the British Parliamentary papers bound set, 1801–1950*, 1958.

Pemberton, J. E. *Bibliographic control of Official publications*, 1981.

Pemberton, J. E. 'The case against the sessional indexes', *Library World*, vol. 72, 1970–1, pp. 35–8.

Pemberton, J. E. 'Government green papers', *Library World*, vol. 71, 1969–70, pp. 46–47, 49.

Pemberton, J. E. 'Privileged publications', *Library World*, vol. 71, 1969–70, pp. 210–11.

Smith, B. E. 'British official publications', *Government Publications Review*, vol. 4, 1977, pp. 201–7; vol. 5, 1978, pp. 1–12; vol. 6, 1979, pp. 11–18.

Trewin, J. C. and King, E. M. *Printer to the House: the story of Hansard*, 1952.

Section 2: Ireland

J. GOODWILLIE

HISTORICAL BACKGROUND

From 1801 to 1921 (in the case of Northern Ireland) and to 1922 (in the case of the remainder of the country) there were no separate Irish parliamentary institutions. But the Irish administration was not entirely integrated into that of the United Kingdom. The Chief Secretary's Office in Dublin administered much of Irish affairs, and as the nineteenth century progressed, a tendency towards establishing specifically Irish departments emerged. Thus, the Board of Public Works (Ireland) was established in 1832, the Board of National Education in Ireland in 1834, the Local Government Board for Ireland in 1872, the Irish Land Commission in 1881, the Congested Districts Board for Ireland in 1891, and the Department of Agriculture and Technical Instruction for Ireland in 1900.

As was the case in Britain, the early publications of these bodies were, on the whole, within the structure of parliamentary publishing. Various reports, accounts, and returns were published as House of Commons Sessional Papers. Frank Rodgers's *Serial publications in the British Parliamentary papers* (1971) lists 49 serials which were in progress in 1900, among them *Statistical Tables of the Dublin Metropolitan Police, Judicial Statistics*.

When non-parliamentary publications emerged, they were mostly under the aegis of HMSO. The HMSO catalogues had a specifically Irish section. The HMSO catalogue of non-parliamentary publications in print in 1920 has an Irish list of

14 pages, of which 5 pages are devoted to the Department of Agriculture and Technical Instruction and 3½ to the Local Government Board. The other items include numerous orders, rules, forms and returns.

Even at this stage, some government publications were published directly by the department concerned.

NORTHERN IRELAND

From the establishment of a Northern Ireland administration in 1921, its government publications have been modelled on those of the United Kingdom. The Belfast office of Her Majesty's Stationery Office publishes its own catalogues, although since 1978 its publications have also been listed in the main HMSO catalogues.

Parliamentary publications and equivalent

Official reports of debates have been published for the House of Commons, Senate, Convention, and Assembly (both 1973–4 and 1982–6). Daily parts were issued and cumulated into volumes.

Journals were published for the House of Commons, Senate, and 1973–4 Assembly.

Order papers were published for the House of Commons.

Minutes of the Senate and *Votes and Proceedings of the House of Commons* were issued daily, but do not appear to have been placed on sale after 1949.

House of Commons reports and papers and Senate reports and papers were published in numbered series. Those for which government departments were responsible have been mostly published as Departmental reports and papers since the establishment of direct rule in 1972, but during the existence of the Assembly with a responsible Executive (1974), they were published as Assembly reports and papers. The reports of the Parliamentary Commissioner and Commissioner for Complaints became United Kingdom House of Commons papers from 1972, and certain financial accounts became United Kingdom House of Commons papers from 1974.

Assembly reports and papers relating to standing orders, committees, etc., were published in the 1973–4 period, but were more numerous in the 1982–6 Assembly due to the operation of a developed committee system.

The Rules of Procedure of the Convention were published as NIC2, but no document numbered NIC1 seems to exist.

Command papers were published at the instance of government departments from 1922 to 1975, after which they were replaced by Departmental reports and papers.

Acts, Bills, Measures, Proposed Measures, Orders in Council, Draft Orders in Council, and Proposals for Draft Orders in Council are discussed in Chapter 3.

Belfast Gazette

The *Belfast Gazette* is published weekly, with various supplements and an annual index. It contains various government announcements, public notices, companies notifications, etc.

Departmental reports and papers

There have always been a considerable number of publications originating from government departments, but their number has increased under direct rule through the absorption of command papers and House of Commons papers (see above). Proposals may be made for legislation, either by the central government or by departments, as in the UK. The law may be republished in a more accessible way, for example *The law relating to supplementary benefits and family income supplements in Northern Ireland*, prepared by the NI Department of Health and Social Services, 1983–.

Some types of regulations may be produced as departmental publications, for example Agricultural Wages Orders and Civil Service Pension Schemes.

The Examiner of Statutory Rules issues periodical reports commenting on problems raised by recently-made rules.

Explanatory material is issued to some legislation, for example Health and Safety Agency guides to regulations, and the Department of Health and Social Service's *Supplementary benefits handbook.*

Decisions of the Commissioner in relation to social security and supplementary benefits are published, as are *Industrial Court Awards.*

Statistical publications are issued by various departments, such as the *Northern Ireland Annual Abstract of Statistics* issued by the Department of Finance and Personnel and the censuses of population issued by the Department of Health and Social Services.

Non-*HMSO* publications

Some publishing is carried on by government departments outside the structure of HMSO. The largest category would be the maps published by the Ordnance Survey of Northern Ireland. Other examples are leaflets published by the Department of Health and Social Services and the Department of Agriculture, statistical indexes published by the Department of Economic Development, and publications of the Public Record Office.

Governmental bodies which are not under the direct control of ministers are also responsible for their own publications. Examples are the reports of the Northern Ireland Economic Council, the Labour Relations Agency, and the Fair Employment Agency.

Indexes and bibliographies

The publications of the Northern Ireland office of HMSO are listed in a *Monthly List of Publications*, which is cumulated into an *Annual List of Publications*. These catalogues give title, ISBN, and price, but are not indexed. There were cumulated catalogues, with indexes, for the years 1921–37 and 1938–47. Since 1978, publications have also been recorded in the general HMSO catalogues, where they receive the normal detailed treatment and can be distinguished only by the ISBN which begins with 0 337.

In general non-HMSO material is difficult to trace. Some

publications are listed in the biennial *Ulster Year Book*. There are a couple of departmental catalogues, and some non-departmental bodies have publications listed in the *Catalogue of British Official Publications not Published by HMSO*, 1980–.

There is a selective retrospective index and breviate of HMSO publications, compiled by Arthur Maltby: *The Government of Northern Ireland, 1922–72: a catalogue and breviate of Parliamentary papers*, 1974.

IRISH FREE STATE AND REPUBLIC

The underground Dáil administration of 1919–22 produced a few propaganda publications. The Dáil debates have been published, some contemporaneously and others subsequently by the Stationery Office. There was also a series of reports of the Commission of Enquiry into the Resources and Industries of Ireland.

Following the Anglo-Irish Treaty of 1922, a Provisional Government of Ireland was established, under which was established the publishing structure which has survived to the present day. A Stationery Office was set up on the British model and has retained a more central role in government publishing than HMSO.

Although Irish is the first official language of the state since 1937, almost all government publications are in English – even those with Irish or bilingual titles.

Oireachtas publications

The Stationery Office, in its catalogues, divides its publications into Oireachtas publications and Stationery Office publications, corresponding to the HMSO division between parliamentary and non-parliamentary publications. The exception to this parallel is that all papers originating from government departments are classified as Stationery Office, there being no equivalent either of command papers or of those House of Commons papers not related to Committees of the House.

Oireachtas publications will be discussed first. Each House

of the Oireachtas (Dáil Éireann and Seanad Éireann) issues an order paper, that of Dáil Éireann having the apparent title *Orders of the Day, Questions*, or *At the Commencement of Public Business* according to the particular section which is listed first. Among the items included are lists of Bills in progress and papers laid before the House. The annual subscription for these publications also covers lists of amendments to Bills.

Parliamentary Debates are issued in two series, one for each House. Daily parts are issued unrevised, and are subsequently cumulated into bound volumes after members have an opportunity to suggest corrections. Each volume is indexed and there are consolidated indexes for the period up to 1956 (Dáil) and 1948 (Seanad). Committee debates have also been published occasionally.

Each House also issues a journal of *Proceedings* and lists of *Divisions*.

Reports are issued by Committees of each House and Joint Committees of both Houses. Some of these are temporary committees set up to examine specific topics or Bills, such as the *Report of the Informal Committee on Reform of Dáil Procedure*, published in 1973. Other committees exist permanently, but only issue occasional reports, such as the Committees on Procedure and Privileges. Committees issuing regular reports have increased in number over recent years, *eg* the Joint Committee on Legislation in 1984.

There are also a number of miscellaneous publications in relation to the Oireachtas. Recent ones have been the publications of the New Ireland Forum (1983–4), Seanad election results, standing orders, regulations for allowances to members, and the Constitution.

Stationery Office Publications

Publications originating from government departments are in general classified as Stationery Office or non-parliamentary publications. They can be considered as of a legal, administrative, statistical, economic, technical, or cultural nature.

Legal

Some publications concern the process of formulating legislation. A number of government-appointed committees have issued proposals for reform. Examples are the Company Law Reform Committee (1958), the Committee on the Constitution (1967), the Advisory Committee on Law Reform (1976). The Committee on Court Practice and Procedure, established in 1962, issued 20 interim reports up to 1978.

Proposals can also be made directly by the government. Examples are *Company Taxation in Ireland: Proposals for Corporation Tax*, issued by the Minister for Finance in 1974; and *The Law of Nullity in Ireland*, issued by the Office of the Attorney General in 1976.

Legislation is covered in Chapter 3, but there is one instance of a pre-1922 Act being reprinted and regarded as a Stationery Office publication; namely the Sale of Goods Act, 1893, reprinted in 1983. The Revenue Commissioners issue versions of the Acts concerning taxation: *Law of Value-Added Tax*, and *The Taxes Acts* (formerly *The Income Tax Acts*), with updating and revision services.

In the early years of the State, not all secondary legislation was in the series of Statutory Rules and Orders. Ten Decrees of the Provisional Government were issued in 1922; a Governor-General's Order was issued in 1923; there were 23 Orders of the Executive Council in 1923 and 1924. There were also occasional items published by the Stationery Office for individual departments; for example, the Increase of Rent and Mortgage Interest (Restrictions) Rules, 1923, the Gárda Síochána Pay Order, 1927, and the Trade Union Act Rules, 1942.

Publications are also issued to explain and popularize legislation. The explanatory memorandum which is normally circulated by the appropriate department with each Bill is occasionally re-issued as an explanatory memorandum to the resulting Act *eg, Explanatory Memorandum to ... Statute Law Revision Act, 1983* (1984). Informational documents may outline a scheme, for example the *Scheme of Compensation for Personal Injuries Criminally Inflicted* (1974).

A guide to the Wildlife Act, 1976, was issued by the Forest

and Wildlife Service under the title *Wildlife and the Law*. There have been several editions of the *Guide to Local Government for Councillors* from the Department of the Environment. Regulations or abstracts of Acts relating to factories are issued by the Department of Labour in poster form.

With regard to the implementation of the law, the Revenue Commissioners issue *Irish Tax Cases* and the Employment Appeals Tribunal issues *Reports of Important Decisions*.

International treaties are published in the *Treaty Series* of the Department of Foreign Affairs; this series has its own index up to 1976. Various conventions and agreements are also published outside this series.

Administrative

Some government departments issue annual reports, covering the activities of a department or unit, *eg* the *Report on Crime* of the Commissioner of the Garda Síochána, or the *Annual Report on Prisons and Places of Detention* of the Department of Justice.

Administrative decisions can be published, for example the Censorship of Publications Board's *Register of Prohibited Publications*, or the Revenue Commissioners' *Customs and Excise Tariff of Ireland*.

Forms are issued, in pursuance of legislation, by the Department of Labour and the Censorship of Publications Board.

The official gazette, *Iris Oifigiúil*, published twice a week with an annual index and a weekly companies notifications supplement, lists much government and commercial information.

Statistical

The main source of statistical material is the Central Statistics Office, but some departments have statistical publications of their own.

Departmental publications

As well as using the services of the Stationery Office, some government departments publish material directly, though this field is not as developed as it is in Britain. The largest category of departmental publications comprises Ordnance Survey maps.

The Department of Labour publishes guides and explanatory leaflets and booklets to protective legislation. The Garda Crime Prevention Unit publishes various advisory leaflets. Technical publications are produced by bodies such as the Aeronautical Information Service and the Meteorological Service. The Central Statistics Office produces various statistical series. The National Manpower Service produces *Career leaflets*. Two publications resembling Statutory Instruments, the Night Work (Bakeries) (Exceptional Work for Limited Period) Regulations, 1978 and 1980, have been issued directly by the Department of Labour.

State-sponsored bodies

The term state-sponsored bodies is used to indicate governmental or quasi-governmental bodies outside the civil service structure. They usually have boards appointed by a Minister and the majority are financed by grant, although some are commercially self-supporting.

Of particular interest is the Law Reform Commission, which was established in 1975 to review the law and formulate proposals for reform. It published a *First programme for examination of certain branches of the law with a view to their reform* in 1976. As well as an annual *Report*, it also publishes numerous *Working Papers* and makes proposals in reports numbered LRC1–1981 etc.

Indexes and bibliographies

Publications of the Stationery Office are recorded in a weekly list in *Iris Oifigiúil*, also available as an offprint. The lists record title and price. From 1984 they also record the weight and, where appropriate, the Oireachtas presentation number, which is an abbreviation of the word 'Parliament' followed by a serial number. They are cumulated into quarterly and annual

Catalogues of Government Publications; cumulated catalogues covering several years were produced for the period up to 1960. The catalogues are arranged according to the category of publication, 'Stationery Office Publications' being divided into sections which correspond, with some exceptions, to departments. 'Catalogue numbers' to be used in ordering are printed in the lists and catalogues, but not on the items themselves: they indicate the section in the catalogue to which an item is assigned.

Some of the larger non-Stationery Office publishers issue catalogues of their publications, but in general bibliographic control is difficult. Some publications are recorded in the *British National Bibliography* and the *Irish Publishing Record*.

There are two unofficial indexes to Irish government publications. The Fords' *Select List of Reports of Inquiries of the Irish Dáil and Senate, 1922–72* lists a greater number of papers, but gives merely the title, date and Stationery Office catalogue number. Maltby and McKenna's *Irish official publications* summarises the more important papers and has a name index and some information on serial reports to 1979.

FURTHER READING

Ford, P. and G. *A select list of reports of inquiries of the Irish Dáil and Senate, 1922–72*, 1974.

Goodwillie, J. Ireland, in *Official publications of Western Europe*, vol. 1, 1984.

McKenna, B. 'Irish official publications', *Aslib Proceedings*, 26(7/8), July–August 1974, pp. 304–12.

Maltby, A. *The Government of Northern Ireland, 1922–72: a catalogue and breviate of Parliamentary papers*, 1974.

Maltby, A. 'Ireland's government publications: a note on their character and bibliographic control', *Government Publications Review*, 3(3) 1976, pp. 213–16.

Maltby, A. and McKenna, B. *Irish official publications: a guide to Republic of Ireland papers, with a breviate of reports, 1922–72*, 1980.

Maltby, A. and Maltby, J. *Ireland in the nineteenth century: a breviate of official publications*, 1979.

Richard, S. *Directory of British official publications*, 2nd edn., 1984.

7. Historical Sources

W. W. S. BREEM

It is the purpose of this chapter to deal, however briefly, with almost all classes of legal materials prior to 1800.

A sound general knowledge of historical source material is essential to a proper understanding of legal bibliography. Legal scholars still find medieval and post-Renaissance records the most fruitful amongst which to conduct their researches, whilst the common law system's dependence upon precedent ensures the practising lawyer's continued concern with the written words and decisions of his predecessors. Though the doctrine exists still that legal memory is limited, being fixed at the year 1189 (the year of Richard I's coronation), the fact remains that, in 1922, the presiding judge at the Old Bailey found it necessary to make reference to the laws of Ine, a West Saxon king who reigned *c*. AD 688–725; in the Casement trial (1917) and that of Joyce (1945) lawyers consulted the Parliament Roll and the Statute Roll with reference to the Treason Act of 1352; whilst in the last quarter of the twentieth century both counsel and judiciary have had occasion to consult the medieval Year Books and pre-1800 state trials, in the course of High Court actions. No law book can be said to be useless merely because it is old.

The advent of the photographic reprint and of microfilm has made potentially available to all law libraries not only the rare law books of yesterday, but also early manuscripts and record documents. An understanding of ancient records is therefore no longer the prerogative of the archivist.

Of the satellite subjects listed by Winfield as essential aids to legal historical research, a knowledge of chronology is among the most important for the successful location of data in early material. In England until the thirteenth century the Christian year commenced on 25 December, but in the fourteenth century the practice of dating the year from 25 March became generally accepted. In 1752 the Legal Year was ordered to commence on 1 January 1753. During the period of change preceding this order official records written between 1 January and 24 March often bear a double date: thus February 1671 or 167½. The top figure refers to the old year and the lower figure to the new year. The regnal year, which involves dating the year from the commencement of a sovereign's reign, did not become fully approved till 1189. From then on all government documents and private charters are so dated. Thus, the year 1 of Richard III's reign covers the period 26 June 1483 to 25 June 1484. The most accessible table of regnal years will be found in Sweet and Maxwell's *Guide to law reports and statutes*, 1962. But in this and similar tables the year is calculated according to present reckoning, though all dates between 1 January and 25 March belong by the old reckoning to one year earlier. Thus, Edward IV's reign may be said to have commenced either on 4 March 1460 or 4 March 1461; both versions being correct. For the dating of manuscripts, reference should be made to C. R. Cheney's *Handbook of dates*, 1945. The four law terms owe their origins to the timing of church festivals, the dictates of Canon Law and the economic demands of medieval agricultural society. In 1831 the dates of the terms were defined by legislation as follows: Hilary Term (11 to 31 January); Paschal (Easter) Term (15 April to 8 May); Trinity Term (22 May to 12 June); Michaelmas Term (1 October to 25 November). A Bill intended to reduce the terms from four to three failed during the 1870 session. Parliamentary sessions are the chronological units of parliamentary business and the principal divisions into which the life of a parliament is divided. A session commences the day Parliament is opened and ends the day it is prorogued or dissolved. For a list of parliaments, 1242–1832 refer to F. M. Powicke and E. B. Fryde's *Handbook of British Chronology*, 1986, pp. 525–81.

Prior to the Conquest, legal documents were written in either Anglo-Saxon or Latin. But under the Normans Latin became the official language for the writing of records of administrative and judicial proceedings. After 1166, Anglo-French began to be used in the courts, and became the technical language of the legal profession both for speech and writing, but had become hopelessly corrupted by the first quarter of the sixteenth century. In 1650 an Act (subsequently nullified at the Restoration) was passed which required all judicial reports, resolutions and law books to be translated into English. Though Anglo-French or Law French, as it is also known, was employed as late even as the eighteenth century, it did not recover its former popularity. In 1731 an Act was passed making English the official language of the law, though a later amendment permitted technical phrases such as *quare impedit* to remain untranslated. The records of the courts of common law, however, though not those of equity proceedings were, except during the Interregnum, written in Latin until 1733. The best exposition of Anglo-French remains that of F. W. Maitland (see the 'Further Reading' list for details). Other useful aids for interpretation include J. H. Baker's *Manual of Law French*, 1979, which includes a valuable bibliography at pp. 29–72, and L. W. Stone and W. Rothwell's *Anglo-Norman dictionary*, 1977–. For Law Latin consult R. E. Latham's *Dictionary of Medieval Latin*, 1975–.

In Wales, despite the Conquest by Edward I, the native tongue remained dominant until 1536, when English became the official language for all legal and government business. In 1967, however, the Welsh Language Act decreed that, within the borders of Wales, Welsh should have equal legal validity with English.

ARCHIVES AND MANUSCRIPTS

Sir Edward Coke defined a record as 'a memorial or remembrance in rolls of parchment of the proceedings and acts of a Court of Justice', but this definition was perhaps always too narrow. Certainly the term record has a wider meaning now and may be interpreted as including any document that is specially created as being authentic evidence of a matter of legal importance. Such a definition indicates that legal records are likely to be found in almost any place where manuscripts are deposited.

The distinction between public and private records was not finally clarified until 1838, when the Public Record Office of

England and Wales, which now contains three-quarters of al
public records, was founded. In general, public records are
concerned with the business of the Crown and those publi
records which have never been officially out of official custod
are accorded an authority as evidence in court that is denied al
other records. Those which are held to be 'not of record' mus
first be proved by the testimony of experts before their conten
matter is acceptable. In the Middle Ages and in many series o
records continued into modern times the language of the
records is almost always either Latin or French.

Legal manuscripts of varying degrees of importance will be
found in repositories as variable as public record offices
universities or family muniment rooms. Ownership therefore
may be public, corporate or private and personal. Many collec
tions still have been listed only briefly, if at all; some, o
outstanding importance and in private hands, are not access
ible even upon application; while the printed catalogues o
calendars of others vary considerably as to treatment, accurac
and completeness.

Among major repositories the PRO is pre-eminent. It con
tains legal records dating from the twelfth century and Parlia
mentary records prior to 1497. The Scottish Record Offic
(HM General Register House, Edinburgh) has a continuou
history since the thirteenth century and under the Treaty o
Union preserves the older public records. The PRO, Belfast, an
the Public Record Office, Dublin, cover Irish affairs, particu
larly since 1922, while the House of Lords Record Offic
contains all Parliamentary records post-1497. The Britisl
Library contains perhaps the richest collection of legal manu
scripts, as opposed to purely legal records, but much materia
of importance will also be found in the National Libraries o
Scotland and Ireland, The Bodleian Library, Oxford, the
University Libraries of Cambridge and Edinburgh, as well a
Trinity College Library, Dublin and the Library of Queen'
University, Belfast. Of the Inns of Court libraries, Lincoln'
Inn possesses the works of Sir Matthew Hale and Serjean
Maynard, while the Inner Temple contains the Petyt Collection

County Record Offices were not established till 1924. Thei
holdings normally include records of the courts of quarte
session and of petty sessions; in general these commence *c.* 1590

Despite the apparent riches of the past, few lawyers today leave working records to posterity, the scripts of treatises excepted. The professional writings of a barrister in chambers are the property of the solicitor who engages him – carbon copies of typescript opinions, for example, are rarely made – and such documents must be sought in the archives of solicitors' firms. Notebooks, if preserved, may be located in family muniments.

For details of materials held, reference must be made to the published guides and catalogues of the institutions concerned, the best collection of these being held at London University's Institute for Historical Research. Also to be noticed is the *National Inventory of Documentary Sources in the U.K.* In this expanding microfiche publication commenced in 1983, the content of archives and MS collections in national, central government, university and polytechnic libraries, county, city and borough record offices as well as specialist and private repositories, are all listed, indexed and described in detail.

PRINTED SOURCE COLLECTIONS

Record Commission Publications

In 1800 the Record Commission of Great Britain was established and between 1802–69 issued fifty-six publications concerning the records of England, Wales and Scotland. These included ancient laws, calendars, documents, fine and oblate rolls, parliamentary writs, pipe rolls, records of parliament, and statutes of the realm, together with Acts of the Parliament of Scotland and other important Scottish record material and *writs*. A high proportion of the material has, in consequence, considerable legal interest. The volumes were published in *record* type, a pioneer effort to reproduce by conventional letterpress, specially made, a near facsimile of the original manuscript.

The Commissioners' publications were not issued as a numbered series and for an easily obtainable list of their issued works see HMSO *Publications Sectional List* – no. 24. A fuller bibliographically annotated list is in E. L. C. Mullins' *Texts and Calendars* [1], 1958.

After 1837 the Commission was allowed to lapse and upon the establishment of the PRO the work of continuing publication of state records became the function of the Master of the Rolls.

The Irish Record Commission, established 1810, was dissolved in 1830. A list of publications issued or planned by the Commissioners will be found in Mullins' [1]. For an account of the Commission, see volume 1 of J. Morrin's *Calendar of the Patent and Close Rolls*, 1861–3.

For details of record publications relating to Scotland and Wales, see P. Gouldesborough, A. P. Krupp and I. Lewis, *Handlist of Scottish and Welsh Record Publications*, 1954. This list excludes official publications, for which refer to HMSO SL – no. 24, and Mullins noted above.

Rolls series

This series of chronicles and memorials of Great Britain and Ireland during the Midle Ages was published under the official title of *Rerum Britannicarum medii aevi scriptores* by direction of the Master of the Rolls. Modelled on Pertz's *Monumenta Germaniae historica*, it consists of 99 numbered publications in 251 volumes and was issued between 1858 and 1911, each chronicle or compilation of documents being treated as an individual work and edited by a commissioned specialist. A withdrawn volume was subsequently issued in 1965. The material includes calendars of state papers such as the close and patent rolls, cartularies, charters and year books, as well as parliamentary records. Most of the prominent chroniclers are included, so that the series covers the principal medieval sources of history. A number of works contain both texts and translations and their introductions are valuable for the bibliographical information contained therein concerning the manuscripts consulted. For a complete list of titles issued, see GPSL – no. 24. A fuller bibliographically annotated list is in Mullins' [1] and [11], 1958–83.

Calendars of state papers

In 1854 the State Paper Office and the Record Office were amalgamated and two years later the still-continuing series of calendars was commenced.

The various series include Chancery Records such as the charter rolls, patent rolls, close rolls and liberate rolls, treaty rolls, inquisitions post mortem and chancery warrants, Exchequer Records such as the memoranda rolls, judicial records such as the Curia Regis rolls and ancient deeds (particularly conveyances of land), state papers domestic, foreign and colonial; also documents preserved in foreign archives of Brussels, Simancas, Venice, Vienna and elsewhere relating to the history of Great Britain and Ireland. Calendars of state papers relating to Scotland and Ireland are also included.

Since the commencement of the calendars, over 800 volumes have been published. It is a measure of the richness of this material that only a minority of these series has yet been completed.

The calendars are issued in octavo-size volumes and are, generally speaking, in the language of the original, though in certain instances translations have been effected. Their purpose is to provide catalogues of the series of documents they record and to give summary notes of the contents of each item.

The documents so calendared relate to those held in the principal state secretariat offices from the first quarter of the sixteenth century onwards, excepting only the Chancery, Exchequer and judicial records of the Curia Regis which predate this period. A summary list of titles and volumes published to date will be found in HMSO SL – no. 24. A fuller bibliographically annotated list is in Mullins' [1] and [11].

Historical Manuscripts Commission reports

The reports of the Royal Commission on Historical Manuscripts commenced in 1870. The purpose of the Commission, established in 1869, was 'to enquire what papers and manuscripts belonging to private families and institutions are extant in Great Britain and Ireland which would be of utility in the illustration of history, constitutional law, science and general literature, and to which possessors would be willing to give access'. The Commissioners' administration is centred in the PRO. To date it has reported on the mss of over 600 private owners and institutions, while its published reports on collections now exceeds 250 volumes. These are listed in detail in GPSL – no. 17. This indicates reprinted volumes still available. Historical manuscripts of the House of Lords 1450–1693 were also noted during the Commission's early years.

The reports of the Commission are of three kinds: the Commissioners' Reports to the Crown; Inspectors' Reports to the Commissioners; Reports of the Secretary to the Commissioners.

The Commissioners' Reports are statements of business during the period under review. It is the Inspectors' Reports which contain the essential data on the collections examined. All reports, however, published up to 1920 were issued as *Parliamentary Papers*.

There are three major guides to the location of material, each of which offers slightly varying data. there is the official *Guide to the Reports*, a series divided into two parts. Part I is topographical, covers reports 1870–1957 and was issued in two volumes, 1914–73, the second being described as an index of places. Part II is an index of persons in five volumes: two covering reports 1870–1911 being issued in 1935 and three the period 1911–57 being issued in 1966. Mullins above contains a detailed list of reports issued, with notes on the contents of calendars. The index to this work includes persons and places referred to in the reports. C. Gross's *Sources and Literature of English History*, 1915 at p. 692 contains a list of reports with keyed references to their location in *Parliamentary Papers*, also an index of repositories holding medieval manuscripts. The complicated publishing history and technical composition of the reports may cause difficulties, and so the best brief location guide to collections will be found in HMSO SL – no. 17. This also contains a brief bibliographical statement and a valuable note on the correct citation of references to the collections reported upon. A most important HMC finding list is their *Guide to the location of collections described in the reports and calendar series, 1870–1980*, issued 1982.

This aims to cover the movement of collections but does not claim completion since a proportion has been dispersed.

Rolls of Parliament

These are the most important early records of Parliament and it is to these that the legal historian or practising lawyer must turn if he wishes to see the original authorized text of any statute from 1 Richard III onwards. Until the sixteenth century the rolls also recorded procedural matters relating to both Houses, but these were afterwards recorded in separate minute books, for details of which, see below under *Journals* of the Lords and Commons. In 1849 manuscript enrolment ceased, to be replaced by the deposit of acts printed on vellum.

In 1767 the rolls were ordered to be printed and publication was effected, certainly by 1783, of *Rotuli Parliamentorum* (n.d.) in six volumes, covering the period 1278–1503. A supplementary volume was afterwards issued to supply deficiencies in the Lords *Journals* and, in 1832, an analytical index. The text of this edition was drawn from uncollated transcripts, not the originals. For details of rolls subsequently published but excluded from this edition, refer to Mullins' [I] at pp. 10–11 (item 1.47), p. 268 (item 33.37), p. 270 (item 33.51); and see also *Records of the Parliament at Westminster*, edited F. W. Maitland, 1893, which contains the rolls of 1305.

Journals of the Lords and Commons

At first kept in manuscript, the journals have been printed more or less contemporaneously since 1762 (Commons) and 1819 (Lords). A record of the proceedings of the two Houses, they constitute the collection of precedents by which present-day parliamentary procedure is governed. They are of value therefore to constitutional historians and are the only authoritative source through which failed Bills (sometimes referred to as Acts) may be traced, or early statutes dated.

The Lords journals date from 1510. The early journals are in Latin, but entries in English appear in the sixteenth century.

The manuscript series was concluded in 1830, to be continued for record purposes by a printed journal bound in vellum and kept on deposit in the Victoria Tower. The printed edition, 1510 to date, was first ordered in 1767 and consists of over 200 volumes. From 1820 onwards each sessional volume contains an index. General indexes have also been issued. These cover varying groups of volumes up to 1863. Thereafter indexes are issued decennially.

Of importance is the material relating to judicial powers, exercised since the eighteenth century by Parliament. These include proceedings on original causes, 1621–93, and cases of privilege, of which approximately 700 were heard between 1660 and 1853. Such cases range from the privilege of a peer to have freedom from arrest (except on certain charges) to actions which involve contempt of the House by its members or strangers. For details of record material relating to impeachments and trials of peers, appeal cases and cases in error, (see page 183). For details of notes of proceedings and draft journals readily available in print and which include data edited out of the final journals, refer to Mullins' [1] at p. 253 (item 31.103), p. 258 (item 32.24), p. 269 (item 33.42) and p. 274 (item 33.83).

The Commons journals date from 1547; none, however, is extant for the period 1581–1603. Refer to Sir S. D'Ewes' *Journals*, 1682, which contains extracts from their contents, and Sir J. E. Neale's *Commons Journals of the Tudor Period*. TRHS, fourth series, vol. 3, 1920, pp. 136–70. Those for 1801–33 were destroyed in the fire of 1834 and the series in manuscript does not extend beyond 1800 as a result. Unlike the Lords' archive copies, no printed edition is kept for record purposes, though HLRO keep a printed set on file. The printed edition, 1547 to date was first ordered in 1742 and consists of over 200 volumes, each provided with an index. The quality of the early printed transcripts is variable but their accuracy from 1642 onwards is held to be much improved. Volumes of general indexes have been issued, covering varying groups of volumes to 1900. Thereafter indexes are issued decennially.

The material recorded may be of particular concern to legal researchers. The progress of each Bill is noted in detail, for, in regard to certain specific amendments the text may be set out in full. Similarly, where accounts and papers are presented these are recorded. In the seventeenth and eighteenth centuries the texts of many such papers were noted in full, while between 1801–34 the texts of the more important were printed in full in the appendix to the journal. Thereafter this practice was abandoned and all such papers ordered to be printed will be found in *Parliamentary Papers*. For details of notes of proceedings and draft journals, readily available in print and which include data edited out of the final journals, refer to Mullins' [1] at p. 243 (item 31.31), p. 250 (item 31.81) and p. 255 (item 32.6).

Parliamentary debates

The debates are invaluable as source material for the genesis of a statute. Through them may be traced the original purpose of a Bill and the intentions of its sponsors. Its reception by both Houses and the climate of political opinion, reflecting the social views of the age, which may require its modification may also be discovered. In addition, the debates are useful as biographical records, for through them much may be learned concerning the parliamentary career of a member.

Prior to 1803 the reporting of debates was held to be a breach of privilege, though up to 1682 (in the Commons) and to 1714 (in the Lords) notes of speeches were recorded in the journals upon occasion. Despite this ban, unofficial reporting did take place in the seventeenth and eighteenth centuries and reports of speeches may be located in a variety of apparently unlikely publications. *The Gentleman's Magazine* reported debates from 1733–46, 1749 and 1752–3 and includes the reports by Samuel Johnson for 1740–2. Periodical cumulative indexes were issued. *The Annual Register* contains the reports of debates after 1762 and has importance because of Edmund Burke's connection with it.

Newspaper reporting of debates began in 1768 and a number carried accounts of parliamentary proceedings, notably: the *London Daily Post and General Advertiser* (afterwards the *Public Advertiser*) which contained the 'Letters of Junius'; and *The Daily Universal Register* (afterwards *The Times*).

Numerous collections of early proceedings have been published. Of these the most comprehensive is *The Parliamentary History of England* ... , 1066 to 1803, edited by W. Cobbett and [after 1812] T. C. Hansard, 1806–20. Volumes 1–12 are entitled 'Cobbett's Parliamentary History of England', continued by T. C. Hansard as *The Parliamentary History of England*. This is now held to be the most reliable source for material on debates, particularly in the eighteenth century.

For the continuation of the debates as published by Hansard reference must be made to page 228.

Calendars of manuscripts of the House of Lords

Calendars of the Lords manuscripts, dating from 1450 to 1693 will be located in HMCR, notably series 1–8 and series 17, which contains thirteen volumes. Of concern to legal historians will be volume 7, which includes papers relating to the Act of Uniformity, the Regicides, and the Act of Indemnity; volume 9, which has material relating to the Test Act, Habeas Corpus Act, and the Statute of Frauds; volume 10, which includes the Exclusion Bill; and volume 11, which has material concerning the Bill of Rights. In general, they contain material relating to *Parliamentary Papers* (Lords and Commons) 1531–1714, judicial records such as papers on appeal and cases in error, and failed Bills of the House of Lords.

As from 1900, the series was continued as House of Lords Papers and the first, or volume 14, in continuation of the old series, is entitled Manuscripts of the House of Lords, 1693–5, New Series, volume 1, 1900. The series to date totals eleven volumes in the new series, or twenty-four altogether, and covers the manuscripts up to the first quarter of the eighteenth century. The entire series is listed, with brief notes on the parliamentary material, in M. F. Bond's *Guide to the Records of Parliament*, 1971, pp. 8–10.

Societies' publications

There are over eighty learned societies in England and Wales alone and these may be classified as either national or local, dependent upon their aims and interests. Such societies, financed by private subscription, usually issue quarterly, annual or occasional publications devoted to the issue of previously unpublished manuscript material, edited transcripts of the same, or the re-issue of early printed texts. Alternatively their publications may consist of articles of original scholarship. Much depends upon the nature and purpose of the society.

Almost all publish a certain quantity of material that may be of concern to the legal historian. The Royal Historical Society, founded in 1868 and which in 1897 absorbed the Camden Society, itself founded in 1831, has established a reputation for being 'the principal organization representing English historical scholarship'. Their combined publications number over 250 volumes and include important records relating to parliamentary and constitutional law. The Pipe Roll Society, formed in 1883, has issued to date some eighty volumes dealing with the records of the Court of Exchequer: pipe rolls, feet of fines, ancient charters and the Herefordshire Domesday. Local societies generally publish the assize rolls and quarter session records relevant to their geographical interests. The importance of society publications, therefore, as of the official collections noted above, lies in the fact that printed texts of the material issued by them may not easily be found elsewhere, if at all.

A number of societies, however, deserve special mention; their concern being wholly with legal materials of historic importance.

The Ames Foundation, established in the United States, requires notice since its publications relate wholly to English legal interests. It was founded in 1910 'for the purpose of continuing the advancement of legal knowledge and aiding the improvement of the law'. Seven volumes have been published, 1914–, and these consist of four volumes of Year Books, two bibliographies of law books and a volume of proceedings before JPs in the fourteenth and fifteenth centuries.

The Selden Society was founded in 1888, largely at the instigation of F. W. Maitland, to encourage the study and advance the knowledge of the history of English law. A prime purpose was the publication of volumes (some thirty to date) of previously unpublished Year Books. While all publications are numbered in sequence, the Year Books have a secondary series of sub-numbers. Other material issued includes plea rolls, eyre rolls, select cases in Chancery, Court of Admiralty, Court of Requests, Court of King's Bench, and Exchequer chamber, select charters and early treatises, as well as source material for historical studies of the Inns of Court and legal education. Publication commenced in 1888 and over 100 volumes have been issued to date. The texts of works in Latin and French are often given with English translations.

The Manorial Society was founded to publish material on the manorial and allied courts and twelve monographs were issued 1906–23.

The best general guide to the works of the learned societies of England and Wales remains Mullins' [1] and [11] which contains full bibliographical details relating to each volume published. Those concerned with the Selden Society should refer initially to the *General Guide to the Society's Publications*, compiled by A. K. R. Kiralfy and G. H. Jones, 1960. This gives detailed and indexed summaries of the contents of the introductions to the seventy-nine volumes then published.

The Stair Society was founded in order to encourage the study and learning of Scots law. Publication commenced in 1936 and continues, over thirty-five volumes having been issued to date. These include justiciary cases, treatises, the writings of influential jurists and volumes of miscellany.

Other Scottish societies whose publications include a proportion of legal materials are the Bannatyne Club, the New Spalding Club, the Scottish Burgh Record Society, the Scottish Historical Society, and the Scottish Record Society. Details of materials published will be found in C. S. Terry's *Catalogue of the Publications of Scottish historical ... clubs and societies and of the volume relating to Scottish history by HM Stationery Office, 1780–1908*, 1909. This work is continued by C. Matheson's *Catalogue of the Publications of Scottish historical and kindred clubs and societies ... including the reports of the Royal Commission on Historical MSS, 1908–27*, 1928.

Irish societies issuing occasional legal materials include the Royal Society of Antiquaries of Ireland, the Irish Archaeological Society and the Royal Irish Academy.

Also to be noticed are the Manx Society, who issued publications, 1859–95, and the Société Jersiaise pour l'Etude de l'Histoire, whose publications commenced in 1876.

LEGISLATION

Anglo-Saxon and Welsh

Anglo-Saxon legislation was originally preserved in the form of oral traditions and customs. The earliest recorded laws – enactments or dooms made by King and Witan – did not appear until the coming of St Augustine. The laws now extant cover the period *c.* 601–1020, but there is a gap of two centuries, *c.* 695–890, and there are various additions in private compilations of the eleventh and twelfth centuries. The dooms are not complete statements for they omit much customary law, *ie*, that which was undisputed or common knowledge.

The principal manuscript source material, which is not contemporary but dates from the eleventh century or later, is preserved in the Cottonian and Harleian collections at the British Library, at Corpus Christi, Cambridge, and at the Bodleian.

The most accessible printed edition of the dooms and one which contains most of the private compilations is *Ancient Laws and Institutes of England*, edited by B. Thorp, 1840.

This includes at pp. 300–3, De Institutis Lundoniae, which contains enactments relating to London gate tolls; at pp. 352–7 an ordinance concerning the Dunsaete, a law issued by Edgar (924–40); at pp. 426–30, Pseudo-Cnuts constitutiones de Foresta, a forgery compiled *c.* 1184 which expounds the administration and judicature of the forest temp. Henry II; at pp. 442–62, Leges Edwardi confessoris, compiled *c.* 1130–5, in which English institutions are described as they were prior to 1066 and temp. Henry I; at pp. 466–87, Leges Willelmi Conquestoris, which professes to contain the laws in the time of Edward the Confessor and promulgated by William I; and at pp. 497–631, Leges Henrici primi, which contain the coronation charter of Henry I.

The earliest Welsh laws are contained in a code promulgated by Howel Dda, *c.* 943–50 and ordered in three recensions: the Venedotian Code adopted for north Wales, the Dimetian Code for south Wales and the Gwentian Code for south-east Wales. The legal system formulated by these codes continued in operation until the time of Edward I's conquest of the Principality of Wales and existed in other parts of the country until final assimilation with English laws in 1536. The texts of the Welsh laws were printed in a collection, *Ancient Laws and Institutes of Wales*, edited by A. Owen, in 1841. Unfortunately this work is not wholly reliable and later editions of individual texts are to be preferred. These include A. W. Wade-Evans' *Welsh Medieval Law*, 1909, *Llyfr Blegywryd*, edited by S. Williams and E. Powell, 1942, and *Llyfr Iorwerth*, edited by A. William, 1960.

Magna Carta

There is no original of this charter to the terms of which King John gave his assent: 'in the meadow called Ronimede between Windsor and Staines on the fifteenth day of June in the seventeenth year of our reign.'

The nearest approximation to an original is a parchment containing preliminary draft terms and commences: 'Ista sunt capitula quae Barones petunt et dominus Rex concedit.' It contains articles or heads of agreement in forty unnumbered paragraphs, is cited as 'Additional MSS 4838', bears the King's seal and is held at the British Library.

Four copies of the charter are extant: two in the British Library. One cited as 'Cotton, charters, xiii, 31a', damaged by fire, is in part illegible and bears the mark of the King's seal; the second is cited as 'Cotton, Augustus II 106'. The third and fourth are in Lincoln and Salisbury cathedrals. The first two have corrections or omissions added at the foot of the text. The third and fourth incorporate these corrections in the body of the text. As to size, the Salisbury copy is seventeen inches by fourteen, running to approximately eighty lines.

It is most probable that the copy sealed on 15 June 1215 was in fact sealed on 19 June and antedated to the fifteenth, the day on which the King and Barons agreed the draft terms 'which served as a warrant to the Chancery for drawing it up and sealing it'. The text was not enrolled for eighty years, probably 'because there was no fitting roll for such an unprecedented document, which, though in form a charter, was really a statute, or even a legal code, whose proper place was in the Royal Treasury'. It was to be added to the Statute Roll some years after its re-affirmation in 1297, so that the Charter of the Statute Roll is not that of John, but of Henry III in modified form.

Early printed editions bearing 'Magna Carta' in their titles proliferated, from Pynson's edition of 1508 to Wight's edition of 1618. Unfortunately, all these reproduced the text of Edward I's Inspeximus of Henry III's re-issue of 1225; not the Charter of John. The earliest reliable edition in print is Sir W. Blackstone's *Magna Charta and Charta de Foresta*, 1759. This contains an account of the several originals and of the alterations made from the first granting to their final establishment in 1300. The other reproduction of note is contained in *Statutes of the Realm*.

For an assessment of the most notable of the many commentaries, reference should be made to W. S. McKechnie's *Magna Carta*, 2nd edn., 1914 at pp. 165–82.

Proclamations

From early medieval times the proclamation, a prerogative instrument of the Crown, was employed for two main purposes: firstly to call attention to and enforce thereby the observation of an existing enactment; or secondly to announce formally an executive Act. The use of proclamations as legislative instruments was undoubtedly at its height in early medieval society and decreased correspondingly through the centuries as the means of communication improved and the Royal Authority was diminished by the expanding powers of Parliament.

Writs of proclamation are recorded on the close rolls, patent rolls and the rolls of Parliament. (The last entry on the statute roll is that of 7 Henry V, 1414.) In Tudor times the entry on the patent roll is irregular, but as from 1600 entry is almost always the rule. Proclamations, however, were not so entered during the period of the Civil Wars; but from James II to the death of Queen Anne enrolment is regular and complete. Because of the often transitory nature of their contents few libraries hold anything like a complete collection of printed proclamations. A list of those issued prior to 1641 is contained in E. W. Pollard and G. R. Redgrave's *Short-Title Catalogue of Books Printed, 1475–1640*, 1926 at nos. 7761–9175. The location of proclamations may also be effected by reference to R. Steele's *Tudor and Stuart Proclamations 1485–1714*, 1910. This calendar lists at pp. xliv, xlviii the thirty-three principal collections held in England, Scotland and Ireland, while Sweet and Maxwell's *Bibliography*, vol. 1, 1955 at p. 549 lists four volumes of contemporary collections issued between 1550 and 1618. Full texts may be found in the *London Gazette* (originally the *Oxford Gazette*) November 1665–, proclamations (by Charles II) first being printed in retentive form in the 1680s. (Orders in Council were also printed in the *Gazette* as early as 1688.) More accessible collections of full texts may be located in P. L. Hughes and J. F. Larkin's *Tudor Royal Proclamations*, 1964–9, and in J. F. Larkin and P. L. Hughes' *Stuart Royal Proclamations*, 1973–83. This latter work contains all known proclamations for the reigns of both James I and Charles I.

The best general exposition on the subject is in Steele at pp. ix–cl. For their effectiveness as instruments of government see R. W. Heinze's *Proclamations of the Tudor Kings*, 1976, and F. A. Young's *Proclamations of the Tudor Queens*, 1976.

Statutes

Original sources

The modern definition of a statute as being a legislative Act of the Crown, established since the time of Henry VII, was meaningless to medieval lawyers, for whom no theory existed regarding the division of power between executive, legislative or judicial bodies. Prior to the fourteenth century there was no clear distinction between statutes and ordinances and the terminology for early laws varied accordingly: an assize under Henry II, Richard and John, a provision under Henry III, and a statute under Edward I. The term enactment might cover a bargain or contract, a grant of land, a peace treaty, a proclamation or a writ.

Though the Statute Book commences with the Provision of Merton, 1236, a law passed in the absence of the Commons, the earliest statute rolls commence in 1278, cover the period 6 Edward I to 8 Edward IV (1468), contain the enrolments of statutes of public concern, and are held by the PRO. This series is incomplete; gaps exist for the periods 1431–45 and 1468–89, so reference must be made to texts held in the Exchequer. From 1483 statutes were enrolled in their final form in the parliament rolls but a gap exists for 1483–97. The parliament rolls, classified by HLRO as original acts, run from 1497 to 1850, omitting legislation passed 1642–9, for which see Interregnum below. The texts are in manuscript and the handwriting is English. As from 1849, original acts are printed on vellum; duplicates being placed on deposit at the PRO. The term 'parliament roll' is not to be confused with those records described under Rolls of Parliament above. These – *Rotuli Parliamentorum* – cover the period 1290–1503, include some statutes omitted from the statute rolls and are invaluable for purposes of verification. The final edited and printed texts of Acts prior to 1713 will be located in *Statutes of the Realm* (see pages 268–9). For final texts of Acts, 1714–1797 reference must be made to the appropriate sessional volumes of public Acts. Since 1798 the final texts of all Acts will be found printed in the appropriate sessional volumes. The later collections, known as *Statutes at Large*, contain slightly abbreviated texts of Acts from 1235.

Public Acts

Sessional volumes of public Acts were first officially printed by Machlinia in 1483 and have been issued regularly ever since. Till 1793 the type used was 'black letter' and those volumes printed in this manner are highly regarded, being composed direct from the original Act. Few complete or incomplete sets for the sixteenth and seventeenth centuries are held outside the libraries of the Lords and Commons. Acts for the Commonwealth are excluded from this series.

Until 1814 public Acts were numbered in large roman numerals, from 1814 in small roman numerals and from 1868 in arabic characters.

The first printed collection was *Nova Statuta I Edward III to XXII Edward IV*, a folio edition attributed to Machlinia and printed *c*. 1484. Numerous other editions by various printers followed, including Berthelet's ambitious printing venture, *In this Volume are contained the Statutes Made and Established from the time of Kynge Henry the thirde unto the fyrste yere of King Henry the viii*. This, issued in two editions in 1543, was the first attempt at a complete collection from Magna Carta to date. By 1600 close on 300 editions by differing printers had been issued, the great majority being unauthorized, incomplete and with suspect texts.

Few later editions are free of the criticisms noted above, but the following require notice, since it is upon one or other of these that the majority of law libraries base their own collections which are then continued by the sessional volumes of the eighteenth and nineteenth centuries. The first is *Statutes at Large from Magna Charta to the Union 41 George III (1800)* by T. E. Tomlins and J. Raithby, 1811. The text for the period to 7 George II is based both on Ruffhead's edition of 1726–1800 and on Cay's proofs for an earlier edition by Cay and Ruffhead, issued 1758–1773; for the period 7 George II to 10 George III it is based on Ruffhead, as well as Hawkins' edition of 1734–58; and for the period 10 George III it is based on the King's Printers' copy. Local and Personal Acts were omitted from this edition, the titles only being printed. The second is *Statutes at Large from Magna Charta to 1761*, by D. Pickering [continued to 1806], 1762–1807. Pickering's edition, which contains the same matter as Cay, also omits the texts of Local and Personal Acts. Both Tomlins, and Raithby and Pickering, were continued by a King's Printers' edition. For informative notes on the collected editions of the statutes reference should be made to Sweet and Maxwell's *Guide*, p. 11.

The Statutes of the Realm is the authoritative edition for use when reference is required to statutes prior to 1714, but is known to be imperfect and where doubt arises only the parliament and statute rolls will suffice. *The Statutes of the Realm* [1225–1713] edited by A. Luders [and others], 1810–22, was published by the Record Commissioners, indexes being subsequently issued. It contains a copy of all statutes in force or repealed from the Statute of Merton to 1713, including the 'Statutes of Uncertain Date' (for details of which see below) and excluding only the period of the Commonwealth. A parallel translation is provided of all early statutes not in English. The historical introduction to volume 1, which is reprinted in part in *Select Essays in Anglo-American Legal History*, by various authors, volume 2, 1908 at pp. 169–208, is bibliographically valuable.

Abridgments

In legal bibliography the terms abridgment, digest and encyclopedia are often interchangeable, the terminology in use at a given time owing more to fashion than to science. For those relating to the Year Books (see page 284), and to case-law, (see page 157).

The earliest printed abridgment, and one relating to statutes, was the *Abbreviamentum Statutorum*, printed *c.* 1481 by Lettou and Machlinia. Written in French, and arranged alphabetically, it covered statutes issued to 1455. Others followed, notably J. Rastell's *The Statutes: Prohemium*, issued in 1519. This offered transcripts in English and contained the texts of certain Acts not included in *Statutes at Large*. It is distinguished by the scrupulous care with which the text was edited. Abridgments of sessional Acts also commenced publication in the early sixteenth century, while the first abridgment of statutes wholly or partly in force was edited by F. Pulton and issued in 1606.

One of the first attempts to produce an abridgment of the general law was William Sheppard's *Epitome*, of 1656, subsequently re-issued as the *Grand Abridgment* in 1675. Principally a recension of Coke's *Institutes*, though rearranged under alphabetical heads, it was, because written in English, popular in its day. More memorable abridgments, however, were to follow. Matthew Bacon's *New Abridgment of the Law* was issued in 1736–66, ran to seven editions and is still consulted. Of this work Winfield wrote: 'he did better what Sheppard had failed to do ... combine an exposition of the law with a digest of it.' Charles Viner's *General Abridgment of Law and Equity* proved itself a monumental work. Written in Law French over a period of fifty years, it was finally published in English by the author between 1742–53. It runs to 23 folio volumes, and though the sub-headings lack the clarity of Bacon's, it remains indispensable as a work of reference for historians. A second edition, a supplement and an index were to follow and prove its worth. John Comyns' *Digest of the Laws of England* was published between 1762–7 and was to run to five editions. Similar in construction to Bacon's, it has a more elaborate arrangement of divisions and sub-divisions and is admirably indexed.

Subsequent attempts to encapsule the law into a single work were to be corporate rather than individual.

Private, Local and Personal Acts

The history of both Private Acts (styled Personal Acts since 1948) and of Local and Personal Acts (styled Local Acts since 1868) is bibliographically complicated as a result of changes in nomenclature and classification. It was not until 1539 that the distinction between public and private Acts was, for the first time, specifically stated on the enrolment in Chancery. From then on until 1797, Acts were classified as being either public or private; the latter term being used ostensibly to describe an Act not held to be of general application. Yet much pre-1797 legislation, classified as public, was in fact of a local nature.

Acts of a private or local nature were not enscribed on the statute rolls but were normally recorded on the parliament rolls: the Exchequer series, 1290–1322 and Chancery series, 1327–1850. From 1593 to 1757 the texts of Private Acts, first recorded on the parliament rolls *c.* 1500, were omitted, titles alone being listed. Since such Acts originated as private petitions, reference for the original texts, thirteenth to sixteenth centuries, must be made to: the Chancery records, the parliamentary and council proceedings (Exchequer) and the ancient petitions, in the PRO. For details of the 'original' texts of Private Acts for the seventeenth century, see Bond, page 99. Private Bills (printed) 1705 to date are held by HLRO, but the texts are not necessarily true copies of the final Acts.

Acts of a private, local nature, stemming from private Bills, appeared in the early printed sessional volumes of (Public) Acts and, not being distinguished as such, were so printed until 1539. From 1571 the titles only of Private Acts were printed; arabic numerals being allotted in the title lists of these Acts despite their not being officially numbered. Private printing of the Bills (initially for the benefit of the Lords) was begun in 1705, causing subsequent bibliographical concern since the prints were entitled 'Acts' – which they are not. Between 1802–14 Private Acts were briefly reclassified as Local and Personal Acts but were not ordered to be printed. Indeed no Private Act was officially printed till 1815. From then onwards a proportion, ordered to be printed, was issued in the sessional volumes of Public General Acts. These Private Acts were numbered in a separate series in arabic characters. Those not printed, including divorce, estate, name and naturalization Acts, can only be located by reference to the original record copies in HLRO. Many are available only as Bills printed by the parliamentary agents, copies of which may be obtained from the Copyright Office, House of Lords.

The sessional volumes of (Public) Acts from 1539 also included statutes originating in private Bills but not deemed to be private. These statutes, entitled Local Acts declared Public, were numbered in one series with the Public Acts in large roman numerals. From 1641 they were known as Local and Personal Acts declared Public and, from 1753, were numbered in one series after those Public Acts originating in public Bills. As from 1798 they were reclassified as Public Local and Personal Acts (declared Public and to be judicially noticed) and printed with the Public Acts (now Public General Acts) as a separately numbered series in arabic characters. From 1803–13 they became Local and Personal Acts (to be judicially noticed) and from 1814 Local and Personal Acts (declared Public) numbered now in small roman numerals.

Local and Personal Acts in company with Private Acts were not collected into a separate series in volume form until 1869.

As a result of lack of availability few, except the older libraries (a total of twenty-nine in the British Isles) possess even partially complete runs of these Acts. The most complete is in HLRO as follows:

Sessional volumes of collected Local and Personal Acts, 1798–1875; a series of collected separate prints.

Sessional volumes of collected Local Acts, 1876 to date, in continuation of the above.

Sessional volumes of collected Private Acts, 1815 to date; a series of printed texts of Private Acts not included in the above two series, such as enclosure, tithe and estate Acts.

Two early guides to location require notice. First, the *Analytical Table of the Private Statutes, 1727–1834* by G. Bramwell, 2 volumes, 1813–35. This is arranged chronologically, alphabetically and also according to subject matter. Second, Salt's *Index to Titles*, of 1863. This covers the period Anne to George I inclusive, deals with 2,231 Acts, and was issued privately in three parts. The list in *Statutes at Large* gives the full title of all Private Acts after 1509 and House of Commons sessional paper 399 of 1914 lists completely the special class known as inclosure Acts. *A Chronological table of Local Legislation*, recording the effect on Local and Personal Acts 1797–1973 and Private Acts, 1539–1973 by legislation enacted between 1 January 1925 and 31 December 1973, was issued by the Law Commission in 1985 for limited circulation only. Since Acts passed before 1925 were listed only if an effect is recorded, the work lies outside the scope of this chapter. For details see page 103.

Commencement, jurisdiction, duration and citation

Until 1793, when under 33 Geo. III *c.* 13 it became obligatory to endorse the date of Royal Assent upon an Act, no date was fixed for the coming into force of an Act. Unless otherwise specified, an Act came into force on the first day of the parliamentary session in which it was passed, irrespective of the fact that Royal Assent was still wanting. This rule arose from the convenient fiction that the whole session lasted but one day.

The only effective means of dating the making of an Act is by following its progress through the Lords journals which, until 1752, record the year of grace as commencing on 25 March (old calendar) not 1 January (new calendar) as now.

Statutes of the following Parliaments were held to be in force in England and Wales: the Parliament of England, 1236–1707 (ended by the Treaty of 1707); the Parliament of Great Britain, 1708–1800 (ended by the Act of Union, 1801); and the Parliament of the United Kingdom of Great Britain and Ireland, 1801–1921. For the influence of this legislation on Scotland, Ireland, Channel Islands and Isle of Man, see below. In general, statutes passed since 1707 (Scotland) and 1801 (Ireland) applied to these countries unless excepted. But the Isle of Man was held to be excluded unless specially noticed.

Unlike Scottish Acts, English statutes do not lapse through non-usage.

Difficulty in the location or identification of early statutes may be avoided if it is remembered that the modern system of citation, superimposed upon the entire Statute Book, may create problems, especially when references occur that use a different style. None should arise when the Act in question is one passed in a session that lies wholly within the regnal year and is the only session in that year.

But if two sessions lie wholly within a single regnal year it is necessary to distinguish Acts as 'statute I' and 'statute II'. Thus 13 Charles II, stat. I, *c*. 1. and 13 Charles II, stat. II, *c*. 1. are not at all the same Act. Again, a double citation is used if Acts are passed in a session that covers two regnal years; thus 13 & 14 Charles II, *c*. 23.

Sir Cecil Carr in his article, 'Citation of Statutes' in *Cambridge Legal Essays*, 1926, recommended in the interests of uniformity that it was desirable to cite Acts down to 1713 as in *Statutes of the Realm*. *The Chronological Table of the Statutes* shows the variants between citations in *Statutes of the Realm* and Ruffhead's *Statutes at Large*.

Availability of statutes

The original Acts not Private and Public are kept as from 1497 in HLRO. Until 1850 each Act was on a separate MS roll. Since then, they have been reprinted in block form. The original Acts are numbered consecutively by session regardless of whether they are Public or Private. They may be consulted on application by members of the public who wish to collate the King's Printer's copy with the parliament roll, or the original Act, or the vellum print. A microform service is also provided. In the case of early Acts, variations sometimes occur between printed editions and official records; then reference may be necessary to the printed rolls of Parliament.

The King's Printer

King's (Queen's) Printers have been appointed since the early sixteenth century with the franchise of publishing statutes, Royal proclamations and other public documents. For details of office holders see W. Blackstone's *Reports*, vol. 1, 1828, pp. 103–21. Following publication of the *Statutes of the Realm* (see pages 268–9) the KP copies are the chief printed source for statutes passed since 1713, remaining, however, only *prima facie* evidence. Copies used to be printed in three forms, folio, quarto and octavo until 1835. Since 1849 the KP has made two vellum prints, one kept in the House of Lords, the other in the PRO. In 1882 HMSO became the Queen's Printer of statutory material.

Statutes of Uncertain Date

This is the term given to a group of statutes believed by Maitland to be apocryphal (see Maitland, F. W. *Collected Papers*, 1911, vol. 2, p. 39). They were included in *Statutes of the Realm* between Edward II and Edward III on the grounds that they were issued in the last year of Edward II's reign. For a list of these statutes, forty-four in number, see W. S. Holdsworth's *History of English Law*, vol. 2, 2nd edn, 1936, p. 604. Now, some are considered to be tracts from law treatises, some administrative measures, some ordinances, others rules relating to court procedure. Only a minority is held to be statutes.

The Interregnum: 1649–60

The last Act to receive Charles I's assent was 1640 (16 Cha. I) *c.* 37. But it was not until January 1649 that Parliament assumed sovereignty. During the Interregnum a considerable body of legislation was passed by Parliament but, for historical reasons, little original material has survived. For original source material, reference must be made to the Lords journals and the *Book of Orders and Ordinances*, 1640–95, both held in HLRO. Each contain textual variations in readings and both are essential for comparative purposes.

The term 'ordinance' was adopted to signify a declaration of the two Houses of Parliament, authorized without the sanction of the King. For political reasons the legislation thus passed, 1642–60 alternated in terminology between 'ordinance' and 'Act' six times. During this period enactments were always issued separately, not in sessional volumes. Few complete sets have survived.

Under authority, contemporary collections, not always complete, were compiled; the most notable being those by E. Husband, issued in 1642 and 1646, and that by Henry Scobell, printed in 1658.

The most accessible edition is *Acts and Ordinances of the Interregnum*, 1642–60, edited by C. H. Firth and R. S. Rait, 1911. The less important matter omitted belongs almost entirely to the period 1642–9. The Introduction, pp. iii–xxxviii, in volume 3 contains a full bibliographical statement on the legislative publications of the period.

Scotland

In Scotland, owing to the almost total lack of extant records, the sources of customary law are a matter for conjecture, though Anglo-Saxon as well as Celtic influences are discernible. For the period between 410 and the introduction of feudal law by David I reference should be made to the *Ancient Laws and Institutes of Ireland* (see page 278) and the *Ancient Laws and Institutes of Wales* (see page 264), as well as to *Ancient Laws and Customs of the Burghs of Scotland*, by C. Innes, 1868–1910.

The law of Scotland has developed from a wide variety of sources, absorbing the influence of Mosaic and Roman, French, Dutch and Canon as well as English law. Differing sources and histories created differing systems which the Union has served to emphasize rather than efface. Indeed, owing to the Union with England in 1707 there is more emphasis on the historical aspect of statute law in Scotland, in which country it falls naturally into three parts. The first period lasts until 1424, when James I held his first Parliament after his years of captivity in England; the second covers the period 1424 to 1707; while the third continues from 1707 to date.

In general, original source material will be found in the Acts and decrees and the *Acta Dominorum* held in manuscript in the General Register House, together with the Acts of Sederunt which, while nominally regulating the procedure of the supreme tribunal – the Court of Session – were often held to be of wider application.

The earliest extant statutory records consist of six rolls for the period 1292–3, 1368–9 and 1388–9; no original parliamentary records previous to 1466 surviving in any quantity. Printed Acts relating to this lost period are based principally on transcripts of varying degrees of authenticity and reliability, and for information on which see Lord Cooper's 'Early Scottish Statutes revisited', *Juridical Review*, volume 64, 1952, pp. 197–203.

For a detailed introduction to the period 1124–1423 refer to the introduction by Cosmo Innes in volume 1 of *Acts of the Parliaments of Scotland*, noted below.

In 1960 there was published the first in a projected series of eight volumes entitled *Regesta Regum Scottorum*, 1153–1424. This set aims to bring together in one collection all the authenticated royal documents of Scotland for the period, with scholarly introductions to each volume. Three had appeared by 1984.

Sessional laws were first issued in printed form in 1565 (printing being introduced into Scotland in 1507) but were not issued with such apparent regularity as English sessional legislation, since the early Scottish parliaments met infrequently. For details of these, see Sweet and Maxwell's *Legal Bibliography*, volume 5, 1957. After 1707, the last official Scottish edition of sessional Acts issued 1718–72 was entitled *British Acts from 6 Anne to 12 George III*. This was in fact a binder's title, but is now so known. Subsequently those statutes referring specifically to Scotland were issued as part of the set of British sessional Acts for each regnal year.

The earliest collection of note was the *Actis and Constitutionis of the Realme of Scotland* covering the period 1424–1564 and issued in 1566. This was the third and most important of the eight collections in the series known as the Black Acts because of their black-letter type. Another version, *The Lavves and Actes of Parliament*, collected by J. Skene and covering the period 1424–1597, was published in 1597. Known as Skene's Acts, it has been criticized for its textual errors. A later collection, much cited in the courts was *The Lavves and Acts of Parliament*, collected by Sir T. Murray, of Glendook, and printed in 1681. A reprint of Skene with seventeenth-century Acts added, it was best known simply as Glendook's Acts. The inadequacy of these collections was to result in the publication of *The Acts of the Parliaments of Scotland*, 1124–1707, edited by T. Thomson and C. Innes, 1814–75. Volumes 5 and 6, being unsatisfactory, were replaced in 1870 and 1870–2 respectively. Volume 1 was published with interpolated material resulting in six separate paginations. Repaginated copies in limited quantity were available under restriction, while the general index contains directions for repaginating volume 1. Issued under the direction of the Record Commission, this remains the authoritative edition for Scottish statutes to 1707.

Scottish statutes, unlike English statutes, could fall into desuetude, either in whole or in part, and this doctrine is still held to apply to statutes promulgated prior to 1707. It is thought that the United Kingdom Parliament has power to repeal pre–1707 Acts, subject to certain restrictions imposed by the Treaty of 1707.

Acts passed by the Parliament of Scotland prior to 1707 are cited by the calendar year and chapter serial number. The serial number, however, varies between the two most commonly cited editions; the Record Commission edition of 1814–75 and Murray of Glendook's edition of 1681.

Digest Practicks

The term Practick means a precedent but not necessarily a binding precedent. The Practicks may be divided into two classes: those known as Decision Practicks (for details of which see page 169); and those known as Digest Practicks. The latter were later in composition but included not only notes of decisions but also excerpts from statutes and the 'auld lawes', as well as much early material drawn from the registers. They were thus digests or encyclopedias of the law, not dissimilar to English abridgments and exercised a considerable influence on the institutional writers (see below). In general, the later Practicks were ordered alphabetically, their contents grouped under subject heads. James Balfour's *Practicks*, issued 1754 but written *c.* 1580, included Supreme Court decisions, aimed to cover the whole field of law and was based wholly on practice. It was to be recognized as 'a work of undoubted authority'. Robert Spotiswoode's *Practicks*, issued in 1706, is noted for its accuracy and is still much cited in court. Thomas Hope was the author of two works: firstly the *Minor Practicks*, written prior to 1634 and first issued in 1726 which is, in content, a treatise on different legal topics and so belies its title; and secondly the *Major Practicks*, not printed till 1937–8 by the Stair Society. It is a major work on seventeenth-century Scots law still virtually unknown to the profession.

Ireland

The earliest known Irish law is found in two major codes, the Senchus Mor, a code of legal usages compiled perhaps in the ninth or tenth century and dealing with civil law, and the Book of Aicill, a survey of the criminal law, both codes having a continuing influence till the end of the fifteenth century. Their texts will be found in *Ancient Laws and Institutes of Ireland*, edited by W. N. Hancock and A. G. Richey, 1865–1901. Volumes 1–3 contain the Senchus Mor, volume 3 also containing the Book of Aicill; volumes 4–5 contain the Brehon law tracts, and volume 6 contains a glossary to the other volumes. The text is in Irish with an English translation. This edition is held to be unreliable. Of more value is D. A. Binchy's monumental *Corpus Iuris Hibernici*, issued in the vernacular, 1978. This is a collection of the records of native Irish law which have been preserved in the manuscripts emanating from the professional schools. The basic structure of this law was pre-Christian, for Irish legal sources cover a span of almost a thousand years.

While certain English statutes were enforceable in Ireland as early as the last quarter of the thirteenth century, the Irish Parliament in Dublin, established in the same period, was subservient to the Parliament in London, and was principally concerned with ratifying such English statutes as could be held to be applicable to Ireland. In 1495 under Poynings' Law, 10 Hen. VII *c.* 22 (Ir.) it was held that all English statutes of general application should apply to Ireland. In 1782 the Irish Parliament achieved independence until self-abolition in 1800, when the new United Kingdom was formed.

The earliest extant Irish legislation dates from 1278. For published statute rolls see *Statutes and Ordinances and Acts of the Parliament of Ireland, King John to [22 Edward IV]*, edited by H. F. Berry and J. F. Morissey, 1907–39. Issued under the direction of the Irish Record Office, these contain transcripts with English translations of the Latin and French texts.

The confused history of the English conquest is reflected in the uncertainty that exists concerning full bibliographical details about sessional publications. The earliest recorded are the *Statuta, Ordinationes, Acta et Provisiones*, covering the period 1584–5 and issued by C. Barker sometime after 1585. No Parliament thereafter was summoned for twenty-seven years, while not till 1603 did English authority reign supreme. Parliaments were held intermittently between 1559 and 1713, only eleven being summoned, but were thereafter held regularly, with lapses of not more than twelve months between each, until 1800. Sessional laws are recorded for the period 1634–1800 and for details of these see Sweet and Maxwell's *Legal Bibliography*, volume 4, 1957 at p. 89. Until 1782 sessional laws are in general re-enactments of such statutes already in force in England, but which could suitably be held applicable to Ireland.

The first collection of statutes was printed to Tottell in 1572 and covered the period 10 Hen. VI to 14 Eliz. I. Other collections were subsequently published, the principal and most accurate being *Statutes at Large passed in Parliaments held in Ireland*, 1310–1767, issued between 1765–69. A later collection, not however titled *Statutes at Large*, was published between 1786 and 1801, covering the years 1310 to 1800.

Channel Islands and Isle of Man

In Jersey the common law stems directly from the customary law of the ancient Duchy and the leading authority on this law remains a work compiled in, probably, the thirteenth century. Numerous extant editions were printed in the years between *c.* 1483 and 1578, but the 'authorized' text normally cited in the Royal Court remains *Le Grand Coustumier du pays et duché de Normandie*, composées par Guillaume le Rouillé d'Alencon, 1539. An annotated edition of this work was issued in 1831 by W. L. de Gruchy, which gives both Latin and French texts but this has not superseded a much earlier work: G. Terrien's *Commentaires du Droit Civil*, 1574. The principal authority for the maintenance of customary law will be found in Privy Council decisions (see page 180). Reference must also be made to the sixteenth-century *Coutume Réformée de Normandie* which expounds the Norman law of that period. There are a number of commentaries upon this work, the most notable being Bérault's *Coutume réformée* 2nd edn. of 1614, Godefroy's *Commentaires* of 1626 and Pesnelle's *Coutume* of 1704. For a historical survey see R. G. Le Herissier's *Development of the Government of Jersey*, 1771–1972, 1974.

Legislation has customarily been enacted by the States, the central legislative body. Refer to *Lois et régléments*, 1771 to date; part of the text of the early volumes is in French and the binder's title reads 'Recueil des Lois'.

In Guernsey the civil law of the island is based in part only upon the 'Ancienne Coutume de Normandie' and, as a result, the principal authority for citation in court remains the commentary by Terrien, noted above. Similarly reference must be made to the *Coutume Réformée* and, in particular, the commentaries most frequently cited in court. These are Bérault's, also noted above, and H. Basnage's *La coutume réformée du païs et duché de Normandie*, 1678–81. For legislation prior to 1800 reference must be made to *Recueil D'Ordonnances de la Cour Royale de L'Isle de Guernsey*, covering the period 1533–1932 and issued between 1852–1933; also to *Actes des Etats*, covering the period 1605–1845 and issued between 1851–1938.

In the Isle of Man, legislation has always been enacted by the Tynwald, a legislature that dates from the time of the Norse Kings, who conquered the island in the ninth century. Except for C. Briscoe's *Statute Laws of the Isle of Man*, 1797, the bulk of Manx legislation is available only in post-1800 works, for which see page 120.

REPORTS OF CASES

Plea rolls

The extant medieval records of the early superior courts are best known by the term 'plea rolls', which describes their form and function. Their genealogy is confusing owing to the complicated history of their classification and arrangement, but the historical origin of some dates from the last quarter of the twelfth century. Among the most important are the curia regis rolls of the courts *coram rege* and *de banco*, later the King's Bench and Common Pleas. The plea rolls contain a succinct summary of each case, recording the place and date of trial, the names of the parties, the nature of the proceedings and the judgment awarded.

In 1884 Sir Paul Vinogradoff discovered a collection of cases drawn from the plea rolls. This was subsequently published as *Bracton's Notebook*, edited by F. W. Maitland, 1887. It contains approximately 2,000 cases and provided the raw material upon which Bracton drew for his celebrated treatise, *De Legibus*, noted below. The value of the plea rolls to the historian lies in the data they record, omitted by the Year Books (see below).

At least forty volumes of select pleas have been printed since the nineteenth century – by the Record Commission, the Pipe Roll Society and others, principally the Selden Society. For details of these refer to Sweet and Maxwell: *Legal Bibliography*, volume 1, 1955, pp. 70–4.

References to printed decisions are made as to the page of a treatise in the normal manner, thus: Select Cases in the Court of King's Bench (S.S. 1936–9) ii, 415.

Year Books

These are the 'law reports' of English medieval society. They differ from the modern concept of reporting in that they are not simply factual and objective, but highly subjective. As a result, they are invaluable to both legal and social historians, whilst their language, for speeches are reported verbatim, provide an untapped source for the philologist. Written in Law French, they run in an almost unbroken sequence from the reign of Edward I to Richard III and thereafter intermittently to 27 Hen. VIII, when they end. Excepting the plea rolls, they are the only extant accounts of legal doctrine as laid down by judges of the fourteenth and fifteenth centuries and, being contemporary reports, are of the utmost value. The reason for their compilation – whether as notes for students or as aids for practitioners – is still obscure; a topic for scholarly disputation.

A considerable quantity of manuscripts is still extant, though few are originals and the majority are to be located in libraries at Oxford and Cambridge and in London. No complete list of these exists, though attempts have been made at compilation, *eg*, J. Nicholson's *Register of Manuscripts of Year Books Extant*, 1956. Nicholson, though useful, is incomplete and occasionally inaccurate in defining ownership, L. W. Abbott's *Law Reporting in England, 1485–1585*, 1973, pp. 257–305 lists Year Books for the period in question, whilst J. H. Baker's *English Legal Manuscripts*, vol. 1, 1975–, aims at completion.

Numerous printed editions exist. A number were first issued by William de Machlinia, *c.* 1481; Richard Pynson printed fifty editions of various terms; while Richard Tottell, to whom 225 editions are attributed, commenced printing these in 1553.

The 'standard' edition is Maynard's. This may be entitled *Year Books; or Reports in the following reigns [1 Edward II to 27 Henry VIII], with notes to Brooke and Fitzherbert's Abridgments* [edited by Sir J. Maynard], 1678–80. The language is Law French, the volumes are folio size, the print is black-letter, and each part has a table of the principal matters. Two parts are usually bound together, but the parts are not numbered and only part one contains matter not previously printed. The coverage of the regnal years is incomplete.

Other editions require notice:

First: the Rolls Series edition, edited by A. J. Horwood and L. O. Pike between 1863–1911 and covering the years 20–22, 30–35 Edward I and 11–20 Edward III. This was made up of previously unpublished material and is notable in that the reports are compared with the original plea roll entries.

Second: the Selden Society, issued as part of that society's publications and edited by F. W. Maitland and others. Over thirty volumes of Year Books not previously printed have been issued and a modern English translation is given against the original text.

Both editions are equipped with extensive and informative introductions.

The black-letter editions of the Year Books omit any identification of the speaker and this is best rectified by reference to E. Foss's *The Judges of England*, 1848–64 and J. H. Baker's *The Order of Serjeants at Law*, 1984.

Cases are cited by the regnal years and the law term in which the plea was heard, and the number of the plea is also given.

Abbreviations are commonly used. Thus, YB 11 Hen. 6; Hil. pl. 10; or Pasch. pl. 1. Where references contain a capital A or B this is usually to Maynard's edition. In this, the A at the head of the page indicates where the recto of the earlier folio (edition) begins; the B, halfway down, indicates where the verso of the earlier folio (edition) commences. With the modern editions reference is made thus: (RS) and (SS).

Excepting reprints, the last Year Book to be printed covered part of 1535–6 and was issued by Myddylton before 1547.

Thereafter, though Year Books in manuscript continued to be produced, and some are extant for the later years of Henry VIII, none was published. Their eclipse was due not to the advent of printing but to other causes; a change in the style of reporting which, in Plowden's hands, was to prove immensely successful; the needs of authors to protect their reputation in an age lacking the certainties offered by a copyright Act; the commercial advantage to be gained by both author and publisher through a personalization of the reporting; and a growing realization that the year book format no longer met satisfactorily the changing needs of the profession. Their language had fallen into desuetude and their emphasis upon the arguments leading to the formulation of the issue in a case lost its value as a result of the change from oral to written pleadings. Legal interest was developing a concern with the decisions themselves. The period 1556–71 is a period of curious if expectant silence, but at the end of it the birth of law reporting took place (see page 135).

Abridgments

The order of arrangement in the Year Books was chronological and, side notes apart, it was difficult to locate the desired information in the mass of material available in manuscript and print. Abridgments digesting the essential under suitable heads were needed and provided. Statham's *Epitome*, of c. 1490, and the *Abridgment of the Book of Assizes*, of c. 1509, deserve mention. The latter is known to modern bibliographers as *Liber Assisarium*, but is not to be confused with the title of the same name in the Year Book series. Two major works, however, require special notice, since their authors did much to enhance the art of the abridger. The first is Sir Anthony Fitzherbert's *La Graunde Abridgment*, issued by Rastell in 1516. This records 14,039 cases under 260 titles alphabetically arranged. Invaluable as an epitome of case-law, it is noted for its accuracy and its system of arrangement, while its structure established a pattern for future writers. Robert Brooke's *La Graunde Abridgment* was published by Tottell in 1573. Based on Fitzherbert, it records over 20,000 cases under 404 titles and abridges the Year Books of Henry VII and Henry VIII. Both works include matter not contained in the Year Books.

It must be noted that the term 'case' covers notes, opinions and points drawn from cases.

TREATISES

England

The early treatise was either an exposition upon a statute or a collection of like statutes, designed to illuminate a particular branch of the law, or it was a book of practice to inform the lawyer as to the necessary expertise required for the conduct of his craft. Treatises were books on the law rather than books about the law – though there were exceptions – and they were written by practitioners for practitioners, rarely for the edification of the student.

In general, such treatises could not be regarded as literary sources of law for they contained only opinions as to the state of the law, not the law itself; thus they were not books of authority and could not be cited in court. But a rule was formulated which made permissible the citing in argument of the works of dead authors, though not those living. In practice, only a minority of works acquired a prestige that made them acceptable to the justiciary almost without question.

The construction of early treatises is at variance with that of the modern textbook, which assumed its present shape in the nineteenth century. They were descriptive rather than creative and the amount of exposition was at first very small. The realization that principles might be deduced from cases, and the cases in turn cited, was slow to develop, so that it is often hard to know where fact ends and comment begins. Systematic exposition was uncommon, texts lacked coherence and authors enjoyed digressions, too often uncritical of material cannibalized from other writers. Intellectual discipline was wanting. The lack of copyright protection did not help. New editions were likely to be edited by printers who altered texts unhindered; while a lack of uniformity in spelling, combined with indifferent proof-reading, did little to assist the establishment of standards for accurate texts and references.

The earliest treatise on English common law was written in the twelfth century by Ranulph de Glanvil. Compiled in Latin between 1187–9, his *Tractatus de legibus* was printed by Tottell *c.* 1554 and 'presents a vivid image of the importance of land law and of procedure in mediaeval England'.

In the thirteenth century a number of anonymous tracts were circulated dealing with procedure, as well as the earliest extant manuscript of the *Registrum Brevium* or Register of Writs afterwards printed in 1531. In the middle of the century a great work was written describing the law and practice of the King's courts and of the judicial commissions: H. de Bracton's *De Legibus et consuetudinibus Angliae*, printed by Tottell in 1569. Bracton contains 500 references to decided cases, fathered a number of epitomes, and remains a monument to medieval jurisprudence.

The first law book to be printed was a masterpiece: Thomas Littleton's *Tenures*, printed by Lettou and Machlinia, *c.* 1481. It was in French, but an English translation was issued before 1538. By 1628, eighty-two editions or variants of editions had been printed. Justly praised for its brevity and lucidity, it remains still a model of the art of treatise writing.

Works published between 1475–1603 include formula books, precedents of pleading (known then as 'books of entries'), readings of the Inns of Court and tracts containing selections of writs. There were works for lay judges dealing with the functions of justices of the peace, manorial courts, courts baron and courts leet, as well as books on special topics such as Admiralty and the law merchant. Others dealt with special jurisdictions such as the palatinates of Chester, Durham and Lancaster.

In 1628, Edward Coke had published the *First Part of the Institutes of the Lawes of England*. Three further parts followed, the last being printed in 1644. Coke surveyed the entire field of law and restated it for his age, but he did more; he asserted the supremacy of the law with an authority that was overwhelming and which remains to this day. A modern edition, however, is needed since a proportion of his citations is known to be uncertain.

The seventeenth century also saw notable works by Heneage Finch, Francis Bacon, John Selden and Matthew Hale, as well as a stream of treatises by lesser men in response to the growing complexities of the law.

The eighteenth century saw a technical improvement in the standard of treatise writing and the volume of output increased though, with the exception of Gilbert, writers individually were less prolific and their work undistinguished. Yet the age produced a classic work aimed originally at academics not practitioners: William Blackstone's *Commentaries on the Laws of England*, 1765–9. Notable for its learning, its clarity and its style it ran into thirteen editions before 1800 and is still cited as a book of authority.

For highly select lists of notable treatise writers refer to the following: *Bibliography of British history*, Tudor Period, 1485–1603, editor, C. Read, 1959, and the companion volumes for the Stuart Period, 1603–1714, editor, M. F. Keeler, 1970, and the Eighteenth Century, 1714–1789, editors S. Pargellis and D. J. Medley, 1951. More comprehensively balanced lists will be found in the *New Cambridge bibliography of English literature*, ed. G. Watson at columns 2277–2286 in vol. 1 (600–1660), 1974 and at columns 1911–1916 in vol. 2 (1660–1800), 1971. J. N. Adams and G. Averley's *Bibliography of eighteenth century literature*, 1982 is a subject and author catalogue including law treatises and all law-related literature in the main legal collections in England. *The eighteenth century short title catalogue: the British Library collections*, edited by R. Alston, 1983–, must also be noticed. This microfiche edition records over 150,000 letterpress items held, and an index of selected genres is included. *ECST* is also available as an online database on BLAISE-LINE together with the catalogues of the British Library's Department of Printed Books (DPB). A valuable aid to identification is W. H. Bryson's *Dictionary of sigla and abbreviations ... in law books before 1607*, 1975. This provides citations both to MSS and printed books.

Scotland

The earliest treatises are the 'Buikes of the Auld Lawes' written before 1500. The first is the *Regiam Majestatem*, a collection of medieval royal and feudal laws with other treatises added, two-thirds of the whole consisting of Glanville's *Tractatus*, suitably modified. The second is the *Quoniam Attachiamenta*, a series of 'statutes' attributed to early kings. Both works are anonymous, deal with court procedure, and were published together in 1597 under the title of the former. Skene's edition of 1609, issued in both Latin and Scottish remains the authoritative edition.

It is impossible to offer a precise definition of an institutional writer. It is perhaps sufficient to say of those under review that their work, owing much, perhaps, to the influence of Roman law writings, have a scope and depth not to be found in even the best of treatises, and all are held to be of high authority. Thomas Craig, author of the *Jus Feudale* published in 1655, was the first. He has been described as 'the first systematic writer on Scots law' and his work remains the standard authority on feudal law; a disquisition of enormous learning which in form provided a model for his successors. James Dalrymple, Viscount Stair, issued his *Institutions of the Law of Scotland* in 1681. It ran to five editions and a tercentenary one, of which the two published in 1826 and 1832 are those now normally cited. Stair was a great scholar, a profound thinker and a fine judge. His intellect was formidable and it did not fail him as a writer. His *Institutions*, which did so much to create the Scottish legal system, is one of the great legal books of the world. George Mackenzie's *Institutions*, 1684, was a slighter work which ran to eight editions and is still consulted, while Andrew McDouall, Lord Bankton's *Institute*, issued 1751–3, is a comparative work designed for the instruction of Scottish and English lawyers. John Erskine's *Institute* was published posthumously in 1773 and ran to seven editions, while his *Principles*, an epitome of the former, issued in 1754, ran into twenty-one editions. These were academic works, the latter designed for students.

Major treatises on the criminal law were Sir George Mackenzie's *Laws and customs of Scotland in matters criminal*, 1678 (it includes twenty-eight pages on witchcraft) and Baron David Hume's *Commentaries on the law of Scotland respecting ... crimes*, 1797. The latter's work has been highly regarded. Hume's *Lectures* were subsequently published by the Stair Society in six volumes between 1939–58 and are now regarded as of quasi-institutional authority.

For notes on select treatises, refer to the *Bibliography of British History*, noticed above.

Ireland

The enforcement of English law upon Ireland till 1782 sterilized the production of major treatises, since it was primarily to English textbooks that the profession of necessity turned for guidance. The output of treatises was inevitably small and though the publications of the eighteenth century more than doubled those of the seventeenth, the range of topics dealt with was not dissimilar. Works on practice and procedure, the duties of justices of the peace and petty constables, landlord and tenant, master and servant, and the corn law appeared in equal proportion with treatises on sovereignty and the constitution, as well as tracts touching upon religious problems.

For a detailed list of treatises see Sweet and Maxwell, *Legal Bibliography*, volume 4, *Irish Law to 1956*, 1957.

Channel Islands and Isle of Man

Since in the Channel Islands customary law is dominant, there is little treatise material available except the commentaries already noted above. The principal treatises date from the seventeenth century but were not printed till much later: J. Poingdestre's *Les lois et coutumes*, 1928, and P. Le Geyt's *Les Manuscrits sur la Constitution*, 1846–7 both relate to Jersey, the latter being held by the Privy Council in 1846 to be the authoritative work. For Guernsey, see T. Dicey's *Historical Account of Guernsey*, 1751.

Treatises on the Isle of Man are equally sparse. Its early history may be studied in A. Ross's *Mona, or the History, Laws and Constitutions of the Isle of Man, c.* 1744, and in H. R. Oswald's *Vestigia Insulae Manniae Antiquiora*, 1860, dealing with similar topics.

FURTHER READING

GENERAL WORKS

Baker, J. H. 'Sources of English legal history', Law Librarian, vol. 11, no. 1, 1980, pp. 6–8.
Ball, J. T. Historical Review of the Legislative System Operative in Ireland, 1172–1800, 3rd edn., 1891.
Cairns, J. W. 'Institutional writings in Scotland reconsidered' in Kiralfy, A. and MacQueen, H. A. New Perspectives in Scottish Legal History, 1984, pp. 76–117.
Holdsworth, W. S. Sources and Literature of English Law, 1925. The early chapters dealing with the statutes, the year books, the reports and abridgments, the register of writs, text books and books of authority are the most valuable for the librarian.
Holdsworth, W. S. History of English Law, various edns., 17 vols., Methuen, 1936–72. See especially vols. 4 and 6 (1485–1700), pp. 310–3 and 312–3 respectively, on chief abridgments of the statutes; vol. 2 (449–1485), pp. 525–56 for the year books; vol. 5 (1485–1700), pp. 378–412 on literature of the common law, pp. 460–72 on the writings of Edward Coke; vol. 11 (1701–1875), pp. 287–387 on statutes: vol. 6 (1485–1700), pp. 574–613 and 614–9 on law books; vol. 12. (1701–1875), pp. 331–43 on treatises; vol. 13 (1701–85), pp. 444–96 on law books.
An Introductory Survey of the Sources and Literature of Scots Law, by various authors, ed. H. McKechnie, 1936.
Paton, G. C. H. 'Scots legal bibliography: a historical outline', Law Librarian, vol. 5, no.3, 1974–5, pp. 39–40.
Plucknett, T. F. T. Early English Legal Literature, 1958.
Windram, W. J. and MacQueen, H. L. 'Sources and literature of Scots law ... 1936–1982' in Kiralfy, A. and MacQueen, H. A. New Perspectives in Scottish Legal History, 1984, pp.1–20.
Winfield, P. H. Chief Sources of English Legal History, 1925.

CHRONOLOGY

Cheney, C. R. Handbook of Dates for Students of English History, 1945.

Poole, R. L. *Medieval Reckonings of Time*, 1918.
Powicke, F. M. and Fryde, E. B. *Handbook of British Chronology*
3rd edn., 1986.

LEGAL LANGUAGE

Baker, J. H. *Manual of Law French* 1979. Contains at pp. 29–37
a list of relevant philological works.
Latham, R. E. 'Coping with medieval Latin', *Amateur Historian*,
vol. 1, 1952–4, pp. 331–3.
Maitland, F. W. 'Of the Anglo-French language in the early
Year Books' *in Year Books 1 & 2 Edw. II*, Selden
Society, 1903, *Selden Society Publications*, vol. 17, pp.
xxviii–lxxxi.
Pollock, F. *First Book of Jurisprudence*, 6th edn., 1929. Contains
information on reading Law French at pp. 299–302.

ARCHIVES AND MANUSCRIPTS

Baker, J. H. 'Unprinted sources of English legal history', *Law
Library Journal*, vol. 64, no. 3, 1971, pp. 302–13.
Bond, M. F. 'The formation of the archives of Parliament, 1497–
1691', *Journal of the Society of Archivists*, vol. 1, 1957, pp. 151–8.
Denholm-Young, N. *Handwriting in England and Wales*. 2nd
edn., 1964.
Galbraith, V. H. *An Introduction to the Use of the Public Records*,
1934.
Galbraith, V. H. *Studies in the Public Records*, 1948.
Jenkinson, Sir H. *A Manual of Archive Administration*,
2nd edn., 1937.
Le Hardy, W. 'How to read 16th and 17th century handwrit-
ing', *Amateur Historian*, vol. 1, 1952–4, pp. 146–54.
Livingstone M. *Guide to the Public Records of Scotland in HM
General Register House*, 1905. A supplementary list of acces-
sions to 1946 is contained in *Scottish Historical Review*, vol. 24,
no. 101, 1947.
Madan, F. *Books in Manuscript*, 2nd edn., 1920.
Maitland Thompson, J. *The Public Records of Scotland*, 1922.
Paton, H. M. *The Scottish Records*, 1933.

PRINTED SOURCE COLLECTION

Aspinall, A. 'The reporting and publishing of the House of Commons Debates 1771–1834' *in* Pares, R. and Taylor, A. J. P. *Essays presented to Sir Lewis Namier*, 1956, pp. 227–57.

Cobb, H. S. *The Journals, Minutes and Committee Books of the House of Lords*, 1957.

Knowles, M. D. 'The Rolls Series', *Royal Historical Society Transactions*, 5th series, vol. 11, 1961, pp. 137–59.

Menhennet, D. *The Journals of the House of Commons*, 1971.

Neale, J. E. 'The Commons Journals of the Tudor Period', *Transactions of the Royal Historical Society*, 4th series, vol. 3, 1920, pp. 136–70.

LEGISLATION

Beale, J. H. 'The early English statutes', *Harvard Law Review*, vol. 35, 1922, pp. 519–38.

Bond, M. F. *Acts of Parliament*, 1958.

Edwards, Sir G. 'The historical study of the Welsh law books', *Royal Historical Society Transactions*, 5th series, vol. 12, 1962, pp. 141–55.

United Kingdom Record Commission, 'Historical survey of ancient English statutes' *in Select Essays in Anglo-American Legal History*, 1908. vol. 2, pp. 169–205.

REPORTS OF CASES

Bolland, W. C. *The Year Books*, 1921.

Bolland, W. C. *Manual of Year Book Studies*, 1925

Holdsworth, W. S. 'The Year Books' *in Select Essays in Anglo-American Legal History*, 1908, vol. 2, pp. 96–122.

Luther, P. 'The Year Books', *Law Librarian*, vol 13, no. 2, 1982, pp. 19–22.

Simpson, A. W. B. 'The circulation of year books in the fifteenth century', *Law Quarterly Review*, vol. 73, no. 4, 1957, pp. 492–3.

8. Commonwealth and United States

Section 1: Commonwealth

J. R. WINTERTON

THE COMMONWEALTH AS A WHOLE

The Commonwealth is a free association of independent countries. This survey does not cover those countries which have withdrawn from the Commonwealth – the Republic of Ireland, South Africa and Pakistan – nor those countries over which Britain exercised limited jurisdiction at some time and which never became members of the Commonwealth. The member countries of the Commonwealth are listed in the *Year Book of the Commonwealth*, published by HMSO, which gives general information and brief details of constitutional development. The few territories which remain dependencies are also listed.

Relations between member countries

The Commonwealth acts as an international organization providing a forum for communication and consultation. Legal relationships between the member countries, apart from their participation in the Commonwealth consultative process, are now governed by treaty and international law as between other countries; see J. E. S. Fawcett's *The British Commonwealth in International Law*, 1963, on this topic.

The Commonwealth as a whole produces little literature of legal interest. There is no legal document that contains a constitution of the Commonwealth. There are, however, several significant documents which define the organization and its function: the London Declaration of 1949, the Singapore Declaration of 1971 and the Lusaka Declaration of 1979 in particular. These documents are reproduced in full and commented on in *The Modern Commonwealth* by Sir William Dale. Declarations, statements and agreed memoranda are issued by the Commonwealth's main forum, the Heads of Government meetings, normally held every two years. These meetings were called Commonwealth Prime Ministers' meetings from 1944 to 1969. All communiqués of these meetings, including the documents mentioned above, are published as United Kingdom command papers and appear in the subsequent *Year Book of the Commonwealth*; they are also published in various forms by the Commonwealth Secretariat. In addition to the Heads of Government meetings, there are meetings at ministerial level which include the Commonwealth Law Ministers' meetings, held every three years, and meetings of law officers on a regional basis; documents relating to these meetings are often published by the Commonwealth Secretariat.

The Commonwealth Secretariat was established in London in 1965 and one of its functions is to promote the exchange of information between member countries. The Secretariat pub lishes the official documents of the Commonwealth, described above, and individual studies and reports on legal topics. The Legal Division of the Secretariat produces the *Commonwealth Law Bulletin* which is a major current source for all legal developments in the Commonwealth.

Unofficial organizations which operate on a Commonwealth-wide basis include a few law-related professional associations from whom publications are available. The Commonwealth Lawyers' Association, recently established in London, publishes the *Commonwealth Lawyer* and has assumed responsibility for the Commonwealth Law Conference. The Conference is a major event now held every three years whose proceedings have usually been published in the host country.

Evolution of the Commonwealth

Relations between members of the Commonwealth in the past have been mainly concerned with the changing constitutional relationships between Britain and the various other countries. The literature documenting these relationships remains important, in particular to the former Dominions. The major work which should be consulted is *Commonwealth and Colonial Law*, 1966, by Sir Kenneth Roberts-Wray which contains the relevant statutes and leading cases with detailed commentary and an opening chapter which defines the numerous terms such as colony, dominion, protectorate and settlement.

The constitutional status of a dependent territory may be decided by the manner of acquisition, and so the early history of that territory will continue to be relevant. The legal and constitutional history of dependent territories may be found in appendix I of Roberts-Wray and in the *Year Book of the Commonwealth*. Many territories were acquired by treaty and many of the instruments are in the major treaty collections such as *Hertslet's Treaties* and *British and Foreign State Papers*.

Each dependent territory to some extent received existing English law as part of its own law. In settled colonies, where there was no established system of law, the whole body of English law was adopted in the form in force on a certain day, usually the date of first settlement. The date of reception of English law is often given in a local statute. Where systems of law already existed, such as religious systems of personal law and local customary law, these were largely retained and remain influential (see Chapter 13 for religious systems of law). English law was specifically adopted to deal with matters, such as shipping, trade and commerce, which were not covered by local law.

The United Kingdom exercised jurisdiction by virtue of royal prerogative or by authority of statute. Among the few major Acts of general application are the British Settlements Acts and the Foreign Jurisdiction Acts which confirmed and clarified the jurisdiction of the United Kingdom in dependent territories. From a very early stage most dependent territories made their own laws and gradually built up their own body of law. The United Kingdom legislated directly for its dependencies mainly on constitutional matters.

Law made in the United Kingdom was contained in various instruments including Acts of Parliament, Letters Patent and Orders in Council. Acts of Parliament which do not expressly extend to a colony may have been extended by an Order in Council. The reception of English law and the extension of English law are dealt with in volume six of *Halsbury's Laws of England*, 4th edition, under 'Commonwealth and dependencies: the extension of English law', paragraphs 1194–1202. The *Statutory Instruments* series, and its predecessor *Statutory Rules and Orders*, contains Orders in Council and Letters Patent in the numbered sequence if they were made under statutory authority. Prerogative instruments are published in the *London Gazette* and appear unnumbered in an appendix at the back of the bound volumes of Statutory Instruments. As this legislation formed part of the law of a territory it was normally included in consolidations or revised editions of the laws of that territory. Some countries have enacted Interpretation Acts or Application of Imperial Law Acts to clarify what English-made law remains in force.

The gradual constitutional shift to self-government and to the independence of the former Dominions of Australia, Canada and New Zealand is documented in a number of sources, many of which are accounts of the consultative process leading up to the Statute of Westminster 1931 which established the independence of the Dominions in law. The only major statutes are the Colonial Laws Validity Act of 1875 and the Statute of Westminster of 1931. These and other relevant Acts are in the general section of Group 26 of *Statutes in force*: 'Commonwealth and other territories'.

Reports and official papers relating to the Dominions and other dependent territories can be found in the same way as United Kingdom official publications on other subjects. A major report is the *Durham Report* (HCP no.3 of 1839) into uprisings in Upper and Lower Canada which led to constitutional Acts for the future Dominions, mainly in the 1850s, establishing responsible self-government. The various conferences which began as a regular occurrence with the Colonial Conference of 1887, renamed Imperial Conference from 1911, are valuable sources; reports of the proceedings were published as command papers. The *Report of the Imperial Conference* of 1926 (Cmd. 2768) contains, at the start of the report of the Inter-Imperial Relations Committee, the Balfour Declaration on the constitutional nature of the Commonwealth, of Britain and the Dominions, 'They are autonomous communities within the British Empire, equal in status, in no way subordinate one to another in any aspect of their domestic or external affairs, though united by a common allegiance to the Crown, and freely associated as members of the British Commonwealth of Nations.'

There are also documents of other meetings, round tables, letters from Governors, speeches and contemporary accounts. Many documents are conveniently gathered in *Speeches and Documents on the British Dominions, 1918–31* edited by A. B. Keith which is continued by *Documents and Speeches on British Commonwealth Affairs, 1931–52* edited by Nicholas Mansergh.

There is less material on the independence of all the other countries since 1931. Unlike the Dominions, other countries achieved independence by a single direct grant with the severance of all earlier constitutional links. Normally an Independence Act was passed and the new constitution scheduled to an associated Order in Council. Usually the only other documents of specific interest regarding the independence are the constitutional conferences which took place when the new constitution was being drafted; these are published as command papers. *From dependence to statehood in Commonwealth Africa* by H. H. Marshall is a collection of documents on the constitutional history of the British protectorates and colonies in Africa from the First World War to independence. A similar work is *Constitutional development of the West Indies 1922–68: a selection from the major documents* by Ann Spackman.

Final appeal from any colonial court was to the Judicial Committee of the Privy Council, subject to appeal in the highest court in the colonial country. Many cases considered by the Privy Council have involved constitutional problems. In some countries the provision for appeal to the Privy Council has been carried beyond Independence. The judgments are in various series of the *Law Reports*; most of the relevant earlier series are reprinted in the *English Reports* volumes 12–20. Several countries have published collections of cases heard on appeal by the Privy Council and most have included the reports in their own major series.

INTERNAL LAW OF MEMBER COUNTRIES

General

The types of legal literature which exist in Commonwealth countries will be largely familiar as they are normally based on English counterparts. In general Australia, Canada, New Zealand and India have an extensive and sometimes complex legal literature. To varying degrees the legal literature of the other countries does not have the same range or depth of coverage. Some general characteristics of the literature and sources of information are described below and primary materials are described in more detail under the individual countries or regions. Indexes and bibliographies of the materials described will be found in Chapter 9.

Constitutions

All Commonwealth countries, except for the United Kingdom itself and New Zealand in part, have written constitutions. Some constitutions are still based on the version contained in United Kingdom legislation and adopted on independence. Many constitutions, however, have been replaced or considerably amended since independence and reference should normally be made to the legislation of the individual country. Some countries produce an updated version of their constitution in booklet form from time to time. A convenient source for the current text of constitutions is the looseleaf *Constitutions of the countries of the world* by Blaustein and Flanz which includes a bibliography for each country. *The modern Commonwealth* by Sir William Dale is a recent study of constitutional government in the Commonwealth countries.

Many members of the Commonwealth have a federal system of government. In these countries the federal authority and each part of the federal structure produces its own body of statute and case-law. The actual jurisdictions of the federal and state authorities vary from country to country according to the provisions of the constitution. Much important case-law has been generated, particularly in Canada and Australia, on the division of power. As the constitutions have been the subject of considerable study, early documents of the drafting and development of the constitution are also important.

Legislation

All the countries publish legislation as it is enacted. A few publish each piece of legislation for sale separately as in the United Kingdom. The primary and subsidiary legislation of most Commonwealth countries appear firstly in, or as supplements to, their government gazette, with little or no indexing. Primary legislation is usually termed Acts, Laws or Statutes or, in dependent territories, Ordinances; subsidiary legislation is normally termed Statutory Instruments, Regulations or Orders but is often part of a numbered series of legal notices or government notices in gazettes. The gazette often contains material of only local or ephemeral interest and, where it is possible to extract and retain the legislation separately, law libraries often discard the gazette itself. A few countries do not issue legislation in any other form. Many countries do reprint their legislation in annual or sessional volumes with the addition of tables and indexes but there may be a delay of several years.

Bound revisions or consolidations of all laws in force at a certain date have been published for most jurisdictions; sometimes subsidiary legislation in force was also included. They were major projects and were never frequent even in the larger jurisdictions; they are now rarely published in bound format. Various methods have been adopted to maintain an up-to-date version of revised laws, the most common being to adopt a looseleaf format.

The Legal Library of the Foreign and Commonwealth Office contains the most comprehensive collection of Commonwealth legislation. The collection is kept up to date and a subject index to the primary legislation is maintained by the Library. Personal callers can make photocopies of individual items of legislation. The legislation and other government publications received by the Foreign and Commonwealth

Office are listed in *Technical Co-operation: a monthly bibliography of Commonwealth official publications*, published by the Overseas Development Administration; details of a postal photocopying service for listed items are given in each issue. The *Commonwealth Law Bulletin* lists recent legislation of interest giving a summary of its provisions.

Law reports

Commonwealth countries have law reports similar in format to those in the United Kingdom. Many countries, however, have no statutory body responsible for law reporting and, where there are official series, they are often published by commercial publishers in receipt of direct government subsidy. It is common for a jurisdiction to have only a single series and a number of countries have no current series of law reports. *A study of law reporting in the Commonwealth* by T. Gregory Kane contains more production and publication details.

There are few sources which gather reports on a Commonwealth-wide basis. The *Commonwealth Law Bulletin* contains notes of recent cases of general interest from all over the Commonwealth, many of which are otherwise unreported or very late in publication; 'many Commonwealth courts accept citations from the Bulletin of cases reported in it' (Dale, *Modern Commonwealth*, p. 79). A series entitled *Law Reports of the Commonwealth* started publication in 1985 and will consist of annual volumes of cases on constitutional law, commercial law and criminal law.

A recent development is the inclusion, in early 1985, of *New Zealand Law Reports* on LEXIS, the computerized legal information retrieval system, forming the first part of a 'LEXIS Commonwealth Library'. There is no indication at present of what further material may be added but the widespread publishing interests of Butterworths make the appearance of Australian and Canadian material on LEXIS a possibility. Details of the existing automated legal information retrieval systems in Australia and Canada, QUIC/LAW and CLIRS, are given under the individual jurisdictions. The

Online Information Centre in London publishes a brief guide, *Law Databases*.

Many countries have digests, although only the largest have frequently updated services. *The English and Empire Digest*, now known as *The Digest*, aims to digest 'the whole case law of England together with a considerable body of cases from the Courts of Scotland, Ireland, Canada, Australia, New Zealand, and other countries of the British Commonwealth . . .'.

Encyclopedias

One of the most widely used works in the Commonwealth has been *Halsbury's Laws of England* but the separate development of the law of Commonwealth countries has rendered Halsbury's and other major works on English law of less use than formerly. Series were published to complement Halsbury's with references to local law for Australia, Canada and New Zealand and these series have become major works in their own right: *Halsbury's Laws of England, 3rd edn., Canadian Converter*, the *Australian Commentary on Halsbury's Laws of England* and the *New Zealand Commentary on Halsbury's Laws of England*. These works summarize statute and case-law under the same headings as Halsbury's; they show where local law corresponds to English law and give references and a brief description where local law differs. Apart from these series the only major legal encyclopedias in the Commonwealth are published in Canada. The *Canadian Encyclopedic Digest, Ontario*, 3rd edn., describes federal and Ontario law in 34 looseleaf volumes. A similar work, the *Canadian Encyclopedic Digest, Western* covers the four western provinces.

Treatises

There have been several series of monographs, in addition to many individual works, published in Britain on the law of Commonwealth countries. The most recent is the *Commonwealth Law Series* currently being published by Butterworths. At its announcement in 1983 it was noted that legal writers had given little attention to the Commonwealth in recent years. Many of the major treatises appeared up to twenty years ago when the number of countries becoming independent reached its peak. A notable series of that period is the *British Commonwealth: the development of its laws and constitutions*, 1952–67. A large number of countries were each covered by a volume in this series and, for certain countries, that volume remains the most recent general treatise available.

There was widespread use of treatises on English law until quite recently even in Australia and Canada. In the 1980 edition of *Using a law library*, Margaret Banks writes: 'Until recently there were relatively few Canadian legal treatises' (p. 165). Publication of legal treatises is now comparatively prolific in Australia, Canada, India and to a lesser extent in New Zealand. There is a scarcity of secondary materials of all sorts in most other countries of the Commonwealth and there are few locally published treatises. Legal publishing has developed in Nigeria in recent years but many secondary materials for Commonwealth Africa are still published by British publishers. Papua New Guinea and the Pacific islands have attracted the interest of Australian publishers. Publishing of secondary, and sometimes primary, materials in the smaller jurisdictions and some African countries has often been the result of initiatives by universities such as the University of the West Indies and the University of Papua New Guinea.

Law reform

The reports of law reform bodies are of importance in themselves and in some countries they may contain the most recent or authoritative survey of an area of existing law. The *List of Official Committees, Commissions and other bodies concerned with the Reform of Law* published by the Institute of Advanced Legal Studies contains details of current projects and published work; this has not appeared since 1979. *Law reform in the Commonwealth: law reform proposals and their implementation*, published by the Commonwealth Secretariat since 1979, lists matters under consideration by permanent law reform bodies and their published work; it also shows what legislation has resulted. Both publications will help identify organizations and provide addresses; they also give guidance on the availability and price of publications. Law reform news is reported extensively in the *Commonwealth Law Bulletin*.

Periodicals

Journal publishing in the larger Commonwealth countries is similar to the UK with many journals for both the academic and the practitioner including a growing number of subject journals. University law reviews hold a more important place than in Britain. In general, periodical literature in many other parts of the Commonwealth has appeared infrequently and irregularly, usually in the form of a single national law journal produced by a university law faculty or a regional journal such as the *Melanesian Law Journal* or the *West Indian Law Journal*. The School of Oriental and African Studies, University of London, produces the major regional periodical on Africa: the *Journal of African Law*. Reference is still made to the *Annual Survey of Commonwealth Law* which was one of the most important periodicals on Commonwealth law before publication ceased in 1977.

Africa

Since Independence, African countries have undergone considerable constitutional change. The subject has attracted several treatises on Commonwealth Africa in general, such as the series of three monographs by B. O. Nwabueze, *Constitutionalism in emergent states*, *Presidentialism in Commonwealth Africa* and *Judicialism in Commonwealth Africa*.

The main source for legislation is the government gazettes. There is a long delay before legislation is incorporated into the looseleaf revised editions of laws which exist for some countries such as Kenya, Malawi and Zambia. Legislation and other legal publications suffer from short print-runs and inadequate distribution facilities and supply is often insufficient to meet even initial demand. Legal publishing, at least of federal material, has expanded rapidly in Nigeria in the last ten years and in this respect it is the exception in Commonwealth Africa. There is no looseleaf revision for Nigeria but the 1958 revised edition of the laws has been reprinted by Professional Books.

Finding aids are not usually available for African legislation. The *African Law Digest* was published from 1965 as part of a project, started at the African Law Center at Columbia University, to digest gazetted legislation from all African countries and to establish a document center at the University of Addis Ababa in Ethiopia. The project came to an end in 1974 but efforts are being made to renew publication. The *Nigerian Current Law Review* is the only publication of its type in Commonwealth Africa; it appears quarterly containing digests of legislation and important cases, articles and book reviews but it is severely delayed in publication.

There are influences at work apart from English common law and local customary law. The law of the southern African states of Zimbabwe, Botswana, Lesotho and Swaziland was heavily influenced by the Roman-Dutch basis of law in the colonies which were to form the Republic of South Africa.

The major series of law reports prior to Independence mainly corresponded to the jurisdiction of regional courts of appeal, East Africa, West Africa and the Federation of Rhodesia and Nyasaland in Central Africa. The East African Court of Appeal, established in 1909, survived after the independence of the countries under its jurisdiction until 1975 and, at one time, its jurisdiction extended to Kenya, Uganda, Tanganyika, Zanzibar, Aden, Somaliland, the Seychelles and St Helena.

Most African countries produce a single national series of law reports in annual volumes which appear after a long delay. In Nigeria there are several series of law reports, both officially and commercially published, covering federal and state courts including monthly reports of the Supreme Court and Federal Court of Appeal. According to G. Ezejiofor[1] 'practically all the series do not report cases until three, sometimes four years from the date on which they were decided'.

---

[1] 'Sources of Nigerian Law', *Introduction to Nigerian Law*, ed. Okonkwo, p. 40.

The African Law Reports, now based at Trinity College Oxford and renamed Law Reports International in 1984, is a non-profit organization which has published law reports in a number of series covering countries such as Malawi and Sierra Leone and a subject series, *African Law Reports: Commercial,* covering several African countries. Its intention is to transfer national series to local publication once established. The organization also acts as an agent and distributor for locally published law reports.

Australia

Constitution

The Constitution, which came into effect on 1 January 1901, formed the Commonwealth of Australia by the creation of the federal government and the federation of the six separate colonies which are now states. Effectively there are six state legal systems with separate and different bodies of law and a further federal or Commonwealth system covering the whole of Australia within the terms of its jurisdiction; each of these systems has a fully developed legal literature associated with it.

'Notwithstanding the notable activity of law reform agencies throughout Australia nearly all the law of everyday life in Australia is common law, and most of it is state law. Federal legislation has little to do with ordinary commercial transactions, property or personal relations except in Federal Territories.'[1] The Constitution limits the jurisdiction of federal government to certain subjects and the states retain all residual jurisdiction.

The history of the federalist movement and the drafting and enactment of the Constitution is dealt with in considerable detail in the opening sections of 'Sources and literature of Australian law, part 1' by R. J. Watts, *Lawasia* (NS) 2, 1982–3, pp. 115–54. The Constitution appeared as the first item in the

[1] T. B. Smith, 'Reception of the common law in the Commonwealth: scope and extent in the older Commonwealth', in *Proceedings and Papers of the Sixth Commonwealth Law Conference,* p. 119.

1973 reprint of Commonwealth Acts and is reprinted in pamphlet form with its own index from time to time. The Attorney-General's Department in Canberra has produced the *Australian constitution annotated* which conveniently gathers relevant documents and gives references to the important case-law. Most state constitutions date from mid-nineteenth century Imperial Acts or Orders in Council and the amended versions are contained in state constitution Acts.

Legislation

The latest complete statement of the federal law at a single date was the *Acts of the Australian Parliament 1901–1973*. Since then the Commonwealth, Western Australia and Queensland have followed the lead of Victoria in reprinting all Acts in pamphlet form for insertion into binders in preference to a new bound volume reprint. Replacement pamphlets are issued as part of a continuous updating process. These 'pamphlet reprints' are the most convenient source to consult at the start of a search for legislation. Although the reprints are published officially, they are not passed by Parliament in that form and, in case of dispute, reference is made to the original Act and amending Acts. Details on bringing state and federal statutes up to date can be found in Chapter 9 of *Legal Research Materials and Methods* by E. Campbell *et al.* which is an essential guide to all aspects of Australian legal literature.

Subject access to legislation of the Commonwealth and some states has been limited. Often an alphabetical list of short titles has served instead of a true subject index. There is no official subject index to the 1973 federal consolidation nor to the Commonwealth pamphlet reprint currently being published. The main work is commercially published: *Subject Index to the Acts and Regulations of the Commonwealth of Australia*, compiled by B. M. Wicks, which appears annually.

The federal government administers several territories. The external territories are islands which were formerly British dependencies, one of which was Papua New Guinea, prior to its independence. There are two internal territories: Australian Capital Territory and Northern Territory. Ordinances for the ACT are published by the Commonwealth, being a form of federal subsidiary legislation. The Northern Territory has been self-governing since 1978 and publishes its own legislation.

A database has been compiled by the Attorney-General's Department of the Commonwealth government called SCALE (Statutes and Cases Automated Legal Enquiry). The database contains full-text Commonwealth Acts and regulations and ACT legislation in reprint form, the *Commonwealth Law Reports* and reports of the Administrative Appeals Tribunal. A commercial firm CLIRS (Computerized Legal Information Retrieval System) is adding state material to SCALE including Acts and regulations of New South Wales and Victoria and the decisions of their Supreme Courts, both reported and unreported. CLIRS began to market the service from early 1985 in Australia. The CLIRS General Manager, A. H. Gould, describes the service in 'CLIRS Australia', *Australian Law Librarians' Group Newsletter* no. 62, 1984, pp. 2–6.

Law reports

The High Court is the supreme federal court and is also the highest court of appeal in Australia for the State Supreme Courts. The only authorized reports of the High Court are the *Commonwealth Law Reports*, published since 1903, which now fill several volumes each year in a consecutively numbered sequence. The *Federal Law Reports* which started in 1956 do not report the High Court; they covered the Federal Court until the end of 1983 and continue to report other federal courts, a growing number of important tribunals and state courts acting in federal capacity. From 1984 the *Federal Court Reports* has been the authorized series of the Federal Court of Australia. The federal court system is complex and, although bibliographic works give an outline, reference may be needed to a treatise such as *The federal judicial system of Australia* by H. E. Renfree.

The *Australian Law Reports,* which continues a long series originally begun in 1895, covers the federal courts and also major decisions of State Supreme courts. Another important general series is the *Australian Law Journal Reports* which has appeared from 1958 as a separately paginated section in the *Australian Law Journal*. The territories have their own supreme courts and reports of cases in them are published in the *Australian Law Reports* in separate sections and also in the *Federal Law Reports*.

Each state now has one major series of law reports of long standing which is published by, or by authority of, the Incorporated Council of Law Reporting for the state. The states, but not the Commonwealth, still retain the right to refer cases to the Privy Council with certain limitations; this practice is likely to end in the near future.

The CLIRS information retrieval service is mentioned above in the section on statutory material and details of the case-law it contains are given there.

The main reference work for case-law is the *Australian Digest* which is nearing completion of its second edition in approximately 40 volumes. The four volume citator will be the first complete citator for Australian cases and the current volume has looseleaf updating. The *Australian Legal Monthly Digest* uses the same subject arrangement as the *Australian Digest* and provides updating between annual supplements to the *Digest*. The *Australian Legal Monthly Digest* and *Australian Current Law* both provide current information on statutes and law reports, federal and state, and contain references to recent articles.

Canada

Constitution

The Canada Act 1982, c.11, enacted by the United Kingdom, gave Canada full control over its own Constitution. The Constitution Act 1982, contained in Schedule B of the Canada Act, was enacted in Canada; it renamed the earlier British North America Acts and other constitutional instruments as the Constitution Acts 1867–1982 and it contained the Charter of Rights and Freedoms. A large number of textbooks, annotated texts and specialized law reports have appeared as a result of these developments. The Department of Justice of Canada has produced *A consolidation of the Constitution Acts 1867–1982* which includes all relevant texts. The looseleaf *Constitutions of Canada: federal and provincial* edited by C. L. Wiktor and Guy Tanguay collects all documents which form the federal Constitution. When complete it will also contain the constitutions of the ten provinces of Canada and the two federal territories.

Areas of Canada were originally colonized by France but were ceded to Britain in the Treaty of Paris 1763. Legal publications of the federal government and Quebec, New Brunswick and Manitoba are published in both English and French, each equally authoritative. The primary language for legal writing in Quebec is French.

Legislation

The *Revised Statutes of Canada* 1970, cited RSC 1970, arranged by short title in bound volumes, is the latest official statement of the statutes in force incorporating amendments. Most of the provinces, starting with Manitoba in 1970, are now publishing continually updated collections of statutes in looseleaf form often referred to as continuing consolidations in Canada. A new edition of federal statutes is planned for 1986 with a new subject index prepared by the Canadian Law Information Council; this edition is likely to be in looseleaf format. Acts are issued in sessional volumes which contain an updated version of the table of public statutes giving a list of all Acts in force with references to all amendments since revision. The *Canada Gazette*, Part III, contains new Acts and irregular updates to the table of public statutes.

There are a number of convenient commercial publications for updating statutory material. The looseleaf *Canada Statute Citator* lists Acts in force and gives the text of amendments. *Canadian Current Law* covers federal and provincial jurisdictions and contains a section on statutes amended, repealed or proclaimed. A series of detailed articles which originally appeared in the *CLIC Legal Materials Letter* have been gathered into a pamphlet entitled *Updating statutes and regulations for all*

Canadian jurisdictions (as of December 1984) by M. J. T. Sinclair; their work is very helpful.

Criminal law is under federal jurisdiction embodied in the Canadian Criminal Code. The Code is included in RSC 1970 and amendments can be found in the normal way through the official publications but there are a number of complete commercial services in the form of annual annotated criminal codes.

A group of legal databases from various sources, official and commercial, is made available for online searching by QL Systems of Ontario and is called QUIC/LAW. The Department of Justice maintains the full text of all federal statutes and regulations in force on QUIC/LAW; case-law contents are described below. A constituent database, CAN/LAW, is also available from the producer Canada Law Book Inc. which publishes major series of law reports.

Quebec has a mixed system of law; common law covers areas of public law and civil law, with a civil code and a code of civil procedure based on the French codes, covers private law such as family law and contract. Several commercial versions of the codes are available in looseleaf bilingual editions.

Law reports

The two official authorized series of federal reports are the *Canada: Supreme Court Reports* and the *Canada: Federal Court Reports*. Both series originally began in 1876. Earlier titles were *Canada Law Reports: Supreme Court* and *Canada Law Reports: Exchequer Court*. Since 1975 all Supreme Court cases have been reported in the official series, but only selectively before that date. There is some delay in publication and reports appear more quickly in commercial series. The Department of Justice has made available on QUIC/LAW the head-notes of the *Supreme Court Reports* since 1876 and of the *Federal Court Reports*.

The *Dominion Law Reports* which began in 1912 is the only general series which covers both federal and provincial courts. Now in its fourth series, cited DLR (4th), it appears in 12 volumes per year and has its own digest and cumulative annual volume of annotations. The DLR reported some

Supreme Court cases not reported in the official series before 1975. Head-notes of the *Dominion Law Reports* from 1955 onwards are available on QUIC/LAW.

Ontario and Quebec, formerly Upper and Lower Canada, have large numbers of older reports. They both have one series of reports published without break since the last century, now entitled *Ontario Reports* and *Recueils de Jurisprudence du Québec*. Although most of the other provinces had a provincial reporter by the early years of this century, most had ceased publication by the 1940s and had been replaced by regional reporters. The most widely known is the still-published *Western Weekly Reports* which began in 1911 covering the western provinces. The eastern provinces were covered by the *Maritime Provinces Reports* which ceased publication in 1968. The recent trend has been back to individual provincial reporters and most of these have started publication since the end of the 1960s.

The individual provincial reporters are not all on QUIC/LAW but the *Atlantic Provinces Reports* which reprints individual reporters for the eastern provinces and the *Western Weekly Reports* are available in head-note form. The major gap in coverage of the common law provinces on QUIC/LAW was the absence of the *Ontario Reports* which was remedied in late 1985 by a database produced by the Law Society of Upper Canada.

The Quebec government established a publishing firm in 1975 called SOQUIJ or Société Québecoise d'Information Juridique, which acts for the Editeur Officiel. Among other publications it took over production of the main series of law reports, the *Recueils de Jurisprudence du Québec* in series for the Cour d'Appel, Cour Supérieure and, from 1975, a third series covering several special courts and tribunals. From 1892 to 1966 this series of reports was entitled *Rapports Judiciaires du Québec*. Most reports in these series are in French.

There is a large and growing number of specialized subject series of reports published in Canada. A few are long established such as those dealing with the criminal law but the majority have appeared since 1970. They may also contain articles on the subject they cover.

Canada possesses one of the most fully developed examples of a digest, the *Canadian Abridgment*, which covers all aspects of both federal and provincial case-law although only decisions of general application from Quebec. *Canadian Current Law* appears monthly with the same subject arrangement and updates all sections of the *Canadian Abridgment*. The use of these two works is described in detail in *Using a law library* by M. Banks. There are other services which specialize in the rapid notification of cases in advance of reporting such as the *All-Canada Weekly Summaries* for civil cases and the *Weekly Criminal Bulletin* which are not normally found in libraries outside Canada but are both available on QUIC/LAW.

Commonwealth Caribbean

The Commonwealth Caribbean includes Belize and Guyana on the mainland and Bermuda and the Bahamas in the Atlantic as well as the fourteen islands or groups of islands in the West Indies which were or are British colonies. Some of Britain's earliest colonies are in the Commonwealth Caribbean and most were subject to political changes caused by the colonial powers from the seventeenth century onwards. The only island where a substantial civil law influence remains from French occupation is St Lucia.

Several groupings or federations of islands were established during the colonial period. The last of these, the Federation of the West Indies, was dissolved in 1962 after Jamaican secession and the larger islands, Barbados, Jamaica and Trinidad and Tobago became independent soon afterwards. The smaller islands of the Federation became self-governing in free association with the United Kingdom and were known as the West Indies Associated States. Most of the Associated States have since become independent. Some of the smallest islands remain as separate dependent territories.

Revised editions of laws have been published for most of the individual islands but only at long intervals. More recently, loose-leaf editions have been published for the larger territories, some by the government printer such as those for Guyana and Jamaica, several in co-operation with the government printer by Sweet and Maxwell – such as those for Barbados, Bermuda, Trinidad and Tobago and St Vincent. Despite being looseleaf, most of these are only infrequently updated.

For many islands it used to be necessary to look through legislation from the official gazettes for which there is often no index. Since 1976, however, the West Indies Legislative Indexing Project at the Faculty of Law of the University of the West Indies has been publishing mimeographed booklets containing consolidated indexes to the laws and subsidiary legislation for each island. They contain tables of all the statutes in force with references to the gazetted legislation, any subsequent amendments and any subsidiary legislation made under the statute. Many libraries lack a set of gazette legislation for some islands, or have an incomplete set. An initiative by the same Project has led to the re-publication of some gazetted legislation for the first time in bound volume form.

The main series of law reports is the *West Indian Reports*; this is a regional reporter published in the United Kingdom by Butterworths in bound volume format only. Its coverage is rather narrow and there is considerable delay in publishing judgments. *Legal literature and publishing in the Commonwealth Caribbean: a working paper* by V. Newton includes a critique of this major series in its full description of legal literature in the area.

Considering the relatively long colonial history few law reports have been published and only three territories have had any continuity in law reporting: Guyana, formerly British Guiana, Jamaica, whose reports are published outside the area by Butterworths, and to a lesser extent Trinidad and Tobago. These series contain reports, not published elsewhere, of the regional courts such as the West Indian Court of Appeal, which existed from 1919 to 1957. Barbados has recently begun publication of a regular series of reports and retrospective publication of volumes covering earlier years. Other series have been sporadic and short-lived and some states such as Belize have only published occasional judgments in their gazette.

India

Constitution

H. C. Jain opens his book, *Indian legal materials: a bibliographical guide*, 1970, p. 3, by explaining that 'India with a federal structure has only one Constitution. The states are part of the federation and do not have their own Constitution'. The Constitution of 1949 sets out the powers of both central and state government and came into force in January 1950. The records of the debates and drafts of the Constitutent Assembly were published by the official publisher, the Controller of Publications, New Delhi and were reprinted in 12 volumes in 1966. The Constitution has been much amended and the latest version is reprinted by the Controller of Publications every two or three years. Amendments to the Constitution are printed in the *Gazette of India*. One of the most widely used works on the Constitution is *Commentary on the Constitution of India* by D. D. Basu which gives the text and detailed commentary and annotations.

Legislation

In the early nineteenth century confusion existed due to the inconsistent application of English law. This led to one of the particular aspects of Indian law: the codification of law on a number of subjects notably the Indian Penal Code of 1861 and also the Indian Succession Act 1865, the Criminal Procedure Code 1861, the Indian Contract Act 1872 and the Indian Evidence Act 1872. It is important to distinguish between these codified laws, in the proper sense of the term, and the codes mentioned below which are in fact reprints of laws in force incorporating amendments.

The *India Code* is the official reprinted version of the central or federal statutes and is updated in India by correction slips between new editions. State official publishing closely follows central government practice. The most common code in use is a commercial version by the publishers All India Reporter Ltd. The *A.I.R. Manual*, 3rd edition, contains all the Acts in force at the end of 1974 with a commentary and has better indexes and tables than the official version. Although Indian courts are not bound to accept any other than the official text, the AIR and some other commercially produced versions are invariably accepted. Commercially produced reprints of statutes with commentary are only available for some of the states although the number is growing. There are many commentaries published containing the reprinted text of individual codified laws or other legislation with annotations.

By their nature, bound reprints may be considerably out of date. Acts and regulations are published currently in the *Gazette of India* and collected in annual volumes. This process is mirrored in the states. More details are contained in 'Using a law library' by H. C. Jain in *Journal of the Indian Law Institute* 24, 1982, pp. 575–91, which elaborates on some points made in his earlier bibliographical guide.

The *All India Reporter,* from which the publishing company takes its name, is a monthly publication containing the central Acts and is probably the most convenient publication to consult first for recent material. Each state has at least one similar publication from a commercial publisher containing its state Acts and relevant central Acts. These publications, usually entitled journals, are a feature of Indian legal literature. They are published weekly, bi-weekly or monthly and contain Acts and law reports, and most also include articles and book reviews. They form complete services to the legal profession and they are more up to date than official publications, especially for law reports, with broader coverage and better indexing.

Religious systems of law in India, Hindu and Islamic, are dealt with in Chapter 13.

Law reports

Older reports to which reference is still made are mainly reports of cases on appeal to the Privy Council. These are contained in collections of cases, in particular *Moore's Indian Appeals,* 1836–1872, reprinted in the *English Reports;* following these the *Law Reports. Indian Appeals,* 1873–1950, were published in England by the Incorporated Council of Law Reporting.

The Supreme Court is the highest Court of Appeal; appeal to it is from the High Court in each state which is supreme within its territorial jurisdiction. No lower courts are normally reported. The *Supreme Court Reports* are the monthly official series of reports published since 1950, when the Supreme Court was established. The official series of reports for the High Courts in the states are the *Indian Law Reports* in a separate series for each High Court: ILR Bombay, ILR Calcutta for example. The series for the Bombay, Calcutta, Madras and Allahabad courts were established in 1876 following the Indian Law Reports Act of 1875. These four courts, known as the chartered High Courts, were particularly important as they were the final courts of appeal in British India before cases went to the Privy Council. Series have followed for other states at later dates, for example Lucknow in 1926, Punjab in 1948, Delhi in 1968.

M. P. Jain in an article, 'Law Reporting in India' in *Journal of the Indian Law Institute* 24, 1982, pp. 560–74 gives a detailed historical account and a critique of the current 'plethora of law reports' (p. 572).

The *All India Reporter,* already mentioned for its statutes content, includes cases from both the Supreme Court and the High Courts. The state 'journals' described above report cases in the High Courts and several, particularly those established to report the chartered High Courts, have been published for many years, for example the *Madras Law Journal* which started in 1891. There are similar journals which cover specific subject areas of law.

Malaysia and Singapore

Constitution

The Malay states were brought under British influence over a long period and were combined in several groupings and federations over the years such as the Straits Settlements, the Federated Malay States, the Malayan Union and the Federation of Malaya. This was achieved almost entirely by treaty and these treaties are a particularly important source. *A Collection of Treaties and Other Documents affecting the States of Malaysia 1761–1963*, edited by J. de V. Allen *et al.* effectively supersedes several earlier collections and includes Singapore.

Malaysia was formed in 1963 by the joining of the Federation of Malaya, independent in 1957, containing all the mainland Malay states with the newly independent states of Sabah (formerly North Borneo), Sarawak and Singapore. Brunei is a separate jurisdiction although in the past it has been administered with Sabah and Sarawak. Singapore withdrew from Malaysia in 1965 and is now a separate independent jurisdiction.

Legislation

There is no consolidation or complete reprint of legislation for Malaysia but each year several important Acts are individually reprinted incorporating amendments, for example reprint no. 10 of 1982 was the federal Constitution. The Acts of Parliament and the federal subsidiary legislation are contained in annual publications which comprise the relevant parts of the federal gazette reprinted and filed in binders. There is no official index to the legislation but Malaysian Law Publishers have produced a *General Index of Acts, Enactments, Ordinances, etc. as at 30 April 1983*. An annual *Survey of Malaysian Law* has been published since 1977 summarizing developments in statutory and case-law by broad topic with a complete list of legislation for the year.

A *Revised Edition of the Laws of Singapore 1970* was published in bound volumes. Annual supplements have been published from 1970 but they take the form of annual volumes of laws and are not incorporated or cumulated in any way with the revised edition. The *Tables of written laws of Singapore* edited by Molly Cheang in their 1982 edition are in looseleaf format but have no regular supplementation. 'Sources and literature of Singapore law' by G. W. Bartholomew in *Lawasia* (NS) 2, 1982–3, pp 1–49, is a detailed account which also includes references to essential Malaysian legal literature.

Law reports

There has been intermittent law reporting in Malaya in the past. Several official series were published but were short-lived.

The only current general series of reports for Malaysia and Singapore is the monthly *Malayan Law Journal,* originally conceived as the only all-Malaya law reporter. It also carries a large number of articles but these are still paginated as preliminary pages. In 1982 the first few cases were published in the Malay language but the large majority of cases are still in English. In 1940 the founding editor of the *Malayan Law Journal,* B. A. Mallal, also began the only major digest of Malayan case-law. Publication of the 3rd edition of *Mallal's digest of Malaysian and Singapore case law 1808–1965* is still continuing; there is no supplementation.

New Zealand

Constitution

New Zealand is a unitary state with a simpler legal literature than many Commonwealth countries. Although provincial governments were set up, they were abolished in 1875. Some provisions of the Constitution are in the New Zealand Constitution Act, based on an Imperial Act of 1852, and in other statutes. As in the United Kingdom the Constitution is not wholly to be found in written sources and is in part contained in common law and constitutional convention. *New Zealand: the development of its laws and constitution* edited by J. L. Robson should be consulted on this subject. New Zealand has administered a number of island dependencies, the majority of which are now self-governing in free association with New Zealand.

Legislation

There is no looseleaf reprint of the statutes of New Zealand. Since 1979 a new series of *Reprinted Statutes of New Zealand* has been published in numbered volumes in brown binding. The preface states that a further reprint of all statutes in force at a certain date like the 'blue series', the *Reprint of the Statutes of New Zealand 1908–57* which is now largely redundant, could not be contemplated because of the difficulty and expense. One or two reprint volumes are published each year and the series will continue indefinitely. Eventually all Acts will be represented and further reprints will appear so that every Act has a version no more than ten years old. More important Acts appear earlier in the series and Acts substantially amended or in common usage may be reprinted at much shorter intervals.

Acts are arranged alphabetically in each volume of the reprinted statutes but there is no overall order to the series and it is essential to look up the location of the most recent reprint of any particular Act. This can be done in the annual softcover booklet, *Tables of New Zealand Public Acts and Statutory Regulations in Force,* which also gives the location of any subsequent amendments. *Butterworths annotations to the New Zealand Statutes,* 2nd edition, a looseleaf service updated monthly, also gives the location of the latest reprint and contains the full text of any amendments as well as case annotations.

A guide to the New Zealand primary sources in the Davis Law Library 1979 by Kathleen Shawcross is a brief guide but lists law reports and legislation comprehensively and contains valuable additional information.

Law reports

An account of the historical development of the court system can be found in the *Report* of the Royal Commission on the Courts in 1978 which contains details of important changes which were subsequently implemented. The *New Zealand Law Reports,* published since 1883, are the official series and contain reports of a selection of cases from the High Court, formerly called the Supreme Court, and most cases from the Court of Appeal. The *New Zealand Law Reports* from 1970 to date were made available on LEXIS in 1985.

Appeals to the Privy Council are reported in the *New Zealand Law Reports* and a collection entitled *New Zealand Privy Council Cases 1840–1932,* originally published in 1938, was reprinted in 1970. Many cases in the lower courts such as the District Courts, formerly the Magistrates' Courts, have been reported and a few subject series are published covering areas such as tax, local government and the work of various tribunals and commissions with special jurisdictions.

Recent Law is published by the Legal Research Foundation at the University of Auckland Faculty of Law. Although it contains articles, it is mainly devoted to brief digests of recent cases in advance of reports. A service is offered to supply copies of individual unreported judgments. *Butterworths Current Law*, which used to be issued as a supplement to the *New Zealand Law Journal*, is a weekly digest of recent cases and statutory regulations with a cumulative index.

The major digest is the *Abridgement of New Zealand Case Law* which has annual supplementation. It contains a complete subject digest modelled on the *English and Empire Digest* and includes case annotations. In 1963 H. Jenner Wiley, the editor, wrote in the preface to volume 1, 'with the consolidation of the New Zealand Statutes, the launching of New Zealand Forms and Precedents and the publication of the Abridgement of New Zealand Case Law the Legal Profession of this country is amongst the best equipped in the world.'

Other jurisdictions

The majority of the remaining territories are small islands, many recently independent. The territories range from Gibraltar and the Mediterranean islands to Fiji and the other Pacific islands. Legal systems other than English common law have affected some islands, for example Roman-Dutch law in Sri Lanka and French civil law in the Seychelles.

Very little legal literature even of a basic kind is available for many of these territories. The Commonwealth Secretary-General wrote in his *Report* covering 1981–3, p. 48, 'A considerable number of small jurisdictions are very poorly served in respect of publications, some even lacking such fundamental legal tools as law reports and indices to their statutes.' Other difficulties are lack of reliable means of supply, lack of up to date material, lack of finding aids and annotations and scarcity of secondary material. The Caribbean and some larger jurisdictions including African countries share similar problems.

Although statute law is hard to obtain in revised form,

external publishers in co-operation with local governments have produced a few publications such as the looseleaf revised editions of laws of Kiribati and Tuvalu published by Sweet and Maxwell. Established and long-running series of law reports are the exception rather than the rule and owe their long existence to the courts of appeal for neighbouring territories and regions which were situated on particular islands such as Fiji and Mauritius. Cases for a large number of islands may only have been reported if they appeared in one of these series. Several wholly new series of locally produced law reports from small jurisdictions have appeared in recent years such as the *Kiribati Law Reports* and the *Solomon Islands Law Reports* both published with the support of the Commonwealth Secretariat. Recent series of law reports from Gibraltar and the Seychelles include a considerable amount of retrospective reporting.

Conventional legal publishing is often not viable because of the size of the potential market. In many areas unpublished treatises, indexes and compilations of teaching materials at universities are available locally but are never published or available elsewhere. The problems and needs of small jurisdictions in the production of legal literature have been the subject of study in recent years and a starting point is *Legal literature in small jurisdictions* edited by William Twining and Jenny Uglow which includes some country studies of existing legal literature and a select bibliography.

FURTHER READING

THE COMMONWEALTH AS A WHOLE

Dale, Sir William. *The modern Commonwealth*, 1983.
Elias, T. O. *British colonial law: a comparative study of the interaction between English and local laws in British dependencies*, 1962.
Fawcett, J. E. S. *The British Commonwealth in international law*, 1963.
Marshall, H. H. 'United Kingdom dependent territories', in *International encyclopedia of comparative Law*, vol. I, pp. U107–U130.

'Reception of common law in the Commonwealth' [various papers], in *Proceedings and Papers of the Sixth Commonwealth Law Conference*, Lagos, Nigeria, 17–23 August 1980, pp. 105–214.

Roberts-Wray, Sir Kenneth, *Commonwealth and colonial law*, 1966.

Wheare, K. C. *The Constitutional structure of the Commonwealth*, 1960.

INTERNAL LAW OF MEMBER COUNTRIES

General

British Commonwealth: the development of its laws and constitutions, 14 vols., 1952–67.

De Smith, S. A. *The New Commonwealth and its constitutions*, 1964.

National reports [on various countries], in *International Encyclopedia of Comparative Law*, vol. I.

Africa

Allott, A. N. *Judicial and legal systems in Africa*, 2nd edn., 1970.

Allott, A. N. *New essays in African Law*, 1970.

Cotran, E. 'African law', in *International encyclopedia of comparative law*, vol. II, chap. 2, pp. 157–68.

Vanderlinden, J. *An introduction to the sources on contemporary African laws*, 1975.

Australia

Australian Law Librarians' Group Newsletter, 1973–.

Borchardt, D. H. (ed.) *Australian official publications*, 1979.

Campbell, E. *et al. Legal research materials and methods*, 2nd edn., 1979.

Watts, R. J. 'Sources and literature of Australian law' (Part I [federal law]), *Lawasia* (NS) 2, 1983, pp. 115–54. Part II, *Lawasia* (NS), 1985, pp. 1–47.

Canada

Banks, M. *Using a law library: a guide for students and lawyers in the common law provinces of Canada*, 4th edn., 1985.

Bishop, O. G. *Canadian official publications,* 1981.
Canadian Association of Law Libraries Newsletter, new series, vol. 1–, 1975–.
Le May, D. *La recherche documentaire juridique au Québec,* 1984.
MacEllven, D. T. *Legal research handbook,* 2nd edn., 1986.

Caribbean

Newton, V. *Legal literature and publishing in the Commonwealth Caribbean: a working paper,* 1979.
Patchett, K. and Jenkins, V. *A bibliographical guide to law in the Commonwealth Caribbean,* 1973.

India

Jain, H. C. *Indian legal materials: a bibliographical guide,* 1970.
Jain, H. C. 'Using a law library', *Journal of the Indian Law Institute,* vol. 24, 1982, pp. 575–91.

Malaysia and Singapore

Bartholomew, G. W. 'Sources and literature of Singapore law', *Lawasia* (NS) 2, 1982–3, pp. 1–49.
Zakaria, S. 'Legal documentation and information retrieval in Malaysia', *Malayan Law Journal,* [vol. 2, 1979], pp. cxlvii–cli

New Zealand

Shawcross, K. *A guide to the New Zealand primary sources in the Davis Law Library 1979,* 1979.

Other jurisdictions

Elliot, J. 'Legal information needs of Papua New Guinea and the Pacific', *Australian Law Librarians' Group Newsletter* no. 58, 1983, pp. 3–11.
Twining, W. and Uglow, J. (ed.) *Legal literature in small jurisdictions,* 1981.

Section 2: United States

P. NORMAN

The sheer size and complexity of American legal literature make it impossible to give more than a brief outline in this *Manual*. The research guides listed under 'Further reading' are all substantial works (Cohen nearly 800 pages, Jacobstein over 600 pages) with copious illustrations, and must be consulted for further detail.

Having its origins as a group of British colonies, the United States inherited the common law of England, although in the seventeenth century remoteness and the lack of a trained Bench and Bar meant that the complicated English legal system of the time was only sketchily adopted. At the Revolution however, most colonies followed the example of New York in adopting English common and statute law as it then stood. Blackstone's *Commentaries on the laws of England* published 1765–70, were a great influence, to the point of being the model for James Kent's *Commentaries on American law* which appeared between 1826 and 1830. As the country expanded westward so an American version of common law was carried across the continent.

Apart from some vestiges of Spanish influence in the south west, the major exception to this trend was, and remains, Louisiana which was sold to the USA by France as late as 1803. Here a system based on the civil law of continental Europe still prevails. The civil code of 1825 was modelled on the French civil code of 1804. Thus, Louisiana stands in similar relation to the rest of the United States as does Quebec to common law Canada.

PRIMARY SOURCES

Legislation

Constitution

As the United States is a federation, the fundamental basis of its legal system is the Constitution of 1789. Among other things, this lays down the composition and powers of the three branches of the federal government – legislative, executive and judicial – and its relationship to the governments of the constituent states of the Union.

There are several publications in which the text of the Constitution appears. It is included in both official and unofficial editions of the United States Code (see p. 327), and was published separately by the Library of Congress in 1973 under the title *The Constitution of the United States of America: analysis and interpretation, annotations of cases decided by the Supreme Court of the United States to June 29, 1972.* In 1962 appeared a looseleaf collection edited by the Legislative Drafting Research Fund of Columbia University: *Constitutions of the United States: national and state.* A second edition appeared in 1978 and now comprises seven binders. There are at least two supplements per year.

Acts of Congress

Acts of the legislature as officially published are similar in character to British Acts of Parliament. There are both public and private Acts, and each are issued first as separate pamphlets, known in the USA as 'slip laws', and then collected into bound volumes in a series entitled *Statutes at Large,* abbreviated in citation to Stat. Citation of an Act is by the number of the Congress enacting it (that meeting in 1983–4 was the 98th) and then a running number in two sequences, one for public and one for private laws. Thus the Trade and Tariff Act 1984 is Public Law no. 98–573 or P L 98–573. Private laws are cited Priv. L.

Before the 85th Congress (1957), citation is by Congress and chapter number, both public and private laws being numbered in a single sequence. Moreover, until 1935, numbering began again for each of the two annual sessions of Congress so that the session number has to be included in the citation.

As well as official editions, the public statutes are issued by the two major legal publishers. Lawyers' Co-op issue a monthly supplement to their *United States Code Service* which contains session laws. The West Publishing Co. began its *Congressional and Administrative News* in 1941 with the first session of the 77th Congress. This contains not only public laws, but presidential executive orders and proclamations. These two are loosely comparable to British Orders in Council, being instruments having statutory authority, issued by the President in the exercise of powers delegated by Congress.

Also included in the *Congressional and Administrative News* is what is known as legislative history. This comprises selected reports of Senate or House committees during the passage of a Bill.

In contrast to the United Kingdom, statutory construction by reference to Congressional intent is both permissible and frequent. Debates on Bills are to be found in the American equivalent of Hansard, the *Congressional Record*, published since 1873. This has fortnightly and annual cumulative indexes. Its predecessors were the *Annals of Congress*, 1789–1824, the *Register of Debates*, 1824–37 and *Congressional Globe*, 1833–73. A comprehensive abstracting and indexing service for Congressional documents is provided by the *Congressional Information Service*, published annually since 1970 with monthly and quarterly supplements. Documents indexed can also be supplied on microfiche.

Consolidations

Most countries have at some time published their statutes in a consolidated edition, being a compilation of all the public general Acts of the legislature in force on a particular date.

In the United States this process began with the publication of the *Revised Statutes of the United States,* first issued in 1875 and containing Acts in force on 1 December 1873. The arrangement is under 74 subject headings or 'titles', but with a single sequence of section numbers running from one to 5601, so that the standard form of citation is *eg*, RS §4931. A second, corrected edition appeared in 1878. The *Revised Statutes* is important as it was enacted by Congress into positive law, so that its content supersedes and replaces the *Statutes at Large* version. It is the only official, authentic codification of the laws of the United States.

United States Code

This is an official compilation of the 'general and permanent laws of the United States in force', first published in 1926, re-issued every six years and updated by annual cumulative supplements. Like the *Revised Statutes* it is divided into subject titles, numbered one to 50, each of which, dependent on size, may be divided into part, chapter and section. Only the title and section number is given in citation, *eg*, 15 USC §23.

It must be noted that only nineteen of the titles have been enacted into positive law and are in that sense authentic. The other titles remain only *prima facie* evidence, and the original *Statutes at Large* or *Revised Statutes* version remains the authentic text. This is not usually of practical significance.

The compilation of both the *Revised Statutes* and the *United States Code* has meant re-grouping parts of Acts of Congress in order to fit the subject arrangement. To some extent this has happened in the British *Statutes in Force*, the taxation statutes being an example.

As well as the official edition of the *Code*, both the major law publishers issue a version. That of West is the *United States Code Annotated* (*USCA*), and that of the Lawyers' Co-operative Publishing Company the *United States Code Service* (*USCS*). The latter originated in 1936 as the *Federal Code Annotated*. While *USCA* follows closely the text of the *Code*, *USCS* prints the original wording of the *Statutes at Large* version, though in *Code* sequence. Each edition is heavily annotated to decisions in the federal and state law reports, but naturally each refers to related publications of the same publisher. Thus, *USCA* refers to *Corpus Juris Secundum* (akin to *Halsbury's Laws*) and uses the unique West key digest system. On the other hand *USCS* refers to *American Jurisprudence 2d* and the *American Law Reports*.

Both services are kept up to date by annual pocket supplements inserted in the back of bound volumes, and by periodic supplementary pamphlets arranged in *USC* title order.

Subordinate legislation

The American equivalent of British Statutory Instruments, namely delegated legislation made by the president, state governors or federal government departments, is published in the *Federal Register*, issued every working day since 1936. Appearance in the *Register* is a condition of the validity of such documents. An index by subject and by government department appears monthly, quarterly and annually.

Just as primary legislation has been compiled into the *United States Code*, regulations are published in codified form in the *Code of Federal Regulations (CFR)*. This is similarly divided into 50 titles, frequently, though not necessarily, corresponding to the *USC* titles. It is revised annually in quarterly instalments, and is consequently issued in paperback rather than in bound volumes. A useful guide to government departments is the *United States Government Manual*, issued annually. This gives not only names and addresses but a brief outline of functions and major publications of each department.

Court rules

The federal rules of civil and criminal procedure are promulgated by the Supreme Court for itself and for the lower federal courts, though in the latter case they may be supplemented by other rules to meet local circumstances. They are most easily found in the *United States Code*, title 18 (criminal) and 28 (civil), but also appear in the Supreme Court digests published respectively by West and Lawyers' Co-op.

Treaties

The international agreements of the United States, if formally concluded and signed by the President and approved by a two-thirds majority of the Senate, have the force of law under Article VI of the Constitution. A similar instrument not requiring Senate approval is the executive agreement, made by the authority of an Act of Congress.

For modern practical purposes, the sources for US treaties are as follows:

Treaties and Other International Agreements of the United States 1776–1949, published by the Department of State under the editorship of Charles I. Bevans.

This is a collection of treaties, executive agreements and other agreements in 13 volumes. Volumes 1 to 4 contain multilateral treaties in chronological order and 5 to 12 bilaterals in country order. Publication began in 1968 and ended with volume 13 the index in 1976.

Treaties and other International Acts Series, cited *TIAS* and beginning with number 1501 of December 1945.

This is the equivalent of the United Kingdom *Treaty Series* as issued in pamphlet form. The first number was obtained by adding together the numbering of its two parallel predecessors, the *Treaty Series (TS)* and *Executive Agreement Series (EAS)*. Beginning with *TIAS* number 2010 (January 1950), treaties are bound into volumes of *United States Treaties and other International Agreements,* cited *UST*. There are usually several 'volumes' per year, each in perhaps three separate parts. There can be four years' delay in the appearance of these volumes; a useful source for some more recent multilateral treaties is *International Legal Materials,* published by the American Society of International Law.

Indexes to treaties

The most important current index is the annual *Treaties in Force* issued by the Department of State since 1950. It is divided into bilateral and multilateral sections, giving current status and citations not only to American official sources, but to the *United Nations Treaty Series* etc., as appropriate.

A series of indexes covering first Bevans and then the *UST* series is edited by Igor I. Kavass *et al.* and published by W. S. Hein. This too is arranged chronologically, by country and by subject.

The states

The federal government legislates in areas of law of nation-wide concern – personal rights and freedoms, defence, taxation, trade regulation, administration of federal government departments. However, private law – domestic relations, property, corporations etc. – is governed by state legislation, though in some areas, particularly commerce, some uniformity has been achieved as between the states. Criminal law is mainly state regulated but there is some federal criminal law involving obviously such subjects as national security.

State legislation

State constitutions are most conveniently to be found in the publication mentioned above, *Constitutions of the United States: national and state*. They can also be seen in the codified versions of state statutes.

Unlike federal statutes, state session laws are seldom widely distributed as 'slip laws', but all states issue bound volumes of session laws. Most are in chronological order like the *Statutes at Large*, but some are arranged in conformity with the current statutory compilation.

Codified versions of state statutes follow more or less the principle of the *United States Code*, but range in approach from only a rearrangement in subject order of session laws to more radical codification. Generally speaking, it is of little value to consult only session laws, not only for reasons of amendment and repeal common to any jurisdiction, but because such a large proportion of such amendments are of a code rather than of previous individual statutes.

A comprehensive guide to editions of state legislation is M. G. Pimsleur's *Checklists of basic American legal publications*.

Subordinate legislation

The expense of maintaining up to date collections of American law means that regulations published by the respective states are unlikely to be found in libraries outside the United States. It should be noted, however, that over 70 per cent of the states publish editions of their regulations in either bound or loose-leaf format. Since, in other states, information must be obtained from the agency concerned, this is probably the best way to obtain such documents. A useful bibliographic guide is the *Monthly checklist of state publications* issued by the Library of Congress.

Uniform laws

Despite the relative autonomy of the states, it has long been thought desirable to create uniformity in certain areas of law. The regulating body is the National Conference of Commissioners on Uniform State Laws.

Of several laws drafted, approved and adopted in the various states, the most important is the Uniform Commercial Code, which first appeared in 1952 and has been adopted, with minor variations to meet local circumstances, by all states except Louisiana. This, and all other uniform laws on commerce, domestic relations and criminal procedure, have been collected in *Uniform laws annotated,* of which the second edition was published on behalf of the Commissioners in 1976 by West. Like their other publications it is thoroughly annotated, and contains reference tables showing which states have adopted a law, at what date, and the citation to the state statutes.

Another major piece of uniform legislation, the *Model penal code,* was issued by the American Law Institute in 1962.

Law reports

Just as there is distinct federal and state legislation, so are there two distinct court systems, federal and state. The pattern of law reporting reflects this duality.

Federal courts

At the top of the hierarchy is the Supreme Court of the United States, the main business of which consists of challenges to federal or state laws as unconstitutional, disputes between state and federal government and cases involving parties in different states.

There are currently three versions of the reports of the Supreme Court. The official series is *United States Reports,* and runs in unbroken sequence from 1790. The first ninety volumes are still cited by the names of their reporters and were only numbered retrospectively in 1875. Thus volume 1 of Wallace's reports is both 1 Wall. and 68 US. Conversion tables appear in the standard guides to United States legal literature and digests.

Prior to the appearance of the bound volume, there are both 'slip opinions' – pamphlet copies of single decisions issued at most two weeks after the decision and sent to subscribers – and 'advance sheets' – paper parts containing several cases like the British *Law Reports.*

The Lawyers' Co-operative Company publishes the *Lawyers' Edition* of the *Supreme Court Reports.* This series, cited L.Ed., or for the second series L.Ed.2d, covers the entire series from the beginning. As well as the text of the decision, a summary of the case and head-notes related to the publishers' own digests are provided, but more importantly some cases are given very full annotations (one might say scholarly essays) perhaps tens of pages long.

The other unofficial series is the *Supreme Court Reporter,* cited S.Ct., and published by West as part of its *National Reporter System.* It begins with 106 US (1882).

The most striking difficulty with both these sets is that volume numbering in no way corresponds to the official edition, though each prints the US volume number(s) in smaller letters on the spine.

Lower federal courts

The lowest federal courts having original jurisdiction are the district courts, of which there is at least one in each state.

Populous states such as California and New York have two or more. Appeal from these courts lies to the Courts of Appeals (formerly known as Circuit Courts of Appeals) and from there to the Supreme Court. The country is divided into thirteen circuits, each having one Court of Appeals.

From time to time, other federal courts have been created by statute to deal with special matters, for example the Court of Customs and Patent Appeals and Court of Claims (together reconstituted as a Court of Appeals for the Federal Circuit in 1982), Emergency Court of Appeals (for suits arising from wartime regulations, dissolved 1962), Temporary Emergency Court of Appeals (for cases involving the economic stabilization laws since 1971) and Court of International Trade.

Reports of cases decided in all these courts are to be found in the various federal units of the *National Reporter System*. The first to appear was the *Federal Reporter* (1880), cited F. or F. 2d, which contains cases in the Courts of Appeals and Temporary Emergency Court of Appeals. Cases in the district courts also appeared here until they were transferred to a new series, the *Federal Supplement,* cited F. Supp., which began in 1932. Decisions of the Court of Claims appeared, first selectively in the *Federal Reporter*, then from 1932 to 1960 in the *Federal Supplement,* then again in the *Federal Reporter* until 1983, when its appellate jurisdiction was transferred to the Court of Appeals for the Federal Circuit.

The federal group of the *National Reporter System* is completed by *Federal Rules Decisions,* containing cases, mainly from the district courts, which construe the Federal Rules of Civil and Criminal Procedure. Unusually, it also contains articles on the subject of procedure. It began in 1940 on the adoption of the Rules.

State reports

Within each state there is a hierarchy of state courts, ranging from a Supreme Court through intermediate appellate courts to trial courts of limited or specialized jurisdiction. In general it is the decisions of the supreme and appellate courts which are reported, as in the UK.

Most states issue official reports, though some have handed over the responsibility of reporting to commercial publishers. For practical purposes outside the United States the only source is again West's *National Reporter System*. This covers, in a number of regional units, the decisions of the Supreme Courts of all the states plus several intermediate appellate courts. The arrangement is:

Atlantic Reporter (Atl., A.2d)	1885–	Conn., Del., Me., Md., N.H., N.J., R.I., Vt., D.C.
North Eastern Reporter (N.E., N.E.2d)	1885–	Ill., Ind., Mass., N.Y., Ohio
North Western Reporter (N.W., N.W.2d)	1883–	N.Dak., S.Dak., Iowa, Mich., Minn., Neb., Wis.
Pacific Reporter (Pac., P.2d)	1883–	Alaska, Ariz., Cal., Colo., Hawaii, Idaho, Kan., Mont., Nev., N.M., Okla., Ore., Utah, Wash., Wyo.
South Eastern Reporter (S.E., S.E.2d)	1887–	Ga., N.C., S.C., Va., W.Va.
Southern Reporter (S., S.2d)	1887–	Ala., Fla., La., Miss.
South Western Reporter (S.W., S.W.2d)	1887–	Ark., Ky., Mo., Tenn., Tex.

All of these *Reporters* have begun a second series, and it will be noted that the form of citation varies in some instances.

Two other series complete the system: the *New York Supplement*, with coverage from 1847 (Court of Appeals) and lower courts from 1888, has also begun a second series (citation N.Y. Supp., N.Y.S.2d). The *California Reporter* (Cal. Rptr.) began in 1960 and is still in its first series. Each of these two covers decisions not found in the corresponding regional reporters.

As the entire *National Reporter System* now comprises over 7,000 volumes, it is comforting to know that the first series and a large part of the second are now available on ultrafiche from the publishers.

Other general series of reports

The *American Law Reports Annotated* published by Lawyers' Co-operative Publishing Co. reports selectively from both federal and state courts. The first series runs from 1918 to 1947 (175 vols., ALR) the second 1947 to 1965 (100 vols., ALR 2d), the third 1965 to 1980 (100 vols., ALR 3d) and the fourth 1980 to date. Since 1969, federal cases have been published in a new series, *ALR Federal*. The main feature of ALR is its lengthy and scholarly annotations which are similar to those in the *Lawyers' Edition* of the *Supreme Court Reports* mentioned earlier. Often two or three cases are grouped together by topic and treated in a joint annotation. Cross-references are given both to official citations for a given case and to other publications of Lawyers' Co-op., notably *American Jurisprudence*, their encyclopedic digest. The whole system is kept up to date by a 'later case service' though the pattern has varied in detail from one series to another.

For the period before the inception of the *National Reporter System* the only fully reliable source for state cases is the official state reports, which are however rarely to be found in libraries outside the United States. A number of selective series were published in the nineteenth century and contain state reports of general interest.

Three series, known together as the Trinity Series, were *American Decisions*, to 1886 in 100 volumes; *American Reports*, 1869–87, 60 volumes; *American State Reports*, 1887–1911, 104 volumes. The predecessors of *American Law Reports Annotated* were *Lawyers' Reports Annotated*, 1888–1918, 146 volumes in 2 series, and *American and English Annotated Cases*, 1906–1911, 21 volumes, which was continued by *American Annotated Cases*, 1912–1918, 32 volumes.

Specialized law reports

In this field the leading publishers are undoubtedly Commerce Clearing House with its 'topical law reports', and the Bureau of National Affairs. CCH reporters take the form of a current set of looseleaf volumes with recent news, government circulars etc., as well as court decisions, all updated sometimes weekly, and then a set of bound volumes of cases. Topics range widely: taxation, accountancy, food and drugs, labour relations and many more. Similarly the BNA produces a large number of looseleaf services, among them the *United States Patent Quarterly* and *United States Law Week*. Other series sometimes referred to in the UK are *American Maritime Cases*, 1923– and *United States Aviation Reports*, 1928–.

Digests

Digests in the United States perform the same function as in other common law jurisdictions, giving subject access to cases by means of very brief summaries of the principles involved. The dual court system and large number of jurisdictions means that the number of digests is also large. Thus there are individual digests for each state and for each regional unit of the *National Reporter System*, and digests covering only federal cases.

The most comprehensive digest is the *American Digest System* published by West. This consists of the Century edition, covering the period 1658 to 1896, and then a number of decennial digests, each in at least 25 and sometimes 50 volumes in an alphabetic subject arrangement with tables of cases and of words and phrases. Because of the increasing volume of cases, the most recent decennial is being issued in two fiveyear sections, 1976 to 1981 (38 vols.) and 1982 to 1986. The decennials are cumulated from the *General Digest* which appears first as a monthly pamphlet, then cumulated every four months into an A–Z bound volume. There may be 30 or more of these bound volumes before the next decennial cumulation, making it laborious to find recent cases. It must be borne in mind however that computerized legal information retrieval has largely removed this problem, and that lawyers dealing with the law of their own state would use a state digest which is less bulky.

From the first decennial onwards, each of the main subject headings is analysed into smaller topics and finally into specific points which are key numbered. It is thus possible, having found this number, to search the entire system to find the same precise point, though of course topics have been revised and new ones added from time to time.

For federal cases only, there are the *Federal Digest*, covering the period to 1938, the *Modern Federal Practice Digest* from 1939 to 1961 and *Federal Practice Digest 2d*, 1962 to date; all are published by West and use key numbers.

Supreme Court decisions are digested in *Digest of the U.S. Supreme Court Reports, L.Ed.* published by Lawyers' Co-op and related to their *L.Ed., ALR* and *American Jurisprudence,* and West's *United States Supreme Court Digest.*

Citators

As in Britain, it is important to find the current status of a case by seeing what later decisions have referred to it, whether by following, distinguishing or overruling it. The most comprehensive system is *Shepard's Citations* published by a company with the same name. As with digests, there are state editions, regional editions corresponding to the units of the *National Reporter System,* and federal editions. Each consists of two or three large bound volumes, with annual and quarterly paperback supplements.

Unlike the citator volume in the British *Current Law,* all these volumes are purely tabular, arranged by source citation: name of report series, volume number, page reference, without name of case. Each entry consists of a column of citations, beginning where applicable with the same decision in other series of reports, or a subsequent appellate decision in the same case. Treatment of the decision in later cases is indicated by a code letter. There are detailed user guides in the preliminary pages of each set.

Shepards are so central to American legal research that to 'shepardize' is the standard word for finding legal citations.

SECONDARY SOURCES

Legal encyclopedias

Those familiar with *Halsbury's Laws of England* will find its American counterpart in two publications, West's *Corpus Juris*

Secundum and the Lawyers' Co-op *American Jurisprudence 2d*. Each, as its title implies, constitutes a second edition of an earlier work, and each is arranged alphabetically by about 400 subject headings divided into sub-sections. Each claims to give a comprehensive statement of both state and federal law by reference to decided cases, and is kept up to date by annual pocket supplements and re-issued volumes as necessary. They are keyed to the sister publications of their respective publishers. *Corpus Juris Secundum* is in over 150 volumes plus 5 index volumes, while *American Jurisprudence 2d* is in 93 volumes plus 8 index volumes. A useful extra in Am. Jur. 2d is its 'Desk book', a collection of legal documents, charts, statistics and tabulations, *eg* Bar admission requirements.

Restatements

The American Law Institute was founded in 1923 'to promote the clarification and simplification of the law ... and to encourage and carry on scholarly and scientific legal work' (Certificate of Incorporation). These objects are in part achieved by the publication of a series of *Restatements of the law*, which set out, in the form of articles in a code, the principles of the common law of the United States. Each restatement is prepared by an eminent legal expert in the field as 'Reporter', with the assistance of consultants. Preliminary versions of particular sections, 'Tentative drafts', are submitted for consideration and approval before being incorporated into the final version. In style, the *Restatements* are comparable to Dicey and Morris' *Conflict of Laws,* with each 'rule' in bold type being followed by extensive comment, suggestions for change or improvement. There is more citation of other sources in the more recent editions. Subjects covered have been agency, conflict of laws, contract, foreign relations law, judgments, property, restitution, security, torts and trusts. There have been second editions of several, and they are all kept under review. While not of binding authority, the *Restatements* are extensively cited in court (over 80,000 times by April 1983). The series *Restatement in the Courts* forms a digest of such citations, and is in several bound volumes, with now annual supplementary volumes. There is also a unit of *Shepard's Citations* devoted to the *Restatements,* beginning in 1976.

Textbooks

These play a similar role to textbooks in British law, being aimed at a similarly wide range of readers – students, practitioners, scholars, non-lawyers. There are established standard works on particular subjects which, though not binding authorities, are frequently cited in the courts. Examples are Wigmore on *Evidence* (Little, Brown, 11 vols.), Williston on *Contracts* (Lawyers' Co-op, 22 vols.), Collier on *Bankruptcy* (Matthew Bender, 11 vols. looseleaf) and Fletcher's *Cyclopedia of Corporations* (Callaghan, 30 vols.)

There is of course a great deal of literature related to particular states, often issued by a publisher based in the area. Callaghan of Chicago produce local books for Illinois, Michigan and Wisconsin and Little, Brown of Boston for Massachusetts and Connecticut. The two giants, West and Lawyer's Co-op cover large numbers of states country-wide.

For student use there are single-volume textbooks giving the salient points of law and referring to landmark cases. West's *Hornbook Series* is of this type. However, a major feature of American legal education is the 'case method' whereby rather than being taught legal principles directly through lectures, students are encouraged to deduce principles by reading key cases on a subject. Hence the popularity of the 'casebook' – a collection of leading cases, and nowadays often of other materials such as statutes or government reports, on a particular subject. The two major series are West's *American Casebook Series* and the *University Casebook Series* of the Foundation Press.

Law reviews

By far the greatest proportion of legal periodicals in the United States is published by the university law schools. An integral part of legal education is the requirement to write and publish articles. While most of these law reviews are general in content, there are some which reflect the particular interest of the school; in other cases there is both a general and a specialized journal such as the *Columbia Law Review* and the *Columbia Journal of Transnational Law.*

As to practitioners' journals one might mention the publications of the American Bar Association. As well as the *American Bar Association Journal*, there are several special interest groups – 'sections' – which produce, as well as a brief newsletter, journals with in-depth articles on a subject. Examples are the *American Criminal Law Review, Antitrust Law Journal* and *Family Law Quarterly.*

Computerized legal research

The United States pioneered the development of computerized information retrieval and there are now several operational systems. The two main commercially available services for law are LEXIS and WESTLAW. LEXIS is operated by Mead Data Central of Dayton, Ohio and WESTLAW by West, the publishers of the *National Reporter System.* Each system is founded on a 'full text' database, in that the computer stores the actual word-by-word text of documents rather than only keywords or abstracts. Both systems offer extensive coverage of American case-law and federal statute law. As is usual with such systems, the most recent material has been 'loaded' first, though retrospective addition continues. For example, the LEXIS file of state reports goes back to the 1960s, although the *U.S. Supreme Court Reports* are present from the beginning.

Mead Data also provides a general news database, NEXIS, with files of the major American and British newspapers, general interest weeklies and 'wire' services.

WESTLAW has the advantage of the West summaries and head-notes to cases prepared as part of its hard copy publishing programme.

Until recently the two services had taken opposing views as to hardware. LEXIS permitted only dedicated equipment having the advantage of over 30 special function keys to speed up operation, plus an integral printer on its 'de luxe' machine.

WESTLAW on the other hand allowed access on a number of different types of terminal. However, LEXIS can now be accessed using IBM and Televideo machines, and WESTLAW is providing customized terminals.

LEXIS is available in the UK and is operated by Butterworth Telepublishing. Constant growth of databases and changes in technology mean that up to date information is best obtained from the suppliers.

FURTHER READING

Campbell, D. and Hepperle, W. *The US legal system: a practice handbook*, 1983.

Cohen, M. L. and Berring, R. C. *How to find the law*, 8th edn., 1983.

Downey, J. A. *US federal official publications: the international dimension*, 1978.

Jacobstein, J. M. and Mersky, R. M. *Fundamentals of legal research*, 2nd edn., 1981.

Price, M. O. *et al. Effective legal research*, 4th edn., 1979. (Known as Price and Bitner).

9. Reference Sources: Common Law Systems

D. M. BLAKE

ENGLAND AND WALES

Bibliographic sources

Reference sources provide librarians with the means of assisting readers and supplying information, whether by answering everyday queries or pointing the way to other sources and further research. In law libraries, reference sources include guides to legal literature, bibliographies, indexes to periodicals, union catalogues, lists of research, dictionaries, encyclopedias, biographical sources and directories.

The most recent additions to this list are the sources that are available online. Since the first edition of the *Manual* in 1976, a vast and ever-growing range of online sources has become accessible. The law database most familiar to British law librarians is LEXIS which is discussed in Chapter 16. A wide range of bibliographic databases provide secondary source material, and the law librarian will find that many general sources, such as the *British National Bibliography* (BNB), or legal sources, such as the *Legal Resource Index*, are available online on BLAISE and DIALOG respectively. But how does one find out what is available, whether and how it can be accessed, and how much it will cost? These are questions requiring the most up to date answers and any detailed information given here would soon be overtaken by the rapid developments taking place in the creation of new databases or alterations to existing ones. In Britain the Aslib Online Information Centre provides guidance for both new and experienced users of online sources. The Centre offers subscribers an enquiry service, its own publications, and a monthly newsletter *Online Notes*, which carries news of databases, hosts and producers, meetings, training courses, and notes of new publications. A useful booklet, *Law databases*, was produced by the Centre in 1983, and this describes each database, its content, period of coverage, host, and so on. More detail is provided by the *Handbook of legal information retrieval*, 1984, edited by J. Bing, which includes a brief history of legal information retrieval and an informative survey of systems by country. A section on international organizations is also included.

Other useful publications covering online databases generally are issued regularly. Examples are the *Directory of Online Databases*, the *European Database Guide*, and the *Eusidic Database Guide*. The *Eusidic* guide gives separate alphabetical lists of organizations, databases, and subjects covered. There is an index to networks, a geographical index, and a full index to everything referred to elsewhere in the volume. It covers services provided within Europe. Access to foreign national bibliographic databases from the UK is not yet possible but is a future probability.

Despite the rapid increase in online information retrieval, there are many law librarians in libraries where local circumstances or the costs of installation prevent the introduction of online systems. Where systems have been installed, they are mostly used to complement rather than replace the traditional reference sources, and it is these traditional sources which form the subject matter of the following pages.

Guides to legal literature

The study of law is a library-based subject and an introduction to the various types of law books and how to use them is the starting point of most undergraduate courses. The publications by D. J. Way, *The students guide to law libraries*, 1967, and Glanville Williams, *Learning the law*, 11th edn., 1982, have now been joined by J. Dane and P. Thomas *How to use a law library*, 1979. *Learning the law* is an excellent introduction to the study of law, and *The students guide to law libraries* describes the layout and contents of a law library for students outside the academic environment. However, Dane and Thomas's book (with six optional tape-slide presentations) provides both new law students and newcomers to law librarianship with a basic introduction to the literature of English law. The book is a valuable elementary reference work, but more detailed information and guidance for legal research must be sought elsewhere, and the authors include a list of further reading in their introduction. Three of the books listed warrant mention here since they are all library research manuals of established reputation though not originally designed for British users: *Legal research: materials and methods*, 2nd edn., 1979, by E. Campbell *et al.*, where the emphasis is on Australian materials; M. A. Banks *Using a law library: a guide for students and lawyers in the common law provinces of Canada*, 4th edn., 1985; M. O. Price and H. Bitner *Effective legal research: a practice manual of law books and their use*, 1953, where the subject matter is primarily American.

In 1973 the Institute of Advanced Legal Studies published *A Bibliographical guide to the law of the United Kingdom, the Channel Islands and the Isle of Man*, 2nd edn., by A. G. Chloros; the first edition in 1956 was edited under the direction of F. H. Lawson. Originally intended as a guide for overseas lawyers unfamiliar with the legal system of the British Isles, it also filled a gap for lawyers in this country. It includes chapters on all the major topics of English law, on other UK legal systems, and on international law, the Commonwealth, jurisprudence, Roman law, canon law, and, new for the 2nd edition, a chapter on Common Market law. Each chapter is written by an expert in the field and has a commentary on the literature followed by a select bibliography. A somewhat similar approach to the literature of the legal systems of the British Isles excluding England and Wales is to be found in *Law publishing and legal information: small jurisdictions of the British Isles*, 1981, edited by W. Twining and J. Uglow, which is referred to in more detail below under each of the jurisdictions it covers.

Another publication to guide the newcomer through the complexities of British legal literature is A. R. Blunt's *Law librarianship*, 1980. This is one of the 'Outlines of Modern Librarianship' series designed to give library school students an introduction to specialized librarianship, but in this case also providing help to any librarian confronted by a collection of legal materials for the first time. For such a slim volume a large amount of detailed information is contained in its 126 pages, 80 being devoted to legal literature. Its brief survey of other legal systems of the British Isles is particularly useful for the non-lawyer.

Bibliographies of legal bibliographies

Bibliographies which themselves list legal bibliographies are an invaluable aid to research. The most recently published bibliographies will be included in the current awareness sections of journals such as *The Law Librarian*, the *International Journal of Legal Information*, and the *Law Library Journal*. References may also be found in general legal bibliographies, in indexes to legal periodicals, and in book reviews.

The annual *Legal Bibliography Index*, first published in Louisiana in 1978, aims to collect together English language legal bibliographies published during the year and 'typically received by U.S. law libraries'. This imposes some limitations on the comprehensive coverage of this excellent publication. Each annual volume is in five sections: subject headings used, regularly published legal bibliographies, serial publications received by US law libraries which feature bibliographic sections, legal bibliographies covering more than one subject, and an alphabetical list of bibliographies arranged by subject and jurisdiction. This last section is the largest and contains cross-references. Each entry gives author, title, publisher, date, pagination, and frequency of publication.

Its straightforward approach makes the *Legal Bibliography Index* a useful *quick* reference tool. Older, but none the less of importance as a guide to bibliographies published before 1943, is W. L. Friend's *Anglo-American Legal Bibliographies*, 1944. The work also provides a useful historical survey.

National bibliographies

The law librarian will find it useful to refer to this type of bibliography when tracing 'fringe' materials, or when not all details of a publication are known.

The *British National Bibliography* (BNB), first published in 1950, is currently issued weekly with cumulations monthly, four monthly, and annually. Six cumulative indexes cover the period 1950–73, BNB is also accessible on BLAISE.

British Books in Print lists books available from British publishers. Formerly issued only annually in two volumes, it is now offered in monthly microfiche and on BLAISE. Whitaker's series of publications listing British books in print or forthcoming are useful sources in both hard copy and online forms. Two of several American publications which include British books are *Books in Print* and the *Cumulative Book Index*.

Legal bibliographies

A good bibliography is of immense value in any library as a reference tool. It enables the reader to check quickly the details of a particular work or discover what has been written upon a topic. When evaluating a bibliography the following factors should be borne in mind: the extent of the coverage, the accuracy and detail of the entries, the logic of their arrangement, the presence of annotations for the entries, and adequacy of indexing.

General

An essential bibliography for any law library is Sweet and Maxwell's *A legal bibliography of the British Commonwealth of Nations*, 2nd edn., 1955–64, 7 volumes. Volumes 1 and 2 cover English law (including Wales), the Channel Islands and the Isle of Man to 1956; volume 3 covers Canadian and British-American colonial law to 1956; volume 4 Irish law to 1956; volume 5 Scottish law to 1956, together with a list of Roman law books in the English language; volume 6 the law of Australia, New Zealand, and their dependencies to 1958; volume 7 the law of the British Commonwealth to 1962, excluding the forementioned countries, India and Pakistan. India and Pakistan were to be covered by a projected volume 8 but this was never published.

Volume 1 has a subject arrangement with author and subject indexes, but otherwise arrangement is by author with subject indexes. Entries are brief: author (surname and initials only), title, and date – an attempt is made to list the dates of all known editions. No publishers are mentioned and rarely the place of publication; a few entries are annotated, mostly in volume 1 which covers the early literature. Although published more than 20–30 years ago, this bibliography still remains a valuable guide to the older literature.

Editions of *Where to look for your law* were published for over half a century; the final 14th edition by C. W. Ringrose appeared in 1962. It provided brief details of current legal literature including lists of the important law books, command papers and law reports, together with a long list of abbreviations of reports and journals. Known familiarly as the 'yellow book', an attempt to update the work in the late 1970s came to nothing.

The most recently published general legal bibliography is *Lawyers' Law Books: a practical index to legal literature*, 2nd edn., 1985, by D. Raistrick. The major drawback to the first edition was the absence of publishers' names; this has been rectified in the 2nd edition for textbooks and monographs, but not for all entries. Also still omitted are the ISBN and place of publication, although the country of publication is included for some entries. The bibliography is arranged in alphabetical subject order with cross-references to other subject headings, and there are both author and subject indexes. Entries give surname and initials, title, edition, publisher and date. A most useful feature is the inclusion under each subject heading of references to the appropriate volumes of major legal encyclopedias such as *Halsbury*, and to relevant journals and reports. Coverage is mainly British but also includes a wide range of material from other common law jurisdictions, and English language publications from the member countries of the Community. Most entries are of recent origin, but older and still useful titles are also included.

The bibliographies referred to above list material published over a wide span of years up to a certain date. There is no British publication devoted specifically to current legal bibliography which periodically lists all material as soon as possible after publication. For this, one must turn to the various American series which adequately cover British output.

Law books in print, first published in 1957, attempts to list all English language legal texts in print. The current 4th edition published in 1982, lists books published worldwide in print at the end of 1981. The list now fills five volumes: volumes 1 and 2 are arranged by combined author and title entries, volumes 3 and 4 by subject, and volume 5 by publisher and series. Primary materials, government publications, and periodicals are omitted. Since 1970, *Law books in print* has been supplemented by *Law Books Published* which is currently issued three times a year, the third issue being cumulative.

The *Bibliographic Guide to Law* began publication in 1969 as the *Law Book Guide* but changed its title in 1975. The main entries are arranged alphabetically by author and include full cataloguing details. It is based on Library of Congress catalogued items and includes a subject sequence which groups books by country or geographical area, and provides a title index. It is published monthly with an annual cumulation.

A third publication in this category is *Bowker's Law Books and Serials in Print*, previously issued in 1982 and 1983 as *Law Information* and from 1976 to 1981 as *Law Books*. This aims to cover English language legal literature worldwide. It includes government, United Nations, and pamphlet material as well as books, listed by author, by title and by Library of Congress subject headings. Serials are indexed by title and subject. Each entry provides full bibliographic details and publication frequency information for serials. The 1986–7 edition is in three volumes and is supplemented by an *Update* issued ten times each year; the *Update* was first published in 1983 as *Law Information Update*.

Apart from these specialist series there are other sources which serve as current bibliographical tools. The monthly issues of *Current Law* (see Chapter 4) list recent books, usually on the inside back cover, and these lists are cumulated by subject in *Current Law Year Book*. Details of author, title, edition and price are given and the ISBN is quoted in preference to the name of the publisher.

The annual catalogues of the leading law publishers and book-sellers form bibliographies in their own right. The law catalogues of Butterworths, Sweet and Maxwell, Blackwells, and Hammicks for example, should be kept in that section of the library.

Early law books

To place in context the books and materials which make up the framework of legal history, the librarian will need to turn first to an introductory survey which will provide a basis on which to judge the subject matter or assess the relative importance of a text. Three scholarly surveys of early English legal literature originate from lecture series. Of first importance is P. H. Winfield's *The chief sources of English legal history*, 1925, which includes many bibliographic annotations within the text in addition to several chapter bibliographies. Although dated, the chapter on bibliographical guides is still of use. Other topics include statutes, public records, case-law, abridgments, textbooks and books of practice. A similar range of topics is covered by W. S. Holdsworth's *Sources and literature of English law*, 1925, but it lacks the annotations of Winfield. The third survey, by T. F. T. Plucknett, *Early English legal literature*, 1958, is narrower in scope but makes useful background reading, especially on Bracton.

Most English legal history texts comment upon the nature and importance of early legal literature. The standard work is W. S. Holdsworth's *History of English law*, 17 volumes in various editions 1903–72; the final volume is an index. The publications of the Selden Society should not be overlooked.

A basic checklist or bibliography for early law books is provided by Sweet and Maxwell's *Legal bibliography*, vol. 1, which covers English law to 1800. For the certain identification of a particular edition it is necessary to consult a descriptive bibliography.

Law books printed in England up to 1600 are covered by J. H. Beale's *A bibliography of early English law books*, 1926. This is reinforced by R. B. Anderson's *A supplement to Beale's bibliography*, 1943. The supplement contains additional entries and corrections, but does not extend the scope of the work beyond 1600. The table of entries in Beale serves as a kind of index and records copies in selected libraries.

A more specialized work containing very detailed descriptions is J. D. Cowley's *Bibliography of abridgments, digests, indexes and dictionaries of English law to the year 1800*, 1932. The introduction is informative on the history and textual matter of the works included. Each entry is followed by a list of locations.

Older legal bibliographies are scarce and the following three works were reprinted in 1953: R. W. Bridgman's *Short view of legal bibliography*, 1807, which is very selective but has detailed notes; J. G. Marvin's *Legal bibliography*, 1847, which is more complete but omits editions not deemed to be of interest to American lawyers; C. C. Soule's *Lawyers reference manual of law books*, 1883, which is more helpful on reports than treatises. Details of early law books may also be checked in the printed catalogues of older law libraries (see p. 352).

Because books on, or relevant to, law formed a high proportion of early printing output, general bibliographies of early literature are helpful. For basic purposes the field is adequately covered by E. W. Pollard and G. R. Redgrave's *A short title catalogue of books printed in England, Scotland and Ireland and of English books printed abroad 1475–1640*, 1926, and D. G. Wing's *Short-title catalogue of books printed in England, Scotland, Ireland, Wales and British America and of English books printed in other countries, 1641–1700*, 1945–51, 3 volumes. They are commonly abbreviated to STC and Wing, and revised editions of both are in progress. Volume 2 (I–Z) of the STC was published in 1976, volume 1 (A–H) 1986, and an additional volume 3 containing an index of printers and booksellers is planned. Volumes 1 and 2 of Wing were published in 1973 and 1982 respectively; volume 3 has yet to appear. Each entry is allotted an identifying number and gives details of author, short title, printer, date, and a selective list of locations in major British and American libraries. Unfortunately the numbers in the new Wing do not always correspond to entries in the earlier edition as a result of the insertion of new material.

Covering the legal literature of one century is J. N. Adams and G. Averley, *A bibliography of 18th century legal literature: a subject and author catalogue of law treatises and all law-related literature held in the main legal collections in England*, 1982. As the title states, the bibliography includes much law-related literature which extends the value of the work to social historians and others. The fact that most entries relate to works held in English libraries enables locations to be given; other details include edition, date, and place of publication. The entries are arranged by subject in a classification system devised for the bibliography and somewhat resembling Dewey. An outline of the system is followed by a detailed list of subject classes, but there is no alphabetical list of subjects to speed location of required topics, nor any running class numbering at the head of each page. The author index is contained on six microfiche filed in a pocket at the back of the volume – not exactly convenient for those without a fiche reader. Although the bibliography contains a wealth of material it is not easy to use, and this is a major drawback to so detailed a work.

Law library catalogues
Printed library catalogues are useful for locating individual copies of a book, for indicating the relative strength of a particular library's stock, and for bibliographical purposes. A comprehensive list may be traced through Sweet and Maxwell's *Legal bibliography*, volume 1, p. 2. With the modern development of photographic techniques and computerized printing there has been a resurgence of interest in the printed catalogue, a form neglected since the nineteenth and early twentieth centuries.

The last of the great traditional English law library catalogues was *A catalogue of the printed books in the library of the Honourable Society of the Middle Temple*, 1914, 3 vols., compiled by C. E. A. Bedwell. A supplement by H. A. C. Sturgess was published in 1925. Also notable are catalogues of the libraries of Inner Temple, Gray's Inn, Lincoln's Inn, and the Law Society, but in view of the losses during the Second World War there is no guarantee that items listed actually exist today.

The first of the modern catalogues was published in 1974 – the *University of Cambridge Squire Law Library catalogue*, 15 vols. This classified listing of more than 60,000 volumes in one of the major British law libraries was made possible by computerization. In 1978 the *Catalogue of the Library of the Institute of Advanced Legal Studies*, 6 vols., was published, followed in 1979 by the *Library Catalogue of the Radzinowicz Library*, Institute of Criminology, Cambridge, 6 vols. Both were produced by photoreproduction of catalogue cards. The IALS catalogue lists entries by author (vols. 1–3) and subject (vols. 4–6), with command papers and theses included in volume 6. The Radzinowicz catalogue has a similar author and subject distribution between volumes but adds periodicals to volume 3 and an alphabetical subject index to volume 6.

Subjects

Specialized bibliographies on various legal topics are often published in journals, but there are many published as separate works which are of interest and value to the law librarian. There is space here for only four examples. D. Campbell *et al. Annotated bibliography on the legal profession and legal services 1960–78*, 1980, has entries arranged within eight chapters in chronological order by subject and cross-referenced. There is a brief synopsis of each entry and an indication by letter-notation of the type of subject matter, *eg*, H – historical perspective, R – reform proposal. Coverage is England and Wales. It is interesting to note that the provision of law libraries is not included as an ancillary service for the legal profession. R. W. M. Dias's *A Bibliography of jurisprudence*, 3rd edn., 1979, is arranged by subjects and lists book chapters and periodical articles. There are excellent annotations. B. A. Hepple *et al.*, *A bibliography of the literature on British and Irish labour law*, 1975, with 1981 supplement listing material omitted from the main work and extending the coverage to 1978. Subsequent updating appears regularly in the *Industrial Law Journal*. The main work lists entries under two headings, 'General Works' and 'Special Subjects', and attempts to include all relevant literature from the eighteenth century to 1972 and includes some early entries as far back as 1542. Entries are cross-referenced and there is a table of cases, and both author and subject indexes. The fourth example is L. Radzinowicz and R. Hood's *Criminology and the administration of criminal justice: a bibliography*, 1976, which won the 1977 Joseph L. Andrews Bibliographical Award of the American Association of Law Libraries for excellence in bibliographical achievement.

From time to time librarians need to be aware of the value of the books in their libraries or the price likely to be asked for out of print or rare material. R. Adamiak, *The law book price guide: a market value reference for antiquarian, out of print and rare law books and documents and other law related materials*, 1983, reprints extracts from the recent catalogues of seven specialist dealers, three English, three American and one Canadian. This provides a means of valuing existing items in a collection, or indicating the cost of acquisition. Annotations to some of the entries give useful comments.

Periodicals

Directories or lists

The most convenient directory of legal periodical titles is the IALS *Union list of legal periodicals* (see p. 357) which gives details of place, publisher and dates.

The American *Index to Legal Periodicals* lists in each issue all those periodicals covered by the *Index*, and gives details of price, frequency, and the publisher's address. Not all British journals are indexed, a limitation which also applies to the American *Legal Periodicals in English*. This ceased publication in 1974 and is now of use only for checking the completeness of back sets.

A comprehensive general directory of periodicals in print is *Ulrich's International Periodicals Directory*, 23rd edn., 1984, 2 vols. and quarterly issues; it is also available on DIALOG. Some series of law reports are included. Also useful as a general directory is the *British Union Catalogue of Periodicals* (BUCOP) now replaced by *Serials in the British Library* (see p.357).

Indexes of articles

Most periodicals have their own volume indexes, and some have cumulated indexes covering a number of volumes such as the *Law Quarterly Review* index to vols. 1–100. There are also indexes which cover a large number of periodicals, but none of these is devoted solely to British legal periodicals or English law and most are American publications.

The earliest in the field was the *Index to Legal Periodical Literature* (the 'Jones-Chipman index'), published in 6 volumes and covering 1803–1937. Coverage included the main Anglo-American legal journals of the time. The arrangement was alphabetically by subject with an author index. The first three volumes, covering the period to 1907, are still invaluable, but the later volumes are less comprehensive than the *Index to*

Legal Periodicals, which commenced in 1908. This has annual volumes for the years to 1925, since when the annual volumes have been cumulated triennially. At present the *Index* is issued monthly (except September) and cumulated quarterly, annually and triennially. It indexes over 400 journals which regularly publish legal content of high quality in the United States, Canada, Great Britain, Australia and New Zealand. It has a combined subject and author sequence, but the main entries are under subject, and the author entries are merely cross-references. There has been a separate table indexing case-notes since 1917, and a table of book reviews since 1940. One disadvantage of the *Index* is that items for inclusion are not selected just by quality but also by length. Excluded are those articles of less than five ordinary pages, and case-notes and reviews of less that two pages. The relatively compact style and format of British journals means that some worthwhile items are thereby not indexed; nevertheless this fact should not obscure the merits of the *Index*. Both hard copy and online forms (on WILSONLINE) are available.

Since 1960 a complementary service has been provided by the *Index to Foreign Legal Periodicals*; 'foreign' in this sense denoting journals dealing with international law, comparative law, and legal systems other than those with a common law basis. Coverage is worldwide and is not restricted to English language journals. Since 1963 the contents of selected volumes of essays and Festschriften have been indexed. The *Index* is published quarterly, the fourth issue of each year being cumulative. The annual volumes are cumulated triennially. The *Index* currently covers about 370 titles and indexes articles of at least four pages in length and book reviews of at least two-and-a-half pages. The main sequence is arranged by subject, with sub-headings for countries under each topic. Articles on the laws of a particular country may be traced through the geographical index. Other features are indexes of authors and book reviews.

The American *Current Law Index* (CLI) began publication in 1980 and covers over 700 law journals in English throughout the world. It includes all those listed in the *Index to Legal Periodicals* but puts no restriction on the minimum number of pages an article must cover before it is indexed. It is issued eight times a year with three quarterly cumulations and an annual cumulation. It offers an author/title index, a subject index with cross-references, a table of cases, and a book review index – it is also more expensive than the *Index to Legal Periodicals*. The CLI is also available on microfilm or online on DIALOG; in this form it is entitled *Legal Resource Index*. The database comprises the CLI journals plus some newspapers and monographs and government reports from the Library of Congress MARC database. The LRI database is updated monthly. There is subject coverage of United Kingdom law.

British legal periodical literature is indexed in *Current Law*. In the monthly issues, articles are listed at the end of the entries under each subject heading, but in the *Current Law Year Book* they are grouped by subject in a separate sequence. Details are given of the title and journal reference of the article with the author's name in brackets.

Some articles on legal subjects published in non-legal journals may be traced through the *Index to Periodical Articles Related to Law*, which selectively indexes articles of research value which do not appear in the *Index to Legal Periodicals* or the *Index to Foreign Legal Periodicals*. The arrangement is by subject with an author index, but since 1979 coverage has been confined strictly to non-legal journals. A more general index which lists articles in non-legal journals is the *British Humanities Index*. It should also be remembered that many bibliographies list articles in periodicals.

Abstracting services

Abstracts provide brief synopses of articles, essays, books and theses. The main purpose of each synopsis is to indicate the scope and level of the item rather than to give a critical review of the contents.

There is no abstracting service which satisfactorily covers British legal literature. We have no equivalent to the American *Legal Periodical Digest*, published in looseleaf form from 1928 to 1962, which abstracted selected articles in English language periodicals. It was mainly of interest to American lawyers.

Some subjects peripheral to law are well served by abstracting services; two examples are *Criminal Justice Abstracts* and *Sociological Abstracts*, the latter being also available online on DIALOG.

Union catalogues

British law libraries are well provided for in this field by the series of five union catalogues published by the Institute of Advanced Legal Studies. The most widely used is the *Union List of Legal Periodicals*, 4th edn., 1978. Nearly 3,000 titles are listed from 114 libraries, 69 of which are outside London (including 10 in Scotland and two in Northern Ireland). The entries are arranged alphabetically by title. The list includes nearly all periodicals taken by specialist law libraries in the United Kingdom and some titles for which no holding is recorded, but generally excludes law reports, legislation, and non-legal periodicals. The *Union List of Air Law Literature*, 1956, was issued in a revised edition in 1975 to include space law. It lists over 450 items with holdings in 22 libraries in London, Oxford and Cambridge. The list includes books and pamphlets, international conferences and treaties, international organizations, laws and regulations, and periodicals and reports. There is a subject index. The remaining three catalogues are discussed elsewhere: the *Union list of Commonwealth and South African law*, 2nd edn., 1963 (below p. 394), the *Union list of United States legal literature*, 2nd edn., 1967 (below p. 394), and the *Union list of West European legal literature*, 1966.

No published list satisfactorily provides locations for UK law reports though the need for such a list is keenly felt. The growth of computerized cataloguing, shared cataloguing systems and the possibilities of producing union lists by computer are factors which will influence the publication of any future union lists. Production by completely manual methods is unlikely.

One general union catalogue which includes law journals is the *British Union Catalogue of Periodicals* (BUCOP), 1955–8, 3 vols. Three supplements cover the period to 1973 and annual cumulations of quarterly issues provide further information since 1973. The actual locations given are selective, but it does provide some means of tracing sets of British law reports. Since 1981 BUCOP has been superseded by *Serials in the British Library* which lists new titles in the British Library and about sixteen other British libraries.

Legal research finding aids

Legal research is conducted for several purposes and at different levels. It may state the law as it is, provide facts to ascertain how the law is working, or suggest reform. It can be conducted in the universities and polytechnics for higher degrees, or as the basis for future publications; on a regular basis by government departments and committees, in particular the Home Office and the Law Commission or its equivalent elsewhere; by *ad hoc* committees and commissions set up to investigate a particular subject, such as the Royal Commission on Criminal Procedure, which published background research papers as well as its report; and by independent bodies to further their own aims, such as the Statute Law Society.

Publication of the research is often by the sponsoring body. Some sponsors have easily identifiable series, such as the Home Office Research Studies, but most theses for higher degrees are not published.

A comprehensive source for research in progress in government departments throughout the British Isles, and selectively for the Commonwealth, is the Institute of Advanced Legal Studies *List of official committees, commissions and other bodies concerned with the reform of the law*, which used to be revised annually but was last issued in 1979. Completed government legal research, if published, should appear in the indexes to government publications described in Chapter 6. Among the government publications *Sectional Lists*, the most useful for published government legal research are the *Home Office List*, the *Miscellaneous List* which includes the Lord Chancellor's Department and the Law Commission, and *Reports of Royal Commissions*, as these are often the starting point for law reform. The *Sectional Lists* are revised frequently.

Academic research in progress is listed regularly in both *Scientific Research in British Universities and Colleges*, vol. 3, which covers thoroughly the research interests of academic staff and belies its title to include government departments and other institutions, and in the IALS annual *List of Current Legal Research Topics*. Details of completed research can be found in the IALS

Legal Research in the United Kingdom, 1905–1984, 1986. Aslib *Index to Theses* has a law section but the IALS list is more complete.

Research, either in progress or completed, which has been sponsored by independent bodies, is not listed regularly, although details of some projects appear in *Scientific Research in British Universities and Colleges,* vol. 3. A recent American publication of value to legal historians is the occasional *Check-list of Research in British Legal Manuscripts,* 1974–, edited by Sue Sheridan Walker. The pamphlet-size volumes provide an alphabetical list of researchers with details of work in progress and publications.

Miscellaneous

Other bibliographical sources of value to law librarians include the *Index to Legal Essays,* 1983, edited by B. Tearle, which lists English language legal essays in Festschriften, memorial volumes, conference papers and other collections, 1975–9. Arrangement is mainly by geographically subdivided subjects listed in alphabetical order. There is also an author index, subject index, geographical index, and a list of the collections in which the essays were published. It is hoped this excellent publication will be updated.

Trials in Collections, 1983, by J. M. Ross, is an index of famous trials throughout the world to 1980. It lists 322 collections and each item is numbered. An alphabetical list of defendants refers to the number(s) of the appropriate collections(s) in which the trial is to be found, and a subject index of offences lists defendants by country. The alphabetical list of defendants is cross-referenced and is useful for tracing trials known by popular name or fictitious name, *eg,* Great Train Robbers, and 'Winslow Boy'.

The publication of pamphlets, books, reports, and statistics by government departments that are not sold by HMSO has increased in recent years. Valuable guides to these publications are *Bibliographic sources for non-HMSO official publications,* 1983 edn., 1984, and the Chadwyck-Healey *Catalogue of British official publications not published by HMSO,* published bimonthly since 1980 and with annual cumulations.

Dictionaries

General language dictionaries

The *Oxford English Dictionary* is the authoritative source for definitions, etymology and examples of use of the English language, including legal terms. As such, it is always consulted by the courts when questions of interpretation of legal and non-legal words arise. However, for normal library use, the *Shorter Oxford English Dictionary*, 1959, is sufficient.

General bilingual dictionaries complement legal bilingual dictionaries for foreign language legal work. Several – Harrap's *New Standard French and English Dictionary* and the *Cambridge Italian Dictionary* – have a high reputation for the accuracy of their definitions of foreign legal terms. But law has a special terminology in every language and for legal purposes general dictionaries should be used with special caution.

Legal dictionaries

English legal dictionaries have several characteristics, whether they deal with the whole range of law, or a special aspect. Unlike general language dictionaries where the entries are of one word, law dictionaries reflect the concepts, terms and institutions of the subject, which may be expressed in one or more words. When the terms and explanations are long, the dictionary resembles an alphabetically arranged digest. They may contain old Anglo-Saxon, Law French and Law Latin terms drawn from ancient deeds and charters, although there is a tendency to excise obsolete terms from new dictionaries or new editions of established dictionaries. The terminology of the law is constantly developing, so it is important to know to what date a dictionary is current. The citation of the authority for a definition is necessary to understand its context and to assess its accuracy.

As well as exhibiting these characteristics, legal dictionaries fall into two categories, the explanatory and the interpreting dictionary. Historically, the development of explanatory legal dictionaries went through several stages.

The first legal dictionary to be published in England was *Expositiones terminorum legum anglorum* in 1527, better known in editions from 1624 as *Les termes de la ley*. Lists of difficult legal words already existed but the novelty of this first dictionary was its alphabetical arrangement. It was intended for the use of students and contained contemporary legal terms with explanations in English. Later editions were larger than the first pocket-size ones because they had words from the early word lists added. Altogether, it was used for over 300 years in twenty-nine editions.

The next dictionary to be published was J. Cowell *The Interpreter* in 1607, which differed from *Expositiones terminorum legum anglorum* in several respects. It included civil, canon and common law terms, and it cited authorities for its definitions. Later editions included antiquarian terms. The seventeenth century legal dictionaries seem to have been either scholarly antiquarian compilations – H. Spellman *Archaeologus*, 1626, and T. Blount *Nomo-lexikon*, 1670; or inferior products, often intended for students – E. Leigh *Philologicall commentary*, 1652, and *The Law-French, Law-Latin dictionary*, 1701. The additional characteristics from this period are the reference to authorities for definitions and the inclusion of many non-legal words. The latter characteristic occurred partly because, according to Cowell, the lawyer 'professeth true philosophy' and should understand any obscure word which he encounters.

A change in the nature of legal dictionaries can be seen in G. Jacob's *New-law dictionary*, 1729. He claims to include 'derivations and definitions of words and terms used in the law, likewise the whole law, with the practice thereof, collected and abstracted'. From Jacob onwards, the better legal dictionaries concentrated on legal terms. In the nature and length of their definitions they became almost digests of the law itself. This encyclopedic characteristic is most pronounced in T. Cunningham *A new and complete law-dictionary*, 1764–5, and W. Marriot *A new law dictionary*, 1798. In an abbreviated form, the encyclopedic law dictionary continued with J. J. S. Wharton *Law lexicon*; C. Sweet *Dictionary of English law*, 1882; W. J. Byrne *Dictionary of English law*, 1923, and W. Jowitt *Dictionary of English law*, 2nd edn., 1977 and supplement 1985. The more recent of these encyclopedic dictionaries endeavour to reduce the number of obsolete terms, but Byrne, Wharton and Jowitt include those Anglo-Saxon, medieval Law French and Latin terms, which may still be used.

Of the dictionaries used today, Jowitt is the major one. The introduction states that it is not only a 'dictionary of legal terms' but also 'a compact encyclopaedia of law and it may be used to get a quick, accurate summary of a topic and as an index to the whole of English law'. The terms range from concepts such as 'tort' to institutions such as the 'Law of Property Act 1925', and many historical words are included. The definitions contain etymology, present meaning and examples of use, arranged chronologically, with reference to the authority of statutes, cases, and the classic textbooks.

The pocket-size dictionaries, P. G. Osborn *The concise law dictionary*, 7th edn., 1983, and H. N. Mozley and G. C. Whiteley *Law dictionary*, 9th edn., 1977, are similar in scope, but only a fraction the size of Jowitt. Their value for students lies in their concise, authoritative definitions and their more recent publication. New editions, although not published with the frequency of major textbooks, are produced occasionally, compiled from primary sources to take account of legal developments. A pocket-size law dictionary added to the Oxford series in 1983 is the *Concise dictionary of law*. It is designed for those without legal qualifications who require some legal knowledge in their working life, and for this reason omits many references to sources and avoids abbreviations in the text. Entries are detailed – 'conveyancing' is allotted $2\frac{1}{2}$ columns – and range from Norman French and Latin terms to 'bomb hoax'. It is cross-referenced.

The second category of legal dictionaries is the interpreting dictionary. These work on a different principle from the explanatory category. They define ordinary and legal words and phrases in the context in which they have been used in the courts and in legislation. Legislation and judicial interpretation are continuous activities and the same words may be defined in different ways, depending upon their context. Therefore it is important to have up to date information on legislative and judicial functions.

F. Stroud *Judicial dictionary of words and phrases judicially interpreted*, 1890, was the first interpreting dictionary to be published in England. The present edition, the fourth, 1971–4, refers to cases, statutes and textbooks for the authority for its definitions. Most of the citations are from English sources, but Scottish, Irish, Commonwealth and American cases are also cited. A similar work, *Words and phrases legally defined*, 1969–70, is arranged alphabetically in broad subject headings with sub-divisions for terms and jurisdictions (England, Scotland, Ireland, Canada, Australia and New Zealand). Its definitions quote directly from law reports and, to a lesser extent, from statutes and textbooks. In order to take developments into account, both Stroud and *Words and phrases* have supplements.

For both retrospective and current judicial definitions, the indexes to legal encyclopedias and the frequently published indexes to law reports can be used. Most have alphabetically arranged 'words' or 'words and phrases' sections. In some, this section is part of the subject index, in others it is a separate sequence. The words and phrases list in *Halsbury's Statutes* is confined to statutory definitions.

Welsh legal dictionaries are of two distinct types: those of medieval Welsh terms (T. Lewis *Glossary of medieval Welsh law*, 1913) now only of historical use; and those of today which attempt to provide a vocabulary of modern legal terms for use by Welsh speakers in the courts (R. Lewis *Termau cyfraith, Welsh legal terms*, 1973).

Bilingual and multilingual legal dictionaries

To use bilingual and multilingual legal dictionaries effectively, the user must have a good knowledge of both languages and legal systems. Great care is necessary as, even between two similar legal systems or the same language used in two jurisdictions, the same term can have different meanings. With two languages and two different legal systems the problems are greater. Many of the concepts of the civil law and common law systems differ although linguistically the words used appear to be the same, *eg* 'jurisprudence' or 'domicile' in French and English law.

Several factors should be borne in mind when using bilingual dictionaries. The first is whether the English language part is biased towards English or American law. Th. A. Quemner *Dictionnaire juridique*, indicates the appropriate jurisdiction in individual entries where necessary. The second is whether the definitions in each language are brief one-word translations themselves drawn from secondary sources such as other legal or general dictionaries, *eg*, J. Jéraute *Vocabulaire français-anglais, anglais-français*, 1953, or whether the dictionary has been compiled from original sources, *eg*, Prischepenko *Russian–English law dictionary*, 1969, where the preface claims that it was compiled from source material, although the sources are not quoted in the entries.

A number of dictionaries are multilingual. Some provide one-word translations, lack of space alone preventing any additional information. An example of this is E. Le Docte *Dictionnaire des termes juridique en quatre langues*, 3rd edn., 1982, which covers terms in French, Dutch, English and German in one volume. R. Herbst *Dictionary of commercial, financial and legal terms*, 1968–82, is in three volumes and covers English, German and French. Each volume takes one of the three languages as the main entry and gives definitions in the other two, including combinations of words.

Adequate translation into the context of another legal system often requires long explanations. The dictionaries which attempt this thoroughly are often not dictionaries but glossaries of terms in special subjects. An example is the series of glossaries published under the title *European glossary of legal and administrative terminology*. These are small works containing only a few hundred terms in a special subject area such as the law of establishment, and each confined to two languages only out of a list that so far includes French, German, Italian and English.

Legal subject dictionaries

Dictionaries of special legal subjects are frequently found in those areas of law which have strong connections with other disciplines. Thus, there are subject dictionaries for parliamentary terms (L. A. Abraham and S. C. Hawtry *A Parliamentary dictionary*, 3rd edn., 1970), and the many branches of commerce have dictionaries of terms associated with one particular branch, as well as general dictionaries of commercial legal terms. Some are straightforward defining dictionaries, but others contain long explanations and provide a digest of the subject. Subject specialization also extends to bilingual and multilingual dictionaries such as A. Romain and D. Rutter *Dictionary of legal and commercial terms*, 1984, 2 vols. (German and English) and F. J. Kase *Dictionary of industrial property: legal and related terms*, 1980 (English, Spanish, French and German).

One result of the early use of Latin as the language of the law has been the growth of the legal maxim, a summary of principle of law described as 'the wisdom of many and the wit of one'. Translations appear in most legal dictionaries but little explanation is given. For that, H. Broom *A selection of legal maxims*, 1939, must be used. Broom is not a dictionary although it has an alphabetical index of the 500–600 maxims which are collected, translated and explained with reference to cases, under ten headings dealing with different branches of the law.

The language of the law has also included Law French, and many of its terms still in current use are found in legal dictionaries. For further study, an excellent introductory work is the *Manual of Law French*, 1979, by J. H. Baker, which provides an annotated bibliography of dictionaries and aids to interpretation. A glossary of all words still in use by mid-Tudor times forms the main part of the book.

Abbreviations

Every newcomer to legal literature experiences the difficulty of identifying the abbreviations scattered liberally throughout texts and footnotes. Varied lists of these abbreviations with their meanings are often included in legal dictionaries, encyclopedias, and reference works such as *Current Law* or the 'yellow book' *Where to look for your law* (referred to above p. 348). The publication of the *Index to legal citations and abbreviations*, 1981, compiled by D. Raistrick, brought together in one compact volume thousands of abbreviations and also listed the many alternative meanings of the same initial letters, *eg*, CLJ (11 versions), CC (22 versions). Geographical coverage is broadly the common law countries of the UK, the Commonwealth and the USA.

Although the *Index* includes citations it does not explain how they should be set out in legal writing. This is illustrated in the *Manual of legal citations*, 1959, 2 vols., published by the Institute of Advanced Legal Studies. Volume 1 covers material relating to the British Isles and volume 2 British Commonwealth publications. Each volume contains selected lists of appropriate abbreviations.

Encyclopedias

General

Encyclopedias covering the whole of English law have appeared in single- or multi-volume form for hundreds of years. *Halsbury's Laws of England, Halsbury's Statutes of England, Halsbury's Statutory Instruments, The Digest* (formerly the *English and Empire Digest*), the *Encyclopaedia of forms and precedents*, and Atkin's *Encyclopaedia of court forms in civil proceedings* are discussed in detail in other chapters. These major multi-volume general legal encyclopedias form a law library in themselves.

The *Oxford companion to law*, 1980, by D. M. Walker, is a one-volume encyclopedic dictionary containing thousands of entries which will provide answers to as many queries. The author has set out 'to make available as concisely as possible information about some of the principal legal institutions, courts, judges and jurists, systems of law, branches of law, legal ideas and concepts, important doctrines and principles of law, and other legal matters which ... any person whose work or reading in any way touches on legal matters may come across'. The result is a wealth of material in eminently readable form. The main text is an alphabetical arrangement of entries each explained in appropriate detail which ranges from a few lines (DPP) to several pages (United States law, – nine pages). The biographical entries include both ancient and modern, dead and living persons connected with the law from all common law countries and Western Europe. The heading 'legal literature' includes a brief survey of the law reports of Australia, Canada, England, France, Germany, Italy, Scotland, and the United States. References to further reading are given at the end of entries, but not all bibliographical details given are accurate. Two appendices are provided, the second of which lists basic legal literature familiar to most law librarians. The first appendix provides lists of holders of various legal offices since 1660, and these invaluable lists include judges of the various courts of England, Ireland, Scotland, the United States Supreme Court, the Permanent Court of International Justice, the International Court of Justice, and the Court of Justice of the European Communities.

Subjects

The comparatively recent proliferation of looseleaf encyclopedias enables the law librarian to sympathize fully with the sorcerer's apprentice as one-volume works become two, three, four and more volumes, and the increasing quantity of legislation and other material needed to update the original text fills binder after binder. Looseleaf is a convenient format for publications on topics that are subject to frequent changes in the law – taxation is a typical example. It is easier to keep works of this nature up to date by regular filing of supplementary pages or 'releases' than to issue a hardback volume with subsequent bulky supplements. The reader has the advantage of consulting one up-to-date work instead of several, and the encyclopedia usually also contains the texts of relevant statutory publications, circulars, statistics, and other significant material. The subject range is considerable: pollution, social security, VAT, road traffic, food and drugs, housing, and many more. Each encyclopedia is serviced several times a year and instructions for filing accompany the new pages. The advantages of the format have been mentioned, but there are also disadvantages. To the reader these are lost or wrongly filed pages, but to the law librarian the greatest disadvantage is the inordinate amount of staff time required to update the many binders filling the shelves.

Biographical sources

Many lawyers appear in the *Dictionary of National Biography*. Its entries are long in comparison with the legal biographical dictionaries, but sometimes inaccurate on matters of detail, such as dates of admission or call for barristers. The entries end with references to sources and further biographies and are signed. A supplementary source of biographical information for those who died between 1851 and 1900 and are excluded from the *Dictionary of National Biography* is F. Boase's *Modern English biography 1851–1900*, 1892–1921. Its subjects, chosen from a wider but lower section of society, are nevertheless notable or interesting people. A quick reference source, particularly useful for a person's official appointments, is *Who Was Who*.

Oxford and Cambridge were the only universities in England until the early nineteenth century. Their teaching of law was confined to the civil law until the 1850s, except for a short period when Blackstone gave his lectures at Oxford from 1753 to 1765. Thus the dictionaries of students at Oxford and Cambridge include only civilians up to 1850, but of course many students who subsequently became lawyers read other subjects. Oxford is covered by A. B. Emden *A biographical register of the University of Oxford to AD 1500*, 1957, and a second volume for 1500–41 published in 1974; and J. Foster *Alumni Oxoniensis: the members of the University of Oxford, 1500–1714*, and a second series for 1715–1886. Emden's works, although relating to the earlier period, contain more information than Foster's. For Cambridge, Emden prepared a similar *Biographical register of the University of Cambridge to 1500*, 1963, and the later years are covered by J. Venn *Alumni Cantabrigiensis: a biographical list of all known students, graduates and holders of office . . . from the earliest times to 1900*, 1922–54. All give information on academic and subsequent careers quoting sources for the statements.

Biographical material in the form of books, essays or articles can be traced through the normal bibliographical tools. For articles, the heading 'biography' in the *Index to Legal Periodicals* is useful. *Biography Index* includes books, essays and extracts from newspapers as well as periodical articles. With both there is a bias towards Americans and American publications, but items on British lawyers are included.

Historical

The historical biographical sources of information about lawyers, other than general sources, emanate almost entirely from the professional bodies.

The Inns of Court, which have been in existence since the fifteenth and sixteenth centuries, maintain, and have published, registers of their students. J. Foster *The register of admissions to Gray's Inn 1521–1889*, 1889, and *Students admitted to the Inner Temple 1547–1660*, 1877, were both privately printed. For the other two Inns there are *Admissions from AD 1420 to AD 1893*, 1896, for Lincoln's Inn, and H. A. C. Sturgess *Register of admission to the Honourable Society of the Middle Temple from the fifteenth century to the year 1944*, 1949. All these lists are arranged in chronological order of admission. The amount of information varies, but generally only the student's name appears during the early period. Later, parents and place of origin were added. Several of the registers have been selectively annotated for publication with details of subsequent offices held and date of death.

More biographical information has been published by the Inner and Middle Temples about their prominent members. In addition to the type of information in the admission registers, further details of Benchers' legal careers can be found in *Masters of the Bench of the Honourable Society of the Inner Temple 1450–1883*, 1883, and in its two supplements for the periods 1883–1900 and 1901–18. Although these books are arranged chronologically, the second supplement contains an alphabetical index to the three volumes. The Middle Temple has published two works with a large amount of biographical information about its members. The *Middle Temple Bench book*, 2nd edn., 1937, is a chronological list with biographical notes of the Middle Temple Benchers from 1463–1937. It also has a list of all Masters of the Temple since the Reformation. By far the most detailed biographical source for any of the four Inns is J. Hutchinson *A catalogue of notable Middle Templars*, 1922. It is the first source so far discussed to be arranged alphabetically. The entries, spanning 400 years, are mostly taken from other published sources and cover career at the Bar, on the Bench, or in other walks of life, and the subject's publications.

Several sources cover lawyers generally and those who have attained high judicial office in particular. J. Foster *Men-at-the-Bar*, 1885, is an alphabetically arranged dictionary of 7,000–8,000 barristers alive in 1885. It gives extensive information on their lives and careers and, as in Hutchinson's book, includes those whose subsequent careers have not been in the law.

For the identification of judges a useful source is E. Foss *Tabulae curiales*, 1865. It shows the rank attained and the reign during which office was held since 1066. A separate regnal list shows the judges who sat in each court. In the biographical dictionary field, E. Foss *Biographica juridica*, 1870, includes all the judges of England from 1066 to 1870. His other biographical work, *The judges of England*, 1848–64, is praised by Holdsworth for its 'solid quality of learning and accuracy', in contrast with the biographical works for the same period by Lord Campbell. Besides narrating the lives of the judges he also lists serjeants and QCs for the period.

Three different works collectively cover biographical sources for Lord Chancellors from 1066 to 1940. J. Campbell *The lives of the Lord Chancellors*, 1845–69, takes them from 1066 to George IV's reign. Various sources note that, while readable, Campbell's work cannot be relied upon, but Heuston records his admiration for the work as a whole and only faults the later volumes. The history of the Lord Chancellors is continued in J. B. Atlay *The Victorian Chancellors*, 1906–8, which covers Lords Lyndhurst to Herschell. R. F. V. Heuston *Lives of the Lord Chancellors 1885–1940*, 1964, commences with Lords Halsbury and Herschell, who were included in the previous work, and finishes with Lord Caldecote. The last two works give a straightforward narrative account of the lives and careers of the Lord Chancellors with some assessment, against their political and legal backgrounds.

A biographical work of a different kind was published in 1984 – A. W. B. Simpson's *Biographical dictionary of the common law*. This is a selective collection of persons no longer living who had achieved prominence before 1939. Although drawn mainly from England and Wales, a few notables are included from Eire, the Commonwealth and the United States. A few entries are of people whose names are associated with the law, such as Charles Dickens. Each entry is written by one of a team of mostly academic contributors and references are given at the end of each entry to sources of further reading, and where a likeness of the subject can be seen. The entries are only introductions to fuller biographies, and range from a few lines to a few pages. Nevertheless this compact volume provides lively descriptions of a wide range of familiar legal figures including Blackstone, Halsbury, and Dicey, together with likenesses of fifty-three of the subjects.

The *Oxford companion to law* contains some biographical entries for persons connected with the law in a common law country or in Western Europe.

Current

There is no biographical publication covering present members of the legal profession. Some of sufficient standing will be included in *Who's Who* and some living persons are included in the *Oxford companion to law*, but the available professional lists or directories carry few personal details.

Until it ceased publication in 1976, the *Law List* was the best means of tracing legal practitioners. It appeared annually from 1841 and provided accurate lists of members of the legal profession. A detailed description of its contents is contained in the first edition of this *Manual* at p. 408.

In 1977, the *Bar List of the United Kingdom* made its first appearance and continued to provide annual information similar to that in part of the *Law List* until 1983, when it, too, ceased publication.

The *Solicitors' Diary and Directory*, also annual and formerly based on the *Law List*, became (after 1976) the main source of information that previously had been included in the solicitors section of the *Law List*. With the disappearance of the *Bar List* in 1983, the one-volume *Solicitors' Diary and Directory* was reorganized to include information about the Bar and, in 1984, was published in two volumes entitled *Solicitors' and Barristers' Directory and Diary*. Volume 1 contains a 15-month diary and three sections of information: courts and offices (UK, Isle of Man and Channel Islands); taxation in England and Wales; barristers (listed by chambers' location and also alphabetically), with a separate list of QCs and information on the Senate of the Inns of Court. Volume 2 has four sections: The Law Society and legal aid, College of Law, and general information concerning solicitors; a geographical list of firms arranged alphabetically under each town, plus an index of individual solicitors cross-referenced to the main geographical list; legal executives; Commonwealth High Commission and consular offices, embassies, and an international lawyers section arranged by country. This annual A4 work is authorized by the Law Society and the Senate of the Inns of Court as the 'official' directory of the legal profession.

Hazell's Guide to the Judiciary and the Courts, with the Holborn Law Society's List of Barristers by Chambers was published for the first time in 1985. It is divided into five main sections: the Judiciary; the Courts; barristers by chambers and alphabetically; a combination of these sections separately for Northern Ireland, Scotland, Isle of Man, Jersey and Guernsey; police forces. It is not designed to give biographical information and includes only dates of admission and Inn for members of the Bar and academic qualifications for Scottish advocates.

Butterworths Law Directory and Diary, 2 vols., also appeared for the first time in 1985. Volume 1 is mainly diary but also includes blue pages of information on courts and offices, probate fees and registry, taxation, conveyancing and legal aid. The far larger volume 2 contains lists of practising barristers and solicitors, but these cover only England and Wales.

The *International Law List*, annual since 1866, lists selected firms of solicitors worldwide arranged alphabetically under the relevant country. For complete coverage of the practitioners in any country it is always best to refer to the local list if one is available. The *International Law List* also includes a useful list of principal law societies and Bar associations, and patent offices. *Kime's International Law Directory* provides similar information.

Other lists of practitioners have been published in *The Lawyer's Diary, Unilaw Lawyers Directory and Diary*, and *Lawyer's Law Directory, International edition.* Each contains some information unique to itself and some common to other publications. Only the individual user can decide which provides the information best suited to his needs.

Academic lawyers in the British Isles teach in universities and polytechnics. Many are barristers or solicitors, although this is not essential. If barristers, they may be listed in the appropriate professional directory; those who are solicitors are only listed if they hold a current practising certificate. All academic staff are listed in the calendar of the university or polytechnic in which they teach. The amount of personal information in these calendars varies, but subjects taught and works published may be shown.

There are two associations to which academic lawyers may belong, the Society of Public Teachers of Law and the Association of Law Teachers, which cater for university and polytechnic teachers respectively. They both publish, for private circulation only, directories of their members with information on their qualifications, appointments held (with dates), and teaching interests. The SPTL *Directory of Members* is issued annually and includes a long list of associate members teaching overseas. The ALT *Directory of Members* is issued occasionally and has less detail in its entries. Both publications list the officers of the associations.

The *Academic Who's Who*, published in 1973 for 1973–4, aimed to include all university teachers throughout the British Isles who had more than five years' teaching experience, thereby not providing complete coverage of academic lawyers. A second edition was issued for 1975–6 but no subsequent editions have been published.

Besides practice and teaching, many lawyers work in other fields, for example in central and local government, Parliament, and industry. Several directories for these bodies include the legal staff. Civil Service lawyers were listed under department or ministry in a section of the *Law List*; a similar section is included in volume 1 of the *Solicitors' and Barristers'*

Directory and Diary but with less detail than formerly given. The *Civil Service Year Book* includes senior grades and covers government departments in England and Wales, Scotland and Northern Ireland. Chief legal officers in local government appear in such directories as the *Municipal Year Book*, and local authorities and nationalized industries with legal employees are listed in the geographical section with firms of solicitors in volume 2 of the *Solicitors' and Barristers' Directory and Diary*.

Lawyers who sit in Parliament are included in the general directories of members, such as *Dod's Parliamentary Companion*, which gives some biographical information including parliamentary career.

Legal organizations

Courts

The same sources that list legal practitioners also list courts and officials, usually following the list of judges for each court. However, a directory solely concerned with courts is *Shaw's Directory of Courts in the United Kingdom* which overlaps and complements the court information in the various British practitioners' directories mentioned above. *Shaw* has been published annually since 1973 and originally covered only England and Wales; this has been extended to include Scotland and Northern Ireland, but references to the Isle of Man or the Channel Islands must be sought in *Hazell* or the *Solicitors' and Barristers' Directory and Diary*.

Additional information about jurisdictional areas of county courts is provided by two directories published by the Lord Chancellor's Department. The *London County Courts Directory* lists, in alphabetical order, streets in the London postal area and gives the county court district in which they fall. A similar index of places, *County Court Districts (England and Wales)*, gives like information country-wide.

Legal associations

There are many organizations of, or for, lawyers, or connected with the law. Some are official bodies, others voluntary associations. They range from those connected with the legal profession, such as the Inns of Court, or formed for some general purpose, such as the International Bar Association, to those having a limited function, like the College of Law, the Howard League for Penal Reform or the Criminal Injuries Compensation Board. There are also many associations whose purpose is related to some aspect of law, such as the Association of Official Shorthand Writers.

Many are listed in the law directories already mentioned and in the *Lawyer's Remembrancer*, which is valuable for the addresses of Law Society area secretaries for legal aid areas. Many voluntary associations, but not public offices or educational establishments, are listed in the *Directory of British Associations and Associations in Ireland*.

Law libraries and librarians

Two problems arise for the potential user of a law library. The first is to locate specialized collections; and the other is to obtain admission to a library, as many leading law libraries belong to private societies. The *Directory of Law Libraries in the British Isles*, 2nd edn., 1984, provides an invaluable source for the answers to these problems. Under the regional areas of England, Wales, Scotland, Ireland, Channel Islands, and Isle of Man, entries are arranged alphabetically by town. The name, address and telephone number of the library is given, together, wherever possible, with a named contact to whom potential users should write, since many of the libraries are private and prior permission to use the library is essential. Further information includes opening hours, admission of non-members for reference, services available to non-members, size of the collection, number of legal serials taken, and notes of any special collections, co-operative schemes, or other information. There are three indexes: libraries or institutions by name; libraries or institutions grouped by type; and a personal name index of the contact in each library or institution.

General guides often include some reference to legal collections, such as the Library Association regional guides to library resources in England and Wales, or the *Aslib Directory*. The *Guide to Government Departments and other libraries* includes libraries such as the Law Commission, the Supreme Court, the Radzinowicz Library in Cambridge, and the Police Staff College.

Information on overseas library resources may be needed and the International Association of Law Libraries *European law libraries guide*, 1971, covers 522 of the major law libraries in 18 countries, and gives the address, size, facilities and specializations of each library. Directories relating to law libraries in individual common law countries are mentioned below.

Associations of law librarians publish lists of their members either for private circulation or public reference. The British and Irish Association of Law Librarians publishes a list of members in the December issue of *The Law Librarian*. Details include name, qualifications, position held, and business address. The list is updated by membership news items in the journal. The International Association of Law Libraries publishes a list of its members from time to time. Many British law librarians are members of the appropriate national Library Association and thus appear in the *Library Association Year Book*.

SCOTLAND

Bibliographic sources

Guides to legal literature

The legal system of Scotland has evolved from both civil law and common law sources. The newcomer to Scots law will find indispensable the detailed account by D. M. Walker *The Scottish legal system*, 5th edn., 1981, which includes a helpful chapter on Scottish legal literature. Two chapters in *Law publishing and legal information: small jurisdictions in the British Isles*, 1981, edited by W. Twining and J. Uglow, are devoted to Scotland.

The first chapter covers the current provision of legal literature, both primary and secondary sources, whilst the second
covers the legal information needs of Scottish solicitors in
private practice. The five pages covering Scotland in A. R.
Blunt *Law librarianship*, 1980, provide a brief but comprehensive survey of Scottish legal literature and are a useful starting
point for further research.

Legal bibliographies

The bibliographies of legal bibliographies and the national
bibliographies mentioned above (pp. 346–7) include coverage
of Scottish legal literature. There is no recently published
separate bibliography of Scottish legal materials. Sweet and
Maxwell's *Legal Bibliography of the British Commonwealth of
Nations* vol. 5, lists material published on Scots law to 1956, and
the selective bibliography in the book edited by Twining and
Uglow aims to update the secondary material in volume 5 to
1981. A valuable source of information is the IALS *A Bibliographical guide to the law of the United Kingdom, the Channel
Islands and the Isle of Man*, 2nd edn., 1973 (p. 345) which
concentrates on modern Scots law, briefly describing each
branch and providing a select bibliography after each description. *Lawyers' law books*, 2nd edn., 1985, lists selected
publications by subject and author, and current information
can be found in *Scottish Current Law*, the weekly *Scots Law Times*,
and the bi-annual *Juridical Review*. The publications of Green
of Edinburgh are included in the annual catalogue of Sweet
and Maxwell.

Early law books
Early Scottish legal literature is described in detail in the Stair
Society's *Introductory survey of the sources and literature of Scots
law*, 1936, which forms volume 1 of the publications of the
Society. This work has four main sections: native sources, non-
native sources, indirect sources, and special subjects. The four
sections each include a list of source material, commentary on
the sources and literature, and a bibliography. A select critical
bibliography of material published between 1936 and 1982 is

contained in the *Journal of Legal History*, vol. 4, no. 3, and reprinted in *New perspectives in Scottish legal history*, 1984, edited by A. Kiralfy and H. L. MacQueen. This bibliography, compiled by W. J. Windram and H. L. MacQueen, follows the headings used in the Stair Society's *Introductory survey*, but does not profess to be a complete guide to material published on Scottish legal history since 1936.

General bibliographies of early literature, Pollard and Redgrave (STC) and Wing, and the printed catalogues of the older law libraries are all means of checking details of early works.

Law library catalogues

A brief but comprehensive list of law library catalogues may be found in Sweet and Maxwell's *Legal bibliography*, vol. 5, pp. 20–1. When dealing with Scottish catalogues it should be remembered that the great Scottish law libraries contained much general literature. The catalogues fall into three categories: those in which law books are not differentiated, those in which law books are listed separately, and those which consist exclusively of law books. A good example of this last category is the *Catalogue of the law books in the Library of the Society of Writers to Her Majesty's Signet in Scotland*, 1856, compiled by W. Ivory. Examples of all three types may be found in the catalogues of the libraries of the Faculty of Advocates, the Society of Writers to Her Majesty's Signet, the Society of Solicitors in the Supreme Courts, and the Royal Faculty of Procurators in Glasgow.

Periodicals

The sources described for England (p. 354–6) apply also to Scotland, and *Scottish Current Law* provides references to articles in its monthly and annual issues.

Union catalogues

Sources described on p. 357 also cover Scotland, *eg*, the IALS *Union List of Legal Periodicals*, BUCOP and its sequel *Serials in the British Library*.

Legal research finding aids

The work in progress by the Scottish Law Commission and any other relevant bodies is included in the IALS *List of official committees, commissions and other bodies concerned with the reform of the law*. Academic research is covered by sources referred to above.

Dictionaries

Legal dictionaries

In Scotland the first legal dictionary was compiled by J. Skene and was entitled *De verborum significatione*, 1597; this contained explanations, sources and examples of use of legal and some non legal 'difficill wordes' drawn mainly from his *Regiam majestatem*, 1597, and previous legislation. The explanations, in English, of each term often occupy several pages. Although published nearly a century ago, the last edition of R. Bell's *Dictionary and digest of the law of Scotland*, 1890, is still used. It displays the encyclopedic characteristic to a greater extent than any of the modern English dictionaries, *eg*, the entry for bankruptcy is explained under several sub-headings and takes up nine pages. The explanations refer to the institutional writers, legislation, cases and textbooks. *A Dictionary of words and phrases judicially defined*, 1946, compiled by A. W. Dalrymple and A. D. Gibb, belongs to the interpreting category of dictionaries. It has judicial, not statutory, definitions from 1800 to 1944 and refers to the cases in which the terms were defined and, if relevant, the Acts in which the words occur. Unlike many legal dictionaries, Dalrymple and Gibb contains a list of statutes and cases. Two dictionaries were published in 1982: J. A. Beaton *Scots law terms and expressions*, and A. D. Gibb *Student's glossary of Scottish legal terms*, 2nd edn. Beaton successfully aims to provide a glossary of Scottish legal terms for non-lawyers; the entries are full, some of several lines, and the coverage extensive. Gibb's *Student's glossary* was first published in 1946 and substantially revised for the 2nd edn. to include many words no longer in current use or which have been replaced by others.

Encyclopedias

The *Encyclopaedia of the laws of Scotland* and the complementary *Encyclopaedia of Scottish legal styles*, were last updated in 1952 and 1954 respectively. Both are discussed fully in Chapter 5.

Biographical sources

Historical

A general source of information is the *Dictionary of National Biography*, but in Scotland several of the professional societies have published their histories which include some biographical information about their members. The *Register of the Society of Writers to Her Majesty's Signet*, 1983, and Sir F. J. Grant's *The Faculty of Advocates in Scotland 1532–1943*, 1944, attempt to list all their members with genealogical and biographical notes.

Several books deal with Scottish lawyers who have held office. G. W. T. Omond *The Lord Advocates of Scotland*, 1883 and 1914, gives 'historical sketches ... rather than a series of complete "lives", to trace the history of the Office' from 1483 to 1880. For the judiciary, a biographical dictionary arranged in chronological order is available in G. Brunton and D. Haig *An historical account of the Senators of the College of Justice, from its institution in MDXXXII*, 1849. The introduction relates its establishment and the development of the offices of Lord Chancellor, Lord President and the judges of the Court of Session. The biographical entries, of varying length, cover family, offices, and political career. The lives of the Lord Chancellors from 1124 to 1708 are narrated, with reference to sources in S. Cowan *The Lord Chancellors of Scotland*, 1911, which has some assessment of the careers of the later ones. These sources emphasize the political more than the legal activities of their subjects.

Current

For current information the *Scottish Law Directory* lists legal practitioners but does not include any reference to personal details, or previous career. The solicitors' list, like the English one, is of certificated practitioners and is also classified by town with alphabetical lists of solicitors and firms. Academic lawyers who are members of the Society of Public Teachers of Law appear in that Society's list of members. Some Scottish academic lawyers are included in the *Academic Who's Who*.

Legal organizations

Courts

Judges and court officials in Scotland are listed in the *Scottish Law Directory* and volume 1 of the *Parliament House Book*, although the arrangement in each differs. The *Scottish Law Directory* gives the dates of circuit sittings of the High Court of Justiciary and the *Parliament House Book* the Sheriff Court days. Days and sittings of Scottish courts are included in *Shaw* and *Hazell*. Since 1982 the *Parliament House Book* has appeared in looseleaf form; the work is discussed fully in Chapter 3.

Legal associations

Reference should be made to the two Scottish publications just mentioned and to the *Directory of British Associations and Associations in Ireland*.

Law libraries and librarians

The location and details of law libraries in Scotland are given in the *Directory of law libraries in the British Isles*, 2nd edn., 1984. The Scottish Library Association publishes the comprehensive

Scottish library and information resources, 5th edn., 1984. Government libraries are included in the *Guide to Government Departments and other libraries* published annually by the British Library.

Law librarians who are members of the British and Irish Association of Law Librarians are included in the members' list published in the December issue of *The Law Librarian*. Members of the Scottish Library Association are included in the *Library Association Year Book*.

IRELAND

Bibliographic sources

Guides to legal literature

The history and development of the legal systems in both the Republic of Ireland and in Northern Ireland are dealt with in Chapter 2. However, the newcomer to Irish legal literature may also find it useful to read the relevant sections in three works already referred to which give brief introductions to the law: *A Bibliographical guide to the law of the United Kingdom, the Channel Islands and the Isle of Man*, 2nd edn., by A. G. Chloros, 1973 (Northern Ireland p. 201); *Law publishing and legal information: small jurisdictions of the British Isles*, 1981, edited by W. Twining and J. Uglow (Republic of Ireland p. 44, Northern Ireland p. 83); *Law librarianship*, 1980, by A. R. Blunt (Republic of Ireland p. 83, Northern Ireland p. 85).

Similarities between Irish and English legal materials are sufficient to enable the guides to English legal publications to be applied to Irish ones.

Legal bibliographies

Coverage of Irish legal literature is included in most of the general and legal bibliographies already mentioned in the

English section; there is no separate Irish legal bibliography. Sweet and Maxwell's *Legal bibliography*, vol. 4, lists Irish law to 1956, and bibliographies for Northern Ireland and the Republic, which aim to update the Sweet and Maxwell volume to 1981, are included in *Law publishing and legal information*. These form a valuable source of information on both older and more recent publications.

Other bibliographies are selective in treatment: the IALS *Bibliographical guide* contains useful select bibliographies for each subject covered in the chapter on Northern Ireland; and *Lawyers law books* includes 'useful titles' from publications issued since 1935 for the Republic and since 1925 for Northern Ireland. Law-related topics are given fairly comprehensive coverage in the *Social sciences bibliography of Northern Ireland 1945–1983*, 1983. It includes a section on the criminal justice system and gives references to journal articles, books, government publications and theses.

Some new publications are listed in *Current Law* and journals such as the *Northern Ireland Legal Quarterly* and the *Irish Jurist*. The catalogues of the Queen's University of Belfast Servicing the Legal System (SLS) programme, provide details of available and forthcoming publications. For the Republic, the publishing houses of Sweet and Maxwell and Professional Books now include Irish law texts in their catalogues. Hitherto the chief publishers have been the Institute of Public Administration in Dublin, the Incorporated Law Society of Ireland, and the Incorporated Council for Law Reporting of Ireland.

Early law books
Early literature may be checked by reference to general bibliographies such as STC or Wing. Of the older legal bibliographies, Irish law books are included in Marvin's *Legal bibliography*, 1847, and Soule's *Lawyers reference manual*, 1883. Bibliographies of works covering Irish legal history may be found in the *American Journal of Legal History* volumes for the years 1960, 1964 and 1969 (entries cover both books and articles), and in each annual issue of the *Cambrian Law Review*.

Law library catalogues
Printed catalogues may be traced through volume 4 of Sweet and Maxwell's *Legal bibliography*. Some Irish material will be

included in the printed catalogues of the larger English law libraries.

Subjects
The *Bibliography of the literature on British and Irish labour law*, 1975, is referred on p. 353.

Periodicals

The outstanding work in this field is the comprehensive index of articles, compiled by P. O'Higgins, *A bibliography of periodical literature relating to Irish law*. The main work was published in 1966 and supplements issued in 1973 and 1983. References are given to articles in periodicals throughout the world and cover both Northern Ireland and the Republic. Articles are arranged by subject, with cross-references, and there is also a subject index and an author index.

Legal research finding aids

The IALS *List of official committees, commissions, and other bodies concerned with the reform of the law* includes work in progress in both Northern Ireland and the Republic. Completed government research published as parliamentary or departmental publications should be included in the indexes described above. The bibliography for the Republic in *Law publishing and legal information* provides a useful list of Irish government publications, including the reports of commissions, reports of committees, Law Reform Commission publications, advisory and community group publications, and other Irish government publications.

Academic research in progress in Northern Ireland is included in the IALS *List of Current Research Topics*. Research in the Republic may be traced through the *Register of Current Social Science Research in Ireland*. This is published annually by the Economic and Social Science Research Institute and includes a section 'Crime; law; deviance'.

Aslib *Index to Theses* includes some reference to completed legal research in Ireland.

Biographical sources

Historical

There are no biographical dictionaries of the Irish judiciary but several collected biographies have been published. F. Ball *The Judges in Ireland 1221–1921*, 1927, makes an original approach and is nearest in form to a biographical dictionary. The chapters deal with legal developments, but each group of chapters is followed by chronological lists and a catalogue of the judges of the period. The catalogue contains the type of information usually found in biographical dictionaries. Two works deal with the Irish Lord Chancellors: O. J. Burke *The history of the Lord Chancellors of Ireland from AD 1186 to AD 1874*, 1879, and J. O'Flanagan *The lives of the Lord Chancellors*, 1870 reprinted 1971. Both are arranged chronologically and the latter has references to original sources, as well as quoting from them and from contemporaries of those whose lives he narrates. A number of Irish lawyers are included in A. W. B. Simpson *Biographical dictionary of the common law*.

Current

Lists of current members of the judiciary, the Bar and solicitors in Northern Ireland are included in the *Solicitors' and Barristers' Directory and Diary* and, excluding solicitors, in *Hazell's Guide to the Judiciary and the Courts*. The *Handbook of the Incorporated Law Society of Northern Ireland* contains lists of judges, barristers and solicitors. This is a looseleaf publication with supplements, but unfortunately these are issued infrequently and the lists are not always up to date.

For the Republic, the annual *Law Directory*, published by authority of the Incorporated Law Society of Ireland, includes lists of judges, practising barristers and solicitors. Also included is a separate register of Northern Ireland solicitors, and a selective international law list.

Irish academic lawyers who are members of the SPTL are listed in the annual *Directory*. The Irish Association of Law Teachers, which has a membership from universities and other third-level institutions both in the Republic and in Northern Ireland, publishes a directory of members and associate members about every two years.

The *Civil Service Year Book* includes lawyers of senior grade in government offices in Northern Ireland. The *State Directory* provides similar information for the Republic.

A general source for current information about people should not be overlooked. *Thom's Commercial Directory*, published annually, contains a 'who's who in Ireland' which includes entries for some members of the legal profession and the judiciary. *Who's Who in Ireland – the influential 1000*, 1984, can also be useful.

Legal organizations

Courts

Courts and officials for Northern Ireland are listed in *Hazell's Guide* and the *Solicitors' and Barristers' Directory and Diary*. Complementary information is provided by *Shaw's Directory of Courts in the United Kingdom*. *Hazell* and *Shaw* give days and times of sittings. The *Law Directory* includes similar information for the Republic.

Legal associations

Legal associations are frequently listed in the directories and guides already mentioned. A useful list of addresses of law-related bodies in Northern Ireland forms an appendix to B. Dickson *The legal system of Northern Ireland*, 1984, and voluntary associations are listed in the *Directory of British associations and associations in Ireland*.

Law libraries and librarians

The *Directory of law libraries in the British Isles* provides locations for law collections in Ireland. The *Guide to Government Department and other libraries* includes Northern Ireland, whilst the *Directory of libraries in Ireland,* 1983, lists libraries in both Northern Ireland and the Republic.

Irish members of the library and law library associations are included in the appropriate lists.

ISLE OF MAN

Bibliographic sources

Guides to legal literature

Useful introductions to legal literature as well as to Manx law are to be found in *A bibliographical guide to the law of the United Kingdom, the Channel Islands and the Isle of Man,* and in *Law publishing and legal information* edited by Twining and Uglow.

Legal bibliographies

The legal publications of the Isle of Man are relatively few. Sweet and Maxwell's *Legal bibliography,* vol. 2, and the *Bibliographical guide* contain lists of publications on Manx law. Twining and Uglow have incorporated these lists into one bibliography which attempts to include *all* published material to 1981, whether originating in the island or elsewhere, and covers both books and periodical articles (see *Law publishing and legal information,* pp.175–8). Relevant items have also been drawn from W. Cubbon *A bibliographical account of works relating to the Isle of Man,* 1933. *Lawyers law books,* 2nd edn., 1985, includes a selection of useful titles with one or two published since 1981. The *Manx Law Bulletin,* published twice a year since 1983, serves as a current awareness bulletin for new publications.

Periodicals

The articles listed in the bibliography in *Law publishing* include those in both legal and non-legal journals.

Biographical sources

Present members of the legal profession are listed in the *Solicitors' and Barristers' Directory and Diary* and in *Hazell's Guide*. The *Tynwald Companion* provides a guide to the legislature and government, and includes useful addresses, chairmen of Boards of Tynwald, and names and telephone numbers of government and local government officials.

Legal organizations

Sources already mentioned in the English section are relevant.

CHANNEL ISLANDS

Bibliographic sources

There is no separately published legal bibliography. Sweet and Maxwell's *Legal bibliography*, vol. 2, lists publications to 1957, and select bibliographies for Jersey and Guernsey are included in *Bibliographical guide*, 1973. A further ten publications may be gleaned from *Lawyers law books*, 2nd edn., 1985. The Channel Islands are omitted from *Law publishing and legal information*.

Biographical sources

Current lists of members of the legal profession may be found in the *Solicitors' and Barristers' Directory and Diary*. *Hazell's Guide* gives days and times of sittings.

Legal organizations

Addresses of the Guernsey Bar Association and the Jersey Law Society are listed in the *Lawyers Law Directory, international edition 1984–85*, 1985.

BRITISH COMMONWEALTH AND THE UNITED STATES

Bibliographic sources

The legal systems of the common law countries of the Commonwealth and the United States have their origins in English law. In consequence much of the legal literature of these countries is markedly similar in form to English counterparts. Many of the reference works already discussed include information relating to the Commonwealth and the United States: bibliographies, periodical indexes, union catalogues, dictionaries, and so on. Literature guides designed specifically for one common law jurisdiction may contain sufficient information on another to serve as a guide to the other's literature. This is well illustrated by the three works long used by British law librarians (see p.345).

The following pages aim merely to provide signposts to some of the reference sources designed for individual common law countries of the Commonwealth and the United States. Detailed descriptions of these sources must be sought elsewhere.

Guides to legal literature

Information on legal online sources available in some Commonwealth countries and the United States, is included in the *Handbook of legal information retrieval*, 1984, edited by J. Bing.

Australia
An indispensable guide is E. Campbell *et al. Legal research: materials and methods*, 2nd edn., 1979. This comprehen-

sively covers the entire range of Australian legal materials and gives good coverage of the legal literature of England, New Zealand, Ireland, Scotland, Canada, and the United States.

Canada

Of value here is M. A. Banks *Using a law library: a guide for students and lawyers in the common law provinces of Canada*, 3rd edn., 1980 (fourth edition in preparation). Although designed for users in Canada, English legal materials are described first before Canadian ones. Chapters cover all primary and secondary materials of both countries and the third edition also provides an annotated bibliography, and includes a chapter on automated legal research in Canada. Emphasis on computerization is evident in D. T. MacEllven *Legal research handbook*, 1983. This is aimed at students and lawyers and covers Canadian primary and secondary sources, both old and new. It includes a chapter each on researching the law of Quebec, England, America, Australia and New Zealand.

Commonwealth Caribbean

Three publications in the 1970s between them provide comprehensive coverage of the legal literature. K. Patchett and V. Jenkins *A bibliographical guide to law in the Commonwealth Caribbean*, 1973, which is updated by V. Newton *Legal literature and conditions affecting legal publishing in the Commonwealth Caribbean: a bibliography*, 1979. Both works are complemented by V. Newton *Legal literature and publishing in the Commonwealth Caribbean*, 1979, a working paper which includes an historical survey.

India

Both old and more recent materials are covered in H. C. Jain *Indian legal materials: a bibliographical guide*, 1970. The older material forms the second part of the bibliography and includes an historical note on Indian law reports. Recent materials, divided into primary, secondary and periodicals, form the first part of the work.

Malaysia and Singapore

Lawasia (NS) 2, 1982–3, contains an article by G. W. Bartholomew 'Sources and Literature of Singapore Law', and this includes references to the basic legal literature of Malaysia.

United States

Guides to American legal literature are many and varied, from general works covering the whole range of legal materials to detailed studies of one specific topic. A general work that has long been used by British law librarians is M. Price and H. Bitner *Effective legal research: a practical manual of law books and their use,* 1953. Subsequent reprints and editions have appeared, but some of these are shortened versions of the original and omit some historical material, the bibliographic appendices, and some of the legal abbreviations. Nevertheless the quality of the work has made it a valuable reference tool not only for American but also English legal materials.

Other guides of some standing include F. C. Hicks *Materials and methods of legal research,* 3rd edn., 1942; J. L. Andrews *et al. Law in the U.S.A.: a selective bibliographical guide,* 1965, and E. H. Pollack *Fundamentals of Legal Research,* 4th edn., 1973.

More recent publications include references to the use of computers in legal research. *How to find the law,* 8th edn., 1983, by M. L. Cohen and R. C. Berring, provides coverage of the basic elements of legal bibliography as well as including information on new materials and techniques.

National bibliographies

These may be traced through general bibliographic sources. Examples are the *Australian National Bibliography* and *Canadiana.* Several of the major general bibliographies of American publications include a wide range of books from other English-speaking countries, and these bibliographies are regularly found in British libraries. Two notable examples are the *Cumulative Book Index* (CBI), also on WILSONLINE, and *Books in Print* (BIP), also on DIALOG.

Legal bibliographies

Africa

The most comprehensive guide to African legal publications is J. Vanderlinden *African Legal Bibliography 1947–66,* 1972.

This covers more than fifty African countries. It has been updated by retrospective supplements in the *Annual Survey of African Law* covering 1966–72, and by a separately published supplement covering 1977–80. Annual supplements have been issued since 1981.

Australia

Coverage to 1958 is provided by Sweet and Maxwell's *Legal Bibliography*, vol. 6, and later works may be traced through *Law Books in Print* or *Lawyers law books*. New publications are noted monthly in both *Current Law* and *Australian Current Law*, and in the quarterly *Current Australian and New Zealand Legal Literature Index*.

Canada

A major source of information on Canadian legal materials is R. Boult *A bibliography of Canadian law*, 2nd edn., 1977, with 1st supplement 1982. This covers primary and secondary sources. Articles, treatises and texts are grouped by subject; periodicals are listed by title with dates.

Three supplementary volumes to the *Canadian Abridgment* were issued in 1981 entitled *Index to Canadian legal literature*. This includes books and journal articles from the start of Canadian legal literature to the present, arranged under headings complementary to the *Canadian Abridgment*. It is updated by an annual cumulative supplement, by the quarterly looseleaf updating of the *Abridgment*, and by the relevant section of monthly *Canadian Current Law*. Specialist bibliographies are issued by the Canadian Law Information Council (CLIC).

Commonwealth Caribbean

Older material may be traced through Sweet and Maxwell's *Legal bibliography*, vol. 7. Reference should also be made to the works listed in the section on legal bibliographies. More recent publications may be listed in *Law Books in Print*.

India

In addition to the bibliographical guide by H. C. Jain, a smaller work C. H. Alexandrowicz *A bibliography of Indian law*, 1958, covers the literature of the day and retrospectively to 1933.

Malaysia and Singapore

Sweet and Maxwell's *Legal bibliography*, vol.7, covers earlier literature. Recommended holdings of legal materials for Malaysia and Singapore are published in the *Malaya Law Review*, vol. 25, 1983, pp. 225–49.

New Zealand

The *Index to New Zealand legal writing*, 2nd edn., 1982, spans 1954–81, and aims to include all books, articles, dissertations and theses both published and unpublished.

United States

Some American legal bibliographies have already been referred to because of their wide geographical coverage. Others include *Current Publications in Legal and Related Fields*, and *Law Books in Review*. The *National Legal Bibliography* made its first appearance in 1984. It aims to provide similar information to the Harvard *Annual Legal Bibliography*, which ceased publication in 1981. The NLB collects references to new publications from 1980 in monthly and annual issues.

Law library catalogues

A useful reference tool is the *Catalog of the law collection at New York University*, 1953, edited by J. J. Marke. This lists a good selection of titles with annotations and critical quotes. On a far larger scale is the comprehensive *Dictionary catalog of the Columbia University Law Library*, 1969–77, 28 vols. and supplements. The *Catalog of the Library of the Law School of Harvard University*, 1909 reprinted 1967, 2 vols., is also now in a microfiche edition that covers 1817–1981.

Periodicals

Directories or lists

The IALS *Union list of legal periodicals* provides British locations for many Commonwealth and American journals. The BIALL *Guide to the law reports of the British Commonwealth* (in preparation) aims to cover a wide range of old and new series.

Indexes of articles
Commonwealth legal periodicals were well covered by the
Index to Commonwealth Legal Periodicals, 1974–81. Since its
demise, the *Current Law Index*, the *Index to Legal Periodicals* and
the *Index to Foreign Legal Periodicals* provide selected coverage.

The Nigerian Institute of Advanced Legal Studies *Index to
Nigerian Legal Periodicals, 1946–81*, 1983, is a useful African
source.

The *Current Australian and New Zealand Legal Literature Index*,
1973–, aims to index the contents of many legal periodicals as
well as including articles on Australian and New Zealand law
which appear in journals published elsewhere.

In addition to the *Index to Canadian Legal Literature* references
to articles may be traced in the *Index to Canadian Legal Periodical
Literature*, issued quarterly with cumulations since 1963.

The *Index to Indian Legal Periodicals*, 1963–, is published
twice a year and covers about 100 Indian journals. Entries are
in a single subject and author index.

Union catalogues

The IALS series of union catalogues includes the *Union list of
Commonwealth and South African law*, 2nd edn., 1963, which is a
useful basic guide to legislation, law reports and digests held
by fifty-one UK libraries. It is arranged by country.

A *Union list of law reports held in Australian law libraries* has
been compiled by Monash University Law Library.

The *Checklist of Law Reports and Statutes in Canadian Law
Libraries*, which is both a bibliography and union list, is published by the National Library of Canada.

The IALS *Union list of United States legal literature*, 2nd edn.,
1967, covers federal and state legislation, reports and digests,
held in nine libraries in London, Oxford and Cambridge.

Legal research finding aids

Reference should be made to the sources mentioned above.
The *Commonwealth Law Bulletin* includes information on law
reform and law revision.

The Australian Law Reform Commission has issued a *Law reform digest*, 1983, covering the reports of law reform agencies in Australia, New Zealand and Papua New Guinea from 1910 to 1980.

Dossier is an annual inventory of current legal research in Canada and covers government, academic, and professional research currently in progress.

V. Newton *Law in Caribbean society: an annotated guide to University of West Indies Law in Society dissertations 1973–77*, 1980, includes periodical articles, books, official publications and unpublished research.

Dictionaries

In addition to those referred to above some compilations emphasise the terminology of a particular jurisdiction. Examples for Commonwealth countries are S. E. Marantelli *Australian legal dictionary*, 1980; J. A. Yogis *Canadian law dictionary*, 1983; and the *New Zealand law dictionary*, 3rd edn., 1979, compiled by G. W. and M. S. Hinde and based on Mozley and Whiteley.

The major United States work is *Black's law dictionary*, 5th edn., 1979, which may also be searched through WESTLAW. A *Dictionary of legal abbreviations used in American law books*, 2nd edn., 1985, compiled by D. M. Bieber, is a comprehensive list from a wide range of legal literature. The *Uniform system of Citation* gives guidance on correct usage.

Encyclopedias

Multi-volume works such as the *Australian Digest, Canadian Abridgment*, and the American *Corpus Juris Secundum*, are discussed in Chapter 8.

Biographical sources

Some Commonwealth and American lawyers are included in A. W. B. Simpson *Biographical dictionary of the common law*.

Individual or collected biographies may be traced through the appropriate national or legal bibliographies.

Select coverage is provided in general directories such as the *International Law List*, or the international section of the *Solicitors' and Barristers' Directory and Diary*. Commonwealth and US members of the SPTL are included in the *Directory of Members*.

The *Australian and New Zealand Law List* ceased publication in 1975. Regional lists are issued such as the *Queensland Legal Services Directory* or the *Legal Directory* (New South Wales).

Who's Who in Canadian Law and the annual *Canadian Law List* provide current biographical and professional information.

The *Commonwealth Caribbean Law List*, 1976, is published for the Organization of Commonwealth Caribbean Bar Associations; the *Directory of Legal Personnel in Barbados as at June 1983*, compiled by J. A. Braithwaite, is produced by the Faculty of Law Library, University of the West Indies.

The major directory of American lawyers is the *Martindale-Hubbell Law Directory*, an annual multi-volume work. *Who's Who in American Law* gives current biographical information. Academic lawyers are the subject of the *Directory of Law Teachers* where entries are biographical.

Legal organizations

Many of the directories mentioned above also list courts and officials. Something of the legal system, court structure and legal profession of individual countries may be gleaned from *Law and judicial systems of nations*, 1978, edited by C. S. Rhyne. Some updating is possible by reference to the *Lawyers Law Directory, international edition 1984–85*, 1985. The *International Law List* includes names and addresses of local law societies and bar associations.

Organizations concerned with the law are listed in the *Australian Legal Directory*.

Bar and law societies of Malaysia and Singapore are included in the *Lawasia Directory*, 1982.

Law libraries and librarians

The International Association of Law Libraries provides a forum for law librarians worldwide. The IALL *Directory*, 1980, lists members by country and by name, and thereby acts as a directory of many Commonwealth law libraries.

A *Directory of law libraries in Australia and Papua New Guinea*, 1979, compiled by R. Finlay, and a *National survey of law libraries in Australia*, 1984, published by the Australian Law Librarians Group, give locations of libraries and an indication of individual library holdings.

A general survey of law librarianship in Canada by Marianne Scott is included in *Law librarianship: a handbook*, 1983, 2 vols., with a useful bibliography. Many members of the Canadian Association of Law Librarians are included in the *Directory of Law Libraries* AALL and this serves as a directory to Canadian law collections.

A *Directory of law libraries in Singapore*, 3rd edn., 1983, includes government, court and law firm libraries with size-able holdings.

The annual *Directory of Law Libraries* issued by the American Association of Law Libraries, lists libraries geographically with indication of size, and provides an alphabetical list of individual librarians. A *Biographical Directory* is issued irregularly.

FURTHER READING

GENERAL

Cooper, B. D. 'Anglo-American legal citation: historical development and library implications', *Law Library Journal*, vol. 75, 1982, pp. 3–33.

Danner, R. A. 'Reference theory and the future of legal reference service', *Law Library Journal*, vol. 76, 1983, pp. 217–32.

Jain, H. C. 'Using a law library', *Journal of the Indian Law Institute*, 1982, pp. 575–95.

Kenny, P. H. *Studying law*, 1985.

Information sources in law, Logan, R. G. (ed.)1985.

Sweet and Maxwell Ltd *Guide to law reports and statutes*, 4th edn., 1962.

UNESCO *Register of legal documentation in the world*, 2nd edn., 1957.

Walford, A. J. *Guide to reference material*, vol. 2: 'Social and historical sciences, philosophy and religion', 4th edn., 1982.

Legal system of Scotland, 3rd edn., 1981.
Grimes, R. H. *Introduction to law in the Republic of Ireland*, 1981.

BIBLIOGRAPHIES

Gillissen, J. *Introduction bibliographique à l'histoire du droit et à l'ethnologie juridique*, 1963–. Vol. C includes Britain and Ireland.
Jegede, O. *Nigerian legal bibliography: a classified list of materials related to Nigeria*, 2nd edn., 1983.

Early law books

Cohen, M. L. 'Administration of rare materials' *in Law librarianship: a handbook*, ed. H. P. Mueller *et al.* vol. 2, 1983.
Mersky, R. M. *et al. Collecting and managing rare law books*, 1982.

Periodicals

Reynolds, T. H. 'Indexing of legal journal literature and the history and development of the *Index to Foreign Legal Periodicals*', *The Law Librarian*, vol. 15, 1984, pp. 38–46.

BIOGRAPHIES

Hicks, F. C. *Men and books famous in the law*, 1921.

LAW LIBRARIES AND LIBRARIANS

Law librarianship: a handbook, Mueller, H. P. *et al.* (eds.) 2 vols., 1983.
Roalfe, W. *The libraries of the legal profession*, 1953.
Sprudz, A. 'The International Association of Law Libraries and its 25 years of activities', *The Law Librarian*, vol. 15, 1984, pp. 50–3.
The Bulletin, Journal or Newsletter of associations such as the American Association of Law Libraries, Australian Law Librarians' Group, British and Irish Association of Law Librarians, Canadian Association of Law Libraries, Caribbean Association of Law Libraries, International Association of Law Libraries, New Zealand Law Librarians Group.
These publications also carry bibliographies of specific topics.

Part III Legal Literature of Other Legal Systems

10. European Communities

A. NOEL–TOD

INTRODUCTION

As the product of a legal system with national, supra-national and international dimensions, European Community law will be present in almost any law library. In many law libraries, particularly those allied to libraries designated as European Documentation Centres (see p. 426), the legal literature will be only part of a wide-ranging collection of documents. Indeed, in signposting the literature of Community law it is important to remember how interwoven it is with documentation of a non-legal nature. The collection of essays edited by Hopkins, *European Communities information: its use and users,* 1985, illustrates the variety of procedure and policies documented in the Community's publications, and the greater variety of publications and databases available for bibliographic control of legal and non-legal documentation.

This chapter has to create an artificial division in its concentration on the legal literature, and its emphasis on the connection with the legal literature of the United Kingdom and the Republic of Ireland. The national dimension of Community law is easier to understand with some knowledge of the wider political and economic aims of Community membership, and this is succinctly provided in the Central Office of Information's *Britain in the European Community,* 1981.

Most guides to the bibliography of Community law can deal only briefly with the working of the legal system and the actual operation of substantive law. Nevertheless library and information work with Community law will frequently suggest recourse to such expositions, and so details of two good, introductory textbooks by Lasok and Bridge, and Collins, have been included in the Further Reading list for this chapter.

THE EUROPEAN COMMUNITIES

The European Communities is in fact a portmanteau title for three separate Communities: the European Coal and Steel Community (ECSC), the European Economic Community (EEC) and the European Atomic Energy Community (EAEC or Euratom). Each was established by a separate treaty, so that even in the present merged Community there remain the different legal identities created by the various treaties.

The European Coal and Steel Community, which included Belgium, France, the Federal Republic of Germany, Italy, Luxembourg and the Netherlands, was established by the treaty signed in Paris in 1951, with the treaty entering into force in 1952.

The European Economic Community (the 'Common Market') comprising the same countries, was established by the Treaty of Rome, signed in 1957 and taking effect in 1958.

The European Atomic Energy Community (Euratom) was established at the same time as the EEC, and all three Communities shared the institutions of the European Assembly and the Court of Justice; other institutions such as the Council of Ministers remained separate to each. In 1965 the six member states signed the Treaty establishing a single Council and a single Commission of the European Communities (the 'Merger' or 'Fusion' treaty) which came into effect in July 1967 and replaced the three separate Councils with a single Council of Ministers and created the Commission of the European Communities in place of the ECSC High Authority and the EEC and Euratom Commissions.

In 1973 the United Kingdom, Denmark, and Ireland ratified the Accession Treaty of 1972. Greece became the tenth member of the Community in 1981, and the membership of Portugal and Spain was ratified in 1986.

SOURCES OF LAW

A recent publication of the European Commission, *The European Community's legal system*, 2nd edn., 1984, listed three written sources of law. The primary legislation can be considered to be the treaties establishing the Communities; the secondary legislation is represented by the various categories of regulations, directives, decisions and recommendations which are issued by the Community institutions as provided for in the treaties; and the third written source is the wide range of international agreements concluded between the Community and non-member states or other international organizations. For the purposes of legal bibliography and research it is practical to include a fourth written source: the decisions of the Court of Justice. Though the Court's role in interpreting and applying Community law differs in many respects from the pattern of precedence and authority that shapes much common law case-law into a source, its jurisdiction is in effect a potent force in Community law, and to exclude its decisions from the primary sources is a correct legal classification that is contradicted by the use of the literature.

Primary legislation

The treaties establishing the European Communities are the primary legislation, or basic law; policy is formulated and action undertaken in pursuit of the principles set out in the treaties, and secondary legislation is created and other legal decisions taken in consideration of one or more articles of the treaties.

The text of the treaties has been issued in various collected editions. The current official edition was published in 1978 in all the official languages including Irish: *Treaties establishing the European Communities; treaties amending those treaties; documents concerning the accession*; in 1982 a supplement was published following the accession of Greece, and in 1985 the Council published a collection of texts relating to the accession of Spain and Portugal: *Instruments concerning the accession ...* , 3 volumes. The English version of the previous official edition of 1973 is still of use as it includes certain annexes not reproduced in 1978 and for which no text is available in the English version of the *Special Edition* of the *Official Journal*. The English texts of the treaties have also been published by HMSO as command papers in the United Kingdom *Treaty Series, eg,* the 'Act concerning the condition of accession ... ' is published as United Kingdom *Treaty Series* no. 1 (1973) Cmnd. 5179 I and II.

Though commercial reprints of primary legislation cannot be considered as official translations, and so lack legal standing, it is often such versions that are consulted first, and there are various commercially published editions that include the text of treaties and related instruments. Sweet and Maxwell's *European Community treaties*, 4th edn., 1980, gives the text of the treaties together with many of the related protocols, conventions, decisions and declarations, including those concerning the accession of the United Kingdom. The Sweet and Maxwell collection reprints the English language texts as issued by the Community's Official Publications Office; a more selective edition based on the texts in the United Kingdom Treaty Series is *Basic Community Laws*, edited by B. Rudden and D. Wyatt.

Annotated and updated texts of the treaties are available in any of the looseleaf encyclopedias described in that section (see p. 422). Smit and Herzog's *Law of the European Economic Community*, 1976–, is arranged around the 1957 Treaty of Rome, so that the text of each of the treaty's articles is accompanied by details of implementing measures and court decisions, a legal commentary, and a bibliography of books and articles. The 'B' volumes of the Sweet and Maxwell *Encyclopedia of European Community law* restrict the annotation to analysis and citation of relevant secondary legislation and case-law.

National implementation of the treaties

In all the member states the treaties have been implemented by national legislation (or by amendment of the constitution) to have direct legal effect. The European Communities Act 1972 is the main statute providing for the implementation of Community law in the United Kingdom; apart from the official and unofficial texts available in statute collections, ar annotated edition of the Act by E. H. Wall has been published as a reprint from *Butterworths Annotated Legislation Series* (see Further Reading).

Legislative history

The main legislative bodies of the European Communities are the Council of Ministers (the Council) and the Commission of the European Communities (the Commission). In certain matters the Commission may act on its own, but more often it initiates legislative proposals for enactment by the Council. A detailed explanation of all stages of the process is given in Chapter 1 of M. Hopkins' *Policy formation in the European Communities: a bibliographical guide ... 1958–1978*, 1981. The legislative background to much of the primary and secondary legislation emanating from these bodies can be found in the COM (Commission) and SEC (Secretary General) documents issued by the Commission. These include both the Commission's legislative proposals (proposals and draft instruments) for Council regulations or directives, and reports to the Council or the European Parliament (communications and memoranda). COM documents are made available free to European Documentation Centres, and to others by subscription.

Those legislative proposals (preparatory Acts) that require an opinion from the European Parliament are published in the 'C' series of the *Official Journal*; others appear in the 'L' series once enacted. Though it is intended that the period from final draft to enactment should be brief, many COM documents, especially those of a controversial nature, remain 'current' for long periods. Since 1981, Euroinformation has published an annual *Index to Documents of the Commission of the European Community*, compiled by G. Pau. In 1983 the Commission began to publish its own annual index, *Annual Catalogue of COM Documents*, with non-cumulative issues throughout the year, *Periodic Catalogue of COM Documents*. Both these indexes have subject and numerical sections. The House of Commons *Weekly Information Bulletin* also contains a list of COM documents newly received.

A useful index and digest to over 600 major COM and SEC documents issued between 1958 and 1978 is the work by M. Hopkins, described above. For further investigation of legislative history the Hopkins digest can be usefully supplemented by J. Neilson's *Reports of the European Communities, 1952–1977: an index to authors and chairmen*, 1981, which covers documents other than COM, SEC, or *Working Documents* of the European Parliament (for the latter category see p. 421).

The citation of COM and SEC documents is by the relevant prefix followed by a date code and document number, the suffix 'final' indicates that it is the final draft so far as the Commission is concerned: *eg* COM (84) 7 final.

Secondary legislation

Secondary legislation is categorized as legal Acts made by the Council and the Commission under the powers conferred on them in the provisions of the treaties. Secondary legislation can be of an obligatory or non-obligatory nature. Obligatory Acts are regulations, directives and decisions. Regulations ('decisions' as defined by the ECSC Treaty) are binding in their entirety and normally directly applicable in all member states. Directives are binding as to the result to be achieved upon each member state to which they are addressed (in the ECSC Treaty they are known as 'recommendations'); thus they are normally issued with a stated time within which the member state must implement the requirements of the directive by means of appropriate national legislation. A decision is binding in its entirety upon those to whom it is addressed, and that may be individuals, member states or corporate groups. Non-obligatory Acts are recommendations provided for under the EEC and EAEC Treaties, and the opinions provided for under all the treaties. Their role is well described by Lasok and Bridge as 'persuasive and constructive in the formulation and execution of the policies of the Community. Though they cannot be formally cited as sources of Community law they ought to be regarded, in the light of their potential, as auxiliary elements of the law-making process of the Community.' It should be remembered that the legal standing of Community legislation is not necessarily determined by its nomenclature; instances exist where 'according to the case-law of the Court in the determination of the legal nature of a sovereign measure only the substance of it matters' (Attorney-General Roemer in Case 40/64: *Sgarlata v. EEC Commission* [1965] I ECR 215 at 231).

An important instance of this ambiguity in form and status of some Community secondary legislation is encountered with Commission decisions. These decisions (not to be confused with the use of the term to describe regulations made under the ECSC Treaty) are classified as legislation, and indeed general decisions have been described as 'quasi-legislative acts'. However the majority of Commission decisions are determinations of specific cases addressed to individuals or corporations within the Community. To that extent such decisions (largely concerned with restrictive practices) can be classified as case-law, and are included in many citators and indexes to Community case-law, including the *Gazetteer of European Law*. All decisions are published in the 'L' series of the *Official Journal*, and most are reported in the *Common Market Law Reports*. Citation practice for decisions is illustrated in the section on the citation of secondary legislation.

Publication of secondary legislation

The *Official Journal* is the official gazette of the European Communities, and as such carries the text of all Community primary and secondary legislation. Its particular importance to law libraries is that it is the comprehensive source for the official text of secondary legislation; and the greatest volume of Community law is contained in the secondary legislation.

The *Official Journal* is issued almost daily in two main series as separate issues, and is available in paper copy or microform. It is published in all the official languages, with the occasional issue in Irish.

The *Legislation* series, known as the 'L' series, publishes the text of all legal Acts, divided into obligatory and non-obligatory Acts. The relative importance of the legislation in any issue is indicated by the use of bold and light typefaces and asterisks against the titles on the contents page.

The *Information and Notices* series, known as the 'C' series, carries different categories of information, not all of which will be present in any one issue. These include: procedural business of the European Parliament, as well as issues devoted to written questions and answers; details of new actions, recent judgments and requests for preliminary rulings in the Court of Justice; and a miscellany of information and public communiqués arising from Council and Commission business.

At the accession of the United Kingdom, Ireland and Denmark in 1973 a *Special Edition* of the *Official Journal* was published in Danish and English versions, which reprinted in chronological order the legislation enacted from 1952 to 1972 and still in force as at January 1973. This contained over 2,000 Acts whose publication was obligatory in the *Official Journal*. A second series of the *Special Edition* was published in ten subject issues containing relevant Acts in force whose publication was not obligatory.

As well as the 'L' and 'C' series the *Official Journal* appears in two further parts. Since 1978 there has been a *Supplement* which carries commercial information concerning public contracts, tenders and project approval arising mainly from the European Development Fund.

Since 1968 the full text of the debates of the European Parliament has been published in a series described as the *Annex* to the *Official Journal*; an English text has been available since no. 157 of 1972–3. Further details are given in the section on the European Parliament. The publishing history of the *Official Journal* since 1952 is complex, but a good guide to all its variants up to 1979 can be found in Jeffries' *Guide*, pp. 20–30.

Indexes to the *Official Journal*

The *Official Journal* is voluminous. In 1983 the 'L' series contained the text of 3,762 obligatory Acts and 675 non-obligatory Acts, as well as several hundred corrigenda to earlier legislation. The index appears in monthly parts with an annual cumulation. It is issued in two parts, the alphabetical table and the methodological table. The methodological table is an arrangement by document number and so is useful when that is known (see the section on citation of secondary legislation).

Prior to 1984 the alphabetical table was in fact a classified index arranged by a selection of terms that required a good knowledge of the subject structure of Community business and the idiosyncracies of Community terminology; as such it was an unspecific means of retrieval for many items. From 1984 the alphabetical index has been based on keyword analysis of each document by use of the vocabulary in the EUROVOC thesaurus. Each document can now have up to five keyword entries, which has made the alphabetical index a more useful and usable index.

Because of the previously intractable nature of the alphabetical index, the subject indexes to works such as Sweet and Maxwell's *Encyclopedia of European Community law*, or the lists and noter-up in the cumulative supplement to volume 42A of the 3rd edition of *Halsbury's Statutes* are often the first point of referral in a subject search for legislation.

The lack of a cumulation of the annual indexes to the *Official Journal* has been remedied to a certain extent by the existence of the *Guide to EEC-Legislation*. This was first published by North-Holland in 1979, with revision of the basic volumes in 1982–5. It comprises three basic volumes indexing all community legislation from 1958 to 1982, with updating by cumulative supplements and a telex service to the T.M.C. Asser Institute at the Hague for recent information. The first edition was updated by microfiche supplements as well as paper copy. As with most indexes to Community secondary legislation, it excludes some of the regulations relating to agriculture but, that apart, it is one of the most comprehensive single indexes to current and lapsed legislation and legislative history. Another more recent bibliography that includes indexing of the *Official Journal* is the *EC Index* which is described on page 429.

The legislation published in the *Official Journal* is searchable in full text on CELEX, which is the database created by the Commission's Integrated Information Systems division (known by its French acronym SII) and available to subscribers via the Euronet–Diane network.

Secondary legislation in force

To discover the current situation with regard to secondary legislation is not an easy task; there is no equivalent to *Statutes in Force* or *Halsbury's Statutory Instruments.* Since 1979 there have been annually revised editions of *Directory of Community Legislation in Force,* which is based on the files of CELEX. Volume I, the 'Analytical Register', gives details of legislation arranged in subject groupings similar to the arrangement of the pre-1984 alphabetical tables to the *Official Journal* with final ordering by the CELEX document number; amendments and other details are indicated also. Volume 2 contains a keyword index to the 'Analytical Register' and a chronological list of CELEX document numbers which is of use in tracing amendments back to their principal Act. The *Directory* is updated with a half-yearly supplement.

At the accession of the United Kingdom an attempt was made to compile a collection of all secondary legislation then in force and keep it up to date. The Statutory Publications Office issued *Secondary legislation of the European Communities: subject edition,* 1973, which was a rearrangement in 41 subject volumes of the legislation contained in the *Special Edition* of the *Official Journal.* The work was provided with an index (vol. 42) and updated by 'Subject lists and table of effects', in monthly parts and annual cumulation. Publication ceased at the end of 1979, but this is still a useful work in tracing legislation in force between 1973 and 1979.

A selection of the secondary legislation in force at December 1972 with amendments to January 1974 was published as volume 42A of *Halsbury's Statutes of England,* and titled *European Continuation Volume I, 1952–1972*; it includes the text of the treaties. The volume is updated by a 'European Supplement' published as part of the annual cumulative supplement to the main work; this includes amending annotations and a selection of full texts and excerpts of new legislation.

The 'C' volumes of Sweet and Maxwell's *Encyclopedia of European Community Law* reproduce a wider selection of texts with the more integral revision allowed by the looseleaf format.

Citation of secondary legislation

Council and Commission regulations are identified by document number, preceded by the providing treaty and followed by the year; since 1963 the numbering of regulations has recommenced annually. Thus Reg. (EEC) 3035/84. OJ 1984, L287/27 is the citation to the *Official Journal* text of Commission regulation (EEC) No. 3035 of 30 October 1984, published in issue 287 of the 'L' series, the text commencing on page 27 of the issue. Fuller citation (as favoured in the *Official Journal*) will include the publication date of the issue, thus: OJ No. L 287, 31.10.84, p. 27. Acts printed in the *Official Journal* whose publication is not obligatory are identified by the sequence of year, document number and governing treaty. Thus a Commission decision of 18 July 1984 on an aid proposal by the Irish Government is cited as: Dec. 84/498/EEC. OJ 1984, L 276/40. In the case of citation to official texts of pre-1973 legislation the French text of the *Journal Officiel* (*JO*) should be preferred, followed by citation to the relevant issue of the English *Special Edition*, if available. Prior to 1967 there was no 'L' and 'C' division, so earlier references just give the page number: Dec. 65/362, JO 1965, 2184; OJ 1965–66, 77. There is little uniformity in the citation of Community secondary legislation in either primary or secondary sources. A useful summary of practice, 'Identification of secondary legislation', was included as part of the introduction to the Statutory Publications Office's *Secondary Legislation of the European Communities: subject edition*. The usage suggested in the Harvard Law Review's *Uniform System of Citation*, 13th edn., 1981 (the 'Harvard Blue Book') differs from general practice in the United Kingdom.

National implementation of secondary legislation

Though regulations of the Council or Commission are directly applicable in member states and binding in their entirety, they often provide for further detailed implementation by appropriate municipal law or administrative procedure, and so are often transformed into some form of domestic legislation. Directives, being binding as to the result to be achieved in the member states concerned, are intended to be transformed into appropriate national legislation within a specified period; the intention being to effect approximation of municipal law in that subject throughout the Community.

In the United Kingdom the implementation of Community legislation is by statute and Statutory Instrument. Relatively little Community legislation is implemented by statute; mainly matters of constitutional significance, such as the 1978 European Assembly Elections Act, and matters requiring major reform of existing law to achieve the necessary result: the Companies Act 1981 was the implementation of the Fourth Directive on company accounts (Dir. 78/660/EEC). Most implementation is by Statutory Instrument and, as with other delegated legislation, there is parliamentary scrutiny of Community legislation and its implementation which is reported in the appropriate series of Parliamentary papers. From 1972–6 there was a House of Commons Select Committee on European Secondary Legislation, retitled in 1976 as the Select Committee on European Legislation. In 1980 a new Standing Committee on European Community Documents was set up to which Community proposals and consultative documents could be referred; scrutiny is also undertaken by the Select and Joint Committees on Statutory Instruments. The major parliamentary committee for the scrutiny and investigation of Community policy and its legal, economic and social consequences is the House of Lords Select Committee on the European Communities; its reports, together with the minutes of evidence, are published as House of Lords papers, and provide extensive documentation on a wide range of topics, including many legal ones: the 23rd Report of the 1979–80 session is on the European Court of Justice (1979/80 HL (101)). Since 1981 this Select Committee has also issued *Progress of Scrutiny* reports which list, in various categories recent Community proposals and any committee action to be taken. A subject list of all reports published since 1974 was issued in 1983 as an annex to a *Progress of Scrutiny* report (no. D8–iii, 26.7.83). The purpose and procedure of the various scrutiny committees is set out in Erskine May's *Treatise on the Law of ... Parliament* and a survey of their activity and documentation can be found in the articles by T. Bates and D. Englefield listed in the Further Reading section.

To discover whether a particular piece of Community legislation has been implemented in a form of national legislation is not easy; there is no single comprehensive concordance with egular updates. Since 1973 the Council has published *List of laws and regulations adopted in the member states in application of acts adopted by the Communities*, but, as this work is issued in parts with a broad subject arrangement and no indexes or cumulations, it has been rightly described as 'almost worthless'. For implementation in the United Kingdom, the 'A' volumes United Kingdom Sources) of Sweet and Maxwell's *Encyclopedia* provide details of all domestic legislation implementing Community legislation, as well as the text of the most important measures. The equivalent service provided in the European Communities section of *Halsbury's Statutes* is more selective in its coverage.

The process of scrutiny and implementation of Community legislation in Ireland is largely similar to that in the United Kingdom. With some exceptions the Statutory Instrument is the legal instrument for domestic implementation, and the drafting and legislative process is scrutinized by the Joint Committee on the Secondary Legislation of the European Communities. An account of the process can be found in the article by M. T. Robinson listed in the Further Reading section.

International agreements

This third source of Community law is not distinct from primary and secondary legislation in that it is composed of a mixture of those sources. However its texts are often treated as a separate source, and since it portrays the Community as an entity having international personality and entering into agreements governed by international law it has a special claim for its dual importance as international and Community law. Two Community publications provide collections of texts of agreements between the European Communities and non-member states and other international organizations.

Collection of agreements concluded by the European Communities is issued as a companion series to the collected edition of the main treaties. The five main volumes reprint the texts of agreements from 1952 to 1975, with a subject and contracting parties index in volume 5; continuation is by annual volumes.

Collected Acts is an updated looseleaf collection of the agreements arranged by country or international organization groupings, with the texts being straight reprints from the pages of the *Official Journal*. In 1985 the format was changed from looseleaf to brochure form.

The Commission's Treaties Office issues a bi-annual list (alternatively in French and English) showing the current status of agreements: *Agreements and other bilateral commitments linking the Communities with non-member countries*. This includes details of some minor agreements not published in the *Official Journal*. The Commission also publishes *The European Community: international organizations and multilateral agreements* which gives detailed information on negotiation history as well as the text of major agreements and ratifying documents; it also has a useful introduction explaining 'the legal bases of the Communities' multilateral relations and the rules governing its participation in the work of international organizations'.

Case-law: the Court of Justice

The Court of Justice of the European Communities (commonly referred to as the 'European Court of Justice' or just 'the European Court') is a single court situated at Luxembourg and composed of thirteen judges, and assisted by six advocates-general elected by the governments of the member states. Cases can be heard in chambers of three or five judges, or in a sitting of the full Court. All matters relating to the interpretation, legality, compliance or enforcement of Community legislation can be brought before the Court, as can cases relating to restrictive commercial practices and cases concerning Community staff. The most important area of jurisdiction with regard to the legal systems of member states is the Court's ability to give preliminary rulings on the interpretation of Community law. In 1982, 94 of the 185 judgments were cases referred by courts in the member states for preliminary rulings. 'Preliminary' is a slightly misleading description for, as Lord Denning emphasized, in 'a question of interpretation or validity ... the European Court is supreme. It is the ultimate authority. Even the House of Lords has to bow down to it' (*H. P. Bulmer Ltd. v. J. Bollinger SA* [1974] 2 CMLR 91 at 113).

The official edition of the Court's procedure was last published by the Court in 1975, *Selected instruments relating to the ... procedure of the Court*. An amended version in codified form was published in the *Official Journal* in 1982 as *Codified versions of the rules of procedure* but, though convenient, this later version has no official status so reference must be made to the separate texts of post-1975 amendments in the *Official Journal*. Commercially published editions of the Court's rules, with annotation, are now available: such as *European Court Practice*, by J. A. Usher, 1983. English courts' rules with regard to the procedure for preliminary rulings to the Court of Justice are included in standard practice books such as the *Supreme Court Practice* and *Atkin's encyclopaedia of court forms*.

A useful textbook on the history, organization and procedure of the Court of Justice is that by Brown and Jacobs listed in the Further Reading section.

Law reports

The decisions of the Court of Justice are published in an official series, *Reports of Cases before the Court*, which is also titled *European Court Reports* and cited as such (ECR). This is the authoritative series for citation, with the only authentic text being that in the procedural language of the case (despite the fact that the judgment is normally drafted in French and then translated into the procedural language). There is an unofficial English translation of cases for 1953 to 1972 in twenty volumes; for citation to an official text of a pre-1973 decision it is usual to refer to the French text: *Recueil de la Jurisprudence de la Cour* (Rec.).

The *European Court Reports* are slow in publication, and that, together with other disadvantages such as the lack of a proper cumulative index and the sparse provision of head-notes and other annotations, makes the *Common Market Law Reports* a more popular series with both practitioners and academics. The *Common Market Law Reports* (CMLR) is an unofficial series published by the European Law Centre and contains translations of decisions since 1961. It appears weekly and, as well as being well indexed and annotated, it includes a selection of decisions from national courts as well as all those of the Court of Justice and the European Commission. Since 1970 *Common Market Law Reports* has given the text of the Court's judgment in the procedural language of the case as well as in English.

Another commercially produced series of Court of Justice decisions is published as part of Commerce Clearing House's looseleaf encyclopedia *Common Market Reports* in a sub-series titled 'Common Market decisions'.

A collection of translations of the Court's judgments up to the end of 1960 can be found in Volume 2 of D. G. Valentine's *The Court of Justice in the European Communities*, 1965, and reference to these texts is included in the *Gazetteer of European Law*.

Though Irish is recognized as a procedural language, all Irish cases so far have been presented to the Court of Justice in English; national decisions of Irish courts on Community law are published in the *Journal of the Irish Society for European Law*.

Recent cases

Brief details of recent judgments and new actions before the Court are published in the 'C' series of the *Official Journal*; judgments usually appear there within six weeks of their delivery. The Registry of the Court of Justice provides on subscription offset copies of the Court's judgments and the Advocate-Generals' opinions prior to their publication in the *European Court Reports*. The Court's Information Office issues weekly a detailed summary of recent judgments, *Proceedings of the Court of Justice*; these are collected together in a quarterly bulletin, *Information on the Court of Justice*.

Since 1982 Elsevier has published the *European Court of Justice Reporter* which carries detailed digests and commentary as well as other court information such as lists of pending cases. It is issued ten times a year with a cumulative case index and is one of the major commercially published awareness services for recent case-law. Others include the reports section of Commerce Clearing House's *Common Market Reports*, the occasional shortened report in *The Times* law reports section, in a sub-series titled '*The Times* European Law reports', and a case and legislation insert in the *New Law Journal*, though the latter is often a survey of only one topic, *eg* C. Sherliker 'Merger regulation in the EEC', *New Law Journal*, vol. 134, 1984, pp. 809–12. Digests of recent cases appear in the *Financial Times European Law Newsletter*, and the 'Current Survey' section of the *European Law Review* appears frequently enough to be considered a useful alerting service.

Structure and citation of Court of Justice reports

In structure the Court of Justice reports differ from English law reports in that the judgment is a unanimous one, usually a brief statement divided into the reasons and the ruling. The opinion of the Advocate-General submitted to the Court is a much fuller text and has a closer resemblance to an English court's judgment; it usually forms the basis of the judgment, and so may be regarded as a commentary on the latter. An illustrated explanation of a Court of Justice decision can be found in J. H. Farrar and A. M. Dugdale's *Introduction to Legal Method*, 2nd edn., 1984, pp. 196–9 and 266–73. The reports follow the European tradition of being identified by the case numbers as well as the names of the parties, *eg* Case 152/78: *EC Commission v. France re Advertising of alcoholic beverages* [1980] ECR 2299, [1981] 2 CMLR 743, is identified as case number 152 in 1978. The precedence in citation is to the official series, and thereafter to an alternative such as *Common Market Law Reports*. In American legal literature it is common for the alternative citation to be to the *Common Market Reports*, *eg*, Case 88/79: *Ministère Public v. Grunert* [1980] ECR 553; [1979–1981 Transfer Binder] Common Mkt. Rpt. (CCH) ¶8680.

The case number is an important identifier as often the case name is no more than a formula title in its recurrence: *EC Commission v. France* is the title of over fifteen different decisions, and translated titles can mislead: 'Ministère Public v. Grunert' files as 'Public Prosecutor v. Siegfried Grunert' in *Common Market Reports*. Many cases have nicknames; for example, *Rewe Zentral AG v. Bundesmonopolverwaltung für Branntwein* is better known as the 'Cassis de Dijon case'. Some citators and indexes attempt to include nicknames, but due to the vagaries of translation no list is exhaustive. Some are given in the *Gazetteer of European Law*, and useful lists are given in the third and fourth editions of *Leading cases on the law of the European Communities*, 1980 and 1982, compiled by D. J. Gijlstra *et al.* (the fourth edition omits certain agriculture and competition cases).

Indexes and digests to Community case-law

The fullest index and citator is the *Gazetteer of European Law . . . 1953–1983*, 1983, published by the European Law Centre. It includes all decisions of the Court of Justice and Commission decisions on competition matters (together some 2,150 decisions); it also indexes a large selection of decisions from courts in member states and some from non-member states, and relevant decisions of international tribunals such as the GATT panels or the European Commission of Human Rights. Volume 1 is the master list of Court of Justice cases by case number and separate lists of Commission and national decisions by letter and date codes; volume 2 contains alphabetical and subject indexes, a chronological index of Court of Justice judgments, and a 'case search', *ie* cases referred to in later judgments. In the master list in volume 1, each citation includes reference to the text in all the official language series, and for foreign national decisions includes a reference to any English translation. Thus an entry for a decision on Community law in a German court reads: D 690227 27 February 1969 (Bundesgerichtshof – KZR 3/68) Re 'Yoga' Fruit Juices. Eng: [1969] CMLR 123; Ger: [1969] BB 692, [1969] GRUR 501, [1969] NJW 978, [1969] WuW 504. The *Gazetteer* is based on the indexes compiled for the *Common Market Law Reports*, and as such supersedes that series' cumulative index for 1962–73 and the annual indexes for 1973–83. However, in one important respect the annual indexes of both law report series are superior to the *Gazetteer*. They both contain a table of Community legislation listing cases arising under particular treaty articles, regulations, directives, conventions, etc., forming part of Community law.

Since 1981 the Court of Justice has published a looseleaf

digest, *Digest of case-law relating to the European Communities*. It is issued in four series: 'A' is for case-law common to the three Communities as the distinct law of the EEC, ECSC and EAEC; 'B' is cases before national courts; 'C' is cases concerning Community officials; and 'D' covers cases on the 1968 Brussels Convention on jurisdiction and the enforcement of judgments in civil and commercial matters. At present the largest section of the *Digest*, the 'A' volume, commences in 1977, as that was the first year not covered by an earlier digest series that also related cases to particular legislation: the *Compendium of case law relating to the European Communities, 1953–1976*, edited by H. J. Eversen and H. Sperl. For the period 1953 to 1972 the Eversen and Sperl digest was only published in French and German and is usually cited by its French title: *Repertoire de la jurisprudence relative aux traités instituant les Communautés Euro-péenes*.

Both the Court of Justice's *Digest* and that by Eversen and Sperl are indexed to allow a search to be made for cases relating to specific Community legislation.

From 1969 to 1983 the Court published *Synopsis of the Work of the Court of Justice*, an annual digest that included details of procedural changes as well as cases heard.

Since 1981 *The Digest* (formerly the *English and Empire Digest*) has included a section on the case-law of the European Communities. The main section appeared in volume 21 (Green Band re-issue) and contained some 3,000 entries for cases to 1980, and this has been updated in the annual cumulative supplement. The most comprehensive digest of Community and related national case-law since 1973 is the *European Law Digest*, which is arranged on the same multiple-entry basis as *The Digest* and brings together both Court of Justice and national courts' decisions as well as details of legislation.

A companion work to the *Guide to EEC-Legislation* is the *Guide to EC Court Decisions*, which contains annotated digests of most decisions for 1954–82, as well as details of Commission decisions; the work is supplemented in the same manner as the *Guide to EEC-Legislation*. A digest of decisions on Community matters in national courts for 1958–82 was published by the Commission's Legal Service, *National decisions concerning Community law*. It provides texts of digests in all the official languages, but, with no cumulative index to its 26 parts, it is difficult to use; references to most of the national decisions it contains are more easily located in the *Gazetteer of European law*.

The availability of LEXIS in a law library allows for extensive searching on UK decisions and legislation relating to Community law, as well as on citations of Court of Justice cases and Community legislation. CELEX includes the full text of Court of Justice cases, and decisions of national courts are being added to the database.

THE EUROPEAN PARLIAMENT

Established in 1952 as the Common Assembly of the European Coal and Steel Community, the European Parliament now consists of 518 members directly elected by universal suffrage in the member states, with national seat-allocation reflecting a compromise between population size and representation within the Community. The United Kingdom has 81 members, Ireland has 15. Unlike most national legislatures the European Parliament cannot initiate or pass legislation, but it has an important consultative role in the drafting of Community legislation. Its opinion is necessary on draft legislation prior to enactment by the Council; though the Council may ignore that opinion. Furthermore, consultation and conciliation procedures can be invoked for disagreements between the Council and the Parliament over Acts with significant financial implications. Though the Parliament has a power of censure over the Commission, its real influence over both the Council and the Commission lies in its power to reject the annual budget proposal and thus delay or limit community policy in certain areas. This budgetary power is based on a detailed and complex procedure that is deployed in a process described as 'invariably complex, often protracted and acrimonious'.

The Parliament's sessional year runs from March to March, within which it normally meets for one week each month in plenary session at Strasbourg. The business of the standing committees and political groups is conducted mainly in Brussels, while the Secretariat is situated in Luxembourg.

The main documents of the European Parliament comprise the debates; the minutes, opinions, resolutions and oral questions; and the *Working Documents*. Since 1968 the debates have been published in the official languages in a supplement to the *Official Journal* entitled the *Annex*. Like the main text of the *Official Journal* the *Annex* is available in hard copy or microform. The *Annex* is published less frequently than the *Official Journal*, and so to mitigate the consequent delay in the publication of debates there are various summaries and a provisional version also available, and these are described in detail in the article by A. S. Reid listed in the Further Reading section. The *Annex* includes an annual index to the debates, arranged under names of speakers and subjects, and also a list of *Working Documents* (see below). The 'C' series of the *Official Journal* publishes the minutes of proceedings, opinions and resolutions, and written and oral questions. The written question is an important method of exerting influence and maintaining supervision of the activities of the Council and the Commission. All parliamentary business published in the 'C' series is indexed in the monthly and annual indexes to the *Official Journal*.

The text of written questions and adopted resolutions is searchable on CELEX.

The *Working Documents* of the European Parliament cover the whole range of Community activity, including both documents presented to the Parliament and documents arising out of its business. Many *Working Documents* are the COM documents forwarded by the Council for Parliament's opinion, and so they will also be found in both the *Official Journal* and their original series. The reports of the European Parliament's specialist committees constitute one of the most important categories of *Working Documents*. The eighteen committees represent the whole range of Community business; their reports deal both with draft legislation and more general proposals, and they also investigate matters of more international concern. *Working Documents*, as with other documentation produced by the Parliament's printing office, are assigned a document number consisting of the number of the directly elected parliament, a running number, and the year of the session: thus the Report of the Legal Affairs Committee on United Kingdom copyright design, published during the term of the first parliament, is identified as: Doc. 1–216/84:7.5.84. As with similar UK official publications, the committee reports are commonly identified by the name of the rapporteur or chairperson, and can be traced by such in the index to the *Annex*.

Information on the Parliament's membership, rules of procedure, and member states' electoral laws is contained in the *Official Handbook of the European Parliament*, a looseleaf work that has been published for the Parliament since 1980 by Dod's Parliamentary Companion. The Parliament's Directorate-General for Research and Documentation has issued a comprehensive survey of the Parliament's activity for 1952 to 1982: *Forging ahead: thirty years of the European Parliament* includes detailed descriptions of procedure and practice as well as various statistical and historical information, and is a useful companion volume to the *Official Handbook*.

The electoral law of the United Kingdom relating to the European Parliament is incorporated in both statutes and delegated legislation. The European Assembly Elections Act 1978 makes provision for delegated legislation on the conduct of the elections, and most of the general electoral law governing the conduct of such elections is collected in the 1983 consolidation of the Representation of the People Acts. The relevant parts of all such legislation are collected in the 'A' volumes of the Sweet and Maxwell *Encyclopedia*, and new editions of treatises on electoral law are now taking account of the European dimension; an example is *Schofield's Election Law*, 9th edn., 1984.

SECONDARY SOURCES OF LAW

Legal encyclopedias and surveys

In many law libraries the commercially published looseleaf encyclopedia is often turned to first to trace Community legislation, as it collates information on documents often widely scattered and inadequately indexed in the primary sources. Three of the most popular titles are mentioned here; further description of their particular uses has been incorporated into the relevant sections of this chapter. Sweet and Maxwell's *Encylopedia of European Community law* is a multi-volume, looseleaf work in three series, all with extensive annotation and commentary: the 'A' volumes, titled 'United Kingdom sources', contain the text of national legislation implementing Community primary and secondary legislation; the 'B' volumes contain the text of the treaties, the rules and governing statutes of the institutions, and the text of international agreements; the 'C' volumes reproduce the text of a large selection of the current secondary legislation, arranged in subject groupings. The work is well-indexed with both subject and case indexes and finding lists of legislation; each series is updated when appropriate, amounting approximately to a quarterly update of the whole text.

Commerce Clearing House's *Common Market Reports* (formerly *Common Market Reporter*) is an American publication designed for the business lawyer, and is popular with law firms and legal departments dealing with European and international business. Its commentary is more discursive than that provided by Sweet and Maxwell, including a bibliography of books and articles, and it includes the text of Court of Justice decisions. A separate volume, 'Doing business in Europe' provides legal and commercial surveys of individual European countries. The work is updated fortnightly and also provided with a weekly bulletin, 'Euromarket news'. The general arrangement of the main volumes of *Common Market Reports* is for secondary legislation and analysis to accompany the relevant articles of the treaties, and this arrangement is also followed by Smit and Herzog's *The law of the European Community: a commentary on the EEC Treaty*. The latter work is structured around the 248 articles of the Treaty of Rome, with the analysis including bibliographies relating to particular Treaty articles.

The Community itself publishes no equivalent encyclopedia, but there are several publications useful for obtaining an overview of legal activity in a particular area. The annual report of the Commission, *General Report on the Activities of the European Communities*, indicates legislative developments in all areas and the chapter on Community law is also available as a separate pamphlet. The annual report of the Council, *Review of the Council's Work*, is a similar work. *Europe Today* is an annual survey of Community activity produced by the European Parliament, which includes synopses of, and references to the 'most important legislative acts of the European Community, including the opinions and reports of the European Parliament, in their most recent form'. Its documentation of both policy and legislation makes it, as Jeffries points out, 'a digest of the secondary legislation of the European Communities'. The *Bulletin of the European Communities*, which is published eleven times a year with an annual index, can act as an update to a work such as *Europe Today* as it reports on current business with references to textual sources such as the *Official Journal*.

There is a wide range of commercially published bulletins and information services providing surveys of current Community developments, and many of them are listed in *Alerting services covering European Community documentation*, compiled by the British Library's Official Publications Library and reprinted in their *European Communities publications*, 1983 and also in the *Law Librarian*, vol. 14, 1983, pp. 47–9. Some of the alerting services with a legal bias have been mentioned in the relevant sections of this chapter.

Textbooks

Though Community law has always generated a substantial body of monographic literature, as witnessed by the substantial bibliographies listed in the Further Reading section, it has only been since the accession of the United Kingdom that it has begun to feature significantly in English law publishers' lists. Many monographs and some casebooks on special aspects are still only published by continental English language publishers.

The growth of the literature and the interest therein has meant a division in both monographs and casebooks between those treating the 'substantive' law of the Communities (agriculture, competition, social policy, etc.) and those dealing with general legal issues and the structure of the institutions.

Casebooks on Community law tend to follow the American 'cases and materials' pattern; not only because of the need to include extracts from the treaties and secondary legislation involved in the courts' decisions, but also because the Court of Justice adopts the continental legal method of allowing the citation of 'doctrine' and 'travaux préparatoires' in legal argument and judgment. Doctrine is normally the writings of jurists to be found in textbooks and periodicals; travaux préparatoires include much from the *Working Documents*, opinions, and debates that feature in the Community's legislative process, and 'it is universally accepted that judges may turn to them for information in order to clarify the thoughts of the legislator' (Lasok and Bridge, p. 120).

Periodicals

Articles, case-notes and commentary on Community law are published in a wide range of periodicals, as evidenced by the entries for the European Communities in the *Index to Legal Periodicals* and the *Index to Foreign Legal Periodicals*, and by the substantial list of journals abstracted for *ELLIS*.

The *European Law Review* appears six times a year and includes a current survey section for cases and legislation that is useful for current awareness; it is indexed with cumulative tables of cases and legislation. The *Common Market Law Review*, published quarterly, includes a subject index and a current bibliography of articles from other English language and European legal periodicals. *Legal Issues of European Integration* has two issues a year and concentrates on lengthier studies, some of which are reprinted as monographs. The *Journal of Common Market Studies* has a more general coverage with the emphasis on political and economic analysis and relatively little on law.

The 1974 'Statement of minimum holdings of the law of the European Communities . . .' by the Society of Public Teachers of Law includes titles of the major French, German and Italian periodicals on Community law which should be considered for an academic library.

OFFICIAL PUBLICATIONS: BIBLIOGRAPHIC CONTROL AND
LIBRARY PROVISION

Though there is an Office for Official Publications of the
European Communities at Luxembourg, publication still remains largely with the various institutions and not all the titles
published are included in the current publishing information
put out by the Office.

Publications of the European Communities is a monthly cata-
logue issued both separately and as an insert to the *Bulletin of
the European Communities*. It includes monographs, serial titles
and current periodicals and cumulates in an annual volume.
All aspects of the policy and operation of the Office for Official
Publications are described thoroughly in the article by
D. Perry, 'The role of the Office for Official Publications of the
European Communities' which is listed in the Further
Reading section.

HMSO is a sales agent for many Community publications and
so new titles appear in the *Daily List*, the *Monthly Catalogue*, and
the annual catalogue of *International Organisations Publications*
which is published as a supplement to the *Annual Catalogue of
Government Publications*.

The Commission also provides access to documentation and
information through a network of libraries and information
offices. The Central Library and the Central Documentation
Service (SCAD) in Brussels are responsible for a range of
printed catalogues, indexes, abstracting services, and bibliographies, all of which are described in the chapter by E.
Gaskell in Hopkin's *European Communities Information*, 1985
(see Further Reading). In each member state the Commission
maintains information offices. A list of the Information
Offices is given in Morris and Boehm's *The European Community: a practical guide*.

Since 1963 a system of European Documentation Centres
and Depository Libraries has been promoted by the Commission. Over forty libraries in the United Kingdom, and six in
Ireland, are designated EDCs, which means they receive free
copies of Community publications. The majority of these EDCs
are in universities or polytechnics. The decentralized nature
of Community publishing and the inadequate bibliographical
control mean that EDCs are not comprehensive collections but
they do contain the greater part of the Community's output.

All the Community publications described in this chapter are likely to be held at an EDC.

Though many publications are common to the holdings of both EDCs and Depository Libraries (DEPs) the latter also receive many documents in the different Community languages, including those only available in the original language, as well as documents with limited distribution and others of a semi-public or semi-official nature. DEPs have larger historical collections, particularly of the founding institutions: it is likely that the BLLD's holding of Euratom documentation is the most comprehensive in existence.

While the main concern of the EDCs is to serve their immediate clientele, the purpose of the Depository Libraries is 'to serve the needs of the general population'. The Lending and Reference Divisions of the British Library both have depository status, with much of the Reference Division's collection being available in the Official Publications Library or the Science Reference Library. *European Communities publications: a guide to British Library resources*, 1983, lists all the serial publications together with their particular location within the British Library. This guide also includes a list of the EDCs in the United Kingdom and the smaller number of libraries designated as European Reference Centres. The latter receive a much smaller selection of basic documents, mainly general and annual reports, and general information series. A list of EDCs and Depository Libraries worldwide is given in Jeffries' *Guide*, pp. 254–83.

It should be remembered that not all EDCs will be complemented by a collection of commercially published titles on Community law necessary for proper legal coverage and, conversely, that there are other libraries without EDC status that maintain strong collections of Community law with both official and commercial publications.

REFERENCE SOURCES

Guides to legal literature

Law is not often treated as a discrete subject within the activity of the Community, and guides to the legal literature usually cover non-legal areas as well. The most useful general guide including description of the Community's legal publications is still Jeffries' *A guide to the official publications of the European Communities*, 2nd edn., 1981. This can be supplemented by the same author's essay on 'Sources of information on the law of the European Communities' in Hopkins' *European Communities information: its use and users*, 1985. The article by T. Kearley: 'An American researcher's guide to European Communities law and legal literature' in the *Law Library Journal*, vol. 75, 1982, pp. 52–97, covers much the same ground as Jeffries but attempts to describe documents in the context of the Community's legal system.

A guide to the documentation of the legislative process is provided by Hopkins' *Policy formation in the European Communities: a bibliographical guide to Community documentation, 1958–1978*, 1981. Hopkins' bibliography is confined to primary material, and so can be usefully expanded by a work concentrating on the secondary literature, such as Lodge's *The European Community: bibliographical excursions*, 1983.

Legal bibliographies

A useful bibliography covering both primary and secondary sources of Community law is that by C. M. Germain: 'European Community law: a selective bibliography of publications in English, French and German with annotations' in the *International Journal of Law Libraries*, vol. 8, 1980, pp. 239–81. Monographic literature from all the member states was surveyed by G. J. Dahlmanns: 'European Communities law: a selective bibliography with annotations. Part two: secondary sources, monographic literature' in the *International Journal of Law Libraries*, vol. 3, 1975, pp. 215–72; equivalent parts for primary sources and periodical literature were never produced. Another general bibliography including textbooks and articles on Community law is Szladits' *A bibliography on foreign and comparative law*.

In the absence of a current bibliography devoted exclusively to all forms of Community law and its commentary, recourse can be had to various bibliographies produced by the Commission.

The Office for Official Publications issues the *Documentation Bulletin* which is produced in three series by the Commission's Service Central des Archives et de la Documentation (SCAD). Series A is a weekly abstracting bulletin including both Community documents and periodical articles on Community matters; it is arranged in 28 subject sections with a subject index in French. The B series comprises over 30 subject bibliographies which are re-issued periodically in revised editions. They include topics such as company law (B15), promotion of consumers' interests (B10), and the law of the sea (B28), and give detailed legal documentation, legislative history, and commentary in books and articles. Series C is a smaller, irregular series of bibliographies based on the entries in Series A since the latter's last cumulation.

A product of the Commission Library's automated cataloguing system is the monthly *Recent Publications and Documents of the EC received by the Library*. This is a classified catalogue with author and title indexes that cumulates annually into a catalogue representing accessions since 1978. As well as Community documents it includes other monographs and a small selection of articles from periodicals and year books. Since 1981 a number of special subject bibliographies have been produced as a by-product of the main listing.

Most law libraries will probably find that reference to the specifically legal sections of the general bibliographies produced by the Commission (including the catalogues of the Office for Official Publications) sufficient for their current bibliography. However, for those working extensively with Community documents, an ambitious current bibliography began publication in 1985. The *EC Index*, published by Europe Data, combines bibliographical listing with title keyword indexing and an abstracting service. Issued monthly with quarterly and annual cumulations, it covers some 7,000 Community items a year, with abstracts for nearly a third. Abstracts are included for COM documents, European Parliament *Working Documents*, Court of Justice judgments and Advocates'-General opinions, preparatory Acts in the 'C' series of the *Official Journal*, and all the 'bold type' entries in the 'L' series.

For online searching for bibliographic detail there is the database SIGLE (System for Information on Grey Literature in

Europe). This is a bibliographic database available in the United Kingdom since 1984 via the British Library's BLAISE-LINE. The input for SIGLE is provided by major national centres for European documentation, including the British Library Lending Division and the Institute for Industrial Research and Standards in Ireland. Grey literature is interpreted to include 'report literature, discussion and policy documents, working papers, theses, some official publications and local government publications'. SIGLE is described in an article by J. Gibb and M. Maurice in *Aslib Proceedings*, vol. 34, 1982, pp. 493–7.

Periodicals

Until recently there was no specific indexing service for Community law. In 1985 Europe Data began publication of *ELLIS: European legal literature service*. This indexing and abstracting service covers some 450 legal journals, as well as selected Festschriften, theses, conference proceedings, research papers, and some official publications. It is published in ten issues a year, cumulating in a year book. ELLIS includes a 'Cited legislation' index and a 'Cited master case list' to help trace commentary on specific Community law. For general law libraries including Community law the high subscription cost is likely to be a deterrent.

Legal research

Community law is not the exclusive subject of any bibliography of theses or directory of research in progress. There are a number of more general works treating the European communities, and these are all described in the section on scholarly literature in Hopkins' 1985 essay, 'European Communities information and its use in British universities and polytechnics'.

Dictionaries

The linguistic problem in a legal system employing eleven official languages is considerable, and one of which the law

librarian should be aware. The situation is graphically described in the section on 'The language of Community law' on
pages 62–85 of Lasok and Bridge. The activity in translation
and interpretation has meant that the Community's institutions are one of the main publishers of dictionaries and glossaries to aid equivalence in legal language. The second edition
of the *European Treaties Vocabulary* began publication in 1983,
Part One being parallel English and Irish texts. The prevailing
influence in the language of Community law is French; indeed
the ECSC Treaty is only authentic in the French language
version. The need to refer to French texts for authentic
versions of pre-1973 legislation means that a French-based
glossary is a necessary part of a Community law collection. The
best glossary for the specific terms of Community law and
policy is the *European Communities Glossary: French–English*,
prepared by the English Division of the Council's Translation
Department. The glossary indicates which English expressions occur in an authentic English translation in the *Official
Journal*, and the supplement includes an index of those terms
corrected since the publication of the main work. A dictionary
based on the French texts of Community treaties and Council
of Europe conventions up to 1969 is the *French–English
Glossary of French Legal Terms in European Treaties*, by R. J. B.
Anderson and R. J. Deckers. Of more general application is
the 1977 edition of Quemner's *Dictionnaire Juridique* which
includes commercial as well as legal terms. The linguistic
problems of equivalence in form and meaning in drafting are
covered in the Council's *Manual of precedents drawn up by the
legal/linguistic experts of the Council* ... , 2nd edn., 1983, and
terms relating to multilateral agreements are given in a multilingual glossary, *ACP–EEC Glossary*, which is based on the
phraseology of the Second Lomé Convention and related
texts, and has indexes in French and English.

Apart from the Commission and Council's own publications, there are only a few English-based subject glossaries
suitable for specific areas of Community law. Between 1969
and 1980 there appeared a series generally entitled the *European glossary of legal and administrative terminology*, published
under the auspices of the International Institute for Legal and
Administrative Terminology. The majority glossed between

two European languages; the few that encompassed English were co-published by Sweet and Maxwell.

There are as yet no subject dictionaries specifically for Community law, and only a small proportion of the Community's legal terms, procedures and institutions receive adequate definition in existing English legal dictionaries.

The European Community: a practical guide and directory for business, industry and trade, 2nd edn., 1985, by B. Morris and K. Boehm includes entries for legal topics (*eg*, Cassis de Dijon case, harmonization, lawyers, etc.) and cites the legal basis for such topics by reference to the 'L' series of the *Official Journal*. The *Dictionary of the European Communities*, 2nd edn., 1982, by J. Paxton, confines itself to a more conventional format. *A Dictionary of the European Communities* by G. and B. Parker is a shorter work suitable for students.

The lack of coverage of Community law in English legal dictionaries extends to abbreviations. Even Raistrick's *Index* includes only some of the more common abbreviations. The best work is the Commission's *Multilingual glossary of abbreviations*, 1983.

Encyclopedias

A useful compendium of information on the European Communities is D. Overton's *Common Market Digest: an information guide to the European Communities*, 1983. Though arranged thematically, it is well indexed and the entries are documented both with bibliographical references and citation of relevant legislation.

The Community's own annual surveys and reports can often serve an encyclopedic function; those most useful for legal information work are described at p. 423.

Legal organizations

All the Community's institutions can to some extent be described as legal organizations, and an annual directory listing all the institutions and their staffing, as well as details of related organizations, pressure groups, etc., is the *Yearbook of the European Communities and of other European Organizations* published by Editions Delta. The *Yearbook* includes some background information on the workings of the institutions and the main areas of Community policy, and that aspect is well covered in the directory by B. Morris and K. Boehm: *The European Community: a practical guide and directory for business, industry and trade*, 2nd edn., 1985.

The Council and the Commission

Both these institutions publish their own directory. The Council's *Guide to the Council of the European Communities* is published twice yearly, while the Commission's *Directory of the Commission of the European Communities* appears three times a year.

The European Parliament

The Parliament's looseleaf *Official Handbook of the European Parliament* includes a general directory and individual biographies for all MEPs.

The Court of Justice

Information on the Court, its composition and procedure, is reprinted in each issue of the quarterly case-digest *Information on the Court of Justice*. From 1969 to 1983 the Court published an annual *Synopsis of the Work of the Court* that included statistical information on the Court's case-load and other administrative detail.

Both particular cases before the Court and general information and commentary on the Court's history and procedure are treated in the bibliography produced by the Court's Information office: *Bibliographie de jurisprudence européenne* covered the period 1953 to 1976, and it has been continued by *Bulletin bibliographique de jurisprudence communitaire*. A useful bibliography for the period prior to the United Kingdom's accession is that by I. Kavass: 'The Court of Justice of the European Communities: an annotated bibliography, 1951–1973', in the *Vanderbilt Journal of Transnational Law*, vol. 8, 1975, pp. 523–650.

FURTHER READING

INTRODUCTION

Central Office of Information *Britain in the European Community*, 1981.

Collins, L. *European Community law in the United Kingdom*, 3rd edn., 1984.

Dahlmanns, G. J. 'European Communities law: a selective bibliography with annotations. Part two: secondary sources, monographic literature', *International Journal of Law Libraries*, vol. 3, part 3, 1975, pp. 215–72. No other parts published.

Fitzgerald, F. N. and Emringer, L. 'Principal source material on European Community legislation: a bibliographic note', *International Journal of Law Libraries*, vol. 3, part 3, 1975, pp. 208–14.

Germain, C. M. 'European Community law: a selective bibliography of publications in English, French and German with annotations', *International Journal of Law Libraries*, vol. 8, part 6, 1980, pp. 239–81.

Hopkins, M. (ed.) *European Communities information: its use and users*, 1985.

Jeffries, J. *A Guide to the Official Publications of the European Communities*, 2nd edn., 1981.

Jeffries, J. 'Sources of information on the law of the European Communities', *in* Hopkins, M. (ed.), *European Communities information: its use and users*, 1985, pp. 227–40.

Kearley, T. 'An American researcher's guide to European Communities law and legal literature', *Law Library Journal*, vol. 75, no. 1, 1982, pp. 52–97.

Lasok, D. and Bridge, J. W. *An introduction to the law and institutions of the European Communities*, 3rd edn., 1982.

Lodge, J. (ed.) *The European Community: bibliographical excursions*, 1983.

SOURCES OF LAW

Bates, T. 'The drafting of European Community legislation', *Statute Law Review*, 1983, pp. 24–34.

Borchardt, K.-D. *The ABC of Community law*, 1984.

Englefield, D. 'Parliament and the European Communities', *in* Hopkins, M. (ed.), *European Communities Information: its use and users*, 1985.

European Communities, Commission *Thirty Years of Community Law*, 1983.

Groux, J. and Manin, P. *The European Communities in the International Order*, 1985.

Jeffries, J. 'CELEX', *Law Librarian*, vol. 11, no. 3, 1980, pp. 60–1, *and* vol. 12, no. 1, p. 13.

Page, A. C. 'Community law', *in* Dane, J. and Thomas, P. A. *How to use a law library*, 1979, pp. 133–8.

Robinson, M. T. 'Irish parliamentary scrutiny of European Community legislation', *Common Market Law Review*, vol 6., no. I, 1979, pp. 9–40.

Wall, E. H. *European Communities Act 1972*, 1973.

Warner, J-P. 'European Community legislation: the view from Luxembourg', *Statute Law Review*, 1982, pp. 134–42.

COURT OF JUSTICE

Brown L. N. and Jacobs, F. G. *The Court of Justice of the European Communities*, 2nd edn., 1983.

European Communities, Commission *The Court of Justice of the European Communities*, 3rd edn., 1983.

Kavass, I. I. 'The Court of Justice of the European Communities: an annotated bibliography, 1951–73', *Vanderbilt Journal of Transnational law*, vol. 8, 1975, pp. 523–650.

EUROPEAN PARLIAMENT

European Communities, Parliament *The European Parliament: its powers*, 1983.

European Communities, Parliament *Forging ahead: thirty years of the European Parliament*, 1983.

Reid, A. S. 'European Parliament information' *in* Hopkins, M. *European Communities information: its use and users*, 1985, pp. 77–90.

OFFICIAL PUBLICATIONS: BIBLIOGRAPHIC CONTROL AND
LIBRARY PROVISION

The following essays from Hopkins, M. (ed.) *European Communities
information: its use and users*, 1985:
> Gaskell, E. 'The library and documentation services of the
> Commission of the European Communities', pp. 91–101.
> Pau, G. 'The general information policy of the European Com-
> munities', pp. 47–57.
> Perry D. 'The role of the Office for Official Publications of the
> European Communities', pp. 25–46.
> Verheyden, W. 'The publications policy and programme of the
> European Communities', pp. 13–23.

Hopkins, M. *Publications, documentation and means for their dissemination in the Commission of the European Communities*, 1981.

Jeffries, J. 'Legal information from European Documentation
Centres', *Law Librarian*, vol. 11, no. 3, 1980, pp. 57–9.

11. International Law and Organizations

Section 1: International Law

C. MISKIN

DEFINITION AND FUNCTION

Classical definitions of international law describe it as 'a body of rules governing the relations between states'. In modern times this definition has been expanded to include the concept of international law regulating the relationships not only between states, but also between international organizations and individuals. For example, Akehurst in his *A modern introduction to international law*, 2nd edn., 1984 defines it as follows:

'International law is the system of law which governs relations between States. At one time States were the only bodies which had rights and duties under international law, but nowadays international organizations, companies and individuals also sometimes have rights and duties under international law; however it is still true to say that international law is primarily concerned with States.'

In Cheng's *International law, teaching and practice*, 1982, Rosalyn Higgins describes the various functions of international law as follows: 'to some it is simply the neutral application of existing rules; to others it is the promotion of international co-operation and functional interpretation; yet to others it is, more negatively, a system for restraint of state behaviour; while to another group, it is the promotion of a world order that is compatible with notions of individual dignity.'

Origins

International law has existed in a rudimentary form since the days of the Greek city states. Although Europe is generally considered to be the place where international law as we know it today had its origins, medieval Europe was not divided into states in the modern sense of nations having undisputed political control over their own territories and being independent of any external political control. This concept of the state began to emerge in Europe in the sixteenth and seventeenth centuries, but it was not until after the First World War that international law became universal. The origins of international law are also closely linked to the writings of the great classical writers on international law, such as Hugo Grotius, Vitoria and Gentili.

Public international law should be distinguished from private international law or conflict of laws, which deals with the interrelationship of the domestic municipal laws of different states, rather than regulating the relations between different foreign states.

Sources

The most generally accepted definition of the sources of international law lies in Article 38(1) of the Statute of the International Court of Justice which states that:

'The Court, whose function is to decide in accordance with international law such disputes as are submitted to it, shall apply:
   a) international conventions, whether general or particular, establishing rules expressly recognised by the contesting states;
   b) international custom, as evidence of a general practice accepted as law;
   c) the general principles of law recognised by civilised nations;
   d) ... judicial decisions and the teachings of the most highly qualified publicists of the various nations, as subsidiary means for the determination of rules of law.'

Definition

In his book on treaties, *Law of treaties*, 1961, Lord McNair defines a treaty as 'a written agreement by which two or more states or international organizations create or intend to create a relation between themselves operating within the sphere of international law'.

Thus the 'conventions' referred to in the Statute of the ICJ actually means treaties and these are an extremely important source of international law. According to Akehurst in *A modern introduction to international law*, 2nd edn., 1984, published versions of treaties entered into by the UK in 1892 filled 190 pages; those entered into in 1960 filled 2,500 pages. The growth of modern technology, improved communications and international trade have made states much more interdependent and treaties on a vast range of subjects have been made over the past century.

Not every agreement between states is intended to create international legal obligations and such agreements are not therefore treaties.

International law does not prescribe a particular form which a treaty should take, and it does not even have to be in writing, though treaties almost always are. Treaties are usually made between states, between heads of states, between governments or between particular ministers, and they are variously described as treaties, conventions, declarations, protocols, and acts, final acts, general acts, accords, exchange of notes, covenants and concordats. For the purposes of this chapter, the term 'treaty' is defined in the widest possible sense (see Glossary).

Treaty publishing is best considered from four different viewpoints: general collections; historical collections; national collections; and specialized (usually subject) collections.

General collections

Collections of texts of treaties generally begin with the year 1648 which was the end of the Thirty Years' War and is used as a convenient date to mark the beginning of the modern nation-state system. The three important general collections are:

The Consolidated Treaty Series, edited by Clive Parry, vols. 1–231, 1969–. This collection begins in 1648 and ends in 1920, when the League of Nations series began. It attempts to reprint the original text and official translations of all treaties. The arrangement is chronological with French or English translations where available. Summaries are given where no translation is available. There is also a multi-volume *Index – Guide to Treaties*, which is divided into the *General Chronological List, 1640–*, and the *Special Chronology 1648–1920* of which five volumes have so far appeared. The general chronological list gives information on the date of each treaty, its title, the names of the parties and, where available, the place of signature, plus information as to the source of each treaty, and details of any other published locations for it.

League of Nations Treaty Series: Treaties and International Agreements registered with the Secretariat of the League, 1920–1946. This 205-volume set contains 4,834 treaties in both English and French. It covers not only treaties between members of the League, but also those between members and non-members. There are index volumes interspersed between the text volumes and these are divided chronologically and by subject.

United Nations Treaty Series: Treaties and International Agreements registered or filed and recorded with the Secretariat of the United Nations 1946–. In December 1946, the UN started publishing the text of every treaty entered into by any of its members. By article 102 of the Charter of the United Nations, all treaties must be registered with the Secretariat and published. Treaties appear first in their official language, followed by English and French translations if necessary. They appear, not in order of signature or ratification, but in order of registration with the UN, making them difficult to locate. So far over 1,000 volumes have been published in this series and they appear at the rate of over 40 volumes a year. In early 1985, the volumes to 1976 (vol. 1007) had been published. Thus, this series is well in arrears and not useful for current treaty research. A Cumulative Index arranged chronologically and alphabetically by subject is produced for every fifty volumes, but this also is seriously in arrears. Indexing for later treaties is left to commercial publishers. Volumes 1–700 of this series are available on microfilm from Oceana.

In an interesting article entitled: 'Problems with sources of information in international law and relations: the case of the worldwide treaty jungle', *International Journal of Law Libraries*, vol. 9, no. 5, 1981, p. 195, Adolf Sprudzs describes the United Nations Treaty Information System (TIS) which was a project to computerize the publication of treaties and thus to speed the whole process up. In fact, there are still severe delays in publication not only of the treaty volumes, but also of the monthly *Statement of Treaties and International Agreements Registered, or Filed and Recorded* which is supposed to be a current awareness service but is actually running two years in arrears.

Historical collections

It is not proposed to discuss in depth the historical collections. for fuller details the reader is referred to the first edition of the *Manual*. Apart from the *League of Nations Treaty Series* and the *Consolidated Treaty Series* already mentioned above, there is one other work which should be mentioned briefly. This is G. F. de Martens', *Recueil des Principaux Traités d'Alliance, de Paix etc.* There were five series of this work, extending between 1760 and 1943, and it is an important source for information on nineteenth-century treaties.

National collections

In recent years many countries have established their own national treaty collections. Of most interest to us are the UK and US treaty series.

United Kingdom

The United Kingdom *Treaty Series* is the official series prepared by the Foreign Office. Treaties of all types are contained in this series, but they are published here only after ratification. They may have appeared earlier in the command paper series and this will be indicated in the top left-hand corner of the title page. The heading on the top right-hand corner gives the name of the country involved if the instrument is a bilateral treaty and the subject matter if it is a multilateral treaty. The *Treaty Series* forms a sub-series to the command papers and every treaty has both a command paper number and a *Treaty Series* number, followed by the year of issue. There is a new numerical sequence every year for the *Treaty Series* numbers.

Each year there are three or four issues of the *Supplementary List of Ratifications, Accessions, Withdrawals etc.*, and there is an *Index to Treaty Series* arranged by *Treaty Series* number and by subject and country (in one sequence). The terms used here are those appearing on the title page top right-hand corner. There is also a *General Index to Treaty Series* which cumulates every three years' indexes. The latest issue is that for 1977–9, which was not published until 1983, and states that it 'is the last General Index to be published'.

United States

The United States is one of the most important participants on the international stage and, for this reason alone, brief note should be made of the major US sources for treaty materials. Also, the US government has a policy of keeping the public informed on its international relations and this means that the texts of US treaties can often be located quickly after they have been ratified.

The first widely circulated official version of treaties which have entered into force appears in pamphlet form in *Treaties and other International Acts Series* (TIAS), published by the Department of State since 1945. Each treaty is issued as a separate item and numbered consecutively although not necessarily published in that order. TIAS is cumulated into, and replaced by, *United States Treaties and other International Agreements* (UST), published by the Department of State since 1950 when the publication of the text of treaties in *Statutes at*

Large was stopped. The texts of treaties are published in the original language and English and keep the same numbers as allocated to them in TIAS. Each volume has an index by subject and country.

For retrospective treaty research, the latest series of *Treaties and other International Agreements of the US*, 1776–1949, edited by C. E. Bevans and published by the Department of State in 13 volumes between 1968 and 1976, is the major source. It includes the English texts of all treaties which were published in *Statutes at Large* between 1776 and 1949. There is an index volume.

Subject collections

In recent years more and more collections of treaties covering particular subject areas have been published. They are frequently produced in looseleaf form for ease of updating. The major publisher in this area is Oceana. One of the most relevant collections for the UK reader is by W. H. and D. B. Diamond *International tax treaties of all nations*, 1975. This multi-volume work contains: 'English language texts of all tax treaties between two or more nations in force on July 1, 1975'. There is also Series B, which covers tax treaties not yet published by the UN. All texts have a short introductory explanation and annotations and are published in English. There is also a very useful looseleaf index listing all the treaties made by each country.

Another subject series is C. Schmitthoff, *International commercial arbitration*, 1974. This series contains a great deal of useful material including both national arbitration rules and various specialist treaties, *eg*, commodity agreements. It is unfortunately extremely difficult to use as the material is not arranged in a readily understood order.

Indexes

Apart from the indexes within each series, there are various indexes to treaties. The largest commercially published comprehensive index to treaties is: Rohn's *World treaty index*, 2nd edn., 1984–5. This is the most important product of the Treaty Project located in the Treaty Research Center at the University of Washington in Seattle. The second edition is now published and a detailed review of the first edition can be found in the *American Journal of International Law*, vol. 71, 1977, p. 800. Another useful general index is that by Mostecky: *Index to multi-lateral treaties: a chronological list of multi-partite international agreements from the sixteenth century through 1963*, 1965, with citations to their text. This index is based on Harvard Law School's treaty collection.

The third general index is J. and R. Vanbery *Cumulative list and index to treaties and international agreements registered or filed and recorded with the Secretariat of the United Nations*, 2 vols., 1977.

Another useful general index is the Harvard Law School's *Index to multilateral treaties*, 1966. This lists 3,859 treaties covering the period 1596–1963, and is reasonably comprehensive for the period up to 1960. Section 1 of this work indexes more than 3,000 items dating between 1969 and 1974 which have appeared since the last UN official index of 1970.

An interesting work is *Multilateral treaties: index and current status*, by M. J. Bowman and D. J. Harris. It is a product of the Treaty Centre of the University of Nottingham. This is a Centre which contains a fairly comprehensive collection of treaty materials and whose activities are concerned with the collation of information on treaty status, the techniques of treaty making and studies of the operation of multilateral treaties. The aim of the *Index* is to offer, in a single publication, status information about the main multilateral treaties as to whether they are in force or not and who the parties are. The work covers over 800 treaties. The material in the book is arranged chronologically and each treaty is given a unique number for the purposes of the publication. Other information given includes the date the treaty was concluded (adopted), its bibliographical locations, its date of entry into force, its duration and the parties to it. There is also a brief abstract for the entry giving subject details, where the content is not fully apparent from the title. It is intended to publish regular supplements to keep the book up to date and it should prove to be an extremely useful aid to treaty research. There are also indexes devoted to national treaty collections, but it is only proposed to consider the English and American publications here.

Apart from the *Index to Treaty Series* the other major index of UK treaties is Parry and Hopkins' *An index of British treaties 1101–1968*. This is a three-volume work, one of whose main purposes is to serve as a complete consolidated index to the UK *Treaty Series*. As it was published in 1970 this work only covers treaties concluded up to 1968 and this limits its usefulness for current research. It is divided into various sections, of which the major section is the chronological list. This list gives the title of the treaty, together with its date of signature, date of entry into force, details of any amendments or modifications, plus bibliographical details of all of its locations. There is a subject index of the multilateral treaties, whose usefulness is somewhat marred by the awkward way in which it is laid out. There are also indices to the bilateral treaties by both country and subject. Within the limitations mentioned above, this is a most useful index.

The best-known American index is the *Treaties in Force* published annually by the Department of State. It lists all treaties and agreements which the US considers to be in force on 1 January of each year. Part I lists bilateral treaties by country and subject and Part II lists multilateral treaties by an alphabetical subject arrangement, indicating those states party to the agreement. In order to facilitate use of *Treaties in Force*, Kavass and Sprudzs have produced a *Guide to the United States Treaties in Force*, 1982. This is a new numerical list and subject index to *Treaties in Force*. The guide helps the researcher by enabling him to find, for example, all bilateral treaties relating to shipping. To do this research using TIF only would mean going through it country by country looking for any listings under that particular subject heading. In Kavass and Sprudzs the researcher merely has to look in the subject index to find all relevant treaties listed. The numerical list is also useful in that it shows all agreements in force by their file number. Part II of the guide deals with multilateral treaties. References are also given to the location of the texts in the various treaty series. This publication is an invaluable aid in ascertaining treaty status and is a very useful general research tool.

Igor Kavass and Adolf Sprudzs have also produced the *United States Treaties and Other International Agreements cumulative index 1950–70, 1971–75*. This gives access to treaties in the *UST* by *TIAS* number, by date of signature, by country and by subject.

Igor Kavass and Adolf Sprudzs also produce the *Current Treaty Index: cumulative index to the United States slip treaties and agreements*. As its long title suggests, this is a cumulative index to the United States slip treaties and agreements. It is a useful quick reference source for treaties and agreements entered into by the US with other countries and international organizations during recent years. It contains cumulated information arranged numerically, chronologically, geographically, by the name of the parties and by subject about current treaties which are available only in slip form during the lengthy period of time between their publication and their eventual incorporation in the bound volumes of UST. The information contained in the index is eventually incorporated into the UST *Cumulative Index*. The *Current Treaty Index* appears in paper covers and it is the editors' intention that it should appear annually. It is an extremely useful source of up-to-date information about recent US treaties.

Other treaty sources

Tracking down treaties can be a difficult task and other general sources of information should be noted.

Official gazettes are usually the first source of declarations, treaties and other official announcements and will frequently contain the most up to date text of a treaty long before the other tools mentioned in this section have caught up with it. Some gazettes have a special section devoted to the texts of international treaties. For example, the German *Bundesgesetzblatt, Teil 11* has a regular supplement, *Fundstellennachweis B: Völkerrechtliche Vereinbarungen* which publishes German treaties. The British Library, Official Publications Library, has the best collection of such gazettes in the UK.

A journal such as *International Legal Materials* gives information on treaties. It reproduces the texts of many relatively obscure treaties and other agreements before they are officially available elsewhere.

It should also be noted that government bulletins, press releases and circulars may often contain the texts of treaties shortly after they are signed. The US Department of State Bulletin is published weekly and has a special section entitled 'Treaty information'. This is compiled by the US equivalent to the English Treaty Records Office and provides information on current developments concerning US treaties. It has weekly and six-monthly indexes. *The U.N. Chronicle*, the *Trachtenblad* (Netherlands) and the *Information Bulletin on Legal Activities within the Council of Europe* are other good examples of bulletins containing treaty information.

The two major textbooks on treaties are Lord McNair's *Law of treaties*, 1961 and Elias's *The modern law of treaties*, 1974. There are some books and articles devoted entirely to dealing with problems in treaty research. Probably the most useful single booklet is by Adolf Sprudzs: *Treaty sources in legal and political research: tools, techniques and problems, the conventional and the new*, 1971.

LAW REPORTS

There is still discussion in scholarly circles as to when international law reporting really began. One favoured date is 1764 when, in the case of *Triquest v. Bath*, Lord Mansfield first judicially affirmed the idea that international law is part of the law of the land. The other most popular date is 1794 when Great Britain and the United States signed the Jay Treaty. This was the beginning of a long practice of arbitral settlement between the two countries and, with it, the start of true international arbitration.

Most series of international law reports begin their coverage in the twentieth century. Because it is difficult to isolate cases relating to international law from the mass of domestic cases published each year, various series of specialized international law reports have been started. These reports cover not only decisions of domestic courts on points of international law, but also decisions of the specially constituted international courts and tribunals.

General collections

The most important series of cases covering more than one country or court are the *International Law Reports*. These started life as the *Annual Digest of Public International Law Cases* in 1929, when they were edited by Lauterpacht and McNair. It was intended to start coverage in 1919 and publish the decisions of international and national tribunals of as many countries as possible. The series commenced publication in 1929 and covers reports of international law cases heard by national and international courts and tribunals, the first volume covering the years 1925–6. Over the years the abstracts grew longer and this was reflected in a change of title in 1940 to *Annual Digest and Reports of Public International Law Cases*. In 1950, with the publication of volume 17, the title of the series was changed again to *International Law Reports* and complete texts of judgments are now always published. The aim of the series is 'to provide within a single series of volumes comprehensive access in English to judicial material bearing on Public International Law'. The material is presented in its original form and, where necessary, translations of foreign judgments are provided. There is the addition of an editorial summary. Some volumes cover a particular topic, others cover several topics. For example, volumes 63–65 were devoted exclusively to foreign sovereign immunity and volume 50 was devoted to one arbitral award. There are regular consolidated tables and indexes to *International Law Reports*.

There has been some criticism of the editorial policy of printing full judgments of, for example, the World Court, as these are published contemporaneously with its decision by the Court itself. See Green 'Raw Materials of International Law', *International and Comparative Law Quarterly*, 1980.

National collections

United Kingdom

The idea of producing a series of United Kingdom international law reports was first suggested by Lord McNair to the

British Institute of International and Comparative Law which, with the International Law Fund, undertook to finance the project. The series was edited by Clive Parry and entitled *British International Law Cases*, 1964–73. It was decided to exclude private international law and the law of prize, but within these limits, the series attempts to cover all international law cases decided in the British Isles between medieval times and 1970. As yet coverage does not extend to cases on war and neutrality, or to the decisions of British courts overseas.

This series is designed to complement the *International Law Reports*. Cases are published in full and unlike the *International Law Reports*, no system of catch-words or cross-references is involved, nor are head-notes added. Each volume of the series contains a cumulative list of the cases published within it, giving full reference to the original reports. Each volume also contains a subject index and there is a cumulative index available for the first eight volumes. The cases are classified as far as possible by the same scheme as is adopted in the *International Law Reports*. Publication of the series has been halted at Supplementary Volume 9, 1966–1970, published in 1973 and there must be considerable doubt as to whether any further volumes are likely to see the light of day in the immediate future.

United States

The major series in America is the *American International Law Cases* which is in the course of publication. After spending many years browsing through hundreds of volumes of United States federal and state law reports, Francis Deak conceived the idea of producing a series of law reports devoted to international law and these volumes are the result. Volumes 1–20 were edited by Francis Deak and volumes 21–28 by Frank Ruddy. Volumes 1–21 cover the period 1783–1968 and subsequent volumes so far published cover 1969–78. There is a separate looseleaf index volume covering the period 1783–1968 which gives full details of the contents of every volume.

Different subjects are covered by different volumes: thus volumes 1–3 cover international law in general and volumes

6–8 cover jurisdiction. The series does not cover the decisions of regulatory agencies. Within each section the cases are grouped in parts: first, United States Supreme Court decisions, second, decisions of lower federal courts and third, state court decisions. In each part, the arrangement is chronological. Each decision, although it may cover more than one topic, is printed only in the chapter which appeared to the editor to be the primary subject of the case and there is extensive cross-referencing from other subjects. The cases also have editors notes which endeavour to give full and uniform information about the treaties or other legislation involved.

Particular courts

Permanent Court of International Justice

The Permanent Court of International Justice was established by its statute in 1920 and came into being in 1921. Its judges were elected by the League of Nations. The Court was dissolved at the same time as the League of Nations in 1946. Until 1 January 1931 the Court issued six series of publications: A, Judgments; B, Advisory Opinions; C, Acts and Documents concerning the organization of the Court; E, Annual Reports; F, Indexes.

In 1931 the PCIJ decided to combine in a single series (A/B) the judgments, orders and advisory opinions delivered by it which had hitherto been divided into A and B. Difficulties sometimes arise with the identification and location of reports in series A, B and C following these changes. The fascicules in both series A and B were renumbered retrospectively in a single sequence which was continued unbroken into the new series A/B, the first fascicule of which became no. 40. In series C all volumes or parts were henceforward numbered consecutively instead of sessionally and previous issues renumbered retrospectively. Thus no. 19 (in 5 volumes) of the old numbering, issued for the 19th session of the Court, is followed by no. 52 which is the first volume in the new numbering, and the apparent gap 20–51 in series C is not really a gap at all. Tables of the renumbered series are in the 8th *Annual Report*.

A convenient collection of the judgments, orders and advisory opinions of the court is Hudson's *World Court Reports, 1922–42*. This four-volume work collects together in full all the judgments of the PCIJ. The first volume also contains the texts of the various instruments setting up the Court and other useful information about it. All the texts are reproduced from official publications and English texts have been given in all cases in which they are available (the official languages of the Court being both English and French).

International Court of Justice

The Court is one of the six principal organs of the United Nations and its Statute, which is very similar to the Statute of the Permanent Court of International Justice, is annexed to the charter of the United Nations, so that all members of the United Nations are automatically parties to the Statute. The Court consists of fifteen judges, five being elected every three years to hold office for nine years. Judgments of the Court are binding on the parties concerned. The Court can also give advisory opinions which, although not binding, are generally complied with.

The publications of the International Court of Justice can be found in four main series. Of these, the most important is the *Reports of Judgments, Advisory Opinions and Orders*, which are issued in fascicules and then form an annual volume with a subject index. The second series is the *Pleadings, Oral Arguments, Documents* which appears on an irregular basis and comprises the documents filed in each case heard by the Court. The Court also publishes a *Yearbook*. This began publication in 1947 and provides information concerning the organization, jurisdiction and activities of the Court. The *Yearbook* is prepared and published by the Registrar of the Court, and is not the responsibility of the Court itself. It contains information about the organization of the Court, biographies of its members and a summary of the work of the Court during the year under review, including abstracts of each case, giving all the salient details succinctly.

Because it is a permanent institution, the Court has been able to create, in a continuous manner, a coherent body of case-law and thus contribute widely to the development of international law. It was set up with the intention of being an instrument for settling disputes, rather than a scientific academy and this rationale is reflected in its decisions.

Arbitration reports

International arbitral awards have always been of importance as a source of international law, but until the Secretariat of the United Nations and the Registry of the International Court of Justice began publication of the *Reports of International Arbitral Awards* in 1948, no systematic collection of these awards had been published.

As a guide to the sources of arbitration reports, A. M. Stuyts's *Survey of international arbitrations, 1794–1970*, 1972, is a most useful publication. It gives details of each arbitration between 1794 and 1970 arranged in chronological order. Each entry gives the bibliographic locations for the arbitration plus basic details of parties, subject matter and the award.

There have also been some historical non-comprehensive collections published by individual scholars of which the most important are those by La Fonteyn, *Pasicrisie internationale, histoire documentaire des arbitrages internationales, 1794–1900* and La Pradelle and Politis: *Recueil des arbitrages internationales 1798–1855*, 2 vols., 1856–72.

The *Reports of International Arbitral Awards* cover only international decisions, *ie*, those rendered between states. Awards between a private individual or body and a state have been omitted, as have the judgments and advisory appeals of the Permanent Court of International Justice, though the decisions of the Permanent Court of Arbitration given since the First World War have been included. The decisions are published in chronological order, starting in 1918 and each decision is preceded by a summary.

Other specialized reports

It is not intended to discuss either the various series of War Crimes Trials reports or the reports of cases in prize here. For full information on these reports, the reader is referred to the first edition of the *Manual*.

One recent series which may be of more interest is the Grotius Publications reports of the Iran–US Claims Tribunal. The tribunal was set up under the Claims Settlement Declaration made in January 1981 by the US and Iranian governments. The reports are entitled *Iran–United States Claims Tribunal Reports*, 1983–, and they contain the texts of all the known decisions and awards made by the tribunal, published in chronological order on the basis of the date on which the awards were signed.

DIGESTS OF CASE-LAW

Although the principle of *stare decisis* does not apply to the International Court of Justice, advocates frequently refer to the Court's past decisions when appearing before it, as does the Court itself. In its early years, bibliographical coverage of the Court's decisions was not as extensive as it is today and it was difficult for parties seeking reliable precedents to find them. Therefore a number of digests began publication.

One of the most important of these is Hambro's *The Case Law of the International Court*, 1952–, a multi-volume work which began publication in 1952 and the latest volume of which was published in 1976. The purpose behind this work was 'to give a complete picture of the Court's pronouncements in the field of international law'. It contains extracts from the decisions of the Court arranged by subject matter, with extensive cross-referencing to allied extracts. Thus the first volume contains twenty-three extracts dealing with the definition of territorial waters. However, in the latest volume, the entries under territorial waters have been greatly expanded to include the continental shelf and fisheries problems. This is a good example of the way in which international law is constantly developing and expanding into new subject areas.

A useful digest is Verzijl's *The jurisprudence of the World Court*, 1965–6. This is a two-volume work containing a case-by-case analysis and commentary on every case heard by the PCIJ and ICJ up until 1964.

Another digest is that by Krystyna Marek: *A digest of the decisions of the International Court*, 3 vols., 1974–8. Volume 1 covers the PCIJ and volumes 2 and 3 the ICJ. The *Digest* contains a summary of every decision of the two Courts. The summary lists the points of law raised both in the Court's decisions and in dissenting opinions, and then gives as concisely as possible the facts of the case, followed by a summary of the judgment.

STATE PRACTICE

This term is generally used to describe the second source of international law – custom. The material sources of custom are many and may include diplomatic correspondence, state legislation, judicial decisions, legal opinions and resolutions. Brownlie's *Principles of public international law* gives a useful description of custom as a source of international law.

It is generally agreed that digests of state practice emanated originally from the United States in the late nineteenth century. In 1964, the Council of Europe passed a resolution recommending that the governments of the member states of the Council: 'publish digests concerning national practice in the field of public international law, insofar as the publication of such a digest has not yet been undertaken by themselves or in any other way which, in the light of principles and methods set forth below, they consider to be satisfactory'.

Digests contain extracts from official documents which illustrate government practice in international law. These documents include diplomatic notes, memoranda, parliamentary reports and debates, judicial and arbitral decisions, treaties and conventions and statements made to international organizations and judicial tribunals.

So far only a few member states have published digests: these include France, Switzerland, the United Kingdom, the Netherlands and the United States.

United Kingdom

The British Digest of International Law is the most up to date statement of state practice in this country, but it is out of date and incomplete. It was originally conceived as a project of the Trustees of the International Law Fund. The editor was Clive Parry and the intention was to produce the *Digest* in two phases, the first volumes covering the years 1860–1914. Later volumes would continue the work from 1914 to date. The *Digest* was to be 'based upon a comprehensive examination of the papers of the Foreign Office, arranged in narrative form and grouped according to subject matter'. Four volumes, 5–8, covering the individual in international law and the organs of states, were published in 1965, and another two covering territory in 1967. It now looks as if this project will never be completed.

An interesting historical source of state practice has recently become available to international law scholars and this is Clive Parry's *Law Officers' Opinions to the Foreign Office 1793–1860*, published in 95 volumes. It is a collection of opinions reproduced from the Foreign Office records in the Public Record Office and comprises some 10,000 reports, principally of the Advocate-General, alone or in conjunction with the Attorney- and Solicitor-General. Its publication, according to the preface, 'has been undertaken in accordance with a plan to make more generally available as much material of this category as possible relating to the foreign and colonial affairs of Great Britain'. The series only runs to 1860, as from this date onwards the Law Officers' reports to the Foreign Office have been published annually. The opinions are published in date order and in the original manuscript form. There is a two-volume index, which contains a calendar, in which the date of each report is given and the names of the Law Officers or other advisers responsible for it, and a brief indication of the substance of the report, plus a reference to any place where the report may have been printed. There is also a brief subject index.

Another useful source of material on UK state practice is the *British Yearbook of International Law*, which has a section in each volume analysing United Kingdom materials on international law published during the year in question. Over the years this section of the *Yearbook* has expanded considerably in scope and it now includes extracts from House of Commons and House of Lords debates, command papers, speeches given by UK representatives at various international meetings, parliamentary answers, evidence to committees, exchanges of notes etc. There is also a sub-section giving details of British legislation during the year which covers international law.

United States

The style of later digests originated from a series of Department of State publications in the late nineteenth century. The earliest notable US digest is the *Digest of the published opinions of the Attorneys-General and of the leading discussions of the Federal Courts, with reference to international law, treaties and kindred subjects* by John Cadwalader. It was originally published in 1877 and is the first subject compilation of official texts on US practice in international law. Another famous digest is that by Francis Wharton, *A digest of the international law of the United States, taken from documents issued by Presidents and Secretaries of State, and from decisions of Federal Courts and opinions of Attorneys-General*, 1886. This is the first true digest of American practice in international law, where the material is arranged by subject. This was followed by John Bassett Moore's *A digest of international law*, 1906, which was an entirely reorganized and expanded version of Wharton's work. It included topics from Wharton but also contained a great deal of extra material. This monumental work was followed by Green Hackworth's *Digest of international law*, 1940–4, which covers the years 1906–39. The most recent digest is that by Marjorie Whiteman, *Digest of international law*, 1963–73, which mainly covers the period 1940–60. This digest follows the pattern of a classified arrangement but unfortunately has rather an irregular coverage, and the volumes were published out of order over a ten-year period, making it difficult on occasion to locate relevant materials.

In the early 1970s the Department of State began a new publication designed to meet the demand for current information on US policy in international law. This is the *Digest of United States Practice in International Law*, 1973–, edited by A. W. Rovine, an extremely comprehensive survey of US practice in international law. No attempt was made to co-ordinate this publication with Whiteman. It is published in annual volumes because the Department of State felt that there was a strong demand for a 'continuous flow of the latest available materials. Yearly volumes should be sufficient to meet the need for a contemporary record.' As in previous digests, all types of documentary sources including judicial decisions, congressional testimony, diplomatic notes and internal memoranda have been used and the material is divided into core subject areas.

Netherlands

International law in the Netherlands, 1978–1980 is a three-volume work published under the auspices of the T.M.C. Asser Institute for International Law to examine Netherlands legislation, court decisions, treaties and diplomatic practice in international law. The essays are contributed by various authors and it is intended that the work should serve the purpose of a digest of state practice.

TEXTBOOKS

Treatises are a leading secondary source of international law and 'the teachings of the most highly qualified publicists of the various nations' are expressly mentioned in the Statute of the ICJ as a source of international law. There is a very distinguished history of academic scholarship in international law. The earliest international law treatise of modern times is that by Legano, written in 1360, but not published until 1477. Other famous scholars include Grotius, Vitoria, Suarez, Gentili, Puffendorf and Savigny. The works of these great writers have been collected together and reprinted by the Carnegie Endowment for International Peace in a series entitled *Classics of International Law*. Each volume contains an introduction describing the historical background of the writer, a photographic reproduction of the original text, and an English translation with explanatory notes.

Amongst more contemporary writers, one or two treatises have acquired particular significance. In Britain, Oppenheim's *International law*, 7th edn., 2 vols., 1952–4, has been described as being 'as nearly official as anything of the kind can be' and its most recent editors, Sir Hersch Lauterpacht and Lord McNair, have both been judges of the ICJ. What is generally considered to be the corresponding work in America is Hyde's *International law chiefly as interpreted and applied by the United States*, 2nd edn., 1945, but this is rather out of date now.

There are many other outstanding modern writers on international law, but they tend to concentrate on particular aspects of what has become an enormous subject area, and it may well be that the comprehensive treatise will become a thing of the past. One interesting book is Sorensen's *Manual of public international law*, which originated in an idea of Francis Deak that there should be an 'international' textbook on international law and the chapters are written by distinguished writers from a variety of countries.

In Great Britain, notable textbooks are those produced by the late D. P. O'Connell on *International law*, 2nd edn., 1970; Brierly's *The law of nations: an introduction to the international law of peace*, 6th edn., 1963; Schwarzenberger's *International law as applied by International Courts and Tribunals*, 1968–76 and *A manual of international law*, 6th edn., 1976, and many other works by the same author.

International law is frequently taught at undergraduate level and there are many good students' textbooks on the subject by English writers including Michael Akehurst's *Modern introduction to international law*, 5th edn., 1984, D. W. Greig's *International law*, 2nd edn., 1976 and Fawcett's *The law of nations*, 2nd edn., 1971.

The American practice of producing casebooks on every legal topic is not quite as popular in the United Kingdom. The outstanding English work of this type is D. J. Harris's *Cases and materials on international law*, 3rd edn., 1983.

SERIAL PUBLICATIONS

Journals

The journal literature of international law originated in Europe with the *Revue de Droit International et de Legislation Comparée* first appearing in 1869 almost 50 years before the American Society of International Law commenced publication of the *American Journal of International Law*, 1907.

Whatever American scholars may have lacked in history they have certainly compensated for in quantity and there are now numerous international law journals published by the American law schools and edited by both students and academics.

The *American Journal of International Law* is probably the leading journal in the field. Other important American journals include the *American Journal of Comparative Law*, and the *Harvard International Law Journal*.

In England, the *International and Comparative Law Quarterly*, published by the British Institute of International and Comparative Law is the premier journal, and in France the *Revue Général de Droit International Public* holds the same position as does the *Rivista di Diritto Internazionale* in Italy.

There are also many periodicals devoted to particular aspects of international law, such as the *Journal of International Law and Economics* and the *International Business Lawyer*. Some subject areas, for example, international taxation, have an enormous literature devoted specifically to their problems.

Newsletters and bulletins

This type of publication is essential to anybody who needs to have up to date information on developments within his subject area. Frequently the first announcements of new treaties, legal decisions and new draft legislation will appear in a bulletin long before the official version is published.

In England, a frequently overlooked but extremely useful source of information is the *Bulletin of Legal Developments* published fortnightly by the British Institute of International and Comparative Law, since 1966. It is a 'fortnightly survey of UK, European, Foreign, Commonwealth and International Legal Events'. Entries are short and give a brief abstract of the subject matter of forthcoming legislation and other legal developments, together with the source of the information. There is an annual index, but its real value lies in the way in which it renders accessible up to date information on international law.

There are numerous other newsletters, but this is the only truly international one. The others tend to cover a particular geographical area *eg, Middle East Executive Reports, American Society of International Law Newsletters, Common Market Reports, Euromarket News* or one restricted to a particular topic *eg, International Copyright Information Centre Bulletin* or *Tax News Service*.

Yearbooks

This type of publication is particularly important as a secondary source of information on international law and can be treated here as a variant of a journal. Yearbooks take the form of collections of articles or documents published at annual intervals. A good example of such a publication is the well-known *British Yearbook of International Law* which contains articles by leading British international law writers as well as shorter notes on topics of current interest. It also contains book reviews, summaries of decisions of British courts involving questions of public international law; decisions of the European Convention on Human Rights; decisions of the Court of Justice of the European Communities and United Kingdom materials on international law, during the period covered by each year book.

Other nations also produce year books. Amongst the better known are the *Netherlands Yearbook of International Law*, which is published in English as is the *Japanese Annual of International Law*. The former, as well as containing articles on international law, also reproduces important documents, and contains a literature survey and reports on Netherlands practice in international law.

Jan Stepan and Frank Chapman have written a useful article surveying the various year books available in *International Journal of Law Libraries*, vol. 8, no. 1, p. 19, which contains a helpful table giving details of the delays in publication for each volume surveyed. This can frequently be so long as to make it seem possible that the year book may have ceased publication.

The *United Nations Juridical Yearbook*, which has been published since 1965, includes details of legal decisions handed down by the ICJ and other international tribunals. It also surveys the legal activities of the UN for that year and the final chapter is a legal bibliography of books and articles about the United Nations and other international organizations. It is a little late in publication and cannot therefore be used for current purposes.

Proceedings

This category includes reports of proceedings of annual conferences or conventions of learned societies and other academic bodies. They usually reproduce the papers presented, plus resolutions etc. adopted and bibliographical information. A good example of this is the *American Society of International Law Proceedings*.

Another outstandingly important publication in this area is the Hague *Recueil des Cours*. The Hague Academy is an institution devoted to the teaching and study of private and public international law and the lectures of the Academy are delivered at the Peace Palace in the Hague by leading authorities from various countries. They deal with the theoretical and practical aspects of the subject including legislation and case-law and their normal duration is six weeks in July and August. There are also additional courses run during the year but there is no permanent teaching staff at the Academy. Lecturers are specially invited and lecture in French or English and these volumes reproduce the texts of the lectures. The number of volumes per year varies as of course do the subject matter and the language. This is a highly respected and scholarly publication.

ONLINE SOURCES

As yet, there is not a great deal of international legal material available online. The UK database LEXIS has little, if any, pure international law online.

In Belgium, the Belgian Ministry of Foreign Affairs has created ORBI (available in Europe through BELINDIS) which is a database on international legal literature. It consists of the documentation system of the Belgian Ministry of Foreign Affairs, which was computerized in 1982. The file contains over 80,000 references, from 1960 onwards, to public international law and the law of international organizations and to domestic legal systems, and contains references from over 620 publications from more than seventy countries.

Another database available through BELINDIS is FALI which is supplied by the Central Library of the Belgian Ministry of Foreign Affairs. It is not a purely legal database but may be of some interest to international legal researchers. It is a bibliographic database containing citations from about 600 periodicals in the areas of multilateral and bilateral external relations, international institutions and international, economic and financial relations.

In France, QUESTEL has a database called LABORDOC which contains some material from the International Labour Organization.

There is also some international law available on US databases. The Information Access Company's *Legal Resource Index*, which is available on Lockheed DIALOG, indexes many of the leading international law journals.

REFERENCE SOURCES

Bibliographic sources

Bibliographies of legal bibliographies

A useful English language bibliography in international law is Howell's *A bibliography of bibliographies of legal materials* which is unfortunately out of print and includes articles and monographs with bibliographic notes, essays and references not indexed elsewhere, as well as books.

Legal bibliographies

The *Bibliographical guide to law*, which is considered in more detail at p. 349, includes materials catalogued by the Library of Congress in the fields of international law and relations and is therefore an extremely useful source of information on international law bibliography.

Another helpful American publication is *Law Books in Print* which is described in Chapter 9.

The literature of public international law is well documented. There are several general bibliographies and a good many more covering particular aspects of the subject. Of the general bibliographies, Merrills's *A current bibliography of international law* and Delupis's *Bibliography of international law* are probably the most useful although the latter is now ten years old.

Merrills's book, although published more recently, in 1978, is also beginning to date. Its emphasis is on periodical literature, published since 1960, in English, although references to important primary sources and significant monographs have been included. The entries are arranged in chronological order and give a brief abstract of the item concerned, together with such useful information as, for example, whether the publication described is available in non-book form. The early chapters deal with primary sources and general works and the nature and sources of international law, and the rest of the book deals with particular topics of the subject, such as human rights and treaties.

The Delupis bibliography covers material published between 1920 and 1974 and although it contains a predominance of material in English, French and German, also includes references in Spanish, Italian, Russian and East European languages. The entries do not contain any abstracts and only the briefest publication details are included. The book has a complicated classification scheme, thus section 7.11.2.2. deals with works on the immunity of consuls but, on finding this section, the reader is referred back to section 7.10.3. However, if the user is not put off by the difficulties of this scheme, there is a good deal of useful material in this publication.

Another book which should be mentioned is that by J. Robinson, *International law and organization: general sources of information*. This book is rather dated now, having been published in 1967. It contains only material which covers the totality of the field of international law and organization and not material concerning the particular 'sources' of international law (treaties etc.) or topics of international law, *eg*, law of the sea. The approach adopted is scholarly in nature and the selection of material is based on a combination of various factors including the reputation of the author and the publication and how great an effect the item has had on the science and practice of international law. The major chapters are devoted to encyclopedias and dictionaries, treaties, bibliographies, bio-bibliographies and year books and serials. Each entry contains full bibliographic details of the work and references to all reviews of it.

A major new project is the *International Law Bibliography*, which is a looseleaf collection of individual bibliographies and other research tools on international law published in two binders. The first volume contains four bibliographies on public international organization; international trade law; global communication and information and the new law of the sea.

Subject bibliographies

It is easy to sub-divide international law into its constituent topics and it is therefore an area of law which lends itself well to being documented in subject bibliographies. As a result, there are several excellent bibliographies. Further information can be found in the general material described in Chapter 9, notably *Legal Bibliography Index*.

Air and space law
The Centre for Research of Air and Space Law at McGill University has commissioned some very useful publications in

this area, including Kuo Lee Li's *Worldwide space law bibliography*, 1978, which contains a comprehensive listing of books and articles published before 1976.

There is also Heere's *International bibliography of air law, 1900–1971*, 1972, with supplement, which covers not only books but also articles and dissertations on the subject. It concentrates on English language publications.

Criminal law

The Université Libre de Bruxelles, Centrum voor International Strafrecht, sponsored De Schutter's *Bibliography on international criminal law*, 1972. This publication indexes over 5,000 books and articles on extraterritorial jurisdiction, extradition, war crimes and international criminal courts. It also contains a list of relevant periodicals. It is supposed to be regularly supplemented, but in fact is currently out of print.

Human rights

This is a rapidly evolving area of international law which is producing a great deal of literature. Much of the documentation is subsumed into the documentation systems of the international organizations, such as UNESCO, which are most closely involved with human rights. However there are also many non-governmental organizations, such as Amnesty International and the International League for Human rights, which are active in this field, and it is difficult to locate much of the material produced. Myrna Feliciano's most instructive article, 'Human rights documentation' in the *International Journal of Law Libraries*, vol. 9, no. 3, 1981, pp. 95–103, is a useful guide to the sources.

In addition the staff of the Centre for the Study of Human Rights at Columbia University have prepared *Human rights: a topical bibliography*. This consists of scholarly books and articles drawn primarily from the disciplines of law, the social sciences and philosophy.

There are also two other current publications which contain bibliographic details of new materials in this area, of which the first, *Checklist of Human Rights Documents*, published monthly since 1976 by the Tarlton Law Library of the University of Texas, is considered as the essential bibliographic tool for researchers in this area. The second publication is *Human Rights Internet Newsletter*, distributed by the Human Rights Internet which is an international clearing house on human rights affairs.

A recent development in this field has been the establishment of the Human Rights Information and Documentation System (HURIDOCS), whose purpose is to promote and protect human rights through the wider dissemination of public information. HURIDOCS was established in 1982 and is based in the Netherlands Institute of Human Rights in Utrecht. Its first project will be to produce a thesaurus.

Law of the sea

Dalhousie University, in Halifax, Nova Scotia, has a special Centre devoted to the law of the sea, which produces an excellent *Marine affairs bibliography*, edited by C. Wiktor and L. A. Farter. There is also a recent bibliography by N. Papadakis and L. Glassner entitled *International law of the sea and marine affairs* which was first published in 1980, with a comprehensive supplement in 1984.

Luke Glassner's *Bibliography on land locked states*, 1980, lists all materials related to access to and from the sea and access to the resources of the sea.

Multinational corporations

This is an area of international law which is of growing importance and is of considerable interest. Browndorf and Rienaer's *Multi-national corporations law: a bibliography of multi-national corporations and foreign direct investment* (2 vols.) is a useful contribution to the subject. It is a compilation of publications in English taken from unpublished material, journals, books and the official documents.

War and peace

There is a useful series of bibliographies published by ABC/CLIO and entitled *War/Peace Bibliography Series*. Recent volumes are Lewis's *Uncertain judgment: a bibliography of war crimes trials*, 1979, and De Vore's *The Arab–Israeli Conflict: a historical, political, social and military bibliography*, 1976.

Law library catalogues

One of the oldest international law library catalogues, which is of use for historical research only, is that of the Peace Palace at the Hague, edited by Molhuysen and Openheim and published by Sijthoff in 1916.

In 1911 the Harvard Law School acquired the collection of the Spanish diplomat, the Marquis de Olivart, who had gathered together probably the most comprehensive collection of international law materials anywhere in the world. The collection contains the standard works of authors from all countries on topics of international law and also large numbers of original documents of international disputes and arbitrations. When the catalogue was printed in 1965 it contained 360,000 cards which attests the size of this library. The *Harvard Law School Library catalog of international law and relations* was published in 1965 in 20 volumes and edited by Margaret Moody.

The Columbia University Law Library is one of the greatest law collections in the United States and by 1967 it held 470,000 volumes. It has a substantial international law collection, which has its own classification scheme, and all the international law holdings are listed in the *Dictionary catalog*.

The best-known English library catalogue of international law to be published is that of the University of Cambridge Squire Law Library, *Catalogue of international law*, 4 vols., 1972, and republished in 1974 as part of the *Law catalogue of the Squire Law Library*.

The Library catalogue of the University of London's Institute of Advanced Legal Studies, 6 vols., 1978, covers the entire holdings of the library including the excellent international law collection.

Periodical indexes

The most important indexes to periodical literature are *Current Law Index*, the *Index to Legal Periodicals* and the *Index to Foreign Legal Periodicals*. Many of the international law journals are indexed in these publications and full descriptions of them are given in Chapter 9.

Another index is *Public International Law: a current bibliography of articles*, published semi-annually by the Max Planck Institute. This publication covers all material received in the Institute's library which is either published as an article in a journal or as a contribution to a Festschrift or other collected work. The bibliography is compiled by scanning over 1,000 journals which cover not only international law but also related topics such as history, politics or economics in which items on international law may appear only occasionally. The aim of the bibliography is to produce as comprehensive a compilation of articles on international law as possible. The items are divided into a subject classification, which has sections on general works; basic problems; history; sources and then specific subjects. There is an index by author and by subject. Where an article covers more than one subject, it is listed under both subjects. The bibliography covers material published in a wide range of languages. The introduction also tells us that, in setting up the bibliography, 'work was facilitated by the use of data processing computers' which have had some bearing on the 'form and organization of the bibliography'. This is an extremely useful source of current information on international law, and is an indispensable aid to any scholar of the subject.

Periodicals directories

Most international law journals are listed in Wypski's *Legal Periodicals in English*, which gives bibliographic details for each title.

Union catalogues

The series of union lists published by the Institute of Advanced Legal Studies includes the *Union list of air and space law literature* which is rather out of date. The second edition was published in 1975. It lists materials held in the libraries of Oxford, Cambridge and London, and other libraries specializing in aviation and astronautical material.

The *University of London List of Serials* (ULS) includes details

of the holdings of libraries within the University in international law and is a most useful location guide.

Dictionaries

The *Dictionnaire de la terminologie du droit international* by J.
Basdevant is a well-known international law dictionary. It is
rather dated now as it was published in 1960. Sponsored by the
International Federation of National Academies of Arts and
Sciences, it took 25 years to produce and was intended to cover
all terms of international law in use at the time. Each term
is accompanied by explanations and examples drawn from
various sources of international law. The text is in French, but
there are vocabulary tables which give the equivalent terms in
English, German, Italian and Spanish.

There is also a dictionary by Haensch, *Dictionary of international
relations and politics*, 1963, which is a multilingual terminological
dictionary, organized by subject matter and alphabetically,
with indexes in English, French, German and Spanish. Despite
its title, it covers the terminology of international law.

The multi-volume Italian language encyclopedia edited by
Morelli, *Enciclopedia del diritto,* 1965, contains a section on
international law, as does the *Nueva enciclopedia juridica*, edited
by C. Mascarenas. A recent dictionary is that published in
Oceana's *International law bibliography*, the second binder of
which contains an *Encyclopaedic dictionary of international law*,
which is 'an up-to-date reference tool ... that brings together
both terminology and pertinent descriptive information. An
intermix of dictionary and encyclopaedia, this unique publication was initiated by the late Professor Clive Parry'. Each
alphabetic letter will appear in an individual looseleaf pamphlet which will be constantly revised and updated. The coverage of the *Dictionary* includes international law terminology,
selected case-law, bibliographical details and information on
important treaties.

Encyclopedias

During this century there have been several proposals for
encyclopedias of public international law, including one by J.
H. Verzijl as long ago as 1926.

The first attempt to produce a comprehensive encyclopedia in English was undertaken by the Max Planck Institute for Comparative Public Law and International Law at Heidelberg and the first instalment of its *Encyclopaedia of public international law* appeared early in 1981. It is a new and independent work, though it owes much to the *Wörterbuch* (mentioned below). It is scheduled to include, in twelve instalments, approximately 1,200 articles by individual authors on all major international legal problems and institutions, as well as the major decisions of international tribunals. Each instalment contains between 45 and 180 entries covering, in alphabetical order, a particular subject area. Once publication of the instalments is completed, a special five-volume edition will be published which will contain all the articles plus supplementary notes, additional bibliographical references, and comprehensive indexes. It will provide a wealth of information.

Mention should also be made here of the *International encyclopaedia of comparative law* which is being published in parts by the International Association of Legal Science under the editorship of Konrad Zweigert.

The new *Encyclopaedia of the United Nations and international agreements* by Osmanczyk, 1985, is a compendium of political, economic, social and legal information about the structure of the UN and other international organizations. Much wider than its title suggests, it contains quick-reference information, detailed explanations and some texts of use for the whole range of international law topics.

There is a French language encyclopedia entitled *Repertoire de droit international* compiled by Dalloz and published in 2 volumes between 1968 and 1969. It consists of a series of signed articles on selected topics by famous academics and also contains some useful bibliographies.

There is also a well-known German language encyclopedia of international law, edited by Strupp and Schlochauer, entitled *Wörterbuch des Völkerrechts*, 2nd edn., 1960–2. It consists of signed articles written by over 150 different scholars in three volumes, with an index volume. There is a table of contents in English and French. This publication is also known as the Strupp–Schlochauer Wörterbuch.

Legal organizations

The *Law and legal information directory* covers associations active in the international law field. Although this directory has a heavy American bias, it does give details of other organizations (*eg*, the International Law Association) which are active in the international law field. The *Europa Yearbook* also has a useful section in its international organizations volume giving brief details, including the address, of several international legal organizations.

Biographical sources

Robinson's book on international organizations contains a useful biographical section giving details of the major figures in international law. The *International Court of Justice Yearbook* gives short biographies of each of its judges.

Section 2: International Organizations

ORIGINS

The origins of international organizations can be traced back through history to the consuls who existed in early Greek and Roman times to safeguard the interests of their citizens who, for whatever reason, were obliged to be resident abroad. The consul represented individuals rather than the state and thus the office of ambassador developed. However, the practice of exchanging ambassadors could really only deal with bilateral problems. With the growth of multilateral problems, such as the negotiating of peace treaties on the conclusion of war, it became necessary to find a method to represent all the countries involved.

The method first used was to convene an international conference. One of the earliest of these conferences resulted in the Peace of Westphalia in 1648, but it was not until the nineteenth century that such conferences became much more important. Because they were organized for a particular purpose, these conferences were found to be unsuitable for dealing with general matters of international importance and, although early in the 1800s the Congress of Vienna acknowledged this fact and had several meetings at regular intervals, it was not until the twentieth century that international organizations as we know them today really began.

The late nineteenth century saw a large number of private international unions develop. These were groupings of non-governmental bodies who felt that their common interests necessitated some kind of international association. Early examples are the International Committee of the Red Cross (1863) and the International Law Association (1873).

As governments began to realize that administrative co-operation was becoming essential in the light of improving communications and increasing international trade and commerce, they also began to set up 'unions', such as the Universal Postal Union (1874), and the European Commission for the Danube (1856). These bodies were considered permanent and had both legislative and administrative organs and they can be regarded as the model for the development of the international political, as opposed to purely administrative, organizations that exist today, the earliest of which was probably the ill-fated League of Nations founded in 1919.

TYPES OF ORGANIZATION

In his book on *International organizations*, 4th edn., 1982, D. W. Bowett says that they can be divided into political, administrative and judicial organizations. They can also be divided into 'global' and 'regional' organizations, into organizations founded in either a treaty between states or a treaty between governments, but there is in fact no agreed scientific classification. The term international governmental organization is usually used to describe an organization set up by agreement between two or more states, as distinct from the term 'non-governmental organization' which is used to describe an organization set up by individuals or groups of individuals.

Recognition as a governmental organization is important as it affects its legal status and its capacity to act under international law. For its public international law status to be recognized, the organization must fulfil three requirements. It must be established by an international agreement, it must have organs and it must be established under international law. Examples of the former are the United Nations, the Council of Europe and the World Health Organization and of the latter, the International Committee of the Red Cross and the International Commission of Jurists.

There are currently in existence over 4,000 international organizations, of which one alone, the United Nations, produces over 180,000 items of documentation a year. The total number of publications produced by international organizations each year is therefore massive. It is proposed to consider mainly the publications of inter-governmental organizations in this chapter and then briefly to describe the publications of non-governmental organizations as the publishing activities of these organizations follow fairly closely those of the governmental organizations and will not therefore be treated separately in detail.

PUBLICATIONS: GENERAL CONSIDERATIONS

The first problem to be faced when dealing with international documentation is the so-called 'fourth dimension', which tends to be overlooked. This is that the same text will frequently be issued in several different languages. For example, the official records of the UN are issued in Chinese, English, French, Spanish and Russian. Selected portions also appear in Arabic and German. Similar problems occur in European Communities' publications where again there are several different official languages, see Chapter 8.

It is convenient initially to divide the material produced by international organizations into two broad physical groups: publications and documents. The first group, publications, includes those materials usually issued in printed form and available to the general public, normally for sale, and produced as part of the publication programme of the organization. These programmes are set up as one of the methods of carrying out the mandate of the treaty establishing the organization, which usually calls for publication of information relating to the organization's objectives, the communication of research findings sponsored by the organization and the distribution of compilations of legal texts. Major reports and studies, conference proceedings, texts of conventions and treaties, periodicals and year books are among the most common types of publication.

The second group, documents, constitutes the major proportion of the material issued in connection with the functioning of the organization including reports, working papers, records of debates, resolutions etc.

The categories mentioned above are not mutually exclusive. In the case of the UN it decides to issue a publication as a sales publication if 'it is of public interest, reaches a standard of intellectual endeavour that reflects credit on the UN and does not substantially duplicate material that has already been published'.

Many UN documents are issued in limited numbers and in draft form and are normally stencilled rather than printed, and in certain areas, made available only to the participants in the particular session or meeting.

Identification of documents

Coding

All organizations use various systems of symbols to identify their documents. Many are based on the system used by the UN, which is described here as an example.

The stencilled documents are identified by symbols consisting of letters and figures, separated by oblique strokes, which identify the issuer. If a document is issued by two or more organs it may well carry the symbols of both organs.

The series elements of the five principal organs are:

A/General Assembly
B/Economic and Social Council
C/Security Council
D/Trusteeship Council
E/Secretariat

The secondary elements denote the subsidiary organ. Thus the documents of such an organ normally carry a symbol consisting of the basic series symbol of the parent body plus one of the following elements:

–/AC	.../–	Ad hoc committee or similar body
–/C	.../–	Standing, permanent, main committee
–/CN	.../–	Commission
–/CONF	.../–	Conference etc.

There can also be a secondary element denoting the nature of the document. Such elements include:

–/MIN.../–	Minutes
–/INF.../–	Information Series
–/WP.../–	Working Paper etc.

For a full list of such symbols see UN document ST/LIB/SER.B/S.

Sales publications

Similary, UN sales publications also receive a sales code, which is found in a box on the reverse title page and back cover. This indicates the language, year, subject category and the number of the individual title. The subject categories are given Roman numerals, plus capital letters where a subject has had to be divided because of expansion over the years. For example, Class II economics has had to be considerably sub-divided as follows:

II.A	– Economics
II.B	– Economic development
II.C	– Trade finance and commerce etc.

Other relevant sub-divisions for legal research are:

IV	– Social questions
V	– International law
XIV	– Human rights

The subject groups are currently sub-divided into groups I to XVII but these categories are not at all uniform, as some subject areas have contracted considerably, whilst others have grown out of all recognition and are overcrowded. Other organizations use similar methods to identify sales publications.

GOVERNMENTAL ORGANIZATIONS

The most important governmental organization is the United Nations and it is therefore proposed to concentrate on discussing the nature of its documentation, as typical of the types of material produced by governmental organizations.

The United Nations was founded in 1945 upon the signing of its Charter, which is a multilateral treaty, establishing the rights and duties of the signatory states, and is also the basic constitutional document of the organization. Membership of the UN is open to all nations willing to carry out the obligations imposed by the Charter and currently stands at over 150 nations. The organization has six main organs, which are the General Assembly, the Security Council, the Economic and Social Council (ECOSOC), the Trusteeship Council, the Secretariat and the International Court of Justice, which has fifteen judges elected by the General Assembly and the Security Council. Its purpose is to achieve peaceful settlement of disputes in conformity with international law. A full description of the organization and functions of the UN is given in Peter Hajnal's book entitled *United Nations: functions and organization*, 1978.

Categories of publication

The publications of most inter-governmental organizations can be divided into several fairly broad types.

Constitutional documents

Many international organizations publish the texts of their enabling documents either singly or as part of a larger collection of administrative and procedural rules. The WHO has issued its Basic Documents and the UN has also issued separately its Charter and the definitive instruments of two of its principal sub-organs – the International Law Commission and the Administrative Tribunal.

Official records

The publishing programme of an international organization is usually closely related to its organizational structure. Official records tend to depend on the hierarchy of the organs which produce them. Their purpose is to provide an official account of the proceedings and decisions of the principal policy-making organs of the organization.

The UN official records consist of the reports of plenary meetings of the major organs, together with papers produced by or for them and resolutions that they have made. For the General Assembly, there is a series of verbatim reports of proceedings of the Assembly itself and also summary records of its six main committees. These appear first as mimeographed documents to which a symbol is assigned but they are subsequently re-published in corrected, edited versions. They are eventually published as volumes for each annual session. These volumes are numbered consecutively from the first session held in 1945.

The other main organs of the UN follow a similar publishing pattern to the General Assembly in their official records.

For quick reference purposes, the printed *Indexes to Proceedings* issued in the Dag Hammarskjöld Library's *Bibliographical Series* are important. They are issued sessionally or annually for the UN's main organs and provide not only a subject index to the proceedings, but also lists of meetings, agenda items and documents arranged by symbols.

Manuals of practice and procedure

Manuals of practice are issued by the larger international organizations to assist members in understanding the organization's constitution and functions. The *Repertory of United Nations Practice* was first issued in 1955, in five volumes, and has required several further multi-volume supplements.

Legal publications

Many of the major inter-governmental organizations have a subordinate organ, usually named a commission or committee, to undertake the organization's legal work. The UN created the International Law Commission, which consists of eminent international lawyers and has its own Statute, regulating its constitution and functions. Its purpose is to 'initiate studies and make recommendations for the purpose of ... (1) encouraging the progressive development of international law and its codification'.

Its records appear initially as mimeographed documents in the UN series A/CN/. The most important of these are later reissued in the *Yearbook of the International Law Commission*, which has been published sessionally since 1949. The work of the Commission consists mainly of drafting the texts of codes or conventions or of making reports on matters specifically referred to it by the General Assembly. One of its most successful projects was its attempts to place the law of the sea onto a multilateral treaty basis. As a result of its work, four conventions were produced and all four have entered into force and been ratified by a number of states.

The United Nations Office of Legal Affairs assists the Legal Counsel in the examination of legal questions referred to him by the Secretary General, UN organs, other international organizations and various governments. It also assists the International Law Commission in drafting and codifying public international law. A survey of the major publications of this office can be found in a most useful article by S. M. Kleckner, 'Major publications of the United Nations Office of Legal Affairs', *Law Library Journal*, vol. 74, 1981, pp. 66–86.

International legislation
Many international organizations have what may be described as a quasi-legislative function. For example, some are the supervisory bodies for basic multilateral agreements in their special field. The International Civil Aviation Organization administers the Chicago Convention of 1944 on International Civil Aviation. The General Agreement on Tariffs and Trade issues a series entitled *Basic Instruments and Selected Documents*, which includes the General Agreement, plus numerous supplements, protocols, ratifications etc. The International Labour Organization publishes the *International Labour Code* which is a systematic arrangement of the Conventions and Recommendations adopted by the International Conference.

Surveys of legislation

Several organizations publish regular surveys of legislation in their specialist field. The ILO has published its *Legislative Series* since 1919. It comprises a selection of the more important texts in the fields of labour and social security legislation. The Food and Agriculture Organization publishes *Food and Agriculture Legislation*, which is a selection of agricultural laws and regulations of international significance. The WHO's *International Digest of Health Legislation* contains a selection of health laws and regulations, a bibliography, and occasional studies in comparative health legislation.

Legal conferences

The proceedings of conferences called by organizations to attempt to achieve international agreement on particular legal topics are sometimes of great importance to the international lawyer. Such publications resemble official records and may be quasi-legislative in nature in that their Final Act may contain a Convention binding on member states. Such conferences are usually *ad hoc* occasional meetings.

Outstanding among these publications are the records of certain major UN conferences covering such diverse subject areas as law of the sea, diplomatic relations and the law of treaties. The official documents are similar, comprising preparatory documents, summary records of the various meetings, the Final Act, and annexes containing the Convention and any protocols or resolutions.

Miscellaneous publications

Most of the larger international organizations publish occasional monographs by individual authors, although the number of legal publications is generally small. The UN series, *International Law* (Class V of Sales Publications), is not restricted to monographs, but includes many legal publications which form serials on their own *eg*, the *Reports of International Arbitral Awards*.

The legal monographs published by international organizations are often comparative surveys of the law on a particular subject in various countries. For example, the UN has published collections of national legislative texts on subjects as diverse as the regime of the high seas, nationality and the conclusion of treaties.

Sponsored publications

Some organizations, especially UNESCO and the Council of Europe, have issued many works through commercial publishers. Legal publications form only a small proportion of UNESCO's output, but in the field of copyright, its principal legal interest, it has published either directly, as with *Copyright Bulletin*, a quarterly review issued since 1948 in various forms, or in an unusual form of collaboration with government departments of two member states. The looseleaf collection, *Copyright Laws and Treaties of the World*, is compiled by UNESCO in co-operation with the Copyright Office of the United Kingdom. Legal publications issued under the auspices of the Council of Europe are particularly numerous in the field of human rights.

Two important series emanating from the Registry of the European Court of Human Rights – Series A, *Judgements and Decisions*; Series B, *Pleadings, Oral Arguments and Documents* are published by Carl Heymanns Verlag of Cologne. Martinus Nijhoff of the Hague has issued, since 1959, the *Yearbook of the European Convention on Human Rights*, containing basic texts, selected documents and decisions of the Commission. Editions Administratives, of Heule in Belgium, has published a bilingual English–French *Digest of case law relating to the European Convention on Human Rights*, 1955–67. Nijhoff again has published annually since 1955 the *European Yearbook*, providing a conspectus of the problems of European integration and organization.

NON-GOVERNMENTAL ORGANIZATIONS

Most non-governmental organizations are established by individuals or associations of individuals, *eg*, the Institute of

International Law and the International Chamber of Commerce. The term 'non-governmental organization', is that which is given to them by the United Nations. This term should not be taken to refer to the membership of the organization: governments or branches of governments are members of many non-governmental organizations. The concept of 'non-governmental organization' refers to the function of the particular organization. They are not endowed with governmental powers and operate under private law rules. There are many non-governmental organizations with international aspects and the Union of International Associations uses seven criteria for classifying them as international non-governmental organizations. Amongst the criteria are that their aims must be international; there must be members with voting rights from at least three countries; the constitution must provide for a formal structure; there must be a permanent headquarters and offices and finance must come from different states. Examples of such organizations are the Inter-Parliamentary Union, Amnesty International, the International Bar Association and the World Peace through Law Centre.

Most non-governmental organizations are not exclusively legal in character and legal publishing forms a small part of their total output. However, there are a few specialist non-governmental legal organizations with their own publishing programmes, which are less well known. Amongst them are the Hague Conference on Private International Law, which has been meeting since 1893 to work for the unification of the rules of private international law. It publishes many draft conventions.

The International Commission of Jurists was founded in 1952 'to strengthen the rule of law in its practical manifestations'. It publishes a *Review* and has issued many reports on some highly topical and controversial matters, in particular the status of law in selected countries.

The International Institute for the Unification of Private Law (Unidroit) undertakes studies of comparative law, prepares drafts of international agreements and uniform laws and also publishes a regular bulletin.

The International Law Association was founded in 1873 for

the study and advancement of international law and publishes regular reports of conferences.

The World Peace through Law Centre promotes the continued development of international law and publishes several directories and journals.

The World Intellectual Property Organization is an intergovernmental body which publishes material in the fields of copyright, patents and trade marks.

REFERENCE SOURCES

It is proposed to consider bibliographic sources of United Nations documentation in this section. It serves as a model for bibliographic control, or lack of it, in the field of international organization documentation.

The story of UN documentation and indexing 'is a clouded and disheartening one with no end in sight. It remains caught in an evolutionary stage. Bureaucrats and librarians, with the best will in the world, seem unable to sustain the indexing impetus. Every new nation admitted to membership represents thousands of pages of harangues, reports, resolutions and studies that must be submitted to some form of bibliographical control. Now even the most experienced bibliographer is daunted by the varied and unrestricted flow of UN documentation, erratically classified and burdened by an almost feckless approach to nomenclature' (T. Reynolds, *Law Library Journal*, vol. 75, 1982, p. 326).

Bibliographic sources

The bibliographic activity of international organizations tends to take one of two forms – subject bibliographies in their own special field, or the recording of their own output of publications and documents.

The UN's Dag Hammarskjöld Library's *Bibliographical Series* includes both classes of work. The libraries in both Geneva and New York publish monthly bibliographies of books, articles and documents which are of current value only, as there are no cumulative indexes.

The *United Nations Document Index* was a monthly publication which listed, described and indexed all documents of the UN and also all printed publications of the International Court. This index ceased publication in 1974 because the flow of documents was becoming overwhelming. The decision was taken to use computer-based indexing systems to try and control the flow and a new index (UNDEX) was started. This system was flawed and had a short time span, being replaced by *UNDOC: Current Index*, which describes itself as a 'key to recent UN documentation, proceedings and publications. It is an essential source of basic information about political questions ... international law ...' It is a product of the United Nations Bibliographic Information System (UNBIS), a computer-based online system. The index is a list of UN documents and publications received by the Dag Hammarskjöld Library at UN headquarters in New York. Each issue of *UNDOC: Current Index* has a standard arrangement, consisting of a checklist of documents and publications which gives full bibliographic citations arranged in alphanumeric order by document series, symbol and session; official records, arranged by official record designator; sales publications arranged by sales number; documents republished; list of new document series symbols; subject index, based on the UNBIS thesaurus.

Amongst commercial publications, *International Bibliography: publications of intergovernmental organizations* is a useful tool. It is a quarterly listing of all publications received by the editorial office of UNIPUB (a Xerox publishing company in the United States). Each document is briefly described and coverage includes sales publications, unpriced material issued by public information offices and selected other unpriced material available to the public. Excluded are working documents, draft texts, press releases and material circulated only to staff. The titles are grouped under broad subject headings, which are arranged alphabetically and may be sub-divided. Within each subject grouping, listings are arranged alphabetically by title, and each entry has a unique number.

Handbooks and guides

There are a number of guides to UN documentation now available. Amongst the most useful is that by Peter Hajnal, *Guide to United Nations organization, documentation and publishing*, 1978. Although it is now 20 years out of date, Brenda Brimmer's *A guide to the use of the United Nations documents*, 1962, is an excellent and informatively written handbook. Theodore Dimitrov of the UN library in Geneva has produced the *World bibliography of international documentation*, 1981, which examines the organization and use of international documents.

Catalogues

Whilst no other international organization approaches the United Nations in the range of its bibliographic activity, most of them provide some sort of guide to their publications. The normal practice is to issue current lists annually and then every few years a consolidated, classified list with indexes.

The UN produces a quarterly checklist, plus special catalogues of its Official Records and periodicals. The Council of Europe produces an annual *Catalogue of Publications* which includes free as well as sales items. The OECD produces a biennial classified catalogue.

A useful commercially produced catalogue is Mary Birchfield's *Consolidated catalog of League of Nations publications for sale*, 1976.

Availability and distribution

Many libraries have become depositories for UN and other international organizations publications. In 1948, there were only twenty depository libraries, while in 1978, there were 310. Many other libraries also acquire material from national distributors of the documentation of the various organizations.

Many of the principal sales publications of several international organizations are available for purchase through

HMSO and are listed in the *Daily List of Government Publications*, the *Monthly Lists* and the annual *International Organisations Publications*.

FURTHER READING

Birchfield, M. E. *The complete reference guide to United Nations sales publications, 1968–78*, 1982.

Butler, W. E. *A source book on socialist international organizations*, 1978.

Commonwealth International Law Cases, 1974–.

Directory of United Nations databases, 1984.

'The UN system', *Guide to the archives of international organizations*, vol. 1, 1984.

Indian Yearbook of International Affairs, 1952–.

International Labour Organization, *Chronological Index of Laws and Regulations, 1919–67*, 1969.

Johnson-Champ, D. S. 'Bibliography: selected readings on teaching international law', *International Lawyer*, vol. 18, 1984, pp. 197–200.

Myers, D. P. L. *Manual of collections of treaties and of collections relating to treaties*, 1922.

Paenson, I. *English-French-Spanish-Russian manual of the terminology of public international law (law of peace) and international organizations*, 1983.

Parry, C. 'Where to look for your treaties', *International Journal of Law Libraries*, vol. 8, 1980, pp. 8–17.

Rosenne, S. *Practice and methods of international law*, 1985.

Schaff, R. 'International organization documentation' [Series in *International Journal of Legal Information*].

Schermers, H. G. *International institutional law*, 1980.

Schutter, B. de *Bibliography on international criminal law*, 1972.

Sprudzs, A. 'The international bookshelf' [Series in *International Journal of Legal Information*].

Syatauw, O. J. *Decisions of the International Court of Justice*, 2nd edn., 1969.

Thompson, L. and Rodrigues, S. 'International administrative tribunals: current status and related bibliography', *International Journal of Legal Information*, vol. 11, 1983, pp. 130–42.

Van Hoff, G. J. H. *Rethinking the sources of international law*, 1983.

Wasserman, P. *Law and legal information directory: a guide to national and international organizations*, 1983.

Whisman, L. A. 'Selected bibliography: articles and cases on international human rights law in domestic courts', *International Lawyer*, vol. 18, 1984.

Wiktor, C. *Canadian bibliography of international law*, 1984.

Williams, J. W. 'International law textbooks: a review of materials and methods', *International Lawyer*, vol. 18, 1984, pp. 173–95.

Williams, J. W. 'Research tips in international law', *Journal of International Law and Economics*, vol. 15, 1981, special supplement.

Winton, H. N. M. *Publications of the United Nations system: reference guide*, 1972.

12. Other Systems of Law: I

Section 1: Comparative Law

P. NORMAN

It is necessary to distinguish the literature of comparative law properly so called, as will be explained below, from the literature covering the law of several jurisdictions without comparative treatment. The distinction is essential, although there are works which straddle both categories.

The literature of comparative law, properly so called, consists of several types of work. There are, first of all, general works on the principles and methods of comparative study. The pioneer work in Britain was H. C. Gutteridge, *Comparative law*, 1949. Among other scholars who have written books on this topic in recent years are Ancel, Constantinesco, David, Derrett, Fikentscher, Rotondi, Schnitzer, Zweigert, Kötz and Rheinstein.

Books of this type tend to be primarily academic; the publications which will be discussed in the following paragraphs vary from primarily academic treatises to works which are intended mainly for use in practice, though no clear distinction can be drawn.

COMPARATIVE STUDY

We must now turn to the numerous works which treat comparatively, either the law of a given jurisdiction in general, *eg*, M. S. Amos and F. P. Walton, *Introduction to French law*, 1967; E. J. Cohn, *Manual of German law*, 1968–71, Kahn-Freund *et al.*, *A sourcebook on French law*, 1979; or a given topic in the law of an individual jurisdiction, *eg*, L. N. Brown and

J. F. Garner, *French administrative law,* 1973; R. David, *Les contrats en droit anglais,* 1973; M. P. Singh, *German administrative law,* 1985; or a single topic on a multi-jurisdictional basis. Examples are H. Nagel, *Die Grundzüge des Beweisrechts im europäischen Zivilprozess,* 1967; P. van Ommeslaghe, *Régime des sociétés en droit comparé,* 1960; I. Szaszy, *International civil procedure: a comparative study,* 1967.

Two major projects of comparative study have been undertaken by Professor M. Cappelletti, initially at the Florence Institute of Comparative Law and later at the European University Institute. These were on the subjects of 'access to justice' and 'constitutional guarantees'. A third series entitled *Integration through law: Europe and the American federal experience* is in course of publication.

Special mention must be made of the *Continental legal history series* 1912–28, and of the *International encyclopedia of comparative law,* 1971–, which is now in course of publication. It contains brief surveys of the legal systems of all jurisdictions, and a large number of essays on individual topics on a multi-jurisdictional basis. Constitutional, administrative and criminal law are, in general, excluded. The work is planned in seventeen volumes, published chapter by chapter. No volume is as yet (1986) complete, though Part 1 of Volume XI, 'torts', appeared as a bound volume in 1983.

Collections

A great deal of the literature of comparative law is to be found in contributions to Festschriften and similar collections. Very few libraries can afford to catalogue these analytically, but indexes exist. German Festschriften, which are very numerous, are indexed in H. Dau, *Bibliographie juristischer Festschriften und Festschriftenbeiträge 1945–61: Deutschland–Schweiz–Österreich,* 1962 (with 3 supplements to 1979). They are now regularly indexed in the *International Journal of Legal Information.* Contributions to collections are indexed or listed in the bibliographical sections of some periodicals, in the general bibliographies such as the *Karlsruher juristische Bibliographie,* and a selection of collections is indexed in the *Index to Foreign*

Legal Periodicals, beginning with 1963. Contributions in English are indexed in Szladits's *Bibliography on foreign and comparative law: books and articles in English*, 1955–. A bibliography of all legal Festschriften from 1868 to 1968, though not an index of contributions, is L. M. Roberts, *A bibliography of legal Festschriften*, 1972.

Valuable material is to be found in the proceedings of international conferences, notably the reports (general and national) to the International Congress of Comparative Law which first convened in 1932 and has met every four years since 1950. There are many general periodicals, such as: *American Journal of Comparative Law*, 1952–; *Annuario di Diritto Comparato e di Studi Legislativi*, 1927–; *Boletin Mexicano de Derecho Comparado*, 1948–; *Comparative Law Yearbook*, 1977–; *International and Comparative Law Quarterly*, 1952–; *Revue de Droit International et de Droit Comparé*, 1908–; *Revue Internationale de Droit Comparé*, 1872–; *Rabels Zeitschrift für Ausländisches und Internationales Privatrecht*, 1927–.

There are some periodicals which deal with the comparative aspects of one or more single topics, *eg*, the *Revue Internationale de Droit Pénal*, 1924– or the *Rivista di Diritto Internazionale e Comparato del Lavoro*, 1953–.

Conflict of laws

It should not be forgotten that the conflict of laws lends itself particularly to comparative treatment, and to a considerable extent demands it. The most important specialized periodicals must therefore be referred to here insofar as they have not yet been mentioned: both those dealing with the conflict of laws only, such as *Revue Critique de Droit International Privé*, 1905–; *Rivista di Diritto Internazionale Privato e Processuale*, 1965–, and those which cover both public international law and the conflict of laws, such as the *British Yearbook of International Law*, 1920–, and *Comunicazioni e Studi*, 1942–.

UNIFICATION OF LAW

A matter of special interest to comparative lawyers is the unification and harmonization of law. This is a matter of importance in federal states, *eg*, The United States, and was also of great importance in some of the successor states of the Austro-Hungarian monarchy which were composed of parts in which different legal systems had been in force before 1918, *eg*, Poland and Yugoslavia. Here it is proposed to discuss international unification and harmonization. With the exception of the European Communities (see Chapter 10), where special considerations apply, the matters which lend themselves most readily to unification are branches of commercial law and cognate matters. Apart from regional unification, *eg*, uniform Benelux laws and uniform laws in Nordic countries, most unification has been the work of the Institute for the Unification of Private Law, established in Rome in 1928 and known as Unidroit, and of numerous international organizations, such as the International Maritime Organization, or the Hague Conference on Private International Law, or of *ad hoc* international conferences such as the Diplomatic Conference on the Unification of Law governing the International Sale of Goods, 1964. Uniform laws have been brought into being by means of conventions concluded at conferences or under the auspices of the organizations mentioned. A great deal of primary and secondary material can be found in the publications and documents of the Rome Institute, in particular *Unification of Law: Yearbook*, 1948–71, *Uniform Law Cases*, 1956–71 (a collection of decisions of national courts applying and interpreting uniform laws), both of which have been superseded by the *Uniform Law Review*, 1973–. The pre-war documents of the Institute were often mimeographed; they were reproduced on microfilm, together with those up to 1970, by Oceana publications between 1967 and 1972. Other sources are the Acts and documents of The Hague Conference of Private International Law, the various treaty series containing the conventions themselves, reprints of texts in the periodicals mentioned above, and K. Zweigert and J. Kropholler (eds.) *Sources of international uniform law*, 1971–80, 3 vols. and supplements. Further references are: Harvard

Law School Library *Index to proceedings and documents of the International Institute for the Unification of Private Law 1928–1965*, 1967 and the *Digest of legal activities of international organizations and other institutions*, compiled by the International Institute. This is a very substantial looseleaf publication, and contains comprehensive information about the law-making activities of international organizations, etc. Many of these tend towards unification or at least harmonization of laws or establishing international standards.

RECEPTION

A matter of great interest to comparative lawyers are the instances in which whole codes of one country have been adopted or substantially adopted by another country. This is a process of respectable antiquity, if we include the reception of Roman law, which admittedly was not codified, in the later Middle Ages and the early post-medieval period. The Code Napoleon was either taken over or closely followed by the civil codes of the countries which formed part of Napoleon's empire. One of the best-known cases is that of the wholesale introduction of the Swiss civil code into Turkey.

COLLECTIONS FROM SEVERAL JURISDICTIONS

Primary materials

There is a considerable body of literature giving information on the law of more than one jurisdiction, both primary texts (mostly legislation) and doctrinal writing. The texts appear frequently in translation. Some periodical collections of texts cover potentially all subjects, *eg*, the *Boletín de Legislación Extranjera* or the *Documentation Juridique Étrangère*, which contains texts as well as secondary material. A series of monographs on topics of interest to international lawyers is the UN *Legislative Series*. Most collections, however, are restricted to one topic or a group of related topics. Examples are the periodical ILO *Legislative Series,* which covers labour law and social security; A. P. Blaustein and G. H. Flanz, *Constitutions of the countries of the world,* 1971–; M. Ferid and K. Firsching *Internationales Erbrecht,* 1969–; A. N. Makarov, *Quellen des internationalen Privatrechts,* 1954–60; M. Ancel and Y. Marx, *Les codes pénaux européens*; Prott and O'Keefe, *Law and the cultural heritage* (projected in five volumes), 1984–; UNESCO, *The protection of movable cultural property: compendium of legislative texts,* 1984 or series of monographs, such as *Aktiengesetze der Gegenwart,* the *American series of foreign penal codes.*

It must always be borne in mind that material of this type is scattered through periodicals, *eg,* an English translation of the Swiss criminal code is to be found in the *Journal of Criminal Law and Criminology,* vol. 30, no. 1, May–June 1939, supplement, and that there are periodicals which exist wholly or partly for the purpose of publishing this type of material. For example, the World Intellectual Property Organization publishes *Industrial Property Law and Treaties* as a regular supplement to its journal *Industrial Property,* 1962–, for insertion in eight looseleaf binders. Collections of this nature of decisions of courts are rarer, but they exist; examples are the ILO *Survey of decisions on labour law,* 1925–38, some series on very specialized topics such as air law, and the *Uniform Law Cases* mentioned above, which are now incorporated in the *Uniform Law Review.*

Secondary materials

There is a good deal of secondary literature, *ie,* not containing the texts themselves. Some of this is global in its coverage and not restricted to any one subject or group of subjects. Sample periodical publications of this type are, the *Annuaire de Législation Française et Étrangère,* 1872– or the *Bulletin of Legal Developments,* 1966–, which is much more summary. Some collections are restricted as to subject, *eg, Income taxes outside the United Kingdom,* or F. Metzger *et al. Das Ausländische Strafrecht der Gegenwart,* 1955–. In some cases, works with similar titles prove to have different form and function. Thus we have Pinner's *World unfair competition law* of which the second edition appeared in 1978 in four looseleaf binders. This contains brief summaries of national laws arranged primarily by subject, with citations to statutory sources. No supplements have appeared since 1979. By contrast Kalinowski's, *World law of competition*, 1979– is now in twelve binders covering North America, Western Europe and parts of Latin America. Extensive commentary is supplemented by appendices of texts of laws, regulations and circulars, sometimes in the original language. By 1985, twenty-eight supplements had appeared. Oceana's *Transport laws of the world*, although now in six binders, contains as yet no national legislation, but only texts of international conventions, with commentary and relevant cases. Examples of works on a single narrow topic, consisting of reports on the position in individual jurisdictions with comparative sections are several works published by the Max-Planck-Institut für Ausländisches Öffentliches Recht und Völkerrecht, *eg*, *Judicial protection against the executive*, 1969–71. A number of series has been produced at the request of the Commission of the European Communities, on the national laws of member states relating, for example, to pollution control and occupational health.

FURTHER READING

David, R. and Brierley, J. E. C. *Major legal systems in the world today: an introduction to the comparative study of law*, 3rd edn., 1985.
Schlesinger, R. B. *Comparative law: cases, text, materials*, 4th edn., 1980.
Zweigert, K. and Kötz, H. *An introduction to comparative law*, 1977. Vol. I: 'The framework'; vol. II: 'The institutions of private law' (translation of their *Einführung in die Rechtsvergleichung auf dem Gebiete des Privatrechts*, 1969–71, of which a second edition appeared in 1984. There are extensive bibliographies for each chapter).

Section 2: Civil Law

P. NORMAN

In the modern world there may be said to exist three major 'families' of legal system: the common law, socialist systems based on the political and social theories of Marx and Lenin, and the civil law family, originating in Western Europe and taken by colonization or reception into many parts of the world including Latin America, francophone Africa and the Far East.

The historical foundation of the civil law is in Roman law, notably the so-called Corpus Juris Civilis of the Emperor Justinian in the sixth century AD. From its rediscovery in the eleventh century this continued to be the basis for academic legal study in European universities.

Despite this common heritage of Roman law, known sometimes as *ius commune*, it must be noted that until the end of the eighteenth century Europe consisted of a large number of small states each with its own legal system based on many sources such as local custom. Even in a large country like France there were effectively two legal systems, the Roman *droit écrit* of the south and a number of separate local *coutumes* in the north.

The pattern of the modern civil law system was set by the *Code civil* of France promulgated in 1804 and known as the Code Napoléon. Other codes followed within the next six years but have not had such worldwide influence.

Codes

The distinguishing feature of civil law systems is that large areas of the law are collected into codes which, though they may be amended from time to time, form a framework for the system itself. Most civil codes deal with the law of persons – legal status, family law; the law of things – ownership and transfer of ownership of property; and obligations including contract and tort.

The usual complement of codes is five; civil, civil procedure, penal, criminal procedure and commercial, but there are variations in number as well as content. In Switzerland, for example, a code of obligations was promulgated in 1881, thirty-two years before the appearance of a federal civil code. In consequence, contract law is absent from the latter. In Italy the provisions of the former commercial code of 1882 have been incorporated into the civil code of 1942.

For daily use by practitioners there are single-volume editions of the codes with only brief references to cases and literature. In France, the *Petits codes Dalloz* are issued annually as 16mo paperbacks for each code. In Germany the publishers, C. H. Beck, issue frequent 'red text editions' (Rote Textausgaben) of the codes and other major laws. The Netherlands, Germany and Austria each have collections of the most often used codes and statutes in A5 looseleaf format. For the Netherlands, Kluwer publish *Nederlandse Wetboeken* (codes) and *Staats- en administratiefrechtelijke Wetten* (constitutional and administrative laws), while Beck issue Schönfelder *Deutsche Gesetzte* and Sartorius *Verfassungs- und Verwaltungsgesetze*, with similar publications for Austria edited by Bydlinski and Schäffer respectively. Finally there are single-volume editions of a group of major codes such as J. A. Fruin, *De Nederlandse Wetboeken*, re-issued about every four years, and M. Fragali, *I cinque codici*, last issued in 1975.

Legislation

Acts of the legislature are usually published in official gazettes, though their style and content vary from country to country. The French *Journal Officiel* is published in five series, of which the first contains laws and decrees, and the second and third the debates of the Senate and National Assembly. By contrast, the German *Bundesgesetzblatt* appears in only two parts, Teil I with laws and regulations and Teil II with treaties. In countries with more than one official language, the gazette may appear either as one edition with parallel columns in two languages (*eg*, the *Moniteur Belge/Belgisch Staatsblad*) or as separate editions such as the Swiss *Feuille Fédérale/Bundesblatt*.

Unofficial editions of legislation which, however, maintain a chronological arrangement are to be found in Belgium and Luxembourg (*Pasinomie*), France (*Bulletin Législatif Dalloz*) and Italy (*Lex*). The last also contains regional enactments.

Apart from the codes, consolidated editions of statutes are rare. In Germany a special part, Teil III of the *Bundesgesetzblatt* was published in looseleaf format between 1958 and the mid-1960s, with a few re-issues, but has not been kept up to date. However, a current looseleaf version is provided in *Das deutsche Bundesrecht* published by Nomos and now in about thirty binders. For Spain, Aranzadi have produced an alphabetic subject collection of statutes in *Nuevo diccionario de legislación* as well as annual volumes of laws. Switzerland has an official looseleaf consolidation, *Recueil Systématique du Droit Fédéral*, published also in the other official languages. This also contains a collection of international treaties.

Law reports

One of the fundamental differences between the common law and civil law traditions is the status of court decisions. In civil law countries there is no doctrine of binding precedent, and the function of the judiciary is seen as solely to interpret and apply the true sources of law – codes, statutes or regulations – to the case in hand. In some countries, such as France, it is expressly forbidden for a judge to make reference to earlier decisions in his judgment.

Despite the fact that there is no 'judge-made law' in the common law sense, court decisions are useful to lawyers in formulating their arguments, and to the judiciary as guides to prevailing principles; in each country therefore at least the decisions of the higher courts are published in some form.

There is usually a hierarchy of courts of general jurisdiction from local trial courts through courts of appeal to a supreme court. Outside this scheme are constitutional courts to judge the constitutionality of legislation and, in federations, to adjudicate between federal and state governments.

In France and the countries most influenced by the Napoleonic codes including Belgium, Italy and the small states of Europe, a separate structure of administrative tribunals exists outside the general hierarchy, with a Council of State as the supreme administrative court. This usually has an advisory as well as judicial function, and despite the theoretical secondary importance of case-law, each has had a strong influence on the development of administrative law in its respective country.

In some countries there are yet more courts having special jurisdiction; Germany has labour courts, finance courts and social insurance courts.

There is wide variation among civil law jurisdictions both in the pattern of publication of judicial decisions and in the style of the decisions themselves. As to style, there are two main groups; in France and countries following its model, judgments are given in a very concise and distilled form and there are no dissenting opinions, nor as already mentioned any reference to previous decisions. By contrast the judgments of German courts are closer in style to those of common law countries, and often refer to previous decisions, particularly of the Supreme Court, as well as statutes and scholarly writings both in major commentaries and periodical literature.

The number of 'official' reports in the Anglo-American sense is often surprisingly small. In France the only really official series are the *Bulletin des Arrêts de la Cour de Cassation* issued in a civil and a criminal series, and the decisions of the Conseil d'Etat. Reliance is placed, for the most part, on general periodicals which are a mixed package of legislation, 'juris-prudence' (law reports) and 'doctrine' (scholarly articles). Examples are the *Recueil Dalloz Sirey* and *Juris Classeur Périodique*, otherwise known as *La Semaine Juridique*. In Germany there are separate series for the specialized courts such as *Entscheidungen des Bundesarbeitsgerichts* (decisions of the federal labour court). However, here also many decisions are to be found in general weekly or monthly law journals such as the *Neue Juristische Wochenschrift* or *Monatsschrift für Deutsches Recht*. A type of law report peculiar to Germany is a looseleaf series arranged in order of the articles of relevant codes or statutes, with new decisions on a particular article added from time to time in numerical order. An example is Hueck, *Nachschlagewerk des Bundesarbeitsgerichts*, of which the full edition is now in over sixty binders. In the smaller jurisdictions of Europe there is usually one general series of reports, such as a *Pasicrisie* for both Belgium and Luxembourg, and the *Nederlandse jurisprudentie* of the Netherlands.

Citation

The citation of statutes varies from country to country. However, it is usual for the major codes to be cited by an acronym, for example the civil codes of France or Italy as c.c. or c.civ., of Germany BGB (for Bürgerliches Gesetzbuch) of the Netherlands BW (Burgerlijk Wetboek). The citation of other statutes and regulations falls into two groups. In Germanic countries it is usual to use an acronym of the title of an Act, sometimes, though not always, with reference to the official gazette in which it appeared. An example is the German 'Gesetz über das gerichtliche Verfahren in Landwirtschaftssachen' (Law on judicial procedure in agricultural matters) cited LwVG vom 21.7.1953 (BGB1.IS.667). The proliferation of such acronyms makes an abbreviations dictionary essential.

By contrast, countries of French inspiration cite statutes simply by type – law, decree, regulation – and date, *eg*, Loi No. 85–705 du 12 juillet 1985, with sometimes an indication of its subject.

Court decisions are always cited by the name of the court

and date of the decision, not by names of the parties. Although there do exist tables by names of parties in some French and Italian series, most German ones have no such table.

SECONDARY MATERIALS

Encyclopedias and digests

The different status of court decisions in the civil law world results in the general absence of digests of the Anglo-American type, though a near equivalent is to be found in the *Jurisprudence Française,* issued first in seven volumes covering the period 1807 to 1967, in an alphabetic subject arrangement. A three-volume supplement to 1976 has appeared. Belgium has the *Recueil Annuel de Jurisprudence Belge,* which also indexes periodical articles. A peculiarity of Italian indexing is the *Massimario,* which reproduces only the head-notes (*massime*) of cases. There are several subject editions.

An approximate equivalent of *Halsbury's Laws* is easier to find, at least in jurisdictions based on the French model. France itself has the *Encyclopédie Juridique Dalloz,* issued in several subject editions known as *Répertoires.* All are looseleaf and updated twice a year. A much larger publication, in over 200 looseleaf binders, in the *Juris Classeur* collection, again in subject groups. This contains not only extensive commentary but also the text itself of codes and statutes. In Belgium we have *Les novelles: Corpus juris belgici,* published by Larcier. This is in some tens of volumes but is not looseleaf, so that some volumes are out of date. The rival publication of Bruylant is the *Répertoire pratique du droit belge,* first issued in seventeen volumes between 1930 and 1967, but with supplements.

German language countries rely less on encyclopedias than on large-scale commentaries on the major codes.

Treatises

As in the English-speaking world, there is a wide range of

treatises aimed at different readership – laymen, students, practitioners and so on.

Student textbooks are a useful introduction for foreign lawyers who can read the language. France has its *Mémentos Dalloz*, Germany its *Juristische Kurzlehrbücher*. At a slightly higher level are the *Précis Dalloz*, the C. H. Beck's *Lehrbücher* and Giuffrè's *Manuali giuridici*.

However, serious study demands the use of multi-volume works which are written by acknowledged experts and carry as much authority as judicial decisions. The framework of codification means that such works are generally based on a particular code. In Germany we have monumental works such as Staudinger's commentary on the civil code which fills about two metres of shelves, and similarly large works on the other codes. Switzerland has two huge commentaries on the civil code, the *Berner Kommentar* and the *Zürcher Kommentar*. All of these works are arranged in the order of the code itself, each article being followed by a lengthy exposition with references to relevant statutes and court decisions, and sometimes a bibliography.

A disadvantage of these works is the length of time between editions which means that changes in interpretation or important court decisions are slow to appear.

In France and the countries influenced by it, works of similar size are not really commentaries but systematic expositions arranged by subject rather than article number. Examples are Planiol and Ripert for France, the Asser series in the Netherlands, and the Italian work edited by Vassalli.

There are three types of scholarly work more prevalent in civil law than in common law jurisdictions. These are doctoral theses, the publications of learned societies and research institutes, and collections of essays in honour of eminent jurists.

It is usual in European countries for doctoral theses to be printed and published, though style of presentation may vary; in France and Belgium they appear as full letterpress paperbacks, whereas in German-speaking countries the format follows the original typescript. A wider dissemination than in Britain provides a potentially wider readership of specialized research papers.

Several universities in the civil law area have institutes devoted to particular fields of law, and these often produce, or support the publication of, specialized monographs. These may be in a numbered series, *eg*, *Kölner Schriften zum Europarecht*. In the case of learned societies, these may publish a journal or the reports of their proceedings. An example of the former is the *Zeitschrift der Savigny-Stiftung für Rechtsgeschichte* (legal history) which appears in three series covering German law, Roman law and Canon law, and of the latter the *Travaux* of the Association Henri Capitant.

Collections of 'essays in honour of ...' are so numerous in the German-speaking world that their word *Festschrift* has come to fill a gap in English vocabulary, though the French *Mélanges* might as easily be used. Such works are usually on topics of interest to the person honoured, and draw their contributions often from internationally known scholars. As a sub-group of this genre one might mention celebratory collections of essays by one person, which can be useful if the original sources – journals or conference reports – are not available.

Legal periodicals

There is a very extensive periodical literature throughout the civil law world. Counterparts of the weekly practitioners' journal, the university law review and the specialist journal are all to be found. The high standing of doctrinal writings, a legacy of university-oriented legal scholarship and education, makes the academic legal journals perhaps more important than in common law countries. Typical of such are the three major French titles: *Revue Trimestrielle de Droit Civil*, *Revue Trimestrielle de Droit Commercial* and *Revue du Droit Public*, which reflect the conceptual framework of the civil law system.

ENGLISH TRANSLATIONS

English language materials on the law of civil law jurisdictions can be grouped into primary and secondary sources. Thus there are verbatim translations of the texts of codes or statutes, as well as an increasing number of treatises and practitioners' guides to a legal system in general or to, for instance, commercial or tax laws.

As to codes, most of the European ones were translated soon after their appearance, but the advent of the European Communities gave new impetus to the issue of modern translations. The Italian civil code was issued in translation in 1969 (Beltramo), while those of Belgium (Crabb), France (Crabb), Germany (Forrester) and Austria (Baeck) have all been published within the last ten years. Criminal codes have appeared in the *American Series of Foreign Penal Codes* published by Rothman; over twenty volumes have appeared.

Commercial codes and related laws are naturally of particular value to firms with trading interests overseas. Until recently there has been a lack of translated texts; publications such as Oceana's *Digest of Commercial Laws of the World* were often too brief to be of practical use. However, the same publisher is now providing regional coverage of actual texts of laws in its *Commercial, Business and Trade Laws of ...* [various countries] in looseleaf format. The major German company and commercial legislation has been published in useful parallel text by Fritz Knapp of Frankfurt. An example is Mueller's *GmbH Law* (Law on limited companies).

The texts of some specialized laws may sometimes be found in series published by international organizations, for example labour laws in the *Legislative Series* of the International Labour Office.

A useful guide to translations of European laws was issued by the Council of Europe in 1967, with a second edition in 1975. This is the *Bibliography of translations of codes and other laws of private law.*

Treatises on the legal system of individual European countries have increased in number since Britain's entry into the EEC, although the classic works such as Amos and Walton's *Introduction to French law*, 1967, Cappelletti's *Italian legal system* and Cohn's *Manual of German law*, 1968, each pre-date this time. A new series is being issued by Kluwer in the Netherlands on the business law of individual countries.

Volumes on Austria (Heller), the Netherlands (Schuit) and Spain (Cremades) have appeared.

AUTOMATED LEGAL RESEARCH

A number of systems for automated legal research have been set up in Europe in recent years. Some of them originated as internal services for courts or departments of justice, while others have been used by the legal profession as a whole.

In Belgium, CREDOC was set up in 1967 by the Union des Avocats and the Fédération des Notaires and there are now six databases including both statutes and case-law. Two of them relate to foreign law: NLEX for Netherlands legislation and LJUS for Luxembourg case-law.

France has five public databases, with varying coverage and style, some in abstract, some in full text. Examples of full-text systems are CEDIJ based at the Conseil d'Etat and used mainly by government departments, and LEXIS, operated by Télécon- sulte in conjunction with Mead Data Central of the United States. Its databases are available to British users of LEXIS.

Italian systems are almost exclusively in the public sector, the two main ones being based at the Chamber of Deputies and the Court of Cassation. Each is a full-text system. In Germany too the main system, JURIS, is organized by the Ministry of Justice.

There are a number of periodicals devoted to the subject, examples being *Datenverarbeitung im Recht* (Germany) and *Informatica e Diritto* (Italy).

A useful listing of databases, though not confined to law, is the *EUSIDIC Database Guide* issued by the European Association of Information Services.

REFERENCE SOURCES

Indexes and bibliographies

In the civil law area, these two groups must be taken together, as they are not usually distinct. Many European countries have produced a national or language-based legal bibliography, but some of these are very old and have not been kept up to date. The French bibliography of Grandin, issued first in three volumes covering 1800 to 1926, received its last annual supplement in 1950. For Belgium we have Bosly's *Répertoire bibliographique du droit belge* covering 1919 to 1970 in 4 volumes. This is continued by an annual bibliography published in the *Annales de Droit de Liège*.

Though now rather old, the Parker School of Foreign and Comparative Law *Guides to foreign legal materials* are very valuable introductions to the structure of both the legal system and literature of the respective countries. The series includes: Szladits on French, German and Swiss law, 1959; Grisoli on Italian law, 1965; and Graulich on Belgian, Dutch and Luxembourg law, 1968. The School's *Bibliography on foreign and comparative law* is also useful, though jurisdictional access is obtained only through the geographic index in conjunction with the item numbers in the contents list. Beginning in the 1950s a series of bibliographical guides was published under the auspices of the International Association of Legal Science; the volumes covering France (David 1952 and 1964), Germany (Gesellschaft für Rechtsvergleichung 1964), Luxembourg (Association Internationale des Sciences Juridiques, Comité National Luxembourgeois 1967) and Scandinavia (Iuul 1961) are noteworthy. However, only the German volume has been kept up to date, with three supplements to 1978. More recently an annual comprehensive German legal bibliography, *Deutsche Rechtsbibliographie* has begun to appear. By contrast, the only source for current French legal publications is provided by lists in the major law reviews. The comprehensive Swiss legal bibliography by Christen (four A4 binders) is supplemented very infrequently, but again the *Zeitschrift für Schweizerisches Recht* devotes a special issue each year to a current bibliography.

For Scandinavia, apart from the comprehensive bibliographies of Søndergaard for Denmark, Reinikainen for Finland and Regner for Sweden, good bibliographies, particularly of works in English, French and German, appear from time to time in the series *Scandinavian Studies in Law*. Some of these have been published separately.

Italy has what is essentially a legal periodical index in Napoletano's *Dizionario bibliografico delle riviste giuridiche italiane*. This first appeared in a large volume covering the period 1865 to 1954, and annual volumes continue to date. Since 1959 it has also contained a subject bibliography of Italian law books published during the year.

The most ambitious European current legal bibliography is the *Karlsruher Juristische Bibliographie* which has appeared monthly since 1965. This not only indexes articles in approximately 700 serials, but also lists recently published books, with ISBN and price. While emphasis is mainly on German materials, a large number of overseas publications, including British ones, are included. There are about 18,000 entries per year.

The *Index to Foreign Legal Periodicals*, 1960–, indexes articles and book reviews in periodicals in languages other than English, covering in consequence most of the major serials in civil law jurisdictions. As a source of bibliographical information on serials, the *Union list of legal serials in selected libraries of the Federal Republic of Germany including Berlin (West)*, 1984, is very useful. It contains nearly 30,000 entries including sub-series.

Of bibliographical guides and guides to legal research designed for the 'home market' one might mention Leurquin-De Visscher's *Documentation et méthodologie juridiques*, 1980 for Belgium, Dunes's *Documentation juridique*, 1977 for France and Walter's *Wie finde ich juristische Literatur?*, 1983 for Germany.

Dictionaries

Single language dictionaries

The importance attached in civil law countries to explanatory dictionaries comparable to Jowitt varies considerably. The closest similarity is found in the German and Dutch pocket dictionaries of Creifelds and Fockema Andreae respectively. These give a brief explanation of terms with much cross-reference, and reference to statutory sources. For France, *Lexique de termes juridiques* of Guillien and Vincent is similar, but with slightly less reference to sources. The Dalloz *Dictionnaire de droit*, 1966 in two volumes, is almost an encyclopedia. The last supplement appeared in 1977. With Spanish dictionaries, one must be sure which of many legal systems are treated. Gomez de Liano's *Diccionario jurídico*, 1979 is indeed published in Spain and refers to Spanish sources, but Rivera Garcia's *Diccionario de terminos juridicos*, 1976, while taking account of the whole Spanish legal world, is based on Puerto Rico, with legal definitions from its Supreme Court. In Scandinavia there are small pocket dictionaries such as Von Eyben's *Juridisk ordbog*, 1982 for Denmark and Eek *et al. Juridikens termer*, 1962 for Sweden.

Bilingual dictionaries

There are three main German–English legal dictionaries: Dietl *et al. Dictionary of legal, commercial and political terms* in two volumes is the most detailed, giving some explanatory notes and footnote references to statutes. Von Beseler and Jacobs *Law dictionary* makes careful distinction between British and American terms, and the English–German volume is nearly twice the size of the German–English. The pocket dictionary is represented by Romain's *Dictionary of legal and commercial terms*, in a series of bilinguals published by Beck and coupling German with Spanish, French, Dutch, Italian and Russian.

French is less well covered, the major work of Quemner, though advertised in recent years, is a reprint of the original 1953 edition. Nichols and Vibes, *Vocabulaire ... de terminologie économique et juridique* is, at 100 pages, too brief to be useful. Although based on EEC texts, the *European Communities glossary* is a valuable word list.

A very thorough encyclopedic English–Italian dictionary is De Franchis, *Law dictionary*, 1984. It is fervently to be wished that the complementary Italian–English volume will give as thorough an account of Italian law to the Anglo-American lawyer.

For Spanish terms, the *Legal and commercial dictionary* of Dios Tejada y Sainz, 1945, and Robb's *Dictionary of legal terms,* 1955, are so old that the best recourse is probably the multilinguals such as Egbert.

There are no large bilingual legal dictionaries of the Scandinavian languages, although small glossaries such as Backe *et al. Concise Swedish–English glossary of legal terms,* 1973, have appeared.

Multilingual dictionaries

The most recent multilingual legal dictionary is Le Docte's *Dictionnaire de termes juridiques en quatre langues,* 1982 covering French, Dutch, English and German in parallel text across a two-page opening. Distinction is made where necessary between *eg,* Belgian and French, or American and British usage. A useful appendix describes court structure in several jurisdictions. Egbert and Morales-Macedo, *Multilingual law dictionary,* 1978, covering English, French, Spanish and German, although less detailed in the treatment of its 6,300 terms, contains an appendix of fuller explanation of selected terms, as well as a useful bibliography of bilingual and multilingual legal dictionaries. Anderson's *Anglo–Scandinavian law dictionary,* 1977, is arranged in separate sections for English, Norwegian, Swedish and Danish, the major part of explanations appearing under the English term, but with much thorough cross-referencing and hints on differences of usage.

Abbreviations dictionaries

There is no single work of this type which would cover all civil law jurisdictions. As has been said above, the most widespread use of abbreviations, particularly of statutes, is in the German-speaking countries of Europe. This merits the comprehensive work of Kirchner, *Abkürzungsverzeichnis der Rechtssprache,* 3rd edn., 1983. As well as the usual listing with explanation and reference to gazettes, an equal proportion of the book is devoted to suggested acronyms for legal materials in general and organizations, official gazettes, periodicals and law reports, and finally of statutes and regulations.

A series of abbreviations lists with only simple expansion of each entry has been prepared by Adolf Sprudzs of the University of Chicago Law School Library. These relate to France, Italy and the Benelux Group. Another finding list for French abbreviations is Leistner's *Abbreviations guide to French forms in justice and administration*, 2nd edn., 1975.

Where no dictionary is available, abbreviations lists may occasionally be found in the major legal journals such as the *Recueil Dalloz Sirey*, or in textbooks.

FURTHER READING

David, R. and Brierley, J. E. 'The Romano-Germanic family' *in Major legal systems in the world today: an introduction to the comparative study of law*, 3rd edn., Part I, Stevens, 1985, pp. 35–154.

Lawson, F. H. *A Common lawyer looks at the civil law*, 1953.

Merryman, J. H. *The Civil law tradition: an introduction to the legal systems of Western Europe and Latin America*, 2nd edn., 1984.

Section 3: Roman Law

B. M. TEARLE

INTRODUCTION

This section gives an account of the sources and literature of Roman law and of its study today.

Roman law has existed for 2,500 years, first as a living system then, since the Middle Ages, as the subject of study influencing ways of thought and the development of European and associated legal systems. Today it has a flourishing international and worldwide body of scholars actively engaged in reconstructing, studying and writing about it. Justification for its study is twofold. It is presented as a complete system in microcosm, exhibiting characteristics of all phases of development, maturity and decline. It also provides an intellectual background to legal thought, especially as employed in civil law systems.

The study of Roman law is required for qualification as a Scottish advocate. Undergraduate and postgraduate courses are also available at some English and Irish universities. Despite its minority position in teaching, there are several Roman law scholars of international repute in the British Isles.

Consonant with its international status, modern literature on Roman law is in many languages. Two linguistic characteristics stand out. Latin is a common language for all its scholars and the librarian will encounter it in the introductions and texts of many reference books and as standard headings in bibliographies and indexes. Secondly, many journals and some monographs are multilingual. Reference here will be made wherever possible to English-language publications, as they are more readily available for purchase and use in English-speaking countries. However, many reference sources are in other languages and will be referred to where they are the standard works.

Few original texts of Roman laws or literature have survived. Our knowledge is derived from inscriptions, later manuscripts or even fragments and non-legal texts. The work of palingenesis has been going on for centuries so that now we have extensive, although still incomplete, reconstructions of many laws and law books. The history of the gradual rediscovery of manuscripts from the ninth to the twentieth centuries, their reconstruction and, from the fifteenth century, their publication is set out briefly in A. A. Schiller's *Roman law: mechanisms of development,* 1978 (hereafter referred to as Schiller). The chance survival of manuscripts, etc. has inevitably resulted in a haphazard and incomplete knowledge of Roman legal literature and a partial view of the substance of Roman law.

ORIGINAL SOURCES

The era of Roman law is divided into several periods, although scholars do not agree on the extent of each. The period of classical Roman law is generally accepted as 150 BC to AD 235 and the last period that of the life of Justinian, AD 527–65. His reign saw the collection, updating and codification of the earlier classical law. Over such a long period of active life, the sources and literature inevitably altered. They are fully described for all periods in F. Schulz's *History of Roman legal science,* 1963.

Pre-Justinian law

During the classical Roman law era the primary sources of law were *leges publicae,* praetorian edicts, *senatus consulta* and imperial enactments. Selections from all categories have survived in fragments or as references in later works. An index to surviving texts of *leges publicae* is provided by G. Rotondi's *Leges publicae populi romani,* 1912, which also contains a brief summary of their contents. The praetorian edict developed over the centuries until its final form was established by Julian under Hadrian's authority in about AD 132 as *Edicta perpetuum Hadriani*. It only survives through references in later works and has been reconstructed by O. Lenel and published as *Das edictum perpetuum*, 1927.

Secondary sources, *ie*, the writings of jurists, fall into several categories: elementary textbooks, collections of legal maxims, commentaries on laws or earlier writings, studies of individual topics and works on the duties of magistrates and on procedure. Most have survived by transmission through references or incorporation in later writings, chiefly in Justinian's *Digest*.

The best known of the juristic sources is Gaius's *Institutes*, an elementary textbook on Roman private law in four books. It was heavily drawn upon in the compilation of Justinian's *Institutes* nearly 400 years later. Of several modern English translations, the most used is *The Institutes of Gaius* by de Zulueta, 1946–53 in parallel Latin and English texts with a commentary.

There are several modern collections of reconstructed sources. Most are in Latin or Greek and several have explanatory notes in Latin. *Fontes iuris romani anteiustiniani* edited by S. Riccobono *et al*. 1940–3 (usually cited as FIRA) has the widest coverage. C. G. Bruns's *Fontes iuris romani antiqui*, 7th edition by T. Mommsen and O. Gradenwitz, 1909 contains *leges* and non-legal writings. Many of the primary sources, and some juristic writings not used in Justinian's works, are collected in P. F. Girard and F. Senn's *Textes de droit romain*, 7th edn., 1967–77. It has the advantage that its notes on sources are in French. These and other collections are described in Schiller and by P. Stein in 'Roman law (sources)' in J. Gilissen's *Bibliographical introduction to legal history and ethnology*, 1965.

The post-classical, pre-Justinian period (AD 235–527) produced other types of literature: abridgments of juristic writings and compilations of imperial enactments. Amongst the latter were the privately compiled *Codex Gregorianus* and *Codex Hermogenianus*, containing enactments from the second and third centuries. The *Codex Theodosianus* was an official codification of imperial enactments from AD 312–438. The standard edition of the reconstructed text is by Mommsen, 1905 and an English translation has been published by C. Pharr as *The Theodosian Code and Novels and the Sirmondian Constitutions*, 1952.

Roman law in the Western Empire was overlaid by that of Germanic invaders during the fifth century but was applied as a personal law. Several official collections were made during the period, *eg*, the *Lex romana Visigothorum* (also called the *Breviarium Alaricianum*) of AD 506, the *Lex romana Burgundionium* and the *Edictum Theodorici*. All three collections are published in FIRA.

Justinian's codifications

Justinian I was Emperor of the East from AD 527 to 565. Soon after his accession he set up a commission of jurists headed by Tribonian to restate and revise the law. They produced three works, the *Digest,* the *Institutes* and the *Code* (in two editions). Justinian's subsequent enactments are known as the *Novels.* The four works were given the collective title in the sixteenth century of *Corpus Juris Civilis* to distinguish them from the *Corpus Juris Canonici.*

Work began on the *Digest* (or *Pandects,* from its Greek title) in AD 530. It was promulgated on 16 December 533 and came into force on 30 December. Its purpose was to codify the law by taking extracts from classical jurists and amending them to reflect contemporary practice. Each text is attributed and the standard edition, Mommsen's *Digesta Justiniani Augusti*, 1870 has a table of derivations. The study of the interpolations of Justinian's Commissioners is an important part of modern textual reconstruction. The *Digest* covers all branches of law and is divided into fifty books.

The *Institutes* were promulgated on 21 November 533 and came into force on 30 December simultaneously with the *Digest.* Although intended as an elementary textbook for students beginning their legal studies, it was given the force of law. It drew heavily upon Gaius's *Institutes* with extracts from some later jurists and Justinianic amendments. It deals mainly with private law with a short summary of criminal law and is divided into four books.

The first version of the *Code* was completed in AD 529 but

was rendered obsolete by Justinian's later enactments. A second version was promulgated in AD 534. It contains pre-Justinian imperial constitutions attributed to the emperor who enacted them. They cover public, private and criminal law and are arranged in twelve books.

The *Novels* are those constitutions which Justinian promulgated after the second *Code*. They deal with public, ecclesiastical and private law and the resolution of difficulties in earlier enactments. They have come down to us in three collections: the *Epitome Iuliani*, the *Authenticum* and a Greek collection. The standard editions combine all three collections. The *Novels* are divided into statutes, chapters and sections.

A brief account of the recovery of texts of the *Corpus Juris Civilis* and the publication of various editions from the fifteenth century onwards is contained in Schiller and in Sass's article 'Research in Roman law', *Law Library Journal*, vol. 56, 1963, pp. 210–33. The standard edition is *Corpus Juris Civilis* in three volumes edited by P. Krueger *et al.* with text and notes in Latin. It was first published in 1872 and the current edition is that of 1954. It is known as the stereotype edition from its method of printing and also to distinguish the volume containing the *Digest* edited by Mommsen from his other edition, *Digesta Justiniani Augusti*, 1868–70 in two volumes, which contains more critical detail.

A complete translation into English was made by Scott and published in 1932 in 17 volumes as *The civil law*, but it is notoriously inaccurate and, if used, must be approached with caution. The *Digest* has been translated by a group of English Roman law scholars under the direction of Alan Watson and published as *The Digest of Justinian*, 1986. It has parallel English and Latin texts, the latter being that of Mommsen's 1878 edition. The latest of many English translations of the *Institutes* is J. A. C. Thomas's *Institutes of Justinian*, 1975 with parallel Latin and English texts and extensive notes in English. Other than Scott's version, there is no translation of the whole of Justinian's *Code* or the *Novels*.

An abbreviated form of reference to the contents of Justinian's works (and other sources) has been used for centuries. The older style is explained in Schiller and in Sass's article. The current method of citation in the English-speaking world follows the numbered divisions and sub-divisions of the texts. Most of Justinian's works are divided into numbered books, titles, laws and finally paragraphs. The *Novels* are divided into numbered statutes, chapters and paragraphs. Citations refer first to the source, usually by its initial letter, then to the numbered divisions and sub-divisions starting with the major one and ending with the smallest, *eg*,

> C.7.6.1.2 = Book 7, title 6, law 1, paragraph 1 of Justinian's *Code*,
>
> D.43.31.1.1 = Book 43, title 31, law 1, paragraph 1 of Justinian's *Digest*,
>
> I. (or Inst. or J.) 2.24.2 = Book 2, title 24, law 2 of Justinian's *Institutes*,
>
> N.118.2.4 = Statute 118, chapter 2, paragraph 4 of Justinian's *Novels*.

Some laws have opening unnumbered paragraphs. They are cited as, *eg*,

> D.41.2.19.,pr. = Book 41, title 2, law 19, opening paragraph.

This pattern of citation is applied to other Roman law sources. The numbered books, titles, etc. are clearly shown in all modern editions. Further information on Justinian's works, translations and methods of citation are contained in Sass's article.

Vocabularies listing words and their occurrences in the *Corpus Juris Civilis* and other sources and indexes of interpolations are important aids to textual study. They are listed in P. Stein's 'Roman law (sources)' in Gilissen, *Bibliographical Introduction to Legal History and Ethnology*. The major publication since that bibliography is T. Honoré and J. Menner's *Concordance to the Digest Jurists*, 1980 which lists occurrences of words, attributes them to jurists and gives their frequency of use. The introduction suggests some ways in which the *Concordance* can be used.

Post-Justinian sources

After the death of Justinian, Roman law continued in use in the Eastern Empire, albeit by the ninth century in a Greek commentary, the *Basilica*, promulgated by Leo the Wise about AD 900. A modern edition with notes is being published under the title *Basilicorum libri LX* edited by H. J. Scheltema *et al.*

In the West, the Empire fragmented, the *Digest* fell into desuetude and the use of Roman law almost died out. It was revived by the discovery in the late eleventh century of a manuscript, later to be called the Florentine manuscript from its place of deposit. With this discovery began the second life of Roman law as a source for *ius commune*, a common law of Europe. From the twelfth century there has been a succession of schools of Roman law. The Glossators during the twelfth and thirteenth centuries annotated or glossed the text of the *Digest*, the most comprehensive edition of which is that of Accursius. The work of the Post-Glossators or Commentators in the thirteenth and fourteenth centuries led to its reception in the German states and the Low Countries, to a lesser extent in France and the Italian states, and gave it some influence in Scotland. The humanist school of the fifteenth and sixteenth centuries sought to reconstruct the original Roman law texts. It was followed by the natural law school of the eighteenth century and the historical school of the nineteenth century, centred on Germany. In the present century the study of Roman law has reverted to a humanist approach, and much historical study, including work on interpolations, has been done to reconstruct texts.

The activities of each school are described in O. Robinson's *European legal history*, 1985. J. A. Clarence Smith's *Medieval law teachers and writers*, 1975 narrates the development of the schools to 1660 emphasizing the work of individual scholars. An elementary account of the application of Roman law in France, Germany and England is given by P. Vinogradoff in *Roman law in medieval Europe*, 1909. A deeper study of the early period has been made by H. Kantorowicz and W. W. Buckland in *Studies in the glossators of the Roman law*, 1938. Until recently the definitive study of the medieval period was F. C. von Savigny's *Geschichte des römischen Rechts im Mittelalter*, 2nd edn., 1834–51, but it is likely to be superseded by a multi-volume, multilingual work, *Ius romanum medii aevi* (IRMA or IRMAE) being prepared by an international group of scholars.

National legal histories will also contain information on the influence of Roman law in their respective countries.

Some of the major works from the various schools published during the fifteenth and sixteenth centuries are obtainable today through the activities of reprint publishers. Similarly, many of the leading works of the last century have been reprinted by the publisher Scientia of Aalen. Reprints of individual works can be traced through the bibliographies referred to at pp. 520–2.

MODERN LITERATURE

Monographs

The monograph literature of Roman law is extensive and growing. English language books are limited to a handful a year, ranging from textbooks (often translations of continental ones), the results of intensive research and translations of sources. Most monographs are published in languages other than English.

An interesting introduction to Roman law in the context of Roman life is J. A. Crook's *Law and life of Rome,* 1967. For its historical development H. F. Jolowicz and B. Nicholas's *Historical introduction to the study of Roman law,* 1972 and W. Kunkel's *An introduction to Roman legal and constitutional history,* 2nd English edn., 1973, are excellent. Several books deal with Roman private law, frequently employing the same arrangement as Gaius's and Justinian's Institutes: W. W. Buckland's *A textbook of Roman law from Augustus to Justinian,* 3rd edn., 1966; F. Schulz's *Classical Roman law,* 1951; M. Kaser's *Roman private law,* 3rd edn., 1980; and B. Nicholas's *An introduction to Roman law,* 1962, all of which are suitable as undergraduate texts. Greater critical evaluation is provided by J. A. C. Thomas's *Textbook of Roman law,* 1976 and a wider perspective by F. Schulz's *Principles of Roman law,* 1936. Among recent scholarly monographs the series by Tony Honoré studies Roman lawyers and legal sources based on an analysis of their style and working methods and that of A.

Watson investigates aspects of private law of the Republican period.

A feature of continental scholarly writing which has been widely adopted in Roman legal scholarship is the Festschrift, a volume of contributions by several authors published to honour a person or institution on an important occasion or as a memorial on the death of a person. Festschriften are widely used in Italian Roman law writing and are frequently multivolume with many contributors. A few Festschriften on a more modest scale have been published in the British Isles, but an alternative method of publication, which is generally preferred in English-speaking countries, is as an issue of a journal. Contributions to Festschriften, like journal articles, may be in a variety of languages.

Conferences are held regularly under the sponsorship of the various bodies, national and international, concerned with Roman law study. Their proceedings are often published as monographs.

For the bibliographical control and retrieval of Festschriften and conference literature see pp. 522–3.

Periodicals

The international nature of Roman law study is reflected in the journal literature, in the nationalities of contributors, the languages in which articles are written and the countries of origin of the journals. The major journals are published in Italy, Germany, France and Belgium. None devoted solely to Roman law is published in an English-speaking country. English-speaking scholars publish their articles in the general English legal journals or in the foreign specialist Roman law journals.

The major current journals are *Bullettino dell'Istituto di Diritto Romano 'Vittorio Scialoja'* (BIDR), *Index, Iura, Labeo, Revue Internationale des Droits de l'Antiquité* (RIDA), *Studia et Documenta Historiae et Iuris* (SDHI), *Tijdschrift voor Rechtsgeschiedenis* (TvR) and *Zeitschrift der Savigny-Stiftung für Rechtsgeschichte, Romanistische Abteilung* (ZSS Rom. Abt.). *Iura*, SDHI and TvR cover other ancient systems of law in addition to Roman law. All the journals have articles. All, except *Labeo* and RIDA, have book reviews. *Iura* and *Labeo* have regular literature indexes (see pp. 522–3), and *Index* and TvR have regular literature surveys or occasional bibliographies. Reports of conferences, seminars and activities of Roman law scholars and associations are noted in all journals except BIDR and ZSS Rom. Abt. The earlier volumes of *Index* contain national surveys of progress in Roman law study. SDHI and TvR have obituaries.

Articles on Roman law are also published in general legal journals. Among the English language ones, the *Cambridge Law Journal, Irish Jurist, Tulane Law Review* and *Acta Juridica* are the most prominent. Journals devoted primarily to classical studies also have occasional articles on Roman law, *eg* the *Journal of Roman Studies*. For indexes to journal articles see p. 523.

REFERENCE SOURCES

Much reference information on Roman law can be obtained from general and specifically legal reference sources. Of the latter the most versatile and useful is A. Berger's *Encyclopedic dictionary of Roman law*, 1953 (hereafter referred to as Berger), which contains dictionary, encyclopedic, biographical and bibliographical information. Despite being both thirty years old and out of print it is an essential tool for serious study.

Bibliographical sources

Guides to the literature

A thorough introduction especially to the original literature is provided by S. Sass's article 'Research in Roman law' in *Law Library Journal*, vol. 56, 1963, pp. 210–33. The bibliographical appendix in W. Kunkel's *An introduction to Roman legal and constitutional history*, 1973, gives an in-depth assessment of the modern literature from Germany, France and Italy. The librarian can glean much bibliographical information from

A. A. Schiller's *Roman law: mechanisms of development*, 1978 although it is not intended as a bibliography or guide to the literature. Most other English language textbooks contain some account of the sources and literature of Roman law.

Books

Bibliographies of bibliographies
There is no separate bibliography of bibliographies of Roman law, but most bibliographies mentioned below have a heading for bibliographies. General legal sources such as *Legal Bibliography Index* and the indexing services referred to on p. 523 must be consulted to keep abreast of new bibliographies of Roman law.

National bibliographies
The most prolific publishing countries for Roman law are Italy and Germany followed by other European countries, South Africa, the South American countries and the USA, with some literature published as far afield as Japan and the USSR. Their national bibliographies should be consulted for bibliographical details or to trace Roman law publications.

Bibliographies
The obvious bibliography for British and Irish librarians to consult is that contained in volume 5 of Sweet and Maxwell's *A legal bibliography of the British Commonwealth*, 2nd edn., 1957, which covers Scottish and Roman law. Its usefulness is limited by its age, the paucity of bibliographical detail, the lack of annotations and its restriction to English language publications. Of similar age but without the other defects are the bibliographies in Berger, in J. Gilissen's *Bibliographical introduction to legal history and ethnology* and in Sass's article. The bibliography at the end of Berger is set out systematically to cover all classes of Roman law literature – reference books, bibliographies, source materials, subject studies – and to include books in many languages. There is some annotation.

Separate sections in Gilissen treat sources, public law, private law and criminal law and medieval Roman law. The annotations, in the style of a narrative connecting the entries, recommend the best sources in each subject. Sass's article contains a selected bibliography of the most important (in 1963) translations of, and books on, the sources of Roman law.

The most thorough, scholarly and recent retrospective bibliography is Manlius Sargenti's *Operum ad ius Romanum pertinentium quae ab anno MCMXL usque ad annum MCMLXX edita sunt*, 1978–83 in 3 volumes, which indexes articles in books, periodicals and Festschriften for the period 1940–70. It includes scholarly and popular works published in many languages.

The usual sources for current legal literature described in Chapter 9 will include Roman law books where they fall within the scope of each bibliography. New books are noted in several sources. Some booksellers' catalogues, *eg*, Brill's and ABI's include new and forthcoming Roman law books from several publishers amongst their more general coverage. Two Roman law journals, *Labeo* and *Iura* have large sections devoted to new literature, both books and articles. Although there is the inevitable delay between publication and listing, these are the best specialist sources for keeping abreast of new publications.

Catalogues
Published library catalogues can be used both as bibliographies, albeit selective, and location tools. The catalogues of the Cambridge Squire Law Library, the Institute of Advanced Legal Studies, and Columbia University Law Library all have Roman law sections.

Theses
Thesis literature is extensive and international. Many French and German doctoral theses have been listed for the period 1851 to 1948 and 1958 respectively in L. Caes and R. Henrion's *Collectio bibliographica operum ad ius romanum pertinentium, series II, 'Theses'*, but no indication is given about publication or where to locate them. Some have been published and can be traced through the national bibliographies. The normal

sources for British and American dissertations and theses described on p. 358 will also include theses on Roman law.

Periodicals

Roman law is one of the most thoroughly indexed of legal subjects. The major indexing services include articles in journals, collections and Festschriften and also books and book reviews. The major service, until it ceased publication in 1978, was L. Caes and R. Henrion's *Collectio bibliographica operum ad ius romanum pertinentium*, series I, 1949–78. Through a policy of retrospective indexing, which is especially noticeable in the first few volumes, it effectively indexes Roman law literature since early last century up to 1975. For subsequent indexing several sources may be used. The journals *Labeo* and *Iura* have extensive indexing sections. *Bibliographie*, 1975–, published annually, covers books and articles on ancient law including Roman law. The index in the allied field of classics, *L'Année Philologique*, 1927–, also contains some references to Roman law articles and book reviews, a few of which have escaped Caes and Henrion.

Lists of Roman law journals are contained in these indexes and in Sargenti's bibliography. There is no separately published list or union list of Roman law journals. For locating them, the general and legal union lists described on p. 357 should be consulted.

Dictionaries

A good Latin–English dictionary such as the *Oxford Latin dictionary*, 1968–76 or C. T. Lewis and C. Short's *A Latin dictionary*, 1879, is indispensable for the serious study of Roman law. Good bilingual dictionaries for French, German, Italian and Spanish into English are also helpful in reading the non – English language modern literature.

Berger's *Encyclopedic dictionary* aims 'to explain technical Roman legal terms, to translate and elucidate those Latin words which have a specific connotation when used in a juristic context ...' and to include 'Latin terms of medieval or modern coinage, unknown to the ancient Romans, but now widely accepted in the Romanistic literature ...' It is the first source to consult for information on Roman legal terminology.

Roman law study has created a large number of abbreviations for journal titles, Festschriften and monographs as well as for the source literature. There is no separate dictionary of them. A few are given in Jowitt's *A dictionary of English law*, 2nd edn., 1977, and the older English legal dictionaries. There are extensive lists in Caes and Henrion's *Collectio bibliographica, series I*, and in Schiller and shorter lists in Berger and in many of the English language textbooks. Since continental European scholarship often uses different abbreviations from those in use in English-speaking countries, continental journals and textbooks should be consulted to identify them.

Encyclopedias

The nearest to an encyclopedia devoted exclusively to Roman law is Berger. At an elementary level *The Oxford classical dictionary*, 2nd edn., 1970, D. M. Walker's *The Oxford companion to law*, 1980, and the *Encyclopaedia Britannica* (most editions) have satisfactory explanations of the main features, personnel and literature. At an advanced level, the great encyclopedias of classical studies, eg, Paulys' *Real-Encyclopädie der classischen Altertumswissenschaft*, 1894–, include Roman law terms, concepts and personnel.

Biographical sources

The encyclopedias mentioned above, with the addition of A. W. B. Simpson's *Biographical dictionary of the common law*, 1984, contain information on classical Roman jurists. The entries in many of them are followed by further reading. The proponents of the medieval Roman law revival appear in some of these sources but are treated more fully in J. A. Clarence Smith's *Medieval law teachers and writers*, 1975.

Biographical information on modern Roman law scholars

may be found in the legal biographical sources appropriate to the person's country. Festschriften usually contain some biographical information and a bibliography of that person's writings. A list of active Roman law scholars with their addresses is given in *Labeo*, vol. 22, 1976, pp. 126–39, 322–36 and 436–8.

Associations for legal history including Roman law are listed in R. Feenstra's *Repertorium bibliographicum institutorum et sodalitatum iuris historiae*, 1980. It includes information about the associations and their publications, although not about their members.

Libraries

The main collections of Roman law in the British Isles are in the copyright deposit libraries with good collections also in the libraries of Edinburgh and Glasgow Universities and University College London.

Section 4: Roman–Dutch Law

B. M. TEARLE

The term Roman–Dutch law was first used to describe the law of the province of Holland by the jurist Simon van Leeuwen in his book *Paratitla iuris novissimi, dat is, Een kort begrip van het Rooms-Hollandts Reght* in 1652.

THE NETHERLANDS

The law about which van Leeuwen and other Dutch jurists wrote was a mixture of local custom, legislation and judicial decisions each influenced by Roman law. Roman law had infiltrated the law of many European countries in the Middle Ages, contributing to the character of Germanic customary law in the states of Germany and the Low Countries. It had gathered momentum in Holland in the fourteenth and fifteenth centuries by way of the authority of the legists (university, therefore Roman law, trained advisers to secular rulers), its application in the territorial high courts and incorporation of many of its rules into local legislation. This resulted in a widespread reception in several countries during the sixteenth century. It was regarded as valid law and was applied by many courts in Holland and the other provinces of what is now The Netherlands (although acceptance by lower courts was slow). Its position is described by van der Linden, one of the last Dutch writers on Roman–Dutch law, in these terms: 'In order to answer the question what is the law in such and such a case we must first inquire whether any general law of the land or any local ordinance (*plaatselijke keur*), having the force of law, or any well-established custom, can be found affecting it. The Roman law as a model of wisdom and equity is, in default of such a law, accepted by us through custom in order to supply this want' (van der Linden, *Rechtsgeleerd, practicaal, en koopmans handboek*, 1806, translated by H. Juta in 1906 and G. T. Morice in 1922). This proposition was examined by van der Keessel in his *Theses selectae iuris Hollandici et Zelandici*, 1806 and further examined and accepted by S. J. Fockema Andreae in his edition of Grotius.

The Netherlands was overrun by the French in 1795 and Roman–Dutch law was replaced in 1809 by Napoleonic codes. After the downfall of Napoleon, the establishment of the Kingdom of the Netherlands in 1815 and the split in 1830 into two kingdoms, The Netherlands and Belgium, Roman–Dutch law was not reintroduced, although elements are found in the civil code adopted in 1838.

Primary literature

The literary sources of Roman–Dutch law, often referred to as the Old Authorities, are commonly described in four categories: legislation, collections of court decisions, opinions of eminent lawyers and treatises.

Legislation consists of *placaaten, ordonnantien* and *diplomata* which had the effect of modifying customary law. It was collected for the period 1097 to 1795 in the *Groot Placaet-Boeck*, 1658–1796 and a selection has been published in Japiskse's *Klein Plakkaatboek*, 1919.

In default of official court reporting, unofficial collections of court decisions were made and published during the seventeenth and eighteenth centuries and are still referred to today in South African courts. Recent and outstanding additions to this literature are Bynkershoek's *Observationes tumultuariae*, 1926–62 continued by Pauw's *Observationes tumultuariae novae*, 1964–7. Although compiled in the eighteenth century, neither was published until the twentieth.

The opinions of eminent lawyers, both professors and practitioners, were influential in developing the law. Amongst the earliest to be published was Nicolaus Everhardus's *Responsa sive consilia*, 1554, but the majority were published during the seventeenth and eighteenth centuries including the most influential, *Consultatien, Advysen, en Advertissementen, gegeven ende geschreven by verscheijde treffelyke rechtsgeleerden in Holland en elders*, 1645–66, known as *Hollandsche consultatien*. Eighty-nine of Grotius's opinions have been extracted and published in translation by D. P. de Bruyn as *The opinions of Grotius as contained in the Hollandsche consultatien en advijsen*, 1894.

While Simon van Leeuwen was the first to use the term in 1652, Roman–Dutch law had been the subject of books since about 1500 and its literature in Holland continued until the early nineteenth century. The most important early book was Hugo Grotius's *Inleiding tot de Hollandsche rechtsgeleertheyd*, 1631, which created a 'synthesis of Roman and customary law' treating it not just as an appendix to Roman law but as a system in its own right. It was written in Dutch and has been translated into Latin and English. The definitive Dutch edition is the 29th, 1952, based on a manuscript discovered in 1948 (*Inleidinge tot de Hollandsche rechts-geleerdheid*, edited by F. Dovring *et al*). It is also available in another Dutch edition by S. J. Fockema Andreae, 1929. A Latin translation by van der Linden in the 1830s, ostensibly to increase its availability to non-Dutch speakers, was only published in 1926 as *Hugonis Grotii Institutiones Juris Hollandici*. Of the several English translations the most used are A. F. S. Maasdorp's *Introduction to Dutch jurisprudence*, 1878 (3rd edn., 1903), which includes Schorer's notes, and R. W. Lee's *The jurisprudence of Holland*, 1926–36. Lee's work has parallel Dutch and English texts in the first volume and a commentary in the second comprising Lee's own notes and references to modern South African statutes and cases and those notes of his predecessors who had written commentaries on Grotius's book – Schorer, Groenewegen, Voet, van der Keessel, Coster, Scheltinga and Fockema Andreae.

Many of the Dutch jurists wrote commentaries on Justinian's works. The most important, which is still cited in South African courts, is Johannes Voet's *Commentarius ad Pandectas*, 1698–1704, a commentary on the *Digest*, in which his comments on the Roman law are followed by notes on its application in contemporary Dutch law. The most reliable edition is considered to be the first, but the fullest is the Paris edition of 1829. Translations into several languages have been made. They are listed in A. A. Robert's *Guide to Voet*, 1933 and his *South African legal bibliography*, 1942. The most used English translation is Mr Justice Gane's *The selective Voet*, 1955–8, which includes all but the obsolete portions of the *Commentarius*. It is kept up to date by supplements which refer to its use in the South African courts.

Among the encyclopedias and dictionaries of the old Roman–Dutch law is F. L. Kersteman's *Hollandsch rechtsgeleerd woordenboek*, 1768, with its supplement, *Aanhangsel*, 1777, by L. W. Kramp. They form an encyclopedic dictionary or alphabetically arranged digest of the law drawing heavily on Voet's *Commentarius* for definitions.

A description of the development of, and principal writers on, Roman–Dutch law is given in H. Hahlo and E. Kahn's *The South African legal system and its background*, 1968, and by P. van Warmelo in 'Roman law and the Old Authorities on Roman–Dutch law', *Acta Juridica*, 1961, pp. 38–57.

Modern literature

General introductions in English to Roman–Dutch law are contained in R. W. Lee's *An introduction to Roman–Dutch law*, 5th edn., 1953 and in Hahlo and Kahn's book. The standard history is J. W. Wessels' *History of the Roman–Dutch law*, 1908, which has several chapters on the literary sources. Several journals carry occasional articles on the history of Roman–Dutch law.

THE SPREAD OF ROMAN–DUTCH LAW

Traders and colonists took the law of their native Holland to the Dutch East Indies, which included Ceylon and the Cape of Good Hope, and the Dutch West Indies, including modern Guyana. When these colonies (with the exception of the Dutch East Indies) were taken over by the British in 1806 (Cape of Good Hope), 1796 (Ceylon) and 1803 (modern Guyana), the continuation of their existing law was guaranteed. Thus, at the time when Roman–Dutch law in Holland was superseded by French-inspired codes, it was transplanted to other parts of the world. Even in the countries of which it is still the common law, it has been substantially altered by legislation and judicial interpretation.

Legislative power for the Dutch East Indies rested with its Council of XVII and the Governor-General and Council in Batavia (now Djakarta), subject to ratification procedures in the United Provinces of The Netherlands. Power was exercised through *placaats* and orders which were eventually collected and published in 1642 as the *Statutes of Batavia* and were applied in Ceylon and the Cape. A revised and updated edition of 1764, the *New Statutes of Batavia*, lacked the authority of the first collection. In 'The expansion of Dutch private law outside Europe in the seventeenth and eighteenth centuries' in *The world of Hugo Grotius (1583–1645)*, 1984, J. Th. de Smidt describes law and law-making during the Dutch colonial period. He also mentions current research into the early history of Roman–Dutch law outside The Netherlands.

Guyana

Roman–Dutch law was introduced by the Dutch settlers in the early seventeenth century, expressly retained in 1803 when the colony capitulated to the British and again in 1831 when the extended colony of British Guiana was set up. It languished for the next 100 years and was replaced by the English common law, except in relation to some aspects of property, by the Civil Law of British Guiana Ordinance of 1916. The Guyana chapter of volume I of the *International encyclopedia of comparative law* describes these events briefly. More detail is contained in the two books by M. Shahabuddeen, *The legal system of Guyana*, 1973 and *Constitutional development in Guyana 1621–1978*, 1978.

Indonesia/Dutch East Indies

Although traders and settlers in the Dutch East Indies took their own law with them, Roman–Dutch law scarcely survives in modern Indonesia. The history and administration of Indonesia under the Dutch is described by John Ball in *Indonesian legal history 1602–1848*, 1982. During the nineteenth century the area continued to be administered by the Dutch government, which introduced codes based on those in force in The Netherlands. Both before and after Independence in 1945 several systems of law were in force: the imported European law, *adat* law and personal religious law. Since 1945 Indonesian law has developed along its own path and produced an extensive literature.

South Africa

The history of legal development in Cape Colony from its foundation in 1652 to its final cession to Britain in 1814 is set out in the first chapter of H. Hahlo and E. Kahn's *The Union of South Africa*, 1960, in Chapter 3 of J. W. Wessels' *History of the Roman–Dutch law*, 1908 and in volume 1 of W. Burge's *Commentaries on colonial and foreign laws*, 1907. They describe the relationship between the Dutch and the Dutch East Indies, of which Cape Colony at first formed a part. They also make frequent and substantial references to the literature of the period and to its authority.

There was no explicit provision in the capitulation of the Cape to the British for the continuance of Roman–Dutch law, but it is a generally accepted principle of English law that colonies acquired by cession or conquest retain their existing law. Not only did this happen in the Cape, but Roman–Dutch law spread with the expansion of the colony itself.

Many factors during the nineteenth century should have led to the gradual eradication of Roman–Dutch law: the introduction in 1827 of English as the only official court language; enquiries into the state of the law in 1826 and 1857 both of which envisaged a gradual replacement of existing law by English law; the staffing of courts with English trained judges; the lack of legal education in South Africa until late in the century; and the actual adoption of English law in some subjects. *The Union of South Africa* contains a chronological table of political and legal events including the dates of adoption of English law, which is described more fully in the text of the book. Despite these pressures Roman–Dutch law survived, mainly with the help of the early British judges who became learned in the Roman–Dutch law which they applied.

Use of Roman–Dutch law was formalized by Bijlage I to the Grondwert (first Annex to the Constitution) of the South African Republic of 19 September 1859 which laid down that van der Linden's *Koopmans handboeck* was the effective law book of the country and, when it failed to deal with a matter, recourse was to be had to van Leeuwen's *Roomsch Hollandsch recht* followed by Grotius's *Inleiding*.

According to A. A. Roberts' *South African legal bibliography*, 1942, the most frequently cited Roman–Dutch law authorities at that time were Justinian's *Corpus Juris Civilis*, the *Groot Placaatboek* and local laws followed by the works of Groenewegen, Grotius, van Leeuwen, Sande, Voet and the *Hollandsche consultatien*. More recently Hahlo and Kahn in *The South African legal system and its background* say that the courts rely mainly on the institutional writers, that Voet (in Gane's edition) is a 'firm favourite' and that van der Keessel's *Dictata*, Bynkershoek's *Observationes tumultuariae* and Pauw's *Observationes tumultuariae novae*, all now available in modern editions or translations, will be increasingly used.

Indigenous South African legal literature got off to a slow start, partly attributed to the non-existence of academic lawyers until late last century. The early literature was of two types: practical handbooks and translations of the Old Authorities. Gradually during this century a fully fledged legal literature of general works, such as *The introduction to South African law and legal theory*, 1980, by W. J. Hosten *et al.*, specialized works and journals, has emerged. Another feature of modern literature is the increase in books written in Afrikaans and parallel English and Afrikaans editions.

Modern South African legal literature now refers to a rich mixture of sources: Justinian's *Corpus Juris Civilis*, later commentaries, the Old Authorities, modern statutes, law reports, journals and textbooks. Roman–Dutch law is just one of the strands which make up the modern law of South Africa, although some subjects, *eg*, persons, are more heavily dependent on it than others, *eg*, procedure.

Efforts have been made since the nineteenth century to make the Old Authorities available in new editions and translations. This has had the support of both the South African Law Revision Committee and its successor, the South African Law Commission.

The modern encyclopedia, *The law of South Africa*, 1976–, refers to the old Roman law and Roman–Dutch law authorities where appropriate, as they are applied in South Africa today. It is similar in arrangement and style to Halsbury's *Laws of England*.

Of the many South African legal journals only the *Tydskrif vir Hedendaagse Romeins-Hollandse Reg* purports to concern itself exclusively with contemporary Roman–Dutch law. The *Annual Survey of South African Law,* by charting developments in different subjects, enables the application and progress of Roman–Dutch law, as one of the constituent strands of South African law, to be followed. This strand will also appear in articles in most journals. Articles on the history and development of Roman–Dutch law in general appear in journals emanating from many countries and can be traced through the sources described on p. 537.

Southern African territories

The three former British High Commission territories of Botswana (Bechuanaland), Lesotho (Basutoland) and Swaziland have 'the law for the time being in force in the Colony of the Cape of Good Hope' as their common law. However they have relied more heavily on English statute law for their development than South Africa and Zimbabwe rather than on Roman–Dutch law.

South West Africa/Namibia, a former German colony, has been administered judicially as a province of South Africa since 1919 and inevitably Roman–Dutch law plays a part.

Sri Lanka

Roman–Dutch law was introduced into Ceylon in 1658 when the maritime districts were won from the Portuguese, confirmed as the law of the land when it was ceded to the British in 1796 and extended to the whole island in 1815. Three factors influenced its application during the nineteenth century: neither Dutch nor Latin was understood by many of the European or indigenous population so that consultation of the Old Authorities was difficult; there was strong pressure to introduce English common law; and the Western systems of law were competing with existing native systems. Nevertheless Roman–Dutch law survived and remains so important a part of Sri Lankan law that it is referred to as the 'residuary law' when other sources fail. These other sources are English law, Muslim law, Kandyan law and Tesawalamai. Roman–Dutch law sources most frequently consulted are the writings of Voet, Grotius, van der Linden, van der Keessel and van Leeuwen and court decisions, because they embody the application of Roman–Dutch law principles into Sri Lankan law.

Good accounts of legal development in Sri Lanka can be found in W. I. Jennings and H. W. Tambiah's *The Dominion of Ceylon: development of its laws and constitution*, 1957 and in *The legal system of Ceylon in its historical setting*, 1972, by T. Nadaraja. The latter covers the period from 1652 to modern times concentrating on the Dutch, then British, administration of the island. The historical approach is also taken by M. H. J. van den Horst in *The Roman–Dutch law in Sri Lanka*, 1985.

Zimbabwe

A series of Orders in Council, proclamations and constitutions, which are detailed in Claire Palley's *The constitutional history and law of Southern Rhodesia 1888–1965*, 1966, laid down that, subject to provisions concerning the application of customary law, the law to be applied in the courts of Southern Rhodesia was to 'be the law in force in the Colony of the Cape of Good Hope on 10th day of June 1891 ...' This has been confirmed by the Constitution of Zimbabwe. Thus the law in force in (Southern) Rhodesia was a mixture of customary law applicable to the black population, Roman–Dutch law plus Cape legislation as of 1891 and subsequent Rhodesian legislation. Despite ties with South Africa, the (Southern) Rhodesian courts have applied Roman–Dutch common law according to their own interpretation where appropriate.

More recent influences on the Zimbabwean legal system are the expansion and formalization of local courts administering customary law and the importance of Marxist political thought. Nevertheless Roman–Dutch law remains the common law.

The country has produced little legal literature, relying heavily on that of South Africa, including the *Law of South Africa* encyclopedia.

REFERENCE SOURCES

Many of the general legal reference and bibliographical sources contain information on Roman–Dutch law. This section comments on their coverage and refers to specific Roman–Dutch law sources. It must be remembered that modern Roman–Dutch law is an integral part of the law of several countries and that therefore the reference and bibliographical sources for those countries should also be consulted.

Bibliographical sources

Guides to the literature

Guidance in the literature of old and modern Roman–Dutch law is provided in several books. Wessels' *History of the Roman–Dutch law* describes the writings of many of the old jurists in detail. While useful for purposes of understanding their authority, his bibliographical detail is poor. Two modern books, Hahlo and Kahn's *The South African legal system and its background*, 1968 and Hosten's *Introduction to South African law and legal history*, 1980 contain accounts of the development of Roman–Dutch law with generous treatment of its literature. Roberts' *South African legal bibliography*, 1942, has an excellent introduction indicating the use of the Old Authorities in nineteenth and twentieth-century South African law.

Bibliographies of bibliographies

The *Bibliography of bibliographies of developing countries*, 1981 by R. Lansky has sections on southern Africa, Sri Lanka, Guyana and Indonesia which may include Roman–Dutch law literature. For current bibliographies consult *Legal Bibliography Index* under the appropriate jurisdictional headings.

General bibliographies

As the principal countries for Roman–Dutch legal publications are South Africa and The Netherlands, the *South African National Bibliography* and Brinkman's *Cumulatieve Catalogus van Boeken* are appropriate sources for obtaining bibliographical details of modern books.

Legal bibliographies

The literature of The Netherlands up to 1800 is listed in R. Dekkers' *Bibliotheca belgica juridica*, 1951. Dutch and South African legal literature is listed in Roberts' *South African legal bibliography*.

Sections of Gilissen's *Bibliographical introduction to legal history and ethnology*, 1961–, deal with The Netherlands, Rhodesia and Nyasaland, Indonesia, British colonization in South and Central America (Guyana), and South Africa.

The Guyana section in Gilissen refers to literature on the replacement of Roman–Dutch law by English law and official publications on, and texts relating to, the Roman–Dutch law in force before 1917. The books by Shahabuddeen referred to on p. 530 also contain bibliographies.

Books on Roman–Dutch law in Indonesia are included in J. Ball's *Bibliography of material on Indonesian law in the English language*, 1981.

The footnote references in Hahlo and Kahn's *The South African legal system and its background* make an excellent bibliography on the Dutch origins of Roman–Dutch law and its establishment in South Africa. The development of nineteenth- and twentieth-century legal literature has been chronicled by A. van Blerk in two articles, 'The growth of South African legal literature' in *De Rebus Procuratoriis*, September 1977, 561–78 and 'The SA attorneys' contribution to SA legal literature' in *De Rebus Procuratoriis*, April 1983, 181–8. Current bibliographies on South African law are contained in the *Annual Survey of South African Law* and *The law in South Africa*. The bibliographies in the latter reflect the currently used literature both old and new. It is kept up to date by supplements published as *The Law in South Africa: Current law*, 1980–, which also has lists of research completed for higher degrees. JUTALEX, the computer database established by the publisher Juta, refers to books and articles on South African Law.

A bibliography of the books and periodicals of the law of Sri Lanka by J. Marikar is contained in *Colombia Law Review*, vol. 4, 1978, pp. 130–43. A good retrospective bibliography from about 1820, including many articles on Roman–Dutch law from the periodicals of Ceylon, is provided by R. Metzger in *An index to periodical articles in the laws of Ceylon*, 1972.

Periodicals

The standard indexes to periodical articles, the *Index to Legal Periodicals, Index to Foreign Legal Periodicals* and *Current Law Index* list Roman–Dutch law articles under the appropriate jurisdiction. Szladits' *Bibliography on foreign and comparative law* has a subject arrangement. Items on Roman–Dutch law can be traced under the heading Roman–Dutch law in the geographical index. Books and articles on southern African law are currently indexed in *African Law Bibliography*, 1947–.

Dictionaries

For modern Roman–Dutch law terminology in South Africa consult any of the standard South African legal dictionaries such as Claassen's *Dictionary of legal words and phrases*, 1975–7. Latin terms with their Afrikaans and English translations and references to their derivation are contained in V. G. Heimst and H. L. Gonin's *Trilingual legal dictionary/Drietalige regswoordeboek*, 1981.

Roman–Dutch legal literature abounds in abbreviations which are listed in many of the textbooks. A good list with guidance on the mode of citation is IALS's *Manual of legal citation: Part II The British Commonwealth*, 1960.

Encyclopedias

Little quick reference information on Roman–Dutch law, ancient or modern, is available either in general encyclopedias or legal ones such as the *Oxford companion to law*.

Biographical sources

The fullest source for biographical information for the Dutch jurists is Wessels' *History of the Roman–Dutch law*, several chapters of which describe the main writers of the sixteenth to eighteenth centuries with information on their careers and publications. Minimal career details precede lists of publications in Roberts' *South African legal bibliography* and Dekkers' *Bibliotheca Belgica juridica*. The latter refers to further sources, mainly in Dutch. A few Dutch jurists are included in the *Oxford Companion to Law*. Roberts also contains brief career details of South African writers and judges from 1828 to 1942. The *Dictionary of South African biography*, 1968, and the smaller *South African dictionary of national biography*, 1966 include lawyers.

Legal organizations

Die Vereniging Hugo De Groot/Society Hugo De Groot of South Africa was established in 1956 to co-ordinate research on Roman–Dutch legal history. It publishes the journal *Tydskrif vir Hedendaagse Romeins–Hollandse Reg.*

The growth of law libraries is reflected in South Africa through the Organization of South African Law Librarians (OSAR/OSALL) which publishes a *Newsletter* about law library and legal bibliography activities in South Africa.

Libraries

The major collections of Roman–Dutch law in the British Isles are concentrated in the copyright deposit libraries with other collections in the Institute of Advanced Legal Studies and Edinburgh University Library.

13. Other systems of law: II

Section 1: Religious Legal Systems

S. M. DOYLE

GENERAL WORKS

Religious laws include those legal systems which claim divine origin, the regulations made by religious bodies for the conduct of their spiritual or temporal affairs, and secular legislation governing religious activities or relating to religious groups. Many of the normal primary and secondary sources of law for a jurisdiction may contain material concerning religious matters, and in addition there are a number of works on comparative law which consider religious legal systems, such as the *International encyclopedia of comparative law*, 1971–. *Introduction to legal systems*, edited by J. D. M. Derrett, 1968, has chapters on Jewish, Islamic and Hindu law, and *Major legal systems of the world today*, by R. David and J. E. C. Brierley, 2nd edn., 1978, has sections on Muslim law and on the law of India. Both have useful select bibliographies. St. J. A. Robilliard's *Religion and the law*, 1984, studies all aspects of the law governing religious activities in Britain, while M. B. Hooker's *Legal pluralism*, 1975, is a wide-ranging study of the interaction between colonial and indigenous legal systems, including Hindu, Buddhist and Islamic law. Comparative law periodicals such as the *International and Comparative Law Quarterly*, 1952–, and the *American Journal of Comparative Law*, 1952–, are also likely sources for articles on religious law.

ROMAN CANON LAW

Primary sources

Legislation

The major source for the canon law of the Roman Catholic
Church is the *Code of canon law*, which came into force on 27
November 1983. The official and binding version is the Latin
text, *Codex iuris canonici*, 1983. A list of corrigenda to this was
published in the *Acta Apostolicae Sedis*, vol. 75, part II, appendix, and further corrections are to be expected. An English
translation has been prepared by the Canon Law Society of
Great Britiain and Ireland, in association with other bodies,
and published in 1983, followed by an index in 1984. A list of
corrigenda to the English translation has been circulated to
members of the Canon Law Society of Great Britain and
Ireland along with the Society's *Newsletter*.

From 1917 to the publication of the 1983 *Code*, the major
source was the *Codex iuris canonici* issued in 1917 as the result
of the immense task of revising and simplifying the vast mass
of historical materials. A permanent Commission for the
interpretation of canon law was set up at this time, and its
decisions are published in the *Acta Apostolicae Sedis*, 1909–, a
publication which appears once or twice a month. Papal legislation subsequent to the 1917 *Codex* and the 1983 *Code* also
appears in the *Acta Apostolicae Sedis*, as do the decisions of the
Congregations – bodies entrusted with expounding the law in
various fields. There are a number of commentaries on the
1917 *Codex*, of which the best known in English is that of T. L.
Bouscaren and A. C. Ellis, *Canon law: a text and commentary*,
3rd revised edn., 1957. This is, however, incomplete, as
several sections of the 1917 *Codex* are omitted, and others
receive only cursory treatment. *Canon law digest*, 1934–, by T.
L. Bouscaren and J. I. O'Connor, is a compilation of documents and decisions for the period subsequent to the *Codex*.
The documents are arranged in the order of the canons to
which they relate, and are in English translation where English

is not the original language. An important development between the 1917 *Codex* and the 1983 *Code* was the second Vatican Ecumenical Council, the Latin text of whose decrees was published in 1966 by the Vatican Press. Various translations are available.

It is also appropriate to mention that the Roman Catholic Church, as an international organization, may enter into legal agreements with temporal governments. Concordats and conventions up to 1954 have been collected in A. Mercati's *Raccolta di concordati*, 1954, and the texts of these agreements are also to be found in the appropriate volumes of the *Acta Apostolicae Sedis*. A study on the Holy See in international law and diplomacy is *The Holy See and the international order*, by H. E. Cardinale, 1976, which includes an appendix of documents.

Law reports

There is no rule of precedent in Roman Canon law, but the decisions of the Sacra Romana Rota are a legitimate guide to inferior courts. They are published in annual volumes, under the title *Decisiones seu Sententiae*, 1909–. For reasons of confidentiality, publication is delayed until ten years after the decisions have been made. More recently, some reports of cases have appeared in *The Jurist*, 1941–, in the *Newsletter of the Canon Law Society of Great Britain and Ireland*, 1969–and in numerous other Canon law periodicals.

Secondary sources

The *New Catholic encyclopedia*, 1967, 15 volumes, is a most useful source of information on all aspects of Roman Catholic belief and practice, though it should be borne in mind that it predates the 1983 *Code of canon law*. Among works written in response to the new code are *The new code of canon law …*, prepared by the Canon Law Society of Great Britain and Ireland, 1983 and *Light for my path: the new code of canon law for religious*, by A. Flannery and L. Collins, 1983. The first major commentary in English is *The code of canon law: a text and commentary*, edited by the American canonists J. A. Coriden, T. J. Green and D. E. Heintschel, 1985. The Canon Law Society of Great Britain and Ireland will shortly publish a practical pastoral commentary on the 1983 *Code* for priests, religious and interested lay people.

Vernacular journals which carry articles and information regarding canon law include *Studia Canonica*, 1967– , and *The Jurist*, mentioned above. The Canon Law Society of Great Britain and Ireland's *Newsletter* has fewer in-depth articles, but carries relevant news, reports of papal addresses, etc. *Catholic Lawyer*, 1955–, is a journal concerned with the ethical and theological aspects of current legal issues, aimed at the legal practitioner rather than the canonist.

Historical sources

There is a great wealth of canon law material pre-dating the *Codex* of 1917. Mediaeval canon law was based on a variety of sources which include bulls and other decrees issued by the Popes, the decretals, *ie*, rulings by Popes on questions brought to them for decision, and the decrees of church councils. In the year 1500 six major collections of these sources of canon law were brought together and issued by Jean Chappuis, of Paris, the most notable item in the collection being the *Decretum* of Gratian. Known as the *Corpus iuris canonici*, this collection became the definitive embodiment of canon law up to that date, and received the offical sanction of the Roman Catholic Church in 1580. The modern standard edition is that of E. Friedberg, published in 1879–81.

For the period following the *Corpus*, the main sources of Roman canon law are the offical acts of the Popes, the decrees of councils and the decisions of the Congregations. A. van Hove's *Prolegomena ad Codicem Iuris Canonici*, 2nd edn., 1945, is a wide-ranging and comprehensive guide to these materials. Bouscaren and O'Connor's *Digest*, already mentioned, presents the documents themselves for the years since the publication of the *Codex*.

THE LAW OF THE CHURCH OF ENGLAND

Primary sources

Legislation

Prior to the Reformation, the major sources of canon law in England were those common to the whole of western Christendom, as embodied in the *Corpus iuris canonici*, together with various enactments relating specifically to the application of canon law in England. At the Reformation, legislative authority became vested in the King in Parliament, although the old canon law remained in force so far as it was compatible with the general law of the land. Thus, much of the law of the Church of England derives its authority from statute. To some extent, however, the power of legislation was delegated to various other bodies. The Convocations, *ie*, the assemblies of clergy, were empowered, subject to certain restrictions, to enact legislative canons. The canons of 1603 have, with minor exceptions, remained in force until the present century. They have now been replaced by the canons of 1969, including those promulgated in 1964, with subsequent additions and amendments. This century has also seen further delegation of legislative authority. In 1919, the Church Assembly was empowered, subject to Parliamentary consent, to pass Measures having the force of Acts of Parliament. In 1970 the Assembly was replaced by the General Synod, which also took over the power of the Convocations to make canons.

Synodical and Church Assembly measures, and subordinate legislation enacted under them, are to be found included in the major collections of Acts of Parliament, both the official publications and commercial ones such as *Halsbury's Statutes*. A volume entitled *Church Assembly Measures Revised* corresponds to the *Statutes Revised*. They are included in *Statutes in Force* in the sections 'Church of England' and 'Church in Wales' and are thus accessible through LEXIS. The *Report of Proceedings* of the Synod is published by the Church Information Office.

Law reports

The system of ecclesiastical courts is governed by the Ecclesiastical Jurisdiction Measure, 1963, as amended, the effect of which is explained in E. G. Moore's *Introduction to English canon law*, 2nd edn., 1985, pp. 143–53. There are briefer accounts in Sir William Dale's *Law of the parish church*, 5th edn., 1975, pp. 103–12 and K. M. Macmorran and K. J. T. Elphinstone's *A Handbook for Churchwardens ...*, new edn., 1983, pp. 31–6. A more technical survey is to be found in *Halsbury's Laws of England*, 4th edn., vol. 14, 1973–, paras. 1259–372. An account of the situation prior to 1963 is to be found in the *Report* of the Archbishops' Commission on the Ecclesiastical Courts, published in 1954.

Early reports of the ecclesiastical courts may be found in various series of reports, covered by vols. 161–7 of the *English Reports*. A full listing may be found in Sweet and Maxwell's *Guide to law reports and statutes*, 4th edn., 1962. For the period 1865–75, ecclesiastical reports are to be found in the Admiralty series of the *Law Reports*, while from 1875 they are published with Probate, and subsequently with the Family Division. The ecclesiastical courts are also covered by such series as the *All England Law Reports*. An *Index of cases in the records of the Court of Arches at Lambeth Palace Library, 1660–1913*, edited by J. Houston, was published in 1972 in the British Record Society's *Index Library* series, and this series also includes many other records of early ecclesiastical courts.

Secondary sources

The title 'Ecclesiastical law' in *Halsbury's Laws of England*, 4th edn., vol. 14 constitutes a comprehensive and authoritative account of the law relating to the Church of England and to other churches in Britain, with some explanation of the historical background. Outlines of English canon law, mainly intended for the non-lawyer are Sir William Dale's *The law of the parish church* and E. G. Moore's *An introduction to English canon law*. Dale's is a concise handbook, Moore's a longer treatment. *A handbook for churchwardens and parochial churc councillors* by K. M. Macmorran and K. J. T. Elphinstone is another compact work which is well suited to the needs of lay people who require information on the legal aspects of day to day church administration. A detailed account of the past and present legislation relating to faculties (authorizations to alter a church or its furnishings), with proposals for reform, is *The continuing care of churches and cathedrals*, 1984, which is the report of the Faculty Jurisdiction Commission of the General Synod. Practitioners' works include H. W. Cripps' *A practical treatise on the law relating to the church and clergy*, 8th edn., 1937, and Sir Robert Phillimore's *Ecclesiastical law in the Church of England*, 2nd edn., 1895. The latter is an invaluable mine of information on the Church's older institutions.

An important source of information as regards the background to synodical Measures is the reports of the Synod's Legislative Committee, which is responsible for liaison with Parliament, in conjunction with an Ecclesiastical Committee of Parliament. These reports are published by HMSO as Parliamentary papers. Among publications of the Synod's Legal Advisory Committee and its predecessor, the Legal Board, are its *Opinions*, 5th edn., 1976, published in looseleaf form. The Acts and proceedings of the Convocations are published in the *Chronicle of the Convocation of Canterbury*, 1859–, and the *York Journal of Convocation*, 1874–. A compilation of these Acts and proceedings, edited by H. Riley and R. J. Graham and covering the period 1921–70 was issued in 1971.

Historical sources

A clear account of the historical development of canon law in England from the earliest times to the date of the report is *The canon law of the Church of England*, 1947, the report of the Archbishops' Commission on canon Law. The principal source for our knowledge of how canon law was applied in England during the Middle Ages is William Lyndwood's *Provinciale*, a gloss and commentary on the provincial constitutions of Canterbury, of which there are many early editions. A reprint from the translation made in 1534, edited by J. V. Bullard and H. C. Bell, was published in 1929. A comprehensive collection of documents relating to canon law in the British Isles is A. W. Haddon's *Councils and Ecclesiastical Documents relating to Great Britain and Ireland*, 3 vols., 1869–78, continued by *Councils and Synods*, 2 vols. in 4, 1964–81, edited by F. M. Powicke. These documents are in the original languages, mainly Latin; many of them are translated in *Documents illustrative of English Church history*, complied by H. Gee and W. J. Hardy, 1896.

OTHER CHRISTIAN CHURCHES

The Methodist Church and the United Reformed Church have both had legislative sanction given to their rules by the Methodist Church Union Act, 1929, and the United Reformed Church Act, 1972, but the other free churches are not statutorily constituted. Information on the law governing religious bodies other than the Church of England can be found in *Halsbury's Laws of England*, 4th edn., vol. 14; paragraphs 1386–435 deal with the free churches. Many of the free churches publish a yearbook or manual which gives some account of their structure, personnel and administrative procedures. The quinquennial *Handbook* of the General Assembly of Unitarian and Free Christian Churches is one publication of this type which includes a section of legal information. For the most part, this kind of publication is to be found recorded in general bibliographies, such as the *British National Bibliography*, 1950–.

IRELAND

Catholic Church

Ireland is covered by the general sources of Canon law, but specifically Irish rules can be found in the *Maynooth Decrees*, 1956. Since that date, the rules promulgated by individual bishops and issued to the clergy in their diocese can be found in such journals as *The Furrow*, 1950–, and the *Irish Ecclesiasti-*

cal Record, 1865–1968. They will be incorporated in the next edition of the *Maynooth Decrees*. For information on the Catholic Church in Ireland there is also the *Irish Catholic Directory*, 1838–.

The Church of Ireland, and other churches

As the Church of Ireland was disestablished in 1869, the statutes are not published in the *Public General Acts*, although the form and terminology of a Parliamentary Act are retained. Legislation is passed by the General Synod, and statutes are found as an appendix in the *Journal* of the General Synod, published annually since 1870. An index and chronological table of statutes are included. The latest edition of the *Constitution* of the Church of Ireland was published in 1978, and the *Church of Ireland handbook*, by J. L. B. Deans, revised edn., 1982, is a useful guide to the organization of the Church, as is *How the Church of Ireland is governed*, by W. G. Wilson, 1963.

As regards the Presbyterian Church, *The Code: the book of the constitution and government of the Presbyterian Church in Ireland* is published by the authority of its General Assembly. The latest edition is that of 1980, updated by looseleaf amendments. *The Minutes of the Assembly and Presbyterian Directory* is published annually.

For the Methodist Church, there is the *Manual of the laws and discipline of the Methodist Church in Ireland*, 1976. Amendments and additional laws are available in looseleaf form, and are also published in the *Minutes* of the Conference, published annually from 1840.

SCOTLAND

Primary and secondary sources

The constitution and powers of the courts of the Church of Scotland are founded on an Act of 1592, and since then legislation has appeared in the *Acts of Assembly*. In 1690, an annual issue was commenced and a volume of Acts appeared each year until 1980, known as the *Principal Acts of the General Assembly*. From 1895, the companion *Reports of the General Assembly* have been issued and in 1981 the Acts were incorporated into the *Reports* series. The standard text is J. T. Cox: *Practice and procedure in the Church of Scotland*, 6th edn., 1976. For biographical and other information, the *Church of Scotland Year Book*, first published in 1886, is very useful.

Since the formation of the Free Church of Scotland in 1843, annual *Acts of the General Assembly* have appeared. Procedure is governed by *The Practice of the Free Church of Scotland in her Several Courts*, revised edn., 1964. After the amalgamation of the United Free Church with the Church of Scotland in 1929, the United Free Church of Scotland (continuing) has issued annual *Reports*, but these do not include Acts. The Free Presbyterian Church of Scotland has issued *Reports* since 1892, but neither do they include Acts.

In 1560 Presbyterianism became the established mode of worship, but the Episcopalian movement, although suppressed on various occasions, continued to flourish. In time it became known as the Episcopal Church in Scotland, now the Scottish Episcopal Church. Various codes of canons have been issued, including P. A. Lempriere's *A Compendium of the canon law for the use of … The Scottish Episcopal Church*, 1903. The latest offical *Code* was published in 1973.

There have been many cases brought about by religious disputes, but the only important reported decisions to have been collected are to be found in *Leading ecclesiastical cases … 1849–74*, 1878. A useful source for ecclesiastical laws, cartularies and records is contained in *A legal bibliography of the British Commonwealth of Nations*, vol. 5, 1957, pp. 33–8.

Historical sources

The whole question of the history and development of both the church and church law in Scotland is a very complex one. Until the Reformation in the mid-sixteenth century, the Roman Catholic Church held sway, and the Roman canon law formed an important element in the early Scottish legal system. Subsequently, although canon law ceased to be widely studied, much of what related to family matters was absorbed into the general law. A concise outline of Canon law appears in D. M. Walker's *The Scottish legal system*, 5th edn., 1981, pp. 57–60. More details and sources may be found in some of the publications of the Stair Society, in particular vol. 1, 1936, pp. 183–92; vol. 20, 1958, pp. 69–89; and vol. 33, 1981, pp. 112–27. There are also relevant articles in the *Juridical Review*, vol. 49, 1937, pp.25–34 and [new series, vol. 2], 1957, pp. 121–37. The laws of the early church may be found in 'The statutes of the Scottish Church, 1225–1559', edited by D. Patrick, and issued as volume 54, new series, 1907, of the *Publications* of the Scottish History Society.

Canon law and the early church courts were closely linked and some Stair Society publications contain descriptive chapters, viz., vol. 1, 1936, pp. 133–62 and vol. 20, 1958, pp. 363–73, while vol. 34, 1982, is entirely devoted to *The Court of the Official in Pre-Reformation Scotland*. A brief but useful summary of ecclesiastical courts is to be found in D. M. Walker's *The Scottish legal system*, 5th edn., pp. 283–4. Much fuller information, although now dated, is in the section entitled 'Church' in the *Encyclopaedia of the laws of Scotland*, vol. 3, 1927, pp. 314–87.

What may be termed 'local' church law is dealt with in W. G. Black and J. R. Christie's *The parochial ecclesiastical law of Scotland*, 4th edn., 1928. The concluding chapter of this book deals briefly with teinds, particularly the changes brought about by the 1925 Act. An earlier work on this subject is N. Elliot's *Teinds or tithes and procedure in the Court of Teinds in Scotland*, 1893.

The Reformation in Scotland, which restored Presbyterianism, may be dated from 1560 and in that year the Church of Scotland became established. At intervals since, various secessions have occurred, the most important being the Disruption in 1843 which brought into being the Free Church of Scotland. In 1900, most Free Church members joined with the United Presbyterians to become the United Free Church of Scotland, and in 1929 this church returned to the fold of the Church of Scotland. However, in 1900 certain Free Church congregations did not join the United Free movement and continued as the Free Church ('the Wee Free' as they are nicknamed); while in 1929 some United Free churches decided to stay out of the Church of Scotland and to call themselves the United Free Church of Scotland (continuing). For the record, there are also still in existence remnants of some of the first seceders, notably the original Secession Church and the Free Presbyterian Church of Scotland. There are individual histories of each of these movements but the best account, for those concerned with the law, is F. Lyall's *Of presbyters and kings: Church and state in the law of Scotland*, 1980.

JEWISH LAW

Primary sources

The Torah

Jewish law derives from a wide variety of sources. Of primary importance is the Torah, a term used narrowly to denote the Pentateuch and laws derived from it by exegesis, though in a wider sense it refers to the entire Bible. Together with the oral law it can refer to the law as a whole. This is supplemented by tradition, regulations and custom. The oldest important compilation of Jewish law is the Mishnah of Rabbi Judah ha-Nasi, written about AD 200, a modern English translation of which is that of H. Danby, 1933. To this was added, in course of time, the Gemara, or commentary of the Palestinian and Babylonian scholars. The Mishnah and Gemara combined constitute the Talmud. An English translation of the Babylonian Talmud, edited by I. Epstein has been published in 35 volumes, 1935–48, and a translation of the Palestinian Talmud by J. Neusner is in progress of publication (*The Talmud of the land of Israel*, 1982–). *The student's guide through the Talmud*, by Z. H. Chajes, 1960, and *Introduction to the Talmud and Midrash*, by H. L. Strack, 1931, are valuable introductions to this vast body of material. During the Middle Ages, further reduction of the legal material deriving from the Talmud became necessary, and a number of codes were compiled, notably the *Mishneh Torah* of Moses Maimonides, of which an English translation is in process of publication (1949–), and the *Shulhan 'Arukh* of Joseph Caro, to which glosses were added by Moses Isserles. *An introduction to the code of Maimonides*, by I. Twersky, was published in 1980.

Responsa

A further important form of Jewish legal literature is the responsa – answers by rabbis to questions submitted to them. For English readers, S. B. Freehof's *The responsa literature*, 1955, is a useful introduction to the field, while the same author's *A treasury of responsa* is a brief illustrative selection from the total literature. Examples of lenient responsa of individual rabbis are Freehof's *Reform responsa*, 1960, and I. Klein's *Responsa and Halakhic studies*, 1975. Notes on important responsa are to be found in the *Jewish Law Annual* (1978–).

Secondary sources

Encyclopedias

The *Encyclopaedia Judaica*, 16 vols., 1972, is an indispensable work for the study of Jewish culture, with extensive articles and valuable bibliographies on legal topics. The specifically legal articles were re-published in 1975 as *The principles of Jewish law*, edited by M. Elon. Less extensive works, such as *The new standard Jewish encyclopedia*, 1970, by C. Roth and G. Wigoder, are useful for explaining Jewish terminology, but do not treat legal matters in the same depth. A specialized Talmudic encyclopedia began publication at the Hebrew University of Jerusalem in 1953, and an English translation of this is *Encyclopedia Talmudica*, edited by I. Epstein and H. Freedman (1969–).

Monographs

Recent years have seen a number of works on the attitude of Jewish law towards modern social developments. *Modern medicine and Jewish law*, by F. Rosner, 1972, and *Judaism and Healing: Halakhic perspectives*, by J. D. Bleich, 1981, both look at the ethical problems raised by modern medical techniques, while *Jewish woman in Jewish law*, by M. Meiselman, 1978, considers feminism from a Jewish viewpoint. A series which includes several studies of this type is Ktav's *Library of Jewish law and ethics*.

Periodicals

An essential periodical for the study of law in Israel, including its religious aspects is *Israel Law Review*, 1966–, which carries notes on cases and book reviews as well as articles such as the series by M. Elon entitled 'The sources and nature of Jewish law' which appeared in vols. 2–4. The *Jewish Law Annual* commenced publication in 1978, and includes essays, a survey of recent literature and current information such as notes on responsa and cases. *Diné Israel* was published from 1969 to 1976; largely in Hebrew, it included some English language material. A more general publication which carries articles on legal topics from time to time is the *Journal of Jewish Studies*, 1948–.

Historical sources

The fundamental sources of Jewish law have already been described, and the consideration of Jewish law in its historical context is of course a matter of as much interest to the historian and theologian as to the lawyer. A work which includes a useful bibliography is *The study of ancient Judaism*, edited by J. Neusner, 1981, while two collections of essays edited by B. S. Jackson, *Essays in Jewish and comparative legal history*, 1975, and *Jewish law in legal history and the modern world*, 1980, are particularly interesting for their discussion of the relationship between Jewish law and other systems.

Jewish law under various jurisdictions

For information on the legal status of the Jews in England at the present day, the section on ecclesiastical law, paras. 1423–32 in *Halsbury's Laws of England* should be consulted, while *Jews and the English law*, by H. S. Q. Henriques, 1908, is an interesting, if not up to date, historical treatment of the topic. The extent to which Jewish law has been recognized by the American legal system is discussed in 'Jewish law in America', by B. J. Meislin, included in *Jewish law in legal history and the modern world*, pp. 147–73, while a more extended earlier study by the same author is *Jewish law in American Tribunals*, 1976.

Since the establishment of the state of Israel, Jewish legal thought has had an extensive influence on the development of the Israeli legal system, in which the rabbinic courts have jurisdiction to administer Jewish religious law in certain fields. *Religious law in the Israeli legal system*, by I. Englard, 1975, is a collection of articles, originally published in the journal *Mishpatim*, on the position of religious law in Israel. An account of the work of the rabbinic courts is to be found in an article by M. Chigier, entitled 'The rabbinical courts in the state of Israel' in the *Israel Law Review*, vol. 2, no. 2, 1967, pp. 147–81. Also concerned with the jurisdiction of the courts is volume 1 of *Jewish jurisprudence: its sources and modern applications*, by E. B. Quint and N. S. Hecht, 1980.

INDIAN RELIGIOUS LAW

Primary sources

Legislation and law reports

The history of Indian law falls into three main periods – the pre-British, the period of British administration and the period following independence. In all these phases it has been recognized by the ruling powers that, in certain areas, such as family law, adherents of different religions should be allowed to follow their appropriate personal law, based on religious principles. A good account of this situation is to be found in D. Pearl's *Interpersonal conflict of laws in India, Pakistan and Bangladesh*, 1981.

During the British administration of India, the Hindu law, based on ancient texts, became modified by the application of British judicial principles, including precedent, and by the operation of statutes. Since independence in 1947, much of this Anglo-Hindu law has been replaced by a series of enactments known as the Hindu Code. Many commentaries on the Hindu Code have been published, including that annexed to Sir Dinshah F. Mulla's *Principles of Hindu law*, 15th edn., 1982, and T. Mahmood's *Hindu law*, 1981. For a fuller listing of primary materials for Indian law than is possible here, reference should be made to H. C. Jain's *Indian legal materials: a bibliographical guide*, 1970.

Secondary sources

In addition to numerous works on specific aspects of Hindu law, such as marriage, there are many general treatises. Prominent titles include Sir Dinshah F. Mulla's treatise mentioned above, N. R. Raghavachariar's *Hindu Law: principles and precedents*, 7th edn., 1980, and N. Diwan's more concise *Modern Hindu law*, 5th edn., 1981. The numerous writings of the distinguished scholar J. D. M. Derrett cover aspects of Hindu law. *An introduction to legal systems*, edited by this author, 1968, and *Major legal systems in the world today*, by R. David and J. E. C. Brierley, 2nd edn., 1978, both have sections on the law of India which provide good introductory treatments. For the many periodicals which cover Hindu law published in India, reference must again be made to Jain's bibliography, while a British journal which carries articles on the topic is the *Bulletin of the School of Oriental and African Studies* at London University, 1917–.

Ancient Hindu law

Hindu law derives ultimately from a large number of very ancient texts known as *śrutis* – that which is revealed – and *smritis* – that which is remembered. The *śrutis*, which include the four *vedas* and the *upanishads*, treat a wide variety of religious and social topics in addition to the legal material that they contain. Among the *smritis*, however, is a class of works dealing specifically with *dharma* – righteousness – the *dharma-śāstras*. The term *dharmaśāstra* is also used to denote the 'science of righteousness' itself. The most important of the *dharmaśāstras* include those known by the names of Manu, Yājñavalkya and Nārada. Springing from the *dharmaśāstras* are numerous commentaries and digests known as *nibandhas*. Leading works in this class are the *Dáyabhága*, a digest by Jimūtavāhana, which gives its name to the school general in Bengal, and the *Mitāksharā*, a commentary on Yājñavalkya by Vijñaneśvara, from which the other major school of Hindu law derives its name. The definitive work on the fundamental sources of Hindu law is P. V. Kane's *History of Dharmaśāstra*, 1930–62, a second edition of which was begun in 1968. F. Lingat's *The classical law of India*, 1973, is a shorter study which includes a bibliography.

Other religious groups

Under the Hindu Code, certain other groups, including Sikhs and Jains, are regarded as Hindus and are subject to Hindu law. The Code, however, gives legal recognition to customary usages in some circumstances, and to this extent the law applicable to these groups may differ from the norm. As regards the position of Sikhs in Britain, the *Sikh Courier*, 1960–, occasionally carries articles relating to the social and legal status of this group.

ISLAMIC LAW

Primary sources

The first sources of Islamic law – the sharī'a – is, of course, the Koran, of which M. W. Pickthall's *The Meaning of the Glorious Koran*, 1930, is a widely accepted English translation. But there is, in fact, very little in the Koran which is directly legal in character. This has led to considerable emphasis on the second source, the *sunna*, or practice of the Prophet as recorded in the *aḥādīth*, or traditions of his actions and words. Of the numerous collections of these traditions, those of Bukhārī, Muslim, Ibn Māja, Abū Dāwūd, Tirmidhī and Nasā'ī are regarded as particularly authoritative. M. Z. Siddiqi's *Hadith Literature*, 1961, is a study of this group of sources from an orthodox Muslim viewpoint. The law also derives from ijmā' or the consensus of learned opinion, and *qiyās*, or analogical deduction from these sources.

This fourfold basis has been subject to many centuries of learned study and commentary, and each particular school has its own authoritative books of *fiqh*, or legal science. The four main schools are the Ḥanafī, Mālikī, Shāfī'ī and Ḥanbalī, and there are numerous groups which are generally regarded as heterodox. Three texts of particular importance on the Indian subcontinent are the *Hedāya* and the *Fatāwa 'Ālamgīrī* (both Ḥanafī) and the *Sharā'i al-Islam*, which is a major text of the Ithnā 'Asharī Shiites. The former has been translated by C. H. Hamilton, while the two latter form the basis of volumes 1 and 2 respectively of N. B. F. Baillie's *Digest of Moohummudan law*, 1869–75, 2 vols., reprinted 1965.

According to traditional Islamic legal theory, no new interpretation of the sources of law has been possible since the 'closing of the gate of interpretation' in the tenth Christian century. In the Indian subcontinent, however, the administration of Islamic law by a British judiciary brought about the development of an Anglo-Muhammadan system in the same way that the Anglo-Hindu law already mentioned came into being. As with Anglo-Hindu law, reference should be made to Jain's bibliography for a full list of legislation and reports. In other Islamic countries the last century has seen a very extensive move towards using legislation and other expedients to meet changed social conditions. Many contemporary laws in the Middle East have been published in Graham and Trotman's *Business Laws Series*.

Secondary sources

The *Encyclopaedia of Islam*, 2nd edn., 1954–, is an essential reference tool for Islamic studies, with numerous articles on legal topics. *The international encyclopedia of comparative law*, 1971–, chapter 1, provides general surveys of the legal systems of a number of Islamic countries, and the annual survey *The Middle East and North Africa* also includes brief notes on the judicial systems of the countries in that area. Treatises on Islamic law as practised on the Indian subcontinent include Sir Dinshah F. Mulla's *Principles of Mohomedan law*, 18th edn., 1977, a leading practitioner's book, and A. A. A. Fyzee's *Outlines of Mohammadan law*, 5th edn., 1985, an excellent introduction for students. A concise treatment is *The Muslim law of India*, by T. Mahmood, 2nd edn., 1982. D. Pearl's *A textbook of Muslim law*, 2nd edn., 1985, concentrates on family laws in the Indian subcontinent but also gives some consideration to other Muslim countries. It includes a useful bibliography and an appendix of select legislation. K. Hodkinson's *Muslim family law: a sourcebook*, 1984, provides extracts of many of the important recent cases from India and Pakistan. There is also an extensive bibliography.

A study of movement towards modernization of legal systems throughout the Islamic world is J. N. D. Anderson's *Law reform in the Muslim world*, 1976, while *An introduction to business law in the Middle East*, edited by B. Russell, 1975, includes a useful compact survey of the historical development of Middle Eastern legal systems and the process of codification. Much more detailed is H. J. Liebesny's *The law of the Near and Middle East: readings, cases and materials*, 1975. This work is in the form of readings accompanied by comment and includes a most useful list of suggestions for further reading.

Commercial law in the Gulf States, by N. J. Coulson, 1984, is an explanation of the fundamental principles of Shari'a law with reference to contract and business transactions, and is aimed specifically at western businessmen and lawyers. *Islamic Law in the contemporary world*, by S. H. Amin, 1985, is especially useful for its select bibliography of materials in European languages and its substantial glossary. The same author's *Middle East legal systems*, 1985, is an invaluable country by country survey of the legal systems of the Muslim nations of the Middle East. It includes Afghanistan, but does not extend to Africa, apart from the Sudan. For each country it gives an account of the development of the legal system, sources of law and present position, with a substantial bibliography.

Periodicals

General orientalist periodicals which carry articles on legal topics include *Muslim World*, 1911– , and the *Bulletin of the School of Oriental and African Studies at London University*, first published in 1917. Reference can also be made to the *Islamic and Comparative Law Quarterly*, 1981– . The standard index of articles in periodicals and other composite works concerned with Islamic studies is *Index Islamicus*, 1958–.

Historical sources

A detailed study of the first two centuries' development is J. Schacht's *The origins of Muhammadan jurisprudence*, 1950, reprinted 1979. The same author's *An introduction to Islamic law*, 1964, reprinted 1982, has a historical section on Sunnī (orthodox) law, and a systematic section on the law of the Ḥanafī school. The bibliography is very extensive and includes material relating to all schools. An excellent account of the historical development of Islamic law is N. J. Coulson's *A history of Islamic law*, 1964, reprinted 1978. T. Mahmood *Muslim personal law: the role of the state in the subcontinent*, 1979, is a survey of the constitutional and legal status of Muslim personal law in India from 1772 to 1976.

REFERENCE SOURCES

Bibliographies

General and religious bibliographies

Specialist bibliographies on religious law are not numerous, and it is often necessary to turn to more general legal or religious publications in order to find the material that one requires. In the fields of Roman canon law, Jewish law, Hindu law and Muslim law a great deal of material is of course published abroad, and the most comprehensive bibliography is *A bibliography on foreign and comparative law books ... in English*, edited by C. Szladite, 1955– , which gives excellent coverage both of monographs and articles in journals and other composite works. This very extensiveness, however, means that there is sometimes a delay before items are recorded.

The gap between publication of a work and its appearance in such a comprehensive bibliography is bridged, at least to some extent, by periodical publications. For Roman canon law the Canon Law Society of Great Britain and Ireland's *Newsletter*, 1969–, *Ephemerides Theologicae Lovanienses*, issued by the Catholic University of Louvain, 1924–, and the *Jurist*, 1941–, are all examples of publications which carry reviews and lists of new works as they appear. As regards the law of the Church of England, the *British National Bibliography*, 1950–, is probably the best source of information. For Jewish, Hindu and Muslim law, general journals with useful bibliographical coverage include the *Journal of Jewish Studies*, 1948–, which carries short reviews, the *Bulletin of the School of Oriental and African Studies*, 1917–, which has extensive reviews of new publications, and *Muslim World*, 1911–, which has book reviews, a list of books received, and a worldwide survey of periodical contents in classified arrangement.

In some cases there are bibliographies concerned primarily with a religion or with a geographical area which include legal topics. *Religious Books and Serials in Print*, 1978– has indexes to sacred works, subjects, authors and titles. An American publication, it is largely Christian and Jewish in coverage. Bibliographies on Anglo-Jewish relations and the position of the Jews in Britain include *Magna bibliotheca Anglo-Judaica*, edited by C. Roth, 1937, and its successors, R. P. Lehmann's *Nova bibliotheca Anglo-Judaica*, 1961, and the same author's *Anglo-Jewish bibliography*, 1973, all published by the Jewish Historical Society of England. A valuable short essay on the bibliography of Islamic law, by J. D. Latham, is to be found on pp. 84–92 of *Middle East and Islam: a bibliographical introduction*, edited by D. Grimwood-Jones, 1979. A further short essay on the bibliography of legal institutions of the Indian subcontinent and Sri Lanka, by J. D. M. Derrett, is included in *South Asian Bibliography*, edited by J. D. Pearson, 1979, pp. 209–11.

Legal bibliographies

Turning to specifically legal bibliographies, a wide-ranging and comprehensive guide to the earlier canon law materials is A. van Hove's *Prolegomena ad codicem iuris canonici*, 2nd edn., 1945. For Israel, E. Livneh's *Israel legal bibliography*, 1963 with its 1965 supplement has little on specifically religious law, but is useful with regard to the Israeli legal system in general. Z. W. Falk's *Current bibliography of Hebrew law and allied subjects*, 1966–9, was absorbed into *Diné Israel*, 1969–76. J. R. Wegner's *A bibliography of Israel law in English and other European languages*, 1972, includes a short but helpful section on religious law, which covers not only Jewish law, but Christian, Druze and Muslim law in Israel. This work is continued by *A bibliography of Israel law in English and other European languages, 1972–79*, compiled by J. D. Wilkenfeld, 1979. Also informative for Israeli law is an article entitled 'Guide to Israel legal bibliography', by E. M. Snyder, in *Law Library Journal*, vol. 70, no. 1, 1977, pp. 14–27. For India, a comprehensive bibliography, including reports, statutes and treatises is H. C. Jain's *Indian legal materials: a bibliographical guide*, 1970, while on Islamic law 'The law in the Near and Middle East', by I. Azzam in the *Law Library Journal*, vol. 57, no. 3, 1964, pp. 234–40 and 'Islamic law bibliography' by J. Makdisi, in *Law Library Journal* vol 78, 1986, pp. 103–89 are of great assistance.

Library catalogues

Published catalogues of major libraries are often an important source of bibliographical information. An extensive collection on Roman canon law is recorded in *The canon law collection of the Library of Congress* ..., compiled by D. C. Ferreira-Ibarra, 1981. It is arranged in classified order with name and subject indexes. An indispensable tool for in-depth study of other systems is the *Library Catalogue* of the School of Oriental and African Studies at London University, published in 22 volumes in 1963 and kept up to date by supplements. Another major bibliography of Asian materials is D. E. Hall's *Union catalogue of Asian publications*, 1971, 4 volumes. For historical aspects of Indian religious law there is the *Catalogue* of the India Office Library, 1888, with its supplements, while the rich oriental collections of the British Library's Department of Oriental Manuscripts and Printed Books are described in lists such as A. G. Ellis's *Catalogue of Arabic printed books in the British Museum*, 1894, with supplements. Legal union lists of materials include the *Union list of legal periodicals*, 4th edn., 1978, which records locations for those legal periodicals which have a religious slant, such as *Catholic Lawyer*, but excludes items not primarily concerned with law. Primary sources for Commonwealth countries are listed in *Union list of Commonwealth and South African law*, 2nd edn., 1963.

Periodicals

Directories

A listing of serial titles in Israeli law is to be found in R. Tronik's *Israeli periodicals and serials in English and other European languages*, 1974, which includes legislation. General directories of periodicals, such as *Ulrich's International Periodicals Directory*, 1932–, are also useful in tracking down publication information for relevant serials. Several of these directories are accessible through DIALOG.

Indexes and abstracts

For information on periodical articles, *A bibliography on foreign and comparative law books* ... is the most comprehensive source. *Index to Legal Periodicals*, 1908–, *Index to Foreign Legal Periodicals*, 1960–, and *Current Law Index*, 1980–, have some material on Christian ecclesiastical law, but are very limited in their coverage of other religious systems. *Index to Commonwealth Legal Periodicals*, 1981–, on the other hand has good coverage of Hindu and Islamic as well as Christian material.

Two specifically religious indexes which may be useful for finding material on religious law are *Religion Index One: periodicals*, 1953–, and *Religion Index Two: multi-author works*, 1978–. From 1975 the former has included abstracts of nearly half the items that it records. A retrospective bibliography of periodical articles on Roman canon law published in the years 1918–34, compiled by G. Moschetti, appears in volume 14 of *Apollinaris*, 1941, pp. 121–45. There is also an abstracting service for Roman canon law, *Canon Law Abstracts*, 1959–, which appears half-yearly and provides abstracts in English of articles in both English and foreign language periodicals.

Institutions with an oriental interest may also hold *Index to Indian Legal Periodicals*, 1963–, and *Index Islamicus*, 1958–. Since 1976 the latter has not only indexed periodicals and composite works, but also includes books. Coverage is wide-ranging and picks up items in publications not obviously of oriental interest such as the *American Journal of International Law*.

Other bibliographical aids

For items in Festschriften and other composite works *Index to legal essays*, 1983, may be consulted. Although its references to religious law are not very numerous, it does pick up some items not recorded elsewhere.

Also worth mentioning is a specialized computerized database for Jewish responsa literature, maintained jointly by the Weizmann Institute of Science and Bar-Ilan University in

Israel. A full description of this by Y. Choueka and others is to be found in *Legal and legislative information processing*, edited by B. K. Eres, 1980, pp. 261–85.

Dictionaries and encyclopedias

There are few specialist dictionaries in the field of religious law, although one such work, in French, for Roman canon law is R. Naz's *Dictionnaire du droit canonique*, 7 vols., 1935. For information on the law of the Church of England it is worth remembering that the earlier works such as Cowell's *Interpreter*, 1607, and Jacob's *New-law dictionary*, 1729, often have entries for historic terms not to be found in more recent works. As regards Hindu law, an interesting though out of date publication is H. H. Wilson's *A glossary of judicial and revenue terms ... of British India ...*, 1855. Most other dictionaries of oriental law require a knowledge of the script, but two works which are worth mentioning for their specialist content, even though they are intended for those with a knowledge of Arabic are H. S. Faruqi's compilation *Faruqi's law dictionary*, 1972, and I. al-Wahab's *Law dictionary: English–Arabic: Arabic–English*, 1972. The glossary of S. H. Amin's *Islamic Law in the contemporary world*, 1985, may also be useful.

General dictionaries of religion which have relevant material include *The Oxford Dictionary of the Christian Church*, 2nd edn., edited by F. L. Cross and E. A. Livingstone, 1974, which is especially useful for its biographical entries and bibliographies. For non-Christian religions there are works such as S. G. F. Brandon's *Dictionary of comparative religion*, 1970, and G. Parrinder's *Dictionary of non-Christian religions*, 1971. A specialized work on Indian religion is M. and J. Stutley's *Dictionary of Hinduism*, 1977.

The *New Encyclopaedia Britannica*, 30 vols., 1980, has substantial articles on Roman and Anglican canon law, both with a largely historical approach. Islamic and Indian law are treated more briefly, while material on Jewish law is dispersed under a variety of headings. The *Encyclopaedia Britannica* is available online through Mead Data International's NEXIS service. *Chambers' Encyclopaedia*, new edn., 1950, unlike the

Britannica, has an extensive section on Jewish law. It also includes material on canon law, the Church of England, Hindu law and Mohammedan law.

The *New Catholic Encyclopedia*, 15 vols., 1967, is an invaluable source of information on all aspects of Roman Catholic doctrine, practice and terminology. It also has helpful articles on Islam, Hinduism and other religions. It should, however, be remembered that, like many of the publications mentioned in this section, it pre-dates the current *Code of canon law*. The *Encyclopaedia Judaica*, 16 vols., 1972, is extremely useful with regard to Jewish law and affairs. It has brief multilingual bibliographies and includes an extensive section on the legal system of Israel. There are also a number of shorter works such as *The new standard Jewish Encyclopedia*, 1970, by C. Roth and G. Wigoder, which provides a helpful introduction to Jewish culture, but does not provide bibliographies and is less informative on specifically legal questions. A specialist encyclopedia on Jewish law is the Hebrew *Ensiqlopediah Talmudit*, 1953, of which an English translation entitled *Encyclopedia Talmudica* is in progress, 1969–. B. Walker's *Hindu World: an encyclopedic survey of Hinduism*, 1968, 2 vols., includes bibliographies and has a useful article on law on pp. 587–92. For Islamic studies the standard work is the *Encyclopaedia of Islam*, new edn., 1960–. Entry is under Arabic terms, but there are some English cross-references. Articles on religion and law from the first edition were re-issued as the *Shorter Encyclopaedia of Islam*, 1953. A rather different slant on a number of issues important to religious law, such as abortion, is to be found in the *Encyclopedia of bioethics*, edited by W. T. Reich, 4 vols., 1978.

Among encyclopedic works of a specifically legal nature, *Halsbury's Laws of England* is an essential source as regards the law of the Church of England. Volume 1 of the *International encyclopedia of comparative law*, 1971–, has very informative introductions to the legal systems of various countries which follow religious law in whole or part, and there is also valuable information on the religious aspects of family law in volume 4, Chapter 11. D. M. Walker's *Oxford companion to law*, 1980, also includes religious legal systems. The article on canon law comprises an extensive historical survey and makes mention of developments in England, Scotland and the United States. It also touches on the canon law of the Eastern Church. There are shorter articles under the headings 'Ecclesiastical law', 'Hindu law', and 'Jewish law'. Further information is to be found under such headings as 'Faculty' and 'Consistory Court'.

Biographical sources

For biographies of the major contributors to the development of Roman canon law, reference should be made to the *New Catholic Encyclopedia*. *Studia Canonica* includes biographical notices of contributors, while the *Catholic Directory*, 1837–, gives names and addresses of priests in England and Wales. The lives of significant figures in the history of the Church of England are recorded in such general biographical sources as the *Dictionary of National Biography*, 1885–, while *Crockford's Clerical Directory*, 1858–, has biographical information on priests of the Church of England, and the Welsh, Scottish Episcopal, Irish and overseas churches. The *Church of England Year Book*, 1963–, includes brief biographies of Synod members, senior clergy and some Synod and Lambeth Palace staff. G. D. Squibb's *Doctors Commons*, 1977, includes biographical notices of a large number of the practitioners in the ecclesiastical courts from the late fifteenth to the mid-nineteenth century. The *Jewish Year Book*, 1896–, also has a 'who's who' section giving brief biographies. In connection with the law of India, there is *India Who's Who*, a biographical dictionary of prominent figures in contemporary India. It has a classified arrangement, the legal section being divided into judiciary and practitioners. For historical biographies there is the Indian *Dictionary of National Biography*, 1972–4, while lives of administrative and legal figures of the British Empire are recorded in C. E. Buckland's *Dictionary of Indian Biography*, 1906.

FURTHER READING

GENERAL WORKS

David, R. and Brierley, J. E. C. *Major legal systems in the world today*, 2nd edn., 1978.
Derrett, J. D. M. *An introduction to legal systems*, 1968.
Hooker, M. B. *Legal pluralism*, 1975.
Robilliard, St. J. A. *Religion and the law*, 1984.

CHRISTIAN LAWS

Roman canon law

Cardinale, H. E. *The Holy See and the international order*, 1976.
Code of canon law, 1983.
Coriden, J. A., Green, T. A. and Heintschel, D. E. *The code of canon law: a text and commentary*, 1985.

The law of the Church of England

Dale, Sir William. *The law of the parish church*, 5th edn., 1975.
Halsbury's Laws of England, 4th edn., 1973– vol. 14, .
Macmorran, K. M. and Elphinstone, K. J. T. *A handbook for church-wardens and parochial church councillors*, 1983.

Ireland

Church of Ireland Handbook, Deans, J. L. B. (ed.) rev. edn., 1982.
The Furrow, 1950–.
Methodist Church in Ireland, *Manual of the laws and discipline*, 1976.
Presbyterian Church in Ireland, *The Code: the book of the constitution and government*, 1980.

Scotland

Cox, J. T. *Practice and procedure in the Church of Scotland*, 6th edn., 1976.

JEWISH LAW

Chajes, Z. H. *The student's guide through the Talmud*, 1960.
Elon, M. 'The sources and nature of Jewish law', *Israel Law Review*, vol. 2, 1967, pp. 516–65; vol. 3, 1968, pp. 88–126, 416–57; vol. 4, 1969, pp. 80–140.
Englard, I. *Religious law in the Israel legal system*, 1975.
Strack, H. L. *Introduction to the Talmud and Midrash*, 1969.

INDIAN RELIGIOUS LAW

Kane, P. V. *History of Dharmaśāstra*, 5 vols. in 8, 1930–62.
Lingat, R. *The classical law of India*, 1973.
Mulla, Sir D. F. *Principles of Hindu Law*, 15th edn., 1982.
Pearl, D. S. *Interpersonal conflict of laws in India, Pakistan and Bangladesh*, 1981.

ISLAMIC LAW

Amin, S. H. *Middle East legal systems*, 1985.
Coulson, N. J. *Commercial law in the Gulf States*, 1984.
Coulson, N. J. *A history of Islamic Law*, 1964.
Fyzee, A. A. A. *Outlines of Mohammadan law*, 5th edn., 1984.
Hodkinson, K. *Muslim family law: a sourcebook*, 1984.
Liebesny, H. J. *The law of the Near and Middle East*, 1975.
Mahmood, T. *Muslim personal law: the role of the state in the subcontinent*, 1979.
Pearl, D. S. *A textbook of Muslim law*, 2nd edn., 1985.
Schacht, J. *An introduction to Islamic law*, 1964.

BIBLIOGRAPHIES

Azzam, I. 'The law in the near and middle east: basic sources in English', *Law Library Journal*, vol. 57, 1964, pp. 234–40.
Bibliography on foreign and comparative law books and articles in English, 1955–.
Hove, A. van *Prolegomena ad Codicem iuris canonici*, edn. 2, 1945.
Jain, H. C. *Indian legal materials: a bibliographical guide*, 1970.
School of Oriental and African Studies, Library, *Catalogue*, 1963–

Snyder, E. M. 'Guide to Israel legal bibliography', *Law Library Journal*, vol. 70, 1977, pp. 14–27.

PERIODICALS

Canon Law Abstracts, 1959–.
Index Islamicus, 1958–.
Index to Indian Legal Periodicals, 1963–.
Ulrich's International Periodicals Directory, 1932–.

DICTIONARIES AND ENCYCLOPEDIAS

Catholic University of America, *New Catholic encyclopedia*, 1967, 15 vols.
Encyclopaedia Judaica, 1972, 16 vols.
Encyclopaedia of Islam, 2nd edn., 1954–.
International encyclopedia of comparative law, 1971–.
Walker, D. M. *Oxford companion to law*, 1980.

Section 2: Socialist Legal Systems

J. BRINE

INTRODUCTION

The following countries may be considered to have socialist legal systems: the USSR; Albania, Bulgaria, Czechoslovakia, German Democratic Republic, Hungary, Poland, Romania and Yugoslavia; Cuba; China; Mongolia, North Korea, Vietnam and Kampuchea.

In view of the USSR's status as a world superpower, and its importance in comparative studies in the West, this note on socialist legal systems will concentrate on the USSR, giving guidance on other socialist states where possible. Priority will be given to English-language sources.

PRIMARY SOURCES

Concise and authoritative articles on sources of law in all the socialist legal systems can be found in the entries for each country in the national reports section of the *International Encyclopaedia of comparative law*.

Constitutions

The socialist legal systems are each based on a written constitution. The constitutions as of the mid-1960s for all the socialist states are conveniently assembled in *Constitutions of the communist party states*, edited by Jan F. Triska, 1969, which also includes the texts of constitutions no longer in force at the time of compilation. For constitutions currently in force, *Constitutions of the communist world*, edited by William B. Simons, 1980, should be consulted. The 1977–8 constitutions of the USSR and its constituent union republics are available in *The Constitutions of the USSR and the Union Republics*, edited by F. J. M. Feldbrugge, 1979; this collection also includes the 1936 USSR constitution. The 1977–8 constitutions for the USSR, the union republics and the autonomous republics can be found in the 'Constitutions' section of Butler's *Collected legislation* ... (see below).

Legislative system

There are a number of features common to the legislative systems of the socialist countries. These include:

a) An elected national assembly, which is in theory the supreme organ of state power. It may be unicameral or bicameral. Generally it meets for just two or three sessions a year, each session lasting only a few days. This assembly passes laws, ratifies legislation enacted by its presidium between sessions, and hears reports from ministers.

b) A presidium, elected by the national assembly and accountable to it, which carries out its business between sessions and can enact legislation which is later ratified by the national assembly.

c) A Council of Ministers, elected by the national assembly, and, in theory, responsible to it. The Council of Ministers issues various types of subordinate legislation relating to matters within its jurisdiction, which is usually very broad. Its enactments do not require ratification by the national assembly.

d) Individual ministries, interdepartmental agencies etc. which enact ordinances and regulations binding upon their subordinate agencies.

e) In several socialist states which are federal (*eg*, USSR Yugoslavia, Czechoslovakia) certain powers are devolved to the legislatures, councils of ministers etc. of the constituent republics.

f) There are in addition various levels of local government agencies which enact ordinances etc. for their locality.

g) In all the socialist states, the work of the legislature and the organs of government is guided by the Communist Party, which does not itself enact legislation or govern the country. The relationship between the Soviet Communist Party and the legal system is described in Chapter 9 of William E. Butler's textbook *Soviet law*, 1983; the same principles apply to the other socialist states. While Communist Party documents are of immense importance in understanding how socialist states are run, they are not of course legislation. Details of post-war Soviet and Eastern European party documents are available in the relevant country chapters of *Official publications of the Soviet Union and Eastern Europe, 1945–80*, edited by Gregory Walker, 1982.

h) In all the socialist states, much legislation is not published in the open press, but is distributed on a 'need to know' basis to the appropriate agencies. This issue is discussed more fully in D. A. Loeber's article: 'Legal rules "for internal use only"' in *International and Comparative Law Quarterly*, vol. 19, 1970, pp. 70–94; he compares the USSR and the GDR with the USA and several West European countries.

The relationship of the Soviet legal system to that of the other socialist states is analysed fully in John N. Hazard's *Communists and their law*, 1968. A very detailed country by country study of the impact of the USSR on the legal systems of the countries of Eastern Europe is provided in *Government, law and courts in the Soviet Union and Eastern Europe*, edited by Vladimir Gsovski and Kazimierz Grzybowski, 1959.

Sources of legislation

This section deals with the USSR alone. For post-war legislation in Eastern Europe, guidance will be found in the relevant sections of *Official publications of the Soviet Union and Eastern Europe*, 1982. For Mongolia, consult William E. Butler's *The Mongolian legal system*, 1982, which includes a bibliography and texts.

Any account of the sources of Soviet law is complicated by

the complex and often unclear hierarchical relationships between the different types of legislative act. The confusion extends to terminology, with over 40 different terms being applied to legislative acts. The different types of legislative acts, and the terminological problems, are dealt with as fully and clearly as possible by Professor Butler on pp. 39–46 of *Soviet law*, 1983. However, one important concept in the Soviet classification of legislative acts should be noted here. This is the division of legislative acts into 'normative' Acts, which are those setting out rules of conduct of general significance, and 'non-normative' acts, which are those having a purely local or personal significance, such as edicts on changes in territorial boundaries, the award of medals, promotions and dismissals of government personnel.

The USSR Supreme Soviet – its national assembly – publishes the proceedings of each of its sessions as a *Stenograficheskii otchet*. It also publishes a weekly gazette, the *Vedomosti Verkhovnogo soveta SSSR*, which contains all the legislation enacted by the Supreme Soviet during its sessions (but not speeches and reports made during the session), and the edicts etc. of the Presidium of the Supreme Soviet passed between sessions of the Supreme Soviet. Major speeches to the Supreme Soviet, and important new legislative acts, are also published in the newspapers, notably *Izvestiia*, which is the newspaper of the Supreme Soviet and the government of the USSR (as opposed to *Pravda*, which is the organ of the Central Committee of the Communist Party of the Soviet Union).

The ordinances, decrees etc. of the USSR Council of Ministers are published in the *Sobranie postanovlenii pravitel'stva SSSR*, which appears every ten to fourteen days. Certain ministries and interdepartmental agencies have their own bulletins of legislation, which are available for export; these include the USSR Ministry of Higher and Secondary Specialized Education and the State Committee on Labour and Social Problems. In addition, since 1972 ministries without a bulletin of their own have published important new enactments in the *Biulleten' normativnykh aktov ministerstv i vedomstv SSSR*. However, much legislation is not properly published, but is circulated to relevant organizations in internal bulletins for official use only.

The RSFSR has a procedure for publishing legislation which is very similar to that of the USSR, except that it has no *Biulleten' normativnykh aktov* ... However, many of the other union republics have a different system. The proceedings of the Supreme Soviets are generally readily available, but only a few of the official gazettes can be obtained abroad. Some republics issue a combined bulletin for the Supreme Soviet and the Council of Ministers. Full details of the Supreme Soviet and government gazettes for the union republics can be found on pages 361–74 of *Official publications of the Soviet Union and Eastern Europe*, edited by G. P. M. Walker, 1982.

Local government legislation varies in availability, but the bulletins and gazettes of local soviets are generally not obtainable abroad. However, they can sometimes be consulted in libraries in the USSR.

From time to time, the USSR and the union republics issue official chronological or systematic collections of laws currently in force, such as the four-volume *Sbornik zakonov SSSR i ukazov Prezidiuma Verkhovnogo soveta SSSR, 1938–75*, 1975–6. These collections are restricted to published texts of laws and edicts of the Supreme Soviets and their presidiums, and do not include the important (and less easily traced) ordinances of the Councils of Ministers. They are therefore often less useful than the unofficial subject collections of laws and normative acts currently in force which are published mainly for the use of trade union officials, delegates to local soviets and lawyers, and are also available to the general public. These subject collections usually include material from a wide range of official bodies, and may contain the first generally available text of a particular piece of legislation previously circulated in an internal bulletin. Many of these subject collections of law and normative acts, and the official chronological and systematic collections, are listed in the chapter on the USSR in *Official publications* ... , 1982, and in V. V. Antonov's *Sovetskoe zakonodatel'stvo*, 1981. These collections can often be obtained on inter-library loan when the official gazettes cannot.

As Professor Butler has observed (in his *Soviet Law*, 1983, p. 58), 'the inconsistent and extensive use of denominations for enactments, the exceptionally large number of entities empowered to "legislate", the need to distinguish between normative and non-normative enactments, and the problems of making enactments physically and linguistically accessible' have made law reform and the creation of an orderly, comprehensive statute book a matter of great urgency. Since the late 1960s, efforts to systematize existing legislation have been given high priority, and this has now resulted in the publication of the first Soviet looseleaf collection of legislation currently in force, the *Svod zakonov SSSR*. This is an official publication of the Presidium of the USSR Supreme Soviet and the USSR Council of Ministers. It includes laws and edicts of the Supreme Soviet and its Presidium, with ordinances of a normative character issued by the Council of Ministers. It is planned that the *Svod zakonov SSSR* will consist of 12 volumes, plus an index, arranged according to a new classification devised for the digest. Each union republic will also issue its own *Svod zakonov*.

Law reports

Although, strictly speaking, court judgments in individual cases are not recognized as providing a precedent for future decisions, still less of creating law, court judgments do nevertheless play an important part in filling gaps in the legislation and in interpreting legislation. The USSR Supreme Court issues a *Biulleten'* with details of its rulings and 'guiding explanations', which are cumulated from time to time. The Supreme Courts of the union republics issue a variety of bulletins and occasional collections of decisions etc. Details of these publications are available in *Official publications* ... , 1982, pp. 312–14. The All Union Institute for Research on Soviet Legislation also issues an annual review of court cases and judgments, called *Kommentarii sudebnoi praktiki*.

Doctrinal writings

The teachings and writings of jurists are not regarded as a source of law in the USSR.

Custom

Customary law officially plays no part in Soviet law. However, traditional customs, especially in family matters, are still strong in certain areas, notably Central Asia and the Caucasus and it seems they are taken into account by People's Courts in such areas.

Primary sources in translation

There are a number of publications which provide translations into English of primary sources of law.

For major new pieces of legislation, the *Current Digest of the Soviet Press* is a convenient and widely available source. Every week it translates or abstracts important and interesting items from Soviet newspapers and, to a lesser extent, Soviet journals. It includes important enactments published in *Izvestiia*, as well as speeches to the Supreme Soviet, debates on proposed legislation and articles about crime and recent court cases. It has thorough name and subject indexes, and from 1985 has been available online on NEXIS.

Translations into German of new legislation from the USSR and Eastern Europe are published in *WGO: Monatshefte für osteuropäisches Recht*.

The translations journal *Soviet Statutes and Decisions* does not aim to provide translations of new legislation. Each volume of this journal is devoted to a particular area of law, such as labour law or the administration of legality. As well as legislation currently in force, court decisions and extracts from commentaries are included, often with detailed and helpful translators' notes.

An extremely valuable new looseleaf service for legislation currently in force is the *Collected legislation of the Union of Soviet Socialist Republics and the constituent union republics*, compiled and translated by W. E. Butler, 1979–. It consists of binders for (a) constitutions; (b) USSR legislation; (c) union republic legislation. The *Collected legislation ...* uses a classification scheme closely modelled on that employed for the *Svod zakonov SSSR*, but the service is not merely a translation of this publication.

Its scope is wider, as it aims to include 'all codes and legislative enactments of interest, whether of legislative, executive, ministerial, departmental or local government origin'. As well as authoritative new translations, there are introductory notes on each document, giving a brief account of its origins, amendments and references to authoritative commentaries.

Many primary documents are available in collections of Soviet legal materials which have been assembled primarily for teaching purposes. W. E. Butler has compiled *Basic documents on the Soviet legal system*, 1983, which provides translations of the major legislative Acts as of 1 August 1983 and incorporates the changes in legislation which followed the new constitutions of 1977–8. It is supplemented by *The Soviet legal system: the law in the 1980s*, by John N. Hazard *et al.*, 1984, which contains translations of some legislative acts, lengthy excerpts from Soviet monographs and articles on the law, court decisions and extracts from Soviet legal commentaries. The collection has been designed to provide material for the study of 'the problems faced in the 1980s by Soviet policy makers and the legal measures taken in an attempt to solve them'. There are several earlier collections which include court judgments, writings by legal experts and a very wide range of legislative acts of all types; although some of this material is no longer in force, the collections are still very valuable. The five main post-Stalin collections of this type are *The Soviet legal system*, edited by W. E. Butler, 1978, the three editions of *The Soviet legal system*, by John N. Hazard *et al.*, 1962, 1969 and 1977, and *Basic laws on the structure of the Soviet State*, edited by Harold J. Berman and John B. Quigley, 1969. Earlier collections are listed in the section on historical sources.

Additional sources of Soviet legal material in English translation are listed in *Official publications* . . ., 1982, and in Charles Szladits's *Bibliography on foreign and comparative law: books and articles in English*, 1955–. The first of these bibliographies also gives information about translations of East European legislation and other official documents, while Szladits covers primary sources of law from all the socialist countries.

SOCIALIST INTERNATIONAL ORGANIZATIONS

The workings of the Council for Mutual Economic Assistance (Comecon) and other specialized international associations are described in Szawlowski's *System of the international organizations of the communist countries*, 1976. This book also covers the Warsaw Pact. Comecon is also described in Schiavone's *The institutions of Comecon*, 1981. A wide range of documents issued by Comecon and other international socialist industrial and economic agencies is available in *A source book on socialist international organisations*, 1978. Comecon issues collections of its documents from time to time in Russian; the fourth edition was published in 1983 (*Osnovnye dokumenty Soveta ekonomicheskoi vzaimopomoshchi*, 2 vols.). For the Warsaw Pact, the two main collections of documents are the Russian *Organizatsiya Varshavskogo dogovora: dokumenty i materialy 1955–1980 gg.*, 1980, and J. P. Jain's *Documentary study of the Warsaw Pact*, 1973.

SECONDARY SOURCES OF LAW

Monographs

The standard English-language monograph on Soviet law today is W. E. Butler's *Soviet law*, 1983. There are chapters on all aspects of Soviet law and the work is supplemented by informative notes on further reading and a table of principal Soviet legislative acts, with references to readily available English translations. For a general account of the legal system in the mid-1960s, prepared for area studies students rather than lawyers, there is Johnson's *Introduction to the Soviet legal system*, 1969. For a fuller treatment of the legal system at that time, see Harold J. Berman's *Justice in the USSR*, 1963; the first edition of this book, called *Justice in Russia*, 1950, gives an account of the Soviet legal system under Stalin. The development of the legal system and the law reforms of the late 1950s through to the 1970s are studied in detail in the three volumes of *Soviet law after Stalin* edited by Donald D. Barry, George Ginsburgs and Peter B. Maggs, 1977–9.

The Documentation Office for East European Law at the University of Leiden issues a monograph series, *Law in Eastern Europe*, which consists of authoritative works on various aspects of Soviet and East European legal systems. Other English-language monographs are listed in the various sources described in the 'Legal bibliography' section below.

Soviet legal monographs are often published under the auspices of research institutes, such as the Academy of Sciences' Institute of State and Law. Most legal publishing is done by the publishing house which specializes in law, Iuridicheskaia Literatura. As well as monographs and textbooks, Soviet lawyers publish detailed commentaries on law codes and individual laws. As well as providing authoritative interpretations of the law, these commentaries can be a useful source of information about unpublished or hard-to-obtain regulations. University publishing houses also issue legal textbooks, including specialist textbooks for students studying other subjects, particularly economics. These textbooks are often accompanied by readers, which contain extracts from relevant legislation. The USSR does occasionally publish English translations of important works on state and law, but most of the books on law published by the USSR in English are more popular (even propagandistic) works.

Periodicals

The major Soviet theoretical journal dealing with the law is *Sovetskoe Gosudarstvo i Pravo*, which is issued by the Institute of State and Law of the USSR Academy of Sciences. The Law Faculty of Moscow University has its own journal, *Vestnik Moskovskogo Universiteta: Pravo*. Staff and researchers from a number of universities and institutes of higher education write in the journal *Pravovedenie*. The USSR Ministry of Justice, Supreme Soviet and Procuracy issue the monthly journal *Sotsialisticheskaia Zakonnost'*, and the RSFSR Ministry of Justice and Supreme Court issue the fortnightly *Sovetskaia Iustitsiia*. Both these journals are intended for practising lawyers and those responsible for law enforcement, and contain articles on the law, its interpretation and administration, legal notes, etc. Articles from these publications are selectively published in English in the translations journal *Soviet Law and Government*. There is also a journal about law and crime intended for the general public called *Chelovek i Zakon*. Several of the union republics issue their own legal journals.

The main Western journals dealing with Soviet law are the *Review of Socialist Law*, issued by the Documentation Office for East European Law of the University of Leiden, *Osteuropa-Recht*, which is published by the Deutsche Gesellschaft für Osteuropakunde, and *WGO: Monatshefte für osteuropäisches Recht*, which is issued by the Abteiling für Ostrechtsforschung of the University of Hamburg. Other articles are published from time to time in the general area studies journals and in journals dealing with international and comparative law.

Details of other law journals issued in the USSR and in Eastern Europe can be found in Leideritz's *Key to the study of East European law*, 1978 and *Official publications . . .*, 1982.

Official publications

In dealing with socialist countries, the term 'official publications' is hard to define. The 'guiding role' of the ruling party in relationship to the government and all aspects of public life means that party documents, while not having the force of law, are extremely important guides to policy and to everyday conduct. In some senses, given party and government control over publishing, all publications not issued illegally could be considered to be 'official'. In practice, the term 'official publications' is generally applied only to those documents issued by, or on the orders of, party and government authorities in the exercise of their responsibilities. The nature of official publication in the Soviet Union and Eastern Europe is discussed more fully by Gregory Walker and other contributors to *Official publications . . .*, 1982.

Official publications of the Soviet Union and Eastern Europe, 1945–1980, edited by G. P. M. Walker, 1982, provides a detailed (but not exhaustive) annotated bibliography for each of the East European states, the USSR and the communist international organizations. As well as legislation, it covers party documents, statistics, leaders' works and foreign policy documents. The introduction to each section gives a concise account of the development of legislative organs in the country and notes particular features of its procedures for issuing official documents, broadly defined. Supplements to this bibliography are now under consideration. For the USSR, a major Soviet guide to legislation has recently been published. This is V. V. Antonov's *Sovetskoe zakonodatel'stvo*, 1981. Unlike *Official publications* ... it covers Soviet legislation for the period 1917–45, but is limited to the USSR and RSFSR. *Official publications* ..., on the other hand, does provide information on the constituent union republics of the USSR, Czechoslovakia and Yugoslavia.

Leideritz's *Key to the study of East European law*, 1978, is a useful supplement to *Official publications* ..., particularly for pre-war Eastern Europe; the bibliographies on Eastern Europe listed in the 'Further reading' section of Chapter 13 will also provide additional material on official publications.

Historical sources

There is no one English language monograph treating the whole of the history of Russian law. For the medieval period, there is David A. Kaiser's *The growth of the law in medieval Russia*, 1980. Various aspects of Russian law from medieval times to the present are discussed in the conference papers published as *Russian law: historical and political perspectives*, edited by W. E. Butler, 1977. There are chapters on the history of the law in several of the major textbooks, notably Butler's *Soviet law*, 1983 and Berman's *Justice in the USSR*, 1963. Many works dealing with Russian history at certain periods also have extensive coverage of legal developments.

A useful collection of the texts of Russian laws up to the time of Peter the Great is *Pamiatniki russkogo prava*, 8 vols., 1952–61. Some of the texts, notably the Pravda Russkaia, are translated by Vernadsky in *Medieval Russian laws*, 1947; *Muscovite judicial texts*, 1966, includes the 1497 and 1550 Sudebniki. Many eighteenth-century legal documents are available in *Russia under Catherine the Great*, edited by Paul Dukes, 2 vols., 1977–8. The great compilation of Russian legislation, the *Polnoe sobranie zakonov Rossiiskoi imperii*, appeared in three series. The first, covering 1649 to 1825, was published in 1830 (45 vols. plus supplements); the second series, covering 1825–81, was issued between 1830–84 (55 vols. plus supplements); the third series, covering 1881 to 1913, was published in 33 volumes in 1885–1916. There is a general chronological index for 1649–1850, and alphabetical name indexes for the first two series. On the basis of the *Polnoe sobranie zakonov* a digest of Russian laws, the *Svod zakonov Rossiiskoi imperii* was first issued in 1832 (15 vols.). Supplements were issued from time to time, and there were several new editions of the *Svod zakonov* through to the end of the Tsarist regime.

For the pre-war Soviet period, the main sources of central government legislation are the *Sobranie uzakonenii i rasporiazh-enii rabochego i krest'ianskogo pravitel'stva* (RSFSR) for the period 1917–22, the *Vestnik TsIKa, SNK i STO SSSR* for 1923–4 and for the period from 1924 the *Sobranie zakonov i rasporiazhenii Raboche-krest'-ianskogo pravitel'stva SSSR*. These publications have a complicated bibliographical history which is set out in *Half a century of Soviet serials*, 1968. A number of early Soviet documents and decrees are available in a more convenient and easily accessible reprint, the *Dekrety sovetskoi vlasti*, 1957–. (The eleventh volume of this series, published in 1983, reached November 1920.) There are also a number of subject and chronological collections of laws issued during the pre-war period; these are listed in Antonov's *Sovetskoe zakonodatel'stvo*, 1981.

Translations of some pre-war legislation are included in Mervyn Matthew's *Soviet government*, 1974, the two editions of *Materials for the study of the Soviet system*, edited by Meisel and Kozera, 1950 and 1953, and in the first two editions of *The Soviet legal system*, edited by John N. Hazard and others. Further guidance on sources of material in translation can be found below.

REFERENCE SOURCES

Bibliographical sources

Guides to legal literature

The main general guide to the legal literature of the USSR and Eastern Europe is Leideritz's *Key to the study of East European law*, 1978. Major bibliographies are also listed in *Official publications of the Soviet Union and Eastern Europe, 1945–1980*, edited by G. P. M. Walker, 1982. For the USSR, the main guide to legal literature is Ksenzova's *Iuridicheskaia literatura*, 1972; for the various countries of Eastern Europe, the bibliographies listed in the 'Further reading' section of this chapter will provide additional information.

National bibliographies

Full details of the national bibliographies of the USSR and the countries of Eastern Europe are provided in *Official publications . . ., 1982*.

Legal bibliographies

In addition to Leideritz's *Key to the study of East European Law*, 1978 and *Official publications . . ., 1982*, there are a number of bibliographies dealing with the legal systems of individual East European countries. Many of these were prepared under the auspices of the Mid-European Law Project, which was based at the Library of Congress in the 1950s and 1960s. The arrangement and coverage of each bibliography is different, but they all provide valuable, detailed information on the country covered. Some, notably that on Poland, have substantial coverage of legal history while others concentrate on the twentieth century. There are also more recent legal bibliographies for Albania, Romania and Yugoslavia. Details of all these publications are given in the 'Further reading' section at the end of this chapter.

The main Soviet legal bibliographies are described by Jenny Brine in *Official publications ...*, edited by G. P. M. Walker, 1982. For the history of Russian law, there is Szeftel's contribution on Russia before 1917, published as section D/9 of *Bibliographical introduction to legal history and ethnology*, edited by John Gilissen, 1966. Many additional works valuable for the study of Russian and Soviet law are described and annotated in the catalogue which W. E. Butler prepared for IDC's microfiche collection, *Russian and Soviet law*, 1976. The printed library catalogues described below are also useful as bibliographies of the history of the law.

The major bibliography of Western-language material about Soviet law published up to the mid-1960s is *Writings on Soviet law and Soviet international law*, 1966, which covers both books and articles. It is supplemented by the exhaustive bibliography on Soviet legal materials in English which appears in the second edition of *The Soviet legal system*, 1969, by John N. Hazard *et al.* The 1977 edition also has a bibliography of books and journals in English on the Soviet legal system, mainly in the post-war period, and a checklist of normative acts then in force available in English translation. This bibliography is updated for 1977–83 in a supplement to *The Soviet legal system: the law in the 1980s*, by John N. Hazard *et al.*, 1984. Butler's monograph, *Soviet law*, 1983, includes a checklist of major Soviet legislative acts, with an indication of where to find translations of some of them. This work also has a most useful 'Further reading' section, which concentrates on material in English.

For all the socialist legal systems, Szladits's *Bibliography on foreign and comparative law*, 1955–, provides good coverage of material in English.

Current bibliographies

New writing in the West on the law of socialist countries is listed regularly in Szladits's *Bibliography on foreign and comparative law*, 1955–. Material about the USSR and Eastern Europe is also listed (albeit some years after publication) in the main area studies bibliographies, the *American bibliography of*

Slavic and East European studies, and the *European biblio-graphy of Soviet, East European and Slavonic studies.*

The major Soviet source for current legal bibliography is *Novaia sovetskaia literatura po obshchestvennym naukam: Gosud-arstvo i pravo,* which is published by the Academy of Sciences' Institute of Scientific Information in the Social Sciences (INION). This is an exhaustive and reliable monthly index covering books, articles and theses. Unfortunately there are no annual indexes, but monthly indexes have recently been introduced. It is now computer-produced.

Law library catalogues

The printed catalogues of major Slavonic and East European collections can be useful in tracing legal materials. Apart from the catalogue of the British Library Reference Division, par-ticular reference should be made to the *Dictionary catalog of the Slavonic Collection of the New York Public Library,* 2nd edn., 44 vols., 1974.

A particularly important printed catalogue for Soviet and East European legal material is that of the Harvard Law School Library, published as *Soviet legal bibliography: a classi-fied and annotated listing of books and serials published in the Soviet Union since 1917 as represented in the Harvard Law School Library* ..., edited by V. Mostecky and W. E. Butler, 1965.

The Documentation Office for East European Law at the Universtity of Leiden, which has large collections of material from the USSR and Eastern Europe, has recently made its systematic catalogue of books available on microfiche. This library also issues a regular accessions list. Another major European collection is that of the Institut für Ostrechtsfor-schung at the University of Hamburg. Its acquisitions are reported in *WGO: Monatshefte für osteuropäisches Recht.*

Union catalogues

In the United Kingdom, lending libraries with holdings of Russian and East European material report their holdings to the Slavonic Union Catalogue at the British Library Lending Division, which operates the *SUC* as part of the normal inter-library loan system. In addition, a union list of Slavonic and East European serials has been under discussion for some years, and much information on serials holdings at major UK libraries has already been assembled. Enquiries for serials locations (but not actual loan requests) should be directed to the Slavonic and East European section of the Bodleian Library, Oxford.

The United States *National Union Catalog* is mainly used for post-1956 imprints, as earlier publications are conveniently listed in the microfiche *Slavic Cyrillic union catalog of pre-1956 imprints*, 1980. The earlier edition of this catalogue, issued on microcard by Readex, is now out of date, but is still useful, as it has a subject sequence not available on the microfiche. *Half a century of Soviet serials*, compiled in two volumes by R. Smits, 1968, is a union list of Soviet serials in US libraries; it is now rather out of date and does not cover pre-1917 publications or newspapers.

Legal research finding aids

New Soviet and East European research on the law is reported to some extent in the legal journals described above. Soviet dissertations on legal matters are most easily traced through *Novaia sovetskaia literatura* ...

Western theses on East European and Soviet law are listed in the usual thesis finding aids and also find their way into the annual area studies bibliographies, described above. American and European research on law in the USSR and Eastern Europe is reported in a special bulletin issued by the Deutsche Gesellschaft für Osteuropakunde, called *International Bulletin for Research on Law in Eastern Europe*.

Computer databases

There are apparently no databases in the West specializing in the law of socialist countries, but this could well change in the next few years. However, INION is now using a computer to produce its monthly indexes of foreign and Soviet legal litera-ture, and this database can be searched online in Moscow. It is also accessible through the International Institute for Applied Systems Analysis in Vienna and, in time, online searches may be available from other centres in the West.

In general, international affairs online services do contain some material relevant for the study of legal developments in socialist countries. Probably the best current affairs coverage, including legal news, is provided by the BBC's *Summary of World Broadcasts*, which is available through the World Reporter service on DATASOLVE. Its four series cover all the socialist countries. The general legal online services, such as the *Legal Resource Index* on DIALOG, do cover English-language material on socialist legal systems. The *Current Digest of the Soviet Press* has been available on NEXIS since 1985.

Dictionaries

The largest general English–Russian dictionary is the *Bol'shoi anglo-russkii slovar'*, edited by Gal'perin, 1972, with its supple-ment (*Dopolnenie*) published in 1980. The main one-volume English–Russian dictionaries are *The Oxford English–Russian dictionary*, edited by P. S. Falla, 1984, and the *Anglo-russkii slovar'*, edited by V. K. Miuller, 18th edn., 1981. The most up-to-date Russian–English dictionaries now available are *The Oxford Russian–English dictionary*, edited by Marcus Wheeler, 1984, and the fully revised 13th edition of the *Russko–angliiskii slovar'*, edited by A. I. Smirnitskii, 1985. These general dic-tionaries are not as full and precise in their coverage of legal terms as more specialized dictionaries.

Specialist dictionaries relevant for work with legal texts include R. E. F. Smith's *Dictionary of Russian social science terms*, 1962, which although now rather outdated does give very helpful concise explanations of Soviet concepts and ter-minology. Prishchepenko's *Russian–English law dictionary*, 1969, compiled under the auspices of the New York Univer-sity School of Law, provides more detailed coverage of the law. The largest and most up to date dictionary is the massive *Mongolian–English–Russian dictionary of legal terms and con-*

cepts, compiled by W. E. Butler and A. J. Nathanson, 1983. There are 11,000 entries defining Mongolian terms, with Russian and English indexes which permit the dictionary to be used to translate from Russian into English and from English into Russian, as well as for Mongolian translating. The introduction to this dictionary has a unique list of legal dictionaries in all the major languages of the USSR.

Russian works are usually full of abbreviations and acronyms; the best modern dictionary for these is Alekseev's *Slovar' sokrashchenii russkogo iazyka*, 3rd edn., 1983.

Encyclopedias

The articles on socialist countries in the national reports section of the *International encyclopaedia of comparative law* provide authoritative coverage of all aspects of their legal systems. For the USSR, the indispensable *Encyclopaedia of Soviet law*, edited by F. J. M. Feldbrugge, 2nd edn., 1985, provides authoritative summaries of Soviet legislation and Soviet legal thought and administration. The first edition was published in two volumes in 1973. For the Soviet view in English translation, the *Great Soviet encyclopaedia*, 1973–82, is useful, despite its confusing use of the Russian alphabet order for the entries.

The major Soviet legal encyclopedia, the *Entsiklopediia gosudarstva i prava*, edited by P. Stuchka, 1925–7, is now useful mainly for the history of Soviet law and the development of legal theory. There are two post-war legal encyclopedias with short entries in alphabetical order; these are the *Iuridicheskii slovar'*, 1953 and 1956, and the *Entsiklopedicheskii slovar' pravovykh znanii*, edited by V. M. Chkhikvadze, 1965. A much fuller, authoritative and up to date encyclopedia was published in 1984; this is the *Iuridicheskii entsiklopedicheskii slovar'*, which is intended for use by legal specialists as well as the general public.

Legal organizations

Professional associations in the Western sense do not operate in the USSR. The only partial exception to this are the colleges of advocates, which administer the affairs of the profession in their locality. The colleges do not appear to have their own journal. The colleges of advocates are described in Butler's *Soviet law*, 1983, pp. 78–84.

News of developments in the legal profession are carried in the major legal journals. From time to time these journals carry obituaries, and biographies of major figures on the occasion of their 70th birthday, or on the award of major honours etc. The journals also occasionally publish profiles of ordinary lawyers whose work and political activity are exemplary.

There is no organization of law librarians, and no journal which carries law library news. Law libraries are briefly described in the two-volume directory, *Biblioteki SSSR: spravochnik*, 1973–4. Major law libraries in Moscow are described by Barbara Tearle in *The Law Librarian*, vol. 15, nos. 1–2, April/August 1984, pp. 3–7.

FURTHER READING

SPECIALIST BIBLIOGRAPHIES ON EAST EUROPEAN LAW

Albania

Arbeitsmaterialen zu einer Landesbibliographie Albanien, herausgegeben von A. Hetzer und V. S. Roman, Heft IV: Recht, 1980.

Baltic states

Klesment, J. *et al. Legal sources and bibliography of the Baltic States*, 1968.

Bulgaria

Sipkov, I. *Legal Sources and Bibliography of Bulgaria*, 1956.

Czechoslovakia

Bohmer, A. *et al. Legal sources and bibliography of Czechoslovakia*, 1969.
Bibliography of Czechoslovak legal literature, 1945–58, 1959.

Hungary

Bedo, A. K. and Torzsay-Biber, G. *Legal sources and bibliography of Hungary*, 1956.
Nagy, L. (ed.) *Bibliography of Hungarian legal literature, 1945–1965*, 1966.

Poland

Siekanowicz, P. *Legal sources and bibliography of Poland*, 1964.

Romania

Bibliographie juridique roumaine, 1944–1968, 1969.
Stoicoiu, V. *Legal sources and bibliography of Romania*, 1964.

Yugoslavia

Blagojevic, B. T. *Bibliographie du droit yougoslave, 1945–1967*, 2nd edn., 1970.
Gjupanovich, F. and Gjupanovich, A. A. *Legal sources and bibliography of Yugoslavia*, 1964.

Part IV Law Library Practice

14. General Administration

E. M. MOYS

This introductory chapter to the section of the volume dealing with law library practice covers policy and general administration, including staffing and accommodation matters. It could have been entitled 'What the chief librarian does', if it were not that, in many law libraries, the same individual is chief librarian and everything else. Most of the general administrative matters are common to a wide range of libraries. They are outlined here for the use of librarians in charge of small or medium-sized law libraries, because practical information about several of the topics covered is not readily available elsewhere.

POLICY AND PLANNING

Purpose

'The purpose of the law library is to provide the organisation to which it belongs with the best possible library and information services within the scope of its activities.' Thus the first of the BIALL *Standards for Law Libraries*, 1981, many of which will be mentioned in this *Manual*, summarizes the aim of any law library. A particular library may wish to expand this statement with more specific aims to suit its own purposes referring, for example, to reference and/or lending services, particular branches of law which are to be covered in special detail, etc.

The position and status of the law library within the organization should be set out clearly. The Third Standard says that 'The law library should be recognised by the parent body, library staff and readers as an integral and essential part of the organisation which it exists to serve'. This should be axiomatic in any law-oriented organization such as a solicitors' firm or law faculty, but may be more difficult to achieve in a more general body such as a large manufacturing firm or a non-legal government office, where the law section forms only a small part of the general library. There, the law librarian, or whoever looks after the legal section (possibly in conjunction with several other subject areas), may well need to rely on the support of 'general' library colleagues. As the Fourth Standard specifies, it is essential to have an organizational framework which sets out clear lines of responsibility and communication, with particular reference to making and implementing policy, financial control, personnel matters and the maintenance of the premises.

Users

The various categories of people entitled to use the library and the level of services, for example lending services or reference use only, which is available to them must be clearly set out and publicized, as specified in Standards Five to Seven.

A policy should be established concerning non-members who apply to use the library for short periods, or who telephone asking for reference or bibliographical information. Whereas a public library is usually required to admit anyone, as is any library which holds a Publishers' Association Licence, a private society or law firm may limit admission strictly to its own members. Between these two extremes there are many possible policies. For example, most academic libraries admit members of other academic or research institutions, especially staff, on proof of membership, on a broadly reciprocal basis.

The library staff should make it their business to get to know as many individual readers as possible – not only their names but their legal interests and specialities and the types of services they need. Readers should be consulted, formally or informally, about development proposals that are likely to affect them, before they are put into effect.

Stock

'All law libraries should provide an adequate collection of primary materials relating to English law, as listed in Appendix VI' according to Standard 33. Libraries in other jurisdictions may, presumably, substitute their own jurisdiction for England. The subsequent standards cover all the aspects of stock policy likely to apply to general law libraries, such as the importance of serial publications, bibliographical and reference materials, etc. Lists of recommended titles were published as an appendix to the Standards themselves in a special issue of the *Law Librarian* in January 1983.

A problem can arise over the provision of duplicate or multiple copies of basic texts. Both BIALL and the SPTL recommend the provision of several sets of law reports in libraries with large numbers of users, a very costly exercise, but necessary if readers, notably students, are to be able to study effectively. Individual treatises are also very expensive, and if library budgets are restricted may be duplicated to only a very limited extent. This is doubly unfortunate since the price of books limits the students' purchasing power too.

Book selection, especially when funds are inadequate, is a delicate business requiring diplomacy and ample consultation with the library users. It should be the responsibility of the librarian. However, in some libraries the library committee exercises partial or even total power over selection. Some form of partnership, at least, is desirable in such cases. The librarian should be authorized to order books up to a specified total each year, or any books costing less than a specified amount per item. Without such an arrangement, urgently-needed material cannot be added to stock quickly and newly-published books could be up to six months old before the committee is able to consider them, by which time they could have gone out of print.

Services

Information services are very important in any law library. Readers need information about the library itself including services and stock available, their location, cost (if any) and how to use any hardware, mechanical or electronic. The library should also provide bibliographic information, not only concerning its own stock but also about other material published and, as far as possible, where it might be found. General information should be available from a general reference collection including such items as local street and telephone directories, maps and atlases, bus and train timetables, directories of legal and other individuals and organizations, foreign language dictionaries, a good general encyclopedia, etc.

In general, the law library consists of legal information, in one form or another. Whilst the library staff can and should direct readers to the most likely sources of the information they need, it is not their function to give legal advice (even if they happen to hold a legal qualification). In presenting information to readers librarians must, of course, avoid any form of discrimination or bias. See also Standards 48 to 54.

Few law libraries lend books on a large scale, as it is essential that all major texts are available at all times to any reader. The major proportion of their stock consists of continuing series and there is a grave danger of sets becoming defective. Not only do many issues of serials go out of print quickly but some multi-volume works can be purchased only as complete sets. Some libraries, including those serving professional associations, are private libraries, specifically constituted as reference libraries and are therefore unable to lend books under any circumstances. Law firm libraries will probably lend to fee-earners and other employees only. In academic libraries, staff and students are usually allowed to borrow treatises but not serial publications.

Any modern library needs to consider the provision of various types of machines for readers' use, such as photocopiers, microform readers or reader-printers, audio-visual hardware and computer terminals. These machines are likely to be fairly expensive and maintenance contracts for them should be considered. Some may need special environments although, fortunately most microcomputers can cope with the normal range of temperature and humidity likely to be experienced in a library. The provision of an ample supply of electric power sockets is an important factor in planning any rooms for library use. See also under 'Equipment', below.

Organization

A basic question in planning a library service is the extent to which the books should be freely accessible to all readers. In most of the English-speaking world, open access is the general rule with collections of rare books or manuscripts being available on special application. Open access has the advantage that readers who know their way about the library can serve themselves for a good proportion of the time leaving the library staff free to deal with the more difficult enquiries. Readers who are not in a hurry can also, in theory, browse along the shelves, finding new material to interest them.

On the other hand, open access requires a rational order of books and shelves, which in turn requires more shelf-space than an arbitrary fixed location system, especially one based on the size of the books. It also means that a little more time must be spent on producing shelf labels, notices, plans, printed guides, etc.

A modified form of closed access may be needed for a limited number of very heavily used books, especially in academic libraries, where they may be issued for short-period loans of a few hours or overnight only. This service can help to overcome problems arising from the library's inability to buy enough copies.

In large organizations, especially universities and polytechnics, the question of decentralization may arise. Most librarians, being largely divorced from the turmoil of departmental teaching problems and interdepartmental rivalries, see very clearly the educational advantages of a large central library to which all students may come, providing them with an opportunity for some degree of cultural cross-fertilization. A large multi-faculty library offers more opportunities for broadening horizons than a series of faculty or departmental libraries, however complete within their own subject areas. This problem may be insurmountable in a multi-site polytechnic, where the undergraduate libraries must be on the same sites as the teaching, however much dispersed.

On the other hand, teachers and students want 'their' material close to hand for classes, moot rooms, laboratories, etc. The desire of many law teachers to have a separate law library, within the law faculty building cannot be ignored. Nevertheless, in some of the newer universities, at least, general academic opinion is in favour of a central library with few, if any, decentralized sections, if only on the very real grounds of economy.

A forceful argument against decentralization is the increasingly interdisciplinary nature of law teaching. For example, students of criminology, sociology of law, jursiprudence and legal history all need to study non-legal texts as well as legal ones. In the reverse direction, legal texts may well be needed by historians, economists, accountants, sociologists and others. There is also the economic factor: a central library requires a smaller number of duplicate copies of frequently used volumes or basic reference works than the total number needed for several faculty or departmental libraries.

In other organizations the predominant need is for instant information. Lawyers in a government department, for example, may be scattered in several buildings, and small groups may be accommodated adjacent to the administrators they advise. They cannot be expected to make a journey of anything up to half an hour for each library consultation. Therefore, the ministry librarian must set up as many branch law libraries, or small office-based collections as are justified by the existence of scattered groups of lawyers, and the ministry must find the finance for the consequent multiple copies.

GOVERNMENT

Most libraries operate under some form of committee government. A small law library probably comes directly under a general committee of the parent body, while a large law library, such as that of one of the Inns of Court, is likely to have a special library committee. Law libraries that are contained within large general libraries, such as those of universities, polytechnics or borough libraries, usually come under the jurisdiction of the general library committee of the organization. The library of an academic law faculty or equivalent organization may report to either the faculty board or the general library committee or, perhaps, to both (a very undesirable arrangement, with the law librarian responsible to two masters).

The libraries of government departments do not normally function under a library committee but under the usual civil service chain of command. The librarian reports to a senior administrator who includes the library among several responsibilities.

The conduct of individual readers is governed by the rules and regulations of the library, which are usually promulgated by the library committee.

Committees

The membership and powers of the library committee are matters over which the librarian rarely has much influence. In some cases, notably in public libraries, these matters are governed by legislation, while committees in the academic and professional worlds are set up under the charters, constitutions or regulations of the individual organizations.

Membership

The library committee of an academic body used to consist almost entirely of senior academic staff. Most have now become more broadly-based 'consumer committees', with the addition of student representatives. The chief librarian of the university, polytechnic or college should be a full member and is now often joined by other library staff members elected by their fellows. As the user representatives usually have large constituencies, such as faculties or the whole students' union, it is probable that the Law Faculty will have one or two members at most and that the law librarian will have to convince the chief librarian of his case for or against a particular proposal, rather than having direct access to the general library committee. If there is a Law Faculty library committee, the law librarian should be a full member so that he can fulfil his functions effectively and maintain full liaison with his readers and their representatives. All representative committee members should report back regularly to their constituents.

Professional bodies tend to be less willing than their academic counterparts to give recognition to the professional status of their library staff and do not always accord even their chief librarians full membership of the library committee. In this respect, some law firms seem to have a better record.

Functions and powers

One of the most important functions of any library committee is to act as a two-way channel of communication between the library users and the library staff. The committee of an academic library, for example, can plan the acquisitions policy needed to cope with changes in the syllabus and any committee may have to deal with disciplinary matters and problems of security.

In general, a library committee's powers should, if legally possible, be confined to establishing broad lines of policy, making regulations, setting the amount of charges and fines and advising the librarian on any other matter he brings before it. Committee members are usually busy people and should not be burdened with the minutiae of daily affairs in the library. The librarian is employed to administer the library, within the policy framework established by the library committee but cannot do so satisfactorily if he is subject to constant interference by the committee in matters which should not be its concern.

Complaints and suggestions, whether from committee members or others, should always be discussed with the librarian before being brought up at a committee meeting. It is both unjust and discourteous to the librarian for complaints or proposals, serious or trivial, to be raised for the first time during a committee meeting, thus giving him no opportunity to investigate and make an informed reply. Many complaints either involve relatively minor errors, such as the misfiling of a card, which can be put right quickly by administrative action, or arise from misunderstandings which can be corrected with tact. Similarly some proposals may seem ideal in theory but would prove unworkable in practice. The committee's time is best reserved for matters involving new principles, problems or developments.

The committee secretary

Whether he is a voting member of the committee or not, the librarian may well be expected to act as committee secretary. He should maintain close liaison with the committee chairman, discussing the agenda with him in advance, and pointing out the items of greatest importance, including those where a decision is essential before a certain date. The secretary usually writes letters on behalf of the committee, but in some organizations it is traditional for the chairman to sign the more important letters.

In academic libraries, in particular, there has been a trend in the past few years for the central administration to provide the secretary for each committee, even the library committee. While this arrangement may seem to be administratively neat and convenient, it can cause great difficulties in practice because of the problems of establishing satisfactory three-way communications between chairman, secretary and librarian. Either the secretary keeps in close touch with the librarian, in which case he forms a sort of barrier against direct contact between the librarian and chairman, or he keeps his counsel, leaving the librarian out of the agenda and minute-taking process almost completely. If, as a third alternative, the librarian and chairman try to maintain their previous close relationship, the secretary becomes a mere shorthand-typist, not an attractive proposition for an ambitious administrator.

It is always easier for a committee to make informed decisions if it has a paper before it, preferably circulated in advance with the agenda. Committee memoranda, and other supporting papers, should be written objectively, setting out all sides of the argument. Having done that conscientiously, the librarian may be allowed to indicate his own preference. In fact, the committee would probably like to receive a positive recommendation from the librarian. If there is any doubt, the chairman should be consulted.

A draft of the minutes should be written as soon as possible, certainly not more than a day or two after the meeting, before the details can fade from memory. It is better to begin with a detailed draft, gradually paring it down to the final text, rather than trying to work in the reverse direction. It is quite common for the secretary to show his final draft to the chairman before sending out official copies to the bulk of the members. The need for later amendments can usually be avoided by this procedure.

Regulations

Every library needs a clear and unambiguous code of regulations governing such matters as: admissions, loans, general discipline (*eg*, prohibition of smoking, bringing bags into the library, etc.), any charges for services such as photocopying and penalties for the breach of the regulations. Some organizations have established disciplinary codes. Where they do not exist and where substantial penalties are allowed, such as exclusion from the library, an appeal procedure must be formulated. If an appeal is made against a disciplinary decision the librarian must, of course, be scrupulous in referring the appeal to higher authority.

It is advisable that library regulations should be promulgated by the library committee. The librarian can find himself in an embarrassing situation if he is (or is thought to be) both legislator and policeman. The committee, being both representative of wider interests and relatively anonymous, can wield more power and, if necessary, bear any opprobrium better than a single administrator.

FINANCE

The sources of library finance vary. A professional library will be financed largely from the general funds of the parent organization, together with income from any investments that may have been earmarked for library purposes. These funds will almost invariably be totally private, owing nothing to either tax or ratepayers, as such. Academic, public and government libraries, on the other hand, are financed mainly from public funds, central or local. Both sources of income may be liable to fluctuations based either on the general business climate of success or otherwise or on the theory and practice concerning public expenditure of the government in power at any particular period.

Occasionally a library may be fortunate enough to receive unsolicited monetary gifts or legacies, although gifts in kind are probably more usual. Certain problems that may be involved in the receipt of gifts of books are discussed in Chapter 17. If funds are needed for a special development, such as the purchase of rare materials or the acquisition of land for a new building, it may be desirable to make an appeal to the members, or to a wider public. The chief librarian should endeavour to ensure that monetary gifts are made directly to the library, rather than to the general funds of the parent body.

Estimates

The librarian is usually expected to produce estimates for the cost of running the service, either annually or for anywhere between two and five years. The details of the estimating procedure and the timetable to be followed will be laid down by the body served. The main areas of expenditure likely to be involved include:

books, periodicals and binding
consumable materials (*eg*, stationery, library forms, catalogue cards)
durable materials (*eg*, shelves, furniture, machines)
maintenance of machines and equipment
subscriptions to computerized information or housekeeping services
building maintenance (including rent, rates, decorating, security)

staff salaries
capital expenditure (new buildings or major alterations)
insurance

Not every librarian will have to cover all of these categories.

Since a very high proportion (probably at least 75 per cent) of the stock of a law library is made up of serial and looseleaf publications, the subscriptions to which tend to rise considerably more rapidly than book prices or national inflation rates, special care must be taken not to underestimate future costs. If any of the published lists of average prices are used as a guide, they must be interpreted with great care, as they may include (or exclude) certain types of material, such as law reports, which are of special importance to the library. It is probably wiser to draw up lists of costs of a representative sample of the actual materials purchased. A librarian who has to buy a fair proportion of second-hand material can obtain help in estimating from second-hand catalogues or publications such as *Book Auction Records*.

An additional complication, especially for libraries with sizeable collections of overseas material, is the fluctuation of exchange rates. It is difficult for a librarian to forecast these movements, but their possible effects should be taken fully into account in estimating likely cost increases.

Costs of stationery, printing, furniture and equipment can be gauged from suppliers' price lists. Most firms are happy to provide quotations or additional information.

Staff estimates must include, in addition to the actual salaries, the employer's contributions to National Insurance and superannuation funds, holiday or any other bonuses and any payroll tax, etc., that may be in force at the time. The parent organization may well have a standard formula for these calculations. An allowance should also be calculated for any possible increase in salary scales, inflation adjustments and, of course, normal scale increments or promotions.

Accounts records

Systems of handling invoices and payments differ according to the practice of individual organizations. The most likely procedure is that the librarian certifies invoices as correct and passes them to the central finance office, which will usually prefer to receive them in regular batches, and may well specify a covering form, setting out information about fund codes, etc. The finance office will prepare and despatch cheques and keep the official account records. Especially if these are kept in a computer, the library should receive regular summaries of expenditure, probably accompanied by details of all paid invoices.

To make the best use of such statements, and to keep track of the library's position between times, it is necessary for the library to keep its own detailed records of actual and committed expenditure, especially on books and serial publications. An independent law library will do this for itself but, in some large organizations, such as universities or polytechnics, the law library's ordering and accounting is likely to be performed on its behalf by the central acquisitions department. The law librarian should receive regular statements of account to enable him to guide the rate of ordering. However, he would be well advised to keep his own records, especially of the total amount committed during the financial year for books and for all types of serial publications.

If a breakdown of figures is required, either by form (law reports, journals, treatises) or by subject or jurisdiction, a printed analysis book with the appropriate number of columns should be used. A simple pocket or desktop calculator will help with the relatively painless production of regular statements of expenditure, easing the problems of keeping proper control over both total annual expenditure and the monthly rate. A simple spreadsheet program on a microcomputer would do the job more quickly.

Suppliers' statements of account should be checked against the library's account records. Any apparent discrepancies should be referred immediately to the supplier or the finance office, as appropriate. If this is not done, the library may later receive urgent reminders or even final demands for sums that are not actually due.

Petty cash

The library should have a small petty cash float, for purposes such as postage (libraries commonly generate mail after the central post room has closed), refunds of postage on inter-library transactions, and other small items. A suitable record of all expenses, together with receipts where possible, should be kept for the accountant's and auditors' inspection.

Audits

Annual auditing of financial records is carried out in most organizations, but the degree to which the library is affected will depend on where the responsibility for official book-keeping rests. Local authority auditors examining library accounts may be assisted by central government officials. Government supported libraries may expect to receive occasional visits from the Exchequer and Audit Department. Private organizations' accounts are usually checked by outside commercial auditors.

Auditors may require the production of stock records, loan statistics, information on the steps taken to recover missing books and security arrangements in general.

Insurance

The librarian should ensure that both the fabric and the contents of the library are fully covered by insurance, and should be prepared to provide average figures for the value of serials and treatises, and to update them regularly. An exception to this may be made for those government and local authority bodies where the cost of complete insurance would be higher than that of replacing actual losses. The chief accountant usually conducts the actual negotiations with the insurance company or brokers.

Some libraries are now considering the idea of insuring fully only the basic core stock, and not covering the special extras, such as rare books or early runs of serials, which are likely to be irreplaceable in practice. If this is contemplated, it is essential to discuss the desired restrictions with the insurance company and have them carefully recorded in the policy. If this is not done, and there is a serious fire or flood, the library could lose the larger part of the intended cover by the application of the rules of average by the insurance company.

LIBRARY ADMINISTRATION

The chief librarian, whether of a one-man library or of a medium or large organization, is responsible to the authorities of his organization, to his readers and to his own staff for the proper running of the library. If he is to exercise this responsibility he must have the concomitant power and authority to do so. He should have, and be seen to have, a suitably high status within the organization. For example, he should be consulted in his own right before any changes are made that will affect the library, its services or its staff and he should be the first person that any member of the organization considers when a bibliographic or information problem arises. Full use should be made of his knowledge and experience in skills ancillary to library work, such as copyright deposit procedures for a publication produced by the organization.

One principle that every librarian should remember is that no one is indispensable. Where there are several staff, the chief librarian must learn to delegate authority, especially when he is away from the library himself. One test of a good leader is that his organization can function quite well, on a day to day basis, without him. At all levels, it is highly desirable that at least two people know how to perform any routine task. For example, it can be disastrous in a law library if no one deals with the incoming serial publications for even one week. In the same way, when the librarian is absent from a one-man library, for any reason, the library must shut down or risk disruption unless arrangements have been made in advance for a relief librarian to be given at least an elementary training.

It is important that the law librarian should keep full records of his activities, decisions and plans. No one is completely safe from sudden illness or accident, and great difficulty could be experienced by the person taking over in an emergency if sufficient records are not available and their organization is not simple and clear. At the same time, superseded papers should either be destroyed or clearly marked as being of historical interest only. Various kinds of library records, and methods of maintaining them consistently, are discussed at appropriate points throughout the following chapters.

There is nearly always a choice of several good methods available for handling any library routine. For example, there are various alternative methods of recording loans to readers each with its own group of advantages and disadvantages. In the abstract, it is impossible to say that any one of these is the best. Each librarian setting up or revising a lending service should examine a variety of issuing systems and decide for himself which best suits the circumstances of his particular library. The same principle applies to most other library procedures.

A general feature of libraries is that they tend to grow. Sooner or later the informal methods, based on the close personal relationships and intimate atmosphere of a small library, are likely to become inadaquate. It will then be necessary to take a hard critical look at the library administration and amend the techniques used, or even substitute new ones. A larger library usually requires more formal arrangements, such as the use of additional forms for various purposes. It may also be sensible to investigate whether the adoption of certain types of automation might be both helpful and economic.

Automation

Computers can be used in libraries for two separate types of work: information storage and retrieval and to perform administrative or clerical ('housekeeping') routines. Outlines of each type of use are given in the following chapters and there is a brief discussion of hardware requirements under 'Equipment' below. It must be remembered that libraries are subject to the provisions of the Data Protection Act 1984.

While computers can be very useful in various ways, it is important to remember that they are only a means to an end, not an end in themselves. They can perform many routine tasks very well, especially those involving mathematical calculations or repetitive clerical work, such as recording and filing loans. But there are still functions, particularly those requiring judgment, which are better performed directly by people. Furthermore, if the procedures concerned are not performed in considerable quantity, manual methods may be both quicker and cheaper than automation. There is a very useful discussion of these questions in Chapter 12 of Norman Higham's *Library in the university*, 1980, which could profitably be consulted by any law librarian contemplating the possibility of automation.

After taking account of these matters, the advantages of computer-based services are such that there seems little doubt that the proportion of law libraries making active use of computer technology will continue to increase. Technical developments, particularly in microcomputers, are coming so rapidly that it is difficult to give information or advice that will not be badly out of date by the time it is printed. A useful overview can be found in Lucy Tedd's *Introduction to computer-based library systems*, 2nd edn., 1984, but anyone seeking the latest position should consult the journal literature. A small selection of current titles is given at the end of the chapter. Useful articles can be traced through indexing services such as *Library and Information Science Abstracts*.

Information is also available from the professional associations, notably Aslib and the Library Association, and from the Library Technology Centre, which is at present housed in the Regent Street building of the Polytechnic of Central London. The various library computer co-operatives, such as BLCMP in Birmingham, SWALCAP in Bristol and SCOLCAP in Edinburgh will be glad to supply information and advice.

Internal organization

Large and medium-sized libraries have been traditionally arranged in departments based on library techniques: acquisitions, cataloguing, lending and reference. The first two are sometimes combined as 'technical services' and the last two as 'readers' services'. More recently in those academic and public libraries which have appointed numbers of subject specialist librarians, subject divisions, such as 'Law', have taken over many of the functions previously covered by all or some of these departments. It is often considered that the most suitable areas of work for such treatment are: information and enquiry work, book selection and possibly subject cataloguing and classification. On the other hand, the actual ordering and accounting are best handled by a single central acquisitions department and it is usually thought to be essential for a library to have a single service point for loans in each library building.

Many law libraries, however, are run by very small numbers of staff each of whom carries the responsibility for a variety of major duties. These librarians may thus enjoy a greater variety of tasks and gain fuller knowledge and experience in one post than their colleagues in larger organizations. On the other hand, in very small libraries they may feel the lack of the stimulus that can be provided by working with several other members of the library profession.

Office organization

If the number of correspondence files is never likely to be large, they can be housed in a deep desk drawer fitted with runners to hold standard manilla filing pockets. Larger collections should be kept in separate cabinets of filing drawers or in a lateral filing unit. All office furniture manufacturers make this type of equipment. The contents of the various files should be clearly shown and a list of files, either in alphabetical order or arranged by a simple home-made classification (*eg*, booksellers, other libraries, staff matters, estimates, etc.) would be helpful to a relief librarian or to the successor to a vacated post.

A policy decision should be taken regarding the normal period of time for the retention of letters and documents. This will depend upon the nature of their contents since some documents, especially those involving financial transactions or staff records, may need to be resurrected after several years. It is noticeable that requests for employment references for members of staff who left long ago cannot be ruled out.

If information is regularly needed from users, a form is often the best method of obtaining the exact type and quantity of details needed. Forms may easily be filed for future reference and should always be as simple as circumstances permit. This does not necessarily mean that they should be as small as possible – a form that provides insufficient blank space for proper answers is tiresome to the reader and nearly useless to the librarian. Any experienced printer will be happy to advise on the design of printed forms and an experienced typist should be entrusted with the details of the layout of a form to be duplicated from typescript, once the objectives have been clearly explained.

Statistics

Library statistics are needed both to tell the librarian what is actually happening, enabling him to take early note of possible new trends, and for use in reporting to the library's governing body and to the general public. Figures can show not only the size and rate of growth of the bookstock but also changes in costs; the growth of the catalogue; increases or decreases in the number of loans, inter-library loans, reservations, online and other enquiries; changes in the number and type of people using the library at various times of day or on different types of days, such as legal vacations; the volume of book losses, etc. Among the uses of the information collected could be: planning developments; estimating, including the need for additional shelving, catalogue cabinets and so on; calculating insurance values and, in the event of a disaster, an insurance claim.

Collecting statistics need not be too burdensome if it is dealt with in frequent small doses. If the daily and weekly figures are cumulated regularly, say once a month, the task of compiling statements for termly committee meetings or the annual report will be less of a chore than adding up long columns of figures at the last minute.

Public relations

No library can make adequate progress without financial and moral support from within its organization and, frequently, from outside as well. Good public relations are therefore an important consideration for the librarian. This is not a matter of advertising or high-powered publicity of the commercial or political variety, but rather of presenting facts in an interesting manner and of keeping the library in the public eye. In many ways the best form of publicity is good service but this reaches only those people who actually use the library. For many law libraries that means virtually all the potential users, but some libraries may still need to attract more people to their services. It is a truism that a good reputation is built up with difficulty and can be destroyed all too easily in a careless moment.

The function of the library committee in public relations has already been mentioned, but the committee is only one strand in the web of the library's relationships. Inside the parent organization are influential people: Benchers, professors, senior administrators, partners and so on, whose goodwill is needed for the promotion of costly new developments and, especially in a period of financial stringency, even for the basic finance needed to maintain existing services.

External relations

Most librarians enjoy showing visitors round and press on them copies of all available guides, book-lists and reports. Some libraries, particularly those of library schools, are delighted to receive other libraries' publications for use both as sources of information and as samples for study. Library schools have also appreciated offers from some law libraries to receive either groups of students on organized visits or single students for fieldwork placings for about a month at a time. Neither of these activities should cost the library anything more than a few cups of tea.

Prospective visitors should be encouraged to make arrangements in advance as unheralded arrivals can cause inconvenience, embarrassment or disappointment.

Librarians, in both their professional and personal capacities, should support their professional associations which provide opportunities for bringing together people with similar interests and problems. They can thus help to develop a common pool of knowledge and experience where all who are interested may share in the advantages which arise from a free flow of information and exchange of ideas.

Librarians should become acquainted with their local booksellers who will usually be happy to put their expertise at the library's disposal. The bookseller's service to the library is almost invariably improved by the establishment of personal contact.

Law publishers also value contact with librarians, which can be brought about either by their travelling representatives or through attendance at BIALL conferences. Publishers are interested to find out librarians' opinions of their books and will look carefully at any suggestions for fresh ventures.

STAFFING

Establishment

The number of people needed to operate a library service depends on several variables including:

the number of hours the library should be open to readers;
the number of users to be served, especially at peak periods;
the rate of acquisition of new material, including issues of serial publications and looseleaf publications;
the amount of servicing of a law branch library performed by the central library (where applicable);
the physical layout, with special reference to:
the number of service points
security problems
putting books away.

The first three are probably the most important. It is usually regarded as essential that the law library should be staffed at all times when it is open. Therefore, a minimum of two staff is recommended in Standard 23 so that closure at, for example, lunch-time can be avoided. Needs for evening or weekend opening must also be considered. Some libraries find it convenient to cover these hours, at least in part, by the employment of part-time staff. It is highly desirable that any such part-time staff should be entirely responsible to the law librarian, rather than being students or other people whose loyalties could be put under strain. If there are two or more essential service points, the number of staff needed will obviously be greater than if the layout permits a single staff desk.

The volume of material of all types coming into the library is probably more important in calculating staff needs than the size of the total stock. For example, a new library being quickly built up from scratch to, say, 15,000 volumes is likely to require more people during its period of rapid growth than a library of twice that size that has settled down to a much slower rate of growth. The solution to this particular situation may well be the employment of one or two people on short-term contracts during a period of rapid build-up or other massive change, such as computerization.

Opinions vary about the correct ratio between the professional and non-professional posts in libraries. It is safe to say that at least one third of the staff should be professional librarians, employed and paid to perform professional library duties (see also under 'Allocation of duties', below). In a law library where readers need a considerable amount of professional bibliographical and information service, a ratio of one professional to one non-professional post would be fully justified. It must be remembered that there will always be a need for non-professional staff to undertake the routine, largely clerical, tasks that abound in any library.

The BIALL Standards set out a formula for calculating staff establishments for libraries which may need more than the basic minimum of two people.

Recruitment

Appointments to publicly-funded posts usually have to be made by open public advertisement. Permanent full-time posts are best advertised in the professional press, notably the *Library Association Record Vacancies Supplement*, which is at present published twice each month, or the *Times Literary Supplement*. Private libraries often use the same journals for advertising vacancies. Law libraries could use legal weekly journals for advertising junior posts, but for professional posts should use journals with a wider circulation among professional librarians.

Non-professional posts, especially those which are either temporary or part-time, may be advertised in the appropriate local papers. Libraries in the centre of London, where there are relatively few local residents, could advertise in one or two of the papers which cover several of the inner London boroughs, such as the *South London Press*. The London evening paper and the national press are likely to be too expensive for most law libraries to contemplate.

Advertisements should be concise, provided they give the essential information such as level of qualifications required and salary offered, and should always specify the closing date for applications. It is usual to prepare a separate sheet giving more details of the organization, the duties of the post, the conditions of service, etc., for distribution on request to potential applicants. This sheet can then form the basis of the subsequent contract of employment, together with the actual offer and acceptance letters exchanged between the organization and the successful candidate.

Some organizations provide application forms and specify the number of copies to be filled in by applicants. This need be only a single copy, as photocopies can be made of the papers for shortlisted candidates. Otherwise, a candidate will be expected to provide his own curriculum vitae. It will help them to do so satisfactorily if the further particulars sheet specifies all the information required about qualifications, previous experience, etc.

Interviews

On or after the closing date, the librarian should draw up a shortlist of candidates to be interviewed, on the basis of criteria already established, most of which will have been published in the advertisement or the particulars. Candidates with inadequate qualifications or experience should be eliminated quickly. There could be a considerable number of suitably qualified candidates, especially for a non-professional post requiring little more than two 'A' levels. If the post is a permanent one, the librarian can look for evidence of commitment to librarianship, or any other relevant criterion to help in selecting four or five people for interview. Confidential references should be sought for all shortlisted candidates, and might be useful in helping to select them in the first place.

For professional posts, at least, formal interviews should be arranged. In addition to the law librarian, the panel should include someone able to speak with authority on salaries and conditions in the organization. If the law library is part of a larger general library, the chair will probably be taken by the chief librarian, but it is essential that the law librarian is present. If a new head for the law library itself is being chosen, and there are no superior librarians in the organization, careful consideration should be given to inviting a suitably qualified librarian from outside to attend as an adviser. Interviews for part-time or non-professional staff can be less formal but the panel must be identical for all interviews for any particular post.

The general shape of a series of interviews should be agreed by the panel before any candidates are seen. It is quite usual for the chairman to take a candidate through all or some of the details of his application to help calm him in an obviously nerve-racking situation. Any gaps in the information provided should be enquired into. The candidate may have been ill, or may have been undertaking some enterprising, non-library activity which is indicative of his general character. It is often necessary to take some time to explain the duties of the post to candidates, but it is vital to give each one a full opportunity to speak for himself. Within reason, questions requiring 'yes' or 'no' answers should be avoided in favour of those requiring the candidate to express preferences or give reasons for his answers.

Letters of appointment must be signed by a duly authorized official of the organization, as they form part of the contract of service. It is highly desirable that each applicant should receive a reply, positive or negative, if the postage funds can be found. A totally unanswered application gives a poor impression of the organization, which could put off good candidates from applying at all for subsequent vacancies.

Qualifications

For professional posts, normal library or information professional qualifications should be held. There is a variety of qualifications available, such as Chartered Librarian, BLib, Postgraduate Diploma in Librarianship or Membership of the Institute of Information Scientists. Full current information should be obtained from the professional associations, as the situation can change. Some law libraries regard a degree in law as a useful qualification, but it is scarcely practicable to insist on one.

Staff in non-professional posts are usually expected to have passed at least two subjects at 'A' level in England and Wales, or the equivalent elsewhere.

Training

There are courses or options in law librarianship to be found at some library schools from time to time. Again, it is advisable to check current details in a changeable situation.

The British and Irish Association of Law Librarians runs one-day seminars and short courses on particular aspects of legal bibliography or law librarianship, which are advertised in the Association's literature. These courses can be useful to both professional and non-professional law library staff, especially people who have not worked in the subject area for very long.

Most training of law library staff takes place within the law library itself. All grades of staff need to learn basic information about legal bibliography as rapidly as possible, as well as the normal everyday routines of the particular library. In the smaller libraries, new staff are likely to pick up most of what they need to know from more experienced colleagues and from appropriate literature, such as this *Manual*. Formal training courses may be possible in a handful of the largest law libraries.

The law library may become involved in a new scheme of training, such as the Licentiate regulations of the Library Association. Advice should be sought from the qualifying body and from colleagues with suitable contacts or experience. Formal in-service training schemes of this type can be useful, but will also be very time-consuming for all concerned and should be approached with some caution before adoption by a small library.

Staff management

The chief librarian is responsible for all aspects of the management of the library and the application of the policies laid down by its governing body. He should ensure that all members of staff are kept informed of developments, plans and decisions and are properly consulted, especially about the practical effects of projected changes. In a small library, or a branch or department of a larger library, it should be possible to achieve these effects by informal discussions, usually with the whole staff together at one time. In a large library, with some people performing shift duties, or working at very busy service points, it may be necessary to hold representative meetings, circulate information bulletins, etc. In either case, staff at any level may make very useful suggestions or constructive criticisms, based on their intimate knowledge of routine procedures and of readers' reactions to them.

Once decisions have been taken, they should be carried out consistently. Continuity of practice, subject of course to necessary improvements, is a cornerstone of efficient library administration, and must be maintained by the successive occupants of each post. One of the best methods of ensuring consistency is the compilation and regular maintenance of a staff procedures manual, consisting of written accounts, illustrated with samples of appropriate forms, catalogue cards, etc., of all the regular routines in the library, in whatever degree of detail appears to be necessary. This applies to large and small libraries equally. The manual should be available for reference to all staff at all times, and could be studied at greater length by new recruits, visiting library students, etc. In a large library, it may be more convenient to have a series of departmental manuals, rather than one large centralized volume.

Timetabling and timekeeping are very important in any library. Most law libraries are likely to be open to their public for longer than normal office hours, so that some form of shift duties will be needed. The staff should be able to see readily the need for keeping to strict duty rotas and for careful planning of holiday arrangements, time off in lieu of shift duties, etc.

Allocation of duties

If there are three or more professional staff, a clear decision should be made as to which person will deputize for the law librarian in his absence. Everyone, including at least the most frequent users, should be informed of the arrangement and the limits to the deputy's authority must be fully discussed with him. The division of permanent responsibilities between chief and deputy in the normal running of the library can be settled between them, according to their particular abilities and interests.

There is fairly general agreement about the different range of duties expected of professional and non-professional staff in libraries, including law libraries. A detailed list is published as Appendix I to the BIALL Standards, under the main headings: 'policy', 'general administration', 'staff', 'stock control', 'acquisitions', 'cataloguing and classification', 'stock maintenance', 'services' and 'buildings'. In small libraries it may not be possible to divide activities so neatly between two or three staff members, and it is probable that in most law libraries, staff members must be prepared to perform any duty that is needed at any time.

Each member of staff should receive a job description. This is often included as one of the documents given to him at the time of appointment, but the possibility of making changes must remain available to the library management. As far as possible, the person concerned should agree to such changes.

ACCOMMODATION

No library can function effectively unless it is housed in suitable accommodation. A space that is barely adequate, awkwardly shaped or inconveniently located within the building cannot be defined as 'suitable' for the library. It is the responsibility of the law librarian to draw his authority's attention to serious inadequacies in the accommodation of his library, preferably well in advance. Because of the expense of radical improvements, not to mention the time required for planning and executing building or adaptation work, he will probably be hammering on the door for a considerable period before results are obtained, but it is imperative that he maintains the effort. Without deliberate effort, poor accommodation can only deteriorate as the library continues its inevitable growth.

Few law librarians are likely to have the opportunity of taking part in the designing and erection of a new free-standing law library building. A number will, however, be involved in the planning of the library section of a law faculty, court, office or other building or the legal section of a general library. The same principles should be applied to any of these possible situations. The need for the librarian and his staff to be closely involved in any accommodation planning cannot be overemphasized.

If the librarian's authority remains unconvinced of the validity of the principles set out in the BIALL Standards, section 8 and Appendices II–V, or the other sources referred to below, the librarian should make every effort to take a group of lawyers or administrators to visit well-planned law libraries and talk to the staff there. Once convinced of the need for better accommodation for the library, the authority is more likely to make serious efforts to provide the necessary funds.

General principles

More has probably been written since 1945 about the principles of academic library buildings than any other single type of library. However, as one of the chief principles put forward is the need for flexibility, it is not unreasonable to recommend that much of what has been said and done in the academic context should be adopted, with any necessary minor modifications, for other types of library buildings, including law libraries.

The original impetus came from the United States, where Dr Keyes Metcalfe, in many articles and his book *Planning Academic and Research Library Buildings*, 1965, advocated flexible modular design. The principles he enunciated have been adopted by many British architects and developed by, among others, Harry Faulkner-Brown. In his review of 'Academic library buildings in the United Kingdom' in *Advances in Librarianship*, vol. 3, 1972, Mr. Faulkner-Brown sets out ten basic principles. The library should be:

'Flexible, with a layout, structures and services which are easy to adapt;

Compact, for ease of movement of readers, staff and books;

Accessible, from the exterior into the building, and from the entrance to all parts of the building, with an easily comprehensible plan, needing minimum supplementary directions;

Extendable, to permit future growth;

Varied in the provision of reader spaces, to give wide freedom of choice;

Organized, to impose maximum confrontation between books and readers;

Comfortable, to promote efficiency of use;

Constant in environment, for the preservation of library materials;

Secure, to control user behaviour and loss of books;

Indicative of its function.'

These principles, or most of them, are widely accepted for application to many types of libraries and are as valid for law libraries as for any others.

Space requirements

Much useful information has been included in the BIALL Standards, section 8, and Appendices II–V. Another valuable source of data is the *New Metric Handbook*, 1979, pp. 293–9, 'Libraries'.

The normal method of calculating space needs used to be to add up the figures for bookstacks, readers' seating and staff working areas, according to standard formulae and add a set percentage for the 'balance area', allowing for stairs, corridors, toilets, plantrooms, etc. These formulae are discussed below and could reasonably be applied to most types of libraries.

With the growing restrictions on public expenditure being applied to academic buildings, the Atkinson report of 1976 set limits for university library buildings on a totally different basis. Atkinson allowed a set area for each student (measured in full-time equivalents) with a very limited addition for future expansion. When the area so calculated was full, the report broadly applied a 'one-in-one-out' philosophy. The same principle is usually applied now to most government-funded libraries.

Books

Law books tend to be thicker than those in many other subjects, so that a standard shelf of 900mm. will hold an average of 15–18 volumes. Most law books need a shelf depth of 200–250mm. and a clear space of 300mm. between shelves. A bay of shelves should not normally be more than 900mm. wide, because of the weight of the books, and a unit about 2,300mm. high should hold seven shelves of average-sized books. Quarto and folio volumes will, of course, mean fewer shelves per bay, and therefore more bays for the same number of books.

The floor space required for 1,000 average-sized law books is 5.4 square metres for open access stacks and 4.6 square metres for closed access shelves. If rolling stacks are employed to house books which are rarely used, considerable savings in floor space can be achieved, but at a considerable cost in convenience. It must be remembered that rolling stacks need a specially strengthened floor.

Calculations should provide for several years' growth of the stock. Any law librarian will wish to allow as much space as possible for the ever-expanding collection of, particularly, the serial publications which are the basis of every law library, but the practical facts of financial and other rules will almost certainly limit ambitions in this direction.

When the limits of capacity of any building have been reached, consideration will have to be given to the possible alternatives, *eg*, physical extension, withdrawal of books from stock or finding a book store outside the main library, either an established depository library or as the private property of the particular library involved.

Readers

Law library users tend to need to gather several volumes for simultaneous reference, thus needing a larger table area for each person than readers in many other subjects. A table space of 0.54 s.m. can be converted into 3.25 s.m. of total floor space per reader, allowing for table, chair and access for other readers to adjacent seats or shelves.

Screened seats, sometimes called open carrels, require much the same space, but enclosed, probably lockable carrels require at least 3.5 s.m. each.

The number of seats provided should be as high as possible. For academic law libraries, a standard of one seat for every two students should be the target. Other libraries should take account of patterns of use. For example, government lawyers who usually take books to their offices need fewer seats than users of libraries where removal of books is not allowed under any circumstances.

Other public areas

Space will be needed for public catalogues, whether manual or automated, online terminals (*eg*, LEXIS), photocopying machines and possibly for audio- or video-cassette equipment, or for typing rooms for readers' use.

Staff

The standard allowance for staff workrooms and offices in academic libraries is 7–9 s.m. per person. This should include space for temporary storage of books in process, book trolleys, etc., adjacent to the desk or table. Where a private office is needed, it should be at least 15 square metres. There may additionally be a need for a sound-dampened room for typewriters, electronic printers, telex terminals, etc.

Balance area

The proportion of space required for ancillary uses is likely to depend on the position of the library in relation to other services provided by the organization. Lifts, internal staircases, toilets, etc., may or may not be necessary within the library area. Spaces may have to be provided for various other activities, such as a loading and unloading bay for goods deliveries, coat and bag deposit room, cleaners' store, staff rest room and lockers, exhibition space and so on.

Environment and services

Heating

For most readers, the comfortable heat level for sedentary study is about 20°–22°C (68°–72°F). For staff working conditions, the same level should be the target, but it should be remembered that the statutory minimum is 16°C (60.5°F), which is uncomfortably low for clerical and similar work. The best storage temperature for books is somewhat lower: 13°–18°C (55°–65°F). Rare and precious books should definitely be stored within this range throughout the year, but more everyday material will probably suffer little from being stored in public reading rooms at the higher temperature recommended for readers.

Ventilation

Older books and manuscripts in particular must be stored in an area where the relative humidity is controlled between 55 and 65 per cent, even if this means setting aside a separate air-conditioned room for the purpose. They should also be protected from direct sunlight and airborne impurities or chemicals.

For readers and staff there should be a complete air change at least three times an hour. This may be achieved in a relatively thin-shaped building by natural ventilation, but in a large deep building (such as a large square) forced ventilation or air-conditioning is essential. If the building has to be insulated against excessive noise or fumes, such as those from nearby roads, railways or factories, the architect will probably specify fixed windows, preferably double-glazed, and air-conditioning throughout.

Lighting

Lighting is naturally very important in a library. The majority of readers or staff feel most comfortable if they can see out of a window, even if it does not provide adequate light inside the building. This psychological effect should be borne in mind when working out floor plans.

A reliable consultant should be asked to advise on current standards, as they may have changed since the BIALL Standards were written, and new lighting equipment is constantly coming onto the market. He should also advise on the best colour of lighting units for the particular building. It is essential that good levels of lighting, not barely adequate minima, are provided both at reading tables and in stack areas, where book spines must be legible at all levels, high and low. Light-coloured finishes can help, as can reflecting surfaces, provided that glare is avoided.

If possible, light fittings should not all be aligned in a single direction. Apart from visual monotony, this type of design can hinder the later rearrangement of furniture or shelving, including the installation of extra shelf units to house a growing stock.

Consideration should be given to emergency lights, operated possibly by batteries or by a stand-by generator. They should light exit signs, stairways, etc., and provide for safe negotiation of all potential hazards.

Noise control

External noise can be reduced by the architect's use of sound-absorbing materials in walls, roofs and double, or even treble, glazing. An acceptable level of internal noise can be achieved by the use of absorbent materials, such as acoustic tiles, carpets and curtains. Noise from air-conditioning or ventilation fans should be not more than a steady hum. Certain noisy machines, notably photocopiers, should be sited with special care in relation to study areas and to noise-carrying areas such as staircases.

Security

Precautions should be taken to secure both the personal safety and the property of readers, staff and the library itself. The architect is responsible for complying with fire regulations, such as means of escape, fire-retarding walls and doors, smoke detectors, fire extinguishers, etc. Sprinklers are not recommended for libraries, or at least for book storage areas.

Water is a great enemy of books and special care should be taken to avoid possible flood damage, either from external sources or from leaking pipes or radiators within the building.

This means that the use of basements for book storage must be carefully thought out in relation to flood levels, etc.

Safety from physical attack, *eg*, mugging, or theft is largely a matter of common sense and constant vigilance. Dark and dangerous corners should not exist in a library, but if entrance to the library cannot be properly controlled, or is legally available to all comers, a closed circuit television system may have to be considered.

External security against break-ins must be dealt with by the parent organization and the architect. Good locks are an obvious precaution, as is a security patrol, but for sensitive buildings or sites a burglar alarm may be desirable.

Mains services

Provision will be needed for water supply, both for everyday use and for fire hoses and external hydrants. The library will need to be connected to the main sewers.

Mains electricity will be needed for lighting and power, and either gas, electricity or oil will be used for heating rooms and water and for any refreshment facilities provided for library staff or readers. It is very important to consider the needs of future library services for a large number of electric power outlets, telephone points for data links, etc., as well as for current use.

An important consideration in planning any new library accommodation is the provision of ducts or trunking to carry various types of cables to all parts of the building: electric power lines, telephone and data lines, TV cables, etc. Any of these may be needed in the future, if not immediately. It is highly desirable that, when building work is undertaken, ducting should be incorporated, as it adds only a little to costs at that stage whereas, if superimposed later on, it is likely to be both costly and unsightly.

Libraries tend to receive a constant flow of parcels as well as letters and journals; most also despatch parcels to other libraries, binderies, etc. Therefore, a library needs easy access to the organization's postroom and the outside world. An independent library building should have direct road access.

Planning and procedures

The long and complex series of operations involved in planning library accommodation, whether in a new or a converted building, are well set out in Godfrey Thompson's *Planning and Design of Library Buildings*, 1973. Brief mentions of some of the main items to be considered by a librarian are given below. The law librarian and his staff should be actively involved at all stages of the planning.

Location

The site for a new building will probably be dictated by external factors, such as ownership of a city centre site by a public or private body, or which areas in an academic campus have not yet been developed. If there is any choice, the law library should ideally be situated either within the general library of the parent organization or adjacent to the accommodation of the lawyers, law faculty, etc., which it is to serve, depending on local circumstances.

If an existing building, room or rooms are to be adapted or converted to law library use, the same general principles should be applied. Any extension of an existing library must be adjacent to the present area, either on the same floor or, if necessary, immediately above or below and connected by an internal staircase. It is essential that the whole of the extended library should be operated as a combined unit, with a single entrance point.

Legal requirements

The law relating to the planning, construction and conversion of buildings should be well known to the architects and the clerk of works. Sometimes the legal requirements, particularly those concerned with means of escape, may conflict with the librarian's operational preferences. In this case, the law will have to prevail.

The local authority may have special requirements concerning traffic planning, parking, sight lines, etc., and neighbours may have rights to light and air ('ancient lights') which must be respected.

The needs of the disabled must also be remembered. For example, access to all parts of the building should be possible for a reader confined to a wheelchair and provision should be made for a blind reader who needs to have a sighted person read aloud to him, possibly for him to make a copy with a braille typewriter.

Architects and builders

The law librarian should be consulted on the selection of architects for a law library project. Previous library design experience, endorsed as satisfactory by the librarian clients, is probably the first criterion of selection, and it is highly desirable that the people responsible for selecting architects should visit several relevant libraries and interview librarians as well as architects.

If the design is to be the responsibility of an architect who has some form of permanent contract or responsibility extending beyond the library project, the law librarian should make the most strenuous efforts to ensure that the architect studies the special needs of law libraries and visits successful buildings, talking to the librarians himself. The architect will not normally need any encouragement to undertake research on these lines.

The law librarian should work closely with the architect in drawing up the design brief, a document setting out the purposes of the project and the types and sizes of spaces required for each of the various activities and services of the library. There should be a true dialogue between architect and librarian, with each helping the other to develop satisfactory final plans.

The builders and specialist contractors will normally be selected by the architects after tendering. Some specialist suppliers, such as shelving contractors, should be selected by agreement between the architect and the librarian.

Conversions

The same principles apply to designing adaptations and conversions as to the design of new buildings. The principles of flexibility, space and environmental needs, etc., will be exactly the same, although fulfilling them may well be much more difficult because of structural or other limitations of the present building.

One factor that needs very careful attention is the adequacy, indeed the safety, of the present floors for library purposes. Floors in a building designed for residential use are unlikely to be suitable for storing books in any quantity unless they are greatly strengthened at a cost which could be prohibitive. It is absolutely essential that advice should be obtained from a structural engineer before a commitment is made to adapt any premises to library use, especially for bookstacks.

Finance

For any library building project, finance has to be found to cover all or most of the following:

acquisition of the site,
demolition of existing building(s),
construction or conversion of accommodation,
professional fees and expenses,
furniture and equipment.

Construction of the shell and fitting it out with services, etc., is likely to be the largest element. Funds in the public sector to cover professional charges and furniture are often calculated as percentages of the basic construction costs.

A typical calculation of allowable costs for a public project might be (at 1985 prices):

	£ per m²
basic building cost	400
London addition @ 20%	80
addition for external works and contingencies	50
total building cost	530
furniture & equipment @ 15%	79.5
professional charges @ 18%	95.4
overall cost limit	£704.9 per square metre.

These are, of course, only sample figures and actual rates of costs and allocations would have to be individually discovered for each project.

Moving in

This could well cause the biggest headache for the library staff. At its simplest, the books and records only would have to be moved from the old furniture into new furniture standing empty and ready in the new area. If necessary, a removal firm with experience of moving libraries could be engaged to perform all the heavy moving, with a member of the library staff at each end to supervise the loading and unloading respectively. This may sound easy, but the operation is rarely as simple as that.

All too frequently, existing shelving and other furniture will have to be emptied for removal to and re-erection in the new rooms. In the meantime, books, journals, records and files will have to be packed into suitable containers to await their turn to be moved and rehoused. Very careful planning of such an operation is absolutely essential and must be completed well in advance of the first day of the actual move. It is also wise to develop in advance contingency plans for dealing with the almost inevitable snags, delays and other frustrations which are likely to occur.

A good removal firm can be very helpful in the planning as well as the execution of the move. Suitable plastic boxes or wire baskets (preferably not tea chests, which are too deep) for storing and moving the books can be hired, if the removal firm does not have enough of their own. Good boxes or baskets hold one or two shelffulls of books, and can be loaded with exactly the right quantity to fit the shelving plan in the new library. If boxes and shelves are accurately labelled to match, the operation should proceed with a fair degree of success.

EQUIPMENT AND FURNITURE

Shelving

It is advisable to obtain shelving for a law library from a supplier who specializes in library shelving. Neither industrial nor domestic shelves are really suitable for libraries. Names and addresses of possible firms can be obtained from the professional associations or the commercial reference section of the nearest large public library system.

Wooden shelving used to be considered cheaper than steel shelving, but this is no longer necessarily the case. Either material can be both sturdy and attractive in appearance. The choice between them, if there is no need to match existing furniture, is largely a matter of taste. In addition, there are now some manufacturers who offer mixed shelving with steel uprights and wooden shelves. A variety of colours and finishes is also available.

The most suitable dimensions for stack shelving, already mentioned, are for bays 900mm. wide, 200–250mm. deep and not more than 2,300mm. high. These can be ranged, single-faced, along any walls that are strong enough to hold their loaded weight, or built up into free-standing double-faced units of the required length. For an open-access bookstack, ranges of shelves should be placed so that their centres are about 1,500mm. apart, but for a closed stack 1,350mm. centres are acceptable. The *New Metric Handbook*, 1979, has many useful diagrams showing possible arrangements of shelves and seats and the recommended dimensions. If space is a problem, better use can be made of what is available by keeping shelves and seats in different (but adjacent) areas.

If very closely placed stacks are needed, it may be possible to install a mobile or rolling stack. These require specially strengthened floors and tend to be expensive to install, but do save a considerable amount of space.

Periodicals and other serial publications can be housed on ordinary shelves, but must be safely and tidily placed in suitable boxes or binders. Many libraries like to display the current issues on a rack, usually with sloping shelves, so that readers can tell immediately which is the latest issue of each title available. Recent back issues *ie*, since the last bound volume, can be kept either in boxes or binders on the same shelves as the main sets or in pigeonholes behind the display shelves.

Furniture

Tables for readers can be obtained from any library furniture supplier. Very few libraries have enough floor space to allow them to provide single tables only. If a table is expected to seat two or more readers, it is often thought desirable for it to have a vertical divider down the centre. Some also have dividers across their width, thus giving a sense of relative privacy to each reader. This type of table is sometimes called an 'open carrel', but the term 'carrel' on its own usually means a small room or study, with furniture for a single reader, and possibly a lockable door.

A large room closely furnished with long tables and ranks of chairs can look uninviting. It is better, if possible, to arrange the reading areas so that there is some variety of view, with a few plants, perhaps, or racks of current serials or, at least, two or three different styles of tables and an armchair or two.

Every law library, however small, is likely to need at least one book trolley. Badly designed trolleys are liable to tip over if loaded on one side only, and any trolley may be difficult to manoeuvre in confined spaces when fully loaded. On the whole, a trolley with wheels at each corner is probably both more stable and easier to manage than one with wheels in the centres of the four sides. Most book trolleys have slightly sloping shelves, backing onto each other, although some have a single row of shelves and yet others have flat shelves, ideal for moving large volumes, such as atlases, or collections of stationery or small items of any sort.

If the size of the rooms available has dictated very high shelves, the law librarian will have to provide steps or ladders. For shelves that are only a little higher than the shorter reader can reach, a movable stool or low step may be sufficient. If the height is too great for these, steps with a small platform and a safety rail may well be desirable for older readers' use, or for lawyers or law students who may need to pick out several volumes at a time for removal to their tables. If, however, a tall ladder is unavoidable, great care must be taken to ensure that it is safe.

Library staff will normally require office desks and chairs of a normal pattern. Service desks or counters can be obtained from library suppliers, either in the form of standard units which can be combined as required, or to special order. Storage cabinets for catalogue cards, microforms and other materials are easily found from library or office contractors, as is display and guiding equipment. Desks and tables specifically designed for computer terminals and printers are made by several office equipment firms.

Automation equipment

If any of the library's housekeeping routines are automated, the make of computer equipment needed will almost certainly be dictated by the supplier of the service, basically the operating programs. The library will need at least one microcomputer (or one terminal to the mainframe computer) and a compatible floppy disk drive. Data can be keyboarded directly into the system or collected by means of a light pen or other unit, such as an ALS book reader.

Output from an automated system can be stored on floppy disks, if small in quantity, or on a hard disk, or transmitted to a mainframe computer for storage. It is very likely that the law library will need printed copies of data input to or produced by the system. Some electronic printers, especially the dot matrix variety, are remarkably cheap. However, the quality of their printing may be unacceptable, and this must be checked before ordering. For booklists or other publications, especially those produced from a word processor, it is advisable to invest in a daisywheel printer, whose print quality is usually superior to that of a dot matrix machine.

The equipment required for online information retrieval may be dictated by the data supplier, as used to be the case with LEXIS, or the library may have a choice of suitable machines. If that is so, many office-type microcomputers are likely to be suitable. A dataline, or at least a 'clean' telephone line will be needed together with an acoustic coupler or, preferably, a modem.

Whenever computer equipment is under consideration, it is absolutely imperative that the library obtains unbiased expert opinion. It is all too easy to select equipment that is not exactly right for the library's purposes, and mistakes can be very costly to correct. At the time of purchase, arrangements must be made for servicing and repair. Even brand-new computer equipment, especially disk drives, can go wrong. Once a system is running, any delays can cause great difficulty.

Other equipment

Photocopying

Almost every library has a photocopying machine. They come in a variety of forms, sizes and prices. Salesmen can be very persuasive and impartial advice should be sought from other libraries. The capital cost of purchase can be high, especially for a small library, and various arrangements for renting or leasing are offered by most companies. It is well worth investigating these as, although the total cost over three or four years may be higher than that of purchase, they usually include 'free' servicing and the costs are spread fairly evenly over the period. In a busy library, these machines lead a hard life and a short one. One minor advantage of a rental or leasing scheme is that the owners can be expected to remove the worn-out machine at the end of the contract period. At least one firm offers a form of credit-card control box as a substitute for coin-box operation. Details of photocopying services and related copyright questions are given in Chapter 15.

Microform readers

Microfilm and microfiche readers will be needed by most law libraries. If users are likely to want to take hard copies away for further study, it is worth thinking of acquiring a reader–printer. They cost considerably more than the plain machines, but may save considerable time and effort as compared to sending films or fiches to a photographic laboratory for printing.

Audio-visual equipment

If the law library is building up a collection of audio- or video-cassettes, etc., machines for using them should be provided on the premises. Loudspeakers will normally be replaced by headphone sets, unless the library is able to install sound-proofed booths for their use.

Office equipment

Typewriters, manual, electric or electronic, are not difficult to find. If the library types its own catalogue cards, it is important to ensure that the typewriters used are fully suitable for the small dimensions and extra thickness of the cards and that the typeface of a new machine matches well with that of the old one. A well compiled catalogue can be spoiled by the use of several different styles of type on the cards. The library may need to have a duplicator or an office photocopying machine, separate from those used by the readers.

LIBRARY CO-OPERATION

Librarians, by tradition and training, are normally of a helpful disposition. At the same time, no library, however large and wealthy, can be entirely self-sufficient. Both factors inevitably lead towards co-operation with other libraries. There is a network of formal and informal co-operation from which any library, large or small, general or special, can benefit, whether or not it is in a position to reciprocate. Any person who is charged with looking after a law library can ask for help and advice from the nearest large library service, public, university or polytechnic, or from any member of BIALL. If the first librarian approached is not equipped to deal with a particular problem, he should be able to pass the enquiry to one who is. The addresses and telephone numbers of likely libraries can be found in the directories mentioned in Chapter 9.

Library co-operation used to be thought of primarily in terms of inter-library loans. While the inter-lending system is constantly being extended and improved, especially by the British Library Lending Division – more details of which are given in Chapter 15 – there are several other areas of regular co-operation which may be relevant to a law library, such as co-operative acquisition, exchanges and storage; co-operative cataloguing and the production of union catalogues; information networks and other co-operative uses of automation. For further details see the following chapters.

LIBRARY RESEARCH

Research into a variety of aspects of libraries is being undertaken in libraries and in library schools. Some research projects are sponsored by official bodies, notably the British Library Research and Development Department, or by professional bodies, such as Aslib, the Library Association and the Cataloguing Research Group. Individual librarians who wish to work for higher degrees are likely to seek registration with one of the library schools where a suitably qualified supervisor may be found.

BIALL has undertaken one or two small investigations, such as the questionnaire on cataloguing and classification practices in libraries with legal collections, circulated in the autumn of 1983 and processed in early 1984. Reports on this and other BIALL projects can usually be found in the *Law Librarian*.

Details of research in progress can be found in *Current Research in Library and Information Science* and particulars of completed projects which have led to publication will be found in *Library and Information Science Abstracts* or *Library Literature*.

FURTHER READING

GENERAL WORKS ON LIBRARY ADMINISTRATION

Blunt, A. *Law librarianship*, 1980.
Handbook of special librarianship and information work, 5th edn., 1982.
Higham, N. *The library in the university*, 1980.
Lock, R. N. *Manual of library economy*, 1977.
University Librarianship, Stirling, J. F. (ed.) 1981.

LAW LIBRARY POLICY AND PLANNING

Magavero, G. 'Circulation policy in law libraries', *Law Library Journal*,
    vol. 69, 1976, pp. 15–25.
Roalfe, W. R. 'Centralized university library service and the law
    school', *Law Library Journal*, vol. 50, 1957, pp. 2–5.
Wilson, J. F. A. 'Survey of legal education in the United Kingdom',
    Journal of the Society of Public Teachers of Law, vol. 9, 1966, pp. 1–
    144.

GOVERNMENT

Cooper, J. 'University library committees', *Journal of Librarianship*,
    vol. 17, 1985, pp. 167–84.
Stockham, K. A. *Government and control of libraries*, 2nd edn., 1975.

LIBRARY FINANCE

Carter, A. M. 'Budgeting in private law firm libraries', *Law Library
    Journal*, vol. 71, 1978, pp. 187–94.
Cooper, A. *Financial aspects of library and information services: a bib-
    liography*, 1980.
Costing and the Economics of library and information services, Roberts, S.
    A. (ed.) 1984.

AUTOMATION

Books and articles

Anderson, M. 'Automation in the law school library', *Law Librarian*, vol. 11, 1980, pp. 11–14.
Davies, J. E. *Data protection: a guide for library and information management*, 1984.
Marek, K. 'Automation in the private law library', *Law Library Journal*, vol. 73, 1980, pp. 134–42.
Tedd, L. A. *Introduction to computer-based library systems*, 2nd edn., 1984.

Journals

Annual Review of Information Science and Technology, 1966–.
Computers and Law, 1974–.
Information Technology and Libraries, 1968–.
Library Micromation News, 1984–.
Library Technology Reports, 1965–.
Online Review, 1977–.
Program, 1966–.
Vine, 1971–.

STATISTICS

Simpson, I. S. *Basic statistics for librarians*, 2nd edn., 1983.

PUBLIC RELATIONS

Harrison, K. C. *Public relations for librarians*, 2nd edn., 1982.

STAFFING

Bull, G. E. 'Education of law librarians in the U.K.', *International Journal of Law Librarianship*, vol. 4, 1976, pp. 3–18.
Casteleyn, M. *Planning Library Training Programmes*, 1981.

Cowley, J. *Personnel management in libraries*, 1982.
Durey, P. *Staff management in university and college libraries*, 1976.
Guidelines for training in libraries. Rev. edn., 1983.
'Problems of non-legally qualified librarians in law libraries', *Law Librarian*, vol. 4, 1973, pp. 21–3.
Slater, M. *Ratios of staff to users*, 1981.

ACCOMMODATION

Faulkner Brown, H. 'Academic library buildings in the United Kingdom', *Advances in Librarianship*, vol. 3, 1972, pp. 107–18.
Metcalf, K. D. *Planning academic and research library buildings*, 1965.
Thompson, G. *Planning and design of library buildings*, 1973.
Vaughan, A. 'British academic library buildings since 1964: a comparative study', *Journal of Librarianship*, vol. 12, 1980, pp. 179–98.

Space requirements

Gt. Brit. Department of Education and Science *Notes on procedure for the approval of polytechnic projects* [Latest edn.].
University Grants Committee, *Capital provision for university libraries*, 1976 (Atkinson report).
University Grants Committee, *Planning norms for university buildings* [Latest edn.].
Way, D. J. 'Atkinson report and its implications for law libraries', *Law Librarian*, vol. 7, 1976, pp. 42–3.

Equipment

'Library equipment: shelving', Supplement to *Architects' Journal*, vol. 147, 1968.

CO-OPERATION

Jefferson, G. *Library co-operation*, 2nd rev. edn., 1977.
Line, M. B. *Universal availability of publications*, 1983.

Sewell, P. H. *Library co-operation in the United Kingdom,* 1979.
Sewell, P. H. *Resource sharing: co-operation and co-ordination in library and information services,* 1981.
Yelland, M. *Local Library co-operation,* 1980.

LIBRARY RESEARCH

Bull, G. E. 'Legal research education in the U.K.', *International Journal of Law Libraries,* vol. 6, 1978, pp. 237–61.
Busha, C. H. and Harter, S. P. *Research methods in librarianship,* 1980.
Research and the practitioner: dissemination of research results with the library-information profession, 1982.

15. Reader Services

S. PHILLIPS

USE OF THE LIBRARY

The law librarian needs to do more than merely put the books on the shelves and wait for people to come and use them. Traditionally, librarians have felt that it is not really dignified to go into the public relations business. There has been a general feeling that the library does not need to be promoted, it was sufficient for it to be there for those who wanted to use it. However it is increasingly being seen as one of the duties of librarians that they must go out and 'sell' their services and actively encourage use of the library. This is reflected in the library school curricula where many students are choosing public relations or promotion-related topics.

In the current economic climate of financial stringency, it is imperative that the value and services of the library are known to, and appreciated by, as many people as possible. If it is perceived by its users to be a positive and dynamic unit vital to the well-being and growth of the organization, it will be easier to persuade those responsible for financial control that it can justify the funds needed to finance future expansion. The library should be regarded as important to the professional interests of its users and they, in return, should respect the professional competence of the library staff. In order to achieve this, the library staff must make itself known to the whole gamut of users and potential users, for example by attending meetings and serving on interdisciplinary committees, and show that they are aware of and planning for, any future developments within the organization.

Physically the library should be a pleasant place to visit, giving a welcoming and friendly atmosphere. Once potential users have entered the library, it is easier to persuade them to take advantage of the services offered. They should not find it a waste of time or unnecessary inconvenience to come to the library.

Orientation

Libraries tend to be confusing places for the uninitiated and library instruction is a topic which has become increasingly important in the last twenty years. It is not enough merely to provide an organized collection of material; some attempt should be made to show the user how to make the best use of the resources offered. The attitudes and behaviour of the library staff are important. They should be approachable and aim not only to provide the information needed at a specific time but also to ensure that the enquirer will know how to find it another time.

It should be remembered that people who come into the law library may well be unfamiliar with a special library of any type and will need to be informed specifically of the various services the library offers. They will expect it to contain books but may not necessarily assume the provision of timetables, newspapers, telephone directories and photocopy machines. They need to know what hours the library is open and how many books they may borrow if any.

When planning library instruction it is necessary to take a number of factors into account – the sophistication of the users, whether they are new students who have never seen a law report or practitioners of many years experience (although a surprising amount of ignorance can be found among the latter) as well as the resources in both staff time and money at your disposal. The needs of the users must be taken into account – they need to be given confidence in the library staff and in their ability to make the maximum use of the library, but it is important not to try to impart too much knowledge – we are not trying to make our users into librarians. In certain special libraries, instruction may be inappropriate as it may be taken for granted that it is for the library staff to find the information required.

It can also be useful to give instruction to secretaries and personal assistants so that they can run simple errands in the library.

Methods

There are many different methods which can be employed to help people to use the library more effectively. The following are the ones mainly used with indications of their main advantages and disadvantages. Most libraries issue some sort of library guide which will contain details of library regulations, loan periods, classification scheme, services offered, special collections, etc. They are given to the prospective users who can then read them at any convenient time and they can be retained for reference to specific points. They are relatively cheap to produce, easy to display and can be picked up and used by casual readers and those too shy to ask for help. Care should be taken to make them as attractive as possible and to avoid jargon. However, too much detail may be confusing and so counterproductive, and the traditional guide covering all aspects of the library service and reprinted annually is not as common as it was. Users will not bother to wade through a long guide to find a specific piece of information.

Such all-embracing guides are often replaced by a series of leaflets each covering a single topic. These can be made available at the point of use and tailored to particular categories or levels of user if necessary, such as notices explaining how to use the catalogue, photocopier, microfiche reader or other technical equipment. They are cheap to update and can be produced quickly and easily as the need arises, and can be extremely effective. Judicious use of this type of material together with effective signposting can obviate much formal instruction.

Tours of the library, either individually or in groups, are probably the most generally used method of library instruction. In many special libraries, it may be the only method as new staff are introduced to the library when they arrive. This provides a good opportunity for personal contact and the information given can be tailored to the particular needs of the individual. However, the physical constraints of the building and the likelihood of disruption to existing users make it impractical for large groups. Tours for large numbers do not give anyone opportunity for personal contact with the library staff or a chance to discover how to use any particular type of material. Locations can be indicated and the most up to date information included but it is extremely time-consuming for the staff.

Some libraries have produced a system of individual guided tours either printed or on a cassette which will guide users round the building showing the main areas and possibly also including practical questions to be answered.

Lectures are a traditional form of teaching. A large group of people can be reached at one time. A good teacher will communicate enthusiasm as well as giving information in a clear and easily understandable fashion and be able to tailor the information to the needs of the curriculum and the resources of the library. An adept use of visual aids such as blackboard and overhead projector will add to the effectiveness of the lecture. However, good lecturers are not easy to find and if the information is put over in a repetitive and uninteresting way the exercise will be counterproductive. In any lecture one of the main aims will be to present an image of the library as a pleasant, friendly place where help can be obtained. Some libraries have made a film or tape/slide show (35mm slides in a carousel slide tray and an audio-cassette tape with silent pulses which automatically synchronizes the narrative with the slides), which can be extremely effective when well done. However a high standard is required as exposure to professional audio-visual material is so great that expectation of this type of material is very high. They are also expensive to produce and quickly go out of date, though individual slides can easily be replaced.

Guiding

Even the smallest library will need some form of guiding and a considerable amount of thought should be given to its form, content and construction. Unfortunately it is often badly done and many library staff have no knowledge of design or expertise in this field. If the library is well laid out and efficiently signposted, an immediate impression of a well organized unit is given. The library staff will spend less time answering questions regarding the location of materials and equipment and users with comparatively straightforward wants will be able to find things for themselves. Someone who has been able to find what he wants quickly and easily will be more likely to come back another time. Ideally, he should be able to find out how the books are arranged and what services are available without undue delay and, if possible, without needing to consult the library staff.

A wide range of materials can be used depending on the size and financial resources of the library. A large face typewriter, stencils or dry transfer lettering can give very professional results and there are also a number of commercially available systems using individual letters. Ideally, all the signs in the library should be planned at the same time and produced in the same style to give a co-ordinated effect. All permanent signs should be consistent in terms of style of lettering, colour, layout, etc. The style of letters should be simple and legible. A mixture of upper and lower case is generally easier to read than a long message all in capitals. There should be plenty of space surrounding the lettering and the final shape should be wider than it is high. They should be placed so that they can easily be seen, directly facing the user and as far as possible at the height of the natural line of vision. A basic principle should be to give the minimum of information – too much will distract the user – and avoiding unnecessary punctuation.

Several different types of signs are needed, not forgetting those in other parts of the building directing potential users towards the library. On the door, or as near to it as possible, should be displayed information about the hours of opening and possibly also extracts from the regulations concerning loans, smoking restrictions, etc. In even a small library it will probably be found useful to have a plan indicating the relative positions of law reports, textbooks, catalogues, etc. These could be colour-coded with different colours representing different types of material, or classification numbers, or have a numbered key. In a multi-storey library, it may be necessary to have one on each floor. These should be so designed that users can easily orientate themselves from the 'you are here' indicator. An alternative aid, or an additional one for a large library, would be a 'directory' of the kind seen in department stores listing the sections of the library facilities in alphabetical order with an indication of their location by stack or floor number. These should give users a basic introduction to the scope and organization of the library.

In addition individual bays, and possibly also shelves, should be labelled giving an indication of their contents. Since these are likely to change quite frequently the method used should be one which can be quickly and easily altered and should be changed whenever stock is moved. They need not be elaborate – cardboard slipped into holders on the ends of bays and shelves for example. Items of equipment, such as a microfiche reader or photocopier, should have clear instructions for use nearby, including what to do if something goes wrong.

Well-designed and well-produced signs are expensive and time-consuming but they are a good investment as they last a long time and fulfil an important need. Obviously the need will, to a certain extent, vary with the users. If the library is used mainly by regulars, fewer signs will be needed than if there is a large number of infrequent users.

Displays

Displays can be a good public relations exercise, making a focal point for users to look at when they visit the library, although legal materials do not readily lend themselves to display. Many libraries display new books in a trough on a convenient table or bookjackets on a noticeboard. It is possible to arrange the latter quite imaginatively, perhaps combining them with suitable cutouts from advertising material. It can also be a useful way of drawing attention to older items which may be little used because no one knows of their existence.

The library could arrange a display in conjunction with a special event organized by the institution to which it belongs. This could consist of books and periodical articles illustrating the subject, plus any manuscripts, documents or other items which may be appropriate. Valuable items should be displayed in a locked case and not exposed to direct sunlight. If items are labelled, the labels should be clear and easy to read, without trying to convey too much information.

LEARNING TO USE LEGAL SOURCES

It is not sufficient merely to tell people how to use the library. Because of the very specialized nature of legal material, it is important to explain both where to find different types of information and how to use the various sources.

Although this section applies mainly to academic libraries, in practice many legal professionals start work with an insufficient understanding of the techniques and sources of legal research. In such cases, however, instruction generally needs to be individual and given on appropriate occasions when it is actually needed, although possibly small groups of new articled clerks could be instructed together. One practical method of instruction could be to draw their attention to some of the published guides to using law libraries listed in Chapter 9.

Academic libraries

The main need for instruction in bibliographical techniques is in academic institutions which experience particular problems with the number of new users at one time who will need to make extensive and in-depth use of the library.

Should law students have a separate introduction or share in the general orientation course of the university as a whole? There is much to be said, especially in a shared building, for the preliminary introduction to be a general one since law students should be encouraged to use the resources of the whole library and not confine themselves to the law library. Who should be responsible for the teaching – library or academic staff? Librarians have a detailed knowledge of the library resources but they frequently lack teaching ability.

The librarian's priority should be to ensure the co-operation of the legal academic staff and he should have a sound knowledge of the curriculum. Academic staff in law are usually more sensitive to the need for bibliographical instruction than their colleagues in other disciplines and it is often included in a legal system or similar course. In such cases the law librarian will give some of the lectures and the course will be integrated with the rest of the teaching programme. In this way the students will realize that the teaching staff appreciate the importance and relevance of the library.

Timing

The timing of instruction needs careful thought. Since students will be expected to use the library immediately they begin their course, the time for orientation is short. The first week of life on campus is so full of new experiences for students that they are unlikely to take in much of what they are told, so it is wise to give at this time only just enough information to meet their immediate needs. They will generally need to register to use the library, and this opportunity can be taken to give a basic video presentation or distribute an introductory handout. A continuous video can be shown near the library entrance during induction week to promote the types of service the library offers and this can be replaced in subsequent weeks with more bibliographical content.

Since law students confront their literature so immediately, the tendency is to fuse orientation and instruction into a concentrated programme. As time is short and numbers large, the law library staff may share the burden of induction with academic staff, but in some institutions library teaching is conducted solely by academic staff with little or no library staff involvement. A balance needs to be struck between general orientation and advanced bibliographical instruction. A detailed account of how to use a specific reference book, which students have not yet realized they need, can be counterproductive as they will 'switch off' and by the time they need the information they will have forgotten what they were told. Another solution is one lecture during the second or third week giving a certain amount of basic information such as how to use the catalogue and a brief introduction to the major sources of law. A second lecture can be given at the end of the first term or the beginning of the second term, once the students are beginning to realize what information they need in order to do the work expected of them. If the timetable permits a more specialized research lecture for final year or postgraduate students can be added.

The precise content of any course of instruction will depend on individual curricula and resources, but the following is the type of material that should be covered. Since the great majority of students will have no experience of legal material, with its division into primary and secondary sources and pattern of citation, it is important that forms of citation for cases and statutes and the use of abbreviation lists are covered very early in the course. It is also necessary to teach students how to interpret reading lists. Many have difficulty in distinguishing references to books and serials, cases, statutes etc. Other topics include use of the catalogue, a brief outline of the classification scheme, the use of legal reference works such as encyclopedias and dictionaries, periodical indexes and current awareness sources together with the main uses, advantages and disadvantages of each, including the subject approach. Handouts giving the basic details of the titles concerned are usually much appreciated.

Methods

The use of a lecture format to convey bibliographic skills remains a problem despite the use of video, slides and overhead projection to give graphic illustration. However two tape-slide programmes have been produced which cover the major sources of English law. *How to use a law library* by Jean Dane and P. A. Thomas which not only takes the students through the main holdings of a law library showing them how to find their way around the specific works but also how to make the best use of them. A more generalized tape-slide programme is produced by Sheffield University Library, entitled *A guide to legal literature*. It consists of a short introductory tape-slide programme for use in induction week and two larger programmes dealing with primary and secondary literature respectively. The programmes are supported by a booklet on legal sources which can be reproduced as a handout to students. These can be shown to a whole class of students at one time and also made available for students to use on their own at a later date, and kept close to the relevant works.

More specific videos and tape-slides can be used near the catalogue, government publications, legal reference works etc. These could be made to play continuously and should be equipped with headphones where noise could create a problem. They can be used to replace or supplement detailed instruction enquiries from the information desk. Alternatively notices explaining how to use particular publications can be left near them or the publishers' 'How to use ...' instructions kept in a prominent position, perhaps hanging from the shelves.

One of the most effective methods of library instruction is individual tuition. A person is most receptive to information when he needs it and a specific request to library staff for assistance is evidence of high motivation. Unfortunately it is also the most time-consuming. Ideally, every opportunity should be taken to point out that library staff can always be approached for help but this is not easy to put into practice. Users cannot be unaware of other pressures such as queues and telephones and are reluctant to admit that they do not understand or to question the staff in depth. If staff resources and teaching time are available, bibliographic skills are best taught in small seminar groups and workshops using actual publications and practical exercises linked to other course teaching. If the content and presentation of workshops is good they need not be compulsory since most students will attend sessions which are beneficial to their overall target of securing a good degree. It is, however, essential to have the support and active co-operation of the teaching staff. Sometimes instruction can be entirely spontaneous – for example if users are seen puzzling over the chart explaining the *English Reports* their attention can be drawn to the index volumes.

Practical exercises

A popular institution in American academic institutions is workbook, a combination of text and appropriate exercise covering basic library skills and knowledge of bibliographic sources used as part of the academic assessment of individual students. Ideally, the participants are actively involved an can work at their own pace and the resulting feedback can be used to assess the effectiveness of instruction provided. A more informal system of practical exercises is used in some British institutions. These are relatively cheap to prepare, though for a large class a number of different sets of questions will be desirable if it is not to become a combined effort. Marking can be time-consuming however and there is also a danger that students will simply consult second- and third-year students.

The University of Aston has produced a game simulating student problems with points being given for completion and sweets as prizes! They claim it produces a better understanding of the library than conventional methods and involves fewer staff.

Sheffield City Polytechnic has produced a checklist as an aid to self-introduction. It poses a series of questions, the answers to which should be readily available in the library. The first section deals with joining the library – how many books can you have on loan, what times is the library open? The second part deals with finding books and information – can you find details of a periodical in the catalogue, where are the reference books? Another part deals with services and environment – how do you reserve a book? The final section deals with bibliographical skills – what are journal indexes? The aim of such publications to to make the users aware of the services offered and can easily be adapted to any circumstances.

Instruction in computer-assisted legal research

The introduction of such systems as LEXIS has given instruction in legal information an added impetus, and there is a growing appreciation that the use of online systems requires a good pre-training in the use of manual information sources. Handbooks and publicity produced by the database publishers can be used to give basic information on each system although these are designed for individual end users rather than as teaching material for topics such as search strategies, database content and retrieval techniques.

Online training for qualified lawyers can be arranged with

the database supplier either on or off the library premises and update training should be arranged to ensure that skills do not lapse. In academic libraries, it is desirable to give students initial hands-on tuition and experience in small groups, and it is therefore advisable that the terminal is in a relatively secluded area. LEXIS has segments of its database for use as a teaching library and a simulation for teaching purposes has been developed by the Department of Law, North East London Polytechnic.

LENDING SERVICES

An important policy decision which has to be made by any library is to what extent the contents will be available for loan. Few libraries now refuse to lend anything, most have a basic reference collection which is never allowed on loan and many do not lend law reports and periodicals. Even libraries which do not lend anything at all will probably need some system to record books removed for an hour or so in emergencies and items sent for binding.

The method used to record loans will depend upon a number of factors, such as the number of people borrowing and the amount of material likely to be away from the library at any one time.

When deciding which issue system (or method of recording loans) to adopt, it is first necessary to decide what information the system is expected to provide, not only at the present moment but also in the foreseeable future since it is expensive to change an existing system. Who has a particular item is the basic question which needs to be answered but it may also be convenient to know further details of the borrower, such as address and what other items are on loan to him, and the date it is due back. One of the chief distinctions between systems is whether it is the borrowers or library staff who are responsible for recording the loan. In a small, closely-knit organization, it can often be left to the members themselves to note items removed from the library. They will be aware of the inconvenience if items are removed without record and if titles are missing, it is usually possible to guess who has it or to conduct an office search. The less work involved in recording the loan, the more likely it is that procedures will be carried out.

Borrowers' register

Depending on the size and complexity of the institution, some libraries may need to limit the number of books borrowed by one person at any one time which may be based on their position within the organization or the type of work done.

It may or may not be necessary to have a central registration of borrowers, depending on such factors as the number of potential borrowers and their geographical location. The type of information required will vary accordingly to the type of institution but may include official address, phone number, department, grade and, if students living away from home, home address. They can then be given either a number of tickets to be used each time a book is borrowed or an identity type card to be used for each transaction. If the register of borrowers is computerized, it will need to be registered in terms of the Data Protection Act 1984. Even if there is no formal register, it is useful to encourage new members of staff to make an early visit to the library to make themselves and their needs known and this opportunity can be taken to introduce them to the library services.

Loan period

Most libraries also limit the period of time for which books may be borrowed, in which case the date the item is due for return should be stamped on a date label inside the book and the loan records should indicate what items are due on any one day. Some sort of system will have to be instituted for the recall of overdue items, either by letter or phone call. The question of fines will apply mainly to academic institutions. Is the deterrent effect worth the sums involved, not to mention the staff time collecting them and subsequent accounting procedures, and the decline in public relations? In small libraries there may be no restriction on the period of loan on the understanding that items will be returned if requested by someone else. In other organizations, items may be retained on permanent loan by an individual or department, for example, a firm's tax collection may be kept in the office of the tax partner.

Other factors to be taken into account when choosing an issue system are the cost and amount of staff time involved. Whatever system is chosen, it should be possible to locate, and if necessary recall, items which have been requested by another reader, and of producing detailed statistics of the number and type of loans which can be used to predict future trends and provide evidence of the use made of the library.

Academic libraries

Law libraries in universities, polytechnics and colleges, even if they are physically separate from the main library, will generally use the same system for issuing books as the parent institution. This means that the law librarian will have little scope to influence the decision. In such libraries the volume of loans and the number of potential borrowers means that regulations concerning the number of books that may be borrowed at one time and the length of time they may be kept, need to be clearly defined and strictly controlled.

Short loans

Most academic libraries will have some form of short loan collection. Students cannot afford to buy all the basic textbooks they need and most libraries can only afford to duplicate these to a very limited extent. In addition, there are also items which are on reading lists of which only parts are relevant to a particular course and it is not therefore reasonable to expect students to buy them. Also students frequently have to read a miscellaneous collection of items – periodical articles, cases, one chapter from a book, part of a government report – for an essay or tutorial. The number of people needing to read the material in a short space of time can place impossible demands on the library unless restrictions are placed on access and loan period. Generally items will be put in the short loan collection on the instigation of a lecturer or by library staff on the basis of their knowledge of students reading habits. The collection may also contain private copies belonging to academic staff that they wish their students to read. The increasing emphasis on independent reading and less dependency on a single textbook makes the short loan collection an important library service.

Items placed in the short loan collection are removed from the open shelves for periods ranging from one or two weeks to a whole year. It will be necessary to put some sort of indication of location in the catalogue and probably also to construct a basic index to the collection. The period may vary with the type of material or demand ranging from one hour to two or three days. Libraries which cater for part-time students may have a special collection of books reserved for them, which are not lent to anyone else and the loan period will take into account the times the students visit the institution.

The system of recording loans will need to reflect the heavy use of the collection at particular times of day, for example the beginning and end of lectures and the time overnight loans are due for return. Possibly a drop box could be provided for returned items to avoid queues. Many libraries charge fines, sometimes quite substantial, to discourage overdue loans. Ideally the system should also enable students to reserve books for a particular period.

Manual methods

The following are some of the main issue systems in use. A basic method for an essentially reference collection from which occasionally items are borrowed for short periods is a simple book in which author/title and borrower are entered and crossed out when returned, and details of defaulters can be transferred elsewhere for further action. But the great majority of libraries require something more than such a single chronological record. A card with the necessary details can be prepared in advance, possibly an additional catalogue card, and the borrower can put his name and any other desired information such as room number or date of issue, on the back. The card will be filed by the library staff.

Another method is the traditional Browne system where a prepared bookcard is kept in the book and is then slipped inside a pocket with the borrower's name on it. Pockets can be kept by the borrower or in the library. This is a particularly useful method if the number of items which can be borrowed by one person at any time is limited. In a more informal organization, blank pockets can be used and the appropriate name written on. The use of pockets bearing the borrower's name and permanent bookcards obviates the necessity of replacing the bookcard regularly if a book is used frequently.

A multiple copy form on self carbon paper can also be used. This involves more effort on the part of the borrower and will probably need to be checked by library staff to ensure that the details are filled in correctly. It will also involve more complicated original processing since the information the borrower has to fill in, such as the form of entry for corporate authors, will need to be clearly indicated on the book. The different copies can be filed under different headings, such as author and borrower or due date, but the more different sequences are used, the more staff time is involved in filing and discharging. Alternatively, second and subsequent copies of the form can be used as overdue notices.

Filing loan records

Various methods can be used to file the loan records. When loans are for a restricted period, the date due is likely to form the primary sequence. If the volume of loans is not very great it may be convenient to change the due date only once a week instead of every day which will give fewer sequences to search Within the date, arrangement may be by author, accession number or possibly borrower. The advantage of filing by accession number, for those libraries which already have them, is that numerical filing by a limited range of five or six figure numbers is easier than filing by author. Where there are several authors with one name and several book. by one author and many copies of one book, not to mention the confusion of corporate authors with perhaps many sub divisions each, the chances of error are innumerable. The main disadvantage of filing by accession number is that in order to trace a particular title it is necessary to look up the accession number in a separate record first.

Automated methods

Microcomputers

Lending systems are an obvious candidate for computerization. Now that microcomputers are becoming cheaper, many smaller libraries are using them for a variety of housekeeping purposes including loan records. The most basic method is to record details of the title and borrower (usually in number form) when a book is borrowed and remove the information when it is returned. However even for small libraries this is time-consuming and would necessitate recourse to other records, such as a register of borrowers, in order to have access to more detailed information such as who has a particular title. The alternative is to have a record of the entire library collection on the computer and to record details of loans against this. Loans can then be recorded either by calling up the book details and keying in the reader's number or name or by means of a light pen passed over barcoded labels on the book and on the reader's ticket. The latter is a much more complicated process to set up because details of every work in the library will need to be recorded and coded before the system can start operating, and will require a greater storage capacity, but is probably better for all except very small libraries. In addition to recording loans, the system should also be able to trap books for reservation purposes, identify readers who already have the allotted number of books out on loan and calculate fines. It may also need to differentiate between different loan periods for different types of material or between varying categories of user.

Ready-made systems
Having decided to computerize, a decision has to be taken as to whether to compile the program in-house or to buy in a ready-made system from outside. Even if an expert programmer is

available, a considerable amount of staff time can be taken up in this exercise, with possibly unsatisfactory results, but the final program should be tailor-made to the library's requirements. Using a ready-made system, however, may lead to some of the library's routines needing to be adapted to fit the program since to make a large number of modifications to a commercial program will be expensive, difficult and dangerous.

There are some commercial software programs, such as LIBRARIAN and MINI-CAIRS, available which will combine the functions of the issue record and a library catalogue and include a full bibliographical description of titles which can be linked to lending information. But such systems often cannot be quickly and easily adapted to any individual library. Anyone contemplating the introduction of a microcomputer system would be wise to seek advice from such organizations as Aslib or the Library Technology Centre at the Polytechnic of Central London and, if possible, also from other similar-sized libraries who have introduced automated systems. They should also ensure that the necessary support service will be available.

Mainframe and minicomputers

Large libraries, such as those in academic institutions, need something more powerful than a microcomputer. Some commercial companies such as GEAC and SB Electronics, have developed systems for mainframe or minicomputers using bar-code labels and light pens or a similar process. The light pens can be adapted to hold a date stamp at the opposite end to facilitate the speedy charging of books. It is also possible to key in numbers if necessary to allow for lost tickets or telephone renewals. They will also trap wanted readers and books. The can also be used to generate reports, such as overdue notices. Some of the co-operative cataloguing projects, such as SWALCA and BLCMP can also be used for loan records.

In addition to reducing drastically the amount of staff time needed to deal with loans, systems can also increase security, for example by making it more difficult for books to be borrowed under a false name. They may also be used in conjunction with an electronic security system.

INTER-LIBRARY LOANS

At some stage, every library will come to the end of its own resources and need to apply for help elsewhere, although it is a good idea to make sure first whether an alternative title might be acceptable. A reader may ask for a specific title because it is the only one he knows on the subject, but be quite happy with another which is in stock. It cannot be emphasized too strongly that whatever system is used for recording loans, especial care should be taken with items borrowed from other libraries, if only in order not to jeopardize any future transactions. Readers should be aware of this fact and any date due for return.

All librarians are likely to have built up a circle of contacts based on geographical propinquity, administrative organizations or similar subject interests and so there may be a first port of call fairly near at hand. If this fails, it is necessary to find out which library has the item you need. Many libraries issue lists of their periodical holdings, ranging from quite elaborate publications to typed lists intended for in-house use but which may be copied for particular recipients. In London the solicitors' firms' libraries have an organization called the City Law Librarians' Group which has issued a union list of holdings. Members will lend books to each other or photocopy articles provided that this does not conflict with their primary duty of providing a service to their own fee-earners.

The Institute of Advanced Legal Studies has published a series of union lists covering legal periodicals and also Commonwealth, United States and West European legal material but these are now all very much out of date. This problem was highlighted in the *Report* of the British Library Working Party on Provision for Law. One of its recommendations was that the British Library should consider, as a matter of urgency, sponsoring a series of guides to resources in law, particularly a directory of the principal legal collections in all types of libraries, a union list of the United Kingdom and overseas law reports, a series of guides to regional law and a short guide to the legal resources of the British Library. Many of the libraries mentioned in the union lists will supply photocopies of periodical articles or law reports against British Library forms or with invoices. Standard textbooks are available on subscription from the Law Notes Lending Library (25–6 Chancery Lane, London WC2A 1NB), where the amount of the subscription paid determines the number and value of books that may be borrowed at any one time.

Local schemes

Some libraries may participate directly in regional co-operative schemes. LASER, covering the London and South East Region, has installed a minicomputer which will give locations by accessing author, title or ISBN. Other regions have COM catalogues arranged by ISBN available to member libraries and the British Library Lending Division and union card catalogues for pre-1977 material. Some regions also organize transport systems with a van service to and from the British Library and individual libraries.

British Library

Failing a local source or definite location, the next resort is likely to be the British Library Lending Division at Boston Spa. The aim of the Division is to provide a speedy supply of loans or photocopies. It has a stock of $4\frac{1}{2}$ million volumes of books and periodicals and about 3 million documents in microform. It attempts to acquire all significant serials (but this does *not* include law reports) irrespective of subject and language (55,000 titles currently received), 'significant' English language monographs (53,000 volumes per year), plus monographs in other languages, reports, conference proceedings and official publications from Britain and the European Community. It does not stock looseleaf services, casebooks or legal encyclopedias and there is frequently a waiting list for standard textbooks. The Lending Division only supplies specific items against request forms. It cannot deal with subject requests or undertake literature searches. Each form covers the loan of one monograph or periodical part or a photocopy of a periodical article up to 20 pages. For full information and a supply of forms, write to BLLD, Boston Spa, Wetherby, West Yorkshire, LS23 7BQ. Registered users of the Lending Division are provided with a free copy of its *Users' Handbook* which explains the procedure in detail.

BLLD forms

The form has three parts, of which B and C are submitted to the Lending Division and A kept for the borrower's records. Since any correspondence refers to the request by the serial number, it is convenient to keep them in this order. As the division averages nearly 11,000 request forms a day (almost twelve feet high!) care should be taken to fill the form in correctly including the source of reference and ISBN number if available. Every effort should be made to ensure that the fullest possible information is given on the form, in particular abbreviations should not be used since it is unreasonable to expect Lending Division staff to be familiar with legal terminology. However, if it is not possible to verify any reference, do not attempt to amplify an abbreviation by guesswork but submit it in the form you received it.

The Division publishes regularly *Current Serials Received* which is also a useful source for the verification of current titles, although it does not include dates of holdings, nor earlier versions for items which have changed their names. But there are always new titles on order and borrowers should not be deterred from applying by the omission of any title from the list.

There is a space on the form for indicating whether either a photocopy or microform is unacceptable and if it is essential that the item should be available for home use (some libraries will only lend for use in the borrowing library). If a photocopy is required, the shaded portion from the top of the B copy should be removed. There is also a place for entering any special requirement such as 'English translation only' and if this is used it is helpful to write it in coloured ink on the B copy in order to draw attention to it.

BLLD searches

If the item is found on the shelves, it will be sent immediately and should arrive within four or five days. Photocopies are sent for retention and books are normally lent for three weeks but can be extended for a further three weeks unless there is a waiting list. If the item is not on the shelves, the next step will depend upon the level of search requested on the form: X, Y or Z which determines the time and effort spent trying to locate a copy of the item concerned. If the item is needed quickly an X search should be requested which can subsequently be altered to a Y search if desired. Forms for unfound periodicals are then returned immediately and forms for monographs are checked in available union catalogues and ISBN location lists. The locations are indicated on the C copy and the requesting library can then send the B and C copies to the first location and they will be routed from one to another until the request is satisfied. There is obviously no guarantee that the item will eventually be supplied but the success rate is approximately 80 per cent.

If the item is not needed urgently, a Y search should be requested. For periodical articles, forms are sent to back-up libraries, large libraries which agree to satisfy requests sent to them from the Lending Division. For monographs, locations are provided if available or in certain circumstances the form may be forwarded to a back-up library although most will not lend books. If this still fails to produce a copy, the Lending Division will try overseas sources for items published abroad. If an international loan is required, the form should be clearly marked for a Z search after it has been returned from an unsuccessful Y search. Such requests can, however, take a very long time to arrive.

In 1981 the British Library set up an *ad hoc* Working Party on Union Catalogues, which recommended that the Lending Division should create a machine-readable file of its English and foreign language monograph stock which should be available as a COM catalogue and in ISBN form as part of the Combined Regional Locations List. This would achieve wider availability of location information and help to prevent libraries being overburdened by requests for material held by the Lending Division and enable them to concentrate on requests for their unique holdings.

If an item is required very urgently, the Lending Division has an urgent action service. A request can be telephoned to Boston Spa and a member of staff will check it individually and telephone back with a report. This service costs two request forms, plus a third if the request is successful.

Automated transmission

Registered users of telex and ARTTEL and BLAISE ADRS can also register to use these services to transmit requests to the Lending Division. This saves postal delay but the requests are not given priority in processing. Requests are not accepted as ordinary messages on the Division's listed telex lines. As costs of transmission equipment decrease and they are more generally available, automatic methods will become more common and the Division is promoting research into this field. Telex probably accounts for almost a quarter of the requests received but the operating costs have risen considerably and are likely to increase. The British Library is also researching into telefacsimile transmission of documents and items requested through the urgent action service can be sent in this way to users with appropriate hardware. Users in Scotland can send BL forms direct to the National Library of Scotland Lending Services, 312–320 Lawnmarket, Edinburgh EH1 2PJ where the Scottish Union catalogue is maintained.

Lending to other libraries

If requests on British Library forms are received from other libraries, send the item with the B copy of the form direct to the requesting library. Attach the issue slip (the perforated section at the bottom right-hand corner of the B copy) to the book and ensure that the correct address is in the 'return to' box. Keep the C copy which can be returned to the Lending Division for a refund, together with forms for unsatisfied requests.

BLLD forms are not only used for requests routed via the Division itself, but are also acceptable currency among a large number of libraries. It is possible to locate an item by phone and then send a form to the library concerned. While the forms may, at first glance, seem expensive (currently nearly £2 each), their use does provide an equitable means of sharing the cost of interlibrary loans. No one library can ever be expected to buy every item needed by its users, even without taking financial and storage restrictions into account, but it is unrealistic to expect the large well-established libraries to bear the whole burden.

PHOTOCOPYING

Sophisticated photocopying machines are now so much a part of everyday life that it is difficult to imagine a time when they were uncommon, cumbersome and difficult to use. Yet that was the state of affairs only thirty years ago when the current copyright legislation was promulgated. Use of all photocopying machines is governed by the law of copyright and it is important that law librarians should be aware of what can and cannot be copied and under what conditions.

Copyright

Basically the Copyright Act 1956 provides that substantial parts of any work may not be copied without the consent of the copyright owner. There are, however, two important provisos. Section 6 concerns 'fair dealing' for the purpose of criticism or review or for 'research or private study'. More important, for libraries, is section 7 and the Copyright (Libraries) Regulations 1957 (SI 1957/868) which concerns any library not established or conducted for profit, which has been interpreted as excluding libraries attached to any profit-making institution.

Such libraries may make one copy of one article in any periodical publication or of a reasonable part of a published work, for a person who requests the copy for research or private study. The Regulations prescribe a form which must be signed by the applicant in person and an amount not less than the cost of making the copy must be paid. In addition, copies should not be made from books if the librarian knows the name and address of a person entitled to authorize the making of a copy or could reasonably obtain it. Similarly such libraries may make copies for other non-profit-making libraries.

Because the Act applies only to 'substantial' parts, it would seem that most small-scale copying that is done is not an infringement of copyright, although 'substantial' has never been defined. In 1970 the Society of Authors and the Publishers' Association suggested that an upper limit of 4,000 words or 10 per cent of the whole work would not be considered 'unfair', but this was withdrawn by the British Copyright Council in 1985 as being no longer appropriate (*Reprographic copying of books and journals*, p. 5). Aslib has suggested in its draft code 'a portion of a work of such size and/or content that a copy of it could render consultation of the complete work necessary; such a copy being capable of use by more than one individual or for more than one purpose'.

For anything further than this, *ie*, more than one copy or a 'substantial' amount, it is necessary to ask the permission of the copyright owner and pay any required royalty. However, legal publishers are not unappreciative of the problems of law librarians and permission is very often given at little or no cost. An extremely helpful article by H. Jones appeared in the *Law Librarian* setting out the policy of one publisher regarding copying by libraries in educational institutions, although when the Copyright Licensing Agency licensing system becomes more widespread, this policy is likely to be modified.

In August 1985, HMSO issued a circular, *Photocopying Crown copyright publications* clarifying the circumstances in which it is necessary to seek permission before photocopying Crown copyright material. Copies of this are obtainable from HMSO, Copyright Section (P 6), St Crispins, Duke Street, Norwich, NR3 1PD.

Recorded cases for infringement of copyright mainly refer to music, but following complaints and legal action brought by the Publishers' Association, the University of Manchester has had to hand over all infringing material, including that used in the library, and warn all staff that they may be held personally responsible for any future infringement. A notice should be displayed by all coin-operated machines giving a brief outline of the relevant provisions of the Act and making it clear that any liability for infringement rests with the individual making the copy.

As a result of technological developments, never envisaged in 1956, authors and publishers have become increasingly concerned about the copyright implications of widespread photocopying. As a result of the apparent reluctance of the government to take any legislative action, the copyright owners started to act on their own. The Copyright Licensing Agency is now offering licences which permit users to copy almost anything they are likely to want without the time and expense of finding and applying to the copyright owner in advance, and agreement on the terms of such licences has been reached with local authority associations in respect of copying in schools and colleges.

In April 1986, the government issued a White Paper, *Intellectual property and innovation,* Cmnd. 9712, proposing new legislation which the Government plan to have on the statute book by the end of 1987. Every encouragement is given to the voluntary licensing schemes although compulsory registration of publishers is rejected. Provisions regarding multiple copying done by educational establishments is based on the assumption that they will have a licence. The present 'fair dealing' clause will be retained, although copying for commercial research will be specifically excluded and there will be no statutory definition of 'fair dealing'. The clauses relating to library exceptions will also remain but libraries will no longer be permitted to make multiple copies of material.

Organizations representing librarians are against a blanket licensing scheme and Aslib, the Library Association and BIALL have all advised their members not to participate. Until new legislation is produced, the provisions of sections 6 and 7 remain in force and libraries and others should think carefully before relinquishing their current rights. The single-copy privilege is regarded as essential for ease of access to information. Too complicated and expensive a system will inevitably lead to dissatisfaction and antagonism, rather than co-operation, among library users and may also result in increased mutilation of library materials. Moreover it should be remembered that the cost involved is likely to be deducted from the library's funds for the purchase of new material.

Meanwhile, the great majority of librarians do want to keep within the bounds of the law, but is not easy to discover where these bounds lie. Until new legislation is produced or a test case is brought, this unsatisfactory position is likely to continue.

Equipment

One important consideration is the type of equipment to be installed. Most of the machines on the market are designed for office use and these frequently have curved printing surfaces or are in other ways unsuitable for library use. It is often necessary to copy from bound volumes which may have a very narrow inside margin, or be so tightly bound that the spine can easily be damaged in an attempt to get a readable copy. Ideally a library machine should have a platen with a completely flat surface extended to the edge of the machine with a horizontal drop so that a volume can be opened at right angles and placed with the spine on the edge of the platen and a copy taken right into the spine of the book.

Most large libraries will need to consider the provision of a coin-operated service and the saving of staff time involved in making copies and writing invoices (with the resultant delay in the production of the copy) outweighs the nuisance value in providing change. In addition, many users will want to copy personal material such as lecture notes.

PUBLICATIONS

Attractive publications will enhance the prestige of the library and therefore care should be taken that any published material emanating from it should be eyecatching and well laid out. Inevitably the method of printing and sophistication of any publication will depend on the resources of finance, time and artistic ability of the library and institution but it is possible to achieve the desired result with a relatively small outlay.

Many libraries produce guides and also accession lists, bulletins, bibliographies, etc. which are lists of books received and guides to the contents of items in the library. Another publication commonly produced by law libraries is a list of periodical holdings which can be distributed to the institution's staff and outside users. Bookmarks, advertising specific services or perhaps giving details of the classification scheme, are likely to be spread around the building and bring the library to the attention of people who may not otherwise use it. Other titles may be prepared by the library staff to fill gaps in existing coverage or to cover matters peculiar to the institution.

If the library has a special collection, this could form the basis for a publication describing the scope of the collection, for both internal and external use and possibly even a catalogue if the collection is particularly important; it may even be possible to interest a commercial publisher in the latter.

FURTHER READING

USE OF THE LIBRARY

Mallery, M. S. and De Vore, R. E. *A sign system for libraries*, 1982.
Reynold, S. L. and Barrett, S. *Signs and guiding for libraries*, 1981.

LEARNING TO USE LEGAL LITERATURE

Fjällbrant, N. and Mallery, I. *User education in libraries*, 2nd edn., 1984.
International Conference on Library User Education, 2nd, Oxford, 1981, *Proceedings*, 1982.
International Conference on Library User Education, 3rd, Edinburgh, 1983, *Proceedings*, 1983.

Lester, R. 'User education in the online age', *Aslib Proceedings*, vol. 36, 1984, pp. 96–111.

Raper, D. 'Training practitioners', *Law Librarian*, vol. 12, 1981, pp. 37–8.

Slade, M. and Gray, R. *The impact and potential of online legal research systems on academic legal education*, 1984. Summarised in: Gray, R. 'Legal research education in an online age', *Infuse*, vol. 8, 1984, pp. 6–11.

LENDING SYSTEMS

Burton, P. F. and Petrie, J. H. *Introducing microcomputers: a guide for librarians*, 1984.

Handbook of special librarianship and information work, 5th edn., 1982.

Look, H. E. 'Evaluating software for microcomputers', *Electronic Library*, vol. 2, 1984, pp. 53–60.

Lovecy, I. *Automating library procedures: a survivor's handbook*, 1984.

INTERLIBRARY LOANS

Barden, P. 'The transmission of interlibrary loan requests: a review of methods, with comments on their use at the British Library Lending Division', *Interlending Review*, vol. 10, 1982, pp. 92–6.

Inter-library lending – practice, politics and prospects, proceedings of a seminar of the Library and Information Research Group, London, November 1983, 1984.

Sewell, P. H. 'Library co-operation', in *British Librarianship and Information Work 1976–80*, 1983.

Smith, M. D. 'The costs of interlending activities', *Interlending and Document Supply*, vol. 11, 1983, pp. 43–7.

Wood, D. N. and Ekers, A. 'Official publications at the British Library Lending Division', *Interlending and Document Supply*, vol. 11, 1983, pp. 17–20.

PHOTOCOPYING

Aslib, *Photocopying and copyright*: supporting document to a draft rights owners and users joint code of photocopying practice for materials other than music, 1984.

Copyright and design law: report of the Committee to consider the Law on Copyright and Designs, Cmnd. 6732 [Whitford Committee], 1977.

Flint, M. F. *A user's guide to copyright*, 2nd edn., 1985.

Jones, H. 'Permission to make multiple photcopies', *Law Librarian*, vol. 15, 1984, pp. 20–1.

Lahore, J. 'Reprographic reproduction', in *Information Technology: the challenge to copyright*, 1984.

Photocopying and the Law: a guide for librarians and teachers and other suppliers and users of photocopies of copyright work, Society of Authors and Publishers' Association, 1970.

Pinnock, K. 'Photocopying and licensing: the publishers' view', *Aslib Proceedings*, vol. 35, 1983, pp. 449–56.

Reform of the law relating to copyright, design and performers protection, Cmnd. 8302, 1981.

Wall, R. A. 'Photocopying rights and wrongs: a Librarian's view', *Aslib Proceedings*, vol. 34, 1982, pp. 113–28.

16. Information Services

J. M. KING and D. E. PERROW

The provision of an information service is a vital function in any organization using legal sources since it is this service which links library resources to library users, acting as a channel between demand and supply of information.

This chapter considers the internal and external information facilities available to the law librarian, the methods he can use to exploit them and the techniques used in communicating information to users.

REFERENCE AND INFORMATION FACILITIES

Published sources

These sources are discussed in detail in Parts I–IV of this *Manual*. The special nature of legal sources means that the law librarian must become accustomed to different techniques from those common in general library practice. In legal literature, conventional subject indexes are supplemented by case indexes and citation indexes which trace case or statute citations in subsequent case-law. Techniques such as noting-up, whereby stickers on a case refer readers to later cases citing it, are unique to law. The looseleaf format, either for a complete work such as *Statutes in Force* or with bound main and supplementary volumes, as in *Halsbury's Statutes* or *Halsbury's Laws of England*, is a common feature in legal material. This may involve the law librarian in search techniques which correlate information from several volumes to establish the current state of law in a subject area.

Bibliographical and reference sources in law, which have more similarity in their use with such sources in other disciplines, are described in detail in Chapter 9. The use of published legal information within the context of reference and information enquiries is discussed later in this chapter.

Internal files

An important part of the resources of a law library are the internal information files and indexes which are built up. This is most likely to happen in a library which has specialized information enquiries and which has the staff time to devote to it. Solicitors' firms' libraries are an obvious example of such libraries. Some of the files will be compiled from publicly available sources such as law reports, periodical articles, etc. Others will be built up from purely internal information and, as such, are private to that organization.

Many libraries not only take copies or cuttings of the law reports in *The Times* and *Financial Times*, but also index them, normally by parties and subjects. The index can be on cards, and entries can be annotated when a published report of a case appears. Some libraries compile an alphabetical index of parties at the front of each volume of the cuttings or photocopies. It should be said that the advent of legal online databases and viewdata services necessitates weighing up the staff time spent in indexing against the cost of checking a reference on one of the computer databases.

Subject information files are a very useful source for library users, and it does not take long to keep them up to date. Subjects for which files are kept should first be decided upon, bearing in mind any particular subject or country interests of the organization concerned, and areas of the law where developments and change are rapid. Items to be collected can include press cuttings, progress of legislation, cases, periodical articles, government Green and White Papers and any internal office memoranda on the topic. Some of these can be gathered comparatively effortlessly whilst the librarian scans newspapers and periodicals for current awareness services, discussed below. It is important to weed these files from time to time to ensure that information is current and that files do not become unwieldy.

Most solicitors' firms' libraries find an index to counsels' opinions both useful and necessary. When a firm seeks an opinion on a matter, it is unique to that firm. But that opinion may need to be referred to sometime in the future; or the information contained in the opinion used again for another matter. Opinions need to be indexed by the name of the person in the firm seeking the opinion, by counsel, by client, subject matter, cases cited and legislation referred to, and indeed by anything else that could be useful.

A similar index can be compiled for details of overseas lawyers that a firm uses. Obvious items to include are name, address etc., by whom used and when, and details regarding their subject areas, expertise etc.

Other indexes could be compiled to cover areas such as office memoranda, linguistic skills within a firm, details of external translators and interpreters, a list of experts or expert witnesses etc. Chapter 9 of P. J. Purton and D. Andrews's *Organisation and management of a solicitors' practice*, 1980, entitled: 'The library and information service', gives further details of the different information files and indexes that can be compiled.

Traditionally indexing such as this has been typed or written on cards. It is probable that card indexes will be around for a long time to come, but libraries are now finding that the new technology offers a number of advantages over traditional methods. Although word processors are not a substitute for a computer they can be used for listing functions and for limited retrieval. However, it is micro- or minicomputers that offer the real advantages for such indexes, with their ability to retrieve through the use of keywords. A database management program, for example, is the computer equivalent of a card index.

External resources

Few libraries are able to be completely self-sufficient. The expense of legal literature, the need for access to materials of other jurisdictions, and requests for non-legal material, all result in the law librarian having to look outside his own library to satisfy certain requests for material or information.

Some of these demands may be satisfied by inter-library loans, discussed in Chapter 15; some from using other libraries; yet other demands may require the use of a commercial information service or broker; and the librarian's own personal contacts are a most valuable source.

Other libraries

It is frequently possible to make good use of other libraries to consult material that is held and obtain photocopies. BIALL's *Directory of law libraries*, 2nd edn., 1984, can be used as a starting point for locating any type of law library anywhere in the country. The reader is also referred to the first chapter of this *Manual* which lists different types of law libraries and briefly describes some of the collections. Any law librarian should familiarize himself with the libraries in his locality and in what ways they may be of use to him.

Information on European Community law may be obtained from the London office of the European Commission. Their information department will provide references, and where available, a copy of a document will be sent. Acccess to EC publications can usually be gained from European Documentation Centres (EDC) and Depository Libraries (DEP), discussed in Chapter 10.

Embassies are a further potential source of information. Their libraries or information departments vary enormously in size and as to how helpful they are, but they may be able to help with statute law and law reports, and trade and commercial information. Most will give information over the telephone.

Commercial information services and information brokers

Commercial information services are an option only for libraries who are willing or able to pay for them. The Financial Times Business Information Service is an example of such a service. An initial payment is made which will provide a certain number of hours of research. When that has been used up a further payment must be made. The BBC runs a similar service called BBC DATA which is based on its extensive library holdings and information files. It will answer queries on a 'one-off' basis.

The use of an information broker is another option. They are a new development in this country though they are widely used in the United States. They can be particularly useful where the librarian is operating in a small unit and perhaps does not have time to spend several hours on a piece of research, or is not able to leave the library unattended for a length of time. The advantage of using an information broker is that they have their own sources of information and contacts; they can work fast and flexibly; and they can be used as a third party for obtaining information without the breaking of confidentiality. It is important to come to an agreement before any work is carried out on how much can be spent in terms of research time, computer search time etc.

Services now exist that will carry out computer searches for firms or organizations that do not have their own retrieval systems. They are sometimes known as mid-user services. Users telephone their request and discuss their information problem with one of the operators. The search is then conducted on one or more of the databases that the service has access to, and the results are telephoned back, or sent by post or electronic mail. Two such services in operation, both based in London, are the Legal Technology Group and London Law Researchers.

Personal contacts

During the course of answering information enquiries a law librarian will build up a network of personal contacts and sources of information. Personal contacts are frequently made initially at professional meetings such as those of the British and Irish Association of Law Librarians and Aslib. Other contacts may be made in the answering of an information query, and it is useful to have a card index, or record of some sort, of those contacts or organizations that provided information. Sometimes there is a need for information in a field that is entirely new to the librarian. A most useful starting point is the CBD Ltd. *Directory of British associations*, 8th edn., 1986, which has a subject index and gives addresses and phone numbers.

THE REFERENCE AND INFORMATION SERVICE

The material which the law librarian acquires or creates, and the external information sources he identifies and accesses, are only the passive elements, the physical artefacts, of the total information service. A library user may solve his information need by direct use of these resources, but from time to time even the most skilled library user will need to seek the assistance of the library staff with an information enquiry.

The legal information officer or reference librarian is the link between the information source and the information seeker. As a librarian he knows the types of information sources which exist: encyclopedias, dictionaries, abstracting and indexing services, etc., how to locate them in the library using the library indexes and classification, and how to translate the enquirer's information problem into index terms which can be answered from the internal arrangement of the information source (contents tables, indexes, etc.). The law librarian adds to this general background an appreciation of the special nature of legal bibliography with its primary and secondary literature, and a familiarity with legal terminology and legal systems.

Reference librarians have always been respected for their knowledge of books, but a modern legal information service requires much more of its staff than bibliographical skill or expertise with online systems. The legal information officer needs personal relations skills, particularly the ability to interview enquirers to identify their real needs and to communicate through the written and the spoken word.

The information desk

Most large libraries have an enquiry desk or information point or points manned by qualified librarians. In large law libraries or general libraries with a subject arrangement legal enquiries will automatically be channelled towards staff with legal expertise. Where only one information point exists in a general library it is necessary for subject enquiries to be routed through the general enquiry desk staff to the law librarian if specialist assistance is required.

In selecting the location of the information desk some considerable thought is needed. Library research has shown that enquiries are frequently directed to library assistants at the counter or to shelving staff because they are often most accessible to the library user when the information need arises. Ideally the information desk should be prominently placed near such points, and this will often mean a location next to the catalogue or returns desk. Similar thought needs to be applied to the telephone system so that enquiries received by phone can be received directly or easily transferred to information desk staff. Once the location of the information point is decided, the service should be properly signed and advertised.

Types of question

Anyone who has worked in a library will appreciate that there are distinctive types of questions asked by library users. Administrative or directional enquiries ('where is the cloakroom?') can be reduced by good signs and library publications. Library enquiries for specific books ('where do I find Clerk and Lindsell on Torts?') or facts ('where was Lord Denning born?') are simply dealt with, and their number can be contained given adequate instruction to users and easily understood library techniques, particularly good catalogues. The enquiries of specific interest to the law librarian are subject enquiries which are open-ended and which require time, discussion with the enquirer and skill in the use of legal sources which the librarian has acquired through training and experience.

All library staff should be able to answer short basic questions, but extra training is required to ensure that library assistants recognize the need, often disguised, for longer or

more difficult enquiries needing the extra skills of the professional law librarian.

Some law libraries receive a large volume of enquiries by
telephone and a telephone enquiry form may be used to take
down the details of the enquirer and enquiry, and to record
the progress of the following research and the answer. These
forms are particularly important where referrals to specialist
law library staff are common, or in busy libraries where shift
changes and lunch breaks are likely to interrupt the answering
of an urgent enquiry.

Subject enquiry forms such as Fig. 1 can be used in all law
libraries, and not necessarily limited to use with telephone
enquiries. These forms prompt library staff to ask relevant
questions during the reference interview, and to check particular legal sources. They can therefore be helpful in training
new staff, and also form a permanent record which can be
used for statistical purposes or to identify sources of information useful in answering particular types of enquiry.

A small proportion of enquiries are received by post, telex
or via a third person. Since no discussion with the original
enquirer is possible here, the law librarian is dependent upon
the precision of the actual words used. Often enquiries received in this form will be given less time since in practice the
librarian finds the subject of the enquiry ill-defined. If possible, the librarian will wish to clarify the enquiry by telephone.
In the case of enquiries via a third person, where a solicitor
sends an office junior or a professor his secretary, the law
librarian must show considerable tact.

Fortunately most legal subject enquiries are face-to-face
encounters between the user and the law librarian. This is
important since, as mentioned below, a great deal about the
enquiry is learned by the observation of the enquirer's ges-
tures and reactions during the reference interview.

The reference process

Enquiry work has been subjected to a great deal of theoretical
analysis. A simplified model of the reference process is used
below to discuss the skills which the librarian should exercise

SEARCH ENQUIRY FORM — LAW	DATE:
NAME OF ENQUIRER	TEL./ADDRESS
SUBJECT OF ENQUIRY	
SEARCH KEYWORDS	INFO. OFFICER

STATUTORY MATERIALS

Bills

Recent: ☐ Daily List/Prestel   Older: ☐ Govt. Publications (monthly/annual)

☐ Weekly Information Bulletin

☐ New Law Journal (Yellow pages)   ☐ Sessional Papers Index

☐ Current Law (Parliament)

Statutes

Chronological:

☐ Statutes at Large

☐ Law Reports Statutes (1865–)

☐ Public General Acts and Measures (1831–)

☐ Current Law Statutes Annotated (1948–)

☐ Chronological Table of the Statutes

Subject:

☐ Statutes in Force

☐ Halsbury's Statutes

☐ Index to the Statutes

☐ Statute Collections (e.g. Butterworths Company Law Handbook)

☐ Lexis

Delegated Legislation

Recent:

☐ Daily List/Prestel

☐ New Law Journal

☐ Current Law

☐ Monthly Index

Older:

☐ Table of Govt. Orders

Subject:

☐ Index to Govt. Orders

☐ S.I.'s to 1961 bound vols.

☐ Halsbury's Statutory Instruments

☐ Subject Encyclopedias

☐ Lexis

CASES

Case name and subject indexes

☐ All England Law Reports

☐ English Reports (Name only)

☐ The Digest

☐ Halsbury's Laws

☐ Times Index
(Daily — Library file)

☐ Law Reports Digest
(1865—1950)/Index (1951—   )

☐ Current Law (Name only)

☐ Lexis

☐ Subject encyclopedias

Titles: individual series

General:

☐ English/Revised
Nominate Reports

☐ The Law Reports

☐ All England Law Reports

☐ Weekly Law Reports

☐ Times/Law Times/
Law Journal, etc.

Subject:

☐ Criminal Appeal Reports

☐ Road Traffic Reports

☐ Tax Cases

etc.

ENCYCLOPEDIAS

☐ Halsbury's Laws of England

☐ The Digest

☐ (Scottish) Current
Law Yearbook

☐ Oxford Companion to the Law

☐ Subject encyclopedias
(e.g. Planning — Heap)

CITATIONS

☐ Raistrick

DICTIONARIES

☐ Jowitt

☐ Stroud

☐ Words and Phrases
Legally Defined

HANDBOOKS

☐ Legal Aid Handbook

☐ Stones' Justices Manual

☐ Supreme Court Practice (White Book)

☐ County Court Practice

DIRECTORIES

☐ Solicitors and Barristers Diary

☐ Miskin — Directory of Law Libraries

FORMS AND PRECEDENTS

☐ Enc. of Forms and Precedents   ☐ Atkin's Court Forms

PERIODICALS INDEXES

☐ Index to Legal Periodicals

☐ Legal Resource Index

☐ Lexis/Lawtel

☐ Current Law

☐ Social Science Citation Index

MONOGRAPHS, etc.

☐ Library Catalogue (Subject/Author/Title)

☐ Law Books Published

☐ Law Books in Print

☐ Index to Legal Essays

☐ BNB

☐ Subject Bibliographies

GOVERNMENT PUBLICATIONS

☐ Annual/Monthly/Daily Govt. Publications Lists

☐ Sectional Lists

☐ COBOP

☐ Index to Chairmen (Stephens)

THESES

☐ Index to Theses

☐ Dissertation Abstracts International (DIALOG)

Figure 1   Specimen Subject Enquiry Form
(Derived from Kent, D. Talbot 'Discipline resource package — law' *in* Doyle, J.M. and Grimes, G.H. *Reference Resources,* 1976, pp. 166-7)

in answering subject enquiries. It is important to realise that this type of theory is merely a vehicle to understanding, and that most practising librarians have an intuitive appreciation of reference skills: the process is experienced rather than learnt.

The initial question

Before the library receives an enquiry the enquirer has to recognize that he has an *information* need and that the library can provide a source or service that can satisfy it. There are several clear alternatives at this stage which will not result in a library enquiry. The user can, for instance, ignore the need. He can try to solve the problem with his own resources, ask a friend, or consult an agency other than a library.

It is important for the information officer to recognize that an enquiry does not necessarily begin when the user approaches the library. The enquirer may have already consulted published sources and agencies which are relevant, and the librarian needs to know this to avoid repeating these efforts.

Equally, this 'prenegotiation stage' may have refined the question and its solution in the enquirer's mind in a way which may mislead the librarian. For instance, an enquirer may ask for the *Oxford companion to the law* thinking this will answer his need. The librarian knows of alternative sources such as *Halsbury's Laws of England*, but unless he is able to retrace the enquirer's thoughts from the initial question to his information need, the enquirer may receive an unsatisfactory answer. The dictum 'the hardest part of answering a reference question is frequently not so much finding the answer as finding the question' must always be borne in mind.

The reference interview

The reference interview is therefore an important stage in the reference process. This discussion between enquirer and librarian reformulates the enquirer's question into terms which allow the librarian to provide an answer from library sources. Personal presence and good training in interview

technique are needed for the librarian to conduct this exchange of information successfully.

The well-conducted reference interview will try to establish
some or all of the following about the subject of the enquiry:

> What does the user want to know?
> Why does he want to know?
> What is he going to do with the information?
> How much does he already know about the subject?
> What form does he want the information in?
> How much information does he want?
> How soon does he want the answer?

This does not mean that the interview will be lengthy or that it
will be by cross-examination. It may take you longer to read
the above questions than to obtain the answers in a particular
situation. In fact a good librarian is merely a good listener and
will prompt the user to express his need by allowing him to talk
relevantly, encouraging the conversation by head nods and
appropriate verbal cues. If the enquirer is not fluent or stum-
bles, he can be encouraged by being posed open questions –
what?, when?, how?, who?, where?, why? – as in the above list.
For the information officer, one of the most useful open
questions is why?, and the most useful why? question is 'Can I
ask why you want this information?' Closed questions – is?,
do?, has?, can?, will? – will give the user closed choices and will
lead to a stilted 'yes and no' conversation.

However, in dealing with enquirers the information officer
must appreciate that only part of the communication takes
place in words. Research has shown that 35 per cent of
communication is verbal and that the majority of the message
is conveyed by paralanguage (accent, intonation, etc.) and
body language. Non-verbal communication has generated a
large literature in recent years. An article by V. Boucher (*RQ*.
vol. 16, 1970, pp. 27–32) outlines the importance of this type
of communication to the reference interview.

The search strategy

At the end of the reference interview the information officer
should have a good understanding of the subject of the en-

quiry. This needs to be translated into a form which can be answered by the information sources he has to hand.

The first stage is to generalize the required information into a type such as a date, abbreviation, bibliographic list or bibliographic details of a particular item, and then to match this to the appropriate information source. Librarians identify particular titles in the relevant subject area by using the library classification scheme or such books as E. P. Sheehy's *Guide to reference books*, 9th edn., 1976; or A. J. Walford's *Guide to reference material*, 2nd edn., vol. 2, 1982. The experienced law librarian will know the sources of law and their library location without frequent recourse to intermediate tools, although it is likely he will deal with UK, Commonwealth and Common Market law more frequently than with civil law jurisdictions. UK law librarians will find that this edition of the *Manual* is their subject specific equivalent of Walford or Sheehy if they need to check on sources in less familiar jurisdictions.

The information store

Once the specific information sources have been identified, whether they are documents or databases, the librarian will exercise diverse skills in extracting the information relevant to the question.

For printed sources, this means a mastery of the indexes, contents pages and arrangement of many different publications, together with an appreciation of their limitations. For online databases it means a knowledge of the contents of the database, search strategy, use of thesauri and, for full text databases, a good understanding of the language of the law and the way the judiciary and legal draftsmen express themselves.

If a complex piece of library research is undertaken the search may range across a number of sources, both primary and secondary, and in a periodical source, such as an index and abstracting journal, the principle of retrospective searching will be used.

Giving the answer

As the librarian conducts his search he will acquire additional information to that supplied by the enquirer. This may prompt him to alter his reformulated question or return to the enquirer with a query about the initial question. In fact, it is common for the librarian and enquirer to work together with sources, although there are certain instances (with online searching, for example) where this might not be considered desirable.

The librarian may at a particular stage be satisfied that what he has found answers his understanding of the initial question. This is his judgment of relevance. The user, however, is exercising a judgment of pertinence to his original need, and if the librarian has incorrectly assessed that need the enquirer may respond negatively to a search result. Quite often the law librarian will find that he misjudges the level of understanding of the enquirer and either produces too specialized or too general a source. If the enquirer is present during the search his comments to particular sources can be monitored and this allows the librarian to fine-tune the search result to the enquirer's need.

Legal research

Intensive legal research is not often undertaken in law libraries because of limitations on staff time. In academic libraries, staff and students undertake their own legal research for sound practical reasons and even in solicitors' firms articled clerks are responsible for legal research rather than library staff.

In certain libraries, however, more in-depth library research is carried out. The library of the House of Commons is one example described by D. Englefield in his book *Parliament and information*, 1981. Individual enquiries from Members of Parliament are often given written answers prepared by one of the five research divisions attached to the library.

Many libraries do conduct library research for groups if not for individuals. Public libraries and some academic libraries prepare bibliographies or factsheets on subjects of topical interest. In the special case of the House of Commons Library this anticipatory work involves the compilation of Reference Sheets and Background Papers on specific topics, many selected after the forthcoming legislative programme is announced in the Queen's Speech.

Public libraries and legal enquiries

Most public library authorities do not have law librarians, and their legal collections will often be fairly limited and concentrated in the central reference library. Frequently a social science or commerce librarian will be responsible for legal enquiries and branch library staff will refer anything beyond the basic enquiry to this person.

The key to public library legal information is training and referral. All library staff need to be aware of the danger of proferring legal advice, and enquiries should be properly referred to the appropriate person and department. If the enquirer's need is identified as one of legal advice rather than information, the librarian will refer the enquirer to either a solicitor (although not specifically to a named firm) or to an agency. A referral file containing names, addresses and other information about agencies will be needed and should be regularly updated. The library staff should also be prepared to provide details of charging (if any) and instructions on how to locate the agency and travel there by public transport. It is often useful to ask for feedback on how successful a referral proves to be, either from the enquirer or the receiving agency.

AUTOMATED LEGAL RESEARCH

Earlier chapters and the preceding section of this chapter have described the use of manual methods and manual research tools for legal research. This section concentrates on the use of automated systems for such research, describing the different types of services available and how they are used.

Automated services for legal research are mounted on a

database. This can be described as a collection of information that is stored in a computer. An online database is accessible to users through a keyboard terminal linked by a telephone line to the computer. A search for information is carried out by interrogating the computer by a question and answer method.

The reader who wishes to learn about the early research and development of computerized legal information systems should read Gillian Bull's article: 'Technical developments in legal information retrieval: a guide for BIALL members', in the *Law Librarian*, vol. 11 (2), August 1980, pp. 34–40.

Manual versus automated

There is no doubt that the advent of online legal information retrieval systems has revolutionized legal research and opened up search possibilities that were not available using manual sources alone. However, the online systems should not be considered a panacea for all research problems: no perfect legal research tool exists, and researchers should normally expect to use several tools and balance them against each other to check the completeness of their research. Moreover, the computer is not a short-cut for the sloppy thinker: the ordering of thought is a prerequisite of a computer search, just as it is for a manual search.

That said, there are searches that computers are particularly well suited to. *Any* word, phrase or number that appears on the database can be used as a keyword to finding a required case. For example, a request for 'a recent passing off case in which Cotswold appears somewhere' would produce no problems for a computer search, but would be virtually impossible to carry out manually. Thus many potentially useful words and phrases are omitted from manually prepared indexes, and only *The Digest* allows for fact-related indexing. The computer overcomes these problems by greatly expanding the number of words and phrases that may be used as a starting point for research.

Secondly, the computer allows a researcher to locate cases that contain arbitrary patterns or combinations of words, phrases and numbers. It will, for example, find all the cases of a given judge in a certain area of law, or retrieve all the cases that cite a named case, contain a particular phrase, or are under a specified statute or section of a statute. A computer would have no problem in locating all the decisions of Mr Justice Sheen on shipping cases relating to collisions in fog, or finding cases under section 23 of the Town and Country Planning Act 1971.

However, a computer cannot assist the researcher in selecting the terms most appropriate to a particular search. It is at this point that manual research may need to be used. A researcher unfamiliar with an area of law might consider commencing his research with textbooks, articles, encyclopedias and printed indexes until he gains familiarity with that area of law, its language and the vocabulary the judges have used.

A further limitation on using computer searches is that of incompleteness of the database. It is important to remember when using any of the online systems, what the limitation is in terms of series of reports, and time – *ie*, how far back the databases go and how current they are. For completeness of coverage earlier decisions must be searched for manually.

In computer searches there is also the difficulty of searching for legal concepts. Although it is true to say that any legal concept has to be expressed in a form of words, the problem is finding that form and every possible alternative. Since the computer searches for word patterns, it will often retrieve a number of cases that contain the specified pattern of words but in the wrong context. Additionally, the computer will normally miss some relevant cases because a particular pattern of words has not been specified. For example, in looking for statutory regulations on the export of petroleum, SI 1982/1000 uses the words 'unless the Minister gives notice of his consent in writing to delivery elsewhere [than the United Kingdom]' to express the concept of export. It is not likely that anyone would have thought of using those particular words in their search.

Despite these disadvantages, research that has been carried out in Canada by M. Iosipescu and J. Yogis and described in *A comparison of automated and manual research: a computer study*, 1981, demonstrates that using computers for legal research can have very effective results. Among the advantages of using automated searches were that manual searches took approximately four times as long as the computer searches over the problems in question; that computer searches were likely to be more accurate because they do not depend on the completeness and exactness of printed indexes, and because of the tendency of researchers to take short cuts and overlook useful sources; and that manual searches were more than three times as expensive as computer searches because of the extra time involved.

Types of automated services

There are a number of different types of database available. A database may give bibliographic references, abstracts or full text. Larger libraries may use online databases as indexes to documents in their stock, but smaller libraries will probably need to obtain hard copy either by inter-library loan or from prints obtained online or supplied by the database producers.

Some databases, for example LEXIS, are made available directly by the database producer. But others, for example CELEX and POLIS, are passed to an organization which runs a computer, and sells access to the databases which are available on its computer. Such system suppliers are known as hosts.

Legal full-text

There were initally two legal full-text information systems available in the United Kingdom, both launched in 1980. However EUROLEX, marketed by the European Law Centre Ltd., was taken over by Butterworth Telepublishing Ltd. in 1985, and some of its database was incorporated into the LEXIS system.

LEXIS originally began in the United States in 1973 and by 1980, when Butterworth Telepublishing launched it in the United Kingdom, there was already a well-developed database of US law covering statute and case-law for both state and Federal systems. This was available to UK users immediately via a satellite link with Mead Data Center's host computer in Dayton, Ohio. In the United Kingdom, LEXIS's original strength lay in the availability of the *All England Law Reports* from 1945 and the early development of a statutory database including all Statutes and Statutory Instruments currently in force. From this base LEXIS developed specialist libraries on such subjects as tax, intellectual property and European law and also entered into an arrangement which allows French law to be made available to LEXIS users. The decision to produce a new text of *Halsbury's Statutes* using LEXIS and linking subscribers to the hard copy into a LEXIS update service marked a movement towards electronic publishing and an integration of the LEXIS operation with Butterworth's traditional publishing role. More recently Commonwealth, Australian and New Zealand case-law has been made available on LEXIS and the full text of many American law school journals has been added to the database.

Another major database entered the UK market in 1982 when CELEX was launched. This database is produced by the legal service of the Commission of the European Communities and covers the whole range of European Community law including the establishing treaties, secondary legislation, the decisions of the Court of Justice and questions to the European Parliament and the Commission. The database is available on the EURIS host, which is owned by Honeywell Bull SA.

Viewdata

In addition to the major full-text databases, there are smaller databases containing legal information. One system provider is Prestel, the viewdata or videotex system provided by British Telecom. This is a computer-based information service publishing information via the telephone system. Users of the service can access many thousands of pages of information, set up as individually numbered 'frames' using a specially adapted television set, which is connected to their telephone by a jack-socket. Prestel sets are supplied with a keypad enabling users to select any particular frame and have it displayed on the screen. The initial page acts as a 'menu' which routes the user through the branching system to the page of information required. Prestel can additionally be accessed from a microcomputer by means of an extra plug-in module.

The user will find a vast amount of useful information on Prestel, *eg*, news, weather, sport, stocks and shares, money rates, travel, etc. An article by D. Raper and L. Stevenson in the *Law Librarian*, vol. 12 (1) 1981, pp. 4–6, describes how Prestel is used in a city firm's library for business and commercial information rather then legal information. There have, in addition, been a number of detailed studies made on the use of Prestel in the public library service, and additional references on this topic are given at the end of the chapter.

Much of the information available on Prestel is free though sometimes the information providers, who set up the pages of information, may wish to make a charge for a particular frame, and in that case the charge is shown in the top right-hand corner of the frame. All this information is available to any Prestel user. There are also closed user groups (CUG's) on Prestel, and to access the information provided by any of these, a subscription is necessary.

LAWTEL is an important closed user group in the legal information field. It has summaries of case- and statute law, quantum of damages, fees information and some Scottish coverage. Unlike the major databases, LAWTEL has a short retrospective file, dating from the late 1970s and provides summary rather then full-text information.

Bibliographic databases

These cover a number of different areas. Parliamentary activity is important to lawyers to warn of impending changes in legislation. Although the legal full-text systems cover Bills such as the Finance Bill, and progress of Bills is given on LAWTEL, the major database for parliamentary information is POLIS. This is compiled by the House of Commons Library and is made available to external users by a commercial host. POLIS dates from 1980 and initially covered House of Commons written, oral and private notice questions, all new public and general Acts, and selected coverage of Hansard and Parliamentary papers. The database is being continually expanded and will cover EEC, OECD, UN and Council of Europe documents in addition to more comprehensive coverage of UK parliamentary activity.

The databases mentioned above have principally covered primary legal materials, whether as full-text or in abstract. LAWTEL covers some British law books and legal periodicals. Unfortunately for British users, the other secondary material is on databases that are American in origin and although they cover UK periodicals, they have a US bias in content. *Legal Resource Index* covers over 600 law journals and *Criminal Justice Periodical Index* over 120. Both these databases are available on the DIALOG host. *Patlaw* covers US law on patents, copyright, trademarks and unfair competition and is available from PERGAMON INFOLINE and DIALOG.

Details of the contents, pricing and availability of all legal databases will be found in the current edition of *Law Databases* published by Aslib.

Commercial and business information

Many law libraries find that they need access to non-legal information from time to time. The information required is frequently of a business or commercial nature. Just as legal online systems have been developed in recent years, so too have online systems which give current political, economic and business information. There are already a number of systems on the market, and this is an area which is earmarked for rapid growth and development as information which was formerly available only in hardcopy is mounted online. Developments in the field are monitored by *Aslib Information* and by their *Online Notes*, together with their editions of *News Databases*.

Some of the databases concentrate on providing news, either in full-text or as an abstract. Mead Data Central have NEXIS as a full-text news database, working on the same search principles as LEXIS. Although primarily consisting of American newspapers and magazines, it has the *Financial Times* and the *Economist* on its database.

Another full-text news and current affairs database is *World Reporter* which is produced jointly by the BBC and Datasolve. Among its sources for the database is the BBC *Summary of World Broadcasts* and the BBC *External Services News*.

Also providing a news and current affairs database is Finsbury Data Services' *Textline*. The information is gathered from over a hundred different sources worldwide, mainly newspapers, translated where necessary, and appears in abstract form rather than full-text. Searching is by the 'free text' approach or by the use of indexing terms.

A further series of databases are those which cover company information. Traditional providers of this information such as Jordans, Dun and Bradstreet and ICC, have now made company news available online and enquirers can find, for example, a company's registered office, directors' names and responsibilities, sales turnover, etc.

Downloading

Libraries which have access to online systems and a microcomputer, can build up their in-house information files by downloading. Allan Foster describes downloading as 'the practice of transferring quantities of data, by electronic means, from a main computer or memory device to a peripheral device where it is then used', *Library Association Record*, vol. 86(9), September 1984, pp. 358–9. Full-text databases, bibliographic databases, and those which provide cataloguing data can be downloaded. It is important to ascertain what permission is necessary for this process, and what royalty charges are payable to the database producer.

Using online databases

There are two ways of searching online databases: by using a controlled vocabulary or thesaurus, or by using what is known as 'free text' or natural language. The purpose of a controlled vocabulary is that only one term should be available to describe a concept. A list of terms is then published as a thesaurus, together with cross-references, so that the appropriate term may be found for use in a database, no matter what word was thought of to express the concept.

'Free text' searching, or the use of natural language means precisely that: any word that occurs in the database may be used as a search term. As we saw previously, this leads to the difficulty of selecting appropriate words and the danger of omitting some useful terms. It is cheaper to produce a database that uses this method of searching, as there is not the expense of compiling a list of indexing terms. Most of the English language full-text systems have chosen the free text approach.

There are some systems that use the free text approach, but have a useful thesaurus-type facility. The European Space Agency, host to a number of databases, has what is known as a 'zoom' command. This is an automated help device which analyses the contents of your current search results and in particular suggests further potentially useful search entries. For example, entering the term 'dock' in the ACOMPLINE database, and using the zoom command, produces the further search possibilities of 'docklands', 'riverside', 'anchorage' and individual names such as 'St Katherine's Dock' and 'Royal Albert Dock', amongst others.

Systems features

When conducting an online search it is important to understand both the way in which search terms operate, and the way in which the computer itself searches. Although different systems operate through different commands, there are a number of features that are common to most online systems.

One of these is what is known as Boolean logic or alternatively Boolean operators. This simply means the use of the terms 'and', 'or', 'not' in a search. Someone might want to search for the terms bike *or* bicycle; or perhaps bike or bicycle *and* car; or car and *not* lorry. Most systems also feature positional operators, or proximity connectors, though these vary considerably from system to system. Another standard feature is the use of right-hand truncation. Instead of entering all word endings as alternatives, a word stem is used as a search term and the computer automatically retrieves all the variants. For example, instead of entering necessary, necessitates, etc. 'necess-' is entered.

A further feature of online systems is the facility to modify and recall a search request at a subsequent level or levels. Most systems have facilities for showing the number of documents retrieved, displaying the search terms in context, and highlighting those terms.

It is useful to understand how the computer itself deals with a search request. When the text of a document is entered onto the database, every word, with the exception of a number of specified common or 'stop' words, is given an address as the system automatically generates an inverted file or concordance. This means that when searching for terms the computer goes straight to the word or words in the concordance with the list of addresses and matches them according to the request. In the LEXIS concordance the word *asbestos* might have an address 346–16–1457 for one of its occurrences. This means that it is the 1457th word in the 16th segment in the 346th document in the file. The request to find the word *cancer* within seven words of *asbestos* would mean the computer checking the lists of addresses in the concordance for both words. The address 346–16–1463 for *cancer* would produce a 'hit'.

Search strategies

Before going online with a search request it is essential to spend some time beforehand working out what search terms to enter. If the user is unfamiliar with the area of law it may be necessary to consult textbooks and other secondary sources first to familiarize himself with the words the courts have used to express a concept.

Once this has been done, or if the user is already familiar with the terminology, the next step is to pick out the keywords that can be used as search terms, and carefully think of any synonyms, opposites, such as admissible or inadmissible, and whether a word is hyphenated or written as one or two words. If necessary the system manual may need to be consulted to see if, or how, plurals and possessives are taken care of, and the truncation facility should be used where appropriate. Equivalents such as numbers and abbreviations should also be allowed for and inserted where the system does not automatically do this.

When this stage has been completed the order of the words and the connectors must be arranged, remembering the order in which the Boolean operators work, and adding positional operators in the way in which the system allows. The user also has to decide whether he will enter the search request at a single level, or at a number of different levels. Finally, the appropriate library or libraries within the database must be selected, bearing in mind any limitations they might have by way of historical date, currency and materials excluded.

Most errors that arise when using one of the online systems can be traced back to the failure to complete one of the above steps correctly. It is, for example, easy to overlook a synonym or to enter a full word instead of a word stem. This inevitably leads to relevant material not being retrieved, and incorrect conclusions being drawn.

Searching for statutory material produces fewer problems. The user may need to refer to published material initially to see what words parliamentary draftsmen have used. Otherwise the main problem is to see how the material is presented on the database, and to master the search techniques.

Equipment

In order to access an online database two pieces of equipment are essential: a terminal for sending and receiving data, and a telecommunications link connecting the terminal to a telephone line. A terminal consists of a visual display unit (VDU), which looks like a small television screen, and a keyboard which resembles a typewriter keyboard but with extra keys for special functions. The telecommunications link consists of a telephone with acoustic coupler or modem. An acoustic coupler is a device into which a telephone receiver is fitted so that data that is received over the telephone line can be converted into the digital pulses that a computer understands. It has the advantage of being cheap and portable, but is prone to general interference unless used on a good quality telephone line. The modem, short for modulator-demodulator, performs a similar function but connects a terminal directly to a telephone line and is considered to be a more satisfactory approach. It is convenient to be able to print out what appears on the VDU, and a printer, which is usually separate from the terminal, is required for this purpose.

Aslib's Information Resources Centre can be approached for technical advice. Their enquiry service offers information, advice and referral on online retrieval, methods and systems. Their editions of *Going online* and *Selecting equipment for online information retrieval* are particularly useful as an introduction for beginners in the online field.

For the first few years of its operation in the UK LEXIS was only available using a dedicated terminal: the equipment supplied by Butterworth Telepublishing and consisting of terminal, telephone link and printer could only be used to access LEXIS. However, following the practice of LEXIS in the United States, it became possible to access LEXIS from a microcomputer in 1985. LEXIS offers a document-delivery service for all material on its database, the service operating from the offices of Butterworth Telepublishing in London.

For those subscribing to other online services there are a number of options available regarding a terminal. A terminal can be purchased, rented or leased from a number of manufacturers. They vary in price and sophistication, but can only be used for online functions and cannot perform any computing or word processing functions by themselves. As such they are sometimes referred to as 'dumb' terminals. An alternative to this is to use a word processor or microcomputer to access an online database. It may be necessary to acquire additional hardware and software in order to make them teletype compatible *ie*, able to access online systems.

Some further technicalities arise over telecommunications. Online systems can be accessed by direct dialling. Non-local users, however, would find it cheaper to dial into their local PSS exchange or IPSS if outside the United Kingdom. The PSS or Packet Switch Stream is a nationwide facility provided by British Telecom to cut down the cost of data transmission over long distances. The PSS breaks up the data information stream into discrete quantities which are wrapped separately in control information and sent through the network as distinct entities called 'packets'. These 'packets' are delivered at the other end in the correct order minus the control information, leaving the data information stream in its original form. This works out cheaper than standard telephone calls, where one data transmission path is constantly maintained throughout the duration of the call. There are PSS nodes in major towns and cities throughout the United Kingdom.

The IPSS or International Packet Switch Stream is the international connection of PSS, linking data networks within the UK to data networks abroad. By this means POLIS can be accessed from abroad via the public telephone system, using public data networks such as EURONET from Europe, and TELENET or TYMNET from the United States.

Another factor to consider when choosing equipment for telecommunications is line speed. The speed of data transmission over the telephone is measured in characters per second which relates to the baud rate of the terminal. 300 baud is 30 characters per second and is a much slower speed than 1200 baud. Lower baud rates increase the cost of telephone calls since it takes longer to transmit the data.

Costs

The cost of using online systems varies a great deal from system to system, and according to the type of user, some database producers operate a cheaper hourly rate for academic users, or allow a certain number of hours' usage for a fixed sum. For commercial users the main difference is between those databases for which there is only an online connect-time charge and those for which there is an additional subscription charge. Some producers require a minimum time usage. Most give discounts for high overall usage, with the commitment normally having to be made in advance of use. Producers also usually provide an offline print service at an extra charge. With a service like DIALOG, which acts as a host to a number of different databases, there are extra royalty charges for printing or downloading. Hosts and database producers generally make a charge for training, and sometimes also charge for the user manual. When signing a contract with a host, a user or user organization is given a password which allows access to all or most of the databases offered. The user normally pays little or nothing in the way of initial charges or subscription, but pays for whatever usage has been made of the databases at the end of the month.

CURRENT AWARENESS SERVICES

Current awareness services aim to inform the library user about material acquired by the library and about relevant developments in a wider context by using externally generated current awareness sources. The services comprise the production of current awareness bulletins, circulation of periodicals and selective dissemination of information, although libraries will not necessarily provide all three services.

Indeed it is not all libraries who are able to provide a current awareness service in an active sense at all. Much depends on resources in terms of staff time and money available, the size of the user group and the working environment of the user. The larger the institution and the user group, the less likely there is to be a fully developed current awareness service. It is, therefore, in the smaller private libraries, government libraries and in public libraries who serve local industry and commerce, all of whom have a well-defined user group, that such a service is most likely to exist.

One of the main benefits of providing current awareness services is that although some library users keep themselves up to date in their own subject areas, the library staff have access on a regular basis to a far wider range of materials than the individual user.

In providing these services the library benefits by keeping its users aware of its existence and by showing itself as an active and informed unit. In the long run the amount of financial and 'political' support a library receives will depend on the attitude of its users, and this will be influenced by the services they receive from the library. In this respect current awareness services can be a very valuable and visible activity for a library.

Current awareness bulletins

Current awareness bulletins are listings which are produced by the library and they can appear in different formats; *eg*, accessions lists, current periodicals contents lists, abstracts of recent periodical articles. Their content may vary enormously according to the needs of the users and to staff time available to produce the service. Frequency can vary from weekly to monthly. Arrangement of the bulletin could be by author, by subject, or by classified arrangement.

General library bulletins can include publicity and announcements such as new members of staff, new phone numbers or the introduction of new services; new books, new periodical titles or law reports; summaries of recent law reports; new Acts and Statutory Instruments; recent Bills and government reports or discussion documents; abstracts of recent periodical articles or listing of titles of articles; counsel's opinions obtained by a firm; transcripts of judgments; announcements of forthcoming meetings and conferences; additions to online databases; new office precedents; internally generated memoranda and practice notes. This can be produced as hard copy or as made available via an electronic mail network.

Many periodicals also have their own current awareness sections, varying in length and style, but all aimed at keeping their readers abreast of new developments. Further information on this can be found in the section on periodicals in Chapter 5.

Periodicals circulation

This is the term used when issues of periodicals are automatically sent to individual library users for perusal. It is normally small private libraries and government department libraries who carry out periodicals circulation. Public and academic libraries rely on periodicals display to keep their readers up to date.

There is debate about the value of circulation of periodicals. It is a slow process when the item is circulated to many people. The issues in circulation are not available for consultation in the library, unless there is a duplicate display copy, and this is an added expense. There may be a need to purchase a number of extra copies of various periodicals to ensure that circulation lists are not too long, again an extra expense. Bad feeling can be caused by the position of individuals on the circulation list. The turnover of staff in an organization, changes of location and users changing their minds about what they want to see results in constant updating of circulation slips. Issues may be mislaid or completely lost during the process of circulation.

However, it may be that some library users are at remote locations and cannot visit the library regularly to read periodicals. Others may have good intentions, but pressure of work detracts from regular library visits. In both these cases the circulation of periodicals is a valuable service. Additionally, it allows an individual to see all the contents of a periodical including news items, editorial comment, etc. which increase his current awareness.

Methods

The names of the recipients of each periodical are generally recorded on slips which are attached to the issues. These slips can be typed and then copied in batches. It is essential to retain a master copy for each circulation slip which will need correcting and updating from time to time.

Word processors can be used for the production of the master circulation slips thus ensuring ease of correction. It is now possible to buy software packages for microcomputers which deal with circulation of periodicals. As an issue of a periodical arrives it is entered into the system and the correct circulation slip is automatically printed out. For further information on traditional circulation methods and problems that may arise, the reader is referred to D. A. Kemp's *Current awareness services*, 1979.

An alternative to circulating the periodicals themselves is to photocopy or type out the contents lists only and to circulate these. Some libraries would then offer a document supply service, and provide a photocopy of items that have been marked up. Public libraries can provide this as a service to local industry and commerce and academic libraries to lecturers.

Academic and public libraries use display of current periodicals instead of periodical circulation. Users know which periodicals cover their field of interest and use a scan of the shelves and new books display as their principal method of current awareness. This might be backed up by the library accessions list and such sources as *Legal Contents*, an American publication which reproduces the contents lists of American and some English legal periodicals, and the current awareness services of the main legal periodicals.

Selective dissemination of information

SDI is generally regarded as the provision of a service whereby the user of the service receives notification of items which match a statement of his requirements, the matching being carried out by a scanner for manual SDI, or computer for automated SDI.

SDI has traditionally been operated most widely in scientific fields, due to the ability to pinpoint search areas and subjects precisely, and because of the need of the research scientist to keep abreast of developments that are reported in hundreds of different sources. The arts and social sciences are more difficult to cover, particularly in using computer searches, where concepts and ideas are less easy to translate into keywords.

However, SDI forms a very important service in many law libraries, with the emphasis on manual systems. For example, a user of the service may wish to be notified of all statutory instruments in a certain category such as company law. Another user might want articles and press cuttings on the progress of a particular piece of law reform such as investor protection. Yet another might wish to be informed of all case reports on, say, arbitration. Others may wish to have information on certain companies in the form of regular press cuttings. It is a service that is time-consuming to operate but one which is of direct benefit to its recipients.

Manual SDI

Manual SDI involves the librarian in scanning, *ie*, examining the accessions of the library and noting material which, in his judgment, may be useful in connection with a user's work. There is much to be said in favour of manual methods of SDI, for the human scanner is able to recognize relevant material not just through keywords, but through the association of concepts and ideas, in a way that a computer cannot. A librarian gradually builds up knowledge and experience not only of his subject, but of individual SDI requirements, which makes the service of increasing use to the recipients.

Such a service normally involves keeping more or less formal records of some sort. The most formal will involve the use of interest profiles for individuals and the compilation of lists of items to be looked for. At the other extreme, a librarian may work from a few informal notes, if he has only a small group of people to work for. The use of records increases the number of people the librarian can serve; they are helpful for the inexperienced, and they facilitate changes in staff and temporary absences. On the other hand, no records are ever complete, and the experienced scanner uses his intuition and past experience for selection of items. Records are expensive to compile and maintain. They may be inconvenient to consult, and the very act of consultation slows down the scanning process. Many scanners use the records they keep to remind themselves of the details of the newer interest profiles, and work from a combination of memory and reference.

Profile preparation

Where fairly formal scanning records are kept, it is necessary to prepare interest profiles. The users of the service are firstly asked to prepare a detailed statement of their interests and needs. This statement is then discussed and modifications made if necessary. Decisions need to be taken about which publications are to be scanned and whether secondary sources such as indexing and abstracting services should be included. Keywords are then selected for each profile. They may include not only subject descriptors but also authors, institutions etc.

Two types of material can be used for scanning for SDI. Firstly, and most commonly, are the primary sources such as journals, textbooks, newspapers, reports, conference proceedings, etc. Secondary materials can also be included for scanning purposes, covering indexing and abstracting services, bulletins and accessions lists from other libraries, bibliographies of newly-published material, etc.

Selection of items to be notified

The techniques of matching items to users' interests can differ markedly, as can the sort of *aide-mémoire* to interest profiles which is kept. The variety of approach differs according to the scanner's knowledge of his subject and his experience with the sources being scanned. The information on the interest profiles is normally transferred to a further record. This may simply be a list of subject interests with names attached. If entered on a word processor such a listing can easily be amended and changed.

Card indexes are widely used, and records kept in this way can quickly be added and withdrawn and alterations made. There is normally a card index by user name that carries a description of the interests of that person, his location and phone number, and the date on which his interest profile was last revised. There is also usually a card index by keywords and phrases giving the users who are interested in those topics.

When relevant material has been found it must then be passed on to the interested party. Very often a photocopy is sent, if for example, a press cutting is involved. Bibliographical references may be passed on in the form of typed lists, or with each item separately listed on a card.

SDI requires a back-up of source material. The minimum requirement should be that the material listed is available for the user to consult. It may be necessary to put all listed items aside for a week or two to enable several people to look at the same item. A document delivery service can be offered to the user by means of a form or tear-off slip accompanying each item or batch of items inviting the user to order a photocopy or reserve an item on loan. When secondary sources are scanned for SDI it is probable that requested items will need either to be purchased or borrowed.

Automated SDI

SDI is a natural candidate for automation: computer systems are logical and precise and the number of profiles and their complexity can be very much greater in computer than in manual systems. Computer SDI can be provided in-house or using external services or used in conjunction with manual SDI, depending on what funds are available for external services and staff time available for manual searching. With the use of computerized cataloguing in many university and public libraries, an SDI service for accessions can be provided as a by-product of the cataloguing procedure, thus giving a service to academic staff, or to selected users of a public library.

When external services are to be used it is important to construct the interest profile very carefully. The same basic steps are used as for manual SDI, but with additional factors to be taken into consideration. If a number of different databases are to be used, will they overlap in coverage and lead to duplication of references? The librarian must know the individual databases and their differing approaches to indexing techniques, and whether controlled or uncontrolled vocabularies are used. The process of selecting keywords needs to be more thorough and precise than for manual SDI. If a database is searched using a thesaurus then this has to be consulted. Free text searching involves selecting all possible synonyms. Different profiles may need to be constructed for different databases.

Examples of SDI run on legal databases include DIALOG and LEXIS. DIALOG offers an SDI service which allows a user to have a search run automatically every time the selected file is updated. The search logic is entered and stored by the computer. For a set price the user then regularly receives a print-out matching his search profile without having to do anything further. A search logic already entered can be modified at any time. Use of the *Legal Resource Index* on DIALOG, for example, would give the user access to a large number of American secondary sources including law journals and law newspapers, legal monographs, government publications and case notes. LEXIS provides a similar service. Up to 80 search requests can be stored on any ID number and items printed out and mailed at weekly, fortnightly or monthly intervals.

FURTHER READING

REFERENCE AND INFORMATION FACILITIES

Miskin, C. *Library and information services for the legal profession*, 1981.
Raper, D. 'The Library and information service', in Purton, P. J. and Andrews, D. *Organisation and management of a solicitors' practice*, Chapter 9, 1980.

REFERENCE AND INFORMATION SERVICE

Crum, N. J. 'The librarian–customer relationship: dynamics of filling requests for information.' *Special Libraries.* vol. 60, pp. 269–77.
Grogan, D. *Practical reference work*, 1979.
Hanstock, T. M. 'Law collections in public libraries: Sheffield City Libraries' example', *Law Librarian*, vol. 11, no. 2, 1980, pp. 31–3.
Jahoda, G. and Olsen, P. E. 'Models of reference: analyzing the reference process', *RQ*, vol. 12, 1972, pp. 148–56.
Jahoda, G. *et al.* 'The reference process: modules for instruction', *RQ*, vol. 17, 1977, pp. 7–12.
Katz, W. A. *Introduction to reference work*, 2 vols., 3rd edn., 1978.
Katz, W. A. and Tarr, A. *Reference and information services: a reader*, 1978.
Taylor, R-S. 'Question-negotiation and information-seeking in libraries', *College and Research Libraries*, vol. 29, 1968, pp. 178–94.

AUTOMATED LEGAL RESEARCH

Iosipescu, M. and Yogis, J. *A comparison of automated and manual legal research: a computer study,* 1981.

Program, vol. 15, no. 3, 1981. Special issue on legal retrieval systems.

Sheldon, A. (ed.) *Prestel in the library context: proceedings of two seminars,* 1982.

Yeates, R. *Prestel in the public library: reaction of the general public to Prestel and its potential for conveying local information,* 1982.

CURRENT AWARENESS SERVICES

Kemp, D. A. *Current awareness services,* 1979.

Whitehall, T. *Personal current awareness service: a handbook of techniques for manual SDI,* 1979.

17. Acquisitions and Storage

D. A. PARNHAM

BOOKSTOCK POLICIES

Policy is mainly influenced by the type of library concerned
and its scope of readership, yet all require certain classes of
material: legislation, law reports, journals and major treatises.
Expansion will be influenced by the following factors: the
automatic growth of serial publications, which increases the
stock held though not, except indirectly, its range; the physical
size of the library area, which may dictate future purchase
policy; and specialized areas of interest resulting in the need to
purchase new titles. Thus a library serving practitioners in
taxation requires different publications in the field of reports,
journals and treatises, from those purchased by one concerned with commercial or property law. Similarly, academic
and educational libraries differ from those used by practising
lawyers, government departments, or the general public. The
setting up of a new library, or the expansion of an existing one,
will be assisted by consultation with other librarians in similar
establishments, and the use of appropriate bibliographies and
publishers' lists. Further aid will be found in the BIALL Standards: appendixes VI–XI, 'Recommended holdings for law
libraries', *Law Librarian*, special issue, 1983.

Although the latest and most important books and recent
issues of periodicals must be stocked, it is of greater value if the
library can offer an additional service. The provision of superseded editions, early printed books and later works long out of
print, complete sets of legislation, law reports and journals,
and fringe publications, which practitioners or students cannot possess, will be of lasting value to readers. Enquiries may
be expected in all libraries regarding publications not held,
or topics not covered, and a good collection of bibliographical works relating to legal topics, and the holdings of other

libraries, is advisable. Information may thus be provided as to the details of publications and their possible location elsewhere. It is important to realize that the service offered by a library need not be confined to the material held.

Selection policy

New acquisitions are normally selected according to the general stock policy, and with consideration for readers' needs. The current state of budget allowances must always be remembered, since the major proportion will be permanently allocated to serials, new editions and supplements. New titles may also be required within these fields. The resultant allocation for individual publications is usually small and great care must be exercised or funds may be used too rapidly; important publications appearing later in the financial year will not then receive consideration until the year following, and it is desirable that readers' needs should be anticipated.

The author's intentions require careful examination, since his book may be written for practitioners or students of either branch of the legal profession, or of another profession; for schoolchildren, or the general public. Thus a work on doctors and the law may expound general legal problems for medical practitioners, or medico-legal problems for lawyers, or present an outline of the layman's rights. Nevertheless, simple expositions of subjects will often assist students, or practitioners working in unaccustomed legal fields, more readily than authoritative specialist works. If doubts arise regarding the possible duplication of items it is advisable to double-check, since offprints of articles in journals, chapters from books, sections of encyclopedic works, and individual volumes from titled series may be published and advertised as separate works.

Opportunities to remedy deficiencies in important collections or series should not be lost, while decisions to purchase all subsequent editions of new works may be reversed if these prove inadequate or unpopular.

Whether librarians purchase books directly, or are required to submit titles to committees for consideration, detailed information should first be acquired through bibliographical searching (see page 717). Wherever possible, publications should be seen and examined. This may be achieved by visiting other libraries holding these items, by calling on suppliers, or contacting publishers. Alternatively, suppliers or publishers may be asked to send copies on approval, though not all will necessarily do so. This practice can, however, create difficulties, as alternative purchasers may not be found for books specially obtained and then rejected. Also, care must be taken to ensure that these books are neither damaged nor retained for an indefinite period for further consideration. Such factors will affect eventual sale elsewhere and, therefore, the suppliers' willingness to accept returns. Should the library be situated beyond the supplier's delivery area, the constant rise in postage costs may prove a further deterrent.

Whether purchases are directed by the librarian's choice, the recommendation of an influential reader, or by the final decision of a committee, certain guidelines may prove valuable. The work of a well-known author or editor, and the productions of a specialist publisher, will always receive primary consideration. Yet it may be that the famous name has been lent to a publication which is mainly the work of other and less expert writers, while publishers occasionally produce books which are principally aimed at other markets. Consultation with an expert academic or practising lawyer can be of value in these instances. Committee members, while usually requiring full descriptions of works under consideration, and often their physical presence, may also prove individually knowledgeable about doubtful items.

Multiple copies

Additional copies of works in constant demand by readers should ideally be provided. The influencing factors of available shelf-space and finance may, however, make compromise a necessity. The SPTL recommendations of minimum holdings for law libraries (rev. edn., 1986) in *Legal Studies*, vol. 6, 1986, pp. 195–215, regarding the ratio of copies required per number of students, give valuable guidance to educational libraries which must also provide for the diverse needs of academic staff. Libraries attached to government departments, and other organizations, such as law firms, are often responsible for supplying a particularly high ratio of copies to meet staff needs. Again, practice libraries which serve students studying for professional examinations must not only supply multiple copies of recommended syllabus reading, but standard practice treatises as well.

Co-operative acquisition

Independent libraries often maintain independence only at the expense of stocking a wider range of material, particularly in regard to reference and bibliographical tools, than is needed in a library that is part of a complex. Co-operation between libraries regarding subject specialization or fringe materials is therefore advantageous, geographical conditions permitting. Duplication of materials may be minimized, and the total shelf-space available be fully exploited to hold the widest possible range of stock.

University library complexes gain when specialized legal departments are instituted. Material such as record publications (see page 253) may be located in the history library, while works concerned with the sociological aspects of law are likely to be held in the sociology library.

Government departmental libraries may assist each other, but while public and educational libraries may participate in local, regional or national loan schemes, these are not often acceptable to libraries which are privately owned and administered. These, of necessity, must be as self-sufficient as possible, and co-operate with each other if feasible, since loan schemes which impose a delay exceeding half a day in supplying titles are largely useless to legal practitioners.

Annual subscriptions, on a personal or group basis, may be advantageous. Organizations such as Law Notes Lending Library can prove invaluable to small units, while demands for historical record material can be supplied by the London Library; both offer postal services. Yet problems

may arise regarding responsibility for items borrowed.
   Outside London, local law societies offer facilities upon
subscription, while many universities are willing to assist practitioners who wish to research materials not available in their
local court or chambers libraries.

ORDERING PRACTICE

Bibliographical searching

It is advisable to watch constantly for the issue of new editions
and other publications of interest. The weekly *Bookseller, HMSO
Daily Lists of Publications*, publishers' lists and advertisements
all give current news. *Whitaker's Books of the Month, Whitaker's
Classified Monthly Book List*, the twice-yearly export number of
the *Bookseller*, and publishers' advance catalogues forecast
future issues, while the *British National Bibliography, Whitaker's
Cumulative Booklist*, publishers' stock lists, and reviews in leading journals supply details of recent and past publications.
British Books in Print and *British Paperbacks in Print* annually
list the availability of older items; American and United
Kingdom publications are represented in the *Cumulative Book
Index, Law Books in Print* and *Law Books Published*, while
[American] *Books in Print* and the *Publishers' Trade List Annual*
are also valuable. *HMSO Catalogues* in monthly and annual
cumulations, together with the *International Organisations
Supplements* and *Sectional Lists* give details of all materials
published and handled by HMSO. Lists of recent textbooks are
given in the monthly issues of *Current Law* but, although series
titles are given where applicable, they do not include the
names of publishers. Titles available on a wide range of given
topics may be located in Raistrick, D. *Lawyers' Law Books*, 2nd
edn., 1985.
   Information regarding older materials, especially early law
books, may be obtained from Sweet and Maxwell's *Legal Bibliography*, 2nd edn., 1955–64, Pollard, E. W. and Redgrave, G.
R. *A Short-Title Catalogue, 1475–1640*, 2nd edn., 1976–, Wing,
D. G. *Short-Title Catalogue, 1641–1700*, 2nd edn., 1972–,

Adams, J. N. and Averley, G. *A Bibliography of Eighteenth Century Legal Literature*, 1982, and Alston, R. (ed.) *Eighteenth Century Short Title Catalogue*, 1983– (microfiche). Also the earlier volumes of the publications noticed above, and the printed catalogues of other libraries will be of assistance.

Reading lists supplied by law faculties, colleges and tutors give basic references to titles required by students. The information given, however, is often dangerously brief, especially in the case of multiple works by one author on one subject, while titles seen in proof stage only, but not yet published, may be recommended.

Law publishers do not generally conform to the accepted principles of publication dates. These cannot be accurately gauged as legislative changes may occur, or be awaited. Also since a high proportion are commissioned from busy practice and academic lawyers, the completion of these publications is often influenced by pressure of work or its unexpected cessation.

Suggestions

It is always good policy to invite suggestions for unstocked titles from readers and staff. Requests should be entered on forms (see sample at Fig. 1) or in a special book. These requests may prove to be held but overlooked, already considered and rejected, outside the stock policy, minor students' aids, ephemera, or expensive works suiting one reader's purpose but of little general interest. Alternately, they may prove well worth consideration.

Suggestion books, if kept in a prominent place, have the advantage that readers may easily see if their suggestions have been accepted, but their disadvantage lies in the need for regular checking and copying of entries by staff, and subsequent annotation.

Forms are portable and many types are available, some of which may also be utilized for orders and intake records. However, their direct use by readers may create problems of legibility. Publishing data will certainly have to be traced and added to most suggestions, while information given will require checking for errors.

```
┌─────────────────────────────────────────────────────────┐
│  The Law Library                                         │
│              SUGGESTION FOR PURCHASE                     │
├─────────────────────────────────────────────────────────┤
│  Author(s)                                               │
│  Title                                                   │
│                                                          │
│  Publisher          Editor              Date             │
│  Price              Number of copies                     │
│  Suggested by                                            │
│  Department                                              │
├─────────────────────────────────────────────────────────┤
│  Catalogue          BBIP        LBIP        BNB          │
│  Order file         BIP         CL                       │
├─────────────────────────────────────────────────────────┤
│  Now available in the library                            │
└─────────────────────────────────────────────────────────┘
```

Figure 1

Ordering methods

Individual and block orders may be entered in duplicate books, on printed forms or on cards and should each contain the maximum publication data. ISBNs and ISSNs may be used as identifying aids, but it is inadvisable to use them alone as extreme care must be taken to list the correct digits, and they may still be misread by the receiver. Also, they are sometimes misprinted in catalogues and book lists. Confirmation orders for material supplied on approval must be equally precise, as this will assist the supplier to forward the correct invoices. Orders may be placed through some computer systems which then provide automatic follow-up services if items are not received. The initial orders will provide the basis for acquisition, processing, and other records.

Standing orders for future issues should be placed with initial orders for new publications if funds permit. New editions, volumes and supplements may be frequent; individual ordering is usually time-consuming and may well create unnecessary delays. Some textbook and most looseleaf supplements are available upon annual subscriptions and should be ordered accordingly (see page 726). Dependent upon the organization, suppliers' records of standing orders may be filed on cards, entered in books, or fed into computers, under either customers' names or publication references. A list may be maintained in the library of all publications on standing order, apart from serials (see page 724). This list should be checked, and imminent new issues noted while conducting bibliographical searching (see page 717), thus reducing the risk of omissions.

Blanket orders placed for all publications on a given subject may be treated similarly to standing orders. Arrangements should, however, be made with suppliers regarding the possibility of returning duplicated items since, for example, a lego-historical work may be supplied for both the legal and the historical collections within the same library.

Faculty members or library staff may, on occasions, purchase books on behalf of the library, preferably by prior arrangement with the librarian. These are usually second-hand items, publications available on special terms to certain individuals, or works published abroad. Receipt of all such material should be recorded and the purchasers reimbursed.

Suppliers (home and abroad)

The number of suppliers retained depends largely upon the range of material stocked. Specialist publishers, such as HMSO, Sweet and Maxwell, Butterworth, Green, and Professional Books maintain bookshops and supply-services. Some specialist booksellers, such as Wildy and Sons and Professional Books also stock second-hand titles, while a general bookseller may be retained to handle quick-reference works and other non-legal publications. The existence of nearby specialist suppliers is extremely advantageous, since they may be visited in order to examine new publications and discuss problems. Alternatively, more distant organizations may be utilized to satisfaction.

Publishers and suppliers abroad may offer large discounts

to direct purchasers, but this fact should be weighed against the advantages offered by home agencies. Language difficulties will inevitably heighten the problems of ordering, errors and returns; individual post or freight charges are usually high, and not all accounts departments are equipped to handle complex foreign payments on a large scale.

The direct purchase of the publications of societies, institutes and similar bodies usually combines economy of cost with speed of delivery, but organizations may prefer to restrict their accounts commitments to a few major suppliers. A substantial discount may sometimes be obtained by joining a society as an institutional member.

Value-added tax

If the organization is in a position to reclaim them, separate records of VAT charges must be maintained. At present, the following items are exempt: books, pamphlets, newspapers, periodicals, maps; also all binders and other articles supplied and charged with them. Items not exempt are plans and drawings for industrial and similar purposes, and all stationery and other materials including microforms and their equipment. Services chargeable are deliveries, postage, telephone, binding, re-binding, and repair of individual items or series. However, the binding of serial publications from pattern boards, including new series, is exempt.

Local authorities may reclaim the payments made by their libraries. Other libraries, dependent on the status of their organizations, may find no way of recovering this expenditure. Those providing and charging for services such as research, photocopying, and book delivery, will generally be required to add the tax to these charges, and must account for this to HM Customs and Excise if their total intake exceeds the current specified annual sum.

Discounts

Under the Net Book Agreement booksellers are not permitted to offer discounts on new publications outside the library licence (see below), except under the following circumstances:

1. If the books have been in stock for a period exceeding one year from the original purchase date, and the publisher has refused an offer to repurchase them at cost price, or at a proposed reduced price.

2. If the books have been purchased second-hand and six months have elapsed since their original date of publication.

Library licence

All libraries which officially grant public access, however limited, are entitled by the Net Book Agreement to apply for a library licence. This permits a discount, usually of 10 per cent, on publications purchased. Librarians wishing to make application may approach a reputable bookseller and enquire as to his willingness to supply them under this system. If he agrees, application must then be made to the Publishers' Association, nominating the bookseller concerned who will then be supplied with the licence.

Additional booksellers may also be nominated upon formal request, but a minimum stated amount a year must be spent with each. However, a notice must be prominently displayed, in or near the library entrance, inviting the public to enter, or stating the conditions under which they may enter for research purposes. Lists of these libraries, by geographical areas, should also be exhibited in public libraries.

Libraries, educational or otherwise, which are privately owned and maintained, and any other libraries which do not or cannot permit public access, are not entitled to apply for this licence.

GIFTS AND EXCHANGES

Donations may or may not prove suitable for inclusion in stock yet some cannot, in the interests of diplomacy, be declined. Potential donors, once rebuffed, may be reluctant to offer more suitable items subsequently, so providing no restrictions are imposed regarding eventual disposal, it is often advantageous to accept unwanted materials in order to gain a few long-sought items. The conditions, if any, of living donors must be strictly observed, during their lifetime at least, but those relating to bequests may have, legally, to be observed in perpetuity.

Publications of readers known to be generous may be deleted from standing orders but, if not forthcoming, they must be re-ordered. The problems created by donations are frequently as great as their benefits, but discretion and tact should be exercised at all times, since many valuable collections have developed from the reluctant acceptance of a handful of apparently extraneous materials.

The receipt of donations should always be formally acknowledged in writing as a matter of courtesy. The details of items presented and retained should, for record purposes, be entered in a special index, together with the name, address and status of the donor. This index will, in future, supply useful information regarding past accessions. Items thus received should be marked with the donors' names and should be retained during their lifetime, as donors enjoy visiting a library to see their gifts and show them to their friends.

Collections or items deposited on loan or permanent loan are often subject to conditions or restrictions. Since these are not part of the library's stock, they cannot be marked or catalogued as such, and are usually retained upon closed or limited access with a separate catalogue or index.

The exchange of duplicate or unwanted materials may be effected informally between two or more libraries, or more formally by subscribing to an organized scheme. In the latter a central authority usually acts as a clearing house for lists of items available, which are supplied by the offering libraries, and distributed to the other subscribers. According to the system in use, requests may be made directly to the library concerned or to the central authority. Allocation is usually made to the first applicant, who arranges for collection or refunds delivery expenses upon receipt of the books.

The British and Irish Association of Law Librarians commenced an experimental exchange scheme in 1972, which is still in operation, issuing lists three times a year. Probably the best-known exchange scheme in the British Isles is that operated by the Gift and Exchange Section of the British Library Lending Division at Boston Spa near Leeds. Both these systems charge modest subscriptions for the consolidated lists of material on offer which they circulate.

SERIAL PUBLICATIONS

Law reports, journals and most legislative materials are usually issued in individual parts which, after completion of a volume, are bound, or replaced by the publishers with bound volumes. Some, however, may be issued directly as volumes only.

New titles may be selected and purchased through the system governing new acquisitions, though careful judgment must be exercised before committing the library to additional annual claims upon its budget.

Subscription agents

Existing suppliers may be requested to handle all administrative matters relating to standing orders for serial publications. Alternatively, if the library's regular bookseller is not equipped to deal with the quantity of titles involved, a separate agent should be sought for this purpose. Direct subscriptions to societies may include free receipt or reduced rates for their publications; additionally, it may prove economical to subscribe directly to publishers and organizations. Nevertheless, this practice may increase staff work, while agents can more easily arrange the return of erroneous or faulty copies, and make representations regarding missing parts. These advantages may well outweigh the cost of handling charges.

Visible indexes

The unusually large proportion of unbound material taken by most law libraries requires careful documentation. Day books, wherein items are recorded in order of receipt, are insufficient for all but the smallest library, and are scarcely adequate to supply rapid answers to complicated queries. Visible indexes, if maintained in detail, will supply immediate information upon the most proliferate of running series and the most occasional of casual series, each on individual cards. These indexes are usually housed in metal cabinets, ledger-type holders or drums, but the size of the collection, space and cost must influence the style and amount of equipment selected. Small coloured tabs are easily obtained for use with these cards to indicate matters such as: date due, material overdue, call-up sent, etc. Use of these tabs on the visible section of the card greatly facilitates the scanning for action needed, such as calling up overdue issues.

Computers can also be utilized for this task, and some library automated issue systems include a serials ordering and recording package, while other major suppliers now offer serials control packs. These hold the records for initial orders, standing orders, and receipt of parts and volumes, together with those of publishers, suppliers, and charges. They can be regularly checked for receipts, alert for claims on missing or damaged items, supply information on the current state of budget allowances against expenditure to date, and maintain binding records (see p. 741).

The larger systems may be stand-alone on minicomputers, or accessed via terminals to the agent's computer, if compatible. Microcomputers will meet simple needs, or the index may be produced on a word processor and stored on floppy disks to conserve space. The volume of acquisitions, record requirements, and available finances will dictate the necessary system. Sophisticated systems generate higher costs, but may also provide wider record services including all orders and acquisitions, fund-accounting, cataloguing, binding, loans, and other library routines. Microcomputers, while considerably cheaper, can currently offer only limited facilities. Advice on the choice of hardware and software can be obtained from the Aslib Information Resources Centre, or the Library Technology Centre at the Polytechnic of Central London.

OTHER MATERIALS

Supplements fall into two separate categories of publication. The first are issued as paper pamphlets, or bound volumes, updating textbooks and multi-volume works, on an occasional or annual basis. These may generally be treated as books, but those acquired upon subscription may be handled with serials. The second consists of supplementary or re-placement sheets, supplied upon subscription to augment looseleaf works (see pages 197–8) and may also be included with serials.

Pamphlets may be ordered and treated as books, those issued as parts of series being placed upon standing order and entered in the serials index, if desired.

Out of print materials may be required to replace items lost or irretrievably damaged, to complete imperfect sets, or to expand collections. A list of works thus required, containing full bibliographical details, should be maintained and standing orders may be placed with specialist second-hand booksellers. When copies become available, and notification is given, prompt action should then be taken to confirm requirement, or they may be offered elsewhere. Catalogues of antiquarian and second-hand booksellers should be searched immediately upon receipt. It is advisable to telephone promptly for wanted items and, if these are still available, reservation may be requested and a confirmation order despatched. Additionally, the catalogues of reprint publishers can be checked, as many of these produce facsimiles of previously rare titles and editions.

Photocopies may also provide a solution to the acquisition problems of out-of-print books, pamphlets and serial parts, also articles of interest and missing pages. These may be obtained from either the original publisher, or another library, but care must be taken regarding infringement of copyright (see pages 668–9).

Microforms offer a currently widening coverage of many types of material, from single titles to long runs of serials. These may be otherwise unobtainable, but many are still available in book format. They are especially valuable to libraries with acute space problems, offering an alternative coverage on long runs of little-used series and newspaper collections, such as *The Times*. Subscriptions may be paid for some serials to be supplied in parts, as issued, and replaced by a microfilm upon completion, while microfiche editions of publications such as *British Books in Print* are also obtainable. However, resistance to use of microforms may well be encountered from readers and staff, since they are time-consuming for quick-reference purposes, and prolonged usage can cause health hazards.

Microforms are issued as films, fiches, cards and prints and are usually purchased directly from the producing organization. These may be repositories issuing material from their own archives, publishers, or other commercial concerns, many of which issue lists or catalogues of items thus available. A catalogue of all available microforms has been projected, largely in order to obviate duplication of materials. If issued, this would be of great assistance in selection and purchase. Video and magnetic tape cassettes are obtainable from specialist suppliers, and are also marketed by some law publishers.

ACCESSIONING

Upon receipt, the contents of all packages should be carefully checked against delivery notes or invoices. Discrepancies should be noted, all relevant items recorded in the serials index, and new receipts checked against orders. Errors and omissions must be promptly followed up, duplicated materials set aside for return and invoices or statements of account passed on for attention.

Accessions registers

Opinions vary as to the value of maintaining accessions registers. Some libraries record all items, others only selected ones. Many regard the practice as a duplication of work and feel that the catalogue provides sufficient record. If this practice is followed, the accessions may be listed in books, on slips, on cards, in computers or word processors. The list may be made either by chronological numbers allocated upon receipt, by authors, titles, subjects, classifications, ISBNs or ISSNs, as preferred. The required data should be entered on a slip or card which accompanies the book until processing is complete. Additional data may be added throughout, as required, prior to entry in the accessions register.

Processing

Collating

Whenever possible all publications should be collated prior to stamping or marking. It is no longer feasible for publishers to undertake this, but they will always exchange faulty copies. This procedure is important since legal publications are consulted rather than read, many books and serial parts go out of print rapidly, and replacement becomes difficult if not impossible should faults subsequently be discovered.

Collating is both tedious and time-consuming, and will only be properly performed by trained staff, who alone may be trusted to conduct this task to satisfaction. Each item should be carefully examined for physical damage, accuracy and completeness of make-up. Pagination sequences of new serial parts should be checked against the preceding part before filing. If a discrepancy exists, but the text is complete, the paper cover may be annotated, thus anticipating readers' or bookbinders' queries. A paper-knife should be used on uncut pages and new or freshly bound books be eased open gently, from the centre outwards, to avoid cracking of bindings. This will render them more flexible and able to withstand heavier usage.

It is advisable to check new microforms upon receipt, especially if they have been made to order. Pages or even volumes may be omitted, while incorrect focusing will result in blurred prints. Faulty copies should be returned for replacement.

Stamping

The use of rubber, brass or embossing stamps to indicate ownership is advisable, particularly in libraries operating loan services. Such stamp impressions may be placed at intervals throughout the text, on the title page, along the top, bottom and fore-edge, and on all illustrations and maps. It is necessary to stamp all separate serial parts, including prelims and indexes, upon receipt, otherwise doubts regarding their provenance may arise when they reach the bookbinders' premises.

Stamps for administrative purposes may also be employed, particularly process stamps to record accession references, location marks, codes denoting suppliers and prices, together with initials of staff who have undertaken various processes on the volume. All stamps should be impressed neatly, care being taken not to mask any portion of the text, and to avoid page edges, which may be trimmed when re-binding takes place.

Side-stamps and tail-stamps bearing the library's insignia may be impressed upon the boards and spines respectively, this usually being undertaken by a professional bookbinder, while embossed stamping of pages or boards may be carried out on the premises, if the necessary equipment is held.

Bookplates and date labels

Bookplates bearing the library's name or insignia may be affixed inside the front boards, unless vital references have been printed there, when they are better placed on the front or reverse of the flyleaf. Lists of rules may be pasted inside the front boards, or on the flyleaf, while in lending libraries they can be printed at the head of date-sheets, which may then be inserted inside the front or back of volumes, together with card-holding pockets, if required. Labels, if necessary, regarding the availability of books for loan, or prohibition of their removal, may be placed inside the volumes or on the front boards. If the library is equipped with a detection device to prevent theft, the appropriate triggers must also be inserted.

Labelling methods

Class numbers or location marks may be placed on the spine as required. The following methods are in current use:

1. hand-lettering in white or indelible ink;
2. transfer-lettering, written manually with an electric stylus;
3. adhesive labels, typed or written.

These methods are relatively cheap, and should be undertaken only by someone with a flair for art work. Care and practice is required to maintain maximum legibility and a bookholder should be used. To ensure permanence and minimize torn labels and smudged lettering, all should be overlaid with transparent material.

4. Embossed labels are quickly produced and clear to read, but may become detached eventually.
5. Alternatively, one may use the Se-lin system of typing on special tape, which is then laminated and heat-sealed to the book.
6. The most permanent method is stamping with a hot iron on gold foil but this requires the expertise of a professional bookbinder.

If possible, all lettering should be placed at a given height above the base of the spine or, if this is impracticable, in the bottom left-hand corner of the front board. On books with narrow spines the lettering may have to run lengthwise and a decision as to whether it runs up or down should be made and permanently adhered to, since variation will create difficulties for readers and staff.

STORAGE

Since most law libraries must retain the bulk of their holdings in perpetuity, and since a large percentage of their stock is in constant demand, great attention must at all times be paid to the care and storage of materials. Books should be shelved according to the library's system and, if space permits, all stacks should contain one or two empty shelves to preclude excessive movement when interpolating. Books should never be laid flat on top of standing volumes on packed shelves. A minimum clearance of one inch between the head of the tallest book and the underside of the shelf above is essential. All shelves should be under- rather than over-filled, or damage to bindings will result. Books on partly-filled shelves require support, and shelving should be easily adjustable, since tall books should never be placed on their fore-edges. This form of stacking weakens bindings and makes location difficult.

Over-size books should be shelved in a separate sequence adjoining their section, or together in one sequence placed apart, in stacks with suitably spaced shelves. Elephant-size folios require extra deep shelves in narrow or partitioned stacks for upright filing. Alternatively, they may be placed flat upon specially designed separate shelves. All items filed outside the sequence of their section should bear an identifying symbol on their spines.

Storage temperature should average 55.4–64.4 degrees F. (13–18 degrees C.) and relative humidity 50–60 per cent, or paper may become brittle and bindings, especially leather, will dry, crack and crumble. The necessity for reasonable working conditions, however, will require compromise in respect of items on open access. A temperature of 45–55 degrees F. is ideal for stock preservation, but is illegal for staff conditions under the Factories Act, 1961. An air-conditioning system with non-electrostatic filtering, assisted by humidification and dehumidification units, should be installed. Light should be clear but diffused, as strong sunlight may render paper yellow and brittle, while binding dyes will fade. Excessive temperature changes and extreme dampness should be avoided. Volumes showing traces of bookworm should be isolated for treatment, and vermin discouraged by forbidding food to be eaten or left on the premises. Fire risk should be minimized by the enforcement of rules banning smoking, the igniting of matches or lighters, use of candles or any form of ignited lamps or heaters. Automatic heat or smoke detection equipment linked to alarm bells may be installed; immediate attention should be given to defects in all electrical installations, and CO_2 or *Sargom* fire fighting extinguishers be made readily available. These cause less damage to books than water or the contents of ordinary extinguishers.

Serials

If suitable storage racks (see below) are not available, or not considered feasible, individual parts of serials may be filed in loose binders, unless the parts are too thick or consist of single sheets, when boxes may be preferred. Specially blocked or blockable binders may be obtained from publishers or purchased through stationers. 'Cordex' or 'Easibinders' are frequently employed for this purpose; spring-back folders will hold single items or small collections of documents, and all will keep parts clean and relatively free from loss or damage.

If preferred, boxes may be employed to house all serials, and may be specially made to match the bound series volumes, but this method is expensive. Box-files with spring-clips, record cases with overlapping front covers, or transfer cases with hinged lids will protect little-used or infrequently published items from dust. However, spring-clips may damage paper, and hinged lids wear and break off. Open-topped boxes may suffice for popular and prolific series, and it is advisable to stock several basic sizes to accommodate a variety of publications.

Alternatively, serials may be piled flat on open shelves, but in this position they may become vulnerable to damage, especially if piled too high. Fuller protection is offered by cupboards with adjustable shelving, or steel shelving with adjustable vertical partitions for upright filing.

If space permits, the most recent issues may be displayed in special racks. Some are designed with hinged partitions covering a space which houses all previous parts. Current issues on display require the protection of transparent plastic or perspex holders.

Binders or boxes containing loose parts of current volumes are more easily located if they are shelved with the bound series. These may be together in one area, filed by title, accession or class number. Alternatively, they may be appended to their various subject sections.

Other materials

Supplements to textbooks, if size permits, may be fitted into slits or pockets inside the back boards, while stiff folders may be provided to protect the thicker ones. All current supplements must accompany the main works at all times.

Pamphlets may be stored in vertical cabinet files, by accession or class number; boxed and shelved in a separate section; or apportioned to their subject sections. If retained, it is advisable to have them bound, either as single items or in collected volumes.

Opinions may be filed by given numbers, key words, or subjects, according to cataloguing treatment, in boxes carefully labelled as to contents.

Press cuttings and articles from journals may be placed in envelopes and filed in cabinets, mounted upon sheets in ringbinders, or pasted into press-cutting books.

Newspaper files may be retained for set periods of time and then discarded, but are sometimes bound in volumes. The copies for general consultation may be held in weekly or monthly batches, on open racks, in large loose binders, or in clamping devices. Binding copies should be stored flat, in the dark, at a constant temperature not exceeding 64.4 degrees F. (18 degrees C.), with a relative humidity of 50 per cent. They should never be handled until bound.

Maps and plans may be stored flat within acid-free paper or polyester film envelopes in large shallow drawers. They should not be folded, but large items may be rolled round cardboard cylinders in an acid-free cover and stored horizontally. The practice of storing upright on shelves is not recommended. Wherever possible, it is advisable to have maps linen-backed, and if large ones are to be folded and bound in a volume they should be cut and jointed by a bookbinder.

Photographs and illustrations may be mounted on lightweight card or thick paper, using photographic corners or cement for photographs, and starch-paste for other items. They should be stored flat to prevent buckling, but this may prove impractical. Small collections may be mounted in albums, filed in cabinets, or in transfer cases, unmounted items having first been placed in envelopes.

Manuscript materials require special care and, if valuable, should be housed in a fire- and burglar-proof strong room. Air conditioning to maintain an even 55.4–64.4 degrees F. (13–18 degrees C.) temperature, and 50–60 per cent relative humidity, should be installed, but parchment and vellum require a higher relative humidity; daylight should be diffused or eliminated. Unbound manuscripts should be unfolded and stored in boxes lying flat, or mounted on guards into stout folders, which may then be filed in upright boxes. The filing order should duplicate the entries in their catalogue, usually by volume number within a titled or numbered class. Strict rules should be drawn up, printed, and adhered to, regarding the use of manuscripts for research purposes.

Microforms

Storage of films and microfilms requires stringent precautions, and regulations are periodically issued by the Home Office, appearing as Statutory Instruments. Older film stock is cellulose-nitrate based, inflammable, and subject to government regulations, but modern triacetate-based film materials are very slow-burning or non-flammable and not subject to the regulations. Deterioration is very slow, but is hastened if fungi or bacteria attack the gelatin of the emulsion. Films should be stored in special rooms with a steady temperature within 50–60.8 degrees F. (10–16 degrees C.) and 30–50 per cent relative humidity. A temperature of 85 degrees F. with 85 per cent humidity must be avoided, as encouraging the incubation rate of fungi and bacteria. Film becomes brittle in excessive dryness and heat, and condensation, forming mould, will result from extreme fluctuations of temperature. Microfilm may be stored at any temperature not exceeding a maximum of 70 degrees F. (21 degrees C.) with 15–40 per cent relative humidity. As a medium for permanent storage it has not been in existence long enough for precise certainty as to its average lifetime, and this will be further affected by the variability of standards in film stock and storage conditions. At the present stage of knowledge, archive films are currently given 25 years before recopying becomes advisable, although they are expected to outlive this; while 50 years is the limit laid down as a cautious maximum estimate.

Individual strips of film may be filed in transparent pockets attached to sheets inserted in looseleaf binders and shelved. They may alternatively be inserted in specially prepared cards with apertures, and filed in standard card cabinets. Rolls of film wound on reels should be placed in metal boxes with loose-fitting lids, and stored flat in metal cabinets, the film resting on its edge. They should not be filed vertically, since it is damaging for the film to rest on its surface. Shelves with raised edges will prevent containers being dislodged. All films stored in open or loose boxes should be subject to the foregoing conditions, but if this is impossible they should be placed in closed, airtight boxes. Cardboard should never be used for storage, as it may exude damaging gases. Filing by accession numbers has much to recommend it, since numbers may be marked clearly and easily, but filing by the system used for books and other materials may be thought less confusing. The leading edge of the film can be marked with an electric stylus, the reel itself with white enamel, and the container with a gummed label to which may be added the title and a summary of contents.

Microfiches, cards and prints are not subject to the storage conditions for films. Fiches and cards, placed in individual opaque envelopes with the tops cut away in front to display headtitling, may be filed in card-index drawers or steel cabinets, but care must be taken with those microcards which bear photographic emulsion on one side only; these should be very tightly packed or they will curl. Stiff plastic folders containing cut-out slits provide a portable storage for microfiche series. Vertical files or pamphlet cases will hold microprints adequately.

Magnetic and video tapes

The British Standards Institution (BS. 5454) recommends that magnetic tapes should be stored between 39.2–60.8 degrees F. (4–16 degrees C.) with a relative humidity of 40–60 per cent, in containers of non-corrodible metal, cardboard or inert plastic. These should be placed in polyethylene bags and stored vertically on metal racks. Tapes should be rewound once a year.

The BSI suggest consultation with specialists regarding the preservation and storage of video tapes and magnetic computer tapes. The former should be rewound every three months.

Co-operative storage

Apart from the natural progression of co-operative acquisition, storage on a co-operative basis mainly applies to reserve stocks and superseded materials. Several libraries may resolve to maintain one joint collection of these items, or divide the classes between them, housing the collection on the premises of one or more of the libraries concerned or elsewhere as required. Such a decision is only wisely made if the storage area is within easy reach of all concerned, for services to readers will be seriously hampered if materials cannot be supplied without excessive delay.

The many and various libraries within the University of London maintain a co-operative depository library at Egham in Surrey, which has been in operation since 1961. Books are deposited on the understanding that they will be entered in the depository's union catalogue and be available for loan to any other library in the country. Others are permitted to rent private storage space. The University Library operates a van delivery and collection service.

PRESERVATION AND CONSERVATION

Print orders for legal publications are small and seldom repeated. Yet no law book ever becomes entirely outdated; all remain of value for reference purposes by historians, academics and practitioners. It is therefore important that the utmost vigilance be observed to prevent damage to stock which has to last a lifetime.

Librarians working in long-established libraries, with stock ranging over several hundred years, have become increasingly aware of the problems engendered by brittle or poor-quality paper, and the growing effects of environmental pollution, increased lighting, heating and ill-usage, on both paper and bindings. In recent years supreme efforts have been made to enhance general awareness of the situation and provide guidelines for remedies and preventions. These, inevitably, are costly in terms of expense and staff time, but should be attempted wherever possible. F. W. Ratcliffe, *Preservation policies and conservation*, 1984, gives the facts relating to current practice and recommends appropriate action. The National Preservation Office has been created by the British Library to promote awareness of problems and provide information on preservation issues, amongst other aims. The Conservation Departments of the Public Record Office and the College of Arms will also undertake work and give invaluable advice. Some major binding firms now advertise similar services.

Protection against environmental conditions has been noted above (see page 497). Protection against human hazards, caused through wear and tear, is best effected initially by basic care on the part of staff and readers. Strict observation of regulations for the easing of books (page 728) and shelving conditions (page 731) will reduce strain upon bindings. Books should never be placed open and face-downwards on tables, piled open on top of one another, used as a writing pad or reading stand, nor closed upon any thick object substituting for a book mark. The marking of leaves in pencil or ink should be forbidden to all except staff authorized to make official annotations.

The photocopying machine has become the most dangerous immediate hazard when allied with single-minded readers possessed of a determination to obtain as near-perfect a copy as possible. The results of this endeavour are broken stitching, cracked spines, snapped-off boards, and torn or loosened pages. Binding and repair cost rise or, if these are limited, many volumes rendered useless must be withdrawn to await eventual repair, or to be discarded.

Repairs

In general, all repair work is best undertaken by professionally qualified craftsmen, but some minor repairs may be safely undertaken by experienced staff observing the limitations noted below.

Torn sheets may be repaired by using approved materials such as bookbinders' gummed paper, but care must be taken not to mask any portion of the text. Invisible repairs with tissue will not withstand heavy usage, and self-adhesive tapes are not recommended.

Loose pages or illustrations may be reinserted after a narrow application of paste along the inner edges.

Brittle paper, resulting from production faults or exposure to wrong conditions, must be laminated by an expert.

Water-soaked sections should be parted and each leaf smoothed and dried by pressure. Subsequent re-sizing to remove stains, reassembly and rebinding is best undertaken professionally. As a result of recent experiments by RHM Research, badly soaked books and documents may now be deep-frozen to prevent movement of inks or paints, and subsequently freeze-dried.

Ink may be removed by the application of a commercial ink remover, provided it is not indian ink, or that from a ball-point pen. Commercial products available for the removal of the latter are unsuitable for the treatment of paper, and this problem should be referred to the British Library Preservation Service or the Public Record Office Conservation Department.

Stains caused by mould and mildew may be removed by wiping with ethyl alcohol, provided the penetration is not deep, and the printed surface is avoided. The removal of oil, grease and 'foxing' should not be attempted.

Insects may be discouraged by the application, to all surfaces of boards and spines, of formaldehyde compounds combined with insecticides.

Ink lettering may be removed from spines by gentle rubbing with a damp cloth, or by scraping with a sharp knife. The latter, combined with an application of acetone, will remove letters made by an electric stylus.

Dirty leather bindings may be washed with saddle soap, but the protective salts must be restored thereafter by the application of a solution containing seven per cent potassium lactate.

All washed or little-used leather-bound books should be treated with recommended leather dressings at two-yearly intervals. Frequently consulted volumes will require only occasional treatment, since the human hand provides its own grease. The application of leather dressings keeps hinges supple, prevents major cracking, and retards the effects of use or atmospheric conditions, particularly on wrongly-tanned leather which absorbs sulphuric acid, thus causing eventual decay.

Vellum bindings do not absorb sulphuric acid, but require a temperature of 55.4–64.4 degrees F. (16–18 degrees C.) with 60–70 per cent relative humidity, to prevent their becoming brittle and cracking. They may be cleaned with a damp sponge, dried quickly at room temperature, and given a sparing application of a leather dressing.

Torn microfilms should be heat-spliced, since old film stock will tear. Finger-marks on microforms should be treated with film-cleaning solution and wiped with a duster.

Queries and doubts regarding treatment of books or binding should be raised with a bookbinder, while those relating to microforms should be taken to a photographic expert.

Binding

Binding or re-binding of any kind should be undertaken only by a professional bookbinder, and must be of the highest quality consistent with the financial resources available. The concept of 'perfect binding' is a misnomer, and true economy lies always in having an item well, not cheaply, bound.

Hand-bound books are almost always stronger and more durable than those bound by mechanical means. A leather-bound book will last longer than any other, and this style of binding is always to be recommended where cost is of secondary importance and permanence of a high order is required. Owing to a number of factors, amongst which a change in the process of tanning may be noted, the manufacture of durable leather is more variable than was formerly the case yet, if the use of approved leather is insisted upon, the problem of powdery decay will be minimized, if not eliminated. Further assistance should be gained from the project of the British Leather Manufacturers' Research Association to restore vital properties in both new skins and older leather bindings. Buckram, however, is also extremely hard-wearing and, if leather can be afforded for books requiring extreme durability, provides an excellent substitute for those of lesser importance, which may correspondingly receive less use. Cloth is less durable and is best reserved for books of least importance. Synthetics such as rexine have proved as hard-wearing as buckram, but suffer from the major defect that it is impossible to stamp efficiently by hand the required lettering upon the spine.

There is a limit to the number of times a book may be rebound, for its length of life is finally determined by the quality of the paper and its ability to withstand use. Under hard and continuous wear it may become pulpy or perhaps brittle, the sewing may give way under strain and the inside edges of the sheets become ragged. The book becomes tighter with each resewing until the print in the margins cannot be read except with difficulty, while the sewing thread finds no purchase in the paper. Repair work then becomes impossible and the book, as a book, is rendered useless. If retention for use is desirable the sheets must be specially treated, guarded and then rebound. Alternatively the treated sheets may be kept loose but boxed. In either case it will be advisable to keep the item on closed access. It is important, therefore, that all law books which perhaps receive more hard wear from readers than any other class of literature, should be bound as infrequently as possible, consistent with the need to protect their sheets.

Considerable variety exists as to the manner in which books may be bound. Spines may be flexible or hollow-backed, while raised bands and head-bands may be required; leather bindings may be decorated with blind or gold tooling, and coloured lettering pieces giving greater clarity on all binding materials. Split, matching or contrasting boards may be preferred, while plain, antique or marble end-papers may need reinforcement by linen guards. Whatever the choice, written instructions should accompany each item sent for binding or re-binding. They should be both precise and unambiguous and, subject to contrary advice from the bookbinder, their exact execution should be insisted upon. Law books or periodicals made up of different sections, each with its own pagination, may cause problems over re-assembly when the book or parts have been stripped for sewing. It is advisable in such instances to attach to the work a sheet enumerating the make-up of its contents, unless the bookbinder already holds a pattern-board giving exact guidance as to all requirements of make-up and binding. These are essential for serial publications, in order to ensure exact continuity of style. Orders may be entered in duplicate books, or upon printed cards or forms. Computer systems which hold acquisitions and serials registers may also encompass records of binding orders, pattern instructions, and current binders' prices. They will also alert for claims of outstanding items.

STOCK-TAKING

Stock should be checked with regularity, if possible, either completely or by sections. This practice, if performed systematically, is of value for obtaining the following data:

1. Total number of volumes held. Comparisons with previous checks will then enable accurate figures to be compiled of the annual accession rate, from which in turn it may be possible to calculate future growth.

2. Items missing and therefore requiring replacement.

3. Items previously missing, but now unofficially returned.

4. Mis-shelved items, formerly presumed lost.

5. The current state of loan systems.

6. An accurate survey of stationery possibly requiring fresh stocks, and equipment which may need repair or replacement.

Stock-taking also provides an opportunity for the accurate re-ordering of books by sections, and a close survey of those requiring repair or re-binding.

The most practical aids to efficient stock-taking are shelf-lists of classified or subject sections.

Withdrawals and disposal

Superseded works and those rendered out of date by subsequent legislation can mislead the unwary reader. They should be withdrawn from open shelves and transferred to reserve storage. If these works are to be retained, location marks on the books, catalogue, subject and other indexes and guides require amendment. Duplicate copies will be rendered superfluous and may be discarded.

The University Grants Committee *Capital provision for university libraries*, 1976, recommended that older or little-used titles should be regularly withdrawn from their stocks, that they should co-operate to form single collections of these works, and dispose of the extraneous copies. This practice, although saving of space and reducing over-duplication, could cause serious problems in matters of conservation and the need for intensified security.

Libraries attached to law firms or government departments frequently offer copies to their general staff. Dependent upon policy, saleable items may be offered to specialist second-hand booksellers, or to libraries subscribing to duplicate exchange schemes (see page 723). Each book marked for disposal should bear a stamp officially authorizing this fact. Waste paper merchants will dispose of unwanted material upon request. These should first be broken to prevent unauthorized circulation of publications bearing the library's stamp.

FURTHER READING

GENERAL

British and Irish Association of Law Librarians 'Standards for law libraries', *Law Librarian*, vol. 12, part 3, 1981 [special pull-out section].
Handbook of special librarianship and information work, 5th edn., 1982.
McElroy, A. R. (ed.) *College librarianship*, 1984.
Reynolds, T. H. *Rare books for law libraries*, 1983.
Stirling, J. F. (ed.) *University librarianship*, 1981.

ACQUISITION

Adamiak, R. *The law book price guide*, 1984.
Astbury, R. *Libraries and the book trade*, 1968.
Bloomfield, B. C. (ed.) *Acquisition and provision of foreign books by national and university libraries in the United Kingdom*, 1972.
Dewe, M. *Library supply agencies in Europe*, 1968.
Dickson, L. E. 'Law library book orders: an analysis of current practice', *Law Library Journal*, vol. 73, 1980, pp. 446–50.
Logan, R. G. 'Bibliographical guides to early British law books', *Law Librarian*, vol. 4, 1973, pp. 9–12.
Melcher, D. *Melcher on acquisition*, 1971.
Mersky, R. M. and Ferguson, S. (eds.) *Collecting and managing rare law books*, 1981.
Moody, M. A. 'Library administration of historical materials: part 1 Acquisitions', *Law Library Journal*, vol. 69, 1976, pp. 314–17.
Spiller, D. *Book selection: an introduction to principles and practice*, 3rd edn., 1980.
Way, D. J. 'Book selection', *Law Librarian*, vol. 4, 1973, pp. 25–7.
Wulfekoetter, G. *Acquisition work: process involved in building library collections*, 1962.

AUTOMATION

Burton, P. F. *Microcomputer applications in academic libraries*, 1983.
Chen, C. and Bressler, S. E. *Microcomputers in libraries*, 1982.
Gates, H. (ed.) *Directory of library and information retrieval software for microcomputers*, 1985.
Gillman, P. and Peniston, S. *Library automation*, 1984.
Lovecy, I. *Automating library procedures*, 1984.
Rowley, J. *Computers for libraries*, 2nd edn., 1985.
Tedd, L. A. *Introduction to computer-based library systems*, 2nd edn., 1984.

MICROFORMS

Barnes, P. M. *Microfilming and the archivist*, 1973 [privately printed for limited circulation].
British Standards Institution *Recommendations for the processing and storage of silver-gelatin-type microfilm*, 1975.
Celluloid and Cinematographic Film Act, 1922.

Diaz, A. J. (ed.) *Microforms in libraries*, 1975.

Dowlin, K. E. *The electronic library*, 1984.

Fair, J. H. (ed.) *Microforms management in special libraries*, 1980.

International Journal of Micrographics and Video Technology, vol. 1–, 1982–.

Microform Review, 1972–.

Surrency, E. W. 'Library administration of historical materials: part 4 Microforms', *Law Library Journal*, vol. 69, 1976, pp. 326–8.

Teague, S. J. *Microform, video and electronic media librarianship*, 1985.

Walsh, P. M. (ed.) *Serials management and microforms* 1979.

SERIALS

Davinson, D. E. *Periodicals collection*, 2nd edn., 1978.

Grenfell, D. *Periodicals and serials: their treatment in special libraries*, 1965.

Jacobs, R. 'Focal point; a composite record for the control of periodicals using a visible signalling device', *Journal of Documentation*, vol. 6, 1950, pp. 213–28.

Mayes, P. (ed.) *Periodicals administration in libraries*, 1978.

PRESERVATION AND CONSERVATION

Banks, P. N. *A selective bibliography on the conservation of research library materials*, 1981.

Barker, N. J. 'Conservation 1983', *Law Librarian*, vol. 14, 1983, pp. 39–43.

Baynes-Cope, A. D. *Caring for books and documents*, 1981.

The British Leather Manufacturers' Research Association *The conservation of bookbinding leather*, 1984.

British Standards Institution *Recommendations for repair and allied processes for the conservation of documents*, 1973–80.

British Standards Institution *Recommendations for the storage and exhibition of archival documents*, 1977.

British Standards Institution *Specification for portable fire extinguishers*, 1980.

'Court records – review, preservation, storage and access', Panel at the 73rd annual meeting of the American Association of Law Libraries, November 1980. *Law Library Journal*, vol. 73, 1980, pp. 997–1013.

Cunha, G. M. 'Preservation and conservation of legal materials', *Law*

Library Journal, vol. 69, 1976, pp. 300–2.

Cunha, G. M. and Cunha, D. G. *Library and archives conservation: 1980's and beyond*, 1983.

Middleton, B. C. *The restoration of leather bindings*, 2nd edn., 1984.

Petheridge, G. (ed.) *Conservation of library and archive materials and graphic arts*, 1985.

Plenderleith, H. J. *Preservation of leather bookbindings*, 1970.

'Preservation of law library materials and disaster planning', Panel at the 73rd annual meeting of the American Association of Law Libraries, November 1980. *Law Library Journal*, vol. 73, 1980, pp. 831–52.

Ratcliffe, F. W. *Preservation policies and conservation in British libraries*, 1984.

Shep, R. L. *Cleaning and caring for books*, revised edn., 1984.

Society of Archivists, Conservation Section Committee, *List of suppliers of materials used by record offices*, 1985.

Storage and display, British Library Reference Division, The Preservation Service, *c*. 1984 (a leaflet available upon request).

PROCESSING

Collison, R. L. *Treatment of special material in libraries*, 2nd edn., 1955.

STOCK-TAKING

University Grants Committee, *Capital provision for university libraries: report of a working party* [Chairman: Professor R. Atkinson], 1976.

18. Cataloguing and Classification

M. BIRCH

INTRODUCTION

It is not proposed to discuss general principles of bibliographic organization in this chapter, as these are covered in general textbooks such as *Cataloguing* by E. J. Hunter and K. G. B. Bakewell, 2nd edn., 1983, and A. C. Foskett's *The subject approach to information*, 4th edn., 1982.

Sources of information on law cataloguing and classification are not numerous. A concise account is given in A. Blunt's *Law librarianship*, 1980, pp. 109–14, and a fuller account of the state of the art in United States law libraries can be found in P. L. Piper and C. H. L. Kwan's chapter in *Law librarianship: a handbook*, 1983. The introductory essay in the first edition of E. M. Moys's *A classification scheme for law books*, 1968, states the principles of law classification. Articles on aspects of law cataloguing and classification are published occasionally in the *Law Librarian*, and, looking further afield, in the *Law Library Journal* (United States), the *Canadian Association of Law Libraries Newsletter/Bulletin*, and the *Australian Law Librarians' Group Newsletter*.

Within the British and Irish Association of Law Librarians, the Standing Committee on Cataloguing and Classification provides a focus for law cataloguing and classification, and there are similar committees in the Anglo-American countries. During 1984 the BIALL Standing Committee carried out a Survey of cataloguing and classification practice in British and Irish law libraries, and some of the information in this chapter has been gathered from the results of the survey (so far unpublished).

The main difficulty in writing a general account of law cataloguing and classification in the British Isles is that practice varies very widely with the size of law libraries and with their function, *ie*, whether they serve academic lawyers and their students, or barristers, solicitors, the courts, etc. In making statements and suggestions it has therefore generally been indicated to what type of law library they are applicable.

CHOICE OF CATALOGUING SYSTEM

For many law librarians there is no choice of cataloguing system. It is a matter of making the best of existing catalogues. However, circumstances may sometimes indicate that a fresh start is desirable. In a small law library, for instance, catalogues may be out of date or non-existent. In a larger library, a card catalogue may have become so large that it is difficult and expensive to maintain.

The librarian of a small library may have some freedom to decide on a new system. For the law librarian of a university or polytechnic, the opportunities to influence the choice of a new cataloguing system may be limited, but he should be able to advise on what is suitable for his subject.

Whatever the circumstances, the choice of a cataloguing system should not be rushed, because it is a decision not easily reversed, and will contribute to (or detract from) the library's efficiency for many years.

Manual or automated

A choice between a new manual system or a new automated system is likely to arise only in small law libraries where the existing catalogues are totally inadequate or there are none. In this situation a new manual catalogue would involve only a small capital expenditure and be simple to produce and maintain. An automated catalogue would be a possibility if the organization served by the library could make existing facilities available, for example a microcomputer used primarily for 'housekeeping' routines. Factors influencing such a decision would be comparative costs with a manual system, availability of suitable software, ease of access to equipment and ease of production of an acceptable physical form of catalogue.

A decision more commonly made by librarians (especially academic) in recent years is choosing between continuation of an existing manual system or changing to a new automated system. The necessity of reducing cataloguing costs has made automation seem an attractive proposition. Labour costs for time-consuming tasks such as manual filing of a card catalogue have been rising faster than the cost of computer hardware, software and processing. Other attractions of automation have been the production of multiple copies of catalogues, ability to produce union catalogues, and the possibility of shared cataloguing.

Automated cataloguing does not of itself produce a better catalogue and a more efficient system. A great deal depends on the skill with which the librarian analyses the defects of the existing system and plans a realistic automated alternative. The many factors to be considered at the stage of planning for automation have been well documented in the professional literature and need not be repeated here. Possibly the most important thing is that the system should be capable of adaptation to changing technology. This involves an awareness on the part of the librarian of the considerable resources needed for development, without which an automated system may become obsolete.

The Survey of cataloguing and classification practice in British and Irish law libraries by BIALL (1984) showed that approximately 38 per cent of replying libraries used automated cataloguing. University and polytechnic libraries did so far more than other types of library.

In-house or external

The choice of whether cataloguing should be done in-house or using an external cataloguing service is closely linked to the choice of a manual or automated system. Manual systems in the United Kingdom are now almost always in-house, whereas automated systems may be either in-house or use an external service.

The great advantage of an in-house system, whether manual or automated, is independence in making cataloguing decisions. The whole content, form and style of the catalogues can be decided on the basis of the needs of users and the requirements of the type of material being catalogued. For law libraries, this is very valuable because of the special nature of legal publications.

Automated in-house systems for medium- to large-sized law libraries would seem a very suitable choice, but few have so far made it, one difficulty being the lack of suitable ready-made computer software. However one such system running on a microcomputer is in use at the Denning Law Library, University of Buckingham, and has been described by the librarian John E. Pemberton in his article 'Selecting software for a micro-based library catalogue' in the *Law Librarian*, vol. 14, 1983, pp. 35–8.

Another difficulty of in-house automated systems generally is that there may be no provision for support and development of the system. Even large general libraries have changed from an in-house system to using an external service, for that reason. If, as seems likely, future developments make in-house automated cataloguing systems a more practical option, law libraries could benefit.

The advantages to a general library of using an external cataloguing service (BLCMP, OCLC etc.) are most marked in the areas of system support and development, and in provision of ready-made catalogue entries, but there are disadvantages for law libraries. External services impose cataloguing standards which may not be suitable. Amendment of records is time-consuming and cancels out the advantages of taking ready-made records.

External services are most successful for a basic law collection, say of undergraduate textbooks. The BIALL Survey shows that the largest group of law libraries using them are the polytechnic law libraries. They are less satisfactory for law libraries wishing to obtain records for foreign language material, rare or very specialized books, older material and serially published works. There is no database specifically for law yet available from which satisfactory records can be obtained.

Full or simplified cataloguing

The arguments for and against simplified or short-entry catalogues have been fully explored in *Full and short-entry catalogues*, by Alan Seal *et al.*, 1982, based on work at the Centre for Catalogue Research. The benefits of a short-entry catalogue are likely to be savings in time spent on descriptive cataloguing; saving of space needed for catalogue entries, leading to cost savings (especially for large COM catalogues); some improvement in speed and accuracy of catalogue use. A major finding was that for monographs, 97 per cent of reader and staff needs would be satisfied by the inclusion of the following bibliographic elements, as appropriate. MARC format tags are shown in brackets:

Record control number (001)
Personal name main entry heading (100)
Corporate name main entry heading (110)
Conference, congress, meeting, etc. name main entry heading (111)
Uniform title (240)
Title proper (245 $a)
Other title information (245 $b)
Multipart item: number and title of volume or part (248 $g $h)
Edition statement (250 $a)
Date of publication (260 $c)
Edition and history note (503)
Personal name subject heading (600)
Corporate name subject heading (610)
Conference, congress, meeting, etc. name subject heading (611)
Personal name added entry heading (700)
Corporate name added entry heading (710)
Conference, congress, meeting, etc. name added entry heading (711)
Title added entry heading (745 $a)
References (9XX).

This list could be used as a starting point for the catalogue of a general law library, though with a few additions. A statement of responsibility for the edition (250 $c) should be added, as the original author of a standard legal treatise may have been superseded and the work rewritten by the editor. Librarians, if not their customers, may prefer to include the complete imprint not just date of publication (260 $a and $b) and have an added entry for the name of a monographic series (440). Larger law libraries might consider short-entry cataloguing for their standard works, while providing fuller entries for rare or unusual items, though it may be argued that this produces a lack of uniformity in the catalogue.

Libraries using an external cataloguing service may not have much choice of what bibliographical elements are in the records they receive. It may be less costly to accept records with more details than are really necessary than to spend time editing them. Also, libraries in co-operative cataloguing schemes may be obliged by the standards of the group to create records with more detail than they really require. It has usually been easier for groups to agree on a full cataloguing standard than a simplified one.

Physical forms of catalogue

The physical form of a library catalogue affects its efficiency to a considerable extent. It should be easy to use with clear instructions provided where necessary, for example how to operate a microfiche reader. The layout and length of catalogue entries also contribute to (or hinder) ease of use. For the librarian the most important considerations are economy, flexibility and speed in adding to and amending the catalogue.

Cards

Card catalogues have been the commonest form in law libraries, with typing as the method of production. They are still a practical choice for a small law library. However large card catalogues become slow to use, are expensive to maintain and take up much floor space. They are essentially a one-copy form, involving much extra labour to produce additional copies, say for the law library of a university. The expense of

maintaining them has been a factor in the decision of many
academic libraries to use an automated system with a different
physical form of catalogue, most often COM fiche. It is possible
to have catalogue cards produced as output from an automated system, but filing still has to be done manually.

Sheaf and book catalogues

Sheaf catalogues have similar advantages and disadvantages
to card catalogues. Space requirements are less, but filing is
somewhat slower. Book-form catalogues have the advantage
that multiple copies are easy to produce and they are easy to
scan. They are quite inflexible except when produced from
computer output with frequent updating.

COM fiche

The BIALL Survey of cataloguing and classification practice
showed that over 50 per cent of the law libraries which had
changed the physical form of their catalogue had changed to
COM fiche. Manual filing is eliminated and multiple copies of
the catalogue are easy and cheap to produce. Regular updating is economic until the file becomes very large, when
supplements may have to be produced between annual cumulations. The frames of the fiche are reasonably easy to scan,
and readability can be improved by careful format and layout
of entries.

Online catalogues

The same survey showed that a significant percentage of law
libraries, mainly academic, had changed to an online catalogue. This type should ideally be part of an integrated library
system which is able to give the user details of items on order
and on loan in addition to normal catalogue functions. Their
main advantages are that they should provide very up-to-date
information, and that users like them especially when the

system is designed to provide guidance through the catalogue. The best systems are tolerant of complex queries from users in a way not currently possible with any other physical form of catalogue. It is likely that further developments in the form of catalogues will be in this area, and that academic law libraries which are part of a larger library system will be most able to participate in these developments.

Cataloguing codes

The BIALL Survey showed that out of 175 law libraries replying to the question 'What cataloguing rules are used?' 105 used AACR2, with university, polytechnic and public libraries predominating. The next largest group was of libraries who used their own codes, followed by smaller numbers using AACR 1967, the ALA Code 1949 and the *Anglo-American Code* 1908.

An account of the cataloguing rules of special interest to law librarians in the earlier codes is given in the first edition of the *Manual of Law Librarianship*, 1976, pp. 512–16. The history of the origin of AACR 1967 and its roots in the 'Paris principles' still has relevance for current practice. AACR2 continues rather than supersedes the earlier code, and in some ways is closer to the 'Paris principles', notably in the use of uniform titles for laws and treaties.

ANGLO-AMERICAN CATALOGUING RULES, SECOND EDITION, 1978

By 1974 a new edition of AACR was being planned to take account of developments such as increasing automation in libraries, growth of centralized and co-operative cataloguing, development of national library services and the use of non-book materials. Published in 1978, AACR2 incorporated all changes and amendments to AACR 1967 which had already been agreed, and reconciled the British and North American texts into one version. Minor amendments have been published from 1982 onwards. The new edition was intended to be a contribution to the development of an international cataloguing code, and its wide adoption has given it something of that status.

The code is divided into Part 1, 'Description' and Part 2, 'Headings, uniform titles and references'. These are followed by Appendices on capitalization, abbreviations, etc. all of which are to be treated as rules.

Descriptive rules

The descriptive rules are comprehensive and well organized, and can provide a high degree of consistency in descriptive cataloguing. Their very size and complexity however can make their use rather slow. The distinctive punctuation of AACR2 (which some may consider intrusive) and the order of the elements of description derive directly from the *General International Standard Bibliographic Description*, ISBD(G).

Chapter 1 contains general rules for all types of material; Chapters 2 to 10 contain rules for specific types of material including non-book material; Chapters 11 to 13 contain 'rules of partial generality', *ie*, microforms, serials and analysis. The chapters are generally used in combination depending on the item being catalogued, for example a serial published on microfiche would be catalogued using Chapter 1 'General rules', Chapter 11 'Microforms' and Chapter 12 'Serials'. As a mnemonic aid the various elements of description are given the same order and numbering within each chapter.

Three different levels of description, of varying fullness, are possible. The intention is that either a library should use only one level or use different levels for varying types of material. Small law libraries should find the first level of description adequate for their needs. It is similar to the description included in the simplified catalogue entry discussed on p. 751. Larger law libraries may wish to use the second level normally and reserve the third, fullest level for rare and bibliographically interesting items. If a combination of levels is used there should be clear guidelines for cataloguers as to the level used for each type of publication.

Examples of description of legal materials using AACR2 may be found in *Cataloging legal literature* by Peter Enyingi *et al.*, 1984. It covers in admirable detail many problems familiar to the law cataloguer. These include statements of responsibility preceding the title proper; notes indicating a change in title from the immediately preceding edition; notes on other related works; 'mixed' editions *ie*, where one volume of a multi-volume work is one edition and another volume is another edition; linking notes to identify relationships between serials; supplementary items and looseleaf publications. The cataloguing practice described in *Cataloging legal literature* is that of the Library of Congress. There is no comparable guide to British Library cataloguing practice for law, though their *Cataloguing Practice Notes* provide general guidance on their interpretation of AACR2.

Entry rules

Part 2 of AACR2 contains rules on headings and uniform titles which are to be added to the description of an item established using the rules in Part 1. Chapter 21 deals with the choice of main and added entries, and includes special rules for legal publications. Chapters 22 to 24 deal with form of headings, Chapter 25 with uniform titles and Chapter 26 with references.

For the law cataloguer there are three main areas of interest: firstly those general rules which are constantly applied to legal publications; secondly the special rules for 'certain legal publications', rules 21.31–21.36; thirdly uniform titles, Chapter 25.

General rules applied to legal publications

Rule 21.1B2 is the general rule covering main entry under corporate body, and applies to serials as well as monographs. Entry is restricted to the listed categories, otherwise it is under title. Category b of 21.1B2 is the general rule authorizing the entry of laws, decrees, administrative regulations, treaties, court decisions and legislative hearings under corporate body. It refers the cataloguer to the special rules 21.31–21.36 except that legislative hearings are covered by the general rule 21.4B.

Rule 21.12 deals with revisions of texts or revised editions, a common feature of many legal treatises. The deciding factor in determining the main entry is whether the original author is still considered responsible for the revised work. Most legal treatises tend to follow the pattern of indicating the responsibility of the original author prominently, as in the example given under rule 21.12A:

> Salmond on the law of torts. – 12th ed. / by R. F. V. Heuston
> Main entry under the heading for Salmond
> Added entry under the heading for Heuston

Rule 21.12B covers the opposite case where the original author is no longer considered responsible for the work. Then entry is under the reviser with an added name/title entry for the original.

Rule 21.13 deals with texts published with commentary. Legal publications such as codes, individual laws, constitutions and court rules which have a commentary or annotations are covered by this rule not the special rules. Entry is under the heading for the author of the commentary (rule 21.13B) or under the heading for the original text (rule 21.13C) depending on the presentation in the chief source of information, usually the title page. Legal examples are given under both sections of the rule. Rule 21.13D provides for the chief source of information to be ambiguous, preferring entry under the heading for the original text in cases of doubt. This rule can be a source of inconsistency in choice of main entry so a record of decisions made, with examples, should be kept.

The form of heading used can affect catalogue consistency as much as choice of main entry heading. Rule 24.18 for example covers the form of heading for government agencies entered subordinately. They may be entered as a sub-heading of the name of the government or in some cases directly under their own name depending on the type of name. Following type 2 a royal commission may be entered as:

> Canada. Royal Commission on Banking and Finance

Where the name of the government is included in the name of the commission however the heading takes the form:

> Royal Commission on Higher Education in New Brunswick.

Similarly law reform commissions may be entered as:

> Australia. Law Reform Commission

or
Law Reform Commission of Canada

Catalogue users including librarians are unlikely to appreciate the cataloguing theories which make entries unpredictable. Matters may be further complicated by an inconsistent use of exact form of name by the government body itself.

Special rules for legal publications

The special rules are:

Rule 21.31 Laws, etc.
Rule 21.32 Administrative regulations
Rule 21.33 Constitutions, charters and other fundamental laws
Rule 21.34 Court rules
Rule 21.35 Treaties, inter-governmental agreements, etc.
Rule 21.36 Court decisions, cases, etc.

They prescribe the choice of main and added entries and the use of uniform titles, but the cataloguer is referred to rules 25.15–25.16 for the form of uniform titles for laws and treaties.

Primary legislation

Rule 21.31A limits the scope of the main rule on laws to primary legislation only, subordinate legislation being dealt with in rule 21.32. Rule 21.31B covers Laws of modern jurisdictions and 21.31C covers ancient laws, certain medieval laws, customary laws, etc.

The main rule 21.31B1, 'Laws governing one jurisdiction', prescribes entry under the heading for the jurisdiction governed by the laws. No form sub-heading such as 'Laws, statutes, etc.' is used as in previous codes. Instead a uniform title is added to the heading for the jurisdiction. Provision is made for cases where 'the laws are enacted by a jurisdiction other than that governed by them' (p. 326). Here an added entry is made for the enacting jurisdiction. This is usually satisfactory, but not in the case of United Kingdom Local Acts which should, strictly speaking, be entered under United Kingdom (or Great Britain whichever is generally used) rather than the locality.

Rule 21.31B2, Laws governing more than one jurisdiction, directs such a work to be entered as a collection, generally with title main entry, following the general rule 21.7 under which some legal examples may be found. Rule 21.31B3, Bills and drafts of legislation, distinguishes between Bills which are entered under the heading for the appropriate legislative body and other drafts of legislation to which the general rules 21.1–21.7 are applied.

Rule 21.31C, ancient laws, certain medieval laws, customary laws, etc. needs care as to what is included. All customary laws for example, both ancient and modern are included, but some medieval laws which were promulgated by a jurisdiction on modern lines, such as Italian city states, should be treated as modern jurisdictions. The rule directs main entry to be under uniform title or the title proper.

Subordinate legislation

It is perhaps in rule 21.32, administrative regulations, etc. that the difficulty of devising a set of rules and terminology suitable for cataloguing material from many jurisdictions can be seen most clearly. Cataloguers in the United Kingdom for example would find 'subordinate legislation' or 'secondary legislation' a more helpful term than 'administrative regulations'.

The rule is divided into 21.32A covering regulations which are promulgated by government agencies as in the United States, 21.32B, those which are laws as in the United Kingdom or Canada, and 21.32C which covers collections. The rule is satisfactory enough when cataloguing material from familiar jurisdictions but is more difficult to apply to unfamilar jurisdictions when it may not be clear whether 21.32A1 or 21.32A2 applies. This is only likely to occur in specialist law libraries who may be helped by a list of which rule the Library of Congress applies to various jurisdictions, in *Cataloging legal literature*, Chapter 8.

Constitutions and charters

Rule 21.33 covers constitutions, charters and other fundamental laws. 21.33A deals with constitutions etc. of a single jurisdiction, which are entered under the heading for the jurisdiction, as are amendments to a constitution. As with rule

21.31B1 for laws, if the constitution is issued by a jurisdiction not governed by it, main entry is under jurisdiction governed with added entry for issuing jurisdiction. In the examples, the United Nations is treated as a jurisdiction.

In contrast to previous codes no sub-heading for constitution is used and neither is a uniform title required as a matter of course under rule 21.33. Under the general rules in Chapter 25, however, a uniform title may be used and it is generally more satisfactory to do so.

Rule 21.33B deals with two types of constitution. Firstly, those emanating from a jurisdiction but applying to a body other than a jurisdiction. The example given is:

Charter of the Franklin Bank of Baltimore
(An act of the Maryland legislature)

Entry is according to the 'type of document', so if it is a law, rule 21.31 for laws is followed. Presumably the cataloguer should deduce from this that if the document is a regulation rule 21.32 applies. Secondly, constitutions which neither apply to nor emanate from a jurisdiction, such as those of learned societies, are mentioned as being entered according to the general rules 21.1B and 21.4B.

Draft constitutions are treated in rule 21.33C similarly to draft legislation in rule 21.31B3. There is no rule for collections of constitutions in 21.33, but an example is given on p. 300 under rule 21.7B for collections:

Constitutions of nations/[compiled by] Amos J. Peaslee
Main entry under title
Added entry under the heading for Peaslee

Admittedly the examples in AACR2 are 'illustrative not prescriptive' (p. 4), but, in the absence of more definite guidance, the cataloguer can hardly be expected to refrain from using them as rules.

Court rules
Rule 21.34A deals with the court rules for a single court, which are entered under the heading for the court. As with rule 21.32 for administrative regulations, it is difficult to have rules which apply equally well to all jurisdictions. In the United Kingdom, court rules are Statutory Instruments and the

courts are not the authors of their rules, so that following the rule produces a heading more in the nature of a subject heading. However an added entry is prescribed for the enacting jurisdiction with a uniform title for the law, so there will be an entry under the strictly correct heading.

Rule 21.34B covers court rules governing more than one court of a single jurisdiction. 'Collection of rules' is here used in the sense of a unified set of rules governing more than one court. If the rules are laws, rule 21.32 is applied; if not, they are entered under the promulgating agency. There is a parallel with administrative regulations in that it may be difficult to ascertain whether court rules are laws or not when dealing with unfamiliar jurisdictions.

Rule 21.34C is on 'collections' in the more usual sense. The court rules may be from different jurisdictions or promulgated by more than one agency. In either of these cases the cataloguer is referred to the general rule for collections, rule 21.7, which prescribes title main entry.

Treaties, etc.

The two main parts of rule 21.35, treaties, inter-governmental agreements, etc. cover firstly international treaties in 21.35A and secondly agreements contracted by international inter-governmental bodies in 21.35B. There follow two special rules, for agreements contracted by the Holy See and by jurisdictions below the national level, in 21.35C and 21.35D. Finally protocols, amendments, etc. and collections of treaties are dealt with in 21.35E and 21.35F. There is no form sub-heading for treaties. As for laws, a uniform title is prescribed for which the cataloguer is referred to rule 25.16.

Rule 21.35A1 describes choice of entry for treaties between two or three national governments. Main entry is under the heading for one of the governments with added entries for the others. Guidance is given as to which to choose as main entry. The home government however is not given any preference here. Rule 21.35A2 prescribes title proper or uniform title main entry for a treaty between more than three national governments, thus keeping consistency with the general rules where more than three persons or corporate bodies are involved. Added entries are made for selected signatories –

home government, government publishing the item and government named first. As the first example under this rule (p. 333) shows, important signatories may be left out in an arbitrary way:

> The definitive treaty of peace and friendship between His Britannick Majesty, the most Christian King, and the King of Spain: concluded at Paris, the 10th day of February, 1763: to which the King of Portugal acceded on the same day.
> (France, the United Kingdom, Portugal and Spain are signatories)
> Main entry under the uniform title for the treaty
> Added entry under the heading for the United Kingdom with uniform title for the treaty.

In 21.35B, agreements contracted by international inter-governmental bodies, the cataloguer is referred back to rule 21.35A. Choice of main entry again depends on the number of parties involved. The only difference in 21.35B is that a uniform title is not added to headings for jurisdictions other than national governments and for other corporate bodies.

For agreements contracted by the Holy See, rule 21.35C, main entry depends on which party's heading comes first in English alphabetical order, and therefore is not always under the heading for the Catholic Church. In rule 21.35D agreements contracted by jurisdictions below the national level, the cataloguer is referred back either to 21.35A and 21.35B or to the general rule 21.6C for works of shared responsibility. Protocols, amendments, etc. covered in rule 21.35E are entered under the same heading as the basic agreement, but have a special addition to the uniform title to distinguish them.

Collections of treaties in rule 21.35F1 are entered in the same way as single treaties if all are contracted by the same two parties. In the case of a collection between one party and two or more parties on the other side, entry is under the heading for the one party (rule 21.35F2). In both cases, the compiler of the collection if named is given an added entry. In 21.35F3, collections of treaties which have no one party common to every treaty, entry is according to the general rule for collections, 21.7, and will generally be under title.

Law reports, etc.
Rule 21.36, Court decisions, cases, etc. deals not only with law reports in the formal sense, covered by rule 21.36A, but also with citators, digests and indexes to law reports in rule 21.36B. Rule 21.36C deals with proceedings of particular cases, both in full and in part.

Rule 21.36A, law reports, deals firstly, in 21.36A1, with reports of one court. In deciding on main entry, this complex rule mentions various criteria which may be summarized as follows:

If the reports are not ascribed to a reporter but are issued under the authority of the court, enter under court.
If the reports are neither ascribed to a reporter nor issued under the authority of the court, enter under title.
If the reports are ascribed to a reporter, enter under court or reporter depending on accepted legal citation practice in the country concerned.

The second of these applies to many modern series of law reports and the third provides for early nominate reports.

Secondly, rule 21.36A2 is about reports of more than one court. Here, main entry is under reporter or title, depending on how many reporters are involved and whether the reporter was responsible for all the cases. The names of the courts involved appear as added entries. Rule 21.36A seems very complicated. An approach based on citation of law reports in their country of origin would be simpler, with guidance as to entry when citation practice is unknown.

Rule 21.36B, citations, digests, etc. prescribes entry under the person responsible for them if openly named, otherwise under title. A special rule seems unnecessary as the general rule 21.28, Related works, covers such works and includes, unlike 21.36B, an added entry for the work to which it is related. There is no equivalent special rule for citators and digests other than those to law reports, so the general rules should be applied for a digest of legislation, for example.

The first three sections of rule 21.36C cover the full proceedings of a particular case, while the following sections 21.36C4 to 21.36C8 cover the various parts of the records of a case. Rule 21.36C9 covers collections of proceedings. Only official proceedings are included in 21.36C. Popular accounts of trials should be catalogued according to the general rules. Again the rule seems unnecessarily complicated, for example, 21.36C4 to 21.36C8 could be simplified by entering all parts of a case under the heading for the whole case.

Uniform titles

The third area of special interest to law cataloguers is Chapter 25, 'Uniform titles'. The use of the whole chapter can be regarded as optional, as rule 25.1 states 'Although the rules in this chapter are stated as instructions, apply them according to the policy of the cataloguing agency' (p. 442).

It is likely that a small law library with a basic collection of treatises and law reports would wish to omit uniform titles completely. At the other end of the scale, the catalogue of a large research collection of law needs a method of organizing the file, especially under headings for jurisdictions.

There are special uniform titles for legal materials covering laws and treaties only. These are rules 25.15 and 25.16 respectively, and they are used in conjunction with rules 21.31 and 21.35 for choice of entry. Also, certain parts of the general rules in Chapter 25 are constantly used by law cataloguers.

Legislation

Rule 25.15 deals with uniform titles for laws and is divided into 25.15A for modern laws and 25.15B, ancient laws, certain medieval laws, customary laws, etc. Rule 25.15A is further subdivided into 25.15A1 covering collections of laws and 25.15 A 2 covering single laws.

The uniform title prescribed to be added to a jurisdiction heading for collections of laws is 'Laws, etc.', but this applies only to general collections, not subject compilations. From the examples on page 455 it may be seen that general consolidations of laws like *Halsbury's Statutes of England*, general codes of laws such as the *United States Code*, and partial collections such as sessional volumes of statutes all have the uniform title 'Laws, etc.'.

A general collection of laws arranged by subject should not be confused with a subject compilation which deals with a particular subject area of law, for example a collection of business and trade laws. It is worth noting while studying the examples under rule 25.15A1 that sessional volumes of statutes are not likely to be catalogued individually as in the third example on p. 455. Law libraries, if indeed they catalogue legislation at all, generally treat sessional volumes as serials, with an open entry for the whole set. The uniform title for such a set would still be 'Laws, etc.'.

Subject compilations are dealt with in the second paragraph of rule 25.15A1. Codes on a particular subject area are included here provided they are collections of Acts rather than a single legislative enactment. The uniform title prescribed is the citation title, if there is one. If not the cataloguer is referred to the general rule 25.3, in which 25.3B is the most likely part to be applied, using the title proper as the uniform title. Rather than having identical title proper and uniform title, the most satisfactory solution is simply to omit the uniform title completely, for example, use:

> Singapore
> Handbook of Singapore tax statutes

not

> Singapore
> [Handbook of Singapore tax statutes]
> Handbook of Singapore tax statutes.

Rule 25.15A2 covers uniform titles for single laws. Codes on a particular subject area come into this category if they are single legislative enactments. European codes such as the French *Code Civil* and German *Handelsgesetzbuch* are included here. The uniform title prescribed is, in order of preference, the official short title or citation title; the unofficial short title or citation title; the official title; any other official designation such as number or date. The date of enactment is included when it is part of the citation title, or it may be added to distinguish different laws with the same title.

The rule for ancient laws, etc., both collections and single laws, 25.15B is used in conjunction with 21.31C. The uniform titles are formulated according to the general rules 25.3 or 25.4 depending on the date of the work. Rule 25.4A, the general rule for works created before 1501, will apply to the ancient laws most commonly found in academic law libraries, such as *Corpus iuris civilis, Sachsenspiegel*, etc.

Treaties

Rule 25.16 covers uniform titles for treaties, dealing with collections in 25.16A and single treaties in 25.16B. The three paragraphs of 25.16A are used in conjunction with 21.35F1 to 21.35F3. The basic uniform title for collections, under a heading for a jurisdiction, is 'Treaties, etc.'. It is used alone for collections of treaties between a single party and two or more other parties, and used with the addition of the other party's name for collections of treaties between two parties. The third paragraph of 25.16A appears to be a special application of the rule for collections of treaties with no one party in common. These are normally entered under the title of the collection and do not require a uniform title.

The uniform title rule for single treaties deals firstly in rule 25.16B1 with those between two or three parties which may be national governments, international governmental bodies, etc. 'Treaties, etc.' is again the uniform title, under a heading for a jurisdiction, with detailed instructions given for adding the name of the other party where two parties only are involved, plus the date of signing.

Secondly, for single treaties with four or more parties involved, the uniform title is 'the name by which the treaty is known'. The jurisdiction heading is not used here, simply the name of the treaty. An English name is preferred if there is one. The title proper of a treaty may be used as a heading following rule 21.35A2, but often it is too long so a uniform title is preferable. The date of signature is added to the uniform title.

Protocols and amendments to treaties have the special designation 'Protocols, etc.', followed by date, which is added to the uniform title for the original treaty, as specified in rule 25.16B3.

Constitutions and charters

There is no special legal rule for the uniform titles of constitutions, but examples on p. 445 and 448 in Chapter 25 indicate that they are used under the general rules. However no collective uniform title like 'Constitution, etc.' is prescribed. The language of the original document is preferred in rule 25.3, so the uniform title will often be the equivalent of

'Constitution' in that language. *Cataloging legal literature* includes a list of uniform titles for constitutions of unfamiliar jurisdictions in Appendix D.

It is a matter of cataloguing policy whether to apply a uniform title to constitutions immediately, or to wait until there are several versions from one jurisdiction and to add a uniform title retrospectively. For a law library which collects foreign law extensively, the former course is preferable.

Revised editions

One further area of interest to law cataloguers in Chapter 25 is the apparent prohibition on the use of a uniform title for revised editions, except where different language editions are involved. In rules 25.2, 25.2A and 25.2B, revised editions are specifically excluded from the application of uniform titles and a legal example is given on p. 443. Revised editions of treatises which have changed title proper therefore have to be connected by notes. If strict alphabetical filing order is adhered to, revised editions of the same work may not file in edition number order, and they may also be interfiled with other works of the same author.

Conclusions

It is the filing order produced by uniform titles, or the lack of them, in AACR2 which is the least satisfactory aspect of the code for law libraries, particularly when a large sequence of uniform title entries builds up under the heading for a jurisdiction. Uniform titles for single laws, not necessarily in English, interfile with the collective uniform titles 'Laws, etc. and Treaties, etc.'. Constitutions may be found anywhere in the sequence depending on the language of the original. Works entered under the jurisdiction alone with no uniform title may also be interfiled.

AACR2 is intended to produce an alphabetical catalogue, and systematic arrangement should in theory have no place there. It is recognized however that systematic arrangement is needed in areas other than law. For instance, the *BLAISE Filing Rules* (British Library, 1980) include special schemes for the systematic filing of 'complex' authors and for filing the books of the Bible in canonical order. Why not a systematic arrangement for law?

Law libraries which use uniform titles and are able to take independent decisions on their catalogue entries may decide to modify AACR2 to file satisfactorily or to use different uniform titles. A list of filing titles for legal materials was published by BIALL in the *Law Librarian*, vol. 7, p. 9. It includes, in this order, constitutions, legislation, treaties, court rules and law reports. It is much less easy for law libraries who belong to co-operative cataloguing schemes or use ready-made catalogue records to find a satisfactory solution. They may be obliged to use AACR2 uniform titles as they stand, so for this reason it is important that there should be a recognized alternative filing system for law. There is a genuine conflict here between a widely accepted standard, AACR2, and the needs of a specialist group.

SUBJECT CATALOGUES

While standardization in author/title cataloguing has had an impact on law libraries, subject cataloguing has remained much more individual. For example, although Library of Congress subject headings are available on UK MARC and LC MARC records, only twelve libraries in the BIALL Survey of cataloguing and classification practice reported using them.

The type of subject work undertaken varies widely. Small and highly specialized law libraries such as that of a firm of solicitors dealing mainly with taxation or company law, have much in common with other special libraries in their approach. The emphasis is on subject access to current information, often in the form of journal and newspaper articles, pamphlets, Statutory Instruments, etc. Subject indexes may be made for these and other special collections such as counsels' opinions and memoranda. Indeed the subject approach in this type of library may be more important than author/title access.

In academic law libraries the two traditional types of subject catalogue, classified and alphabetical, still predominate. The advantages of both forms are dealt with fully in A. C. Foskett's

The subject approach to information, 4th edn., 1982, and summarized in Hunter and Bakewell's *Cataloguing*, 2nd rev. edn., 1983. Only those aspects especially relevant to law libraries are mentioned here.

Classified catalogues

In the BIALL Survey the classified catalogue and associated alphabetical subject index was by far the most used form of subject catalogue. The arrangement of the classified sequence will reflect the advantages and disadvantages of the classification scheme used. A scheme which has jurisdiction as its primary facet will separate books on particular legal topics, for instance material on tax havens will be split between the various jurisdictions. The alphabetical subject index can however bring together subjects dispersed in this way.

In an automated cataloguing system, a classified catalogue and its index may be computer-produced in the same form as the author/title catalogue, most commonly on microfiche. The suitability of the classifications scheme's notation for machine filing is important here. The major general classification schemes and Moys' *Classification scheme for law books*, 2nd edn., can all be filed by machine, whereas local schemes or variations on a general scheme may have introduced illogical elements. Online catalogues also have the ability to present a classified sequence to the user, though there is still two-stage access to the classified sequence via the alphabetical index.

A classified catalogue is only a practical proposition where the whole or most of the library is classified by a scheme adequate for law. If all, or a major part, is unclassified or the scheme is very broad, an alphabetical subject catalogue is more suitable.

Alphabetical subject catalogues

While these have been less popular in Britain than in the United States, they are in use by a substantial number of law libraries. As the vocabulary of law is fairly well defined, they work well provided that the headings used have adequate specificity and currency.

Control of subject vocabulary

Most alphabetical subject catalogues in law libraries use a controlled vocabulary, either a published list of subjects or their own list. Very specialized libraries dealing with only a small subject area will often wish to compile their own list for use in subject cataloguing and indexing. Published lists are not sufficiently detailed or current for their needs. For libraries collecting more widely in the subject area, several published lists are in use but none is generally accepted as a standard. It is common practice to use a published list as a basis and adapt it to local needs.

Library of Congress subject headings, microfiche edition

This is the major general subject headings list, of which law is only a part. It is unlikely that many law libraries would wish to use the standard list when there is a special list for law by Krieger, based on it. However, a law library which is part of a general library may be obliged to use the standard list if that is the policy of the library as a whole, especially where ready-made catalogue records containing the subject headings are available. In this situation, the American spelling and terminology may be accepted rather than amended, and ideally only a small proportion of the subject cataloguing need be done in-house.

As the list is entirely based on the collections of the Library of Congress, the legal headings are substantial, especially for common law jurisdictions. Public international law subjects are well covered, but private international law and comparative law headings are more limited. The list is most appropriate for a large law library which collects extensively over a wide range of jurisdictions and legal systems.

There are several publications which provide a guide to the often complex principles and application of the subject headings. A general guide is *Library of Congress subject headings: principles and application* by Lois Mai Chan, 1978, which includes a section on law in Chapter 11. *Cataloging legal literature* contains a detailed exposition of the headings for law in part 4, 'Subject cataloging', and is essential reading for the specialist law cataloguer. In fact anyone studying law subject headings could profit by reading it, as it analyses types of headings including those for primary materials such as legislation and treaties. The Library of Congress's own application of the subject headings may be checked in the *Bibliographical Guide to Law*, published annually by G. K. Hall, or LC MARC records may be checked online via BLAISE-LINE.

Subject Headings for the Literature of Law and International Law, and Index to LC K Schedules, 3rd edn. compiled by Tillie Krieger, 1982

This list is derived from the 9th edition of *Library of Congress Subject Headings*, and is intended primarily for use in law school libraries of the United States. These are often large comprehensive collections and the list reflects this in its coverage. It is a good basis for a subject headings catalogue of a comparable collection in the United Kingdom or Ireland.

Its main advantage over the standard *Library of Congress subject headings* is that it is compact and easy to use. It can be used as a guide to the legal headings in the standard list, though it is not identical. Some terms from Library of Congress classification schedules which are not authorized subject headings are included, and some references are omitted. Subdivision is simplified, and the introduction includes notes on geographical sub-division and a list of form and subject subdivisions which may be applied to any heading. Headings for treaties are also described in detail.

The drawback for British and Irish law libraries is once again the American spelling and terminology, and also currency, though new headings may be obtained from the standard list in microfiche and the Library of Congress's *Cataloging Service Bulletin*.

Legal Subject Headings for Libraries, by Ian M. Sainsbury, 1974

In contrast to the previous lists discussed, this was based on the subject headings used in the English Inns of Court libraries, and as such use English rather than American terms. It is most suitable for use with a collection of English law, though international law is included. The inclusion of many terms of 'lawyer's law' makes it especially suitable for libraries used by practising lawyers.

Thesauri

The nearest approach to an English-language thesaurus for law is the index-thesaurus to Moys' *Classification scheme for law books,* 2nd edn., 1982. Although it is not a full-scale thesaurus as broader and narrower terms have been omitted – they may be found in the schedules – other thesaurus features such as the ability to combine terms are present, and some related terms are shown. Compound terms which are well-established have been retained as such, and English terminology is preferred to American. It is hoped that the classification scheme and index-thesaurus will be updated by supplements to be published in the *Law Librarian.* It is a systematic and easy-to-use list which should not be overlooked by law librarians considering a subject headings catalogue.

A full-scale multilingual legal thesaurus has yet to be published. The cumulative volumes of the *Index to Foreign Legal Periodicals* contain a broadly classified sequence in English, French, German and Spanish, followed by separate alphabetical lists in each of the four languages, with English translation of the foreign terms.

CHOICE OF CLASSIFICATION

Whether to classify

The classification of law libraries has long been a subject of controversy. Many, particularly those serving professional ocieties, declare that they are not classified. In a strict sense, his is rarely true; law reports, statutes and so on are almost nvariably separated from the treatises, and materials on oreign or international law are kept apart from those on the ocal jurisdiction. It is usually more appropriate to say that hese libraries are classified very broadly by jurisdiction and orm, but that the treatises within a jurisdiction are not classified by subject.

One of the lawyer's first objections to subject classification is hat he knows his books particularly well by author and that lphabetical arrangement is therefore most efficient. This is rue of the classic texts, such as *Chitty on Contracts* or *Ryde on Rating*. But the law is changing rapidly and new subjects are onstantly arising, such as environmental protection, for which the old standard treatises are inadequate. In an unlassified collection, the lawyer will have to make enquiries, list he authors of books which might help him, and collect the olumes together from their dispersed shelves in order to ssess them. A subject arrangement should have all available olumes on adjacent shelves, enabling the lawyer to browse hrough them easily and quickly to make his selection. It vould also enable him to trace a chapter on a very new topic in more general book, before specialist volumes had been vritten. These arguments apply more strongly if the reader is student or a research worker.

One of the disadvantages of classified arrangement is that nore shelf-space is needed to maintain the collection in orrect classified order and to allow space for a reasonable umber of new additions. Books which are allocated fixed ocations need less space, but shelving alphabetically by author equires the same sort of expansion and insertion allowance as oes subject arrangement. Other objections are based on the nadequacies of particular classification schemes. While it s true that some schemes are unsuitable for specialist law braries, better schemes do exist, see below.

A collection may be classified either broadly into a relatively mall number of large categories, such as contracts, commercial law, criminal law, etc., or closely with each such class ivided and sub-divided into detailed topics, such as the law of notor vehicle insurance or the law of expert medical evidence.

For a large research library, there can be little doubt that a detailed classification, closely linked with good catalogues, is the best solution. They will together enable both the practitioner with a complex case and the advanced student preparing a thesis to locate the materials needed in the most efficient manner.

The BIALL Survey mentioned above showed that, of the 192 libraries which replied to the questionnaire, 160 use some sort of classification scheme:

83 Dewey Decimal Classification
7 Universal Decimal Classification
7 Library of Congress
3 Bliss Bibliographic Classification
29 Moys
1 Other published scheme (not specified)
30 Libraries' own schemes

Undoubtedly, many of these 160 law libraries are parts of larger, more general libraries, whose parent bodies more or less dictate the use of a particular scheme, whether or not it is really suitable for a law library. Nevertheless, it would appear that the 'unclassified' law library is now in the minority in the British Isles.

Criteria of classification

It is fairly generally agreed that the two basic criteria for law library classification are the importance of the legal system and the distinction between primary and secondary sources. Both these principles should be incorporated in the structure of the classification scheme used in any law library. It is also advisable to consider various more practical aspects of the scheme, such as its notation, provision for updating and the index. Another factor that an increasing number of librarians will need to consider is the scheme's suitability for use in automated systems of operation.

It must be emphasized that the problems involved in devising even a simple classification scheme are very considerable. It is a task that should be undertaken only by a very experienced classifier, who should be aware of the pitfalls. Anyone else, including subject experts with limited knowledge of the technicalities of constructing library classifications, is most strongly advised to make use of one or other of the schemes discussed below.

The legal system

Almost anyone using a legal collection is concerned at any particular moment with one system of law, be it English law, Scots law, Australian law, French law, Hindu law or public international law. A reader who says that he is looking for books on conveyancing can be assumed to be concerned with the law of conveyancing applicable to the jurisdiction within which the library is situated. Similarly, a book entitled 'Law of conveyancing' will almost certainly relate to the jurisdiction in which the author lives and works. If this is not the case, in either example, the reader or the author will almost invariably specify the jurisdiction with which he is concerned. The vast majority of law books, including serial publications, deal with the whole or part of the law of a single jurisdiction. Most classifiers are accustomed to a citation order that puts first the detailed topic, such as transistors, wages, football or computers, with the facets of purpose, place, time and so on following in a suitable order. This procedure is not valid for a collection of legal materials. For the reasons explained above, and in the bibliographical chapters, the first step in the arrangement of a law library is to group the volumes according to the facet of 'legal system' or 'jurisdiction'. The classification scheme used should provide for this simply and unambiguously. Most modern legal jurisdictions are much the same as the political jurisdictions in up to date place tables, such as California, Canada and Cuba. But additional provision is needed to cover books dealing with those legal systems, such as classical Roman law, Islamic law and public international law which do not correspond with any modern political jurisdiction, and with subjects such as jurisprudence, criminology and comparative law.

Primary and secondary sources

In dealing with a problem in any of the common law jurisdictions (see Chapter 2) the distinction between books containing the law itself (primary sources) and those commenting on the law (secondary sources) is also of vital importance. In legal systems based on the civil law, the distinction may be somewhat less important, but it can usually be clearly seen in the literature and can still be useful to readers.

Some general libraries prefer to place the text of an individual statute with the treatises on the subject, for example putting an Education Act with the books on education in general, at some distance from the law section of the library. Any law library, on the other hand, and any general library which maintains a complete set of the jurisdiction's legislation, will find it essential to keep its complete sets of statutes and other primary materials all together, especially those that are serially published, and to treat the secondary materials separately.

The classification scheme should provide for separate treatment of primary and secondary materials under each jurisdiction. Primary sources are usually most suitably arranged by legal form; legislation, law reports, etc., with the digests, indexes and citators close to the volumes to which they refer. Secondary materials are usually classified, if at all, by subject content, *ie*, by topic, within the jurisdiction.

Practical considerations

Notation
One of the most immediately obvious characteristics of a classification scheme is its notation. Most schemes use notation made up of either letters or numbers or a combination of the two, as code symbols to represent the subjects and concepts in their schedules. For example, the English law of evidence in criminal proceedings is represented by SECAN in Bliss 2; by 344.2056 in Dewey 19 (jurisdiction-first option); by KD 8371 in Library of Congress and by KM 600 or 346.96 in Moys.

The chief function of notation is to reflect the order of the classes and concepts in the scheme. If possible, it should also help to show the structure of the scheme, the subordination of classes, and the changes of facet and phase. Both numbers and letters carry an obvious sequential meaning. If any other symbols, such as punctuation marks are used, not only their meaning but also their order in the sequence must be made absolutely clear.

As the notation is likely to be used on the spines of books and pamphlets, as well as in catalogue entries, brevity is an obvious advantage. It is also helpful, both to librarians and to readers, if class marks can be easily spoken and remembered. An alphabetical notation, with its potential base of 26 characters, will usually produce the shortest class symbols. On the other hand, a group of numbers or a mixture of numbers and letters is often thought to be easier to remember than a non-syllabic group of letters; it is especially difficult if upper – and lower-case letters are used with different meanings.

Updating

Even in a relatively conservative subject area such as law, new jurisdictions and new topics arise fairly constantly. An example of the former was the change in the Pacific, where the Gilbert and Ellice Islands separated into the two nations of Tuvalu and Kiribati, and an example of the latter was the invention of the hovercraft, which is neither a ship nor an aircraft but has some of the characteristics of both, and whose legal status had to be settled by the passing of the Hovercraft Act 1968. The classification scheme should make provision for new subjects and other changes by providing hospitality for them in its notation as well as in the schedules. Supplements or newly revised editions should be published at reasonable intervals.

Index

The need for a good subject index to the schedules should be self-evident. Almost all published schemes provide indexes of some sort. The index should be as full and as specific as possible, including a wide range of synonyms and near-synonyms which the user is likely to encounter. There should be only one number in the schedules for a topic, but as many index entries to that number as may be needed. The broader the classification scheme, the more important it is for specific terms to be indexed. For example, if a single number is allocated to landlord and tenant, the index should include entries to that number for a list of several terms, such as: dilapidations, dispossession, distress (rent), eviction, fixtures and fittings, furnished premises, ground rent, improvements, *landlords, leases, rent,* repairs, security of tenure, *tenancy,* tenants, unfurnished premises. Some of these terms are too specialized to be needed in a general library, but at least those printed in italics should be included in the index.

CLASSIFICATION SCHEMES

There are two or three general classification schemes covering the whole range of knowledge which are likely to be used by large academic, public or other general libraries which have legal sections (see Chapter 1). In these schemes, there is always a law class which contains, at the very least, provision for arranging legal primary materials and for treatises on some legal topics, especially 'lawyers' law'. But there are some topics of considerable importance to a law library which may, in a general scheme, either be placed in other classes, *eg,* trade union law, banking law, public health law, or may be given specific places in the law class.

However, in a general classification, there will always be a number of subjects ancillary to legal studies which must remain in other classes, such as political and social history, general sociology, ethics, philosophy, etc. Thus, law students using the legal section of a general library may have to be directed to other parts of the building for books on ancillary subjects. But a separately housed law faculty library should contain a suitable selection of books on related subjects and will normally give them the same class marks as they would have in the main library. An independent law library that uses one of the general schemes should follow the same procedure.

In addition to the general schemes, several special law classification schemes have been devised. Many of these schemes were tailored to the needs of particular libraries and would be likely to require considerable adaptation before they could be used elsewhere. Specialist schemes usually provide places for the ancillary subjects mentioned above and also for general materials, such as bibliographies and dictionaries which are found in non-legal sections of the general classification schemes.

Dewey Decimal Classification

The nineteenth edition of this well-known scheme was published in 1979 in three volumes. It includes some minor revisions of the 'phoenix' schedule for law first published in 1971 in the eighteenth edition, and incorporates the optional alternative citation order first authorized in 1973. In fact three basic options are offered:

Preferred option:
base number 34, indicating 'law';
single digit, indicating 'branch of law' (see below);
area notation (from the tables);
o (zero) plus one or more digits to indicate the specific topic.
Option A:
base number 34;
single digit for 'branch of law';
notation for specific topic (not preceded by zero);
(this option to be used without area notation, to give preference to a specified jurisdiction).
Option B:
base number 34;
area notation (i.e. jurisdiction);
o (zero) followed by digit for 'branch of law';
notation for specific topic (not preceded by o).

Yet another option, C, is provided for those libraries which wish to treat law as a sub-division (026 from the tables) of a main subject.
The 'branches of law' used by DDC are:

2 Constitutional and administrative law

3 Miscellaneous public law
4 Social law
5 Criminal law
6 Private law
7 Civil procedure and courts
8 Laws (statutes), regulations, cases.

Digits 1 and 9 have been left clear for 'non-local' laws: 341 being international law and 349 being 'law of individual states and nations', *ie*, foreign law.

An example is given in the schedules: 'criminal procedure in Australia', where the elements of the class mark are:

34 law
  5 criminal law and procedure
05 criminal procedure
94 Australia

The resultant numbers would be:

Preferred option	345.9405
Option A	345.05 (in an Australian library)
Option B	349.4055

Similarly, 'law of education in Scotland' would be:

34 law
  4 social law
07 education
411 Scotland

Preferred option	344.41107
Option A	344.07 (in a Scottish library)
Option B	344.11047
Option C	370.26

In assessing the value of Dewey to law libraries it must be said that it should be possible to find one or other of the three optional citation orders which suits most individual requirements. It may be noted that the British National Bibliography has adopted Option B, partly, perhaps, on the recommendation of BIALL.

For a small law library with little foreign material, Option A would provide a reasonable compromise, with a brief notation for most material relating to the home jurisdiction. The Preferred Option cannot be recommended to law libraries under any circumstances. The citation order: subject – jurisdiction – subject, being totally unsuitable.

While the treatment of subject treatises in classes 340 to 347 is generally satisfactory, according to W. A. Steiner's review in *Law Librarian*, vol. 4, 1973, pp. 14–15, that of primary materials in class 348 is less so. There are 90 potential numbers between 348.01 and 348.099, but only 20 of these are specified. Further sub-division could be undertaken by individual law libraries, but this would have to be at the risk of being overtaken by later official amendments.

The scheme's general tables are very full and useful, notably the area table and the table of sub-divisions for bibliographical forms, the latter being used wherever required. For example, a periodical (05) on negligence in English law would be 344.2063205, using Option B.

The notation, as the name suggests, is entirely numerical. Every class number contains at least three digits, followed, if there are further digits, by a decimal point as shown in the examples above. The structure of the scheme is clearly reflected in the notation and changes in the criterion of division are usually indicated by an intervening zero, especially in the tables of standard sub-divisions already mentioned. Class numbers tend to be long, because of the inevitable limitations of a base of ten. The same difficulty affects every decimal scheme. For example, the German law of criminal procedure, 344.3055 in Dewey, would be 349.43059 in Moys, which is even longer.

New subjects are catered for by the publication, about every five to seven years, of a complete new edition. The fact that thousands of libraries use the scheme, and must buy each successive edition, alone makes this publication programme economically possible. Except when a 'phoenix' schedule is produced, such as that for class 340, law, in the eighteenth edition, new numbers usually have to be fitted in by sub-dividing existing numbers. Relatively minor amendments are published, in the mean time, in the bulletin of 'Additions, notes and decisions'.

The published index to the whole scheme is very large and

generally satisfactory. Even so, a law library is likely to find the detail insufficient, but this would probably apply equally to the index of any all-embracing classification scheme.

Universal Decimal Classification

This scheme was developed, primarily on the continent of Europe, from the earlier editions of Dewey. It has grown steadily further and further away from Dewey until the resemblance is now only superficial. The UDC was one of the first attempts to produce a faceted classification, and uses a variety of punctuation or mathematical symbols to indicate various facets and phases, such as:

=	language
(1) to (9)	place
(1) to (9)	time
:	relationship

The new 'medium' edition gives the outline:

34	Law. Jurisprudence
340	Law in general
341	International law
342	Public law. Constitutional law. Administrative law
343	Criminal law. Penal offences
344	Special criminal law. Military, naval, air force law
345–6	[vacant]
347	Civil law
348	Ecclesiastical law. Canon law. Religious law
349	Special branches of law. Miscellaneous legal matter

This scheme, with its decimal base and its structure of auxiliary tables, almost invariably produces long class marks. But it does provide, in its full and medium editions, more detail than any of the other general schemes, with the possible exception of the Library of Congress.

Supplementation, or rather notification, of occasional revisions, comes in bulletins of 'Extensions and corrections' published annually, and cumulated every three years. The index to the new version has not yet been published (late

1985), but it is understood that FID had plans to produce a computerized index which, incidentally, probably accounts for the large number of synonyms and near synonyms in the schedules.

Library of Congress Classification

Although class K was assigned to law when the Library of Congress's mammoth classification was being compiled at about the turn of the century, no part of it was published until 1969, when 'Sub-class KF, Law of the United States' appeared in a preliminary edition. Several other sections have been published since, notably: 'KD, United Kingdom and Ireland', 1973; 'KE, Canada', 1976; 'K, Law (general)', 1977; 'KK–KKC, Germany', 1982.

The main divisions of class K are expected to be:

K	Generalia; periodicals; philosophy of law; comparative law
KB	Ancient law; Roman law; theocratic legal systems
KD	United Kingdom; Ireland
KE	Canada
KF	United States
KG–KH	Latin America, West Indies
KJ	Europe; EEC; Western Europe
KK	Central Europe
KL	Southeastern Europe; Northern Europe
KM	Soviet Union
KP–KQ	Asia
KR	Africa
KT	Australia; New Zealand; Antarctica
(KX)	Optional alternative to JX for international law

According to the annual reports of the Librarian of Congress, several sections of KG, KH and KJ are being applied to the Library's bookstock, preparatory to publication.

It can be seen that primacy has been given throughout to the jurisdiction. The classes so far published contain very full schedules for all the major jurisdictions covered, together with detailed tables for arranging materials for individual states, provinces, cities, etc. There is a clear distinction made between primary and secondary materials and the schedules for each jurisdiction are given in meticulous detail.

The scheme is designed for the arrangement of the Library of Congress's own very extensive collection and is enumerative rather than being based on an analysis of the facet structure of law. Inevitably the terminology has an American bias but care was taken in class KD to add or substitute British terms when this was thought to be necessary. Some of the 'Americanisms' in the placing of specific topics, such as public property and commercial law, mentioned by Moys in her review of class KF (*Law Librarian,* vol. 1, 1970, pp. 24–7) have been anglicized in class KD.

The notation is the usual Library of Congress mixture of letters and consecutive numbers. A slight modification from other classes in LC is that three letters are used to denote some relatively small jurisdictions, such as Scotland, the Channel Islands and the individual states and territories of the United States. The notation system produces fairly short class marks, for example, the English law of fire insurance is KD 1885; the law of education in New York City is KFX 2065. As the numbers run consecutively, they do not demonstrate the structure of the scheme as clearly as do decimal numbers, but hospitality to new topics is easier to achieve by the simple expedient of leaving groups of numbers unused at likely points in the schedules.

Supplementation is by means of LC's quarterly bulletin of 'Additions and changes' and, ultimately, by the publication of updated editions of the schedules. It is more than likely that new editions of the earliest sub-classes will be needed before the whole of class K has been printed. The Library of Congress can still give no firm date for this to be achieved.

Each published sub-class has its own index, which is full and thorough. For example, the KF schedules take 277 pages in well-spaced single column format, while the index occupies 55 pages of closely printed double columns.

The American Association of Law Libraries publishes two looseleaf works based on sub-class KF, 'Law of the United States'. These are a *Cumulative Schedule* first published in 1984 and a *Cumulative Index,* first published in 1982. Both publications incorporate the Library of Congress additions and changes and seem to bear the same sort of relationship to the official edition as do the lawyers' editions of the US Constitution, Supreme Court Reports, etc. (see Chapter 9). A similar *Cumulative schedule and index* for sub-class KD was published in 1985.

When the Library of Congress Class K Classification is completed, it will undoubtedly be the largest, most scholarly and best organized law classification ever seen. It is possible, though, that its very size and degree of detail may militate against its use by many libraries in the United Kingdom and Ireland.

Bliss Bibliographic Classification

The first edition of this scheme was compiled in the United States and completed in 1953. Its outstanding feature was the carefully worked out order of the main classes, based on an explicit theory of gradation in speciality.

The second edition, radically revised and greatly enlarged, is being prepared by the Bliss Classification Association, which maintains the scheme, under the editorship of Mr. Jack Mills, formerly of the Polytechnic of North London. Work started in 1970 and since the publication of BC2 commenced in 1977 about half the projected eighteen volumes have been published. Classes R and S, political science and law, will together form one volume to be published in mid-1987. The outline of Class S, Law, will be as follows (but some of the notation is provisional):

S	Law
S2	Common sub-divisions for form and subject
S3	Study and research, comparative law
S9B	Primary materials (general)
S9E	Jurisprudence, natural law, conflict of laws
SA	Practice and procedure, administration of justice, courts
SAX	Subjects of law, substantive law (general)
SB	Private, civil law
SBX	Public law (general)
SC	Criminal

SCR	Constitutional and administrative (alternative, preferred in R)

Jurisdictions
(each jurisdiction may be qualified by all preceding facets S2/
S9 and SA to SC)

SDB	By period (By political authority)
SDD	International law (alternative, preferred in R)
SDT	National, municipal law (general)
SEX	Common law systems (general)
SE	England and Wales
SE9B	Primary materials
SE9E/SED	Secondary materials (by topic)
	Rest of British Isles. Commonwealth, USA
SSX	Civil law systems (general)
ST	France, Spain, Italy, Germany
SY	Home country (if desired)
SZ	Religious jurisdictions

It seems certain that the main requirements for a fully faceted law classification scheme will be met by BC2, both in the concepts and in the notation, which is primarily literal, but with some numerals, notably for the common subdivisions.

Updating of the computer-held schedules is provided by the *Bliss Classification Bulletin.* A computer-generated alphabetical index will also be published.

Moys Classification Scheme for Law Books

Unlike the schemes discussed above, this one originated in academic libraries. It was not, however, tailored to a particular library or group of libraries. It is intended to be suitable for use in various types of libraries, academic, professional or public, anywhere in the English-speaking world. To this end, the same basic schedule has been provided with two different notations. The original was a Library of Congress type class K, and the optional alternative is a Dewey style 340. The outline is:

K version 340 version

General and non-national legal systems

Journals and reference books	K	340.01–9
Jurisprudence	KA	340.1
General and comparative law	KB	340.3–6
International law	KC	341
Religious legal systems	KD	342
Ancient and medieval law	KE	343

Modern national legal systems
  Common law
    Primary materials

British Isles	KF	
Canada, USA, West Indies	KG	} 344
Australia, New Zealand	KH	

    Treatises

General	KL	345
Public Law	KM	346
Private law	KN	347

  Other modern legal systems

Own country (optional alternative)	KP	348
Africa	KR	349.6
Latin America	KS	349.8
Asia and Pacific	KT	349.5
Europe	KV	349.4
European Communities (optional alternative)	KW	349.4

Non-legal subjects   KZ

There is careful separation of legal systems, but not on a strictly jurisdictional basis. A consensus of law teachers consulted at the time of compilation was in favour of keeping together all material from the main common law jurisdictions, which were defined rather narrowly as: England and Wales, Canada, Australia, New Zealand and the United States. From this decision arose a number of anomalies, particularly affecting Scotland and other Commonwealth jurisdictions such as India, which were fully discussed in the introduction to the first edition. Some of the anomalies can be overcome by the use of class KP (348) for any jurisdiction, or group of jurisdictions that may be desired. It could, for example, be used for a single jurisdiction, such as Scotland, or for a federal system like Canada and its provinces, or for non-common law countries, such as the continental members of the European Communities.

Primary and secondary materials are clearly separated, and there are detailed schedules for the English and United States primary materials and for legal topics in classes K to KE and KL to KN inclusive.

The scheme is at least partially faceted in construction. Nine tables are provided after the main schedules:

    IPrimary materials
    IISubjects of law
    IIIDates
    IVCommon law jurisdictions
    VCourts
    VISpecial legal forms and topics
    VIIPersons
    VIIINon-legal forms and treatments
    IXEuropean Communities law

The use of the tables to build up class marks from the various facets of a subject is fully explained in the volume's introduction, with several examples of each, *eg*:

Land tenure in Kenya
Kenya	KR3101–50(C)	OR	349.6762
Land tenure (table II.C)	29.2	(table II.F)	071
Full number	KR3129.2	OR	349.6762071

Constitution of Canada
Canada	KG1–60(A)	OR	344.71
Constitution (table I.A)	14	(table I.E)	019
Full number	KG14	OR	344.71019

English legal history
Common law treatises	KL–KN	OR	345–7
Legal history	KL401–19		345.94–99
England (table IV)	1		(DDC) 42
Full number	KL401	OR	345.942

Procedure in juvenile courts
Procedure, by court	KN361–9	OR	347.921–9
Juvenile courts (table V)	7.1		7.1
Full number	KN367.1	OR	347.9271

Casebook on income tax			
Income tax	KM337.11	OR	346.531
Casebooks (table VI)	.Z2		.Z2
Full number	KM377.11.Z2	OR	346.531.Z2
Women in trade unions			
Trade unions	KN195	OR	347.48
Women (table VII)	.Q2		.Q2
Full number	KM195.Q2	OR	347.48.Q2
EEC farm prices			
EEC	KV1–50 OR KW1–150	OR	349.4
Farm prices (table IX.B)	32 (IX.A) 114		(IX.C) 081
Full number	KV32 OR KW114	OR	349.4081

The two notations follow closely the methods of the Library of Congress and Dewey classifications respectively, with the advantages and disadvantages mentioned above. The allocation of three whole classes to legal topics in the common law system enabled numbers there, in both notations, to be kept fairly short, although it must be remembered that the notation does not indicate the specific jurisdiction concerned. The law of television in England, for example, is KN344 or 347.877 in Moys, 344.2039946 in Dewey, KD2915 in Library of Congress. Both notations are provided for all subjects, except in a few places where users of the decimal notation are instructed to use DDC tables, notably the area table.

The first edition was published in 1968 and the second (1982) incorporated a considerable expansion, in both the schedules and the tables. It is hoped to produce occasional supplements and any plans are likely to be announced in the *Law Librarian*.

There was a substantial alphabetical index to the first edition, compiled on conventional lines. For the second edition it was converted into an index-thesaurus, occupying 162 of the 344 pages of the volume. It follows the format recommended in BS 5723:1979 for thesauri, except that broader and narrower terms were omitted (being indicated by the classification schedules) as were topics which did not appear at all in the schedules. Both notations are fully indexed.

PRACTICAL CATALOGUING AND CLASSIFICATION

Although few law libraries in the British Isles are large enough to have a separate cataloguing department, it can be helpful to read general articles on the management of cataloguing, in order to see the operation as a whole and its links with other library functions. Chapter 10 of Hunter and Bakewell's *Cataloguing,* 2nd rev. edn., 1983, discusses management techniques, and A. Jeffrey's article 'Management in cataloguing services' published in *Catalogue and Index* no. 46, 1977, pp. 2–4, deals with practical problems arising from automated cataloguing.

Assuming that sound basic decisions on choice of cataloguing system and classification have been made, as outlined above, the main tasks of management are to maintain an efficient flow of work, to control the quality and consistency of cataloguing and classification and to ensure that the staff involved are well trained and informed. The more suitable the cataloguing system is for the library concerned, the better will be the flow of work, which can be adjusted and improved as the librarian's experience of the system grows. The chief aids to controlling quality and consistency in the catalogues are authority files, filing rules and certain practical points with regard to classification. Staff training can be assisted by a good practice manual which, if kept up to date, can save the librarian's time in staff instruction and keep consistency in details of practice. It can also improve continuity when, as is often the case, the one person cataloguing and classifying the law library leaves and another takes over.

Authority files

An authority file has been defined by J. Hudson in 'Bibliographic record maintenance in the online environment' (*Information Technology and Libraries,* vol. 3, 1984, pp. 388–93) as a file which 'collects, records and maintains the authorized forms of headings to be used as access points and those headings which act as *see* and *see also* references to lead the user to the authorized heading'.

The amount of authority work done in law libraries

depends on the size and complexity of their catalogues. In those which are part of a general library it may be done by the central cataloguing section, while the smallest libraries may keep a simple card file of decisions taken. In general, the larger the collection, the more important are the authority files for keeping consistency in headings and avoiding cross-classification.

Any law library which uses cataloguing rules, classification scheme and subject headings list will find useful a master copy used as an authority, and annotated with major decisions such as which options or alternative rules are used, and any other decisions of principle. In addition separate files may be kept for decisions on individual headings and class numbers. Additional information may be included such as scope notes in subject files and notes on changes of names of jurisdictions in name files.

It should be decided what type of headings are to be included, for example, are all headings to be included, or just those which require cross-references? For a law library, all corporate bodies including names of jurisdictions and all uniform titles should be included, and all titles of monographic series if they are used as access points. Personal names could perhaps be limited to those requiring cross-references.

There are differences in authority file work in manual and in automated cataloguing systems. In manual systems the work is done both at the time of cataloguing and classification, and later if inconsistencies appear when filing new entries in the card or sheaf catalogues. Automated authority files vary in their operation. For example, they may provide a print-out of conflicting headings, or automatically change such headings in the catalogues. One very desirable feature is the capacity for 'global' changes, in which the authority file is linked to the bibliographic records, so that amending the authority file amends every record containing that heading. Some less sophisticated automated systems lack authority controls, and are unsuitable for all but the smallest catalogues. Authority control is particularly necessary in shared cataloguing systems where the records originate from a variety of sources.

Published authority files are available, notably the British

Library's *Name authority list* and the *Library of Congress authority file*. They are useful for checking headings but cannot provide an effective substitute for a local file in a specialist library.

Filing rules

There is no generally accepted system for filing catalogues in the British Isles. AACR2 does not include filing rules, though the rules for uniform titles do provide a filing arrangement under names of jurisdictions, which has been discussed above. Before deciding on a code of filing rules, some consideration should be given to the types of entry to be included in the catalogues. For instance, should names, both personal and corporate, used as subjects be included in the author–title catalogue or the subject headings catalogue? Some names used as subjects found in law library catalogues, for example names of Acts like:

> Great Britain
> Banking Act 1979

(used as a subject heading for a treatise on the Act) seem out of place in a subject headings catalogue and are probably best included in a name–title catalogue. Alternatively a dictionary catalogue combining name–title and subject heading catalogues is worth consideration, though the filing is more complex. Large law libraries may also wish to consider producing separate catalogues of primary material or journals, especially if their production can be facilitated by automated means.

Whatever the size of library, a code of filing rules should be used for both author–title and subject headings catalogues. The filing of classified catalogues is according to the notation of the classification scheme used. It is also vital to look at a catalogue, preferably of a law library, filed by each of the various codes, if a decision to begin a new catalogue or to improve the filing of an existing one, is made. The filing of entries under names of jurisdictions and other corporate bodies is particularly important.

Automated cataloguing systems dispense with the chore of

manual filing but may restrict the law librarian's ability to change unsuitable filing sequences. Some of the large co-operative cataloguing schemes have developed their own rules for machine filing, such as BLCMP and BLAISE LOCAS, and here there is no possibility of amending the filing to suit the individual library. It is worth mentioning the importance of accurate coding in preparing catalogue entries for machine filing, as inaccuracies can result in entries becoming irretrievably lost. It is probable that online catalogues will be easier to use as they depend less on the user having some knowledge of the filing system than do conventional card or microfiche catalogues.

Codes of filing rules published in recent years have been produced with machine filing in mind. These include the *ALA Filing Rules, Library of Congress Filing Rules,* and *BLAISE Filing Rules,* all published in 1980.

Practical classification
Determining the subject of the document

There is one golden rule that should be observed by all classifiers: never classify by title alone. Many authors and publishers take considerable care to ensure that the title of a book closely reflects the actual subject content, but others are less careful, and a few employ misleading or whimsical titles. But even meticulous authors tend to omit from their titles the name of the legal system about which they are writing, especially if it coincides with the political jurisdiction in which they live and work.

The classifier should analyse the total subject of the document by legal system (jurisdiction), legal topic(s), form of publication and any other relevant facets, such as period, special group of persons aimed at, etc., bearing in mind the construction of the classification scheme in use.

In addition to the information given on the title page, help in determining the subject can be obtained from the other parts of the book, notably the list of chapters, the preface, foreword or introduction, the concluding section, the major topics featured in the index, or even the publisher's blurb (though less reliance can be placed here than on the author's own statements). If the detailed legal topic of the book is clear, but its place in the field of legal literature is not known to the classifier, help can be found in legal dictionaries or the indexes to classification schemes. Valuable guidance can also be obtained from subject bibliographies. For current material, the *British National Bibliography* gives DDC numbers and the United States *National Union Catalog* gives both DDC and LC numbers. Cataloguing-in-publication data is useful as a guide but should not be relied upon absolutely as it is prepared prior to publication.

Assigning the class mark

The class mark, in the narrow sense of the total subject symbol, is found from the classification scheme in the manner described above. The classifier will need to make frequent reference to the index of the scheme his library uses, but it must be emphasized that books must never be classified solely on the basis of an index entry. It is vital that the classifier should turn to the schedules at the number or numbers suggested in the index and examine their total subject content before deciding on the final class mark.

Location symbols are needed to lead readers to any collections of books that are detached from the main sequence for any reason, such as short-loan collections, rare book collections and stacks containing superseded editions. These symbols are usually based on appropriate words for example RB for rare books. If symbols are required for alphabetical arrangement of authors, etc. within a single class mark, they can be simple abbreviations of the name, or they can be taken from a table of Cutter numbers.

Recataloguing

The need for recataloguing arises in varying circumstances, such as inadequate cataloguing in the past, or the decision to adopt a new cataloguing code. It may also arise from the adoption of an entirely new cataloguing system involving a change in the physical form of the catalogue.

For a very small law library, the improvement and amendment of a card catalogue by recataloguing may be worthwhile, but for libraries above that size, the expense of the labour involved would be prohibitive, even if only the headings were amended and the rest of the entries left untouched. Many recataloguing projects have arisen in recent years from the need to convert card catalogues to machine-readable form after a new computer-based catalogue has been started. Multiple catalogues are unsatisfactory for library users, and pose problems, especially with serial publications, in deciding whether or not to close the old catalogues completely. Also the problem of whether to provide links between old and new catalogues arises.

Retrospective cataloguing may be approached in a variety of ways, largely depending on the funding available for the project. It may be done by a commercial organization from a catalogue or shelf-list supplied by the library, or done in-house, or a mixture of the two. In either case ready-made records from databases may be utilized where they are available. These records vary in quality, and specialist law libraries may also find that they are not available for a proportion of their stock. It should be easier to control the quality of records resulting from an in-house operation, but it is likely to be slower than using a commercial service unless adequate extra staff can be employed.

The details of a retrospective cataloguing project need as much advance planning as the change to an automated system, and there is advice available in the professional journals. If there is not sufficient funding for a complete recataloguing, priorities should be established, such as whether primary sources or treatises or simply everything in the open access library should be recatalogued first. Even after conversion to current standards, further upgrading of records may be necessary in the future (AACR3?), but this should be less arduous for records in machine-readable form than the conversion of card catalogues.

Reclassification

Reclassification is generally undertaken for one of two reasons: the scheme in use may be judged inadequate and a better one adopted, or a new edition or revision of the scheme in use is published. In smaller law libraries, a high proportion of the active bookstock is serially published, and, even if they need reclassification, it should not be a major operation. That leaves a fairly small number of treatises to be reclassified. However in larger, and especially research, law libraries with reserves of older monographic material, the question of how much to reclassify will arise. Older books may not, for instance, fit easily into a new classification schedule. A possible arrangement for larger collections is to reclassify everything in the open access library but not the closed access stacks. The most used stock will then always be classified by an up to date scheme and the older stock may be shelved in an unclassified order but be accessible through the catalogues.

There are two main methods of effecting the physical rearrangement of the books and the catalogues. It is possible to assign new class marks to all books and records gradually, while leaving them in their original order until the reclassification is virtually completed. It is then probably advisable to close the library to readers so that the books can be rearranged in their new order. This method requires two class labels for each volume. Alternatively, it is possible to operate two parallel sequences, old and new. With either method, extra staff will have to be recruited to complete the reclassification in a reasonable time.

FURTHER READING

INTRODUCTION

Blunt, A. *Law librarianship*, 1980.
Foskett, A. C. *The subject approach to information*, 4th edn., 1982.
Hunter, E. J. and Bakewell, K. G. B. *Cataloguing* 2nd edn., 1983.
Moys, E. M. *A Classification scheme for law books*, [1st edn.] 1968 [out of print].
Piper, P. L. and Kwan, C.H. L. 'Cataloging and classification' in *Law librarianship: a handbook*, ed. H. P. Mueller *et al.*, vol. 1, 1983, Chapter 10.

CHOICE OF CATALOGUING SYSTEM

Centre for Catalogue Research *Introducing the on-line catalogue ...* , ed. A. Seal, 1984.
Favret, L. 'Some implications of on-line circulation for cataloguing', *Catalogue and Index*, no. 70, 1983, pp. 4–8.
Massil, S. W. 'Standards for sharing in bibliographic systems', *Catalogue and Index*, no. 65, 1982, pp. 1–6.
Seal, A. *et al*. *Full and Short Entry Catalogues: library needs and uses*, 1982.
also: Foskett, pp. 288–97; Piper and Kwan, pp. 366–73.

AACR2

Ayres, F. H. 'The code, the catalogue and the computer: an assessment of AACR2', *Vine*, no. 32, 1980, pp. 3–13.
British and Irish Association of Law Librarians 'AACR2 and legal materials', *Law Librarian*, vol. 12, 1981, pp. 56–60.
British and Irish Association of Law Librarians 'Memorandum to the Library Association Cataloguing Rules Committee on the revision of AACR, 1967', *Law Librarian*, vol. 5, 1974, pp. 9–13.
British and Irish Association of Law Librarians 'Supplementary memorandum on the revision of *AACR*, 1967', *Law Librarian*, vol. 7, 1976, pp. 7–9.
Enyingi, P. *et al*. *Cataloging legal literature: a manual on AACR2 and Library of Congress subject headings for legal materials, with illustrations*, 1984.

Glasson, T. 'New cataloguing rules for legal publications', *Australian Law Librarians' Group Newsletter*, no. 31, 1979, pp. 1–9.

Hu, S. S. 'The problems with AACR2 rules 21.32 and 21.34', *Canadian Association of Law Libraries Newsletter/Bulletin*, vol. 5, n.s., 1979–80, pp. 143–6.

'Implications of the AACR2 for law libraries: panel discussion', *Law Library Journal*, vol. 72, 1979, pp. 690–706.

Marion, P. C. 'Planning for a change: AACR2', *Law Library Journal*, vol. 71, 1978, pp. 673–80.

also: Hunter and Bakewell, Chapter 3; Piper and Kwan, pp. 331–48.

SUBJECT CATALOGUES

Chan, L. M. *Library of Congress subject headings: principles and application*, 1978.

'Legal subject headings', *Australian Law Librarians' Group Newsletter*, no. 55, 1983, pp. 2–3.

Miskin, C. 'The solicitors' law firm library', *Law Librarian*, vol. 9, 1978, p. 41.

Scott, A. 'Private law firms in the city', *Law Librarian*, vol. 9, 1978, pp. 3–4.

also: Enyingi, part 4; Foskett, Hunter and Bakewell, Chapter 4.

CHOICE OF CLASSIFICATION

Bakewell, K. G. B. 'Cataloguing and classification', in *British librarianship and information work, 1976–1980*, vol. 2, 1983, pp. 173–99.

Gilchrist, A. 'Classification and subject indexing', in *British librarianship and information science, 1971–75*, 1977, pp. 57–64.

Maltby, A. *Classification in the 1970's*, 1972.

Sayers' Manual of classification for librarians, 5th edn. by A. Maltby 1975.

also: Foskett.

CLASSIFICATION SCHEMES

Dewey Decimal Classification

Steiner, W. A. F. P. 'Dewey decimal classification: law' [book review], *Law Librarian*, vol. 4, 1973, pp. 14–15.

Sweeney, R. 'Dewey in Great Britain and Northern Ireland', *Catalogue and Index*, no. 76–77, 1984–5, pp. 1–7.
Trotter, R. 'The use of Dewey in BNB', *Catalogue and Index*, no. 41, 1976, pp. 3–6.
Vann, S. K. 'The Dewey decimal classification', in Maltby, A. *Classification in the 1970's*, pp. 87–122.

Universal Decimal Classification

Foskett, A. C. *Universal decimal classification*, 1973.
Lloyd, G. 'Universal decimal classification', in Maltby, A. *Classification in the 1970's* pp. 145–66.

Library of Congress Classification

Immroth, J. P. 'Library of Congress classification', in Maltby, A. *Classification in the 1970's*, pp. 123–44.
Library of Congress Classification, class K, subclass KF, Law of the United States: cumulative index, by L. D. Dershem, 1982–.
Library of Congress Classification, class K, subclass KF, law of the United States: cumulative schedule, by L. D. Dershem, 1984–.
Piper, P. L. and Kwan, C. H. *Manual on KF, the Library of Congress Classification for Law of the United States*, 1972.

Bliss Bibliographic Classification

Bliss Classification Bulletin, 1954–.
Maltby, A. and Gill, L. *The case for Bliss*, 1979.
Mills, J. 'The Bibliographic classification', in Maltby, A. *Classification in the 1970's*, pp. 25–50.

Moys Classification

Mills, J. [Review of 1st edn.] *Journal of Documentation*, vol. 24, 1968, pp. 317–19.

PRACTICAL CATALOGUING AND CLASSIFICATION

Ayres, F. H. 'It's not as easy as ABC', *Catalogue and Index*, no. 54, 1979, pp. 1–3, 8.

Hudson, J. 'Bibliographic record maintenance in the on-line environment', *Information Technology and Libraries*, vol. 3, 1984, pp. 388–93.

Jeffreys, A. 'Management in cataloguing services', *Catalogue and Index*, no. 46, 1977, pp. 2–4.

Ludy, L. E. and Rogers, S. A. 'Authority control in the on-line environment', *Information Technology and Libraries*, vol. 3, 1984, pp. 262–6.

Matthews, E. W. 'The making of a cataloging manual at Southern Illinois University', *Law Library Journal*, vol. 76, 1983, pp. 123–6.

Ralls, M. C. 'The evolution of a retroconversion', *Vine*, no. 58, 1985, pp. 31–8.

'Retrospective conversion: a look at some of the services available', *Vine*, no. 58, 1985, pp. 19–25.

'Retrospective conversion: how complete should it be?' *American Association of Law Libraries Newsletter*, vol. 16, 1984, pp. 112–13.

Thomas, C. M. 'Authority control in manual versus online catalogs', *Information Technology and Libraries*, vol. 3, 1984, pp. 393–8.

also: Hunter and Bakewell, Chapters 6 and 10.

Index of Works Cited

INTRODUCTION

This index is intended to include all works discussed in the text except when they are used as examples to demonstrate such matters as cataloguing rules. Bibliographic details for most items are those supplied by the contributors, although some have been amplified as a result of further research. In a few instances, the details given in the index are thought to be more up to date than those printed in the body of the text.

The choice of entry words does not follow any particular cataloguing code, such as AACR, because the practices followed in the many sources from which contributors obtained information vary enormously. As far as possible, different entries for the same work have been amalgamated and a reference has been made from the unused heading, if this seemed desirable. Subject to this, the most likely places to find required items are as follows:

Most serial publications, including legislation and law reports which are issued at fairly regular intervals, are entered under their titles. The older, nominate reports should be found under the name of the reporter(s) and series with titles such as *Annual Report* ... are entered under the body responsible for the work.

Monographs, pamphlets and articles are entered under the author(s), if known, but works produced under editorial direction may be found under either editor or title, according to the information supplied.

Government departments are given as sub-headings under

the name of the country concerned, e.g. Gt.Brit. Lord Chancellor's Department; U.S. Department of State. Non-government institutions with distinctive names are entered directly, e.g. Institute of Advanced Legal Studies; Squire Law Library. Organizations with non-distinctive names, e.g. 'Library', are entered as sub-headings of the parent body, e.g. Harvard University. Law School. Library.

All entries beginning either *Encyclopaedia of* . . ., or *Encyclopedia of* . . . have been interfiled, as the exact spelling is rarely well-known. Similarly, Mc, and Mac are interfiled. Occasionally, the computer may have produced slightly unusual results, especially where punctuation marks are included in entry words.

International Standard Book/Serial Numbers have been included where possible. To save space, the identifying abbreviations, ISBN or ISSN, have been omitted.

Annual Review of Information Science and Technology, 1966– . White Plains, NY, Knowledge Industry Publications. (US 0066–4200) 641

Annual Survey of Commonwealth Law, 1965–77. Oxford, Clarendon Press. 303

Annual Survey of South African Law, 1947– . Cape Town, Juta. (SA 0376–4605) 392, 533, 537

Annuario di Diritto Comparato e di Studi Legislativi, 1927– . Rome, Istituto de Studi Legislativi. (IT 0003–5149) 491

Antonov, V. V. *Sovetskoe zakonodatel'stvo: spravochnik-putevoditel' po osnovnyn izdaniim*. Moscow, Kniga, 1981. 575, 582, 583

Apollinaris, 1928– . Rome, Instituti Utriusque Iuris. 564

Arbeitsmaterialen zu einer Landesbibliographie Albanien, ed. A. Hetzer and V. S. Roman. Heft. IV: Recht. Bremen, Universitätsbibliothek, 1980. 590

Archbold, J. F. *Pleadings, evidence and practice in criminal cases*. 35th ed. Sweet & Maxwell, 1962. 42nd ed. Sweet & Maxwell, 1985. (0 421 32210 1) 190, 199

Armstrong, A. Industrial library news. *New Library World*, vol 76, 1975 p. 64. 216

Aslib. *Photocopying and copyright: supporting document to a draft rights owners and users joint code of photocopying practice for materials other than music*. Aslib, 1984. 673

Aslib Directory. Aslib, 1977–80. 2 vols. (0 85142 104 0, etc.) 376

Aslib Information, 1973– . Aslib. (UK 0305–0033) 696

Aspinall, A. The reporting and publishing of the House of Commons debates, 1771–1834. *In* Pares, R. and Taylor, A. J. P. *Essays presented to Sir Lewis Namier*. Macmillan, 1956. 292

Asser, T. M. C. *Handleiding tot de beoefening van het Nederlandsch burgerlijk recht*. Zwolle, Tjeenk Willink, 1934– . 6 parts in 16 vols. [Various editions] 502

Association International des Sciences Juridiques. Comité National Luxembourgeois. *Bibliographie du droit Luxembourgeois*. Luxembourg, Imprimerie de l'Etat, 1967. 506

Association of Law Teachers. *Directory of members*. Stevens. [Irregular] 373

Astbury, R. *Libraries and the book trade*. Bingley, 1968. (0 85157 009 7) 743

Atkin, J. R. *Encyclopaedia of court forms in civil proceedings*. 2nd ed. Butterworth, 1961. 42 vols. (0 406 01020 X) [undergoing continuous revision] 196, 366, 415

Atlantic Provinces Reports, 1975– . Fredericton, Maritime Law Book. 311

Atlantic Reporter, 1885–1938. St. Paul, Minn., West. 200 vols. 2nd series, 1938– . (*National Reporter System*) 334

Atlay, J. B. *The Victorian Chancellors*. Smith Elder, 1906. Repr. Wildy, 1972. 370

Audio-visual materials in law: a select list of programmes recommended for degree-level use. British Universities Film and Video Council, 1984. (0 901299 9) 209

Australia. Attorney General's Department. *The Australian Constitution annotated*. Canberra, Australian Government Publishing Service, 1980, repr. 1981. (0 642 02796 X) 306

Australian commentary on Halsbury's Laws of England (Fourth edition) Sydney, Butterworths, 1974– . 6 vols. Looseleaf. 301

Australian Current Law, 1963– . Sydney, Butterworths. (AT 0045–0405) 308, 392

Australian Digest. 2nd ed. Sydney, Law Book Company of Australasia, 1963– . 38 vols. Supplements [various, 25 vols to date] (AT 0067–1843) 308, 395

Australian Law Journal, 1927/28– . Sydney, Law Book Company of Australasia. (AT 0004–9611) 308

Australian Law Journal Reports, 1958– . Sydney, Law Book Company of Australasia. (AT 0004–9611) 308

Australian Law Librarians' Group Newsletter, 1973– . St. Pauls, NSW ALLG. (AT 0311–5984) 322, 398, 747

Australian Law Reform Commission. *Law reform digest, 1910–80.* Sydney, Law Reform Commission of Australia, 1983. (0 644 01628 0) 395

Australian Law Reports, 1973– Sydney, Butterworths. (AT 0310–0014) 307, 308

Australian Legal Directory, 1977– . Melbourne, Law Council of Australia. (AT 0155–297 X) 396

Australian Legal Monthly Digest, 1947/48– . Sydney, Law Book Company of Australasia. (AT 0004–0046) 308

Australian National Bibliography, 1936– . Canberra, National Library of Australia. [1936–60 entitled *Annual Catalogue of Australian publications*] 391

Axele-Lute, P. Legal citation form: theory and practice. *Law Library Journal,* vol. 75, 1982, pp. 148–56. 185

Ayres, F. H. The code, the catalogue and the computer: an assessment of AACR2. *Vine,* no. 32, 1980, pp. 3–13. 797

Ayres, F. H. It's not as easy as ABC. *Catalogue and Index,* no. 54, 1979, pp. 1–3, 8. 800

Azzam, I. The law in the Near and Middle East: basic sources in English. *Law Libary Journal,* vol. 57, 1964, pp. 234–40. 562, 569

Backe, T. [and others]. *Concise Swedish-English glossary of legal terms.* Lund, Gleerup; South Hackensack, NJ, Rothman, 1973. (91 40 02754 6); (0 8377 0305 0) 509

Bacon, M. *New abridgment of the law,* 1736–66.. n.p. 5 vols. 270

Baeck, P. L. *The general civil code of*

Austria. Dobbs Ferry, NY, Oceana for Parker School of Foreign and Comparative Law, 1972. (0 379 00025 3) 504

Baillie, N. B. F. *A digest of Moohammadan law.* Lahore, Premier Book House, 1869–75. Repr. New York, Orientalia, 1965. 2 vols. 558

Baker, J. H. *English legal manuscripts.* Zug, Inter Documentation Co. A.G., 1975– . (3 85750 009 3, etc.). [In progress.] 282

Baker, J. H. *An introduction to English legal history.* 2nd ed. Butterworths, 1971. (0 406 55500 1) 70

Baker, J. H. *Manual of Law French.* Letchworth, Avebury Publication Co., 1979. (0 86127 401 6) 251, 291, 365

Baker, J. H. *The order of sarjeants at law.* Selden Society, 1984. (Selden Society, supplementary series, 5) 283

Baker, J. H. Sources of English legal history. *Law Librarian,* vol. 11, 1980, pp. 6–8. 290

Baker, J. H. Unprinted sources of English legal history. *Law Library Journal,* vol. 64, 1971, pp.

Bakewell, K. G. B. Cataloguing and classification. In *British Librarianship and information work, 1976–1980.* Library Association, 1983. Vol. 2 pp. 173–99. 798

Balfour, Sir J. *Practicks: or a system of the more ancient laws of Scotland.* Edinburgh, n.p., 1754. 171, 278

Ball, F. *The judges in Ireland 1221–1921.* New York, Dutton, 1927. 2 vols. 385

Ball, J. *Bibliography of material on Indonesian law in the English language.* 3rd ed. Chatswood, NSW, Oughtershaw Press, 1981. 536

Ball, J. *Indonesian legal history, 1602–1848.* Chatswood, NSW, Oughtershaw Press, 1982. 531

Ball, J. T. *Historical review of the legislative system operative in Ireland, 1172–1800.* 3rd ed. Longman Green, 1891. 290

Ballantyne, G. H. *The Signet Library, Edinburgh, and its librarians, 1722–1972.* Edinburgh, Scottish Library Association, 1979. (*Scottish library studies*, 6) (o 900649 18 6) 34

Banking world, 1880– . Waterlow. (UK 0737–6413) [1880–1982 entitled *Journal of the Institute of Bankers*] 140

Banks, M. A. *Using a law library: a guide for students and lawyers in the common law provinces of Canada.* 4th ed. Toronto, Carswell, 1985. (o 459 37610 1) 302, 312, 322, 345, 390

Banks, P. N. *A selective bibliography on the conservation of research library materials.* Chicago, Ill., Newberry Library, 1981. (o 911028 26 9) 744

Bar list of the UK *see Solicitors' and Barristers' Directory and Diary*

Barclay, J. B. The Society's library. *In The S.S.C. story, 1784–1984.* Edinburgh, Edina Press, 1984, pp. 108–24. 34

Barden, P. The transmission of interlibrary loan requests ... British Library Lending Division. *Interlending Review*, vol. 10, 1982, pp. 92–6. 673

Barker, N. J. Conservation 1983. *Law Librarian*, vol. 14, 1983, pp. 39–43. 744

Barnes, P. M. *Microfiling and the archivist.* Public Record Office, 1973 [Privately printed for limited circulation] 743

Bartholomew, G. W. Sources and literature of Singapore law. *Lawasia* (N.S.) vol. 2, 1982–83, pp. 1–49. 317, 323, 390

Basdevant, J. *Dictionnaire de la terminologie du droit international.* Paris, Sirey, 1960. 469

Basic documents on the Soviet legal system, trans. and ed. by W. E. Butler. New York, Oceana, 1983. (o 379 20833 4) 578

Basic laws on the structure of the Soviet state, trans. and ed. H. J. Berman and J. B. Quigley, Jr. Cambridge, Mass., Harvard UP, 1969. 578

Basilicorum libri LX: series A, textus librorum I–LIX, ed. H. J. Scheltema

& N. van der Wal. The Hague, Nijhoff [etc.], 1955–7. 7 vols. (90 01 77916, etc.) 517

Basnage, H. *La coutume réformée du paiis et duché de Normandie.* Rouen, Lucas, 1678–81. 2 vols. 281

Basu, D. D. *Commentaries on the constitution of India.* 6th ed. Calcutta Sarkar, 1973– . [In progress.] 314

Bates, T. The drafting of European Community legislation. *Statute Law Review*, 1983, pp. 24–34. 412, 435

Baynes-Cope, A. D. *Caring for books and documents.* British Museum, 1981 (o 7141 2006 5) 744

Beale, J. H. *A bibliography of early English law books.* Cambridge, Mass., Harvard UP, 1926. Repr. Buffalo, NY, Dennis, 1966. (o 89941 351 X) 350

Beale, J. H. The early English statutes. *Harvard Law Review*, vol. 35, 1922, pp. 519–38. 292

Beaton, J. A. *Scots law terms and expressions.* Edinburgh, Green, 1982. (o 414 00691 7) 379

Bedford, S. *The best we can do* [trial of J. Bodkin Adams]. Collins, 1958. 185

Bedo, A. K. and Torzsay-Biber, G. *Legal sources and bibliography of Hungary.* New York, Praeger, 1956. 591

Belfast Gazette, 1921– . Belfast, HMSO. 117, 230, 241

Bell, R. *Cases decided in the Court of Session, 1790–5.* Edinburgh, J. Dickson, 1794–6. 2 vols. 169, 172

Bell, R. *Dictionary and digest of the law of Scotland.* 7th ed. Edinburgh, Bell and Bradfute, 1890. 379

Bell, Sir S. S. *Compendium of decisions of the Court of Session from 1808–33.* Edinburgh, Black, 1841–2. 2 vols. 172

Bellot, H. H. Parliamentary printing, 1660–1837. *Bulletin of the Institute of Historical Research*, vol. 11, 1933–4, pp. 85–98. 238

Beltramo, M. and Longo, G. E. *The Italian civil code.* Dobbs Ferry, NY, Oceana, 1969. Supplement

1969–1978. 1978. (o 379 20292 1) 504

Bennion, F. A. R. *Consumer credit control.* Longman Professional, 1976–. 3 vols. Looseleaf. (o 85120 239 X) [Contains *Consumer Credit Law Reports*] 134

Bennion, F. A. R. *Statute law.* 7th ed. Oyez Longman, 1983. (o 85120 802 9) 122

Berault, J. *Coutsume réformée du pays et duché de Normandie.* 2nd ed. Rouen, Du Petit-Val, 1614. 280

Berger, A. *Encyclopedic dictionary of Roman law.* Philadelphia, Pa., American Philosophical Society, 1953. (*Transactions of the ... Society,* n.s., vol. 43, pt. 2) 520, 523, 524

Berman, H. J. *Justice in Russia.* Cambridge, Mass., Harvard UP, 1950. 579

Berman, H. J. *Justice in the USSR: an interpretation of Soviet law.* Rev. ed. Cambridge, Mass., Harvard UP, 1963. 579, 582

Berner Kommentar: Kommentar zum schweizerischen Privatrecht. Bern, Stampfli, 1926–. [8 vols. in about 40; various editions] 502

Beseler, D. von and Jacobs, B. *Law dictionary: technical dictionary of the Anglo-American legal terminology.* 3rd ed. Berlin De Gruyter, 1971–76. 2 vols. (3 11 002187 0, etc.) 508

Bibliographic Guide to Law, 1969–. Boston, Mass., G. K. Hall. (US 0360–2745) [1969–75 entitled *Law Book Guide*] 349, 463, 771

A Bibliographical guide to the law of the United Kingdom, the Channel Islands and the Isle of Man. 2nd ed. Institute of Advanced Legal Studies, 1973. (o 901190 14 4) 119, 345, 377, 382, 383, 387, 388

Bibliographie 1975–. Paris, Centre de Documentation des Droits Antiques. 523

Bibliographie juridique roumaine, 1944–1968, ed. T. Ionascu. Bucharest, Academie de la R.S.R., 1969. 591

Bibliography of British history to 1485 ... 1485–1603 ... 1603–1714 ...

1714–89 ... [Various editors, eds. and dates, repr.] Hassocks, Harvester Press. (o 85527 136 1) 287, 289

Bibliography of Czech legal literature, 1945–58. Prague, Publishing House of the Czechoslovak Academy of Sciences, 1959. 591

Bibliography of Hungarian legal literature, 1945–65, ed. L. Nagy. Budapest, Academiai Kiado, 1966. 591

Bibliography of translations of codes and other laws of private law. 2nd ed. Morgan-Grampian for the Council of Europe, 1975. (o 900865 45 8) 504

Bibliography on foreign and comparative law books and articles in English. 1955–. Dobbs Ferry, NY, Oceana. (US 0067–4329) 428, 491, 506, 537, 561, 563, 569, 578, 585,

Biblioteki SSSR: spravchnik: biblioteki RSFSR. Moscow, Kniga, 1974. 590

Biblioteki SSSR: spravchnik: biblioteki soiuznykh respublik (bez RSFSR). Moscow, Kniga, 1973. 590

Bieber, D. M. *Dictionary of legal abbreviations used in American law books.* 2nd ed. Buffalo, NY, Hein, 1985. (o 89941 347 1) 395

Binchy, D. A. *Corpus Iuris Hibernici ad fidem codicum manuscriptorum recognovit.* n.p., Instituid Ard-Leinn Bhaile Atha Cliath, 1978. 6 vols. 279

Bing, J. *Handbook of legal information retrieval.* Amsterdam, Elsevier Science Publishers, 1984. (o 444 87576 X) 186, 344, 389

Biography Index, 1946–. New York, H. W. Wilson. (US 0006–3053) 369

Birchfield, M. E. *The complete reference guide to United Nations sales publications, 1968–78.* Berlin, De Gruyter, 1982. 486

Birchfield, M. E. *Consolidated catalog of League of Nations publications for sale.* Dobbs Ferry, NY, Oceana, 1976. (o 379 00328 7). 485

Birkenhead, F. E. Smith, 1st Earl. *Judgments, 1919–22.* HMSO, 1923. 140

Birmingham Libraries Co-operative Mechanisation Project. *Code of filing rules*. Birmingham, BLCMP, 1971. (0 903154 00 5) 793

Bishop, O. G. *Canadian official publications*. Oxford, Pergamon Press, 1981. (*Guides to official publications*, no. 9) (0 08 024697 4) 323

Biulleten' normativnykh aktov ministerstv i vedomstv SSR, 1972– . Moscow, Iuridicheskaia Literatura. 574, 575

Black, H. C. *Black's law dictionary*. 5th ed. St. Paul, Minn., West, 1979. 395

Black, W. G. and Christie, J. R. *The parochial ecclesiastical law of Scotland*. 4th ed. Edinburgh, Hodge, 1928. 551

Blackstone, Sir W. *Commentaries on the laws of England*. Oxford, Clarendon Press, 1765–9. 4 vols. 19, 189, 287, 324

Blackstone, Sir W. *Magna charta and charta de foresta*. Oxford, Clarendon Press, 1759. 265

Blackstone, Sir W. *Reports of cases determined in the several courts of Westminster Hall, 1746–1779*. 2nd ed. London, n.p., 1828. 2 vols. 274

Blackwood's Acts [of Scotland, 1707– 1946] Edinburgh, Blackwood, 1876–1947. 93 vols. 113

Blagojevic, B. T. *Bibliographie du droit yougoslave, 1945–1967*. 2nd ed. Paris, The Hague, Mouton, 1970. 591

Blaustein, A. P. and Flanz, G. H. *Constitutions of the countries of the world*. Dobbs Ferry, NY, Oceana, 1971– . 18 vols. Looseleaf. (0 379 00467 4, etc.) 298, 494

Bleich, J. D. *Judaism and healing: Halakhic perspectives*. New York, Ktav, 1981. (0 686 73601 X) 554

Blerk, A. van. The growth of South African legal literature. *De Rebus Procuratorius*, 1977, pp. 561–78. 537

Blerk, A. van. The SA attorneys' contribution to SA legal literature. *De Rebus Procuratorius*, 1983, pp. 181–8. 537

Bliss bibliographic classification. 2nd ed. Butterworths, 1977– . [In progress.] 785

Bliss Classification Bulletin, 1954– . Bliss Classification Association. 786, 799

Bloomfield, B. C. *Acquisition and provision of foreign books by national and university libraries in the United Kingdom*, Mansell, 1972. (0 7201 0299 5) 743

Blount, T. *Nomo-lexikon: a law dictionary*. Thomas Newcomb for John Martin and Henry Hemingman, 1670. 361

Bluett, J. C. *Advocate's notebook, being notes and minutes of cases heard before the judicial tribunals of the Isle of Man*. Douglas, Johnson, 1847. 181

Blunt, A. *Law librarianship*. Bingley, 1980. (*Outlines of modern librarianship*) (0 85157 299 5) 34, 345, 377, 382, 640, 747, 797

Board of Trade Journal *see* British Business

Boase, F. *Modern English biography 1851–1900*. Truro, Netherton and Worth, 1892–1921. Repr. Cass, 1965. 6 vols. (0 7146 2118 8, etc.) 368

Bohmer, A. [and others]. *Legal sources and bibliography of Czechoslovakia*. New York, Praeger, 1959. 591

Boletín de Legislación Extranjera, 1910– . Madrid, Cortes Espanolas. 493

Boletín Mexicano de Derecho Comparado, 1948– . Mexico City, Universidad Nacional Autonoma de Mexico, Instituto de Investigaciones Juridicas. (MX 0041–8633) 491

Bolland, W. C. *Manual of year book studies*. Cambridge UP, 1925. (*Cambridge studies in English legal history*) 292

Bolland, W. C. *The year books*. Cambridge UP, 1921. 292

Bol'shoi anglo-russkii slovar', pod obshchim rukovodstvom I.R. Gal'perina. Moscow, Sovetskaia Entsikloopediia, 1972. 2 vols. Supplement, 1980. 588

British Library. Lending Division. *Current serials received*, 1975–. Boston Spa, BLLD. (UK 0309–0655) 665

British Library. Lending Division. *Users' handbook*, United Kingdom. 4th ed. Boston Spa, BLLD, 1983. 665

British Library. Working Party on Provision for Law. *Report.* The Library, 1983. (o 7123 4105 6) 5, 34, 663

British Library. Working Party on Union Catalogues. *Report.* The Library, 1982. (o 7123 2007 5) 666

British National Bibliography, 1950– . British Library, Bibliographic Services Division. (UK 0007–1544) 222, 248, 343, 347, 548, 561, 717, 794

British Paperbacks in Print, 1960– . Whitaker. (UK 0262–9763) 717

British Standards Institution. *Recommendations for the processing and storage of silver-gelatin-type microfilm.* BSI, 1975. (BS 1153:1975) 743

British Standards Institution. *Recommendations for repair and allied processes for the conservation of documents.* BSI, 1973–80. (BS 4971:1973–80) 2 parts. 744

British Standards Institution. *Recommendations for the storage and exhibition of archival documents.* BSI, 1977. (BS 5454:1977) 735, 744

British Standards Institution. *Specification for portable fire extinguishers.* BSI, 1980. (BS 5423:1980) 744

British Union Catalogue of Periodicals see Serials in the British Library

British Yearbook of International Law, 1920– . Oxford UP. (UK 0068–2691) 455, 460, 491

Brooke, Sir R. *La graunde abridgment.* Tottell, 1573. 2 vols. 284

Broom, H. *A selection of legal maxims.* 10th ed. Sweet & Maxwell, 1939. Repr. 1971. (o 421 16050 0) 365

Brown, L. N. and Garner, J. F. *French administrative law.* 3rd ed. Butterworths, 1983. (o 406 56152 4) 489–90

Brown, L. N. and Jacob, F. G. *The Court of Justice of the European Communities.* 2nd ed. Sweet & Maxwell, 1983. (*Modern legal studies*) (o 421 31400 1) 415, 435

Brown, M. P. *General synopsis of the decisions of the Court of Session including House of Lords appeals, 1540–1827.* Edinburgh, Tait, 1827–9. 4 vols. 171

Browndorf, E. and Rienaer, S. *Bibliography of multinational corporations law … and foreign and direct investment.* Dobbs Ferry, NY, Oceana, 1980. 2 vols. (o 379 20372 3) 466

Brownlie, I. *Principles of public international law.* 3rd ed. Oxford, Clarendon Press, 1979. (o 19 876066 3) 454

Brunker, T. *Digest of cases superior and other courts of common law and admiralty from Sir J. Davies' reports to the present time.* Dublin, Hodges & Smith, 1865. 179

Bruns, C. G. *Fontes iuris romani antiqui.* 7th ed. by T. Mommsen and B. Gradenwitz. Tubingen, Mohr, 1909–12. 2 vols. 513

Brunton, G. and Haig, D. *An historical account of the Senators of the College of Justice, from its institution in 1532.* Edinburgh, Stillie, 1849. 380

Bryson, W. H. *Dictionary of sigla and abbreviations to and in law books before 1607.* Charlotteville, Va., UP of Virginia, 1975 (8139 0615 6) 287

Buckland, C. E. *Dictionary of Indian biography.* Sonnenschein, 1906. Repr. New York, Greenwood, 1969. (o 8183 0277 7) 567

Buckland, W. W. *A textbook of Roman law from Augustus to Justinian* 3rd ed. by P. Stein. Cambridge UP, 1966. 518

Building Law Reports, 1976– . George Godwin. (o 7114 3206 6) 134, 135

Bull, G. E. Education of law librarians in the U.K. *International Journal of Law Libraries*, vol. 4, 1976, pp. 3–18. 641

Bull, G. E. Legal research education in the U.K. *International Journal of*

Law Libraries, vol. 6, 1978, pp. 237–61. 643

Bull, G. E. Technical developments in legal information retrieval: a guide for BIALL members. *Law Librarian*, vol. 11, 1980, pp. 34–40. 691

Bulletin Bibliographique de Jurisprudence Communitaire, 1965– . Luxembourg, Court of Justice. [1965–76 entitled *Bibliographie de Jurisprudence Européenne*] 433

Bulletin des Arrêts de la Cour de Cassation, 1804– . Paris. [Two series: Chambre Criminelle and Chambres Civiles] 499

Bulletin Legislatif Dalloz, 1918– . Paris, Dalloz. 498

Bulletin of Legal Developments, 1966– . British Institute of International and Comparative Law. (UK 0007–4969) 459, 494

Bulletin of Northern Ireland Law, 1981– . Belfast, SLS Legal Publications. (UK 0260–6550) 116, 117, 214

Bulletin of the European Communities [Commission], 1968– . Luxembourg, Office for Official Publications. (EI 0067–5116) 424, 426

Bulletin of the International Association of Law Libraries see International Journal of Legal Information

Bulletin of the School of Oriental and African Studies, 1917– . The School. (UK 0041–977 X) 556, 560, 561

Bulletino dell'Istituto di Diritto Romano 'Vittorio Scialoja', 1888– . Milan, Giuffre. 519

Bundesgesetzblatt, 1949– . Bonn, Bundesanzeiger-Verlag. 446, 498

Burge, W. *Commentaries on colonial and foreign laws*. New ed. Sweet & Maxwell, 1907. 5 vols. 531

Burke, O. J. *The history of the Lord Chancellors of Ireland from A.D. 1186 to A.D. 1874*. Dublin, Ponsonby, 1879. 385

Burnett, J. F. R. *The elements of conveyancing*. 8th ed. Sweet & Maxwell, 1952. 191

Burrow, Sir J. *Reports of cases ... King's Bench, 1756–72*. Worrell & Tovey, 1766–80. 5 vols. 136

Burrow, R. Law reporting. *Law Quarterly Review*, vol. 58, 1942, pp. 96–106. 186

Burton, P. *Cases with the opinions of eminent counsel [1700–75]*. E. & R. Brocke, 1791. 2 vols. 140

Burton, P. F. *Microcomputer applications in academic libraries*. Boston Spa, British Library Lending Division, 1983. (*LIR report* no. 16) (0 7123 3021 6) 743

Burton, P. F. and Petrie, J. H. *Introducing micros: a guide for librarians*. Van Nostrand Reinhold, 1984. (0 442 305999 0) 673

Busha, C. H. and Harter, S. P. *Research methods in librarianship*. New York, Academic Press, 1980. (*Library and information science*) (0 12 147550 6) 643

Business Law Brief, 1972– . Financial Times Business Information. [1972–83 entitled *European Law Letter*] 134, 417

Butcher, D. *Official publications: an outline of modern librarianship*. Bingley, 1982. (0 85157 351 7) 121, 223, 238

Butler, W. E. *The Mongolian legal system: contemporary legislation and documentation*. The Hague, Nijhoff, 1982. (90 247 2685 9) 573

Butler, W. E. *Russian and Soviet law: an annotated catalogue of reference works, legislation, court reports, serials and monographs ...* Zug, Inter Documentation Company, 1976. (3 85750 012 3) 585

Butler, W. E. *A source book on socialist international organizations*. Leiden, Sijthoff, 1980. (90 286 0798 6) 486

Butler, W. E. *Soviet law*. Butterworths, 1983. (0 406 56260 1) 573, 574, 575, 579, 585, 590

Butler, W. E. and Nathanson, A. J. *Mongolian-English-Russian dictionary of legal terms and concepts*. The Hague, Nijhoff, 1983. 588

Butterworths Annotated Legislation Service, 1947– . Butterworths. 89

Butterworths annotations to the New Zealand Statutes. 2nd ed. Wellington, Butterworths, 1982– . 3 vols.

Constitutions of the USSR and the union republics, ed. F. J. M. Feldbrugge. Alphen aan den Rijn, Sijthoff and Noordhoff, 1979. (90 286 0489 8) 572

Consultatien advysen en advertissementen gegeven ende geschreven by verscheyden treffelijke rechts-geleerden in Holland. Rotterdam, Naeranus, 1647–89. [Also known as *Hollandsche consultatien*] 528, 532

Consumer Credit Law Reports see Bennion, F. *Consumer credit control.*

Continental legal history series. Boston, Mass., Little, Brown, 1912–28. 490

Conveyancer and Property Lawyer, n.s. 1936– . Sweet & Maxwell. (UK 0010–8200) 197

Cooper, A. *Financial aspects of library and information services: a bibliography.* Loughborough, CLAIM, 1980. (0 904924 23 8) 640

Cooper, B. D. Anglo-American legal citations. *Law Library Journal*, vol. 75, 1982, pp. 1–35. 185, 397

Cooper, J. University library committees. *Journal of Librarianship*, vol. 17, 1985, pp. 167–84. 640

Cooper, T. M., Lord Cooper. Early Scottish statutes revisited. *Juridical Review*, vol. 64, 1952, pp. 197–203. 276

Copyright Bulletin, 1967– . Paris, Unesco. (FR 0010–8634) 481

Copyright Laws and Treaties of the World, 1956– . Paris, Unesco. (UN 0069–9969) 481

Coriden, J. A. [and others]. *The code of canon law: a text and commentary.* Chapman, 1985. (0 225 66424 0) 543–4, 568

Cornish, W. R. *The jury.* Allen Lane, 1968. (0 7139 0076 8) 71

Coroners handbook [Isle of Man] 237

Corpus iuris canonici, ed. E. Friedberg. Graz. Akademische Druck– und Verlagsanstalt, 1955. 2 vols. 544, 545

Corpus iuris civilis, ed. P. Krueger, T. Mommsen, R. Schoell and G. Kroll. Berlin, Weidmann, 1954. 3 vols. [various editions]. 514

Corpus Juris Secundum, 1936– . St. Paul, Minn., West. [Supplements and replacement volumes]. 328, 337–8, 395

Costing and the economics of library and information services, ed. S. A. Roberts. Aslib, 1984. (*Aslib reader series*, vol. 5) (0 85142 176 8) 640

Cotran, E. African law. *In International encyclopedia of comparative law.* Tubingen, Mohr [etc.], 1972– . Vol. 2, pp. 157–68. 322

Coulson, N. J. *Commercial law in the Gulf States.* Graham and Trotman, 1984. (0 86010 574 1) 559, 569

Coulson, N. J. *A history of Islamic law.* Edinburgh: UP, 1964. (0 85224I 11 9) 560, 569

Council of Europe. *Catalogue of publications.* Strasbourg, The Council. [Annual] 485

County and Municipal Record, 1903– . Glasgow. 168

County Court Practice, 1945– . Butterworth. Annual. 199

Court of Appeal (Civil Division). *Cases on Appeal*, 1951– . [Transcripts of unreported cases, lodged in the Supreme Court Library, London] 142

Court of Appeal (Criminal Division). *Cases on Appeal*, 1951– . [Transcripts of unreported cases, lodged in the Supreme Court Library, London] 142

Court records – review, preservation, storage and access: panel ... *Law Library Journal*, vol. 73, 1980, pp. 997–1013. 744

Coutume réformée de Normandie. [c. 1585] 49, 280

Cowan, S. *The Lord Chancellors of Scotland, from the institution of the office to the Treaty of Union.* Edinburgh, Johnstone, 1911. 2 vols. 380

Cowell, J. *The interpreter.* Cambridge, John Legate, 1607. Repr. Menston, Scolar Press, 1972. (0 85417 647 0) 361, 565

Cowley, J. *Personnel management in libraries.* Bingley, 1982. (0 85157 324 X) 642

Cowley, J. D. *Bibliography of abridgements, digests, indexes and dictionaries of English law to the year 1800.* Quaritch, 1979. (0 91200415 0) 350

Cox, J. T. *Practice and procedure in the Church of Scotland.* 6th ed. Edinburgh, Church of Scotland committee on General Administration, 1976. (0 7152 0326 6) 550, 568

Cox's Criminal Cases, 1843–1948. Butterworth. 31 vols. 133

Crabb, J. H. *The constitution of Belgium and the Belgian civil code as amended to September 1, 1982.* South Hackensack, NJ, Rothman, 1982. (0 8377 0438 3) 504

Crabb, J. H. *The French civil code (as amended to July 1, 1976).* South Hackensack, NJ, Rothman, 1977. (0 8377 0531 2) 504

Craies, W. F. *Craies on statute law.* 7th ed. Sweet & Maxwell, 1971. (0 421 14510 2) 92, 95, 122

Craig, T. *Jus federale, tribus libris comprehensum; quibus non solum consuetudines feudales et praediorum jura, quae in Scotia, Anglia, et plerisque Galliae locis obtinent continentur sed universum jus Scoticum* ... Edinburgh, n.p., 1655. 288

Creifelds, C. *Rechtswörterbuch.* 7th ed. Munich, Beck, 1983. (3 406 09409 0) 507

Cremades, B. M. *Spanish business law.* Deventer, Kluwer, 1985. (90 6544 220 0) 505

Criminal Appeal Reports, 1908– . Sweet & Maxwell. (UK 0070–1521) 133, 134, 158

Criminal Appeal Reports (sentencing), 1979– . Sweet & Maxwell. (UK 0144–3321) 133, 134

Criminal Injuries Compensation Board [Press releases and summaries of cases], 1964– . The Board. 151

Criminal Justice Abstracts, 1968– . Monsey, NY, Willow Tree Press. (US 0146–9177) 356

Criminal Justice Periodical Index, 1975– . Ann Arbor, Mich., University Microfilms International. (US 0145–5818) 696

Criminal Law Review, 1954– . Sweet & Maxwell. (UK 0011–135X) 128, 140

Criminal Statistics, England and Wales, 1857– . HMSO. Annual. 230, 233

Criminal Statistics, England and Wales: supplementary tables, 1980– . Home Office. Annual. 230, 233

Criminal Statistics, Scotland, 1925– . Edinburgh, HMSO. Annual. 236

Cripps, C. A. *Compulsory acquisition of land.* 10th ed. Stevens, 1950. 143

Cripps, H. W. *A practical treatise on the law relating to the church and clergy.* 8th ed. Sweet & Maxwell, 1937. 547

Crockford's Clerical Directory, 1860– 1980/82. Cox. 567

Crook, J. A. *Law and life of Rome.* Thames and Hudson, 1967. (*Aspects of Greek and Roman life*) 518

Crum, N. J. The librarian-customer relationship: dynamics of filling requests for information. *Special Libraries,* vol. 60, 1969, pp. 269– 77. 710

Cubbon, W. *A bibliographical account of works relating to the Isle of Man.* Oxford UP for Manx Museum & Ancient Monuments Trustees, 1933. 2 vols. 387

Cumming, Sir J. *Contribution towards a bibliography dealing with crime and cognate subjects.* 3rd ed. Privately printed, 1935. 185

Cumulative Book Index, 1898– . New York, H. W. Wilson. (US 0011– 300X) 347, 391, 717

Cunha, G. M. Preservation and conservation of legal materials. *Law Library Journal,* vol. 69, 1976, pp. 300–02. 744

Cunha, G. M. and Cunha, D. G. *Library and archives conservation: 1980's and beyond.* Scarecrow Press, Bailey Bros, 1983. 2 vols. (0 8108 1587 7 and 0 8108 0604 0) 745

Cunningham, T. A. *A new and complete law dictionary.* King's Printer, 1764–5. 2 vols. 361

Current Australian and New Zealand

Legal Literature, 1973– . Sydney, Law Book Company. (AT 0310–5415) 392, 394

Current Digest of the Soviet Press, 1949– . Columbus, Ohio, American Association for the Advancement of Slavic Studies. (US 0011–3425) 577, 588

Current Law, 1947– . Sweet & Maxwell. (UK 0011–362X) 80, 102, 104, 117, 128, 143, 150, 159, 161, 162, 164, 173, 180, 206, 215, 349, 356, 365, 383, 392, 717

Current Law Citator, 1947– . Sweet & Maxwell. 161, 162, 163, 174, 180

Current Law consolidation, 1947–51. Sweet & Maxwell. 159, 163

Current Law Index, 1980– . Belmont, Calif., Information Access Co. (US 0 196–1780) 355, 394, 467, 537, 564

Current Law Legislation Citator, 1972–1985. Sweet & Maxwell, 1986 (0 421 36270 7) 88

Current Law Statutes Annotated, 1948– . Sweet & Maxwell. 88, 114

Current Law Statutes Citator, 1947–1971. Sweet & Maxwell. (0 421 19730 7) 88

Current Law Yearbook, 1947– . Sweet & Maxwell. (UK 0011–362X) 159, 163, 173, 349, 356

Current Publications in Legal and Related Fields, 1953– . Littleton, Colo., Rothman. (US 0011–3859) 393

Current Research in Britain, Social Sciences, 1985– . Boston Spa, BLLD. (UK 1267–1972) 208

Current Research in Library and Information Science, 1974– . Library Association. (UK 0263–9254) [1974– entitled *Radials Bulletin*] 639

Customs and Excise Tariff of Ireland, 1963– . Dublin, SO. 246

D'Ewes, S. *Compleat Journal of the votes, speeches and debates, both of the House of Lords and House of Commons throughout the whole reign of Queen Elizabeth,* n.p. 1682. 258

Dahlmanns, G. J. European Communities law: a selective bibliography . . . part two: secondary sources, monographic literature. *International Journal of Law Libraries,* vol. 3, 1975, pp. 215–72. 428, 434

Dahlmanns, G. J. Serving legal information: twenty-five years of IALL. *In Courts, law libraries and legal information in a changing society.* Freiburg, n.p., 1984, pp. 4–23. 35

Daily List of Government Publications from Her Majesty's Stationery Office. HMSO. (UK 0263–743X) 116, 220, 426, 486, 717

Daily Universal Register, 1785–7. n.p. [Afterwards *The Times*] 259

Daintree, D. *The legal periodical: a study in the communication of information.* MA thesis for the University of Sheffield, 1975. 216

Dale, C. W. M. and Lehmann, R. C. *Digest of cases overruled, not followed disapproved* [etc.], 1756–1886. Stevens, 1887. 160

Dale, Sir W. *The law of the parish church.* 5th ed. Butterworths, 1975. (0 406 17401 6) 546, 568

Dale, Sir W. *The modern Commonwealth.* Butterworths, 1983. (*Commonwealth Law Series*) (0 406 17404 0) 294, 298, 300, 321

Dalrymple, A. W. and Gibb, A. D. *A dictionary of words and phrases judicially defined and commented on by the Scottish supreme courts.* Edinburgh, Green, 1946. 379

Dane, J. and Thomas, P. A. *How to use a law library.* Sweet & Maxwell, 1979. (0 421 25250 2) 24, 344

Dane, J. and Thomas. P. A. *How to use a law library: a new teaching aid for law librarians and law students.* Sweet & Maxwell, Butterworths, 1983. [Series of tape-slide programmes] 653

Daniel, W. T. S. *History and origin of the law reports.* Clones, 1884. Repr. Wildy, 1968. 187

Danner, R. A. Reference theory and the future of legal reference service. *Law Library Journal,* vol. 76, 1983, pp. 217–32. 397

Datenverarbeitung im Recht, 1972– .

brief report. *New Zealand Libraries*, vol. 43, 1980, pp. 57–60. 36

Edwards, Sir G. The historical study of the Welsh law books. *Royal Historical Society Transactions*, 5th series, vol. 12, 1962, pp. 141–55. 292

Eek, H. [and others]. *Juridikens termer*. 2nd ed. Stockholm, Svenska Bokforlaget, n.d. 508

Egbert, L. D. and Morales-Macedo, F. *Multilingual law dictionary: English-Francais-Espanol-Deutsch.* Dobbs Ferry, NY, Oceana [etc.], 1978. (0 379 00589 1) 509

Eighteenth century short title catalogue: the British Library collections, ed. R. Alston. BLRD, 1983– . [Microfiche] 287, 718

Elchies, P. Grant, Lord. *Court of Session cases from 1733–54; collected and digested into the form of a dictionary.* n.p., 1813. 2 vols. 172

Elias, T. O. *British colonial law: a comparative study of the interaction between English and local laws in British dependencies.* Stevens, 1962. 321

Elias, T. O. *Modern law of treaties.* Dobbs Ferry, NY, Oceana, 1974. (0 379 00230 2) 447

Elliot, J. Legal information needs of Papua New Guinea and the Pacific, *Australian Law Librarians' Group Newsletter*, no. 58, 1983, pp. 3–11. 323

Elliot, N. *Teinds or tithes and procedure in the Court of Teinds in Scotland*, Edinburgh, Blackwood, 1893. 551

Ellis, A. G. *Catalogue of Arabic printed books in the British Museum.* British Museum, 1894. 3 vols. Supplements 1–3, 1926–77. 263

Ellis, C. J. Law reporting today. *Law Librarian*, vol. 6, 1975, pp. 5–8. 186

Elmes, J. *Ecclesiastical and civil dilapidations.* 3rd ed. Samuel Brooke, 1929. 133

Elon, M. *The principles of Jewish law.* New Brunswick, Transaction Books, 1975. (0 87855 188 3) 553

Elon, M. The sources and nature of

Jewish law. *Israel Law Review*, vol. 2, 1967, pp. 516–65; vol. 3, 1968, pp. 88–126 and 416–57; vol. 4, 1969, pp. 80–140. 554, 569

Emden, A. B. *Biographical register of the University of Cambridge to 1500.* Cambridge UP, 1963. (0 521 04896 6) 368

Emden, A. B. *Biographical register of the University of Oxford to AD 1500.* Oxford, Clarendon Press, 1957–9. 3 vols. (0 19 951105 5, etc.) Supplement, 1500–1541. 1974. (0 19 951008 3) 368

Employment Law Cases, 1984– . Income Data Services, Ltd. 7 vols. Looseleaf. 134

Enciclopedia del diritto, ed. F. Santoro-Passarelli. Milan, Giuffré, 1958– . 469

Encyclopaedia Britannica see New Encyclopaedia Britannica

Encyclopaedia Judaica. Jerusalem, Keter 1972. 16 vols. 553, 566, 570

Encyclopedia of bioethics, ed. W. T. Reich. New York, Free Press, 1978. 4 vols. (0 02 926060 4, etc.) 566

Encyclopedia of European Community Law, ed. K. R. Simmonds. Sweet & Maxwell, 1973– . 3 vols. (0 421 19350 6; 0 421 19360 3; 0 421 20760 4) 404, 409, 410, 413, 422, 423

Encyclopaedia of forms and precedents other than court forms. 5th ed. Butterworths, 1985– . 42 vols. [with service vols.] 196, 197, 366

Encyclopedia of housing law and practice. Sweet & Maxwell. 4 vols. Looseleaf. (0 421 00730 3) 113

Encyclopaedia of Islam. 2nd ed. Luzac, 1954– . 559, 566, 570

Encyclopedia of labour relations law. Sweet & Maxwell. 3 vols. Looseleaf. (0 421 16960 5) 112

Encyclopedia of planning law and practice. Sweet & Maxwell, 1970– . 4 vols. Looseleaf. (0 421 00740 0) 198

Encyclopaedia of public international law ... Max Planck Institute. Amsterdam, North-Holland, 1981. 470

Encyclopedia of road traffic law and practice. Sweet & Maxwell. 4 vols. Looseleaf. 109

Encyclopedia of Scottish legal styles. Edinburgh, Green, 1935–40. 10 vols. 211, 380

Encyclopedia of social security law. Sweet & Maxwell, 1980–5 2 vols. Looseleaf. (o 421 24370 8) 149

Encyclopaedia of Soviet law, ed. F. J. M. Feldbrugge. 2nd ed. The Hague, Nijhoff, 1985. 589

Encyclopedia of the laws of Scotland. 3rd ed. Edinburgh, Green, 1926–35. 16 vols. Supplement, 1931–52. 5 vols. 195, 211, 380, 551

Encyclopedia of value added tax. Sweet & Maxwell, 1973– . 2 vols. Looseleaf. (o 421 17860 4) 198

Encyclopedia Talmudica. English translation ... Jerusalem, Talmudic Encyclopedia Institute, 1969– . 553, 566

Encyclopédie juridique Dalloz. Paris, Dalloz, 1951– . 7 vols in 30. Looseleaf. 501

Englard, I. *Religious law in the Israel legal system.* Jerusalem, Harry Sacher Institute for Legislative Research and Comparative Law, 1975. 555, 569

Englefield, D. *Parliament and information.* Library Association, 1981. (o 85365 570 7) 689

Englefield, D. *Parliament and the European Communities. In* Hopkins, M. *European Communities information: its use and users.* Mansell, 1985, pp. 105–27. 412, 435

English and Empire Digest see The Digest

English Reports, 1220–1865. Stevens, 1900–32. 178 vols. Repr. Abingdon Professional Books, 1974. 138, 163, 171, 177, 179, 297, 315, 546, 654

Ensīqlōpēdiah Talmūdīt. Jerusalem, Talmudic Encyclopedia Institute, 1953– . 566

Entscheidungen des Bundesarbeitsgerichts, 1955– . Berlin, de Gruyter. (GW 0433–7050) 500

Entsiklopedicheskii slovar' pravovykh znanii (sovetskoe pravo), ed. V. M. Chkhikvadze. Moscow, Sovetskaia Entsiklopediia, 1965. 589

Entsiklopediia gosudarstva i prava, ed. P. Stuchka. Moscow, Izd-vo Kommunisticheskoi Akademii, 1925–7. 3 vols. 589

Enyingi, P. [and others]. *Cataloging legal literature: a manual on AACR2 and Library of Congress subject headings for legal materials, with illustrations.* Littleton, Colo., Rothman for AALL, 1984. (AALL publications, no. 22) (o 8377 0120 1) 755, 756, 759, 767, 771, 797

Ephemerides Theologicae Lovanienses, 1924– . Louvain, Catholic University. (BE 0013–9513) 561

Episcopal Church in Scotland. *Code of canons.* Edinburgh, Cambridge UP, 1973. (o 521 159174 1) 550

Eres, B. K. *Legal and legislative information processing.* Westport, Conn., Greenwood Press, 1980 (o 313 21343 7) 565

Erskine May's treatise on the law ... and usage of Parliament. 20th ed. Butterworths, 1983. (o 406 29103 9) 412

Erskine, J. *Institute of the law of Scotland.* Edinburgh, n.p., 1773. 2 vols. 288

Erskine, J. *Principles of the law of Scotland.* Edinburgh, n.p., 1754. 2 vols. in 1. 288

Estates Gazette, 1858– . Estates Gazette, Ltd. (UK 0014–1240) 128, 140, 150

Estates Gazette Digest, 1902–84. Estates Gazette, Ltd. 150, 160

Euromarket News. Chicago, Ill., Commerce Clearing House. (US 0588–649X) 460

Europa Year Book: a world survey, 1926– . Europa Publications. (UK 0071–2302) 471

Europe Today: state of European integration, 1976– . Luxembourg, Office for Official Publications. [Annual] 424

European Bibliography of Soviet, East European and Slavonic Studies,

1975– . Paris, Editions de l'Ecole des Hautes Etudes en Sciences Sociales, Institut d'Etudes Slaves. (FR 0140–492X) 586

European Communities. *Instruments concerning the accession of Spain and Portugal.* 3 vols. 403

European Communities. Commission. *The Court of Justice of the European Communities.* 3rd ed. Luxembourg, Office for Official Publications, 1983. (*European documentation,* 18314) (92 825 3615 7) 435

European Communities. Commission. *The European Community: international organizations and multilateral agreements.* 3rd ed. Luxembourg, Office for Official Publications, 1983. (92 825 3775 7) 414

European Communities. Commission. *The European Community's legal system.* 2nd ed. Luxembourg, Office for Official Publications, 1984. (*European documentation* 5/1984) (92 825 4432 X) 402

European Communities. Commission. *European treaties vocabulary, compiled on the basis of the treaties establishing the European Communities.* 2nd ed. Part 1: English/Irish. Luxembourg, Office for Official Publications, 1983. (92 825 4045 6) 431

European Communities. Commission. *National decisions concerning Community law, 1958–1982.* Brussels, Commission Legal Service, 1958–82. 26 parts. 419

European Communities. Commission. *Thirty years of Community law.* Luxembourg, Office for Official Publications, 1983. (*European perspectives series*) (92 825 2652 6) 435

European Communities. Commission. *Treaties establishing the European Communities, treaties amending those treaties, documents concerning the accession.* Luxembourg, Office for Official Publications, 1978. (92 825 0376 3). Amendments. 1983 (92 824 0008 5) 403

European Communities. Council. *ACP-EEC glossary (and List of States).* Luxembourg, Office for Official Publications, 1984 (92 824 0173 1) 431

European Communities. Council. *Collection of the agreements concluded by the European Communities ... 1952–75.* Luxembourg, Office for Official Publications, 1977–9. (92 824 0002 6). Annual supplements, 1976– . 413

European Communities. Council. *European Communities glossary: French-English.* 8th ed. Luxembourg, Office for Official Publications, 1984. (9 824 0131 6) 431

European Communities. Council. *Manual of precedents drawn up by the legal/linguistic experts ...* 2nd ed. Brussels, The Council, 1983. 431

European Communities. Council. *Multilingual glossary of abbreviations ...* Luxembourg, Office for Official Publications, 1983. (92 824 0115 4) 432

European Communities. Council. *Review of the Council's work, 1959/60– .* Luxembourg, Office for Official Publications. 424

European Communities. Court of Justice. *Codified versions of the rules of procedure, the supplementary rules and the instructions to the Registrar. Official Journal,* no. C 39, 15.2.82, pp. 1–40. 415

European Communities. Court of Justice. *Selected instruments relating to the organization, jurisdiction and procedure of the Court.* Luxembourg, Office for Official Publications, 1975. 415

European Communities. Parliament. *Debates* [Annex to the *Official Journal*]. Luxembourg, Office for Official Publications. (EI 0378–5041) 421

European Communities. Parliament. *The European Parliament: its powers.* Luxembourg, Office for Official Publications, 1983. 435

European Communities. Parliament.

Introduction to legal method. 2nd ed. Sweet & Maxwell, 1984. (0 421 29770 0) 417

Faruqi H. S. *Faruqi's law dictionary: Arabic-English.* Beirut, Librairie du Liban, 1972. 565

Faulkner Brown, H. Academic library buildings in the United Kingdom. *Advances in Librarianship*, vol. 3, 1972, pp. 107–18. 623, 642

Favret, L. Some implications of on-line circulation for cataloguing. *Catalogue and Index*, no. 70, 1983, pp. 4–8. 797

Fawcett, J. E. S. *The British Commonwealth in international law.* Stevens 1963. (*Library of world affairs*, no. 61) 293, 321

Fawcett, J. E. S. *The law of nations.* 2nd ed. Harmondsworth, Penguin, 1971. (0 14 080287 8) 458

Federal Code Annotated see United States Code Service

Federal Court Reports, 1984– . Sydney, Law Book Company. (AT 0813–7803) 307

Federal Digest, 1927–1938. St. Paul, Minn., West. 336

Federal Law Reports, 1956– . Sydney, Law Book Company. (AT 0085–0462) 307, 308

Federal Practice Digest, 2d., 1962– . St. Paul, Minn., West. 337

Federal Reporter, 1880–1924. St. Paul, Minn., West. 300 vols. 2nd series, 1924– . (*National Reporter System*) 333

Federal Rules Decisions, 1941– . St. Paul, Minn., West. (*National Reporter System*) 333

Federal Supplement, 1933– . St. Paul, Minn., West. (*National Reporter System*) 333

Feenstra, R. *Repertorium bibliographicum institutorum et sodalitatum iuris historiae.* 2nd ed. Leiden, Brill, 1980. (90 04 0629 2) 525

Feliciano, M. S. Human rights documentation. *International Journal of Law Libraries*, vol. 9, 1981, pp. 95–103. 465

Feliciano, M. S. Law libraries and legal documentation in the Philippines. *International Journal of Law Libraries*, vol. 4, 1976, pp. 176–87. 36

Ferid, M. and Firsching, K. *Internationales Erbrecht: Quellensammlung mit systematischen Darstellung des materiellen Erbrechts sowie des Kollisionsrechts der wichtigsten Staaten.* Munich, Beck, 1955– . 7 vols. (3 406 08665 9) Looseleaf. 494

Feuille Fédérale de la Confédération Suisse: Bundesblatt der Schweizerischen Eidgenossenschaft, 1849– . Bern. 498

Financial Times, 1888– . London, Financial Times Ltd. 160, 676, 696

Financial Times European Law Newsletter see Business Law Brief

Finlay, J. *Digested index to all Irish reported cases in law and equity from the earliest period.* Dublin, 1830. 178

Finlay, R. *Directory of law libraries in Australia and Papua New Guinea.* Sydney, Butterworths, 1979. 397

Fisher, R. A. *Digest of reported cases, 1756–1870.* [London], 1870. 5 vols. Supplement, 1870–80. 1880. 2 vols. 157

Fitzgerald, F. N. and Emringer, L. Principle source material on European Community legislation: a bibliographic note. *International Journal of Law Libraries*, vol. 3, 1975, pp. 208–14. 434

Fitzgibbon, H. M. *Irish land reports, 1895–1920.* Dublin, Falconer, 1895–1920. 25 vols. 177

Fitzgibbon, H. M. *Irish local government orders and legal decisions, 1899–1919.* Dublin, 1899–1919. 17 vols. 177

Fitzherbert, Sir A. *La graunde abridgment.* Rastell, or de Worde, 1516. 3 vols. Repr. Abingdon, Professional Books, 1983. 2 vols. [Also on microfiche] 284

Fjällbrant, N. and Malley, I. *User education in libraries.* 2nd ed. Bingley, 1984. (0 85157 361 4) 672

Flannery, A. and Collins, L. *Light for my path: the new code of canon law for religious*. Dublin, Dominican Publications, 1983. (0 907271 22 7) 543

Fletcher, W. M. *Cyclopedia of corporations*. Chicago, Ill., Callaghan, 1959–80. 30 vols. [Supplements and replacement volumes] 339

Flint, M. F. *User's guide to copyright*. 2nd ed. Butterworth, 1985. 674

Fockema Andreae, S. J. *Rechtsgeleerd handwoordenboek*. 4th ed. Alphen aan den Rijn, Tjeenk Willink, 1977. (90 6092 700 1) 507

Fontes iuris romani antejustiniani in usum scholarum. 2nd ed. by S. Riccobono [and others]. Florence, S. A. G. Barbera, 1940–3. 3 vols. 513

Food and Agriculture Legislation, 1952– . Rome, Food and Agriculture Organization. (IT 0015–6221) 480

Forbes, W. *Journal of the session containing decisions ... in the most important cases ... from 1705–13 and the Acts of Sederunt made in that time* ... Edinburgh, n.p., 1714. 169

Ford, P. *Select list of British Parliamentary papers, 1955–1964*. Shannon, Irish UP, 1970. 228

Ford, P. and Ford, G. *A breviate of Parliamentary papers, 1900–1916*. Oxford, Blackwell, 1957. 228

Ford, P. and Ford, G. *A breviate of Parliamentary papers, 1917–1939*. Oxford, Blackwell, 1951. Rev. ed. Shannon, Irish UP, 1969. (0 7165 0576 2) 228

Ford, P. and Ford, G. *A breviate of Parliamentary papers, 1940–1954*. Oxford, Blackwell, 1961. 228

Ford, P. and Ford, G. *A guide to Parliamentary papers*. 3rd ed. Shannon, Irish UP, 1972. (0 7165 1418 4) 238

Ford, P. and Ford, G. *Select list of British Parliamentary papers, 1833–1899*. Rev. ed. Shannon, Irish UP, 1969. (0 7165 0574 6) 228

Ford, P. and Ford, G. *A select list of reports of inquiries of the Irish Dáil and Senate, 1922–72*. Dublin, Irish UP, 1974. (0 7165 2254 3) 248

Forrester, I. [and others]. *The German civil code of August 18, 1896, amended as of January 1, 1975*. South Hackensack, NJ, Rothman, 1975. (0 8377 0601 7) 504

Forsyth, W. *Cases and opinions on constitutional law and various points of English jurisprudence*. London, n.p., 1869. 140

Foskett, A. C. *The subject approach to information*. 4th ed. Bingley, 1982. (0 85157 313 4) 747, 768–9, 797

Foskett, A. C. *Universal decimal classification*. Bingley, 1973. (0 85157 159 X) 799

Foss, E. *Biographia Juridica: a biographical dictionary of the judges of England from the Conquest to the present time, 1066–1870*. John Murray, 1870. 370

Foss, E. *Judges of England, 1066–1864*. John Murray, 1848–64. 9 vols. 283, 370

Foss, E. *Tabulae Curiales ... 1066–1864*. John Murray, 1865. 370

Foster, A. Extending the electronic library by downloading. *Library Association Record*, vol. 86, 1984, pp. 358–9. 697

Foster, J. *Alumni Oxonienses: the members of the University of Oxford, 1500–1714*. Oxford, Parker, 1891–2. 4 vols. [Supplement] ... 1715–1886. 1888. 4 vols. 368

Foster, J. *Men-at-the-Bar*. Reeves & Turner, 1885. 370

Foster, J. *The register of admissions to Gray's Inn, 1521–1889*. Gray's Inn, 1889. 369

Foust, J. M. Pennsylvania County law libraries. *Law Library Journal*, vol. 73, 1980, pp. 143–217. 37

Fragali, M. *I cinque codici*. 11th ed. Milan, Giuffre, 1975. 497

Free Church of Scotland. *The practice of the Free Church of Scotland in her several courts*. Rev. ed. Edinburgh, Knox Press, 1964. 550

Free Church of Scotland. General Assembly. *Acts of the General Assembly*, 1843– . Edinburgh, printed for the Church by John Grieg. 550

Free Presbyterian Church of Scotland. *Reports*, 1893– . Glasgow, The Church. 550

Freehof, S. B. *Reform responsa and recent reform responsa.* New York, Ktav, 1973 (0 87068 202 4) 553

Freehof, S. B. *The responsa literature and a treasury of responsa.* New York, Ktav, 1973 (0 87068 212 1) 553

Freeman, C. A. Local authority bye-laws: creation and control. *Law Librarian*, vol. 14, 1983, pp. 19–23. 123

Friend, W. L. *Anglo-American legal bibliographies.* Washington, DC, Library of Congress, 1944. Repr. Littleton, Colo., Rothman, 1966. 346

Fruin, J. A. *De nederlandse wetboeken: zoals zij tot op 1 januari 1984 zijn gewijzigd en aangevuld.* Zwolle, Tjeenk Willink, 1984. (90 271 2134 6) 497

The Furrow, 1950– . Maynooth, Furrow Trust. (IE 0016–3120) 548, 568

Fyzee, A. A. A. *Outlines of Muhammadan law.* 5th ed. New Delhi, UP, 1985 (0 19 561393 7) 559, 569

Galbraith, V. H. *An introduction to the use of the public records.* Oxford UP, 1934. (0 19 821221 6) 291

Galbraith, V. H. *Studies in the public records.* London, Nelson, 1948. 291

Gaskell, E. The library and documentation series of the Commission of the European Communities. *In* Hopkins, M. *European Communities information*, pp. 91–101. 426, 436

Gates, H. *Directory of library and information retrieval software for microcomputers.* Gower, 1985. (0 566 03531 6) 743

Gazette of India, 1864– . Delhi, Manager of Publications. 314, 315

Gazette of the Incorporated Law Society of Ireland, 1907– . Dublin, The Society. 179, 214

Gazette of the Incorporated Law Society of Northern Ireland, new series, 1964– . Belfast, The Society. (UK 0018–3526) 215

Gazeteer of European law ... 1953–1983, compiled by N. M. Hunnings. European Law Centre, 1983. 2 vols. (0 907451 08 X) 407, 418, 420

Gee, H. and Hardy, W. J. *Documents illustrative of English church history.* n.p. 1896. 548

A general abridgment of cases in equity [1677–1744], by A Gentleman of the Middle Temple. Henry Lintot, 1732–56. 2 vols. 157

General Agreement on Tariffs and Trade. *Basic instruments and selected documents*, 1952– . Geneva, GATT. (UN 0072–0623) 479

General Assembly of Unitarian and Free Churches. *Handbook.* The Assembly. [Quinquennial] 548

General index of Acts, Enactments, Ordinances, etc. as at 30 April, 1983 [Malaysia]. Kuala Lumpur, Malaysian Law Publishers, 1983. 317

General Report on the Activities of the European Communities, 1968– . Luxembourg, Office for Official Publications. (EI 0069–6749) [Annual] 423

General Synod Measures, 1920– . HMSO. [1920–70 entitled *Church Assembly Measures*] 97, 545

Gentleman's Magazine, 1731–1868 [over 200 vols in 5 series]. Index to 1731–1818 4 vols. 259

Georgia Journal of International Law, 1970– . Athens, Ga., School of Law, University of Georgia. (US 0046–578X) 1031

Germain, C. M. European Community law: a selective bibliography of publications in English, French and German with annotations. *International Journal of Law Libraries*, vol. 8, 1980, pp. 239–81. 428, 438

Germain, C. M. France: libraries of law and librarians. *Law Library Journal*, vol. 72, 1979, pp. 235–44. 36

Gesellschaft für Rechtsvergleichung. *Bibliography of German law in English and German: a selection.*

Haddan, A. W. *Councils and ecclesiastical documents relating to Great Britain and Ireland.* Oxford, Clarendon Press, 1869–78. 3 vols. 548

Haensch, G. *Dictionary of international relations and politics ... German, English/American, French, Spanish.* Amsterdam, Elsevier, 1965. 469

Hahlo, H. R. and Kahn, E. *The South African legal system and its background.* Cape Town, Juta, 1968. 529, 532, 535, 537

Hahlo, H. R. and Kahn, E. *The Union of South Africa: the development of its laws and constitution.* Stevens, 1960. (*The British Commonwealth: the development of its laws and constitutions*, vol. 5) 531

Hailes. Sir D. Dalrymple, Lord. *Decisions of the Court of Session, 1776–91*, ed. by M. P. Brown. n.p., 1826. 2 vols. 4–41

Hajnal, P. I. *Guide to United Nations Organization documentation and publishing for students, researchers and librarians.* Dobbs Ferry, NY, Oceana, 1978. (0 379 20257 8) 477, 485

Half a century of Soviet serials, 1917–1968: a bibliography and union list ... compiled by R. Smits, Washington, DC, Library of Congress, 1968. 2 vols. 583, 587

Hall, D. E. *Union catalogue of Asian publications.* Mansell, 1971. 4 vols. 563

Halsbury's Laws of England. 4th ed. Butterworth, 1973–85. 50 vols. (0 406 03400 1, etc.) Annual and cumulative supplements, 1974– . Index. 1985. 2 vols. Current service. 65, 95, 105, 117, 122, 132, 139, 143, 158, 194–5, 296, 301, 337, 348, 366, 546, 548, 555, 566, 568, 675

Halsbury's Laws of England. 3rd ed. Canadian Converter, 1965– . Toronto Butterworths. (0 409 80145 3, etc.) 301

Halsbury's Statutes. 4th ed. Butterworths, 1985– . [To total 50 vols.] (0 406 21409 3, etc.) 87–8, 102, 104, 132, 158, 363, 366, 409, 410, 413, 545, 675, 694

Halsbury's Statutory Instruments. Butterworth. [Continually updated] 24 vols. (0 406 04500 3, etc.) 107, 108–9, 132, 366, 410

Handbook of special librarianship and information work. 5th ed. by L. J. Anthony. Aslib, 1982. (0 85142 160 1) 640, 673, 742

[Hannay, R.] *Address to the Right Hon. Lord President Hope and to members of the College of Justice on the method of collecting and reporting decisions.* Edinburgh, David Brown, 1821. 188

[Hannay, R.] *Letter to the Dean of the Faculty of Advocates relative to a plan which has been proposed for reporting the decisions of the Court of Session.* Edinburgh, Bell & Bradfute, 1823. 188

Hannay, R. K. Some questions regarding Scotland and the canon law. *Juridical Review*, vol. 49, 1937, pp. 25–34. 551

Hansard *see Parliamentary Debates* [Hansard]

Hansard's Breviate *see Catalogue of Parliamentary reports and a breviate of their contents ...*

Hanson, A. H. and Walles, M. *Governing Britain: a guidebook to political institutions.* 4th ed. Fontana, 1984. (0 00 636758 5) 121

Hanstock, T. M. Law collections in public libraries: Sheffield City Libraries' example. *Law Librarian*, vol. 11, 1980, pp. 31–3. 710

Harrap's new standard French and English dictionary. Harrap, 1940–72. 3 vols. (0 245 50972 0) 360

Harris, D. J. *Cases and materials on international law.* 3rd ed. Sweet & Maxwell, 1983. (0 421 29270 9) 458

Harrison, E. R. *Tax finder and digest.* 7th ed. Oyez Longman, 1982– . 3 vols. Looseleaf. (0 85120 649 2) 159

Harrison, K. C. *Public relations for librarians.* 2nd ed. Aldershot, Gower, 1982. (0 566 03454 9) 641

NY, Lawyers Co-operative Publishing Company, 1942. 391

Hicks, F. C. *Men and books famous in the law.* Rochester, NY, Lawyers Co-operative Publishing Company, 1921. 398

Higham, N. *The library in the university: observations on a service.* Deutsch, 1980. (0 233 97222 6) 611, 640

Hinde, G. W. and M. S. *New Zealand law dictionary.* 3rd ed. Wellington, Butterworths, 1979. (0 409 60028 8) 395

Historical Manuscripts Commission *see* Gt. Brit. Royal Commission on Historical Manuscripts

Hobart, H. *Reports in the reign of James I, 1603–25.* J. More, 1641. 4–10

Hodkinson, K. *Muslim family law: a sourcebook.* Croom Helm, 1984. (0 7099 1256 0) 559, 569

Holdsworth, Sir W. S. *History of English law* [various eds.] Methuen, 1936–72. 17 vols. 7th ed. Sweet & Maxwell, 1956–72. (0 421 05160 4, etc.) 187, 274, 290, 350

Holdsworth, Sir W. S. *Sources and literature of English law.* Oxford, Clarendon Press, 1925. Repr. Buffalo, NY, Hein, 1983–4. (0 89941 8) 290, 350

Holdsworth, Sir W. S. The year books. *In Select essays in Anglo-American legal history,* compiled by a committee of the Association of American Law Schools. Boston, Mass., Little, Brown, 1908. Vol. 2, pp. 96–122. 292

Holk, L. E. van. Pays-Bas. *In* Gilissen, J. *Introduction bibliographique à l'histoire du droit et à l'ethnologie juridique,* Chapter C/4. 1971. 536

Holland, D. C. The Isle of Man. *In* Keeton, G. W. and Lloyd, D. *The British Commonwealth: the United Kingdom.* Vol. 1, pt. 1. Stevens, 1955. 71

Honore, T. and Menner, J. *Concordance to the Digest jurists.* Oxford, Clarendon Press, 1980. Booklet and 84 microfiches. (0 19 825354 0) 516

Hooker, M. B. *Legal pluralism.* Oxford, Clarendon Press, 1975. (0 19 825329 X) 541, 568

Hope, T. *Major practicks, 1608–33.* Edinburgh, Stair Society, 1937–8. 2 vols. (Stair Society, 3 & 4) 278

Hope, T. *Minor practicks, or treatise of the Scottish law [with] a discourse on the rise and progress of the law of Scotland . . . and an abridgment of the Acts of Sederunt.* Edinburgh, n.p., 1726. 278

Hopkins, M. *European Communities information: its use and users.* Mansell, 1985. (0 7201 1701 1) 401, 428, 434, 436

Hopkins, M. European Communities information and its use in British universities and polytechnics. *In* Hopkins, M. *European Communities information,* pp. 195–222. 430

Hopkins, M. *Policy formation in the European Communities: a bibliographical guide to Community documentation, 1958–1978.* Mansell, 1981. (0 7201 1597 3) 405, 428

Hopkins, M. *Publications, documentation and means for their dissemination in the Commission of the European Communities.* Boston Spa, BLLD, 1981. *(Research and development reports,* 5618) (0 905984 69 2) 436

Hornbook series. St. Paul, Minn., West. 339

Horst, M. H. J. van. *The Roman Dutch law in Sri Lanka.* Amsterdam, VU Boekhandel, 1985. (9 06256 236 1) 534

Hosten, W. J. [and others]. *Introduction to South African law and legal theory.* Rev. repr. Durban, Butterworths, 1980. (0 409 03348 0) 532, 535

Houdek, F. G. *Introducing the American Association of Law Libraries.* Chicago, Ill., AALL, 1983. 35

House of Commons sessional papers of the eighteenth century, ed. S. Lambert. Wilmington, Del., Scholarly Resources, 1975–6. 147 vols. 226, 228

vehendis ... Mediolani, Giuffre, 1901– . 517
Iuul, S. [and others]. *Scandinavian legal bibliography.* Stockholm, Almquist & Wiksell, 1961. 506
Izvestiia Sovetov Narodnykh Deputatov SSSR, 1917– . Moscow [publisher varies]. 574, 577

Jackson, B. S. *Essays in Jewish and comparative legal history.* Leiden, Brill, 1975. (90 04 04333 0) 554
Jackson, B. S. *Jewish law in legal history and the modern world.* Leiden, Brill, 1980. (*Jewish Law Annual, Supplement* 2) (90 04 06254 8) 554
Jackson, R. M. *The machinery of justice in England.* 7th ed. Cambridge, UP, 1977. (0 521 21688 5) 70
Jacob, G. *New law dictionary.* E. and R. Nutt and R. Gosling, 1729. 361, 565
Jacobs, R. Focal point: a composite record for the control of periodicals using a visible signalling device. *Journal of Documentation,* vol. 6, 1950, pp. 213–28. 744
Jacobstein, J. M. and Mersky, R. M. *Fundamentals of legal research.* 2nd ed. Mineola, NY, Foundation Press, 1981. (*University textbook series*) (0 88277 034 9) 341
Jahoda, G. and Olson, P. E. Models of reference: analyzing the reference process. *RQ,* vol. 12. 1972, pp. 148–56. 710
Jahoda, G. [and others]. The reference process: modules for instruction. *RQ,* vol. 17, 1977, pp. 7–12. 710
Jain, H. C. *Indian legal materials: a bibliographical guide.* Bombay, Tripathi, and Dobbs Ferry, NY, Oceana, 1970. (0 379 00466 6) 313, 323, 390, 392, 556, 562, 569
Jain, H. C. Using a law library. *Journal of the Indian Law Institute,* vol. 24, 1982, pp. 575–91. 315, 323, 397
Jain, J. P. *Documentary study of the Warsaw Pact.* Asia Publishing House 1973. (0 210 98156 3) 579
Jain, M. P. Law reporting in India.

Journal of the Indian Law Institute. vol. 24, 1982, pp. 560–74. 316
Japanese Annual of International Law, 1957– . Tokyo, Japan Branch, International Law Association. 460
Japikse, N. and Blecourt, A. S. de. *Klein placaatboek van Nederland.* Groningen, n.p., 1919. 527
Jefferson, G. *Library co-operation.* 2nd ed. Deutsch, 1977. (0 233 96851 2) 642
Jeffreys, A. Management in cataloguing services. *Catalogue and Index,* no. 46, 1977, pp. 2–4. 790, 800
Jeffries, J. CELEX. *Law Librarian,* vol. 11, 1980, pp. 60–1; vol. 12, 1981, p. 13. 435
Jeffries, J. *A guide to the official publications of the European Communities.* 2nd ed. Mansell, 1981. (0 7201 1590 6) 408, 427, 428, 434
Jeffries, J. Legal information from European Documentation Centres. *Law Librarian,* vol. 11, 1980, pp. 57–9. 436
Jeffries, J. Sources of information on the law of the European Communities. *In* Hopkins, M. *European Communities information* ... 1985, pp. 227–40. 434
Jegede, O. *Nigerian legal bibliography: a classified list of materials related to Nigeria.* 2nd ed. Lagos, Nigerian Institute of Advanced Legal Studies, 1983. 398
Jenkinson, Sir H. A. *A manual of archive administration.* 2nd ed. Lund Humphries, 1937. Repr. 1965. (0 85331 072 6) 291
Jennings, Sir I. and Tambiah, H. W. *The Dominion of Ceylon: the development of its laws and constitution.* Stevens, 1952. (*The British Commonwealth: the development of its laws and constitutions,* vol. 7) 534
Jeraute, J. *Vocabulaire français-anglais, anglais-français.* Paris, Pichon, 1953. 364
Jewish Law Annual, 1978– . Leiden, Brill. 553, 554
Jewish Year Book, 1896– . Jewish

Chronicle Publications. (UK 0075–3769)–11/12. 567

Johansson, E. *Current British Government publishing*. AAL, SED, 1978. (o 902248 06 5) 223

Johnson, E. L. *Introduction to the Soviet legal system*. Methuen, 1969. 579

Johnson-Champ, D. S. Bibliography: selected readings on teaching international law. *International Lawyer*, vol. 18, 1984, pp. 197–200. 486

Jolowicz, H. F. and Nicholas, B. *Historical introduction to the study of Roman law*. Cambridge UP, 1972. 518

Jones, C. G. and Proudfoot, R. *Notes on hire purchase law*. 2nd ed. Butterworth, 1937. 143

Jones, H. Permission to make multiple photocopies. *Law Librarian*, vol. 15, 1984, pp. 20–21. 669, 674

Jordan, R. Australian law and law libraries, 1977. *Law Librarian*, vol. 8, 1977, pp. 39–42 and vol. 9, 1978, pp. 5–6. 35

Journal of African Law, 1957– . School of Oriental and African Studies, University of London. 303

Journal of Common Market Studies, 1962– . Oxford, Blackwell. (UK 0021–9886) 425

Journal of Criminal Law, 1937– . Pageant Publishing. (UK 0022–0183) 140

Journal of Criminal Law and Criminology, 1910– . Chicago, Ill., Northwestern University School of Law. (US 0091–4169) 494

Journal of Jewish Studies, 1948– . Oxford, Centre for Postgraduate Hebrew Studies. (UK 0022–2097) 554, 561

Journal of Legal History, 1980– . Cass. (UK 0144–0365) 378

Journal of Library Automation see *Information Technology and Libraries*

Journal of Roman Studies, 1911– . Society for the Promotion of Roman Studies. (UK 0075–4358) 520

Journal of the General Synod of the Church of Ireland, 1872– . Dublin, Hodges, Foster. 549

Journal of the Indian Law Institute, 1958– . New Delhi, The Institute. (II 0019–5731) 316

Journal of the Institute of Bankers see *Banking World*

Journal of the Irish Society for European Law, 1977– . Dublin, The Society. 416

Journal of the Irish Society for Labour Law, 1982– . Dublin, The Society. (IE 0790–0473) 214

Journal of the Law Society of Scotland, 1956– . Edinburgh, The Society. (UK 0458–8711) 211, 212

Journal of the Society of Public Teachers of Law, n.s., 1957–80. Butterworth. (UK 6038–0024) 203

Journal Officiel de la République Française, 1870– . Paris. 230, 498

Journals of the House of Commons, 1547– . HMSO, 1742– . 142, 228–9, 257, 258

Journals of the House of Lords, 1509– . HMSO, 1771– . 142, 183, 228–9

Jowitt, W. Earl. *A dictionary of English law*. 2nd ed. by J. Burke. Sweet & Maxwell, 1977. 2 vols. Supplements 1981 and 1985. (o 421 23090 8, etc.) 361, 362, 524

Judgments of the Court of Criminal Appeal, 1924–78. Dublin, Incorporated Council of Law Reporting in Ireland, 1983. (o 946738 00 9) 175

Judgments of the Royal Court of Jersey and of the Court of Appeal of Jersey, 1950– . Jersey, Bigwoods, etc., 1967– . 156, 180

[Judicial Committee of the Privy Council] *Cases on appeal*, 1840– . [Limited circulation]. 142

Judicial Statistics, England and Wales. HMSO. Annual. [1972–4 entitled *Statistics on Judicial Administration*]. 234–5

Judicial Review: the law journal of Scottish universities, 1889– . Edinburgh, Green. (UK 0022–6785) 212, 377, 551

Juris Classeur Périodique (La semaine juridique), 1927– . Paris. Editions Techniques. (FR 0049–0156) 500

Juris Classeurs, 1905– . Paris, Editions Techniques. [More than 200 looseleaf vols in 10 subject areas]. 501

Jurisprudence Française, 1807/1926– (1953)– . Paris, Editions Techniques. 501

The Jurist, 1837–66. Stevens. 55 vols. 131

Jurist, 1941– . Washington, DC, Department of Canon Law, Catholic University of America. (US 0022–6858) 543, 544, 561

Juristische Kurzlehrbücher. Munich, Beck. 502

Justiciary Cases, 1916– . Edinburgh, Oliver & Boyd. [Also issued as part of *Session Cases*]. 173

Justinian, Emperor of Rome, *see Corpus iuris civilis*

Kahn-Freund, O. [and others]. *A sourcebook on French law: system, methods, outlines of contract*. 2nd ed. Oxford UP, 1979. (0 19 876088 4) 489

Kaiser, D. H. *The growth of the law in medieval Russia*. Princeton, NJ, Princeton UP, 1980. (0 691 05312 X) 582

Kalinowski, J. O. von. *World law of competition*. New York, Bender, 1979– . 12 vols. Looseleaf. 495

Kames, H. Home, Lord. *Remarkable decisions in the Court of Session*, 1716–52. n.p. 1728–66, 1790–9. 2 vols. 169

Kames, Lord and Woodhouselee, Lord. *Decisions of the Court of Session abridged in the form of a dictionary, 1540–1796*. n.p., 1741–97. 4 vols Supplement to vols 3–4. 1804. 171

Kane, P. V. *History of Dharmaśāstra*. Poona, Bhandarkar Institute, 1930–62. 5 vols in 8. Vol. 1: 2nd ed. Philadelphia, Pa., International Publications Service, 1968–75. (0 8002 0928 1) 557, 569

Kane, T. G. *A study of law reporting in the Commonwealth*. Commonwealth Secretariat, 1975. 300

Kantorowicz, H. and Buckland, W.

W. *Studies in the glossators of the Roman law: newly discovered writings of the twelfth century*. Cambridge UP, 1938. Repr. [with changes] Aalen, Scientia, 1969. (3 521 00641 4) 517

Karlsruher Juristische Bibliographie, 1965– . Munich, Beck. (GW 0453–3283) 490, 506

Kase, F. J. *Dictionary of industrial property: legal and related terms*. (English, Spanish, French, German). Leyden, Sijthoff, 1980. (90 286 0619 X) 365

Kaser, M. *Roman private law*. 3rd ed., trans. R. Dannenbring, based on 10th rev. German ed. Pretoria, University of South Africa, 1980. (0 86981 173 8) 578

Katz, W. A. *Introduction to reference work*. 3rd ed. New York, McGraw-Hill, 1978. 2 vols. (0 07 033319, etc.) 710

Katz, W. A. and Tar, A. *Reference and information services: a reader*. Metuchen, NJ, Scarecrow Press, 1978. (0 8108 1091 3) 710

Kavass, I. I. *The Court of Justice of the European Communities: an annotated bibliography, 1951–73*. Vanderbilt Journal of Transnational Law, vol. 8, 1975, pp. 523–650. 434, 435

Kavass, I. I. Law libraries of the United States: development and growth. *International Journal of Law Libraries*, vol. 3, 1975, pp. 25–49. 37

Kavass, I. I. and Sprudzs, A. *Current treaty index, 1984: a cumulative index to the US slip treaties and agreements*. 3rd ed. Buffalo, NY, W. S. Hein, 1984. (0 0731 818 9) 330, 446

Kavass, I. I. and Sprudzs, A. *A guide to the United States treaties in force*. Buffalo, NY, 1982. 445

Kavass, I. I. and Sprudzs, A. *United States Treaties and other International Agreements: UST cumulative index, 1950/70– . Buffalo, NY, Hein, 1973– . 330, 446

Kearley, T. An American researcher's guide to European Communities law and legal literature. *Law*

1900. Berne, Union Inter-Parlementaire, 1902. 452

La Pradelle, A. de and Politis, N. *Recueil des arbitrages internationaux, 1798–1875*. 2nd ed. Paris, Editions Internationales, 1957. 3 vols. 452

Labeo : Rassegna di Dirrito Romano, 1955– . Naples, Jovene. (IT 0023–6462) 519, 520, 522, 523, 525

Lahore, J. Reprographic reproduction. *In Information technology: the challenge to copyright*. Sweet & Maxwell, 1984. pp. 1–40. 674

Lambert, S. Guides to Parliamentary printing, 1696–1834. *Bulletin of the Institute of Historical Research*, vol. 38, 1965, pp. 111–7. 238

Lambert, S. House of Commons papers of the eighteenth century. *Government Publications Review*, vol. 3, 1976, pp. 195–202. 238

Lambert, S. *Printing for Parliament, 1641–1700*. Swift Printers, 1984. (*List & Index Society, special series*, vol. 20) 227

Lambert, S. Printing for the House of Commons in the eighteenth century. *The Library*, series 5, vol. 23, 1968, pp. 25–46. 238

Lands Tribunal Cases, 1972/3–1978. Chichester, Barry Rose, 1974–8. 6 vols. (o 85992 014 3) 149

Lands Tribunal rating appeals, 1950/51–1960/61. Rating and Valuation Association, 1952–64. 10 vols. 149

Langan, P. St. J. Irish material in the State Trials. *Northern Ireland Law Quarterly*, vol. 18, 1967, pp. 428–36; vol. 19, 1968, pp. 48–53, 189–97, 299–309. 181

Lansky, R. *Handbook of bibliographies on law of developing countries*, Frankfurt-am-Main, Klostermann, 1981. (3 3 465 01446 4) 536

Lansky, R. Libraries for law in the Federal Republic of Germany. *International Journal of Law Libraries*, vol. 3, 1975, pp. 49–78. 36

Larkin, J. F. *Stuart royal proclamations, vol. 2: Royal proclamations of King Charles I (1625–1646)*. Oxford,

Clarendon Press, 1983. (o 19 822466 4) 266

Larkin, J. F. and Hughes, P. L. *Stuart royal proclamations, vol. 1: Royal proclamations of King James I (1603–1625)*. Oxford, Clarendon Press, 1973. 266

Lasok, D. and Bridge, J. W. *An introduction to the law and institutions of the European Communities*. 3rd ed. Butterworths, 1982. (o 406 26894 0) 406, 425, 431, 434

Latey, W. *A short history of the Law Reports, 1865–1965*. Incorporated Council of Law Reporting for England and Wales [1966]. 187

Latham, J. D. Islamic law. *In* Grimwood-Jones, D. *Middle East and Islam: a bibliographical introduction*. 1979, pp. 84–91. 562

Latham, R. E. Coping with medieval Latin. *Amateur Historian*, vol. 1, 1952–4, pp. 331–3. 291

Latham, R. E. *Dictionary of medieval Latin from British sources*; facs. 1, A–B. British Academy, Oxford UP, 1975– . 251

Lavves and actes of Parliament maid be King James the First and his successors Kinges of Scotland [1424–1597], collected by J. Skene. Edinburgh, Waldegrave, 1597. 277

Lavves and acts of Parliament made by James I, II, III, IV, V, Queen Mary, James VI, Charles I and II [1424–1681], collected by Sir T. Murray of Glendook. Edinburgh, n.p., 1681. 277

Law, W. *Our Hansard: or the true mirror of Parliament*. Pitman, 1950. 238

Law and Legal Information Directory, 1980– . Detroit, Gale Research. [Biennial]. 471

Law Book Guide see Bibliographic Guide to Law

Law Books see Bowker's Law Books and Serials in Print

Law Books in Print, 1957– . Dobbs Ferry, NY, Glanville. (US 0075–8221) 349, 392, 463, 717

Law Books in Review, 1974– . Dobbs Ferry, NY, Glanville. 393

Miers, D. R. and Page, A. C. *Legislation*. Sweet & Maxwell, 1982. (o 421 27110 8) 122

Millin, S. S. *Digest of the reported decisions of the superior courts relating to petty sessions in Ireland, 1875–98*. Dublin, n.p., 1898. 179

Mills, J. The Bibliographic Classification. *In Maltby, A. Classification in the 1970s*. Bingley, 1972. pp. 25–50. 799

Mills, J. [Review of Moys classification, 1st ed.] *Journal of Documentation*, vol. 24, 1968, pp. 317–9. 799

Milsom, S. F. C. *Historical foundations of the common law*. 2nd ed. Butterworth, 1981. (o 406 62502 6) 70

Mishnah, trans. by H. Danby. Oxford UP, 1933 (o 19 815402 X) 552

Miskin, C. *Library and information services for the legal profession*. British Library, 1981. (*British Library Research and Development Reports*, 5633) (o 905984 73 0) 13–14, 34, 710

Miskin, C. The solicitors' law firm library. *Law Librarian*, vol. 9, 1978, p. 41. 798

Miuller, V. K. *Anglo-russkii slovar'*. 18th ed. Moscow, Russkii Iazyk, 1981. 588

Model penal code. Philadelphia, Pa., American Law Institute, 1962. 331

Modern Federal Practice Digest, 1938–1961. St. Paul, Minn., West. 337

Modern Law Review, 1937– . Sweet & Maxwell. (UK 0026–7961) 202

Moir, E. *The justice of the peace*. Penguin, 1969. (o 14 020963 8) 71

Mokdisi, J. Islamic law bibliography. *Law Library Journal*, vol. 78, 1986, pp. 103–89. 562

Monash University. Law Library. *Union list of law reports held in Australian law libraries*. Clayton, Monash University, 1979. (o 86746 039 3) 394

Monatsschrift für Deutsches Recht, 1947– . Cologne, Schmidt. (GW 0340–1812) 500

Moniteur Belge: Belgisch Staatsblad, 1831– . Brussels. 498

Montagu, B. *Law of set-off*. 2nd ed. Butterworth, 1828. 133

Monthly Checklist of State Publications, 1910– . Washington, DC, Library of Congress. 331

Moore's Indian Appeals, 1836–72. Stevens. 14 vols. 315

Moore, E. G. *An introduction to English canon law*. 2nd ed. Oxford UP, 1985. (o 264 66901 0) 546

Moore, J. B. *A digest of international law ... of the United States*. Washington, DC, GPO, 1906. 2 vols. 456

Moran, C. G. *Heralds of the law*. Stevens, 1948. 186

Morgan, A. M. *British government publications: an index to chairmen and authors, 1941–1966*. Library Association, 1969. (o 85365 121 3) 224

Morgan, A. M. and Stephen, L. R. *British government publications: an index to chairmen, 1967–1971*. Library Association, 1976. (o 85365 468 9) 224

Morison, W. M. *Decisions of the Court of Session [1540–1808] in the form of a dictionary*. Edinburgh, Bell & Bradfute, 1801–15. 22 vols. Supplement, by M. P. Brown, 1826. 5 vols. 171, 172

Morrin, J. *Calendar of the patent and close rolls of Chancery in Ireland, 1514–1633*. Dublin, HMSO, 1861–3. 3 vols. 254

Morris, B. and Boehm, K. *The European Community: a practical guide and directory for business, industry and trade*. 2nd ed. Macmillan, 1985. (o 333 37669 4) 426, 432, 433

Moschetti, B. Bibliographia iuris canonici ex ephemeridibus ab a 1918 ad a 1934. *Apollinaris*, vol. 14, 1941, pp. 121–45. 564

Moys, E. M. BIALL: landmarks of the first ten years. *Law Librarian*, vol. 11, 1980, pp. 3–5. 35

Moys, E. M. *Classification scheme for law books*. [1st ed.] Butterworths 1968. (o 406 30700 8) 17, 747, 797

Moys, E. M. Law libraries. *In British*

library and information science 1971–1975. Library Association, 1977. pp. 224–30. 34

Moys, E. M. Library of Congress classification class KF: a review article. *Law Librarian,* vol. 1, 1970, pp. 24–7. 784

Moys, E. M. *Moys Classification scheme for law books.* 2nd ed. Butterworths, 1982. (0 406 30701 6) 772, 786

Mozley, H. N. and Whiteley, G. C. *Law dictionary.* 9th ed. Butterworths, 1977. (0 406 62524 7) 362

Mueller, R. [and others]. *GmbH Law: German law concerning the companies with limited liability.* 4th ed. Frankfurt am Main, Knapp, 1981. (3 7819 2829 2) 504

Mulla, Sir D. F. *Principles of Hindu law.* 15th ed. Bombay, Tripathi, 1982. 556, 569

Mulla, Sir D. F. *Principles of Mohomedan law.* 18th ed. Bombay, Tripathi, 1977. 559

Mullins, E. L. C. *Texts and calendars [I]: an analytical guide to serial publications.* Royal Historical Society, 1958. (*RHS guides and hand-books,* 12) 254, 255, 256, 257, 258, 259, 262

Mullins, E. L. C. *Texts and calendars [II]: an analytical guide to serial publications,* 1957–1982. Royal Historical Society, 1983. (*RHS guides and handbooks,* 12) (0 86193 100 9) 254, 255, 256, 262

Municipal Year Book and Public Services Directory, 1898–. Municipal Publications. 374

Muscovite judicial texts, 1488–1556, trans. and ed. ... H. W. Dewey. Ann Arbor, Mich., Department of Slavic Language and Literature, University of Michigan, 1966. 582

Muslim World, 1911– . Hartford, Conn., Hartford Seminary Foundation. (US 0027–4909) 560, 561

Myers, D. P. *Manual of collections of treaties and of collections relating to treaties.* New York, Burt Franklin, 1922. (0 8337 2499 1) 486

Nadaraja, T. *The legal system of Ceylon in its historical setting.* Leiden, Brill, 1972. (90 04 03637 7) 534

Nagel, H. *Die Grundzüge des Beweisrechts im europäischen Zivilprozess: eine rechtsvergleichende Studie.* Baden-Baden, Momos, 1967. 490

Napoletano, V. *Dizionario bibliografico delle riviste giuridiche italiane,* 1865–1956(1958)– . Milan, Giuffre. [Annual since 1966]. 507

National Insurance Commissioners' Decisions *see* Social Security Commissioners' Decisions

National inventory of documentary sources in the U.K., 1983– . Cambridge, Chadwyck-Healey. Microfiche. 253

National Legal Bibliography, 1984– . Buffalo, NY, Hein. (US 0739–1951) 393

National Library of Canada. Resources Survey Division. *Checklist of Law Reports and Statutes in Canadian Law Libraries,* 1977– . Ottawa, The Library. (0 662 00442 6, etc.) 394

National Reporter System [US]. St. Paul, Minn., West Publishing Company [Many series, various dates]. 332–4, 335, 336, 337, 340

National reports [on various countries]. *In International encyclopedia of comparative law.* Tuebingen, Mohr, and others, 1972– . 490

National survey of law libraries in Australia. Australian Law Librarians Group. 1984. 397

National Union Catalog: a cumulative author list representing Library of Congress printed cards and titles reported by other American libraries, 1942– . Washington, DC, Library of Congress, Card Division. [1983– published in microfiche]. 587, 794

Naz, R. *Dictionnaire du droit canonique.* Paris, Letouzey, 1935–65. 7 vols. 565

Neale, Sir J. E. The Commons journals of the Tudor period. *Transactions of the Royal Historical*

Omond, G. W. T. *The Lord Advocates of Scotland from the close of the fifteenth century to the passing of the Reform Bill*. Edinburgh, Douglas, 1883. 2 vols. 380

Omond, G. W. T. *The Lord Advocates of Scotland, 1834–1880*. Andrew Melrose, 1914. 380

Online Information Centre. *Going online*. The Centre, 1983. 701

Online Information Centre. *Law databases September 1983*. The Centre, 1983. (0 946663 04 1) 301, 696

Online Information Centre. *News databases*. The Centre, 1985. 696

Online Information Centre. *Selecting equipment for online information retrieval*. The Centre, 1984. 701

Online Notes, 1979– . Online Information Centre. (UK 0144–125X) 343, 696

Online Review: the international journal of online information systems, 1977– . Abingdon, Learned Information. (UK 0309–314X) 641

Ontario Law Reports see Ontario Reports

Ontario Reports, 1882– . Toronto, Canada Law Book. (CN 0030–3089) [1901–31 entitled *Ontario Law Reports*]. 311

Oppenheim L. *International law*. 7th and 8th ed. by H. Lauterpacht. Longmans, 1952–5. 2 vols (0 582 48807 7 etc.) 458

Orders in Council, and other matters of general interest registered in the records of the Island of Guernsey, 1803– . n.p. 120

Orders in Council, Laws, etc. [Jersey], 1951– . Jersey, States' Greffe. 120

Ordinances of the States [of Guernsey], 1533/1800– . Guernsey Herald. 120

Ordres du conseil et pièces analogues enregistrés à Jersey, 1536–1867, ed. H. M. Godfray and A. Messeroy. Jersey, Labey & Blampied, 1897–1906. 6 vols. 180

Organizatsiia Vashavshkogo dogovora: dokumenty i materialy 1955–1980 gg. Moscow, Politizdat, 1980. 579

Osborn, P. G. *Concise law dictionary*. 7th ed. Sweet & Maxwell, 1983. (0 421 29670 4) 155, 362

Osmanczyk, E. J. *The encyclopaedia of the United Nations and international agreements*. Taylor and Francis, 1985. (0 85066 312 1) 470

Osnovnye dokumenty Soveta ekonomicheskoi vzaimopomoshchi. 4th ed. Moscow, n.p., 1983. 2 vols. 579

Osteuropa-Recht, 1955– . Stuttgart, Deutsche Gesellschaft für Osteuropakunde. (GW 0030–6444) 581

Oswald, H. R. *Vestigia Insulae Manniae Antiquiora, or dissertation on the armorial bearings of the Isle of Man … and the original usages … laws and constitutional government of the Manx people*. Isle of Man, Manx Society, 1860. (Manx Society Publications, 5). 289

Overton, C. D. *Common Market Digest: an information guide to the European Communities*. Library Association, 1983. (0 85365 553 7) 432

Oxford classical dictionary. 2nd ed. Oxford, Clarendon Press, 1970. 524

Oxford companion to law, ed. D. M. Walker. Oxford UP, 1980. (0 19 866110 X) 366, 371, 524, 538, 566, 570

Oxford dictionary of the Christian church, ed. F. L. Cross and E. A. Livingstone. 2nd ed. Oxford UP, 1974. (0 19 211545 6) 565

Oxford English Dictionary, ed. J. A. H. Murray. Oxford, Clarendon Press, 1933. 13 vols. (0 19 861101 3, etc.) Supplements, 1972– . (0 19 861115, 3, etc.) 360

Oxford English-Russian dictionary, ed. P. S. Falla. Oxford, Clarendon Press, 1984. (0 19S 64117 6) 588

Oxford Gazette see London Gazette

Oxford Latin dictionary. Oxford, Clarendon Press, 1968–82. 8 vols. 523

Oxford Russian-English dictionary, ed. M. Wheeler, 2nd ed. Oxford, Clarendon Press, 1984. (0 19S 64154 0) 558

Pacific Reporter, 1884–1931. St. Paul, Minn., West. 300 vols. 2nd

appeal from Scotland decided in the House of Lords, 1707–27. Strahan, 1807. 171

Robilliard, St. J. A. *Religion and the law.* Manchester UP, 1984. (0 7190 0956 1) 541, 568

Robinson, J. *International law and organization: general sources of information.* Leiden, Sijthoff, 1967. 464

Robinson, M. T. Irish parliamentary scrutiny of European Community legislation. *Common Market Law Review,* vol. 16, 1979, pp. 9–40. 413, 435

Robinson, O. F. [and others]. *An introduction to European legal history.* Abingdon, Professional Books, 1985. (0 86205 107 X) 517

Robson, J. L. *New Zealand: the development of its laws and constitution.* 2nd ed. Stevens, 1967. 318

Rodgers, F. *A guide to British Government publications.* New York, H. W. Wilson, 1980. (0 8242 0617 7) 121, 223, 228

Rodgers, F. *Serial publications in the British Parliamentary papers, 1900–1968: a bibliography.* n.p., 1971. 228, 239

Rohn, P. H. *World treaty index.* 2nd ed. Santa Barbara, Calif., APC–Clio Information Series, 1983–4. 5 vols. 444

Rolle, H. *Un abridgment de plusieurs cases et resolutions del common ley.* n.p., 1668. 2 vols. 157

Romain, A. and Rutter, D. *Dictionary of legal and commercial terms.* 3rd ed. Butterworths, 1983. 2 vols. [English–German; German–English] (0 406 03810 4, etc.) 365, 508

Rosenne, S. *Practice and methods of international law.* Dobbs Ferry, NY, Oceana, 1985. (0 379 20140 2) 486

Rosner, F. *Modern medicine and Jewish law.* New York, Bloch, 1972. (0 8197 0389 3) 554

Ross, A. *Mona, or the history, laws and constitution of the Isle of Man.* n.p., [c. 1744]. 289

Ross, J. M. *Trials in collections: an index to famous trials throughout the world.* Metuchen, NJ, Scarecrow Press, 1983. (0 8108 1603 2) 359

Roth, C. *Magna bibliotheca Anglo-Judaica.* Jewish Historical Society of England. 1937. 562

Rotondi, G. *Leges publicae populi romani.* Milan, Societa Editrice Libraria, 1912. 512

Rowley, J. *Computers for libraries,* 2nd ed. Bingley, 1985. (0 85157 388 6) 743

Royal Historical Society. *Camden third series,* 1900–56. The Society. 90 vols. 261

Royal Historical Society. *Camden fourth series,* 1964– . The Society. 90 vols. 261

Royal Historical Society. *Transactions,* 1872– . The Society. (UK 0080–4401) [Several series]. 261

Rudden, B. and Wyatt, D. *Basic Community laws.* Oxford, Clarendon Press, 1980. (0 19 876119 8) 404

Rules of the Court of Session. Edinburgh, HMSO, 1965. 115

Ruoff, Sir T. B. F. [Letter] Law Society's Gazette, vol. 80, 1983, p. 2963. 85

Russell, B. *An introduction to business law in the Middle East.* Oyez, 1975. (0 95120 272 1) 559

Russell, W. O. *On crimes and misdemeanours.* 3rd ed. n.p., 1843. 2 vols. 190

Russia under Catherine the Great . . . ed. P. Dukes. Newtonville, Mass., Oriental Research Partners, 1977–8. 2 vols. (0 8925 0104 9, etc.) 583

Russian law: historical and political perspectives, ed. W. E. Butler. Leyden, Sijthoff, 1977. (90 286 0607 6) 582

Russko-angliiskii slovar' . . . ed. A. I. Smirnitskogo. Moscow, Sovetskaia Entsiklopediia, 1985. 588

Ryde's Rating Cases, 1956/7–1976/9. Butterworths, 1957–79. 21 vols. (0 406 89068 4). Index, 1980. 150

Sainsbury, I. M. *Legal subject headings for libraries.* Butterworths, 1974. (0 406 36580 6) 772

Salmond, Sir J. W. and Heuston, R. F. V. *Salmond and Heuston on the law of torts.* 18th ed. Sweet & Maxwell, 1981. (o 421 28700 4) 213

Salt, W. *Index to the titles of 604 private acts passed in the reign of Anne, George I and George II.* n.p., 1863. 272

Sargenti, M. *Operum ad ius romanum pertinentium quae ab anno MCMXL usque ad annum MCMLXX edita sunt: index modo et ratione ordinatus.* Milan, Cisalpino-La Goliardica, 1978–82. 3 vols. 522

Sartorius, C. *Verfassungs- und Verwaltungsgesetze: das öffentliche Recht der Bundesrepublik Deutschland.* Munich, Beck, 1959– . Looseleaf. (3 406 31156 3) 497

Sass, S. Research in Roman law: a guide to the sources and their English translations. *Law Library Journal,* vol. 56, 1963, pp. 210–33. 515, 520

Savigny, F. C. von. *Geschichte des römischen Recht im Mittelalter.* 2nd ed. Heidelberg, Mohr, 1834–51. 7 vols. 517

Sayers' manual of classification for librarians. 5th ed. by A. Maltby. Deutsch, 1975. (o 233 96603 X) 798

Sbornik zakonov SSSR i ukazov Prezidiuma Verkhovnogo soveta SSSR, 1938–1975. Moscow, Izvestiia, 1975–6. 4 vols. 575

Scandinavian Studies in Law, 1957– . Stockholm, Almqvist & Wiksell. (SW 0085–5944) 506

Schacht, J. *An introduction to Islamic law.* Oxford, UP, 1964. (o 19 825611 o) 560, 569

Schacht, J. *The origins of Muhammadan jurisprudence.* Oxford, Clarendon Press, 1950. (o 19 825136 X) 560

Schäffer, H. *Österreichische Verfassungs- und Verwaltungsgesetze.* Vienna, Manz, 1981– . Looseleaf. (3 214 02951 7) 497

Schermers, H. G. *International institutional law.* Leiden, Sijthoff, 1985. 486

Schiavone, G. *The institutions of Comecon.* Macmillan, 1981. (o 8419 0608 4) 579

Schiller, A. A. *Roman law: mechanisms of development.* The Hague, Mouton, 1978. (90 279 7744 5) 512, 513, 515, 521, 524

Schlesinger, R. B. *Comparative law: cases, text, materials.* 4th ed. St. Paul, Minn., Foundation Press, 1980. (o 88277 007 1) 495

Schmitthoff, C. *International commercial arbitration.* Dobbs Ferry, NY, Oceana, 1974. (o 379 00266 3) 443

Schofield's election law. 9th ed. by A. J. Little. Shaw, 1984– . (o 7219 0344 4) Looseleaf. 422

Schonfelder, H. *Deutsche Gesetze: Sammlung des Zivil–, Straf– und Verfassungsrechts.* Munich, Beck, 1931– . [Looseleaf since 4th ed., 1935]. (3 406 30761 2) 497

School of Oriental and African Studies. *Library Catalogue.* Boston, Mass., G. K. Hall, 1963– . 563, 569

Schuit, S. R. [and others]. *Dutch business law.* 2nd ed. Deventer, Kluwer, 1983. (90 6544 122 0) 505

Schulz, F. *Classical Roman law.* Oxford, Clarendon Press, 1951. 518

Schulz, F. *History of Roman legal science.* Oxford, Clarendon Press, 1946. 512

Schulz, F. *Principles of Roman law.* Oxford, Clarendon Press, 1936. 518

Schutter, B. de. *Bibliography on international criminal law.* Leiden, Sijthoff, 1972. 465, 486

Schwarzenberger, G. *International law as applied by international courts and tribunals.* Stevens, 1957–76. [Various editions]. 3 vols. (o 429 3773 1, etc.) 458

Schwarzenberger, G. *A manual of international law.* 6th ed. Abingdon, Professional Books, 1976. (o 903486 26 1) 458

Schwerin, K. The International Association of Law Libraries: its beginnings. *International Journal of*

Legal Information, vol. 12, 1984, pp. 1–6. 35

Scientific Research in British Universities and Colleges, vol. 3, social sciences, 1946– . HMSO. (UK 0080–7745) 358, 359

Scolag: the bulletin of the Scottish Legal Action Group, 1975– . Dundee, Scottish Legal Action Group. 212

Scots digest of appeals in the House of Lords from 1707 and of cases in the supreme courts of Scotland, 1800–73. Edinburgh, 1908–12. 4 vols. 172

Scots digest of appeals in the House of Lords from 1707 and of cases in the supreme courts of Scotland, 1873–1904. Edinburgh, 1905. 2 vols. 172

Scots digest of appeals in the House of Lords from 1707 and of cases in the supreme courts of Scotland . . . [Continuation volumes to 1946/7] 8 vols. 172

Scots Law Times, 1893– . Edinburgh, Green. (UK 0036–908X) 167, 173, 174, 212, 377

Scots Law Times European Court Case Notes, 1984–
—*Lands Tribunal for Scotland Reports,* 1971–4
—*Lyon Court Reports,* 1950–9, 1966, 1978
—*Notes of Recent Decisions,* 1946–
—*Poor Law Reports,* 1934–41
—*Scottish Land Court Reports,* 1964–
—*Sheriff Court Reports,* 1922–68

Scots Law Times Reports, 1895– . Edinburgh, Green. 167, 168, 173

Scots Mercantile Law Statutes, 1949– . Edinburgh, Green. [Annual]. 90

Scots revised reports [prior to 1873] Edinburgh, Green, 1898–1908. 45 vols. 172

Scots Statutes Revised [1900]. Edinburgh, Green, 1899–1908. 11 vols. 113

Scott, A. Private law libraries in the City. *Law Librarian,* vol. 9, 1978, pp. 3–4. 798

Scott, M. Law libraries in Canada. *Law Library Journal,* vol. 64, 1971, pp. 314–22. 35

Scott, M. Law library resources and planning in Canada. *International Journal of Law Libraries,* vol. 3, 1975, pp. 78–90. 35

Scott, S. P. *The civil law, including the Twelve Tables . . .* Cincinatti, Ohio, Central Trust, 1932. Repr. New York, AMS Press, 1972. 17 vols. (0 404 11026 6, etc.) 515

Scottish Criminal Case Reports, 1981– . Edinburgh, Law Society of Scotland. 170

Scottish Current Law, 1948– . Edinburgh, Green. (UK 0265–6159) 173, 377, 378

Scottish Current Law Citator, 1949– . Edinburgh, Green. 174

Scottish Current Law Statutes annotated, 1947– . Edinburgh, Green. 114

Scottish Current Law Yearbook, 1948– . Edinburgh, Green. 173

Scottish Episcopal Church. *Code of canons of the Episcopal Church in Scotland.* Edinburgh, Cambridge UP, 1973. (0 521 15974 1) 550

Scottish Jurist, 1829–73. Edinburgh, Constable. 46 vols. 167, 171, 172

Scottish Land Court Reports, 1913–63. [Supplement to *Scottish Law Review;* continued in *Scots Law Times*]. 167

Scottish Land Court Reports, 1964– . Edinburgh, Green. 167

Scottish Law Directory, 1892– . Glasgow, Hodge. (UK 0080–8083) 381

Scottish Law Gazette, 1933– . Dunblane, Scottish Law Agents' Society. (UK 0036–9314) 212

Scottish Law Reporter, 1865–1924. Edinburgh, Baxter. 61 vols. 167, 173

Scottish law reporter. Digest to volumes 1–32, 1865–95. Edinburgh, Baxter, 1898. 173

Scottish law reports [microfilm edition; over 300 volumes covered]. 1973–4. 172

Scottish Law Review and reports of cases in the Sheriff Courts of Scotland, 1885–1963. Glasgow, Hodge. 79 vols. 167, 212

Scottish Library Association. *Scottish library and information resources.* 5th ed. Glasgow, The Association, 1984. (0 900649 55 0) 382

Seal, A. [and others]. *Full and short entry catalogues: library needs and uses.* Bath, University Library, 1982. *(BLRD report, 5669) (Centre for Cataloguing Research publication)* (0 86197 032 2) 751, 797

Secondary legislation of the European Communities: subject ed. HMSO, 1973. 42 vols. Subject list and table of effects, 1973–79. HMSO, 1974–80. 8 vols. 410, 411

Secretary see Professional Administration

Selden Society. *General guide to the Society's publications, vols 1–79,* compiled by A. K. R. Kiralfy and G. H. Jones. Quaritch, 1960. (0 85423 027 0) 262

Selden Society. *Publications, vol. 1–. 1888– .* Selden Society. Repr. Abingdon, Professional Books. 261–2, 283, 350

Select essays in Anglo-American legal history ... ed. by a committee of the Association of American Law Schools. Boston, Little, Brown, 1907–9. 3 vols. 269

La Semaine Juridique see Juris Classeur Périodique

Serials in the British Library, 1981– . British Library. (UK 0260–0005) [Continues BUCOP. Quarterly, with cumulations on microfiche]. 354, 357, 378

[Session Cases]: *Cases decided in the Court of Session* [five series; various editors], 1821–1906. Edinburgh, Clark, 1822–1906. 84 vols. 165, 172, 173

Session Cases, 1906/7– . Edinburgh, Oliver & Boyd for Scottish Council of Law Reporting. 63, 165, 166, 170, 173, 174

Session Notes, 1925–48. Edinburgh, Clark for the Faculty of Advocates, 1925–48. 6 vols. 166, 173

Sewell, P. H. Library co-operation. *In British librarianship and information work, 1976–80.* 673

Sewell, P. H. *Library co-operation in the United Kingdom.* British Library Research & Development Department, 1979. *(Research and Development Reports,* 5479) (0 905984 38 2) 643

Sewell, P. H. *Resource sharing: co-operation and co-ordination in library and information services.* Deutsch, 1981. (0 233 97342 7) 643

Shahabuddeen, M. *Constitutional development in Guyana, 1621–1978.* Georgetown, n.p., 1978. 530, 536

Shahabuddeen, M. *The legal system of Guyana.* Georgetown, n.p., 1973. 530, 536

Shaw's Directory of Courts in the United Kingdom. Shaw. (UK 0264–312 X) [Annual]. 374, 381, 386

Shaw, P. *Digest of cases decided ... Scotland, 1800–68 and on appeal by the House of Lords, 1726–1868.* Edinburgh, Clark, 1869. 3 vols. 172

Shawcross, K. *A guide to the New Zealand primary sources in the Davis Law Library, 1979.* Aukland, Davis Law Library, University of Aukland, 1979. [Stencilled]. 319, 323

Sheehy, E. P. *Guide to reference books.* 9th ed. Chicago, ALA, 1976. (0 8389 0205 7) 688

Sheffield City Polytechnic. Department of Educational Services. *Basic library skills: a checklist.* Sheffield, PAVIC Publications, 1982. (0 903761 85 8) 655

Sheldon, A. *Prestel in the library context: proceedings of two seminars.* British Library, 1982. *(Library and Information Research Report,* 6). (0 7123 3009 7) 711

Shep, R. L. *Cleaning and caring for books.* Rev. ed. Sheppard Press, 1984. (0 900661 30 5) 745

Shepard's Citations. New York, Colorado Springs, Shepard's Citations, McGraw-Hill. [Many series, covering all sections of the *National Reporter System* and other US reports]. 337, 339

Sheppard, W. *Epitome of all the common and statute laws of this nation in force ...* n.p., 1656. 269

S[heppard], W. *Grand abridgment*

of the common and statute law of England. n.p., 1675. 3 vols. 269

Sheridan, L. A. Channel Islands. *In* Keeton, G. W. and Lloyd, D. *The British Commonwealth: the United Kingdom,* vol. 1, pt. 2. Stevens, 1955. 71

Sheriff Court Reports, 1922– Edinburgh, Green. 168, 212

Sherliker, C. Merger regulation in the EEC. *New Law Journal,* vol. 134, 1984, pp. 809–12. 417

Shorter encyclopaedia of Islam by H. A. Gibb and J. H. Kramers. Ithaca, NY, Cornell UP, 1957. (0 8014 0150 X) 566

Shorter Oxford English dictionary, ed. W. Little. Oxford UP, 1959. 2 vols. (0 19 861105 6, etc.) 360

Siddiqi, M. Z. *Hadith literature.* Calcutta, Calcutta UP, 1961. 558

Siekanowicz, P. *Legal sources and bibliography of Poland.* New York, Praeger, 1964. 591

Sikh Courier, 1960– . Edgeware, Sikh Cultural Society of Great Britain. (UK 0037–511 X) 557

Simon, J. A. *Taxes.* 9th ed. Butterworth, 1970– . 9 vols. Looseleaf. (0 406 06860 7) 197

Simpson, A. W. B. *Biographical dictionary of the common law.* Butterworth, 1984. (0 406 51657 X) 371, 385, 395, 524

Simpson, A. W. B. The circulation of year books in the fifteenth century. *Law Quarterly Review,* vol. 73, 1957, pp. 492–3. 292

Simpson, A. W. B. The rise and fall of the legal treatise: legal principles and the forms of legal literature. *University of Chicago Law Review,* vol. 48, 1981, pp. 632–79. 216

Simpson, I. S. *Basic statistics for librarians.* 2nd ed. Bingley, 1983. (0 85157 352 5) 641

Sinclair, M. J. T. *Updating statutes and regulations for all Canadian jurisdictions (as of Dec. 1984).* Ottawa, CLIC, 1985. (0 920358 77 2) 309–10

Singh, M. P. *German administrative law in common law perspective.* Berlin, Springer, 1985. (3 540 15618 6) 490

Sipkov, I. *Legal sources and bibliography of Bulgaria.* New York, Praeger, 1956. 590

Skene, J. *De verborum significatione.* Edinburgh, Robert Waldegrave, 1597. 379

Slade, M. and Gray, R. *The impact and potential of online legal research systems on academic legal education.* Department of Law, North East London Polytechnic, 1984. [Summarized in Gray, R. Legal research in an online age. *Infuse,* vol. 8, 1984, pp. 6–11.] 673

Slater, M. *Ratios of staff to users . . . and the potential for automation.* Aslib, 1981. (*Aslib Occasional publications,* no. 24), (0 85142 144 X) 642

The Slavic Cyrillic union catalog of pre-1956 imprints, compiled by the Catalog Publication Division, Library of Congress. Totowa, NJ, Rowman and Littlefield, 1980. [Microfiche and booklet]. 587

Smidt, J. Th. de. The expansion of Dutch private law outside Europe in the seventeenth and eighteenth centuries. *In The world of Hugo Grotius (1583–1645)* . . . Amsterdam, APA, Holland UP 1984. (90 302 1284 5) 530

Smit, H. and Herzog, P. E. *The law of the European Economic Community: a commentary on the EEC treaty.* New York, Matthew Bender, 1976– . 6 vols. Looseleaf. 404, 423

Smith, B. E. British official publications. *Government Publications Review,* vol. 4, 1977, pp. 201–7; vol. 5, 1978, pp. 1–12; vol. 6, 1979, pp. 11–18. 238

Smith, J. A. C. *Medieval law teachers and writers: civilian and canonist.* Ottawa, University of Ottawa Press, 1975. (0 7766 2014 2) 517, 524

Smith, J. P. *Reports, King's Bench and Chancery, 1803–6.* Clarke, 1806–7. 3 vols. [Reissue of reports from *Law Journal* [newspaper], 1803–6]. 131

subjects. Washington, DC, GPO, 1877. 456

US. *Federal Register*, 1936– . Washington, DC, USGPO. 328

US. *Revised statutes of the United States in force ... 1873.* Washington, DC, USGPO. 2nd ed. to 1875. 1878. 327

US. *Statutes at Large*, 1789– . Washington, DC, USGPO. [Publisher varies]. 325, 327, 330, 442–3

US. Library of Congress. *The canon law collection ...* compiled by D. C. Ferreira-Ibarra. Washington, DC, USGPO, 1981. (0 8444 0367 9) 563

US. Library of Congress. Processing Services. *Library of Congress filing rules*, prepared by J. C. Rather and S. C. Biebel. Washington, DC, Library of Congress, 1980. (0 8444 0347 4) 793

US. Library of Congress. Subject Cataloguing Division. *Library of Congress classification, class K, Law.* Washington, DC, 1969– . [5 vols to date: K, Law (General) 1977; KD, UK & Ireland, 1973; KE, Canada, 1976; KF, US, 1969; KK–KKC, Germany, 1982]. (0 8444 0231 1, etc.) 783

US. Library of Congress. Subject Cataloguing Division. *Library of Congress subject headings.* 9th ed. Washington, DC, LC, 1980. (0 8444 0299 0). Microform ed., quarterly cumulation. (US 0361–5243) 770

United States Aviation Reports, 1928– . Dobbs Ferry, NY, Oceana. [Publisher varies]. 336

United States Code, 1926– . Washington, DC, USGPO. [Reissued every 6 years, with annual supplements]. 325, 327–8, 330

United States Code Annotated, 1927– . St. Paul, Minn., West. 50 titles in about 250 vols. [Supplements and replacement vols.] 327, 328

United States Code Congressional and Administrative News, 1941– . St. Paul, Minn., West. 326

United States Code Service, 1936– . Rochester, NY, Lawyers' Co-operative Publishing Company. [1936–70 entitled *Federal code annotated*]. 326, 327, 328

United States Government Manual. Washington, DC, Office of the Federal Register. [Annual]. 328

United States Law Week, 1933– . Washington, DC, Bureau of National Affairs. (US 0148–8139) 336

United States Patent Quarterly, 1929– . Washington, DC, Bureau of National Affairs. 336

United States Reports, 1790– . Washington, DC, USGPO. 332

United States Supreme Court Digest, 1754 to date, 1943– . St. Paul, Minn., West. [Supplements and replacement vols.] 337

United States Supreme Court Reports, lawyers' edition, 1790– . Rochester, NY, Lawyers' Co-operative Publishing Company. 332, 335, 337

United States Treaties and other International Agreements, 1950– . Washington, DC, Department of State. 441, 442, 446

Universal Decimal Classification, international medium ed. English text. Part 1: systematic tables. British Standards Institution, 1985. (FID Publication no. 571) (BS 1000M: Part 1: 1985). 782

Universal Register see The Times

University Casebook Series. Mineola, NY, Foundation Press. 339

University librarianship, ed. J. F. Stirling. Library Association, 1981. (Handbooks on library practice). (0 85365 621 5) 640, 742

University of Cambridge. Institute of Criminology. *Library catalogue of the Radzinowicz Library.* Boston, Mass., G. K. Hall, 1979. 6 vols. (0 8161 0242 2) 352

University of Cambridge. Squire Law Library *see* Squire Law Library

University of Leiden. Documentation Office for East European Law. *Systematic catalogue.* Zug,

IDC, 1981. [Microfiche; R–16081]. 586

University of London. Institute of Advanced Legal Studies *see* Institute of Advanced Legal Studies

University of Sheffield. Library. *A guide to legal literature*. Sheffield, University Library and AV/TV Centre, 1980. [Series of tape-slide programmes]. 653

Update to Bowker's Law Books and Serials in Print, 1983– . New York, Bowker. (US 0000–0728) [1983 entitled *Law Information Update*]. 349

Usher, J. A. *European Court Practice*. Sweet & Maxwell, 1983. (0 421 26780 1) 415

Valentine, D. G. *The Court of Justice of the European Communities*. Stevens, 1965. 2 vols. (0 420 39139 4) 416

Value Added Tax Tribunal Reports, 1973– . HMSO. Irregular. 149, 150, 232

Van Hoof, G. J. H. *Rethinking the sources of international law*. Deventer, Kluwer, 1983. (90 654 4085 2) 486

Vanbery, J. and Vanbery, R. *Cumulative list and index to treaties and international agreements registered ... with ... the United Nations*. Dobbs Ferry, NY, Oceana, 1977. 2 vols. 444

Vanderlinden, J. *African legal bibliography: bibliographie de droit africain, 1947–66*. Brussels, Presses Universitaires, 1972. [Supplement 1966–72 in *Annual Survey of African Law*; later supplements published separately]. 391

Vanderlinden, J. *An introduction to the sources on contemporary African laws*. Beograd, Institute of Comparative Law, for the International Association of Legal Sciences under the auspices of Unesco, 1975. 322

Vann, S. K. The Dewey decimal classification. *In* Maltby, A. *Classification in the 1970's*, pp. 87–122. 799

Vassalli, F. *Trattato di diritto civile italiano*. Turin, UTET, 1938– . 15

titles in about 60 vols. [Various editions]. 502

Vatican Council, 2nd. *Documents of Vatican II*. Chapman, 1966. (0 225 27 568 6) 543

Vaughan, A. British academic library buildings since 1964: a comparative study. *Journal of Librarianship*, vol. 12, 1980, pp. 179–98. 642

Vedomosti Verkhovnogo Soveta SSR, 1938– . Moscow, Izd. Verkhovnogo Soveta SSR. (UR 0320–7951) 574

Venn, J. *Alumni Cantabrigiensis: a biographical list of all known students, graduates and holders of office at the University of Cambridge, from the earliest times to 1900*. Cambridge UP, 1922–54. 10 vols. 368

Verheyden, W. The publications policy and programme of the European Communities. *In* Hopkins, M. *European Communities information*, pp. 13–23. 436

Verkhovnyi Sovet SSSR ... sessiia ... sozyv ... goda: stenograficheskii otchet, 1 sessiia, 1 sosyv, 12–19 ianvaria 1938 g. Moscow, Izd. Verkhovnogo Soveta SSSR. 574

Verzijl, J. H. W. *The jurisprudence of the World Court: a case by case commentary*. Leyden, Sijthoff, 1965. 2 vols. 454

Vestnik Moskovskogo Universiteta: seriia 11: Pravo, 1956– . Moscow, Izd-vo Moskovskogo Universiteta. (UR 0130–0113) 580

Vestnik Tsentral'nogo ispolniel' nogo komiteta, Soveta narodnykh komissarov i Soveta truda i oborony SSSR, 1923–24. Moscow, n.p., n.d. 583

Vine, 1971– . Southampton, University. (UK 0305–5728) 641

Viner, C. *General abridgment of law and equity, alphabetically digested under proper titles, with notes and references*. n.p., 1742–58. 24 vols. 19, 270

Vinogradoff, P. *Roman law in medieval Europe*. 3rd ed. Oxford UP, 1961. 517

Voet, J. *Commentarius ad Pandectas*. Lugdoni Batavorum, Verbessel, 1698–1702. 2 vols. 528

Abingdon, Professional Books, 1975. (0 903486 07 5). First supplement, 1975–80. Professional Books, 1981. (0 86205 024 3) 214

Year Book of the Commonwealth, 1969– . HMSO. [Formerly *Commonwealth Office Year Book*; *Commonwealth Relations Office Year Book*; *Commonwealth Relations Office List*]. 293, 294, 295

Year Books, 20–22 and 30–35 Edward I; 11–20 Edward III, ed. A. J. Horwood and L. O. Pike. Master of the Rolls, 1863–1911. 20 vols. (Rolls Series, 31). 283

Year Books: or reports in the following reigns [1 Edward II to 27 Henry VIII] with notes to Brooke and Fitzherbert's Abridgments, ed. Sir J. Maynard. n.p., 1678–80. 11 vols. Repr. Professional Books, 1981. (*Classic Law Texts series*, vols. 69–79). 283

Yearbook of the European communities and of other European organizations. Brussels, Delta. 433

Yearbook of the European Convention on Human Rights, 1955– . The Hague, Nijhoff. (IX 0071–2701) 481

Yearbook of the International Court of Justice, 1946– . Leyden, Sijthoff. (IX 0074–445X) 451, 471

Yearbook of the International Law Commission, 1949– . New York, UN. (IX 0082–8289) 479

Yeates, R. *Prestel in the public library* … British Library, 1982. (*Library and Information Research Report* 2). (0 7123 3003 8) 711

Yelland, M. *Local library co-operation*. Boston Spa, British Library, 1980. (*Research and Development Reports*, no. 5578). (0 905984 62 5) 643

Yiannopoulos, A. N. *Civil law in the modern world*. Baton Rouge, La., Louisiana State UP, 1965. (0 8071 0841 3) 72

Yogis, J. A. *Canadian law dictionary*. Woodbury, NY, Barron's Educational Series, 1983. 395

York Journal of Convocation, 1874– . Church Information Office. (UK 0085–8374) 547

Young, F. A. *Proclamations of the Tudor queens*. Cambridge UP, 1976. (0 521 21044 5) 266

Zakaria, S. Legal documentation and information retrieval in Malaysia. *Malayan Law Journal*, vol. 2, 1979, pp. cxlvii–cli. 323

Zander, M. *Cases and materials on the English legal system*. 4th ed. Weidenfeld & Nicolson, 1984. (0 297 78457 9) 70

Zander, M. *The law making process*. 2nd ed. Weidenfeld & Nicolson, 1985. (0 297 78662 8) 70, 122

Zander, M. *Lawyers and the public interest*. Weidenfeld & Nicolson, 1968. (0 297 17605 6) 72

Zeitschrift der Savigny-Stiftung für Rechtsgeschichte, 1880– . Vienna, Bohlaus. [3 series: Germanistische, Kanonistische and Romanistische]. 503, 519, 520

Zeitschrift für Schweizerisches Recht, 1852– . Basel, Helbing und Lichtenhahn. (SZ 0084–540X) 506

Zulueta, F. de. *The Institutes of Gaius*. Oxford, Clarendon Press, 1946–53. 2 vols. 513

Zürcher Kommentar: Kommentar zum Schweizerischen Zivilgesetzbuch, 3rd ed. Zurich, Schulthess, 1959– . 6 vols in about 30. [In progress]. 502

Zweigert, K. and Kotz, H. *An introduction to comparative law*. [Amsterdam]. North-Holland, 1977. 2 vols. (0 7204 0703 6, etc.) 495

Zweigert, K. and Kropholler, J. *Sources of international uniform law*. Leiden, Sijthoff, 1971–3. 3 vols. (90 218 9131 X, etc.) Supplements. 492

Subject Index

NOTE

Although this volume deals with legal literature from many jurisdictions, both national and non-national, a heavy emphasis has necessarily been placed on the most local jurisdictions: the United Kingdom in general and England and Wales in particular. To avoid a great deal of repetition, there are no headings or sub-headings in the index for those jurisdictions. Material at pages where another jurisdiction is not indicated may be assumed to involve the UK as a whole or England and Wales. The separate local jurisdictions of Scotland, both parts of Ireland, the Channel Islands and the Isle of Man have been indexed.

Most organizations mentioned in the text have been indexed, except publishers and booksellers and references to other bodies solely in their publishing capacity.